Prominent
**Indonesian
Chinese**

ISEAS–Yusof Ishak Institute (formerly Institute of Southeast Asian Studies) was established as an autonomous organization in 1968. It is a regional centre dedicated to the study of socio-political, security and economic trends and developments in Southeast Asia and its wider geostrategic and economic environment. The Institute's research programmes are the Regional Economic Studies (RES, including ASEAN and APEC), Regional Strategic and Political Studies (RSPS), and Regional Social and Cultural Studies (RSCS).

ISEAS Publishing, an established academic press, has issued more than 2,000 books and journals. It is the largest scholarly publisher of research about Southeast Asia from within the region. ISEAS Publishing works with many other academic and trade publishers and distributors to disseminate important research and analyses from and about Southeast Asia to the rest of the world.

Prominent Indonesian Chinese

Biographical Sketches

4th EDITION

Leo Suryadinata

 YUSOF ISHAK INSTITUTE

First published in Singapore in 2015 by
ISEAS Publishing
30 Heng Mui Keng Terrace
Singapore 119614

E-mail: publish@iseas.edu.sg   • Website: bookshop.iseas.edu.sg

All rights reserved. No part of this publication may be reproduced, stored in a retrieval system, or transmitted in any form or by any means, electronic, mechanical, photocopying, recording or otherwise, without the prior permission of the ISEAS–Yusof Ishak Institute.

© 2015 ISEAS–Yusof Ishak Institute, Singapore

The responsibility for facts and opinions in this publication rests exclusively with the author and his interpretations do not necessarily reflect the views or the policy of the publisher or its supporters.

ISEAS Library Cataloguing-in-Publication Data

Suryadinata, Leo, 1941–
   Prominent Indonesian Chinese : Biographical Sketches.
   4th edition.
Formerly published under title: Eminent Indonesian Chinese: biographical sketches
   1. Chinese—Indonesia—Biography.
   2. Indonesia—Biography.
   I. Title.
DS632.2 C5S966   2015

ISBN 978-981-4620-50-5 (soft cover)
ISBN 978-981-4620-51-2 (E-book PDF)

Typeset by International Typesetters Pte Ltd
Printed in Singapore by Markono Print Media Pte Ltd

CONTENTS

Preface to the Fourth Edition (2015)
vii

Introduction
xi

List of Prominent Indonesian Chinese
xix

Biographies
1

Abbreviations and Glossary
409

Select Bibliography
436

Index
471

PREFACE TO THE FOURTH EDITION (2015)

This fourth edition (2015) is the most up-to-date version of my book on Prominent Indonesian Chinese.

The origin of this book was a long paper published by Ohio University in 1972 with the title of *Prominent Indonesian Chinese in the 20th Century: A Preliminary Survey* (papers in International Studies, Southeast Asian Series, Ohio University, it consists of only 62 pages). Six years later, when I worked as a researcher at the Institute of Southeast Asian Studies (ISEAS), I revised the paper and made it into a book and published it in 1978 with a new title: *Eminent Indonesian Chinese: Biographical Sketches*. This was officially the first edition of this book. Two years later, an Indonesian publisher in Singapore, Gunung Agung, expressed his interest to republish the book. But since the book would be sold in Indonesia, I had to come out with two versions, one with the Chinese characters and the other without as the Soeharto regime banned books with Chinese characters for distribution. As a result, I had to remove all Chinese characters from the book and prepare a separate booklet on the list of Chinese characters for readers who were outside Indonesia. I wanted my book to be circulated in Indonesia and I accepted that arrangement, otherwise the book would have not been allowed to be distributed in Indonesia at all. This was the second edition of my book.

The book was out of print for many years. Fifteen years later, many new figures emerged and old ones passed away. An update was needed. I was interested in issuing a third edition and offered it to ISEAS, which was the publisher of my first edition. My offer was accepted and the book was published in 1995 with a new title: *Prominent Indonesian Chinese: Biographical Sketches*. Chinese characters in the book were restored. Within a year, the book was reprinted at least once.

In the last nineteen years, there have been a lot of new generation leaders and the book requires another update. This time, updating of the book becomes more difficult as not only do I need to revise the existing biographies, I also need to add new figures that have emerged in the last two decades. The number of new figures is significant, over 100 persons in total. This book has therefore become much larger. As in the past, the name of an individual in different versions and spellings are provided in the book for easy reference.

After the fall of Soeharto, more information on the Chinese in Indonesia become available. I also take the opportunity to correct some of the mistakes in the book based on newly available information. However, it becomes more difficult to identify the background of the persons as many have changed their Chinese names into Indonesian sounding names. Furthermore, the younger generation born after the 1966 Name Changing Regulation would not have Chinese names, at least officially. In compiling the new addition of this book, I have faced many difficulties to ascertain if the person is of Chinese descent or not. As a rule, if I do not have the original Chinese name or Chinese surname of the individual and even if the person is said to be an Indonesian of Chinese descent, I do not include him/her in this book, i.e. Rusdi Kirana (aviation tycoon) and Indah

Kurniawati (member of parliament). I have also decided to omit Dora Sasongko Kartono (supreme judge) who appeared in the previous edition as I am unable to obtain her Chinese name.

With regard to the names in their original Chinese characters, when available they will be provided together with their pronunciations in *Hanyu Pinyin*. However, when the original Chinese characters are not available, I still provide the names in Chinese characters marked with an asterisk to differentiate them from those which have original Chinese characters. Since these Chinese characters are based on transliteration, the *Hanyu Pinyin* will not be provided.

I have also decided to use some Indonesian Chinese names rather than their Indonesian names as the main entries if the individuals are better known in their original Indonesian Chinese names, or their activities were known when they still used their Chinese names although after 1966 they adopted Indonesian names. For instance, Bong A Lok instead of Suwandi Hamid, Nio Joe Lan instead of Junus Nur Arif, Tan Joe Hok instead of Hendra Kartanegara. However, when a person is equally known in his/her Indonesian name and Chinese name, his/her Indonesian name is used: Soedono Salim instead of Liem Sioe Liong, Mochtar Riady instead of Li Wenzheng.

I would like to thank the coordinator of the Indonesian Studies Group of ISEAS, Dr Hui Yew Foong, for recommending the publication of this revised version. Nevertheless, the contents of the book are solely the responsibility of the author.

Leo Suryadinata
1 October 2014

INTRODUCTION[1]

This work is to present a documented study of Indonesian Chinese in the twentieth century and beyond. The term "Indonesian Chinese" as used here refers to "ethnic Chinese" in Indonesia who have or had Chinese surnames, regardless of their citizenship. Many Indonesian citizens of Chinese descent have adopted Indonesian-sounding names since 1966 — in a few cases, the adoption of such names occurred even earlier than that date — and they prefer *not* to be identified as "Chinese", but for academic purposes, they are still included in this study.

It should also be noted that some Indonesian-born Chinese who migrated elsewhere in their early age and became well-known only in their newly adopted land (for instance, Wang Gungwu and Choo Hoey) will be excluded from this book, but those who migrated after they had made significant contributions in Indonesia will be included in the category of Indonesian Chinese (for instance, Thung Tjeng Hiang and Yap Tjwan Bing).

In fact, the Chinese in Indonesia, numbering about 4 million, are a heterogeneous and complex community. Culturally, they can be divided into Indonesian-speaking *peranakan* and Chinese-speaking *totok*,[2] but the Chinese-speaking group has rapidly declined during the Soeharto New Order period (1966–98); legally they can be classified as Indonesian citizens and aliens, cutting across the above-mentioned cultural divisions; politically, they are split into pro-Jakarta, pro-Beijing, pro-Taipei groups, and others who are not sure of their orientation. The majority, however, remain politically passive. Economically, the Chinese are heavily engaged in, but not confined to, trading activities. As the present study shows, they are found in a wide range of professions.

The division between the *peranakan* and the *totok* has become less useful with the passage of time as most *totok* children by the third generation have become *peranakan* in the sense that they have lost their command of the Chinese language. This is especially true with the Chinese who were born or who grew up after Chinese schools in Indonesia were closed in 1966. However, for the older generation, some of the second generation, and some who have been educated in Chinese-speaking countries/areas, Chinese or Chinese dialect is still used at home as their medium of communication. In such cases, they can still be classified as *totok* in the cultural sense.

Such a division is not entirely useless, however, since ethnic Chinese have used Chinese language or dialect to establish networking for economic purposes. Many Indonesian Chinese who still have a command of the Chinese language or dialect can continue to take advantage of their ethnic connections to promote their economic interests within Indonesia and beyond. It is also true that the *totok* tend to possess more entrepreneurial spirit compared with the *peranakan*.

Nevertheless, sometimes it is difficult to tell whether an individual has become *peranakan* or peranakanized as he/she may be able to shift easily between Indonesian and Chinese when he/she speaks. As the situation of Chinese Indonesians

Introduction xiii

is becoming more complex, it becomes increasingly more difficult to identify a person as *totok* or *peranakan*. Therefore in this new edition, I have stopped providing the prominent Indonesian Chinese with such a label. Nevertheless, when reading their biographical sketches, the reader can still identify their different cultural backgrounds. It should also be noted that it has become more difficult to identify Chinese Indonesians who were born after 1966 as many no longer use their Chinese surnames. To obtain their Chinese names is not easy; those so-called Chinese figures without Chinese names or surnames will not be included in this book.

There are at least nine kinds of prominent Chinese included in these biographical sketches: community leaders, political party leaders, religious activists, writers, journalists, businessmen, academicians, artists, and sportsmen. These categories often overlap. The criteria used to select these prominent ethnic Chinese should be elaborated here. Community and political leaders are those who hold or have held major positions or are known to be influential in one or more of the following areas:

(a) major Chinese socio-political organizations such as the THHK,[3] Siang Hwee, CHH, PTI, KMT (in Indonesia), Baperki, LPKB,[4] Qiao Zong, PBI, INTI, and PSMTI;
(b) major political institutions such as the Volksraad (during the colonial period), the Tjuo Sangi In and BPUPKI (during the Japanese Occupation), and the DPR and MPR(S) after Indonesia's independence and DPD after the fall of Soeharto;
(c) Indonesian political parties (PNI, PKI, Golkar, PDIP, etc.);
(d) Indonesian administrative positions such as mayor, governor, bupati etc.; and
(e) Indonesian major educational, cultural, and religious institutions (such as UI, LIPI, GKI etc.).

In selecting businessmen for inclusion in the Biographies, wealth was one criterion, but this was often taken into consideration together with affiliation with the above-mentioned socio-political organizations, of which many leading businessmen were members. The so-called *cukong* or *Konglomerat*[5] is also included in the category of prominent businessmen.

The criteria used in selecting prominent writers, journalists, artists, and academicians were rather arbitrary. For prominent writers, although publications in book form were considered, equal weight was also given to their impact and reputation among Chinese or Indonesian readers, depending on the language the writers use. The judgment on this was often subjective. Nio Joe Lan's book on *Sastera Indonesia-Tionghoa* [Literature of *Peranakan* Chinese] was also consulted to aid selection here. With regard to journalists, their association with one or more major *totok* and *peranakan* newspapers was an important criterion. Prominent artists and sportsmen were selected on the basis of their national reputation; again, the judgment was a subjective one. In choosing leading academicians, the possession of a PhD was often used as an indicator, but equal weight was also given to publications and positions held by individuals in academic and higher-learning institutions, especially in Indonesia.

Whenever available, I have provided for each individual such information as field of activity, occupation, place of birth, educational and religious backgrounds, offices or positions held, and original Chinese dialect group (speech group) when available.

In the past editions, Indonesian citizens of Chinese descent were entered under their Indonesian names followed by their Chinese names within parentheses. Their Chinese names were also entered separately for cross reference purposes. For alien Chinese or Indonesian citizens of Chinese descent who do not have Indonesian names, their Chinese names were used as

Introduction

entries. However, for this edition, Indonesian names are only used as entries when the individuals are better known in their Indonesian names. For those figures who were better known by their Chinese names (e.g. Tan Joe Hok, Nio Joe Lan etc.) as they became famous before changing their names to Indonesian names, their Chinese names will be used as entries.

All Chinese names are spelt as they appear in Indonesia (that is, Dutch romanized–Hokkien or Dutch romanized–Hakka, and so forth, depending on the individual's ancestral origin). The Pinyin system is used when the Indonesian spelling is unavailable. Chinese characters are also included when known, those Chinese characters which were based on transliteration are marked with asterisk.

The present work is a substantive expansion of my previous study entitled *Prominent Indonesian Chinese in the 20th Century: A Preliminary Survey*, published in Athens, Ohio, in 1972, *Eminent Indonesian Chinese: Biographical Sketches*, published by ISEAS (1978) and Gunung Agung (1981), and *Prominent Indonesian Chinese: Biographical Sketches* (1995). It contains more names and more detailed information and is therefore more comprehensive. It is fully documented and more systematic in its presentation. It is the result of several years of research using both published materials such as newspapers, periodicals, biographies, and handbooks (see the Select Bibliography section) and — whenever possible — correspondence or oral interviews.

It should be noted here that two pioneering works of a similar nature but much more limited in scope were published before World War II. One was Tan Hong Boen's *Orang-Orang Tionghoa Jang Terkemoeka di Java* [Prominent Chinese in Java] (Solo: Biographical Publishing Centre, 1935). This work contains valuable biographical data on over two hundred prominent Chinese in Java before 1935, but it is very sketchy and poorly organized. The other was Liu Huanran's *Heshu*

Dongyindu Gailan [A Brief Introduction to the Dutch East Indies] (Singapore: Nanyang Baoshe, 1939), which contains the biographies of approximately 100 prominent Indonesian Chinese before 1939. Like Tan's biographical study, Liu's book has some valuable information; but unlike Tan's book which confines itself primarily to *peranakan* in Java, Liu's work tends to stress the *totok* community in both Java and the Outer Islands. My present study has benefited from these two pioneering works, as shown in my frequent inclusion of them as a source of information. In recent years, I have also benefited from various Indonesian language publications such as *Apa dan Siapa Sejumlah Orang Indonesia*, especially the 1985–86 edition, a Tempo publication, and the *Tokoh-Tokoh Etnis Tionghoa Indonesia* by Sam Setyautama, which was partly based on the early edition of my book (1995) but has included more recent figures. Unfortunately, Setyautama's book is not only poorly organized but also marred with numerous errors in names and data. The book is weakest in providing the Chinese characters of names.

The collection of materials for this book was made possible by the cooperation over a long period of time of various Indonesian Chinese individuals and scholars with an interest in the field. It is not possible to list the names of all those who had kindly helped me for two reasons: there are too many and some wish to remain anonymous. Nonetheless, I would like to single out the late Mr Tio Ie Soei, who had kindly shared with me his notes on various pre-war *peranakan* writers, journalists, and a few individuals whom he had known personally. I have occasionally cited this information in my study with acknowledgement in the "Source" section.

Over the years I have received many comments and letters from friends and people whom I have never met. Some know the persons mentioned in the book and others are related to the individuals in the book. They have kindly provided me with new information. A study of this kind can never be exhaustive. It needs continuing research and updating. Additional information and corrections are therefore welcome and would be appreciated.

Leo Suryadinata
Singapore
August 2014

Notes

1. This is a slightly revised version of the "Introduction" appeared in the 1995 version of *Prominent Indonesian Chinese: Biographical Sketches*.
2. See Abbreviations and Glossary section for the definitions of *peranakan* and *totok* Chinese.
3. For the meaning of those and subsequent abbreviations, refer to Abbreviations and Glossary section.
4. Strictly speaking this was a mixed organization because it consisted of both indigenous and non-indigenous Indonesians. However, because of the dominant role of the *peranakan* Chinese in the organization and its rivalry with Baperki, it is included here in the category of "major Chinese socio-political organizations".
5. The English term for *konglomerat* is conglomerate, but in Indonesian, the term refers to tycoons rather than the organization itself.

LIST OF PROMINENT INDONESIAN CHINESE

Please note that Chinese characters with an asterisk indicate that their original Chinese characters are not available. The characters included are transliterations.

A

A WU (阿五)
ADIDHARMA (李永隆)
ADMADJAJA, Usman (饶耀武)
ALI, Mohammad (李杰登)
ALIM, Markus (林文光)
AMIEN, Muhammad (陈振文)
ANANTA, Aris (陈连虎)
ANG Ban Tjiong (洪万昌*)
ANG Jan Goan (洪渊源)
ANG Tjiang Liat (洪昌烈*)
ANGKOSUBROTO, Dasuki (吴瑞基)
ANTON, Abah (魏兴安*)
ARBI, Haryanto (洪阿比*)
ARIEF, Jackson (汤泰动*)
AW Tjoei Lan (区翠兰)

B

BARKI, Kiki (纪琦辉)
BE Kwat Koen (马厥群*)

BE Tiat Tjong (马铁宗*)
BONG A Lok (王亚禄)
BUASAN, Bahar (黄才文*)
BUDIANTA, Melani (陈石芯*)
BUDIKUSUMA, Alan (魏仁芳)
BUDIMAN, Arief (史福仁)

C

CHAN Kok Cheng (曾国清*)
CHEN, Bubi (陈埔毕*)
CHENG, David G. (郑大卫*)
CHIAO, Evelyn (赵春琳)
CHU Chong Tong (朱昌东)

D

DANANDJAYA, James (陈士林*)
DARMADI, Jan (霍佐幼)
DARMAPUTERA, Eka (郑运兴*)
DARMAWAN, Hari (陈灿福*)
DARMAWAN, Hendra (黄贵德*)
DARMOHUSODO, K.R.T. Obi (温文英*)
Dawis, Didi (俞雨龄)
DEWI, Utami (梁碧婉*)
DIPOJUWONO, Budi (李宝友*)
DJIAUW Pok Kie (饶博基)
DJIE Ting Liat (徐定烈*)
DJIE Ting Tjioe (徐庭州)
DJOJONEGORO, Husain (朱国盛)
DJUHAR, Sutanto (林文镜)
DURIANTO, Darmadi (林德純)

List of Prominent Indonesian Chinese xxi

E

ERVINNA (爱慧娜)
ESMARA, Hendra (王德美)

F

FADJRIN, Verawaty (黄惠拉*)

G

GAN Choo Ho (颜朱和*)
GAN K.L. (颜国梁)
GAN Koen Han (颜群汉*)
GAUTAMA, Sudargo (吴玉祥)
GINTING, Lo S.H. (罗祥兴)
GO Gien Tjwan (吴银泉)
GO Ing Liang (吴英亮)
GO (GOUW) Tiauw Goan (吴兆元)
GO Tjoe Bin (吴朱民*)
GOEI Poo Aan (魏保安)
GOEY Tiauw Hong (魏朝凤)
GOH Tjing Hok (吴清福)
GONDOKUSUMO, Suhargo (吴家熊)
GOUW Peng Liang (吴炳亮)
GOZALI, Hendrick (吴协和)
GOZELIE, Tellie (李敏东)
GUNARSA, Singgih D. (吴启祥)
GUNAWAN, Andrew H. (魏福义)
GUNAWAN, Mu'min Ali (李文明)
GUNAWAN, Rudy (郭宏源)
GUO Liangjie (郭两捷)
GUO Rongfu (郭荣福)
GUO Yuxiu (郭毓秀)

H

HADI, Abdul W.M. (安禄基*)
HADINATA, Christian (纪明发)
HAKIM, Rachman (许世经)
HALIM, Boediharto (林文华)
HALIM, Rachman (蔡道行)
HAN, Awal (韩浩泉)
HAN Tiauw Tjong (韩兆宗)
HARDJONAGORO, Kanjeng Raden Tumenggung (吴德宣)
Harsono, FX (胡丰文)
HARTONO, Michael Bambang (黄惠祥)
HARTONO, Robert Budi (黄惠忠)
HASAN, Mohammad Bob (郑建盛)
HASSAN, Hadji Mohammad (陈金龙)
HAUW Tek Kong (候德广)
HEI Ying (黑婴)
HIE Foek Tjhoy (许福才)
HIMAWAN, Charles (王查理*)
HIOE Njan Joeng (丘元荣)
HO Liong Tiauw (何隆朝)
HONORIS, Charles (何震康)
HONORIS, Otje (何春霖)
HOO Eng Djie (何英如*)
HUANG Yurong (黄裕荣)
HUSINO, M.H. (胡信丰*)
HUSNI, Arief (王成庆)
HUTOMO, Suryo (柯贵安)

I

IE Tjoen Siang (余春祥)
INJO Beng Goat (杨明月)
IRAWAN, Bingky (傅孙铭)
ISKANDAR, Nathanael (陈源长)

J

JANANTO, Soetopo (叶瑞基)
JAUW Keng Hong (饶庆丰*)
JAYA, David Herman (林万金)
JINARAKKHITA, Bhikku Ashin (郑满安)
JOHAN, Daniel (张育浩)
JUSUF, Ester Indahyani (沈爱玲)
JUSUF, Tedy (熊德怡)

K

KAM Hwat Hok (甘发福)
KAMIL, Iskandar (林开河*)
KAN Hok Hoei (简福辉)
KARIM, Hadji Abdul (黄清兴)
KARMAN, Hasan (黄少凡)
KARTAJAYA, Hermawan (陈求学)
KARWANDY (郭蔡广*)
KARYA, Teguh (林全福)
KENCANAWATI, Cecillia (茜茜丽亚)
KHARMAWAN, Byanti (许绵池)
KHO Liang Ie (许亮宜*)
KHO Ping Hoo (许平和)
KHO Sin Kie (许新基*)
KHO Tjoen Gwan (许俊源*)
KHO Wan Gie (高焕义)
KHOE A Fan (丘亚樊)
KHOE Tjeng Tek (丘清德)
KHOE Woen Sioe (丘文秀)
KOO Bo Tjhan (许茂灿*)
KHOUW Hok Goan (许福源)
KHOUW Ke Hien (许启兴)
KHOUW Kim An (许金安)
KO Hong An (高丰安*)

KO Kwat Oen (高厥运*)
KO Kwat Tiong (高厥忠)
KO Swan Sik (高宣锡*)
KO Tjay Sing (高财盛*)
KOSASIH, Tirtawinata (丘成绍)
KURNIAWAN, Rudy Hartono (梁海量)
KUSUMA, Eddie (伍瑞章)
KUSUMA, Sugianto (郭再源)
KWA Khay Twan (柯凯传*)
KWA Tjoan Sioe (柯全寿)
KWEE Bie Sin (郭美丞)
KWEE Djie Hoo (郭二和*)
KWEE Hin Goan (郭兴源)
KWEE Hing Tjiat (郭恒节)
KWEE Kek Beng (郭克明)
KWEE Oen Liam (郭允廉)
KWEE Soen Tik (郭顺德)
KWEE Swan Lwan (郭碹峦)
KWEE Tek Hoay (郭德怀)
KWEE Thian Hong (郭天丰*)
KWEE Thiam Tjing (郭添清*)
KWIK Djoen Eng (郭春秧)
KWIK Kian Gie (郭建义)

L

LAUW Giok Lan (刘玉兰)
LAUWANI, Siegvrieda (刘英文)
LEE Man Fong (李曼峰)
LEE Teng Hui (李登辉)
LEMBONG, Eddie (汪友山)
LESMANA, Hendrawan (施亨利*)
LI Chunming (李春鸣)

LI Qing (犁青)
LI Xu'nan (李旭南)
LI Zhuohui (李卓辉)
LIANG Chiu Sia (梁秋霞)
LIAO Ziran (廖自然)
Lie Dharmawan (李德美)
LIE Hin Liam (李兴廉)
LIE Ing Tien (李应徽)
LIE, Ivanna (李英华)
LIE Khe Bo (李启茂*)
LIE Kian Joe (李建佑*)
LIE Kian Kim (李建金)
LIE Kim Hok (李金福)
LIE Ling Piao, Alvin (李宁彪)
LIE Mei (李梅)
LIE Oen Hock (李运福)
LIE Oen Sam (李运三*)
LIE Siong Hwie (李双辉)
LIE Tek Tjeng (李德清)
LIE Tjeng Tjoan, John (李清泉*)
LIE Tjian Tjoen (李前俊)
LIE Tjwan Sien (李全信)
LIE Tjwan Sioe (李全寿)
LIEM A Pat (林亚拔*)
LIEM Boen Siang (林文祥)
LIEM Bwan Tjie (林满志*)
LIEM Ho Ban (林和万*)
LIEM Hwie Giap (林徽业)
LIEM Hwie Liat (林徽烈*)
LIEM K.D. (LIEM King Djwan 林庆全*)
LIEM Khiam Soen (林谦顺)
LIEM Khiem Yang (林金扬*)
LIEM Khing Hoo (林庆和)
LIEM Koen Beng (林群明)

LIEM Koen Hian (林群贤)
LIEM Koen Seng (林群盛)
LIEM Kwi Boen (林贵文*)
LIEM Sam Tjiang (林三昌*)
LIEM Seng Tee (林生地)
LIEM Sik Tjo (林锡祖)
LIEM Swie King (林水镜)
LIEM Thay Tjwan (林泰全*)
LIEM Thian Joe (林天佑)
LIEM Tjae Le (林财礼)
LIEM Tjing Hien (林清兴*)
LIEM Tjong Hian (林宗贤*)
LIEM Toan Tek (林传德)
LIEM Twan Djie (林端裕*)
LIM Hiong Tjheng (林香串)
LIM Kek Tjiang (林克昌)
LIM Sui Khiang (林瑞强)
LIN Che Wei (林志伟*)
LIN Qingshan (林青山)
LIN Wanli (林万里)
LING Nanlong (凌南隆)
LING Yunchao (凌云超)
LIONG Sit Yoe (梁锡佑)
LITELNONI, Benny Alexander (李仁强*)
LIU Chun Wai (廖春慧)
LIU Jinduan (刘金端)
LIU Nam Sian (刘南先*)
LIU Yaozeng (刘耀曾)
LIYANTO, Abraham Paul (李树宝)
LOE Ping Kian (吕炳建)
LOHANDA, Mona (赖模娜*)
LUKITA, Enggartiasto (卢尤英)
LUNANDI, Andy (吴伦安*)
LYMAN, Susanta (李尚大)

M

MAH Soo Lay (马树礼)
MANANSANG, Jensen (蔡亚声)
MARCHING, Soe Tjen (黄淑贞*)
MARGA T. (蔡良珠)
MASAGUNG (蒋维泰)
MOCKTAR, Brilian (莫壮亮)
MULJADI (翁振祥)
MULJADI, Kartini (许芬尼*)
MURDAYA, Siti Hartati (邹丽英)

N

Naga, Dali Santun (杨元利)
NG Sim Kie (吴慎机)
NIO Joe Lan (梁友兰)
NIO Peng Liong (梁炳农)
NIO, Threes (梁丽丝*)
NJOO Cheong Seng (杨众生)
NJOO Han Siang (杨汉祥)
NOTOWIDJOJO, Suhendro (施先汉*)
NURIMBA, Adil A. (林英怀)
NURSALIM, Sjamsul (林德祥)

O

OE Siang Djie (邬祥如*)
OEI Gee Hwat (黄义发)
OEI Hui Lan (黄惠兰)
OEI Ik Tjoe (黄奕住)
OEI Jong Tjioe (黄涌洲)
OEI Kie Hok (黄基福*)
OEI Liong Thay (黄隆泰)
OEI Tiong Ham (黄仲涵)

OEI Tjoe Tat (黄自达)
OEI Tjong Hauw (黄宗孝)
OEI Tjong Ie (黄宗诒)
OEI Tjong Swan (黄宗宣)
OEN Tek Hian (温德玄)
OEN Tjhing Tiauw (温清兆*)
OETOMO, Dede (温忠孝)
OEY An Siok (黄安淑)
OEY-GARDINER, Mayling (黄美玲)
OEY Hay Djoen (黄海春)
OEY Hong Lee (黄丰礼)
OEY Hong Tjiauw (黄丰朝*)
OEY Kian Hoei (黄强辉)
OEY Kim Tiang (黄金长)
OEY Liang Lee, Paulus Ignatius (黄良礼*)
OEY Tiang Tjoei (黄长水)
OEY Tong Pin (黄东平)
OJONG, Petrus Kanisius (欧阳炳昆)
ONG, Charles (王查理*)
ONG Eng Die (王永利)
ONG Hok Ham (王福涵)
ONG Hok Lan (王福兰)
ONG Liang Kok (王良国)
ONG Siang Tjoen (王祥春)
ONG Siong Tjie (王尚志)
ONG Tjoe Kim (王梓琴)

P

PANGESTU, Mari Elka (冯慧兰)
PANGESTU, Prajogo (彭云鹏)
PANGLAYKIM, Jusuf (冯来金)
PATROS, Asmin (戴运明)
PHOA Keng Hek (潘景赫)

PHOA Liong Gie (潘良义)
POEY Kok Gwan (方国源*)
POO, Murdaya Widyawimarta (傅志宽)
POUW Kioe An (包求安)
PRAWIROHUSODO (叶基忠)
PRIBADI, Henry (林运豪)
PURNOMO, Nurdin (吴能彬)

Q

QIU Zheng'ou (丘正欧)

R

RAHARDJA, Hendra (陈子兴)
RAHARDJA, Subur (林新水*)
RAHMANATA, A.M. (王宗孝*)
RAO Jian (饶简)
RIADY, James Tjahaja (李白)
RIADY, Mochtar (李文正)
RIDWAN, Ignatius (黄佐音*)

S

SADELI, Eddy (李祥胜)
SALIM, Anthony (林逢生)
SALIM, Soedono (林绍良)
SAMPOERNA, Putera (林天宝)
SANJAYA, Christiandy (黄汉山)
SASANASURYA (丘思谦)
SATJADININGRAT, TKP (陈庆宝*)
SETIABUDI, Natan (陈忠延*)
SETIAWAN, Chandra (黄金泉)
SETIAWAN, Daniel Budi (何明良)

SETIONO, Benny Gatot (许天堂)
Shannu (陈展湖)
SHEN Demin (沈德民)
SIAUW Giok Bie (萧玉美)
SIAUW Giok Tjhan (萧玉灿)
SIAUW Tik Kwie (萧德贵)
SIDHARTA, Myra (欧阳春梅)
SIDHARTA, Priguna (薛碧玉)
SIE Boen Lian (施文连)
SIE, Peter (施添宜*)
SIE Tjin Gwan (施振源*)
SIEM Piet Nio (沈泌娘)
SILALAHI, Harry Tjan (曾春福)
SIM Ki Ay (沈基爱)
SINDHUNATHA, Kristoforus (王宗海)
SOE Hok Gie (史福义)
SOE Lie-Piet (史立笔)
SOEGIARTO, Lita (林丽达*)
SOEJATMIKO, Basuki (林福良)
SOEMANTO, Agoes (陈盛发)
SOERYADJAYA, William (谢建隆)
SOESASTRO, M. Hadi (陈月明)
SOETANTYO, Tegoeh (陈恭立)
SOETO Meisen (司徒眉生)
SOETO Tjan (司徒赞)
SONG Zhongquan (宋中铨)
SUDIN (蔡瑞龙)
SUDJATMIKO, Djoko (李玉孝)
SUDJATMIKO, Prasasto (李玉道)
SULINDRO, Be (马须铃)
SUNUR, Eliaser Yentji (孙炳炎*)
SUPRANA, Jaya (潘国昌)
SUPRATIKNO, Hendrawan (黄正德)
SURIPTO, Ateng (许正理*)

SURYADI, Petrus Aang (洪贤良*)
SURYAWAN, Yoza (杨兆骥)
SUSANTI, Susi Lucia Francisca (王莲香)
SUSANTO, T.L. (林冠玉)
SUTANU, Tommie (陈炳煌)
SUTRISNO, Slamet (朱迪发)
SUWONDO, Gani (李源利)

T

Tahir (翁俊民)
TAN Beng Yauw (陈明耀*)
TAN Boen Aan (陈文安)
TAN Boen Kim (陈文金)
TAN Boen Soan (陈文宣)
TAN Eng Hoa (陈英华)
TAN Eng Hong (陈英丰*)
TAN Eng Tie (陈英智)
TAN Giok Sin (陈玉信)
TAN Goan Po (陈源宝)
TAN Hin Hie (陈兴砚)
TAN Hoe Teng (陈富定)
TAN Hong Boen (陈丰文)
TAN Hwat Tiang (陈发长*)
TAN Joe Hok (陈友福)
TAN Kang So (陈江苏)
TAN Kian Lok (陈建禄)
TAN Kim Bo (1872–1935) (陈金茂*)
TAN Kim Hong (陈金丰)
TAN Kim Kian (陈金建)
TAN Kim San (陈金山)
TAN Koen Swie (陈群瑞*)
TAN Kong Tam (陈光谭*)
TAN Liep Tjiauw (陈立超*)

TAN Ling Djie (陈燊如)
TAN, Mely G. (陈玉兰)
TAN Pia Teng (陈丙定)
TAN Ping Liem (陈炳林*)
TAN Ping Tjiat (陈秉节)
TAN Po Goan (陈宝源)
TAN Siang Lian (陈祥连)
TAN Siong Kie (陈祥基)
TAN, Sofyan (陈金扬)
TAN Swan Bing (陈宣明)
TAN Tek Heng (陈德恒)
TAN Tek Ho (陈德和)
TAN Tek Peng (陈泽炳)
TAN Tik Sioe Sian (陈德修仙)
TAN Tiong Khing (陈忠庆)
TAN Tjeng Bok (陈清木)
TAN Tjien Lien (陈振霖)
TAN Tjoen Hay (陈春海*)
TANDIONO, Ki Anan (陈建安)
TANNOS, W.P.A. (杨伟彬)
TANOESOEDIBJO, Hary (陈明立)
TANOTO, Latif Harris (陈龙虎)
TANOTO, Sukanto (陈江河)
TANUDJAJA, Sukanta (陈大江)
TANUWIBOWO, Budi S. (陈清明)
TANSIL, Eddy (陈子煌)
TANZIL, Haris Otto Kamil (陈添福)
TEDJOSUWITO (郑俊瑞*)
TENG, Benny (邓通力)
TENG Sioe Hie (邓寿喜*)
THE Goan Tjoan (郑源全*)
THE Hong Oe (郑宏宇)
THE Kian Sing (郑坚成)
THE Liang Gie (郑良义)

List of Prominent Indonesian Chinese   xxxiii

THE Neng King (郑年锦)
THE Sin Tjo (郑信作*)
THE Teng Chun (郑登俊)
THEE Kian Wie (戴建伟)
THIO In Lok (张印禄*)
THIO Soei Sen (张瑞生)
THIO Thiam Tjong (张添聪)
THIO Tiauw Siat (张肇燮)
THIO Tjin Boen (张振文)
THUNG Ju Lan (汤友兰)
THUNG Liang Lee (汤良礼)
THUNG Liang Tjay (汤良才*)
THUNG Sin Nio, Betsy (汤新娘)
THUNG Tjeng Hiang (汤清香*)
TILAAR, Martha (徐培玉*)
TIO Hian Sioe (赵贤修*)
TIO Ie Soei (赵雨水)
TIO Kiang Sun (赵江顺*)
TIO Oen Bik (赵温毕)
TJAHAJA PURNAMA, Basuki (钟万学)
TJAHAJA PURNAMA, Basuri (钟万友)
TJAHJADI, Robby (施佳宜*)
TJAN Ing Djiu (曾荧球)
TJAN Kiem Bie (曾金美*)
TJAN Som Hay (曾森海*)
TJAN Tian Soe (曾天赐)
TJAN Tjoe Siem (曾祖沁)
TJAN Tjoe Som (曾祖森)
TJANDINEGARA, Wilson (陈冬龙)
TJEN Djin Tjong (曾仁宗*)
TJEN, Rudianto (曾昭真)
TJHIE Tjay Ing (Hs) (徐再英)
TJHO Lian Sin (曹联信)
TJIA Eng Tong (谢英堂*)

TJIA Giok Thwan (谢玉端)
TJIA, May On (谢梅安)
TJIA Tjeng Siang (谢清祥*)
TJIAM Djoe Khiam, Fredericus Christophorus (詹裕谦)
TJIO Tiang Soey (蒋长瑞*)
TJIOK San Fang, Elsie (石圣芳)
TJIPUTRA (徐振焕)
TJOA Hin Hoey (Mrs) (郭悦娘)
TJOA Keng Loan, Effie (蔡庆鸾)
TJOA Sie Hwie (蔡锡辉)
TJOA Sik Ien (蔡锡胤)
TJOA Tjie Liang (蔡志良)
TJOE Bou San (朱茂山)
TJOE Siauw Hoei (朱晓辉*)
TJOENG Lin Sen (钟林生*)
TJOENG Tin Jan (钟鼎远)
TJOKROSAPUTRO, Handoko (郭汉将*)
TJOKROSAPUTRO, Kasom (郭森作*)
TJONG A Fie (张耀轩)
TJONG Hioen Nji (章勋义)
TJONG Jong Hian (张榕轩)
TJOO Tik Tjoen (曹德崇)
TJUI, Maria (崔妙)
TJUNG See Gan (庄西言)
TJUNTJUN (梁俊俊*)
TONG Djoe (唐裕)
TONG, Stephen (唐崇荣)
TSAI, Frans (蔡华喜)

U

UMBOH, Wim (林炎荣*)
URAY, Burhan (黄双安)
UTOMO, Tirto (柯新标)

W

WAHYUDI, Johan (洪友良)
WANANDI, (Albertus) Sofjan (林绵昆)
WANANDI, Jusuf (林绵基)
WANG Jiyuan (王纪元)
WANG Renshu (王任叔)
WEN Bei'ou (温悲鸥)
WEN, Tony (温金道*)
WIBISONO, Christianto (黄建国)
WIDJAJA, Eka Tjipta (黄奕聪)
WIDJAJA, Mira (黄美拉*)
WIDJAYA, Tjiangdra (黄松长)
WIDYONO, Benny (黄鸿栏)
WIJAYA, Eko (刘顺严)
WIJAYA, Nancy (马咏南)
WIJAYAKUSUMA, Hembing (张鑫铭)
WINARTA, Frans Hendra (陈贤伟)
WINATA, Tomy (郭说锋)
WIRANATA, Ardi (王阿迪*)
WISAKSANA, Panji (潘万鑫)
WITARSA, Endang (林顺佑*)
WONGSOREDJO, mBah (白邦英)
WONGSOSEPUTERA, Jusuf (王振龙*)
WONOWIDJOJO, Surya (蔡云辉)
WONOWIDJOJO, Susilo (蔡道平)
WU Weikang (吴伟康)
WUISAN, Empie (李瑞华)
WULLUR, Jahja (黄振山*)

X

XIE Zuoshun (谢佐舜)
XIE Zuoyu (谢佐禹)

XU Baozhang (徐保璋)
XU Huazhang (徐华璋)
XU Juqing (徐琚清)
XU Zhongming (许仲铭)

Y

YAN Weizhen (严唯真)
YANG Xinrong (杨新容)
YANG Xiulian (杨秀莲)
YAP A Siong (叶亚祥)
YAP Hong Tjoen (叶鸿俊)
YAP Lip Keng (叶立庚)
YAP Loen (叶仑*)
YAP Thiam Hien (叶添兴)
YAP Tjoen Soe (叶存渭)
YAP Tjwan Bing (叶全明)
YAP Yun Hap (叶运合)
YAPUTRA, Albert S. (叶锦标)
YEO Kuei-pin (杨圭斌)
YO Heng Kam (杨恒甘*)
YO Soen Bie (杨纯美)
YOE Tjoe Ping (游子平)
YOUNG, Fifi (陈金娘)
YUAN Ni (袁霓)

Z

ZHANG Guoji (张国基)
ZHANG Zhan'en (张沾恩)
ZHANG Zhusan (张祝三)
ZHENG Roumi'ou (柔密欧·郑)
ZOU Fangjin (邹访今)

A Hok. See **TJAHAJA PURNAMA, Basuki**

A WU (阿五; LI Weikang 李伟康, 1911–2002)
Chinese writer, Schoolteacher, Hakka

A Wu (The Fifth) was the pen-name of Li Weikang. Born in Jakarta (Batavia) in July 1911 to a Hakka migrant family, his young parents moved to Batavia (now Jakarta) when he was a child. His parents opened a *warung* (small grocery shop) in Chinatown. A Wu, a fifth child in the family, completed his primary Chinese school education in Jakarta, and returned to China to study at Jimei school (Amoy), and later entered the Sun Yat Sen University (Guangzhou) to study chemistry. Due to economic difficulty, he did not finish his tertiary education and returned to Jakarta to work as a schoolteacher. He taught at Pah Tsung High School for ten over years and stopped teaching in 1966 when all Chinese schools were closed down.

He began to write in Chinese newspapers such as *Xin Bao* (新报), *Shenghuo Bao* (生活报) and monthly magazine *Zhongxue Sheng* (Secondary School Students 中学生). When he reached eighty years of age, i.e. in the 1990s, he started to publish numerous short stories and essays depicting Indonesian Chinese society. It is interesting to note that towards the end of Soeharto rule, Indonesian Chinese writers started to write again and published their works, but most of these works were published overseas as Chinese publications were still banned in Indonesia. Not surprisingly all of A Wu's books, four in total, were published by Huoyi (获益) Publishing in Hong Kong. These are: *Pu Man* (*Piggy Bank* 扑满, 1993), *Xingzi* (*Apricot* 杏子, 1994), *Hong Shanhu de Gushi* (*The Story of Red Coral* 红珊瑚的故事, 1995) and *Ren yue huanghun hou*

(*Love in the Evening* 人约黄昏后, 1997). Apparently there is a mixture of old and new works in the books but the majority appears to be new. Unfortunately, A Wu did not indicate the year of his writing in the books and this makes it difficult for researchers to study his works. One literary critic noted that A Wu was the most productive Chinese writer of the old generation who is next to Huang Dongping (**OEI Tong Pin**).

Sources: The above-mentioned books; A Wu 阿五, "Wo de xiaozhuan" ("我的小传"), in his *Hong Shanhu de Gushi* (红珊瑚的故事, 1995), pp. 128–57; Dong Rui 东瑞, *Liujin Jijie* (流金季节, 2000), pp. 117–19; Li Zhuohui 李卓辉, *Yinhua xiezuojingying fendou fengyu rensheng* (印华写作精英奋斗风雨人生,2010), p. 175.

Abah ANTON. See **ANTON, Abah**
Abdul HADI W.M. See **HADI, Abdul W.M.**
Abdul KARIM. See **KARIM, Hadji Abdul**

ABDUSSOMAD, H. See **YAP A. Siong**
ABITURIENT. See **GOH Tjing Hok**
Abraham Paul LIYANTO. See **LIYANTO, Abraham Paul**

ADIDHARMA (LIE Eng Liong; LI Yonglong 李永隆, 1930-)
Musician

Born in Jakarta on 25 May 1930, son of Lie Soen Liang (a music teacher), Lie Eng Liong studied at the Conservatory of Music in Amsterdam, majoring in violin and graduated cum laude in 1956. Upon his return to Indonesia, he was appointed Concertmaster of Radio Jakarta-Violin Orchestra. He was appointed Conductor of the RRI Orchestra in 1959, and a member of the Arts Council of the City of Jakarta in 1968. Between 1961 and 1985, he was the leader of Orkes Simfoni Jakarta (Jakarta Symphony Orchestra).

Sources: *TIM*, p. 19; *Apa & Siapa 1985–86*, pp. 21–22; the compiler's notes.

Adil ISMANTO. See **TAN Boen Aan**
Adil NURIMBA. See **NURIMBA, Adil**

ADMADJAJA, Usman (RAO Yaowu 饶耀武, 1946-)
Banker

Born at Tanjungkarang (Lampung) on 3 May 1946, his father Njauw (Rao in Mandarin) Pin Tiong was a small businessman. Yaowu (after 1966 known as Usman) had his primary school education in his hometown but went to Jakarta for his secondary education. He graduated in 1965 from Pah Tsung (Pa Chung, also known as Ya Zhong), a Chinese-language high school in Jakarta. After graduation he studied medicine at Tarumanegara University for a short while. He had to discontinue his education because of economic difficulty.

According to *Apa & Siapa*, Usman began to run his own business in 1966. He established UD Apollo and became the supplier of clothes to PD Fadjar Bhakti, which later became the state company PN Satia Niaga. Then through PN Satia Niaga, Usman became the supplier of clothes, food, and other family appliances to Shell. The business expanded and UD Apollo became PT Kaliraya Sari, specializing in harbour construction. In 1976 he took over Bank Persatuan Indonesia, which was renamed Bank Danamon. In 1986 the bank had eleven branches in Indonesia with 500 staff members. He took over Wisma Sandang Sarana, a big textile company in Bandung. With the help of Citibank, Usman also took over the distribution of Pepsi Cola in both Jakarta and Surabaya. About the same time, he also took over Tungsram, a bulb manufacturer, and PT Bintang Raya, a military boots factory.

According to *Forbes Zibenjia*, in 1981 Bank Asia Afrika merged with Bank Danamon. In 1988 the bank obtained a licence to trade in foreign currencies and went public the following year. It expanded its business overseas, and entered into partnership with a South Korean Bank. In March 1995

Usman was awarded the Satya Lencana Kebaktian Sosial medal for his contribution in building low-cost flats for Jakarta residents.

In the 1997–98 Financial Crisis, Donamon was badly hit by the crisis. It was taken over by the government and recapitalized by the Indonesian Central Bank. Usman was also forced to step down.

Sources: *Apa & Siapa 1985–86*, pp. 27–28; *Forbes Zibenjia*, July 1994, p. 28; *Shijie Huaren Fuhao Bang*, p. 224; *Dananews*, July 1955, p. 48; the compiler's notes.

Ahok. See **TJAHAJA PURNAMA, Basuki**
Al Huina. See **ERVINNA**
Alan BUDIKUSUMA. See **BUDIKUSUMA, Alan**
Albert YAPUTRA S. See **YAPUTRA, Albert S**

ALI, Mohammad (LIE Kiat Teng; LI Jiedeng 李杰登, 1912–90)
Politician, physician, Muslim

Born in Sukabumi on 17 August 1912, he graduated from NIAS (Surabaya) as a physician. After graduation he worked as a government doctor in Curup and Bengkulu, then as a doctor to a mining company at Rejang Lebong. He later served as the director of the Central Planters Hospital in Waringin Tiga. During the Japanese Occupation, he served as the head of the government Health Division. After Indonesia's independence, he was appointed a *dokter keresidenan* (county doctor) in Palembang. He later resigned and went into private practice. In 1946 he was converted to Islam and changed his name to Mohammad Ali. He later became the head of the economic section in the PSII. During the period 1953–55, he was appointed as Minister of Health. According to one report, he later established Rumah Sakit Mohammad Husni in Palembang to serve the local population.

Sources: *Kempen, KP*, p. 33; Li Zhuohui, *Qingshan bulau haoqi changcun* (2008), p. 88.

ALIM, Markus (LIN Wenguang 林文光, 1951-)
Entrepreneur, community leader

Born on 24 September 1951 in Surabaya, Alim Markus is better known in the Chinese-speaking community as Lin Wenguang. He went to a local Chinese school and after receiving only junior school education; he quit school at the age of fifteen to help his father run the family's factory which produced aluminium kitchenware.

At the age of twenty, Alim Markus managed to convince his father to expand the business and succeeded in establishing PT Maspion, with its Chinese names as Jin Feng (金锋 or golden peak) in 1971. Maspion is an acronym for "Mengajak Anda Selalu Percaya Industri Olahan Nasional" (Inviting you to put your trust in national industrial products). He is currently president-director of PT Maspion and Maspion Group which produces plastic ware, glassware, and electrical home appliances. The company has four industrial sites, sixty factories and employs 30,000 people. He and his family were listed in *Forbes* (2006) at no. 38 of "Indonesia's 40 Richest".

Alim Markus has also been active in politics and local Chinese organizations. It was reported that he was an economic consultant to President Abudurrahman Wahid (Gus Dur) as well as consultant to Speaker of the House Agung Laksono. He is the general chairman of the Indonesian Federation of Fuqing Associations (印尼福清社团总会). He also served as the general chairman of the Indonesian Fuqing (Hokchia) Organization, general chairman of the Indonesian Lim Surname Association and permanent honorary chairman of the Indonesian Hakka Association.

Sources: Leo Suryadinata, "Alim, Markus", Suryadinata, ed., *Southeast Asian Personalities*, pp. 7–9; "Alumnus in Conversation: Mr Alim Markus", 29 February 2008; *Quanqiu Jiechu Huaren Huazhuan* (2011), pp. 56–61.

Alvin LIE. See **LIE Ling Piao, Alvin**

AMIEN, Muhammad (CHEN Zhenwen 陈振文, 1937–2014)
Social/political activist, Muslim

Born in Ciawi, West Java, in 1937 (one say 1928), he received Chinese education. He was later converted to Islam. In April 1980, together with Dr KH EZ Muttaqin, a Muslim scholar in Bandung, he established Keluarga Persaudaraan Islam (KPI Jabar), a Muslim Friendship Association, advocating Islam among Chinese Indonesians but at the same time promoting harmony between Chinese and indigenous Indonesians. In 1998 he joined PAN and served as the chairman for the West Java region. He read and wrote Chinese. He was also active in promoting the study of Chinese language in Indonesia. He died in Bandung on 1 May 2014.

Sources: Zhou Nanjing, *Quaqiao Huaren baike quanshu*, pp. 94–95; <http://blog.sina.com.cn/s/blog_5edd46a70100gee7.html> (accessed 26 June 2014); "Tokoh Muslim keturunan M. Amien, Wafat", *Pikiran Rakyat*, Pikiran Rakyat Online (accessed 26 June 2014).

Anang SATYAWARDAYA. See **TJOA Tjie Liang**

ANANTA, Aris (TAN Lian Hou; CHEN Lianhu 陈连虎, 1954-)
Economist and Demographer

Born in Klaten, Central Java on 26 November 1954, he is son of a local businessman. Ananta received his primary school (SD) and junior high school (SMP) education in Christian schools in his birthplace. He moved to a state school, still in Klaten, for his senior high school (SMA) education and graduated in 1972. He was admitted to the University of Indonesia and obtained a B.A. degree in Economics in 1975. In 1978 he got an Msc degree in Social-Economic Statistics from George Washington Universy (USA). He finished his PhD in 1983 from the Duke University (USA) after submitting his dissertation entitled "An Economic Model of Fertility Behavior in Developing Countries: An Indonesian Case".

He joined the Department of Economics, University of Indonesia (FEUI), after returning from the States. He also served as a senior researcher at the Lembaga Demografi (Institute of Demography) at FEUI. In 1995 he was promoted to full professor and became the youngest full professor at UI. His inaugural speech was "Transisi kependudukan di Indonesia: Beberapa masalah dan prospek perekonomian" [Population transition in Indonesia: a few problems and the economic prospect]. From 1988 to 1991, he was head of the research section at FEUI, and between 1992–95, head of the Population Information Section and between 1995 and 1997, he served as the deputy head of the Institute of Demography. Between 1996 and 1998, he was also appointed as the coordinator of the post graduate degree programme at FEUI.

In 1999–2000 he joined the Department of Economics (NUS) as a senior fellow. Since 2001 he is a senior research fellow at ISEAS. He has written and edited many books while at ISEAS, including: *Ethnicity and Religion in a Changing Political Landscape* (2003), *Indonesian Electoral Behaviour: A Statistical Perspective* (2004) and *Emerging Democracy in Indonesia* (2005), all of which were co-authored with Leo Suryadinata and Evi Nurvidya Arifin. His more recent publications are related to the aging population and labour.

Sources: Interview (February 2013); the above-mentioned books.

Andy LUNANDI. See **LUNANDI, Andy**

ANG Ban Tjiong (1910–38) 洪万昌*
Poet

Ang Ban Tjiong was born in Makassar. He received his HCS education in his birthplace. After graduation he worked in a magazine *Favoriet* which was owned by his uncle. However, the magazine did not last long, he then moved to work in the *Pembrita Makassar* as a journalist. He wrote many short stories and articles on theosophy, using his pen-name Mendoesin. Ang was talented. He was able to play all sorts of musical instruments, including piano, violin, and *kecapi* Bugis (Buginese harp). He was also good in tennis and acrobatic sports. However, his greatest achievement was his poems written in the local language (Malay mixed with Makassarese). These poems were very popular and until the 1980s, his poems were still recited/sung by many local entertainers in Makassar. However, Ang had a drinking problem. He said that he rellied on alchoholic drink in order to get inspiration. After a few glasses of drink he was able to sing for the whole night. He died at the age of twenty-eight and left with a collection of his poems entitled *Pantoen Melajoe Makassar*, which consist of 200 Malay-Makassarese poems.

Source: Myra Sidharta, *Dari Penjaja Tekstil Sampai Superwoman* (Jakarta: KPG, 2004), pp. 109–11.

ANG Hian Liang. See **SURYADI, Petrus Aang**

ANG Jan Goan (HONG Yuanyuan 洪渊源, 1894–1984)
Community leader, newspaperman

Born in Bandung on 25 May 1894, he had a good command of Malay, Dutch, English, and, to some extent, Chinese. Ang first went to a Malay school, then to a THHK school in his birthplace. After finishing his primary education, he was awarded a scholarship and continued his schooling at the JNXT in China. However, before he could complete his secondary education, the 1911 Revolution broke out. He returned to Java and became a schoolteacher, teaching at a THHK school in West Java and involving himself in the THHK organization.

Ang was introduced to **TJOE Bou San** in 1918 when the former was still a schoolteacher, and they later became good friends. In 1922 Ang eventually left the THHK school and joined the editorial board of *Sin Po*. In November 1925, Tjoe died suddenly and **KWEE Kek Beng** took over his place as the editor-in-chief while Ang became the director. Ang maintained the position until *Sin Po* ceased publication in 1959. In 1960 he established the Surya Prabha publishing company, which published *Warta Bhakti*, an influential left-wing daily in Jakarta. The newspaper was closed in October 1965. Ang became very ill and eventually retired. In 1967 he migrated to Canada to join his sons. He died in Toronto in 1984. During his stay in Canada he completed his memoirs in English. Although the English version was not yet published, its Chinese translation entitled *Hong Yuanyuan Zizhuan* (洪渊源自传) came out in 1989 in Beijing. It was slightly revised and republished in 2010. Its Indonesian version (*Memoar Ang Yan Goan*) was published by Yayasan Nabil in 2009.

Ang was one of the major figures in Chinese communities. He was a leading member of various Chinese organizations (especially *peranakan* organizations) such as the THHK (Jakarta), Siang Hwee (Jakarta), Persatuan Tionghoa, and the PDTI. He was elected as the treasurer of Baperki when it was established in 1954.

Sources: Tan, *Tionghoa*, p. 186; Kwee, *Wartawan*, pp. 24, 107–8; *Sin Po*, 15 March 1954; *Zhongcheng Bao*, 25 May 1964; *Who's Who in China* (1936), p. 117; Ang Jan Goan's memoirs, the compiler's notes.

ANG Tjiang Liat 洪昌烈*
Community leader, local prosecutor

Originally from Banjarmasin, Kalimantan, Ang worked as a prosecutor (*jaksa*) in Den Pasar, Bali, where he joined Baperki and served as a member of Baperki's Bali-Lombok regional council. In 1957 he served as a member of the DPR representing Baperki.

Sources: Somers, dissertation, p. 153; *Keng Po*, 12 January 1957.

ANG Tjin Siang. See **MULJADI**
ANG Yu Liang. See **WAHYUDI, Johan**

ANGKOSUBROTO, Dasuki (GOW Swie Kie; WU Ruiji 吴瑞基, 1921-)
Tycoon

Born in Malang in 1921, he was involved in the import of rice and other agricultural products. After linking his business with BULOG (National Logistic Board), which was headed by General Bustanil Arifin, Gow's company, Gunung Sewu, later diversified into finance, consultation, and construction. He also owns PT Indo Sanggar Pacific Leasing Corporation, a joint venture with Ayala Philippina, and PT Califa Pratama, a consultant firm in planning and construction. Gow's group has succeeded in building various impressive shopping/office complexes such as Wisma Gunung Sewu and the Chase Plaza. The group also has linkages with the Harapan Group and the Bangkok Bank. Gow is assisted by his sons who were trained in the West.

Sources: *Expo* 2, no. 1 (4 January 1984): 17–18; *Shijie Huaren Fuhao Bang*, p. 229; Setyautama, *Tokoh-tokoh etnis TH*, pp. 62–63.

ANTON, Abah (Mohammad ANTON, GOEI Hing An, 1965-) 魏兴安*
Mayor of Malang, businessman, Muslim

Born on 31 December 1965 in East Java, he graduated from SMK YP 17-2, a state high school in Malang. He was once a taxi driver but later became a successful businessman dealing with sugar cane products. He is the owner of PT Chandra Wijaya Sakti and chairman of Persatuan Islam Tionghoa Indonesia (PITI), a Chinese Muslim organization, Malang Branch. In 2013 he formed a team with Sutiaji, a local PKB leader, contesting the election of Malang's mayor and deputy mayor against three other pairs of candidates. His pair was supported by NU (PKB) and Gerindra and succeeded in defeating the other candidates who were supported by Golkar, PAN and Partai Demokrat. His pair won 47 per cent of the total votes and was elected as mayor-deputy mayor of Malang for five years (2013–18). Before election, he promised to develop the city and also donated his salary to charity organizations.

Sources: "Pertama kali, wali kotaMalang dari etnis Tionghoa", Tempo.Co., 5 October 2013; "Abah Anton Resmi Menang, 35 Persen Golput", *Malang Post*, 5 October 2013.

ARBI, Haryanto (1972-) 洪阿比*
Badminton player

Born on 21 January 1972 in Kudus, his Chinese surname is Ang (or Hong 洪 in Mandarin). Chinese newspapers in Singapore refer to him as Hong Abi. He played the first men's singles in the Thomas Cup Competition in 1994 and defeated Rashid Sidek of Malaysia. He also won the men's singles in the Asian Games XII (1994) in Hiroshima. Abi was well-known for his powerful smash.

Sources: *Media Karya*, June 1994, p. 54; *Zaobao*, 11 May 1994, p. 22; *Sunday Times* (Singapore), 16 October 1994.

Ardi WIRANATA. See WIRANATA, Ardi
Arief BUDIMAN. See BUDIMAN, Arief
Arief HUSNI. See HUSNI, Arief

ARIEF, Jackson (THUNG Thay Tung, 1949-) 汤泰动*
Film Producer, entrepreneur

Born in Jakarta on September 1949, he received his primary school (Chung Shan, 1961) and middle school (Sin Wen, 1964) education in Jakarta. While still in the first year of secondary school, he helped in a shop selling tape recorders. In 1976 he became a film producer. He cooperated with Sjamsuddin Sjafi'i, an Indonesian movie director, to produce local films starring Rhoma Irama. Arief is the general director of Jackson Film Production, and from 1977 the general director of Jackson Records and Tapes. His records company has produced many local talents such as Ebiet G. Ade, Franky and Jane, and Vina Panduwinata. Arief has been active in Buddhist associations. He has served as chairman of the Pluit branch of Majelis Agama Buddha Niciren Syosu Indonesia since 1977.

Source: *Apa & Siapa 1985–86*, pp. 80–81.

ARIF, Junus Nur. See **NIO Joe Lan**
Aris ANANTA. See **ANANTA, Aris**
ARSADJAJA, Jani. See **TJOENG Tin Jan**
Asmaraman SUKOWATI. See **KHO Ping Hoo**
Asmin PATROS. See **PATROS, Asmin**
ATENG. See **SURIPTO, Ateng**
AUWJONG Peng Koen. See **OJONG, Petrus Kanisius**

AW Tjoei Lan (OU Cuilan 区翠兰, better known as Mrs LIE Tjian Tjoen, 李前俊夫人; also known as OUW Tjoei Lan; 1889–1965)
Social-worker, community leader

Born in Majalengka on 17 February 1889, she began to get involved in social work from 1912. Together with her husband she founded "Ati Sutji", a social institution aimed at helping orphans and deserted children. On 31 August 1935 she was awarded the Ridder Oranje Nassau by the Dutch Government for her contribution to the welfare of unfortunate children and women. She died in Jakarta on 19 December 1965 after leading "Ati Sutji" for fifty-one years.

(**Note:** Tan Hong Boen noted the surname of Mrs Lie Tjian Tjoen as **Ouw**, in fact, the tombstone shows that her surname was Aw.)

Sources: Tan, *Tionghoa*, p. 169; Pringgodigdo and Shadily, eds. (1973), p. 730; *Maandblad Istri*, October 1935, p. 1; Picture of Tombstone provided by Marius Roest, October 2013.

Awal HAN. See **HAN, Awal**

Ba Ren. See **WANG Renshu**
Bahar, BUASAN. See **BUASAN, Bahar**

BAI Bangying. See **WONGSOREDJO, mBah**
Bambang SURYONO. See **LI Zhuohui**
BAO Qiu'an. See **POUW Kioe An**

BARKI, Kiki (JI Qihui 纪琦辉, 1939?-)
Community leader, tycoon, coal producer

Born in Bandung of a Hokchia (fuqing) family, he was educated in a Chinese high school in Bandung. He later went to Beijing and completed his secondary school education before continuing his study at the Mining Academy, also in Beijing. After graduation, he returned to Bandung. He first joined his father's textile factory and hotel, later, his family's banking business. In 1976 he joined his friends to engage in coal business. Eventually he succeeded in establishing the Tanito Harum Company and emerged as a major coal producer in the country.

He was identified by *Forbes* as one of the 40 richest tycoons in Indonesia in 2012. It was reported that his company acquired 50.5 per cent of PT Karya Usaha Mandiri, a coal mining enterprise in East Kalimantan. Barki is chairman of the Hokchia association in Bandung and general chairman of the Indonesian Chinese Chamber of Commerce (印尼中华总商会). He was a member of Yudhoyono's trade delegation to China in July 2005.

Sources: "福布斯公布印尼40富豪榜", <http://www.sinchew-i.com/indonesia/node/21037> (accessed 14 December 2012); <http://www.forbes.com/profile/kiki.bar> (accessed 14 December 2012); "纪辉琦: 煤矿巨子,架设中印经贸彩桥", <http://www.hongqiwang.net/detail12.asp?id=635> (accessed 14 December 2012).

Basuki TJAHAJA PURNAMA. See **TJAHAJA PURNAMA, Basuki**

Basuri TJAHAJA PURNAMA. See **TJAHAJA PURNAMA, Basuri**

BE Kwat Koen (1863–1945) 马厥群*
Community leader, millionaire

Son of a *majoor* and personal friend of Sri Susuhunan Solo and Mangkunegoro VII, he was born in Purworejo on 1 December 1863. After moving to Solo, he was appointed a *kapitein*, and later promoted to a *majoor*. Prior to World War II, he was awarded medals by the governments of China, the Netherlands, Germany, and Thailand. In the 1930s he was appointed as the patron of THHK (Solo). He passed away in 1945.

Source: Tan, *Tionghoa*, p. 128; <http://tionghoa.org/index.php/item/2036-bhe-kwat-koen-1863-1945> (accessed 25 April 2013).

Be SULINDRO. See **SULINDRO, Be**

BE Tiat Tjong (1889-?) 马铁宗*
Community leader, engineer

Born into a banker's family in Semarang on 21 December 1889, he was educated at the ELS (Semarang and Magelang) and the HBS (Semarang), and obtained an Ir degree from the THS (Delft, Holland). While he was a student in the Netherlands, he served as the president of the CHH-Netherlands from 1922 to 1923. He returned to Semarang after his graduation and worked for the Be Biauw Tjwan Bank. In 1927 he served as a member of the preparation committee of the CHH congress in Semarang. In 1928 he was elected as a member of the CHH Central Board. In the 1930s he worked for the local government and was a member of the Semarang Municipal Council.

Sources: Tan, *Tionghoa*, p. 130; Suryadinata, *Peranakan politics*, pp. 49 and 109.

Benny Alexander LITELNONI. See LITELNONI, Benny Alexander
Benny Gatot SETIONO. See SETIONO, Benny Gatot
Benny TENG. See TENG, Benny
Benny WIDYONO. See WIDYONO, Benny
Bhikku Ashin JINARAKKHITA. See JINARAKKHITA, Bhikku Ashin
Bingky IRAWAN. See IRAWAN, Bingky
BOE Beng Tjoe. See OEY An Siok
Boediharto HALIM. See HALIM, Boediharto
BOEN Kim (Kin) To. See WEN, Tony

BONG A Lok (also known as Suwandi HAMID; ONG Ah Lok; WANG Yalu 王亚禄, 1918–78)
Community leader, businessman, Hokchia
Born in Putian, Fujian in 1918, he first went to Lampung, Sumatra before World War II, engaging in the export of agricultural products. He was the president of the CHTH (Jakarta) in the 1950s. He assisted **KWEE Bie Sin** to establish *Zhonghua Shangbao* and served as a deputy director. In 1958 he was detained by the Indonesian authorities for his active role in the KMT. He became active again after the 1965 coup. Since 1968 he served as a member of the Presidium of the IBC (Jakarta) and the vice-president of the NDC (Jakarta). He was the director of Bank Dirgahaju (formerly Datong Yinhang, Jakarta) from the 1950s. In September 1968 he represented the NDC at the 6th Overseas Chinese Merchants' Congress in Tokyo. He died in Singapore in 1978.

Sources: *Ribao*, 20 September 1968; *Yinni Zainan* (1959), p. 24; Jiang, "Yajiada", p. 15; *Directory of Chinese Names*, p. 104; *Huaqiao Dacidian*, p. 794.

BONG Hong San. See SANJAYA, Christiandy
BONG Sun On. See URAY, Burhan
BONG Swan An. See URAY, Burhan
BONG Tjhai Bun. See BUASAN, Bahar

Brilian MOCKTAR. See **MOCKTAR, Brilian**

BUASAN, Bahar (BONG Tjhai Bun, 1964-) 黄才文*
Member of DPD, Catholic

Born on 25 March 1964 in Pangkal Pinang, he obtained a Bachelor degree from the Faculty of Technology, Sekolah Tinggi Teknologi Mandala Bandung (2006). He served as director of PT Harlie Kreasi Pratama Bandung (since 1994), commissioner of PT Harlie Farma, Jakarta (since 2005) and president director of PT Harlie Trevelindo, Bandung (since 2007). He was also general chairman of the Indonesian Bandung Management Association (2007–10). He was elected as a member of DPD for Bangka Belting (2009–14) and attempted to contest again for the 2014–19 term but failed.

Sources: *Wajah DPR & DPD 2009–14*, p. 615; Pengurus Pusat Fordeka, *Buku Acuan 2014*, p. 110; the compiler's notes.

Bubi CHEN. See **CHEN, Bubi**
Budi DIPOJUWONO. See **DIPOJUWONO, Budi**
Budis S. TANUWIBOWO. See **TANUWIBOWO, Budis**

BUDIANTA, Melani (TAN Tjiok Sien, 1954-) 陈石芯*
Academic, researcher

Born in 1954 in Malang, Budianta began her career as a volunteer teacher while still pursuing her Bachelor's degree in English Literature at the University of Indonesia. She went on to obtain her master's degree and doctorate in the United States before teaching at the University of Indonesia. She continued to write articles and conduct workshops on teaching Indonesian culture. Her research interests are mainly on gender, ethnicity and the Chinese cultural identity. She is the first Chinese-Indonesian woman to become professor of the School of Humanities (FIB) at the University of Indonesia in 2006.

She has published and presented more than 100 articles and conference papers throughout her career on topics such as Feminism, Postcolonial Studies and Multiculturalism. She is recognized internationally through her trainings, workshops and seminars. Her love and affinity for Indonesian culture have driven her to become a dedicated Indonesian educator and scholar. Budianta is currently professor and head of the University of Indonesia's literary department in the School of Humanities.

Source: Aimee Dawis, "Budianta, Melani", Suryadinata, ed., *Southeast Asian Personalities* (2012), pp. 40–42.

BUDIKUSUMA, Alan (WEI Renfang 魏仁芳, 1968-)
Badminton player

Born on 29 March 1968 in Surabaya, he was the champion of the Germany Open (1992), Indonesia Open (1993), and World Cup (1993). He also took the championship in the Olympic Badminton Competition (1992). He is married to **Susi SUSANTI**, who won the women's singles in the 1992 Olympics.

Sources: *Media Karya*, June 1994, p. 52; *Zaobao*, 13 May 1994, p. 32; *Sejumlah Orang Bulutangkis Indonesia* (1994), pp. 23–25.

BUDIMAN, Arief (SOE Hok Djin; SHI Furen 史福仁, 1941-)
Political activist, public intellectual, writer, psychologist-sociologist, elder brother of **SOE Hok Gie**

Born on 3 January 1941 in Jakarta, he began writing essays while studying at the FPUI. In 1963 he was awarded the Best Essayist prize for his "Manusia dan Seni" [Man and Art] by *Sastra*, a well-known Indonesian literary monthly. In the same year he became a signatory of the Manikebu, an anti-communist cultural manifesto. In 1964 he attended the College d'Europe in Belgium for a semester. When he returned to Indonesia, he was active in student demonstrations, which contributed to the downfall of Soekarno. He was a regular contributor to a number of Jakarta newspapers: *Kompas, Sinar Harapan,* and *Indonesia Raya*. He also served as an editor of *Horison* (1966–72), a leading literary journal of which Mochtar Lubis was the editor-in-chief.

In 1968 he obtained a Drs degree in Psychology from the UI after defending his thesis "Manusia Dalam Persoalan Eksistensiilnja" [Man and His Existential Problem], using the prominent poet Chairil Anwar as a case study. In 1968 he was appointed as first deputy chairman of the Arts Council of the City of Jakarta. In the period 1968–71 he served as a member of the Film Censor Board. In 1970 he became the leader of the Anti-Corruption Campaign. When the general elections were about to take place in 1971, he founded Golongan Putih (or Golput), the "White Group" consisting of liberals and intellectuals who refused to vote in the elections. In October 1972 he left Indonesia and worked in Paris for a year. In September 1973 he went to Harvard for further studies. In 1980 he obtained a PhD in Sociology. On his return from Harvard he joined the Universitas Kristen Satya Wacana (UKSW) in Salatiga. He was also teaching at the postgraduate programme at the above university and was very active in social and cultural activities. In November 1994 he protested against the appointment of the vice-chancellor (*rektor*) of the UKSW for the latter was not properly elected, and Arief was dismissed by the University.

Unable to get a teaching position, he applied to Melbourne University which was looking for an Indonesian professor. He was offered a professorship in Indonesian Studies in 1997 and became the first Indonesian to obtain such a position in the Australian universities. While in Melbourne, he continued to be active and was a frequent commentator on the Indonesian socio-political scene. He retired in 1997.

He is married to Leila Chairani, a psychologist who is an indigenous woman. Prior to marrying her in 1968 he was converted to Islam. It was reported that he also registered their marriage in the civil registration office in 1971.

His publications include *Chairil Anwar: Sebuah Pertemuan* [Chairil Anwar: An Encounter] (Jakarta, 1976), which was based on his Drs thesis; *Pembagian Kerja Secara Seksual* [Division of Work by Sex] (Jakarta, 1981); *Jalan Demokratis Ke Sosialisme: Pengalaman Chili dibawah Allende* [Democratic Way to Socialism: Chili under Allende] (Jakarta, 1987), which is based on his dissertation; *Sistem Perekonomian Pancasila dan Ilmu Sosial di Indonesia* [Pancasila Economy and Social Science in Indonesia] (Jakarta, 1990); and *Indonesia: The Uncertain Transition* (co-editor with Damien Kingsbury, Melbourne, 2001).

Please note that Arief Budiman's Chinese surname *Soe* in Chinese character is 史 (shi), not 苏 (Su).

Sources: Soeprobo, *comp.* (1969), p. 201; Arief Budiman, *Chairil Anwar*, back cover; Teeuw (1970), p. 258; Roeder, *Who's Who*, p. 60; *Intisari* (Jakarta), June 1974, pp. 129–36; *Apa & Siapa 1985–86*, pp. 138–39; <www.tamanismailmarzuki.co.id/.../ariefbudiman.html> (accessed 24 June 2014); the compiler's notes.

BUDIMAN, Daud. See **KWEE Thian Hong**
Burhan URAY. See **URAY, Burhan**
Byanti KHARMAWAN. See **KHARMAWAN, Byanti**

CAHYADI, Robbi. See **TJAHJADI, Robby**
CAI Daoping. See **WONOWIDJOJO, Susilo**
CAI Daoxing. See **HALIM, Rachman**
CAI Huaxi. See **TSAI, Frans**
CAI Liangzhu. See **MARGA T.**
CAI Qingluan. See **TJOA Keng Loan, Effie**
CAI Ruilong. See **SUDIN**

CAI Xihui. See **TJOA Sie Hwie**
CAI Yasheng. See **MANANSANG, Jansen**
CAI Zhiliang. See **TJOA Tjie Liang**
CAO Dechong. See **TJOO Tik Tjoen**
CAO Lianxin. See **TJHO Lian Sin**
Cecillia K. See **KENCANAWATI, Cecillia**
CHAN K.C. See **CHAN Kok Cheng**

CHAN Kok Cheng (K.C. CHAN; pen-name: "Sub-Rosa", 1893–1971) 曾国清*
Journalist, writer, community leader

Born in Penang (or Melaka?) on 27 January 1893, he was educated at an English school in Penang. In 1908 (or 1913?) he migrated to Semarang to work for Java In Boe Kongsie (a printing press). After World War I he went to England to study at the London School of Economics.

Before finishing his studies, he returned to Semarang with the intention of going into business. But in the period 1929–36 he became the editor-in-chief of *Djawa Tengah Review* (a *peranakan* monthly in Malay published by *Djawa Tengah*). When the PTI was founded in Semarang, Chan became a member and was enthusiastic in publicizing its ideas in 1933. He resigned from *Djawa Tengah Review* and became the editor-in-chief of *Soeara Semarang* in 1936–39. His well-known work was on birth control, published in *peranakan* Malay. A former British subject, he became a naturalized Indonesian in 1959. He died in 1971.

Sources: K.C. Chan's letter to Tjoa Tjie Liang, 13 September 1959; Tan, *Tionghoa*, p. 130; Liem Gwan Ging, 23–27 August 1971; Liem Thian Joe, 10 June 1939, pp. 14–15; the compiler's notes.

Chandra SETIAWAN. See **SETIAWAN, Chandra**
CHANG Pi Shih. See **THIO Tiauw Siat**
Charles HIMAWAN. See **HIMAWAN, Charles**

Charles ONG. See **HIMAWAN, Charles**
Charles ONG. See **ONG, Charles**
Charles HONORIS. See **HONORIS, Charles**
CHEN Baoyuan. See **TAN Po Goan**
CHEN Bingding. See **TAN Pia Teng**
CHEN Binghuang. See **SUTANU, Tommie**
CHEN Bingjie. See **TAN Ping Tjiat**

CHEN, Bubi (Buby CHEN, 1938–2012) 陈埔毕*
Jazz pianist

Born in Surabaya on 9 February 1938 into a Tan (陈) family, he received SMA education. He gave private piano lessons for a living. Since 1957 he had been a performer at the Radio Republik Indonesia (RRI, Jakarta). In 1967 he participated in the Jazz Festival in Berlin. He was the chairman of Yayasan Musik Victor Indonesia (Surabaya) and the leader of the Indonesian All-Stars Band. He died in Semarang, Central Java on 16 February 2012.

Bubi had released at least thirty-five albums, including *Bubi Chen and his Fabulous 5* (1962), *Buaian Asmara* (Cradle of love, 1957, 2007), *Lagu Untukmu* (A song for you, 1969), *Jazz the Two of Us* (1996), *Mei Hua San Lung* (1997), *Best of Me* (2007).

Sources: *Sinar Harapan*, 30 May 1970; "Warna Lokal Jazz", *Tempo*, 12 June 1976, p. 49; *Apa & Siapa 1985–86*, pp. 148–49; <http://id.wikipedia.org/wiki/Bubi_Chen> (accessed 24 March 2013).

CHEN Chien-An. See **TANDIONO, Ki Anan**
CHEN Dajiang. See **TANUDJAJA, Sukanta**
CHEN De Xiu Xian. See **TAN Tik Sioe Sian**
CHEN Dehe. See **TAN Tek Ho**
CHEN Deheng. See **TAN Tek Heng**
CHEN Donglong. See **TJANDINEGARA, Wilson**
CHEN Fengwen. See **TAN Hong Boen**

CHEN Fuding. See **TAN Hoe Teng**
CHEN Gongli. See **SOETANTYO, Tegoeh**
CHEN Jian'an. See **TANDIONO, Ki Anan**
CHEN Jianghe. See **TANOTO, Sukanto**
CHEN Jiangsu. See **TAN Kang So**
CHEN Jianlu. See **TAN Kian Lok**
CHEN, Jinfeng. See **TAN Kim Hong**
CHEN Jinjian. See **TAN Kim Kian**
CHEN Jinlong. See **HASSAN, Hadji Mohammad**
CHEN Jinniang. See **YOUNG, Fifi**
CHEN Jinshan. See **TAN Kim San**
CHEN Lianhu. See **ANANTA, Aris**
CHEN Linru. See **TAN Ling Djie**
CHEN Longhu. See **TANOTO, Latif Harris**
CHEN Mingli. See **TANOESOEDIBJO, Hary**
CHEN Qingming. See **TANUWIBOWO, Budi S.**
CHEN Qingmu. See **TAN Tjeng Bok**
CHEN Qiuxue. See **KARTAJAYA, Hermawan**
CHEN Shanhu. See **SHANNU**
CHEN Shengfa. See **SOEMANTO, Agoes**
CHEN Shilin. See **DANANJAYA, James**
CHEN Tianfu. See **TANZIL, Haris Otto Kamil**
CHEN Wen'an. See **TAN Boen Aan**
CHEN Wenjin. See **TAN Boen Kim**
CHEN Wenxuan. See **TAN Boen Soan**
CHEN Xiangji. See **TAN Siong Kie**
CHEN Xianglian. See **TAN Siang Lian**
CHEN Xianwei. See **WINARTA, Frans Hendra**
CHEN Xingyan. See **TAN Hin Hie**
CHEN Xuanming. See **TAN Swan Bing**
CHEN Yinghua. See **TAN Eng Hoa**
CHEN Yingzhi. See **TAN Eng Tie**
CHEN Youfu. See **KARTANEGARA, Hendra**

CHEN Yuanbao. See **TAN Goan Po**
CHEN Yuanchang. See **ISKANDAR, Nathanael**
CHEN Yueming. See **SOESASTRO, M. Hadi**
CHEN Yulan. See **TAN, Mely G.**
CHEN Yuxin. See **TAN Giok Sin**
CHEN Zebing. See **TAN Tek Peng**
CHEN Zhanhu. See **SHANNU**
CHEN Zhenlin. See **TAN Tjien Lien**
CHEN Zhenwen. See **AMIEN, Muhammad**
CHEN Zhongqing. See **TAN Tiong Khing**
CHEN Zihuang. See **TANSIL, Eddy**
CHEN Zixing. See **RAHARDJA, Hendra**

CHENG, David G. 郑大卫*
Cabinet minister

No information is available on him, although one source has it that he came from Hong Kong. He was appointed Minister of City Planning and Construction on 28 May 1965 by the Soekarno government.

Sources: Finch, *Cabinets*, p. 59; *Kabinet* (1970), p. 34.

CHEONG Fatt Tze. See **THIO Tiauw Siat**

CHIAO, Evelyn (ZHAO Chunling 赵春琳**, 1944-)**
Dancer, singer

Daughter of a migrant businessman who came to Indonesia in the 1920s, she was born in Bandung in 1944. At the age of seven she learned ballet from Y. Jaquet; later she studied West Java court dances from R.T. Sumantri and learned singing from Mrs T. Borst, Mrs G. Rovorger, and Ms Yu Yixuan.

Evelyn became famous as a dancer in the 1950s, and as a singer in the early 1960s. She won the Indonesian national singing competition for the *seriosa* category in 1962. During the

Soekarno era she appeared in a number of Indonesian movies and was a member of the Indonesian artist delegation which visited various countries, including Singapore, Malaya, the Philippines, North Vietnam, and North Korea. It was reported that President Soekarno appreciated her talents. After 1965 she left Indonesia and eventually settled in Hong Kong where she works as a trainer for newcomers in Hong Kong Asia Television. She gave a concert in Hong Kong in September 1978, and another in Singapore in 1985.

Sources: *Dipingxian*, no. 6 (August 1979), pp. 12–15; *Zaobao*, 28 July 1985; Setyautama, *Tokoh-Tokoh Etnis TH*, pp. 32–33.

CH'IU Han-hsing. See **QIU Zheng'ou**
CHOW Li Ing. See **MURDAYA, Siti Hartati**
Christian HADINATA. See **HADINATA, Christian**
Christiandy SANJAYA. See **SANJAYA, Christiandy**
Christianto WIBISONO. See **WIBISONO, Christianto**
CHU Ch'ang-tung. See **CHU Chong Tong**

CHU Chong Tong (CHU Ch'ang-tung; ZHU Changdong 朱昌东)
Community leader

Born in Guangdong, he was the vice-consul general of RC in Jakarta prior to 1949. In 1952 he established Qiao Lian under the instruction of the Taiwanese authorities and served as its secretary-general. In the same year he attended the Overseas Chinese Affairs Conference in Taipei. He lived in Taiwan after his expulsion from Indonesia in the 1950s.

Sources: *Huaqiao zhi*, p. 126; Huang, *Geming*, p. 266; *Directory of Chinese Names*, p. 18.

CHUA Chee Liang. See **SATYAWARDAYA, Anang**
CIPUTRA. See **TJIPUTRA**
CUI Miao. See **TJUI, Maria**

DAI Jianwei. See **THEE Kian Wie**
DAI Yunming. See **PATROS, Asmin**
Dali Santun NAGA. See **NAGA, Dali Santun**

DANANJAYA, James (TAN Soe Lin; CHEN Shilin 陈士林, 1934–2013)
Anthropologist, folklore specialist

Born on 13 April 1934 in Jakarta, Danandjaya received his junior education in Malang and Surabaya. According to him, his mother was the one responsible for his pursuit of a higher education. He went to the University of Indonesia in 1963 to study anthropology under Professor Koentjaraningrat, obtained a scholarship to complete his M.A. degree in UC Berkeley in 1971 before returning to the University of Indonesia to earn his PhD in 1977. His dissertation, *Kebudayaan Petani Desa Trunyan di Bali* was published in 1985 by Balai Pustaka. His other book, *Upacara-upacara Lingkaran Hidup di Trunyan Bali*, was also published in the same year.

Although doing research on Bali, he was better known for his folklore works. Danandjaya in fact studied folklore in Berkeley where he submitted an M.A. thesis on "Annotated bibliography of Javanese folklore", and developed his talent in that direction. During his twenty years of professorship at the University of Indonesia, Dananjaya published several books on folklore and serials for children. He is known as the first Indonesian folklore specialist, and is the author of *Indonesian Folklore* (1984), *Japanese Folklore* (1997), and *Chinese Folklore* (2007). For his publication, *Indonesian Folklore*, he received The Best Book Award of 1987 from Yayasan Buku Utama. He also received Satyalencana Kebudayaan in 2002 from the Indonesian Government for his contributions in writing and his development of cultural anthropology and folklore. He was made a professor of emeritus after retirement. He died in Jakarta on 21 October 2013.

Sources: Thung Ju Lan, "Dananjaya, James", Suryadinata, ed., *Southeast Asian Personalities* (2012), pp. 222–24; *Apa dan Siapa Sejumlah Orang Indonesia 1985–86*, pp. 155–57; <http://www.tempo.co/read/news/2013/10/21/173523312/James-Danandjaya-Ahli-Folklor-Tutup-Usia> (accessed 15 February 2014).

Daniel JOHAN. See JOHAN, Daniel
DARMA, Yahya Daniel. See LIE Tjeng Tjoan, John
Darmadi DURIANTO. See DURIANTO, Darmadi

DARMADI, Jan (FOK Jo Jau; HUO Zuoyou 霍佐幼 (佑), 1937-)
Wealthy businessman, member of the Presidential Advisory Council

Born in 1937 in Jakarta, the son of Dadi Darma (Yauw Foet Sen) who ran casinos in Jakarta when Ali Sadikin was the governor. Jan was sent to the United States for studies. In 1971 he received an MA degree in Commerce from New York University. After his return he continued his father's business. When casinos were banned in Indonesia, he moved into the property business and established the Jakarta Setiabudi International. The Jan Darmadi Group expanded its business to include textiles, travel, plastic manufacturing, transport, and banking. The Group had significant shares in Bank Susila Bhakti and Panin Bank. By 1992 the group became one of the 200 largest Indonesian companies: his company was ranked number 15 in 1990 and number 18 in 1991.

Darmadi is still considered as one of the 100 richest men in Indonesia. He joined the Partai NasDem and served as chairman of the NasDem Supreme Council. Upon the recommendation of the party, on 19 January 2015 he was appointed as a member of the Presidential Advisory Council (*wantimpres*) by President Joko Widodo.

Sources: *Forbes Zibenjia*, October 1991, p. 69; July 1994, pp. 28–29; *Shijie huaren jingying zhuan lue: Yindunixiya juan*, pp. 268–77 which is based on the article published in *SWA*, October 1992; "Ini Profil Singkat Jan Darmadi", Kompas.com, 19 January 2015 (accessed 20 April 2015).

DARMAPUTERA, Eka (THE Oen Hien, 1942–2005) 郑运兴*
Religious scholar, church activist, Protestant

Born on 16 November 1942 in Magelang, Central Java, the son of a *warung* shop owner. He received his primary and secondary education at his birthplace. After graduation in 1960 he went to Jakarta to study at Sekolah Tinggi Teologia (STT, Theologian College) He was active in the GMKI (Indonesian Christian University Students' Association) and served in its central committee. In 1966 he graduated from the STT and eleven years later he was sent to Boston College, Massachusetts. In 1982 he obtained a PhD after having successfully defended his dissertation "Pancasila and the Search for Identity and Modernity in Indonesia — An Ethical and Cultural Analysis", which was later (1988) published. Its Indonesian translation was also published (1993). He returned to Indonesia and served in various churches. He was a council member of Persekutuan Gereja Indonesia (1984–89).

His family had lived in Boston for some time and when they returned to Indonesia, his very young son, Arya, asked him in English: "Why do they call me Chinese? I'm not, am I?" Eka answered, "Yes, you are. But more than that, you are an Indonesian."

He passed away on 29 June 2005 after more than twenty years of battling with cyrosis and liver cancer.

Sources: *Apa & Siapa 1985–86*, pp. 166–67; Stephen Suleeman, "Darmaputera, Eka", Suryadinata, ed., *Southeast Asian Personalities*, pp. 227–29.

DARMAWAN, Hari (TAN Tjan Hok, 1940-) 陈灿福*
Retail business king

He was born on 27 May 1940 in Makassar. His father Tan A Siong was a local businessman dealing with agricultural products. After graduating from SMA Darmawan he came to Jakarta to work. He met and married the daughter of the owner of "Mickey Mouse", a small department store in Pasar Baru, then a well-known shopping district in Jakarta. His father-in-law later sold the store to him. Under his management, the store expanded rapidly. In 1968 he bought over the then largest department store in Pasar Baru called *Toko De Zon* (Dutch; The Sun). He changed its name to *Matahari* (Indonesian: The Sun). In the 1980s Matahari established branches in almost every major cities of Indonesia and the store was known as the largest retail chain store in Indonesia. He was even elected as the deputy chairman of Asosiasi Pengusaha Retail Indonesia (Aprindo). During the 1997 monetary crisis, Darmawan's business was affected and incurred great losses. It was eventually bought over by the Lippo Group. Darmawan himself later established a new company called Pasar Swalayan Hari-Hari.

Sources: *Kompas* 7 Juli 1996; Setyautama, *Tokoh-tokoh Etnis TH*, pp. 391–92.

DARMAWAN, Hendra (OEY Kwie Tek, 1918-) 黄贵德*
Accountant

Born in Jakarta on 11 February 1918, he received a Drs degree (majoring in accountancy) from the FEUI in 1955. In 1958 he established his own accounting firm. He is the owner and director of Darmawan and Co., a large certified public accounting firm in Indonesia. He was also one of the founders and a member of the executive committee, Ikatan Akontan Indonesia (Indonesian Accountants' Association), and a part-time lecturer at the FEUI.

Sources: Arief, *Indonesian Business*, p. 105; the compiler's notes.

DARMOHUSODO, K.R.T. Obi (OEN Boen Ing, 1903–82) 温文英*
Court physician

Born in Salatiga on 3 March 1903, Dr Oen Boen Ing was the son of a wealthy cigarette merchant. He first practised in Kediri between 1922 and 1923. Later he moved to Solo and became the head of a private polyclinic, Tsi Sheng Yuan. Since 1944 he was appointed as the personal physician of the Solo (Surakarta) Court (*dokter pribadi Istana Mangkunegaran*). In recognition of his service, in 1975 he was made a court official and bestowed the title Kangjeng Raden Tumenggung (KRT) Obi Darmohusodo ("Obi" is the abbreviation of Oen Boen Ing).

On 31 August 1952 Dr Oen expanded the Tsi Sheng Yuan into a full hospital, which later became the Panti Kosala Hospital. This hospital was established for the local community, especially those who were poor. It was reported that Dr Oen helped many freedom fighters during the revolution. He even supplied penicillin to General Sudirman (Father of the Indonesian Army) when he suffered from tuberculosis.

Dr Oen passed away on 30 October 1982 and was cremated in Solo. Before the cremation, Solo Court officials escorted the coffin from the Panti Kosala Hospital to the crematorium.

Sources: *Suara Merdeka*, 5 November 1982, p. 12; Junus Jahja, *Peranakan Idealis*, pp. 77–83.

Dasuki ANGKOSUBROTO. See **ANGKOSUBROTO, Dasuki**
Daud BUDIMAN. See **KWEE Thian Hong**
David Herman JAYA. See **JAYA, David Herman**

DAWIS, Didi (YU Yuling 俞雨龄, 1945-)
Community leader, entrepreneur, Hokchia

Didi Dawis, a Hokchia, was born in 1945 in Madiun, East Java. His father came from China at the age of eleven. The family later moved to Bandung. Dawis' father established a textile factory, producing 777 brand singlet. Dawis graduated from

Huaqiao Zhongxue, a Chinese-medium high school, in Bandung. He wanted to be a teacher but was opposed by his father.

He then went to Jakarta alone to try his luck. After working for a while, he set up a company selling cements and liquors. In 1974 Liem Sioe Liong established a cement factory and Dawis became one of the agents selling Indo cements. However, his fortune came from his lottery business. Between 1986 and 1993 he obtained a licence to run the lottery in twenty-seven Indonesian provinces and became rich.

Dawis later formed the Ling Brothers, a trading and property company. He also has interests in building materials, real estate development, hotel and banking. In addition, he owns a 9.6 per cent stake in QAF Ltd., a diversified food company listed in Singapore. Dawis also established charity foundations. According to the *Bloomberg Businessweek*, Dawis was one of the 150 richest Indonesians (no. 102, with assets of US$320 million). After the fall of Soeharto, he became active in Chinese organizations. He was the president of the Jakarta Fuqing Gonghui (Hokchia association) and later the president of Shijie Fuqing Shetuan Lianyihui (International Federation of Futsing [Fuqing] Clan, based in Singapore). In early 2014 Dawis was elected as the president of Yinni Fuqing Lianyihui (Indonesian Federation of Hokkian Associations).

Sources: 《新华网记者访世界福清联谊会主席俞雨龄》, 12 October 2013 (accessed 18 June 2014); *Bloomberg Businessweek*, information on QAF: Singapore (accessed 18 June 2014).

Dede OETOMO. See **OETOMO, Dede**
DENG Tongli. See **TENG, Benny**
DENG Zhenning. See **NANGOI, T.**

DEWI, Utami (NIO Pik Wan, 1951-) 梁碧婉*
Badminton player, sister of **Rudy Hartono KURNIAWAN**

Born on 16 June 1951 in Surabaya, she took the women's singles title in the Indonesian national championship in 1968, 1969, and 1971. In 1969 and 1972, she also won the women's doubles title (together with Minarni). In 1972 she was the runner-up for the women's singles title at the Olympic Exhibition (Munich). She was a member of the Indonesian All-England team in 1972, 1973, and 1975.

Sources: *Topik*, 19 April 1972, pp. 14–21; *Tempo*, 31 May 1975, p. 48.

Didi DAWIS. See **DAWIS, Didi**

DIPOJUWONO, Budi (LIE Po Yoe, 1921-) 李宝友*
Politician

Born on 16 February 1921, he was educated in a Dutch primary and secondary school. He graduated from the Mid Handels School (Middle Commercial School) in Bandung in 1937. During the Indonesian Revolution, he assisted the Republican government at Banyumas in the collection and supply of food. He joined the PNI after Indonesia's independence. In 1956–59 he was a member of the DPR representing the Chinese minority and in 1959–66 he represented the PNI.

In the 1971 general elections, he represented the PNI in the Tegal regency (East Java) and was elected as a member of the DPR to serve during the period 1971–76.

Sources: *DPR 1971*, p. 129; *Who's Who in Parliament, 1971–76*, p. 42.

DJIAUW Pok Kie (RAO Boji 饶博基**, also known as Djoko HARJONO, 1910–73)**
Community leader, businessman

He was born on 15 August 1910. During the Indonesian Revolution, he smuggled weapons for Indonesian nationalists (1946). He was later awarded medals for his contribution to the Indonesian Republic (1950s?). In the 1950s he established Bank Asia-Afrika. When the anti-KMT campaign was launched in 1958 he was arrested by the Indonesian authorities for his affiliation with that political party. Eight months later he was released and went to Hong Kong where he stayed until 1966 when Soeharto assumed power. It was reported that he was invited by Sultan Hamengku Buwono IX (formerly the vice-president of Indonesia) to return, and became active again in the banking business. He was director of the Bank Asia Berdjuang in Jakarta, and ran SPNC Tat'ung Chung-hsiao Hsueh-hsiao, which was primarily for alien Chinese children. He died in Jakarta on 17 January 1973.

Sources: Jiang, "Yajiada", p. 16; *Ribao*, 18 and 20 January 1973; the compiler's notes.

DJIE Ting Liat 徐定烈*
Accountant, community leader

Born in Nganjuk, he was educated at a Dutch school in Surabaya before going to a commercial college in Amsterdam, where he majored in trade. After graduation he worked in a private firm in Amsterdam as a practising accountant. When he became a qualified accountant, he returned to Java to work for the Oei Tiong Ham Concern, first, as an accountant and, later, as the head of the accountancy section. In the 1930s he was appointed Trade Commissioner of the Chinese Republic in the Netherlands East Indies. He was active in the CHH and in 1935 was appointed to head a committee to make proposals for the reorganization of the CHH.

Sources: Tan, *Tionghoa*, p. 131; *Panorama*, 12 May 1934; Suryadinata, *Peranakan Politics*, pp. 105ff.

DJIE Ting Tjioe (XU Tingzhou 徐庭州, 1904-?)
Community leader, accountant

Born in 1904, he graduated from the Rotterdam Economic School and practised as a certified public accountant in Malang. In 1942 he became the president of the HCTH (Malang).

Source: *Djawa Nenkan* (1973), p. 464.

DJOJONEGORO, Husain (CHU Kok Seng; ZHU Guosheng 朱国盛, 1949-)
Entrepreneur

Born in Semarang in November 1949, he received primary and middle school education in Medan and Jakarta. He started working at the age of fifteen, first as a salesman. In 1968 he became the director of his father's company, PT International Chemical Industrial Co. Ltd., and produced ABC battery, which became one of the most popular brands of batteries in Indonesia. In addition to batteries, he also moved into other products: soya sauce, syrup, tomato sauce, and orange juice, all using the same brand. His factories are located in Medan, Jakarta, and Surabaya.

Source: *Apa & Siapa 1985–86*, pp. 197–98.

Djoko HARJONO. See DJIAUW Pok Kie

DJUHAR, Sutanto (LIEM Oen Kian; LIN Wenjing 林文镜, 1928-)
Tycoon, partner of **Soedono SALIM** *(Liem Sioe Liong)*

Born in 1928, place unknown. According to one source, Djuhar's father went to Indonesia with **LIEM Sioe Liong** in the same ship. Both of them also lived in Kudus, and Sutanto got along well with Liem Sioe Liong, who was twelve years older. Sutanto was a basketball player when he was young. In the 1950s he established a *batik* factory in Pekalongan. But in the 1960s he and Liem Sioe Liong jointly established the Kencana Group. He was one of the permanent partners of Liem's group. After China introduced an open door policy, together with Liem Sioe Liong, he invested in Fuqing, China, including establishing an industrial park.

However, after 1998 the core friendship between Djuhar Sutanto and Liem Sioe Liong ended unhappily. Disagreement over Anthony Salim's debt settlement with IBRA (Indonesian

Bank Restructuring Agency) led to the Djuhar Sutanto family taking Salim to court in Jakarta, but the lawsuit was soon withdrawn. Despite the case, some Salim-Djuhar business ties remained in place.

Sources: *Forbes Zibenjia*, July 1994, p. 24; Siregar and Widya (1988), pp. 39, 44, 193; Richard Borsuk and Nancy Chng, *Liem Sioe Liong's Salim Group: The Business Pillar of Suharto's Indonesia* (Singapore: Institute of Southeast Asian Studies, 2014), pp. 480–83.

DURIANTO, Darmadi (LIM Tek Tjun, LIN Dechun, 林德純, 1967-)
Member of Parliament, academic

Born in Pontianak on 25 June 1967, Darmadi obtained a PhD in business (name of the university unavailable). He is a lecturer teaching graduate courses at the Kwik Kian Gie School of Business (Jakarta). He is also deputy head of People's Economy Empowerment Body in the PDIP Central Board. He contested the parliamentary election in 2014 and won a seat for the Jakarta constituency (2014–19).

Sources: Pengurus Pusat Fordeka, *Buku Acuan 2014–19*, p. 124; the compiler's notes.

Eddie KUSUMA. See **KUSUMA, Eddie**
Eddie LEMBONG. See **LEMBONG Eddie**
Eddy TANSIL. See **TANSIL, Eddy**
Eka DARMAPUTERA. See **DARMAPUTERA, Eka**
Eka Tjipta WIDJAJA. See **WIDJAJA, Eka Tjipta**
Eko WIJAYA. See **WIJAYA, Eko**
Eliaser Yentji SUNUR. See **SUNUR, Eliaser Yentji**
Empie WUISAN. See **WUISAN, Empie**
Endang WITARSA. See **WITARSA, Endang**
Enggartiasto LUKITA. See **LUKITA, Enggartiasto**

ERVINNA (LIU Lanfang 刘兰芳; AI Huina 爱慧娜, 1956?-)
Pop singer

Born in Surabaya in the middle of the 1950s (1956?), her career as a pop singer began at the age of sixteen or seventeen. In the last eight years or so she produced approximately 150 records, of which forty were in Mandarin, forty in English, and the rest (about eighty) in Indonesian. Popular both in Indonesia and Singapore, she had also performed in many countries, including Taiwan, Hong Kong, Europe, and Australia. In 1978 she co-starred in an Indonesian motion picture *Hujan Duit*. In 1980 she was elected as one of the most popular singers in Southeast Asia; in 1984 her song "Jangan parkir disitu" (Don't park there) won her a golden award given by Cipto Record; the song also received a prize from the Defence Ministry of Indonesia.

Sources: *Xingzhou Ribao*, 27 June 1980; *Nanyang Shangbao* (Malaysia), 25 August 1980; *Kedaulatan Rakyat*, 9 April 1989, p. 1; the compiler's notes.

ESMARA, Hendra (ONG Tek Bie; WANG Demei 王德美, 1935–98)
Economist, university professor

Born in Padang on 13 April 1935, he was converted to Islam when he was young. Later he married an indigenous Indonesian girl. He received a Drs degree from the FEUI in 1961. Initially he served as Dean of the Faculty of Economics, University of Jambi (East Sumatra). He later joined the Department of Economics, Andalas University (Padang, West Sumatra). In 1985 he was promoted to Professor of Development Planning, Faculty of Economics at the same university. In early 1990 he was appointed deputy executive director of the Asia-Pacific Economic Co-operation (APEC) Secretariat in Singapore, representing Indonesia. His extensive publications include *Regional Income of West Sumatra 1966–71* (1972); *West Sumatra: Facts and Figures* (1973); and *ASEAN Economic*

Co-operation: A New Perspective (Singapore, 1988), a volume he edited.

Sources: *Apa & Siapa 1985–86*, pp. 220–21; *Tempo*, 24 August 1991, p. 39; the compiler's notes.

Ester JUSUF. See **JUSUF, Ester**
EW YONG Tjhoen Moy. See **SIDHARTA, Myra**

FADJRIN, Verawaty (also known as Verawaty WIHARJO, 1957-)
黄惠拉*
Badminton player

Born on 1 October 1957 into a Oey (黄, Wiharjo) family, she studied Physical Education at the IKIP. She won many national and international competitions, including women's singles title in Indonesia for a number of years, Asian Games (Bangkok) women's doubles title (together with Imelda Wigoena) and All-England women's doubles title (also with Imelda Wigoena) in 1979. In the same year (1979) she married her schoolmate Fadjrin Syah and was converted to Islam. In 1980 she participated in the Second World Badminton Championship (held in Jakarta) and took the women's singles title. In 1981 she won SEA Games (Manila) women's doubles title.

Sources: *Pembauran*, no. 8 (May 1979), pp. 14–15; *Straits Times*, 1 June 1980; Sabaruddin Sa. *Apa & Siapa Sejumlah Orang Bulutangkis Indonesia*, pp. 48–49; the compiler's notes.

FENG Huilan. See **PANGESTU, Mari**
FENG Laijin. See **PANGLAYKIM, Jusuf**
Fifi YOUNG. See **YOUNG, Fifi**
FOK Jo Jau. See **DARMADI, Jan**
Frans Hendra WINARTA. See **WINARTA, Frans Hendra**
Frans TSAI. See **TSAI, Frans**
FU Sunming. See **IRAWAN, Bingky**

FU Zhikuan. See POO, Murdaya Widyawimarta
FX HARSONO. See HARSONO, FX

GAN Choo Ho (1914-) 颜朱和*
Community leader, leading businessman

Born in Semarang on 10 November 1914, he was educated at a Chinese-English school in Semarang, St Paul's College in Hong Kong, and St John's University in Shanghai. He returned to Indonesia to run his business. In 1955 he served as the president of N.V. CIP in Den Pasar and was a member of the DPRD-Buleleng. He was also the president of Baperki (Bali-Lombok) and participated in the 1955 general elections on its ticket.

Source: *Pedoman Kampanje*, p. 56.

GAN Fafu. See Kam Hwat Hok

GAN K.L. (GAN Kok Liang; YAN Guoliang 颜国梁, 1928–2003)
Kungfu novel translator

Born in 1928 in Amoy (Fujian), Gan was taken by his father to Indonesia in 1938. He first stayed in Purworejo but from 1949 he lived in Semarang. Without a formal education, Gan at first tried many jobs but at the age of thirty he decided to translate *kungfu* novels for *Sin Po*. His first work was *Tjhau Guan Eng Hiong* or *Pahlawan-Pahlawan Padang Rumput*, which was a translation of Liang Yusheng's novel *Saiwai Qixia Zhuan* 塞外奇侠传. One year later, the novel was published in book form.

In the 1970s he began to translate the works of Taiwan's *kungfu* writer, Gu Long (古龙, Khu Lung). Gan's best-known work, *Pendekar Binal* (consisting of fifty-eight volumes), is in fact the Indonesian version of Gu Long's *Juedai Shuangjiao* 绝代双骄. This *kungfu* novel, which tells the story of two twin brothers raised by rival groups and hence having different personalities, was highly praised by a book reviewer. It is believed that it was the only *kungfu* novel ever reviewed in a major Indonesian newspaper, *Kompas*. A spot check of the translation against the original shows that Gan had indeed succeeded in retaining the spirit of the original work. He published more than forty titles.

Gan K.L. died in Semarang on 28 November 2003.

Sources: Suryadinata, *Kebudayaan Minoritas Tionghoa* (1988), pp. 124–32; *Rimba Hijau*, November/December 2004, p. 6.

GAN Koen Han (1916-?) 颜群汉*
Microbiologist, university professor

Born in Purbolinggo on 4 January 1916, he received his PhD in Pathology from the FKUI in 1941(?) and did his post-doctoral work in microbiology in the Netherlands, France, and England. He has an impressive career record. He was a student assistant (equivalent to graduate assistant at the FKUI) from 1934 to 1941. Then from 1941 to 1943 he became a voluntary assistant at the Department of Serology, Eykman Institute (Jakarta). In 1943–46 he worked as a bacteriologist at a private laboratory in Solo, and concurrently as a doctor of the clinic of the Social Welfare Association. In 1947 he served as a ship's doctor and returned to the FKUI in 1949. In 1950–52 he also served as head of the Department of Microbiology at the Leprosy Institute in Jakarta. In 1952–55 he was chairman of the Department of Public Health of the Social Welfare Association in Jakarta. In 1958–59 he was appointed as a research associate at the Virus Laboratory of the University of California. During the period 1963–65, as a member of the WHO Bacteriology-Diarrhoeal Disease Advisory Team, Geneva, he conducted field studies in Iran, Pakistan, and Venezuela. From 1956 to 1969 he was appointed Professor of Microbiology at the FKUI and was head of the Department of Microbiology, also at the FKUI.

Source: Roeder, *Who's Who*, p. 101.

GAN Kok Liang. See **GAN K.L.**
Gani SUWONDO. See **SUWONDO, Gani**
GAO Huanyi. See **KHO Wan Gie**
GAO Juezhong. See **KO Kwat Tiong**

GAUTAMA, Sudargo (GOUW Giok Siong; WU Yuxiang 吴玉祥, 1928–2008)
Academician, lawyer

Born in Jakarta in 1928, he obtained an "Mr" degree from the FHUI in 1950 and a PhD in law from the same university in 1955 for successfully defending his dissertation "Segi-segi Hukum Peraturan Perkawinan Tjampuran" [Legal Aspects of Intermarriage]. In October of 1955 he was a part-time lecturer (Lektor Luar Biasa) at the FHUI. In September 1958 he was appointed Professor of Law at the FHUI and he was concurrently a lecturer at the Air Force Academy, Jakarta. Earlier he was appointed State Lawyer as well. His publications include *Tafsiran Undang-undang Pokok Agraria* (Jakarta, 1960), his dissertation; *Warga Negara dan Orang Asing* (Jakarta, 1962; 2nd ed.); "Marriage and Divorce Laws of Indonesia", in *A Comparison of Marriage Laws of the World*, edited by Miyazaki (Tokyo, 1969); and *Credit and Security in Indonesia* (Brisbane, 1973).

Gautama continued practising and teaching law until he passed away on 8 September 2008 at the age of eighty in Perth, Western Australia where he had spent most of his final years, which probably explains why his passing received minimal attention from the media in Indonesia.

Sources: "Pengantar Redaksi", *Pantjawarna*, 15 September 1956, p. 1; *Bintang Timur*, 30 September 1958; Tapingkae, ed., *Selected Scholars*,

p. 247; *Ribao*, 5 May 1975; Yu Un Oppusunggu, "Gautama, Sudargo", Suryadinata, ed., *Southeast Asian Personalities*, pp. 273–76;

GINTING, Lo S.H. (LO Siang Hien; LUO Xiangxing 罗祥兴, 1921–98)

Political party leader, social scientist, Catholic

Born in Yogyakarta on 13 June 1921, he was educated at the HCS (Yogyakarta) for seven years, and at Xaviers College (1935–41), a multiethnic boarding school in Muntilan.

He studied at Katholik Economisch Hoogeschool (Tilburg) in 1948–55. After obtaining a BA degree in Economics and a Drs degree in Social Sciences in 1955, he joined the Ministry of Labour, RI, and stayed there until 1967.

While in the Netherlands, he was active in the Catholic Party. In 1955 he joined Partai Katholik in Indonesia heading its Biro Perburuhan (Labour Bureau). Later he was elected as a member of the Presidium of Partai Katholik. From 1966 to 1971 he was appointed as a member of the DPR representing the Catholic Party. When Indonesian political parties were simplified, he withdrew from political activities and entered into private business. Apart from his political activities, he was also active in the educational field. He taught at the UGM from 1955 to 1956, and in 1960 was involved in establishing Atma Jaya University in Jakarta. He served as Dean of the Faculty of Social Sciences at Atma Jaya and later as chancellor (*rektor*) until 1971. In 1966 he was adopted as a son by the Ginting (Batak) family. He was the secretary-general of Bakom in the 1970s.

Between 1978 and 1981, he served as the secretary of the Yayasan Prasetya Mulia. He had represented Indonesia to attend various meetings of ILO. Lo died in Singapore on 19 April 1998.

Sources: Daftar Golkar, p. 4; *Buku Pedoman Universitas Katholik Indonesia 1971* (1971), p. 34; interview, 1976; Setyautama, *Tokoh-tokoh Etnis TH*, p. 233.

GO Ge Siong. See **GUNARSA, Singgih D.**

GO Gien Tjwan (WU Yinquan 吴银泉, 1920-)
Community leader, sociologist

Born in Malang on 22 September 1920, he received a Drs degree in Sociology from Rijks Universiteit (Leiden) and a PhD in Sociology from Vrije Universiteit (Brussels, 1962). He had been involved in politics since the Indonesian struggle for independence. From 1945 he was a leading member of Angkatan Muda Tionghoa (Malang); from 1946 to 1947 he was a member of the Council of Socialist Parties. In 1947 he moved to Jakarta to work for the Ministry of Foreign Affairs. At the end of 1947 he left for the Netherlands. In 1948–52 he was elected as an executive member of the Perhimpunan Indonesia Amsterdam branch. In 1952 he became the head of the Antara Amsterdam branch. In the same year he was expelled from the Netherlands.

He returned to Indonesia and in 1955 served as the head of the Antara News Agency and in 1954–55 as the secretary-general of the Baperki central board. In the following years he continued to hold high positions in the organization. In 1963–65 he was a lecturer at the URECA (Jakarta). After the 1965 coup, he left for the Netherlands where he was appointed as a lecturer at Amsterdam University and retired in 1985. He visited the PRC at least five times since 1963. His publications include *Eenheid in Verscheidenheid in een Indonesische Dorp* [Unity in diversity in an Indonesian village] (Universiteit van Amsterdam, 1966), and a few articles on the Chinese minority. In order to reach wider readers in Indonesia, his dissertation was eventually published in Indonesia ten years after the fall of Soeharto, entitled, *Desa Dadap: Wujud Bhinneka Tunggal Ika*. (Jakarta: Elkasa, 2008).

Sources: *Eenheid*, pp. i–vii; *Pedoman Kampanje*, pp. 39–40; *Sin Po*, 15 March 1954; Wen Guangyi, "Wu Yinquan Boshi zai woguo jiangxue",

Dongnanya Xuekan, no. 5 (December 1988), pp. 112–16; *Desa Dadap* (2008); the compiler's notes.

GO Ing Liang (WU Yingliang 吴英亮)
Community leader

Born in Blora, he was educated at the THHT in Blora, the ELS in Blora, MULO in Surabaya, and the Dutch Commercial School in Jakarta. In the late 1920s he was a member of the local council, and in the 1930s, a member of both the Central Java Provincial Council and the Blora Regency Council.

Source: Tan, *Tionghoa*, pp. 67–68.

GO Ka Him. See GONDOKUSUMO, Suhargo
GO Nen Pin. See PURNOMO, Nurdin

GO (GOUW) Tiauw Goan (WU Zhaoyuan 吴兆元, 1890–1956)
Journalist

Born in 1890 in Madiun, he was educated at the THHK (Jakarta). He was awarded a scholarship by the Chinese Government to study at the CNHT (Nanking), and he returned to Java in 1911. He joined *Sin Po* in 1925 and in 1928 became acting (*plaatsvervangend*) editor-in-chief of *Sin Po*. He was interned during the Japanese Occupation. After the war he joined *Sin Po* again, replacing Kwee Kek Beng as the editor-in-chief in 1947. He wrote many articles on China for *Sin Po* and *Pantjawarna*. When *peranakan* Chinese were given the opportunity to choose between Indonesian and Chinese citizenship in 1950, Gouw chose Chinese citizenship. He visited the PRC in 1953 with other Indonesian Chinese. Gouw died in Jakarta on 30 March 1956.

Sources: Nio Joe Lan, April 1956, p. 42; information provided by Tan Ee Liong (1969); Tan, *Tionghoa*, pp. 187–88; *Sin Po*, 9 May 1928.

GO Tik Swan. See HARDJONAGORO, Kanjeng Raden Tumenggung

GO Tjoe Bin (1907-?) 吴朱民*
Physician, community leader

Born in Banjarmasin on 15 May 1907, he graduated from NIAS (Surabaya) in 1936 and joined government service in Kalimantan. In 1946 he was appointed as the Kalimantan delegate to the Pangkal Pinang Conference. In 1948 he attended the BFC (Conference for Federal Consultation) in Bandung. In 1949 he went into private practice. In 1952 he was elected as the president of the IDI (Banjarmasin). In 1954 he was elected as the president of Baperki (Banjarmasin) and contested the 1955 parliamentary elections on the Baperki ticket but was not elected.

Source: *Pedoman Kampanje*, p. 51.

GOEI Hing An. See ANTON, Abah
GOEI Hok Gie. See GUNAWAN, Andrew H.

GOEI Poo Aan (WEI Bao'an 魏保安, 1905–66)
Journalist, father of Andrew GUNAWAN

Born in 1905, Madiun (East Java), he did not have much formal education when he was young. In the late 1920s he moved to Surabaya and attended classes at the Burger Avond School (BAS). He had worked for various *peranakan* Chinese newspapers in Java since 1925, first with *Perniagaan*, later with *Sin Jit Po*, *Sin Tit Po*, and *Mata Hari*. From 1947 to 1965 he was the founder and the director-general of a left-wing *peranakan* daily, *Trompet Masjarakat* (Surabaya). He died in 1966.

Sources: *Almanak Pers*, p. 280; Andrew Gunawan's letter to the compiler, 1995; the compiler's notes.

GOEY Tiauw Hong (WEI Chaofeng 魏朝凤, 1899–1964?)
Expressionistic painter

Born in Menado in 1899, he studied art at the Dutch Royal Academy (the Hague) and the Julian Academy (Paris). In 1920 he was awarded the Vigilius First Prize, and in 1922 the Julian First Prize. He held a number of exhibitions both overseas and in Indonesia. He was the first Indonesian-Chinese expressionistic painter. He died in 1964(?).

Sources: *Sin Po Weekblad*, no. 512 (21 January 1933); C.M. Hsu's notes.

GOH Tjing Hok (pen-name: Abiturient; 吳清福 WU Qingfu, 1919–90)
Newspaperman, community leader

Born in Semarang on 13 April 1919, he was educated at MULO (Semarang, 1935–38) and Middelbare Handelschool (Jakarta, 1939–40). He served as the deputy editor-in-chief of *Sin Min* (Semarang) from 1947 to 1949; editor-in-chief of *Java Post* (Surabaya) in 1950; editor-in-chief of *Liberal* (Surabaya) from 1953 to 1959; and editor of *Liberty* (Surabaya) from 1959 to 1990. A matter interesting to note is that *Liberal* was renamed *Liberty* in 1959 when Soekarno denounced "Liberal Democracy" and introduced "Guided Democracy".

Being outspoken, Goh was detained by the Indonesian authorities three times (1951, 1956, and 1961) for violating the press law. He favoured the PP-10 (1959) regulation banning foreign traders in rural areas, and was critical of Baperki for not supporting the regulation. He believed in assimilationist ideas and was one of the promoters of the Bandungan seminar which generated *Piagam Asimilasi*, of which he was a signatory (1961). He died in Surabaya in October 1990.

Sources: *Star Weekly*, 4 June 1960, p. 2; *Assimilasi*, p. 34; Letter to the compiler, 1976; *Tempo*, 27 October 1990, p. 38.

GONDOKUSUMO, Suhargo (GO Ka Him; WU Jiaxiong 吳家熊, 1926–2010)
Wealthy businessman

Born on 4 August 1926 in Nan'an, Fujian, he came to Indonesia in 1947. In the late 1950s he established the Dharmala Group in

Surabaya(?), which first specialized in the trading of agricultural products (according to another source, he used to export coffee), but in the 1970s it expanded to include other businesses, especially after his eldest son Suyanto (Wu Duanxian) returned from studies in the United States. The Group was involved in real estate (Wisma Dharmala, PT Taman Harapan Indah, and so forth), finance (PT Bank Pasar Warga Nugraha), import, and distribution (PT Mekasindo Dharma International, PT Kayu Eka Ria, and so forth). His companies are multinational, operating in Hong Kong (DMT International Hong Kong), the Philippines, and Thailand. The Group also formed DeMat Investment to invest in China. The Dharmala Group was ranked no. 11 (?) among Indonesian conglomerates in the 1990s. Suhargo died in Singapore on 2 September 2010. He is survived by four sons and one daughter. In fact, his business had been run by his sons and relatives since he retired.

Sources: *Expo 2*, no. 1 (4 January 1984): 17–19; *Indonesian Financial Profile*, p. 37; *Forbes Zibenjia*, July 1994, p. 27; *Jakarta Program Magazine*, no. 87 (August 1994), p. 65; *Straits Times*, 4 September 2010.

GOUW Giok Siong. See **GAUTAMA, Sudargo**
GOUW Loen An. See **LUNANDI, Andy**
GOUW P.L. See **GOUW Peng Liang**

GOUW Peng Liang (P.L. GOUW; WU Bingliang 吴炳亮, 1868–1928)
Journalist, writer, community leader

Born in Jatinegara in 1868, he served as an assistant to the editorial board of a Jakarta-based Malay newspaper, *Bintang Betawi*, around 1900. He soon joined *Sinar Betawi* (Jakarta) and served as a member of its editorial board. In 1907 he became the editor of *Perniagaan*. In 1909 he was promoted to editor-in-chief, a position he held until 1916. In 1917 he bought the newspaper and made himself the director. Two months before he died he sold the newspaper to Liem Tiauw Goan.

Gouw was well-known for his command of Batavian (Jakarta) Malay as well as for his translation works. Among his numerous publications, the following are the better-known: *Lo Fen Koei* (Batavia, 1903); *Boekoe Tjerita Nona Clara Wildenau* (Batavia, 1911); *Tjerita Mohamed Ali Pacha* (Batavia, 1917); and *Kedjoedjoeran Lebi Menang dari Katjoerangan* (Batavia, 1918).

His conservative political view reflected that of the *peranakan* community at that time. He was against Dr Sun Yat-sen's revolutionary movement although after the 1911 Revolution he changed his attitude. Gouw was a supporter of the CHH and came into conflict with *Sin Po*, a major *peranakan* daily newspaper in Jakarta. He died in Jakarta on 20 October 1928.

Sources: *Panorama*, 3 November 1928, pp. 1683–87; *Perniagaan*, 9 August 1909, 30 September 1916; interview with Tio Ie Soei.

GOUW Tiauw Goan. See **GO Tiauw Goan**
GOW Swie Kie. See **ANGKOSUBROTO, Dasuki**

GOZALI, Hendrick (WU Xiehe 吴协和, 1939-)
Film producer

Born on 28 November 1939 in Jakarta, Gozali first went to Sin Hwa Chinese School in Pasar Baru (Jakarta) where he studied until his graduation. He became involved in the film industry in the 1960s when he established Goldig Films (协利电影) film company with his brother Wu Xuejian (吴协建 Alex Gouw). He later formed PT Tekun film to import Hong Kong movies to Indonesia. He started to produce Indonesian films when he became the director of the Garuda Film Company, taking over from an ex-classmate's father.

Gozali went on to become a leading Indonesian film producer with a number of award-winning Indonesian films. Some of his more notable works included *Bonny dan Nancy* [Bony and

Nancy], *Ranjang Siang Ranjang Malam* [The Bed for Day and the Bed for Night], *November 1828* (co-produced with **NJOO Han Siang**) and *Rembulan dan Matahari* [The Moon and the Sun]. He produced many award-winning films and enjoyed many box offices successes during a period of forty years before shifting his attention to making and producing popular television serials in the 1990s. It was also a time when the Indonesian film industry was declining to its lowest point and most of the films produced were of low quality. He has now retired and passed on the business to his son and daughter who are also interested in the film industry.

Sources: Leo Suryadinata, "Gozali, Hendrick", Suryadinata, ed., *Southeast Asian Personalities* (2012), pp. 305–7; *Apa Siapa Orang Film Indonesia 1926–1978* (1979), p. 210; *Apa dan Siapa 1985–1986*, pp. 238, 398–400; "Wu xiehe xishuo rensheng" 吴协和细说人生 manuscript, June 2006.

GOZELIE, Tellie (LIE Men Dong, LI Mindong, 李敏东, 1970-)
Member of DPD, Buddhist

Born in Tanjung Pandan on 10 December 1970, he obtained a Bachelor degree in Economics (Sarjana Ekonomi) in 1995. He was a deputy head of the foreign relations of PSMTI, Central Board. He was elected as a member of DPD in 2009–14 for Bangka-Belitung, and was re-elected as a member of DPD in 2014–19 for the same province.

Sources: *Wajah DPR & DPD 2009–2014*, p. 655; Pengurus Pusat Fordeka, *Buku Acuan 2014*, p. 108; the complier's notes.

GUNARSA, Singgih D. (GO Ge Siong; WU Qixiang 吴启祥, 1934-)
Psychologist, university professor, Protestant

Singgih Dirga Gunarsa or Go Ge Siong is a pioneer in child development psychology and sports psychology in Indonesia. Born in Banyumas on 12 August 1934, he was first educated at HIS Muhammadiyah. After he passed the SMA, he went to the FKUI but a year later he transferred to the FPUI, where he graduated in 1963. Three years later he was awarded a fellowship to study at the Tavistock Clinic, London. In 1975 he obtained a doctorate degree from the UI. He has published extensively. Between 1973 and 1983 he published at least seven books. He taught at the Faculty of Psychology, UI, between 1976 and 1980 as lecturer and senior lecturer. In 1980 he was promoted to Professor of Psychology. Apart from his work at the FPUI, he also serves as a consultant at the Husada Hospital.

He received many awards for his contribution to the Indonesian state and society, including the medal, Satya Lancana Karya Satya Kleas 1 (1989). He retired at the end of 1999 and was made professor emeritus by the UI the following year. While he was teaching full-time at the UI, he served as a member of the Tarumanegara University Foundation (Jakarta). After retirement from the UI he became a full-time staff at the Tarumanegara University. Terumanegara also made him professor emeritus when he was seventy.

He married Juul, a psychology graduate in 1964 and they have three children.

Sources: *Apa & Siapa 1985–86*, pp. 183–84; Leo Suryadinata, "Gunarsa, Singgih D.", Suryadinata, ed., *Southeast Asian Personalities*, pp. 307–9.

GUNAWAN, Andrew H. (GOEI Hok Gie; WEI Fuyi 魏福义, 1933–2009)

Student leader, economist, son of **GOEI Poo Aan**

Born in Solo in 1933, he received a Drs degree from the FEUI. He was active in *peranakan* student movements in the 1950s and early 1960s. He served as the general chairman of the Perhimi central board and represented the organization in the Perserikatan Perhimpunan2 Mahasiswa Indonesia (PPMI). After the 1965 coup Perhimi was banned and Goei was detained. Upon his release he went to Australia to do his graduate studies. He later worked in the commercial sector. His publications include *Research Materials on Indonesia, Available in Australia* (1969), "Honor to a Friend: Bambang Kusnohadi" (1973), and "The Role of Students in the 15 January 1974 Incidents" (1975). Goei, or better known among his Australian friends as Andrew, died in Melbourne on 20 August 2009.

Sources: The above-mentioned publications; Charles Coppel's email, 25 August 2009; the compiler's notes.

GUNAWAN, Mu'min Ali (LIE Mo Ming; LI Wenming 李文明, 1939-)
Banker

Born on 12 March 1939 in Jember, East Java, his father is a small businessman. He went to a primary school in Jember but finished his secondary school in Jakarta in 1959. He first worked as the director of an inter-island shipping company until 1965. Later he moved into the banking business. He was the commissioner of PT Bank Kemakmuran (1968) and Bank Industri & Daya Indonesia (1969). In 1971 he became the director of Bank Industri Dagang Indonesia and from 1971 served as the director of Pan Indonesia Bank (Panin), which is the second largest bank in Indonesia after Bank Central Asia. Mochtar Riady at one time was the general manager of the bank but later left because of disagreement with Mu'min, who succeeded him as the managing director.

After his involvement in the banking business, he studied at the Banking Academy and Indonesian Management Institute, both in Jakarta. In addition to Panin Bank, he also owns Pan Union Insurance, Panin Putra Life Insurance, Green Villa and Green Garden (both real estate companies), and Clipan Leasing.

Panin at one time cooperated with a PRC commercial bank to form an international bank in Amoy, but withdrew soon after.

Sources: *Shijie Huaren Fuhao Bang*, p. 229; *Apa & Siapa 1985–86*, pp. 239–40.

GUNAWAN, Rudy (GUO Hongyuan 郭宏源, 1966-)
Badminton player

Born on 31 December 1966 in Solo, he used to play doubles with Edy Hartono. They won the All-England doubles in 1992 as well as the runner-up in the 1992 Olympic Badminton Competition. After Edy Hartono retired, Rudy Gunawan teamed up with Bambang Suprianto. They won the All-England men's doubles in March 1994, Thailand Open, China Open, and Grand Prix. They were also members of the 1994 Indonesian Thomas Cup Team.

Sources: *Media Karya*, June 1994, p. 54; *Zaobao*, 8 May 1994, p. 24; the compiler's notes.

GUO Chunyang. See **KWIK Djoen Eng**
GUO Dehuai. See **KWEE Tek Hoay**
GUO Hengjie. See **KWEE Hing Tjiat**
GUO Xingyuan. See **KWEE Hin Goan**
GUO Hongyuan. See **GUNAWAN, Rudy**
GUO Jianyi. See **KWIK Kian Gie**
GUO Keming. See **KWEE Kek Beng**

GUO Liangjie (郭两捷, 1889-?)
Community leader, businessman

He was born in 1889 in Pontianak(?), his ancestors having been in Indonesia for a hundred years. He was engaged in the ice, paint, rubber, and shipping businesses, and was acknowledged as the wealthiest businessman in Pontianak.

Prior to World War II, he served as the chairman of various local Chinese associations including Siang Hwee (Pontianak), the Charity Committee of Chinese Refugees, and the Chinese Sanatorium. He also served as a member of the Municipal Council of Pontianak and the Dutch Educational Committee (Pontianak).

Source: Liu, *Gailan*, p. [119].

GUO Meicheng. See **KWEE Bie Sin**

GUO Rongfu (郭荣福; KWEE Eng Hoe(?), 1859-?)
Community leader, businessman

Born in Pontianak in 1859, he was the son of a rich merchant in the area. He worked in the Pontianak Local Government and in 1932 was appointed *kapitein* of Pontianak.

Source: Liu, *Gailan*, p. [113].

GUO Shunde. See **KWEE Soen Tik**
GUO Shuofeng. See **WINATA, Tomy**
GUO Xuanluan. See **KWEE Swan Lwan**
GUO Yunlian. See **KWEE Oen Liam**

GUO Yuxiu (郭毓秀, 1907–97)
Community leader, wealthy businessman, Hokchia

Born in 1907 in Fuqing, he graduated from the Fuzhou Secondary School. He came to Indonesia in 1927, first lived in Bandung and worked as a shopkeeper, selling cloths. In 1946 he raised capital and opened his own shop Nanxing Gongsi (南星公司). In 1948 he opened a branch in Jakarta. After the establishment of the PRC, Guo began to be active in the overseas Chinese community. In 1953 he became the president of Yurong Gonghui (玉融公会, a Hokchia association in Jakarta) and in 1955, as vice-president of Qiao Zong. He was in the reception committees of Premier Zhou Enlai (1955) and President Liu Shaoqi (1964) in Indonesia. It was also reported that in 1967 he joined a procession in Jakarta protesting the death of a PRC national Ning Xiangyu in the Indonesia jail. He was detained for seven months and was eventually released.

He died in Singapore in 1997 but his remains were buried in Jakarta.

Sources: *Singapore Futsing Association* (1980), p. 13; Lin Weimin and Li Shengmu (1999), pp. 298–305; the compiler's notes.

GUO Zaiyuan. See KUSUMA, Sugianto

HADI, Abdul W.M. (1946-) 安禄基*
Poet, former journalist, academic, Muslim

His full Chinese name is withheld by the compiler, his family name is An (安). Born in Madura in 1946 into a Chinese Muslim family, he studied Indonesian literature at the FSUI (1965–67) and Western philosophy at the UGM (1968–71). From 1969 to 1970 he was the editor of the *Mingguan Mahasiswa Indonesia* (Central Java edition). In 1971 he moved to Bandung and served as the editor of the same student newspaper, West Java edition (1971–73). After attending the Nusantara Literature Seminar in Kuala Lumpur in 1973, he participated in the International Writing Program (at Iowa University) as a guest-writer (October 1973 to April 1974). In June 1974 he was invited to take part in the International Poetry Festival in Rotterdam.

Abdul Hadi is a prolific writer. Apart from poetry, he has also written essays, articles, commentaries, and book reviews, ranging from student life, literature, philosophy, to culture. His poems, which have appeared in book form include *Riwayat* [Life story], *Terlambat di Jalan* [Late on the road], *Laut Belum Pasang* [The tide is not high yet], *Potret Panjang Seorang Pengunjung Pantai Sanur* [Portrait of a visitor in the Sanur Beach], and *Anak Laut Anak Angin* [Son of sea and son of wind]. He received the S.E.A. Write Award in 1985 for his poems. He was quoted as saying in an interview that he is "interested in the Far East, including China — my grandfather is Chinese". In 2006 he published his selected poems: *Madura, Luang Prabhang: Seratus Puisi Pilihan* (Jakarta, 2006).

Abdul Hadi was invited to the Universiti Sains Malaysia to teach but at the same time he was also doing his post graduate study and received his PhD degree from the same university. He later returned to Jakarta to teach at the Universitas Paramadina and in 2008 he was promoted to a full professor. His inaugural speech is entitled, "Paradoks Globalisasi: Memikirkan Kembali Arah Kebudayaan Kita" [Paradox of Globalization: Rethinking of Our Cultural Direction].

Sources: Abdul Hadi W.M., *Potret Panjang Seorang Pengunjung Pantai Sanur* (1975), back cover; Gunawan, "Berkenalan Dengan Tokoh-Tokoh Non-Pribumi", *Kompas*, 4 February 1979; *Asia Magazine*, 27 July 1986, p. 28; "Abdul Hadi WM", *Wikipedia Bahasa Indonesia, ensiklopedia bebas*, (accessed 8 February 2013); the compiler's notes.

HADINATA, Christian (JI Mingfa 纪明发, 1949-)
Badminton player

Born in Purwokerto on 12 December 1949, he was educated in his hometown. In 1971 he graduated from the IKIP (Bandung). Initially he played doubles with **TJUNTJUN**, but later teamed up with Ade Chandra and won the All-England men's doubles in 1972. In 1972, 1976, and 1979 he was a member of the Indonesian Thomas Cup Team. Apart from playing badminton, he also likes teaching. In 1980 he worked as a primary schoolteacher.

Sources: *Apa & Siapa 1981–82*, pp. 178–79; the compiler's notes.

HAKIM, Rachman (XU Shijing 许世经, 1950?-)
Community leader, businessman

Born in Belitung to a China-born father who has thirteen children, Rachman is number eight. Received his primary education in Belitung, he came to Jakarta to study at Pah Tsung

(Pa Chung) and only up to the junior high school level when the school was closed down by the Soeharto regime. He went into business and was involved in motorcycle and banking. After the fall of Soeharto he joined INTI. In 2005 he replaced **Eddie LEMBONG** as the general chairman of INTI and continued to hold the position for two terms. In 2013 he stepped down but was re-elected general chairman (2013–17) after INTI amended the constitution allowing the general chairman to serve for more than two terms.

Sources: Pan Changan 潘长安 *Fenzhiwujin, mianjinzili*, 奋志无矜, 勉勤自励, *Fujian qiaobao*《福建侨报》, <http://www.com/Fujian_w/news/fjqb/031024/1_17.html> (accessed 25 January 2014); INTI publications; the compiler's notes.

HALIM, Boediharto (LIEM Boen Hwa; LIN Wenhua 林文华, 1922–76)
Leading textile businessman

Born on 16 May 1922 in Semarang (according to *Shangbao*, he was born in China), he was educated up to secondary school level. Later, he took courses on textiles and management. In 1960 he established a huge company called PT Sandratext in Semarang and in 1970 in Jakarta as well. His company specialized in dyeing, finishing, weaving, and spinning. He died in Hong Kong on 27 November 1976.

Sources: Roeder, "Chinese 'Impudence'", p. 34; *Nanyang Shangbao*, 8 December 1976; Arief, *Who's Who in Indonesian Business* (2nd ed.), pp. 823–24.

HALIM, Rachman (TJOA Toh Heng; CAI Daoxing 蔡道行, 1947–2008)
Tycoon, son of **Surya WONOWIDJOYO**

Born in 1947 in Kediri, he was educated in a local Chinese school. In 1984 he succeeded his father as the general manager of Gudang Garam, one of the largest clove cigarette manufacturers. At one time, Gudang Garam supplied up to 50 per cent of the clove cigarette market in Indonesia. But the decline in cigarette consumption forced Gudang Garam to expand into other fields: finance, restaurants, hotels, and properties. Halim (and his family) was named as the best second-generation entrepreneur. His company employed 41,000 workers. His motto was "employees are the major partners in the entreprise". Like his father, it was reported that he looked after his employees very well. In 2007 he was selected as the richest Indonesian by Forbes. He died on 27 July 2008 in the Elizabeth Hospital, Singapore, but was buried in Kediri.

Sources: *Forbes Zibenjia*, July 1994, pp. 23–24; *Apa & Siapa 1985–86*, pp. 262–63; Indonesia Tokoh.Com (accessed 8 July 2008); Dwidjo U Maskum, "Jelang Pemakaman Bos Gudang Garam...", <http:// tempointeraktif.com/> (accessed 8 July 2008).

HAMID, Suwandi. See **BONG A Lok**

HAN, Awal (HAN Hoo Tjwan; HAN Haoquan 韩浩泉, 1930-)
Leading architect

Born in Malang in 1930, Han Awal had been interested in the art of spatial arrangement since childhood. After graduating from high school (at RK HBS Albertus Malang), he obtained a scholarship from the archbishop of Malang to study at the Technische Hoogeschool in Delft in the Netherlands. However, the conflict between Indonesia and the Netherlands over West Guinea pushed him to leave Delft to pursue his architecture education in Technische Universitat Berlin in Berlin, Germany, then known as one of the centres for the development of modernist architecture in Europe.

During the course of his study in Europe, Han Awal met many committed Indonesian architects and together they constituted a group called ATAP (the roof), which signified their attempt to address issues of identity in architecture and the crisis of housing in Indonesia. He is one of the first Indonesian modernists of the post-colonial era who believe in the power of architecture and space in registering social change. Returning to Indonesia in 1960, he designed many buildings — ranging from individual houses, schools, and churches to hospitals, pharmaceutical factories, and scientific research centres as well as conducted research on housing for the poor, and contributed his knowledge to universities in various cities of Java. At a later stage of his career, starting from the 1980s, when many buildings (of heritage value) had been torn down to make way for the rapid development of the city, he registered the importance of conservation and documentation of important buildings. He also contributed to the founding of the Centre for the Documentation of Architecture.

He is a brilliant architect and a committed educator. He has won three national awards associated with the Indonesian Association of Architects (IAI) for the design of the University of Atmajaya (awarded in 1984), and the conservation of the National Archive Building (2000) and the Bank of Indonesia (2009). He is also the recipient of UNESCO Asia — Heritage Award of Excellence in 2001 (with Budi Lim and Cor Passchier) for his conservation project. In 2007, Han Awal, with Ajie Damais and Wastu Pragantha Tjong, were awarded the Professor Teeuw Award for their contribution to fostering cultural exchange between Indonesia and the Netherlands through architectural conservation of buildings from the Dutch era.

Source: Abidin Kusno, "Han, Awal", Suryadinata, ed., *Southeast Asian Personalities* (2012), pp. 312–14.

HAN Hoo Tjwan. See HAN, Awal

HAN Tiauw Tjong (HAN Zhaozong 韩兆宗, 1894–1940)
Community leader, engineer, shareholder of Indische Lloyd
Born on 1 February 1894 in Probolinggo, his wealthy family background enabled him to attend the ELS in Kraksaan. He

continued schooling at the HBS (Semarang), and in 1911 went to the Netherlands to attend the HBS and Technical College in Delft, where he graduated as a qualified engineer in 1921, and received a PhD in engineering in 1922 after submitting a dissertation on the industrialization of China.

While in the Netherlands he was active in the CHH-Netherlands and became the president of the organization from 1919 to 1920, during which time he criticized the Dutch Nationality Law and favoured Chinese nationality for Indies Chinese. He changed his view after he returned to the Indies in 1923. In 1924 he lived in Pekalongan where he was appointed as a member of the Volksraad and reappointed as a member in 1927. Unlike **H.H. KAN**, who was happy with the Dutch Nationality Law, he criticized the defects of the law and urged the assimilation of the Chinese into European legal status.

Han was one of the founders of the CHH and an executive member of its central board. In 1934 he succeeded in calling a conference of Chinese members of local councils in Central Java and secured their support for the CHH. He died in Semarang in 1940.

Sources: Tan, *Tionghoa*, pp. 132–33; Wal, *Volksraad*, vol. II, p. 712; *Volksraad, 1928–29*, p. 90; *Djawa Tengah*, 25–28 March 1927; *CHHTC*, April 1923, p. 146.

HAN Zhaozong. See **HAN Tiauw Tjong**

HARDJONAGORO, Kanjeng Raden Tumenggung (GO Tik Swan; WU Dexuan 吴德宣, 1926-)
Expert on Javanese culture

Born in Surakarta in 1926, he was a grandson of a leading *batik* manufacturer, Tjan Khay Sing, who was a close friend of Gusti Hadidjojo and Prabuwikoto, two well-known *keris* experts in Surakarta. Go learned a lot about *keris* (*tosan aji*) from these two men. He showed special interest in Javanese culture in general and the *keris* in particular, which led to his entry to the FSUI in 1956. He participated in many Javanese dance performances while he was a student and headed the Cultural Section of the Students' Council at the FSUI. In the 1960s he won a competition in Javanese decorating art sponsored by the Jakarta Municipal Government. He held many exhibitions within and outside of Indonesia on *batik* and the *keris*. In September 1972 he was ordered by the Sultan of Surakarta (Susuhunan Paku Buwono XII) to visit the palace in traditional Javanese dress and was honoured as *bupati anom kraton* (palace regent). He was the first *peranakan* Chinese to obtain that honour for his cultural expertise. In March 1979 he was invited to the United States by the Textile Museum of Washington to give lectures on traditional *batik*. He also went to Saudi Arabia in the same year. In 1984 he went to Mecca to perform a small hadj. He runs a *batik* factory and is the curator of Museum Radyapusaka, a Javanese museum built by a high official during Pakubuwono IX's reign in 1890. His rich experiences have been recorded in his autobiography entitled, *Jawa Sejati, Otobiografi Go Tik Swan Hardjonagoro* [A true Javanese, Autobiography of Go Tik Swan Hardjonagoro] as told to Rustopo, a professor at the Institute of Arts in Surakarta. The book was published in 2008.

Sources: *Kompas*, 13 November 1972; Lee, *Indonesia between Myth and Reality* (1976), pp. 124, 183; *Tempo*, 31 March 1979, p. 31; 24 January 1981, p. 31; 24 August 1991, pp. 39–40; Suryadinata, ed., *Southeast Asian Personalities*, pp. 322–23.

Hari DARMAWAN. See DARMAWAN, Hari
Haris Otto Kamil TANZIL. See TANZIL, Haris Otto Kamil

HARJONO, Djoko. See DJIAUW Pok Kie

HARSONO, FX (OH Hong Boen; HU Fengwen 胡丰文, 1949-)
Founding Member of New Art Movement, artist

Born on 22 March 1949 in Blitar, East Java, Harsono is hailed as one of the most important contemporary Indonesian artists who emerged during the Soeharto period, first as an innovator and social critic, and later as an artist in search of an identity. He studied in two Chinese schools in his birthplace before a government regulation stipulating that from 1958 onwards, Indonesians of Chinese descent (WNI) would not be allowed to attend Chinese medium schools. He was transferred to a Catholic Primary School called Santa Maria where he learned drawing and painting. In 1969, he was admitted to the STSRI ASRI, or the Sekolah Tinggi Seni Rupa Indonesia (Indonesian College of Art), in Yogyakarta where he studied fine arts. It was at this college that he began to develop his talent in art and take an interest in Indonesian politics.

In August 1975, Harsono and a group of young artists held an exhibition in Taman Ismail Marzuki, Jakarta, where they officially announced the formation of the Gerakan Seni Rupa Baru (GSRB New Art Movement), advocating the elimination of the distinctions between painting, graphics, and sculpture, abandoning the elitist view on arts, and creating a new Indonesian art form in which Indonesian characteristics and contents would be highlighted. It was later disbanded in 1979 due to internal conflict. Over the years Harsono and his generation of artists continued to depict social injustice and repression through their art. He produced his works using the new concept of contextual art and new technique. A number of his works such as "The Relaxed Chain" dated 1975, "Power and the Oppressed" dated 1992, and "Voice without Voice/Sign" dated 1993–94, portrayed injustices and military suppression during the New Order. After the 1998 anti-Chinese riots and the fall of Soeharto, many of his works concentrated on Chinese culture in Indonesia.

Harsono began to gain recognition outside Indonesia as one of the nation's top contemporary artists since 1992. He participated in many group exhibitions and held thirteen solo exhibitions since 1994. He is currently teaching at the Faculty of Art and Design, the University of Pelita Harapan, Tangerang, West Java.

Sources: Leo Suryadinata, "Harsono, FX", Suryadinata, ed., *Southeast Asian Personalities* (2012), pp. 324–26; Harsono, "CV FX Harsono 2011"; Harsono, "Washed Away Memories: FX Harsono"; Kolesnikov-Jessop, "FX Harsono's Rebellious, Critical Voice Against 'Big Power' in Indonesia", *The New York Times*, 11 March 2010; Rath, eds., *Re: Petition/Position/FX Harsono* (2010); private communications, April 2012.

Harry Tjan SILALAHI. See **SILALAHI, Harry Tjan**

HARTONO, Michael Bambang (OEI Gwie Siong; HUANG Huixiang 黄惠祥, 1941?-)
Kretek cigarette manufacturer, banker, elder brother of **Robert Budi HARTONO**

Born in Kudus, Central Java, in 1941(?), son of Oei Wie Gwan, who established Djarum, a *kretek* (clove) cigarette manufacturer in 1951. Michael received his education in Kudus. He later went to Diponegoro University but had to return to Kudus when Djarum was burnt down in 1963. He and his yonger brother **Robert Budi HARTONO** re-built the company and made it into the largest *kretek* (clove) cigarette manufacturer in Indonesia. The Djarum Group has established more than ten companies dealing in textiles, electronics, furniture, finance, banking (Bank Hagakita and Hagabank), and property (PT Bukit Mulia). In 1993 the Bukit Mulia began to construct Karawang Industrial Park, which is located in West Java. Michael and Robert Hartono have been listed by Forbes (2013) as the richest Indonesians with the net worth of US$15 billion.

The Djarum Group has been involved in various activities. It has a badminton club which is well-known for training champions. **LIEM Swie King**, **Ivana LIE** and **Susi SUSANTI** were all trained by this club.

Sources: *Forbes Zibenjia*, June 1993, p. 88. Setyautama, *Tokoh-tokoh Etnis Tionghoa*, pp. 264–65.

HARTONO, Robert Budi (OEI Gwie Tiong; HUANG Huizhong 黄惠忠, 1942?-)
Kretek cigarette manufacturer, banker, younger brother of **Michael Bambang HARTONO**

Born in Kudus, Central Java, in 1942(?), he is now the CEO of the Djarum Group. Together with his older brother **Michael Bambang HARTONO**, they succeeded in developing Djarum to become the largest cigarette manufacturer in Indonesia. They later diversified the company and expanded to banking and property. In 1998 the Hartono brothers became the majority shareholder of Bank Central Asia (BCA), the largest private bank in Indonesia which was owned by **Soedono SALIM** (the Salim Group) before the fall of Soeharto. According to one report, the Harotono brothers were able to have 51 per cent of the BCA share through the Mauritius-based Farindo Investments, and 90 per cent of the Farindo Investments shares were controlled by the Hartono brothers. The Djarum Group is still run by the second generation, but the third generation, mainly sons of Robert Hartono, are now gradualy taking over the executive positions.

Sources: *Forbes Zibenjia*, June 1993, p. 88. Setyautama, *Tokoh-tokoh Etnis Tionghoa*, p. 265; Arifin Surya Nugraha & dkk, *10 Orang Terkaya Indonesia 2007* (Yogjakarta: Pustaka Timur, 2007), pp. 2–20.

Hartono, Rudy KUNIAWAN. See **KURNIAWAN, Rudy Hartono**
Hary TANOESOEDIBJO. See **TANOESOEDIBJO, Hary**
Hasan KARMAN. See **KARMAN, Hasan**

HASAN, Mohammad Bob (THE Kian Seng; ZHENG Jiansheng 郑建盛, 1931-)
Timber king, cabinet minister, promoter of sports

Born in Semarang in 1931, he was the president of Apkindo (Asosiasi Panel Kayu Lapis Indonesia), the Indonesian Plywood Association. He was raised as a foster-child by Colonel Gatot Subroto who later became a well-known general. It is said that because of this background, he was close with the military.

According to *Forbes Zibenjia*, he had two groups of companies: the Bob Hasan Group and the Pasopati, the major shareholder of which was Sigit Harjojudanto, President Soeharto's eldest son. *Tempo*, however, stated that Hasan owned and had investments in twenty to thirty companies which included Kalimanis Plywood, PT Pasopati holding company, PT Wasesa Lines, PT Karana Shipping Lines, PT Hutan Nusantara, and PT Lifetime Assembly of Watch and Electrical Equipment. The companies were engaged in a variety of businesses such as chemicals, paper manufacturing, steel, construction, transportation, hotels, and insurance.

Bob Hasan is a sports enthusiast. He has been sponsoring athletic activities in Indonesia and was elected by the Indonesian Journalist Association for being the best promoter of sports (Pembina Olahraga) in 1980 and 1984. He has also served as the chairman of PASI (Indonesian Athletes Association) since 1979. In 1994 he was elected a member of the International Olympic Committee (IOC).

Although popular in the sports arena, Hasan was disliked in business circles. Still President Soeharto, who had refused to appoint Chinese Indonesians to his cabinet, eventually did appoint one — Bob Hasan. In early 1998, a few months before he stepped down under international pressure, Soeharto reshuffled his cabinet and announced the line-up of the new cabinet on 16 March 1998, with Hasan as his new Minister of Trade and Industry. Soeharto was criticized by many domestic and foreign observers who did not think Hasan was capable of salvaging the Indonesian economy which was in crisis then. In fact the cabinet was dissolved after two months and five days, being the shortest Soeharto government ever and coinciding with the downfall of Soeharto on 22 May 1998.

After the fall of Soeharto, Hasan was involved in a series of court cases. He was eventually sentenced to six years in prison and ordered to pay compensations amounting to US$243.7 million. The sentence was first upheld by the Supreme Court and he was sent to Nusakambangan. But later the sentence was reduced and by early 2004 he was freed on parole. Hasan was re-elected as chairman of PASI. In October 2011, an eighty-year-old Hasan launched his book entitled, *Mengapa Saya Sehat* [Why am I healthy?] in Jakarta.

Sources: Roeder, "Chinese 'Impudence'", p. 34; McDonald, *Soeharto's Indonesia*, pp. 30–31; *Apa & Siapa 1985–86*, pp. 292–94; *Tempo*, 20 October 1979; *Forbes Zibenjia*, July 1994, p. 27; *Eksekutif*, no. 194 (August 1995), p. 36; Suryadinata, ed., *Southeast Asian Personalities*, p. 328; the compiler's notes.

HASSAN, Hadji Mohammad (TAN Kim Liong; CHEN Jinlong 陈金龙, 1925-)
Politician, businessman

Born in Tanah Grogot (Kalimantan) in 1925, he completed SMA education, and attended Akademi Wartawan (two years), and Universitas 17 Agustus (Jakarta). In 1956 he was appointed as a member of the DPR representing the Chinese minority. Prior to his appointment, he was a merchant and later a photographer of *Suluh Indonesia*. One source says that he was a member of the PNI (Jakarta branch). He advocated name-changing for Indonesian citizens of Chinese descent in the 1950s and changed his own name to Mohammad Hassan. He was appointed as a member of the DPR in 1959–64 representing the NU. In 1964 he was made Minister of State Revenue, Finance and Audit (RI). From 1962 to ? he was also the general manager of *Duta Masjarakat*, the NU newspaper. In 1967 he left for Hong Kong where he lived for about seven years and in 1974 he returned to his birthplace to engage in cocoa cultivation. He established the PT Hasfarm Product Ltd. to manage his enterprise.

Sources: *Mingguan Sadar*, 23 December 1956, p. 30; Finch, *Cabinets*, p. 55; *DPR*, 1971, p. 653; *Tempo*, 17 November 1979, p. 54.

HAUW Tek Kong (HOU Deguang 候德广, 1887–1928)
Community leader, newspaperman

Born in Jakarta in 1887, he was probably educated at the Anglo-Chinese School in Singapore. In 1913 he became the director of *Sin Po*, holding Chinese nationalist view. In 1919 he was sent to China by *Sin Po* to negotiate with the Chinese Government on the repudiation right of *peranakan* in connection with the Dutch Nationality Law. The Dutch authorities barred him from re-entering Indonesia. He eventually abandoned his anti-Dutch law attitude and was allowed to return to Java in 1922 when he became the editor-in-chief of *Bin Seng*. In 1923 he published a new *peranakan* daily, *Keng Po*, and served as its director. He died in Jakarta on 7 April 1928.

Sources: Suryadinata, *Peranakan Politics*, pp. 35ff; Tio, *Lie Kimhok*, p. 92; *Sin Po*, 23 September 1919.

HE Cunlin. See HONORIS, Otje
HE Longchao. See HO Liong Tiauw
HE Zhi. See HONORIS, Otje
HE Zhenkang. See HONORIS, Charles

HEI Ying (黑婴; ZHANG Bingwen 张炳文; ZHANG Youjun 张又君, 1915–92)
Writer, newspaperman, Hakka

Born in 1915 in Medan, he went to Mei Xian for his early education. At the age of thirteen he returned to Medan to enter an English school while he worked part-time in *Xin Zhonghua Bao*. At the age of thirty-two he went to China again and was admitted to Foreign Language Department, Jinan University. He started writing short stories and essays. In 1933 he published *Diguo de nuer* (Daughter of Empire 帝国的女儿), and in 1935 a collection of his essays *Yibang yu guguo* (Foreign country and motherland 异邦与故国). When the anti-Japanese war erupted in China he returned to Medan again, and worked as chief editor of *Xin Zhonghua Bao*. In 1941 he moved to Jakarta. During the Japanese Occupation of Java he was arrested and interned for several years. He was released after Japanese surrender. In 1945, together with Huang Zhougui 黄周贵 and **Wang Jiyuan** 王纪元, he established *Sheng Huo Bao* (Seng Hwo Pao) and served as the editor-in-chief. During 1946–48 he also taught part-time at Pa Chung (Pah Tsung). He produced many essays, poems, commentaries etc., but his best works were short stories and short novels. In 1947 he published his collection of short stories under the title of *Shidai de gandong* (The Touch of the Era 时代的感动). In 1949 he published a short novel entitled, *Hongbai qi xia* (Under the red-white flag 红白旗下). In 1950 he went to China and worked for *Guangming Ribao*. He died in 1992.

Source: Qian Ren, "Hei Ying shengping jianjie", in Qian Ren, Liang Junxiang, eds., *Shenghuobao de huiyi* (Guangdong: Shijie tushu chuban Guangdong youxian gongsi, 2013), pp. 196–97.

Hembing WIJAYAKUSUMA. See **WIJAYAKUSUMA, Hembing**
Hendra DARMAWAN. See **DARMAWAN, Hendra**
Hendra ESMARA. See **ESMARA, Hendra**
Hendra KARTANEGARA. See **TAN Joe Hok**
Hendrawan LESMANA. See **LESMANA, Hendrawan**
Hendrawan SUPRAKTIKNO. See **SUPRAKTIKNO, Hendrawan**
Hendrick GOZALI. See **GOZALI, Hendrick**
Hendrick SIE. See **Hendrawan LESMANA**
Henry PRIBADI. See **PRIBADI, Henry**

Hermawan KARTAJAYA. See **KARTAJAYA, Hermawan**
HIDAYAT, Basuki. See **TJIA Giok Thwan**

HIE Foek Tjhoy (XU Fucai 许福才, 1892-?)
Community leader, employee of Yung-an T'ang (manufacturer of Chinese medical preparations)
Born in Medan (?) in 1892, he was active in various Chinese organizations in Jakarta before World War II. In 1946 he served as the president of Poh An Tui (Jakarta).
Sources: Tio's notes; a pamphlet on Poh An Tui.

HIM Tek Ji. See **JUSUF, Tedy**

HIMAWAN, Charles (Charles ONG, 1934–2002) 王查理*
Lawyer, university professor
Born in Semarang on 17 April 1934, he obtained his SH degree from the FHUI in 1961. In 1969 he studied at the University of Minnesota Law School as a Fulbright scholar. In 1971 he studied at the Hague Academy of International Law. He continued his graduate studies in the United States. He received his Master of Law (LLM) from Harvard University Law School in 1976, and two years later, he was awarded Doctor of Judicial Science from the same university. He published his dissertation: *The Foreign Investment Process in Indonesia: The Role of Law in the Economic Development of a Third World Country* (Singapore: Gunung Agung, 1980). Apart from the dissertation, he has also published at least six monographs: *Highlights on the Company Law of Indonesia* (Singapore, 1973); *Doing Business in Indonesia* (Cambridge, 1976); The Poverty of Law in Indonesia (Cambridge, 1978); *The Role of Law in Indonesia's Plantation Development* (Jakarta, 1981); and *Peningkatan Peran Ahli Hukum dalam Bisnis* [The Upgrading of the Lawyer's Role in Business] (Jakarta, 1988). In 1980 he was the director of the Centre for the Study of Law and the Economy, FHUI. In April 1991 he was promoted to Professor

of Law at the same university. In his augural speech, he maintained that the Indonesian law was still in deep sleep and it was time to wake it up. Charles was later appointed as a member of the National Commission on Human Rights by the Jakarta government. He liked to read the works of Shakespeare and often quoted Shakespeare in his conversations. He died of a heart illness in Jakarta on 11 May 2002.

Sources: Himawan's dissertation; *Kompas*, 25 April 1991; *Strait Times*, 24 November 1994, p. 28; Charles Himawan, <http://www.tokohindonesia.com/ensiklopedi/c/charles-himawan/index.shtml> (accessed 3 February 2004).

HIOE Njan Joeng (QIU Yuanrong 丘元荣, 1895–1978)
Community leader, businessman, Hakka
Born in 1895 (1897?) in Meixian, Guangdong, he received little formal education, but managed to read and write Chinese very well. He came to Java at the age of eighteen and worked as a clerk. However, he soon became a successful businessman, specializing in textiles and later in many other fields. Like many well-to-do Hakkas in Jakarta, he was a leading member of the KMT. Prior to World War II, he was widely recognized in the *totok* community, especially among businessmen. In 1936–40 Hioe was elected as the president of Siang Hwee (Jakarta). He was elected as the president of Huaqiao Gonghui 华侨公会, a *totok* organization dominated by Hakkas, for the period 1942–46.

Hioe was active in the anti-Japanese campaign. He was the chairman of the China Charity Fund Committee. It follows that when Japan occupied Java, Hioe was detained in the concentration camp. He became active again after World War II, first in the formation of Shang Lian and later the Shang Lian–sponsored Gao Shang School (in the 1950s). He was also the chairman of the board of trustees of a large pro-Kuomintang high school, Chung-shan Chung-hsueh (Zhongshan Zhongxue), prior to 1958. In 1958 he was detained by the Indonesian authorities in connection with the anti-KMT campaign after the Regional Rebellions. He was later released but continued to live in Indonesia. When the Special Project National Schools (SNPC) for alien Chinese children were established after the 1965 coup, Hioe supported the project. He died in Jakarta in 1978.

Sources: Liu, *Gailan* [20]; interview, 1970; *Huaqiao Da Cidian*, p. 796; the compiler's notes.

HO Liong Tiauw (HE Longchao 何隆朝, 1928–2011)
Community leader, Hokchia

Born in Fuqing in 1928, he came to Java at the age of nine. Information on his education is unavailable. He became a leading textile merchant in Semarang, and was later known as King of Plastic. In 1950 he became chairman of the Semarang Textile Merchants Asssociation. In 1952 when he was twenty-four years old he was elected as the president of the pro-Beijing CHTH in Semarang. He held the position until 1965. From 1957 he became chairman of boards of various Chinese medium schools in Semarang. He was also the deputy president of Shijie Fuqing shetuan lianyi hui.

Sources: *Zhongcheng Bao*, 18 February 1964; <http://tieba.baidu.com/p/1245324478> (accessed 28 June 2014); the compiler's notes.

HO Tjek. See **HONORIS, Otje**
HONG Abi. See **ARBI, Haryanto**
HONG Le Hoa. See **SIEM Piet Nio**
HONG Youliang. See **WAHYUDI, Johan**
HONG Yuanyuan. See **ANG Jan Goan**

HONORIS, Charles (HE Zhenkang 何震康, 1984-)
Member of Parliament

Born on 23 July 1984 in Jakarta, he graduated from the International Christian University in Tokyo (2007). He is vice-president of PT Modern Land Realty in Jakarta. He contested and won a parliamentary seat for Jakarta representing the PDIP in the 2014 election.

Sources: Pengurus Pusat Fordeka, *Buku Acuan 2014–2019*, p. 126; the compiler's notes.

HONORIS, Otje (HO Tjek; HE Zhi 何值; HE Chunlin 何春霖, 1922–81)
Wealthy businessman

Born in 1922 in Singapore, he migrated to Sulawesi (Indonesia) when he was one year old. He learned photography and opened a photo studio in Ujung Pandang. In 1965 his son, He Xiaokun (Ho Sioe Koen, Samadikun Hartono), graduated from a Chinese middle school in Ujung Pandang and joined him. In 1971 Otje Honoris established the Modern Group. Both father and son succeeded in getting the sole distributorship rights for Fuji Film in Indonesia, and since then the Group has been expanding. The group has three major companies: Modern Foto Film, which specializes in photo business; Modern Land, which specializes in property; and Modern Bank. In 1985 Samadikun Hartono became the chairman of the Modern Group. According to the Chinese edition of *Forbes Zibenjia*, the Modern Group has thirty-five companies.

Sources: *Forbes Zibenjia*, November 1993, pp. 40–44; July 1994, p. 29; <http://www.plasticstoday.com/articles/productivity> (accessed 25 April 2013).

HOO Eng Djie (1906–62) 何英如*
Poet, singer, songwriter

Hoo Eng Djie was born in Makassar to a poor *peranakan* family. He did not finish his primary schooling due to economic difficulty. By the age of thirteen he worked in the ship which travelled between nearby islands such as Buton, Raha, Ambon and Dobu. He lost his job and returned to Makassar to help in his father's shop. However, during night time he liked to read *peranakan* novels, play guitar and sing. He also began to make friends with street youth and lived like one. He drank, smoked and womanized. He felt in love with the two *peranakan* prostitutes who eventually abandoned him. At one time he went to Dobu to look for his sweetheart who also became a prostitute. Broken hearted, he returned to Makassar and started writing many songs. Between 1930 and 1940 he succeeded in composing around 3,000 songs. Most of his songs depict the experience of life and his bleak future. Some were adaptations from Chinese songs, of which the most famous were *Ati Radja* (King's heart), *Sai Long* (Lion and Dragon Dance), *Pasang Teng* (To light lantern) and *Sio Sayang* (Mutual love). His songs were often played during special occasions such as wedding ceremonies or celebrations. Hoo was so popular that a music firm in Surabaya Firma Ho Soen Ho invited him to record his songs.

Hoo later met a divorcee named Soan Kie and married her. During the Japanese Occupation they lived in the mountainous area and only returned to Makassar after Japanese surrender. Hoo revived his singing career. He taught students music and together with his students and stepson Tajem Choi, they formed an orchestra which performed during various occasions. In 1947 he met **NJOO Cheong Seng**, a well-known *peranakan* film director and producer. Hoo often appeared in Njoo's movies playing some small characters. Nevertheless, Hoo's main interests were still music and songwriting. In 1953 he formed the Singara Kulla-Kullawa (Sparkles of Fireflies) Group and specialized in Bugis and Makassarese music. Nevertheless, many were based on his songs and lyrics. He won the Indonesian National Radio Award in Makassar for his songs and music. It was reported that Hoo also met President Soekarno who liked his music. Hoo died on 7 March 1962 in his house in Makassar. His songs are still popular even after his death.

Source: Myra Sidharta, *Dari Penjaja Tekstil Sampai Superwoman* (Jakarta: KPG, 2004), pp. 112–23.

Biographies

HOU Deguang. See **HAUW Tek Kong**
HSU C.C. See **XU Juqing**
HSU C.M. See **XU Zhongming**
HU Fengwen. See **HARSONO, FX**
HUANG Anshu. See **OEY An Siok**
HUANG Changshui. See **OEY Tiang Tjoei**
HUANG Dongping. See **OEY Tong Pin**
HUANG Fengli. See **OEY Hong Lee**
HUANG Haichun. See **OEI Hai Djoen Tj**
HUANG Hanshan. See **SANJAYA, Christiandy**
HUANG Honglan. See **WIDYONO, Benny**
HUANG Huilan. See **OEI Hui Lan (Mrs Wellington Koo)**
HUANG Huixiang. See **HARTONO, Michael Bambang**
HUANG Huizhong. See **HARTONO, Robert Budi**
HUANG Jianguo. See **WIBISONO, Christianto**
HUANG Jinchang. See **OEY Kim Tiang**
HUANG Jinquan. See **SETIAWAN, Chandra**
HUANG Longtai. See **OEI Liong Thay**
HUANG Meiling. See **OEY-GARDINER, Mayling**
HUANG Qianghui. See **OEY Kian Hoei**
HUANG Qingxing. See **KARIM, Hadji Abdul**
HUANG Shaofan. See **KARMAN, Hasan**
HUANG Songchang. See **WIDJAYA, Tjiangdra**
HUANG Shuang'an. See **URAY, Burhan**
HUANG Yicong. See **WIDJAJA, Eka Tjipta**
HUANG Yifa. See **OEI Gee Hwat**
HUANG Yongzhou. See **OEI Jong Tjioe**

HUANG Yurong (黄裕荣, 1936–83)
Handicapped writer

Born in Meixian, Guangdong, China in 1936, he migrated to Indonesia in 1950 together with his father who was a physician. From young he suffered from tuberculosis (better known as TB) in the spine and his back was rather crooked. In 1952 he underwent an operation and failed. He became paralyzed below his waist. However, he was very determined to live a normal life. By self-taught he was able to finish his education at Xiamen University correspondence course. He wrote short stories, essays, poems, fables and literary critics, published in Chinese magazines in Hong Kong, mainland China and Indonesian Chinese newspapers. He also served as editor of the literary pages of *Zhongcheng Bao* (Jakarta) and series editor of *Feicui Wenyi Xiao Ji* 翡翠文艺小集.

He later published collections of his works, including *Chunfeng de bolang* (春风的波浪 the wave of spring wind, poems), *Yinhua wenyi pinglunji* (印华文艺评论集 a collection of literary critics on Yinhua literature, two volumes). After the 1965 coup, he took the TCM correspondence course from Xiamen University. After he passed away, Jinan University of China published a volume of his work, entitled *Lunyi shang de zhange* (轮椅上的战歌, a battle hymn on the wheelchair).

Source: Pan Yadun 潘亚墩, ed., *Lunyi shang de zhange* (1995), pp. 11–12.

HUANG Zhonghan. See **OEI Tiong Ham**
HUANG Zida. See **OEI Tjoe Tat**
HUANG Zongxiao. See **OEI Tjong Hauw**
HUANG Zongxuan. See **OEI Tjong Swan**
HUANG Zongyi. See **OEI Tjong Ie**
HUO Zuoyou. See **DARMADI, Jan**
Husain DJOJONEGORO. See **DJOJONEGORO, Husain**

HUSINO, M.H. (OH Sien Hong, 1904-?) 胡信丰*
Lawyer, former journalist and teacher

Born on 5 March 1904 in Yogyakarta, he was educated at the HCS (Yogyakarta), MULO (Yogyakarta), and the AMS (Bandung). He later enrolled as a law student at the RHS in Jakarta but left after passing the Candidate's Examination (1927). While at the RHS he served as the secretary of Ta Hsioh Sing Hwee (1926) and the president of the Central Chung Hsioh. From 1925 to 1927 he worked as a teacher at the THHK school (Jakarta). He became the editor-in-chief of *Perniagaan* in 1928, and of *Siang Po* in 1930. He resigned from *Siang Po* in the same year and worked as a schoolteacher again.

After 1945 he was active in the labour movement (Sin Min Lao Kung Hui, which was later renamed Pusat Organisasi Buruh or POB). He represented the RI at ILO conferences several times. In 1952 he conducted a study of the working conditions of Indonesian pearl-divers in Australia. In the same year, he finished his law studies at the FHUI and has been practising law since. He was a member of the PSI but did not hold any political office. During the New Order period, he was a member of the advisory board of Bakom.

Sources: Tan, *Tionghoa*, pp. 201–2; *Sin Po*, 11 October 1926; interview, 1968; correspondence, 1978; the compiler's notes.

HUSNI, Arief (ONG Sin King; ONG Seng Keng; WANG Chengqing 王成庆, ?-1974)
Businessman, banker

He was the director of N.V. Coopa, a leading import-export firm in Jakarta, and the director of Bank Ramayana (PT Bank Rama, according to another source) in Jakarta, owning 50 per cent of the shares. In the late 1960s he was involved in a major BULOG fertilizer scandal. He later moved to Singapore and died in 1974 after falling from a horse.

Sources: *Indonesia Raya*, 4 October and 4 November 1972; Crouch, "Generals and Business in Indonesia", *Pacific Affairs* 48, no. 4 (Winter 1975–76): 534–35; *Straits Times*, 25 April 1995, p. 2; *Lianhe Zaobao*, 25 April 1995, p. 3; the compiler's notes.

HUTOMO, Suryo (KWA Kwie An; KE Gui'an 柯贵安, 1936–97)
Community leader, Confucian

Born in Surakarta on 10 August 1936, he was educated at the Faculty of Law, Universitas 17 Agustus (now Universitas

11 Maret) at his birthplace. In 1964–68 he served as the deputy chairman of the Majelis Agama Khonghucu Indonesia (Matakin). He was the general chairman (*ketua umum*) of Matakin from 1969 to 1987. He also held the following positions: DPP-Golkar, Kosi Agama Khonghucu (since February 1976); Member of Bapilu (Badan Pengendali Pemilihan Umum), Sub-Departemen Agama Khonghucu. Later he stepped down from Matakin and went into business. He was the director of Perguruan Setia Bhakti (Tangerang) between 1992–97.

Sources: Interview, 1976, 1995; *Apa & Siapa 1985–86*, pp. 324–25; *Riwayat Klenteng, Vihara, Litang, Tempat Ibadat Tridharma se Jawa* (1980), p. 121; the compiler's notes.

I

IDRIS, Tahyar. See THE Teng Chun

IE Tjoen Siang (YU Chunxiang 余春祥, 1885–1953)
Community leader, landlord

A fourth-generation Chinese born in Jatinegara on 6 November 1885, he went to a Hokkien school and the ELS (Jatinegara). One source says that he started working at the age of thirteen. Due to his courage and familiarity with Dutch law, he became rich and respected in the local Chinese community. He once organized the local Chinese to petition the reduction of government fee for Chinese cemetery land and succeeded in forcing a Dutch newspaper to apologize for insulting the Chinese. Before 1939 he served as the president of the THHK (Jatinegara) for seventeen years, and the president of the THHK (Jakarta) in 1939. He was a member of a landlord's association and Siang Hwee (Jakarta) prior to World War II. He died in Jakarta on 26 June 1953.

Sources: *Tan, Tionghoa*, p. 188; Liu, *Gailan*, p. [42]; *Fujian*, p. 68; the compiler's notes.

IM Jang Tju. See **TAN Hong Boen**
IM Yang Tjoe. See **TAN Hong Boen**

INJO Beng Goat (YANG Mingyue 杨明月, 1904–62)
Journalist, community leader

Born in Bengkulu in 1904, he was educated at the RHS (Jakarta) and in 1926 served as an executive member of Ta Hsioh Sing Hwee (Jakarta). Before World War II he was a leader of the local T'ien-ti Hui (Tiandi Hui). In the 1930s he served as an editor and in the 1950s(?) as the editor-in-chief of *Keng Po*, an influential *peranakan* Chinese newspaper. In 1948–50 he was an executive member of the PT/PDTI central board. He died in Jakarta on 1 November 1962.

Sources: *Sin Po*, 11 October 1926; *Warta Bhakti*, 2 November 1962; *Sinar*, 1950, back cover; *Sinar*, 1 April 1949, p. 8; *Directory of Chinese Names*, p. 111.

IRAWAN, Bingky (FU Sunming 傅孙铭, 1952-)
Leader of Religious Organization, Confucian

Born in a small town near Surabaya, East Java in 1952, his father was a Chinese migrant and his mother is a Javanese woman. At one time he studied mysticism. Later he was exposed to Confucianism, and in 1985 he joined Matakin. He first became the deputy chairman and later chairman of Boen Bio (Confucian temple) in Surabaya. He believed in the legal rights of Confucianism. In 1995 he was the one who supported Budi and Lany to sue the Civil Registry Office in Surabaya which refused the couple to be registered in a Confucian marriage. Budi and Lany eventually lost the case but Confucianism won a great sympathy from the indigenous Indonesian community, including the Islamic community. Bingky was a good friend of President Abdurrahman Wahid (Gus Dur), it was reported that in 2000 Gus Dur attended the Cap Go Me (Lantern Festival celebration) in Surabaya which was organized by Bingky.

Source: Wang Aiping, *Kongjiao yanjiu*, pp. 133–36.

Iskandar KAMIL. See **KAMIL, Iskandar**

ISKANDAR, Nathanel (TAN Goan Tiang; CHEN Yuanchang 陈源长, 1917-77)
Demographer, university professor, Protestant

Born in Cianjur on 13 March 1917, he received a Drs degree in Economics from the FEUI in 1956, and a certificate in demography from the FEUI in 1970. In 1949-53 he was the principal of a Christian high school in Jakarta. In 1957-59 he was a lecturer at both the FEUI and the UNPAD (Bandung). In 1962-64 he was appointed as a senior lecturer at the FEUI; from 1964 to 1967 and from 1969 to 1977 he was the head of Lembaga Demografi, FEUI. In 1970 he served as the assistant dean at the FEUI. He also served as a member of the board of trustees of Christian University of Indonesia (UKI), a member of the UN Population Commission, and a member of the International Union for the Scientific Study of Population. In June 1977 he was promoted to full professorship at the FEUI. He died from a heart attack on 2 November 1977. His publications include *Perkembangan Penduduk Dunia* (Jakarta, 1969); *Perkembangan Penduduk di Asia Tenggara* (Jakarta, 1969); *Population Projections for Indonesia 1961-2001* (Jakarta, 1970); *Population Dynamics and Economic Development* (Jakarta, 1970); *Some Monographic Studies on the Population in Indonesia* (Jakarta, 1973); and *Masalah Pertumbuhan Penduduk di Indonesia* (Jakarta, 1974).

Sources: The above-mentioned books; *Selected Scholars*, p. 304; *Annual Report of the Christian University of Indonesia 1974*, p. 47; *Kompas*, 3 November 1977; the compiler's notes.

ISMANTO, Adil. See **TAN Boen Aan**
ITEM. See **TAN Tjeng Bok**

Jack OEI. See **OEI Tjong Ie**

JAHJA, Junus (LAUW Chuan Tho; LIU Quandao 刘全道, 1927–2011)
Leader of the assimilationist movement, economist, Muslim

Born in 1927 into the family of a *wijkmeester* (zone-chief) in Jakarta, he was educated at a Dutch school in his birthplace. In 1949 he went to Rotterdam, Holland, where he was active in students' movements. In 1959 he obtained a Drs degree in Economics from the University of Rotterdam.

He returned to Indonesia in 1960, signed the Piagam Asimilasi in 1961, and founded Panitia Penjuluhan Asimilasi. In 1962 he established Urusan Pembinaan Kesatuan Bangsa, which was the forerunner of the LPKB. In the same year he changed his Chinese name to an Indonesian name.

In 1974 he was appointed as a member of the BPKB-DKI. In June 1979 he repudiated Protestantism and became a Muslim. In 1980 he went to Mecca and became a *hadji*. Soon after that he established Yayasan Ukuwah Islamiah, which aimed at spreading Islam among young and educated Chinese Indonesians. Between 1980 and 1990 he was appointed as a council member of Majelis Ulama Indonesia. He has worked with Muhammadiyah to promote economic cooperation between indigenous and ethnic Chinese businessmen. Since 1990 he was appointed as an adviser to the Association of Indonesian Muslim Intellectuals (ICMI).

In August 1998, he was awarded Bintang Mahaputra Utama by President Habibie for his contributions to Indonesia. Some of his published works include *Kisah-kisah Saudara Baru* [The stories of new converts] (1989); *Catatan Seorang WNI Tionghoa* [The diary of an Indonesian of Chinese descent] (1988), an autobiography and *Peranakan Idealis: Dari Lie Eng Hok sampai Teguh Karya* [Idealist *Peranakan* Chinese:

From Lie Eng Hok to Teguh Karya] (2002), a collection of biographies of prominent *peranakan* in Indonesia. In fact, this book is more a compilation rather than his own works. He also edited/compiled books such as *Garis Rasial Garis Usang* [Racial line is obsolete line] (1983); *Zaman Harapan Bagi Keturunan Tionghoa* [Era of hope for Indonesians of Chinese descent] (1984); *Muslim Tionghoa* [Chinese Muslims] (1985); *Nonpri di Mata Pribumi* [Non-indigenous Indonesians in the eyes of indigenous Indonesians] (1991). Junus died in Jakarta on 7 November 2011.

Sources: *Lahirnya Konsepsi Asimilasi*, p. 23; *Inti Masalah "Minorita"* (c.1962), p. 29; *Tempo*, 6 August 1977, pp. 6–7; *Pembauran*, no. 10 (July/August 1979): 2–4; Jahja, *Nonpri di Mata Pribumi* (1991), pp. 349–50; *Suara Merdeka*, 15 August 1998; *Kompas*; the compiler's notes.

Jahja WULLUR. See **WULLUR, Jahja**
James DANANJAYA. See **DANANJAYA, James**
Jan DARMADI. See **DARMADI, Jan**
Jani ARSADJAJA. See **TJOENG Tin Jan**

JANANTO, Soetopo (YAP Soetopo; YAP Soei (Swie) Kie; YE Ruiji 叶瑞基, 1934–84)
Industrialist, wealthy businessman

Born in 1934 (place of birth unavailable), he became known after the New Order era (1965). He had many joint ventures with major Japanese financial groups. Two of these ventures were the Indonesian Bridgestone Tyres Corporation and the CV Berkat Paper Manufacturing Company (which produced 34 per cent of Indonesian bond paper).

Yap's businesses included timber, copper, plantation, import-export, real estate, and banking. He was the general manager of the Berkat Group, the president of the board of trustees of a Hong Kong finance company (Weihao Caiwu Gongsi), the chairman of the Indonesian Bowling Association, and later, the president of the FIQ. A close friend of the Johor Sultan, he was awarded the SPMJ (Dato Seri Paduka Mahkota Johor) by the Sultan in October 1980. He died in Singapore on 25 January 1984.

Sources: *Bangkok Post*, 28 January 1971; *Indonesia Raya*, 4 November 1972; *Nanyang Shangbao*, 30 October 1980; *Zaobao*, 27 January 1984.

JAUW K.H. See **JAUW Keng Hong**

JAUW Keng Hong (K.H. JAUW, 1895-?) 饶庆丰*
Community leader, lawyer

Born in Gorontalo on 15 May 1895, he was educated at Amsterdam University (1920–23) and Leiden University (1923–25). In 1926, one year after receiving an LL D degree from Leiden, he was appointed Judge of the European Court in Semarang, and in 1930–42 Judge of the High Court in Palembang. While in Semarang he worked with **KO Kwat Tiong**. He went into private practice in 1950. During the 1955 general elections, he was a Baperki candidate for South Sumatra.

Sources: *Pedoman Kampanje*, p. 76; Tan, *Tionghoa*, p. 135.

JAYA, David Herman (LIEM Wan King, 林万金 LIN Wanjin, 1952-)
Community leader, entrepreneur

David Herman Jaya was born on 5 March 1952 in Magelang, Central Java. He received his high school education at the SMA Bhineka Tunggal Ika in Yoryakarta. His father was an owner of a car workshop called Las Tiga and David used to help out in the workshop. But David later had his own garment and umbrella business and was quite successful. Nevertheless, he became interested in the manufacturing of cars. In 1976 he established PT Mekar Armada Jaya, a company that specializes in the manufacturing of cars in Magelang. He also succeeded in the manufacturing of buses and his company became a major company producing buses for the domestic market. During the 1982 general election, his company became the sole coordinator for supplying buses for the use by district chiefs (*camat*) for the whole of Indonesia. Between 1999 and 2001 the company exported minibuses to Arabia, Bangladesh, Sri Lanka and Kenya. In 2003 he established another workshop in Tambun, Bekasi (West Java) and by 2008 the company was able to produced 400–500 buses per month.

Apart from car manufacturing business, he also ventured into other related and unrelated sectors. In 1981 he set up PT Bumen Radja Abadi, an official dealer for Mitsubusi cars; in 1987 he set up Volgo Mobil, an official dealer for various Japanese cars such as Daihatsu, Isuzu, and Nissan truck as well as European cars BMW and Peugeot. In 1990 he established Bank Perkreditan Rakyat (BPR) which had seven branches. In 1991 he established Volgo Finance and in 1992, Armada finance. He later moved into the furniture and resort business as well.

David has served as leader in many social organizations: chairman of Kesetiaan Warga Magelang Foundation, general chairman of the Buddhist Council in Central Java, and first chairman of Asosiasi Karoseri Indonesia (Indonesian car body association). He is currently chairman of Paguyuban Sosial Marga Tionghoa Indonesia (PSMTI, 2013–17).

Sources: Kisah Peruangan, "David Herman Jaya membesarkan karoseri New Armada", Tabloid *Kontan*, no. 13, tahun IX, 3 January 2005 (accessed 18 August 2014); "David Herman Jaya Ketua Umum PSMTI 2013–2017", *Minggu*, 6 October 2013, Hall Riau (accessed 18 August 2014).

Jaya SUPRANA. See SUPRANA, Jaya
Jeanne LAKSANA. See YUAN Ni
JI Mingfa. See HADINATA, Christian
JI Qihui. See BARKI, Kiki
JIAN Fuhui. See KAN Hok Hoei
JIANG Weitai. See MASAGUNG
JIN Aiqin. See KENCANAWATI, Cecillia

JINARAKKHITA, Bhikku Ashin (THE Bwan An; ZHENG Man'an 郑满安, 1923–2002)
Buddhist monk

Born on 23 January 1923 in Bogor, he is considered as the person who revived Buddhism in Indonesia. He stayed a long time in Semarang. Holding an engineering degree (Ir) from a Dutch university (*Kompas* notes that he studied physics and chemistry at Rijks University), he spent some time in Burma (Myanmar) where he became a Buddhist monk and changed his name to Bhikku ASHIN Jinarakkhita on 23 January 1954. In 1954 he attended an international conference of the World Fellowship of Buddhists in Rangoon. Upon his return to Indonesia, he specialized in the *vipassana* (insight) meditation and attracted a multitude of followers. He later rejected Sam Kauw Hwee and preferred an organization that was not exclusively Chinese. In 1958 he established Perbuddhi (Perhimpunan Buddhis Indonesia, the Indonesian Buddhist Association), which soon became an influential association.

Bhikku Ashin attempted to Indonesianize Buddhism by proposing the concept of one supreme god. He claimed that in the tenth-century Javanese Buddhist text, *Sang Hyang Kamahayanikan*, there was the concept of Adi Buddha as a supreme god. Hence his Buddhism fits in with the first principle of the Indonesian state ideology, Pancasila — belief in one supreme god.

Bhikku Ashin was also of the view that saints (*orang suci*) can be found anywhere, and that personal religious experience is unique. In other words, every Buddhist can find his/her own enlightenment in accordance with his/her path. When preaching he often quoted various non-Buddhist figures, including the Javanese literary giant, Ranggawarsita. He also expressed great admiration for Sai Baba, a Hindu spiritualist, and Dalai Lama, a Tibetan spiritual leader. His syncretic teachings were controversial and were opposed by some members in the Buddhist Council. Nevertheless, he had many followers, including academicians, both in Indonesia and overseas.

Bhikku Ashin was elected as the chairman (Maha Nayaka) of Sangha Agung Indonesia (1974), which was a component organization of Walubi (Perwalian Umat Buddha Indonesia), the Buddhist Council of Indonesia. Sangha Agung Indonesia later came into conflict with other component organizations. Some leaders in the council did not agree with his style and his teachings. Walubi later experienced power struggle and was dissolved in 1998. That same year, the new Walubi was established while a rival organization KASI (Konferensi Agung Sangha Indonesia) was formed. Jinarakkhita was associated with the latter organization.

He passed away on 18 April 2002 in Lembah Cipendawa near Cianjur (West Java).

Sources: Willmott, *Semarang*, pp. 252–54; "Bangkitnya Klenteng Tirtowinoto", *Tempo*, 29 March 1975, p. 16; Brown, "Indonesian Buddhism", *Kompas*, 22 January 1995; Suryadinata, ed., *Southeast Asian Personalities of Chinese Descent: A Biographical Dictionary* (2012), pp. 383–84; the compiler's notes.

JOHAN, Daniel (ZHANG Le Hao; ZHANG Yuhao 张育浩, 1972-)
Member of Parliament

Born in Jakarta on 10 April 1972, he received a B.A degree from the Universitas Tarumanagara in Jakarta. He is a special staff member in the Ministry of Pembangunan Daerah Tertinggal (Development of Lack Behind Area). He joined the Partai Kebangkitan Bangsa, contested the 2014 election and won the seat for West Kalimantan.

Sources: Pengurus Pusat Fordeka, *Buku Acuan 2014–2019*, p. 159; the compiler's notes.

Johan WAHYUDI. See **WAHYUDI, Johan**
John LIE. See **LIE Tjeng Tjoan, John**
Junus JAHJA. See **JAHJA, Junus**
Junus Nur ARIF. See **NIO Joe Lan**

JUSUF, Ester Indahyani (SIM Ai Ling; SHEN Ailing 沈爱玲, 1971-)
Human rights activist, lawyer

She was born SIM Ai Ling on 15 January 1971 in Malang, a city of pleasant climate in the province of East Java, Indonesia. Ester went to Tirta Marta Primary School where her father was a teacher. She managed to gain acceptance to study law in the Faculty of Law at Universitas Indonesia (FHUI). During her university years, she would always seek to take part in activities that benefited the community. Fired up by youthful enthusiasm, she was very active in fund-raising and organizing programmes for prison inmates; however the outcome of her activities was not always encouraging. She graduated with a law degree in 1996.

Ester was most known as one of the founders of Solidaritas Nusa Bangsa (SNB), a non-governmental organization formed to address social and racial issues after the May 1998 riots. SNB has since been helping the victims of the riots, raising community awareness of the events and their implications, and lobbying the government for legal reform in order to provide better protection for minority groups. Her work in bringing human rights issues to the consciousness of the public was also recognized with various awards; most prominent of which are those from the Human Rights Institute (Lembaga Hak Asasi Manusia or ELHAM) and a Christian magazine, *Majalah Narwastu Pembaruan*. In 2001, Ester was granted a **YAP Thiam Hien** Award, an award named after a leading human rights lawyer. She is currently a practising lawyer and a volunteer at SNB.

Source: Dewi Anggraeni, "Jusuf, Ester Indahyani", Suryadinata, ed., *Southeast Asian Personalities* (2012), pp. 389–91.

Jusuf PANGLAYKIM. See **PANGLAYKIM, Jusuf**

JUSUF, Tedy (HIM Tek Ji; XIONG Deyi 熊德怡, 1944-)
Army general, community leader

Born on 24 May 1944 in Bogor, he is also known as Xiong Deyi. According to published information, Jusuf was first educated at a Chinese medium school in Pa Hwa (Patikuan Chinese School) up to the junior middle school level. He later moved to an Indonesian state school and graduated in 1962 in the science stream.

Jusuf was one of the few Indonesian army generals of Chinese descent during the Soeharto regime. He joined the Indonesia Military Academy in Malang after finishing secondary school and graduated in 1965 as a junior officer. He rose to the rank of Brigadier General in 1994 and was appointed Member of Parliament representing the Indonesian Armed Forces in 1996. He was eventually asked to retire from active military duty in 1999. Nevertheless, during the Soeharto era, he was not known as an ethnic Chinese.

He became active in the Chinese community after Soeharto stepped down. He became the leader of one of the largest Chinese Indonesian social organizations (Paguyuban Sosial Marga Tionghoa Indonesia or PSMTI or 印华百家姓协会 in Chinese) established in 1998. This is the first ethnic Chinese social organization in the post-Soeharto period to have both Chinese-educated and Indonesian-educated Chinese in Jakarta as members. As chairman of PSMTI, he stated that assimilation had failed and hence maintained that integration was more suitable for national unity. Jusuf later stepped down as General Chairman and served as Honorary Chairman.

Sources: Tedy Jusuf, *Sekilas Budaya Tionghoa di Indonesia (SMTI)* (2000); *Musyawarah Keluarga Besar Paguyuban Sosial Marga Tionghoa Indonesia* (28 November–2 December 2000), pp. 22–26; Leo Suryadinata, "Jusuf, Tedy", Suryadinata, ed., *Southeast Asian Personalities* (2012), pp. 391–93.

Jusuf WANANDI. See WANANDI, Jusuf
Jusuf WONGSOSEPUTERA. See WONGSOSEPUTERA, Jusuf

KALIANA, Pita. See **OEY An Siok**
Kanjeng Raden Tumenggung HARDJONAGORO. See **HARDJONAGORO, Kanjeng Raden Tumenggung**

KAM Hwat Hok (GAN Fafu 甘发福, 1887-?)
Community leader

Born in Tegal on 4 March 1887, he was educated in a Hokkien school. While in Tegal he was involved in the THHK, Tiong Hoa Im Gak Hwee, and other Chinese organizations. In the 1930s(?) he moved to Pemalang and became a zone-chief (*wijkmeester*). He served as the chairman of the CHH (Pemalang) and a member of the Regency Council in Pemalang.

Source: Tan, *Tionghoa*, p. 120.

KAMIL, Iskandar (LIEM Kay Hoo) 林开河*
Senior military officer, Supreme Court Judge, Muslim

Born in Semarang, date of birth is not available. Trained as a lawyer (SH), he was a brigadier-general in the Indonesian Army and retired as a major-general. He was head of the Legal Upholding Body (Babinkum ABRI, Center for the Military Law for Indonesia) between 19 December 1988 and 1992; member of DPR between 1993 and 1998. He later served as a Supreme Judge (Hakim Agung) in the Supreme Court of the Republic of Indonesia (Makamah Agung RI).

Sources: *Indonesia* (Cornell University), no. 56 (October 1993), p. 133; *Jakarta*, no. 376 (24 September 1993), p. 76; <https://www.mail-archive.com/rantau.net@groups.or.id/msg03266.html> (accessed 20 October 2014); the compiler's notes.

KAN Hok Hoei (H.H. KAN; JIAN Fuhui 简福辉, 1881–1951)
Politician, landlord

Born in 1881 in Jakarta, he received Dutch secondary education. Initially he was active in Siang Hwees (chambers of commerce) and later in the Municipal Council of Batavia (Jakarta) as well. His wealth and his knowledge of Dutch soon made him the most outspoken *peranakan* Chinese in Dutch circles. He was also well-known among members of local councils and Dutch-appointed Chinese officers.

When the Volksraad was to be formed and the organizations of the Indies Chinese decided not to take part in that new council (1917), Kan accepted the appointment of the governor as a representative of the Indies Chinese. He believed that Chinese interests would be well protected under Dutch colonial rule.

In 1918 a review commission was appointed to probe into the Indies political structure. Kan and two other Dutch members submitted a report that was in favour of preserving the status quo. In 1927 he voted against the proposal for an indigenous majority in the Volksraad, an action which stigmatized him in the eyes of Indonesian nationalists.

When Chung Hwa Hui (CHH) was formed in 1928, Kan was elected as its president. Though the response of *peranakan* Chinese newspapers was not favourable to Kan, he was elected every year until the dissolution of the CHH during the Japanese Occupation.

In 1932 Kan was sent by a local Chinese business firm to tour China. His links with the Consul-General of China became closer after his return to Java. In 1934 the Federation of Siang Hwees of the Dutch East Indies was founded under the instruction of the Consul-General of China, who became the honorary president while Kan was elected as the president. Kan's daughter married a son of the Chinese Consul. The Dutch Governor-General was unhappy with Kan's association with the *totok*-dominated organization, especially Kan's relationship with the Consul-General of China. Kan was eventually forced to resign from the position.

In 1935 he was awarded a medal by the Dutch Government for his "outstanding service" and in the following year he visited the Netherlands to promote closer relations between the Indies Chinese and the Netherlands. Kan continued to support Dutch rule and was imprisoned by the Japanese in 1942 for his anti-Japanese activities. He was released after the Japanese capitulation and died in 1951.

Sources: Suryadinata, *Peranakan Politics*, pp. 156–59; *Directory of Chinese Names*, p. 36.

KARIM, Hadji Abdul (OEI Tjeng Hien; HUANG Qingxing 黄清兴, 1905–88)
Religious and political party leader

Born in Padang on 6 June 1905, he received primary school education. In 1939–52 he served as the chairman of the Board of Muhammadijah (Bengkulu). During the Japanese Occupation, he was appointed as a member of Tjuo Sangi Kai (Provincial Assembly of Counsellors, Bengkulu, 1943), and a member of the KNI (Bengkulu, 1944). After Indonesia's independence, he became the director of the Indonesian Muslim Bank (Bengkulu, 1946). He later moved to Jakarta and was appointed as a member of the DPR representing the Chinese minority from March 1956 to July 1959, and representing Masjumi from July 1959 to June 1960. After the 1965 coup, he served as the chairman of the Persatuan Islam Tionghoa Indonesia (PITI) as well as a member of the central board of Partai Muslimin Indonesia (1968–69). In 1974 he served as a member of the BPKB-DKI (Jakarta). He was a member of the board of executives of the Istiqal Mosque Project (Jakarta), an adviser to Bakom, and an executive member of Majelis Ulama Indonesia. He was also the president of the

Asli Knitting Factory and Central Asian Insurance Company, and the owner of a medical factory, Bintang Tujuh. In 1975 his daughter Iriani Dewi Karim was married to an indigenous Indonesian. Ali Sadikin, the Governor of Jakarta, attended the wedding and delivered a speech in praise of the inter-racial marriage. He continued to be active in the Chinese Muslim community. In 1982 he published his autobiography entitled *Mengabdi Agama, Nusa dan Bangsa*. He died in Jakarta on 13 October 1988.

Sources: Roeder, *Who's Who*, pp. 175, 473; *Tempo*, 5 April 1975, p. 39; *DPR 1971*, pp. 614, 627; Suryadinata, *Mencari*, pp. 173–85.

KARMAN, Hasan (HUANG Shaofan 黄少凡, 1962-)
Politician, ex-mayor, Protestant

Born on 6 August 1962 in Singkawang to a petty merchant family, he has five siblings and is the youngest of all. He attended primary and junior middle schools at his birthplace, but went to Malang, Java, for his senior high school education. Between 1982–88 he studied at the Faculty of Law, UI. After graduation, he worked for the Barito Pacific Lumber Company for eight years. He later studied for an MBA and in 1996 set up his own law firm. In 2004 he began to be interested in politics. In 2005 he served as the deputy chairman of the Perkumpulan Masyarakat Singkawang (West Kalimantan) dan Sekitarnya (Singkawang and surrounding area association). He participated and won the mayorial election. He served as the Mayor of Singkawang from 2007–12. During one of the interviews, he stated that after he looked after his city he would like to continue his study. His eventual objective is to be a lecturer at a university. But in the 2014 election he contested the parliamentary seat for West Kalimantan on the Gerindra ticket but was not successful.

Sources: Dewi Anggraeni, "Hasan Karman: No Stranger to Politics", *Jakarta Post*, 8 February 2008; Li Zhouhui, *Fengxian, Xisheng, Fenjin*,

Jueqi, Jakarta 2012, pp. 289–91; Pengurus Pusat Fordeka, *Buku Acuan 2014*, p. 161; the compiler's notes.

KARTAJAYA, Hermawan (TAN Tjioe Hak; CHEN Qiuxue 陈求学, 1947-)
Marketing guru

Born on 18 November 1947 in Surabaya, East Java, Kartajaya is almost synonymous with the discipline of "marketing" in Indonesia. Not much was known of his early childhood and education. He enrolled at the Institut Teknologi Sepuluh Nopember but did not complete his undergraduate degree. Instead he obtained his degree from the Faculty of Economics, Universitas Udayana, and eventually earned his master's degree (MSc) at the University of Strahclyde, Glasgow in 1995.

Kartajaya started his own consulting firm MarkPlus Professional Service as an education company in 1989 offering marketing related training for executives in Surabaya. The company took ten years to position itself well in Jakarta and Surabaya by offering consultancy in business strategy for private and state-owned enterprises. By the year 2000, MarkPlus has established a solid reputation as a local consultancy firm. MarkPlus continues to grow to become the first ASEAN marketing consultancy group. Currently, he is the chairman of MarkPlus Inc., one of the top-ranking consultancy firms which has grown to encompass MarkPlus Consulting, MarkPlus Insight, MarkPlus Institute of Marketing (MIM) and Markteers. With education as the cornerstone, he began to write books on marketing, imparting the models he developed from his knowledge and experience with MarkPlus. He later collaborated with international marketing experts to publish books related to the 1997–98 Asian Financial Crisis in the late 1990s, marketing ASEAN as a region in the mid-2000s and global marketing in the late 2000s. Several of his publications made it to the list of local and regional bestsellers.

Kartajaya's contribution to marketing sets him apart from the rest as he elevates the marketing discipline at the international level while imparting a unique Asian flavour. He is a testament to the art and science of marketing that he has mastered. Through MarkPlus, he secured the pedestal for being president of the World Marketing Association since 2002, crowning him as the "Asian Marketing Guru". The Chartered Institute of Marketing, United Kingdom (CIM-UK), even dubbed him one of the "50 Gurus Who Have Shaped the Future of Marketing" alongside other international names such as Seth Godin, Al Ries, and Philip Kotler. Kartajaya has built himself a household name with a formidable presence at home, abroad, and on the worldwide web.

Source: Aris Ananta and Nida An Khafiyya, "Kartajaya, Hermawan", Suryadinata, ed., *Southeast Asian Personalities* (2012), pp. 395–97.

KARTANEGARA, Hendra. See **TAN Joe Hok**
Kartini MULJADI. See **MULJADI, Kartini**

KARWANDY (KWEE Tjoa Kwang, 1912-) 郭蔡广*
Supporter of independence movement

Born on 7 July 1912 in Bagan Siapi-Api, he was a Chinese schoolteacher. During the Revolution he joined the Laskar Rakyat (People's Army). Holding the rank of Letnan II (in Batalyon I, Regiment II, Division II), he was given the task of mobilizing ethnic Chinese support in Jambi for Indonesia's independence. Besides that, he also imported weapons from Singapore and Malaya for the People's Army. In 1948 he took refuge in Singapore to escape arrest by the Dutch authorities but continued to supply arms to the People's Army in Jambi. In 1950 he returned to Indonesia. He retired as a member of the Indonesian Armed Forces with the rank of Letnan I. He was also awarded Bintang Jasa by the Indonesian Government.

Sources: Letter of Anthony Quick, 5 April 1983, and relevant documents.

KARYA, Teguh (Steve LIEM; LIEM Tjoan Hok; LIN Quanfu 林全福, 1935-2001)
Playwright, theatre and movie director

Born in Bandegalang (West Java) on 22 September 1935, he was first educated at the Akademi Seni Drama dan Film in Yogyakarta (1956), and continued his studies at the Akademi Teater Nasional Indonesia (Jakarta, 1957-61), specializing in acting, designing, and play-directing. In 1957 he and other Christian *peranakan* founded the Seni Teater Kristen in Jakarta. He was later awarded a scholarship to study drama and film-making at the University of Hawaii.

After his return from Hawaii, he established Teater Populer (with its headquarters in Hotel Indonesia). When Taman Ismail Marzuki was founded, he moved Teater Populer to this cultural centre. In 1975 he established an acting school.

He directed a number of movies. *Wajah Seorang Lelaki* [The face of a man], his first movie made in 1972, was not a success. *Cinta Pertama* [First love], his second movie, won him repute. He was given the award of Best Indonesian Director in 1973 for this movie at the Film Festival of Indonesia. His other movies include *Ranjang Pengantin* [The wedding], which clinched him the Best Director award in 1974; *Kawin Lari* [Runaway marriage]; *Perkawinan Dalam Semusim* [Wedding in a season]; and *Badai Pasti Berlalu* [The storm will be over]. His movie, *November 1828*, a historical epic, won six awards in the 1970 Indonesian Film Festival, including Best Picture of the Year and Best Director of the Year. In the 1980s he directed many more movies, three of which won Best Director awards: *Dibalik Kelambu* [Behind mosquito nets] (1982); *Ibunda* [Mother] (1986); and *Pacar Ketinggalan Kereta* [My love missed the train] (1989).

According to a report, Teguh was very disappointed and shocked by the anti-Chinese violence on 13 May 1998. He suffered a serious stroke and became paralyzed. He then lived for another three more years before passing away on 11 December 2001 in Jakarta. At the Asia-Pacific Film Festival of 2001, Teguh Karya was given the "Life Achievement Award" for his contribution to Indonesian movies. On Heros Day (10 November) of 2002, President Megawati Sukarnoputri presented the Bintang Budaya Paramadharma award, "the sons of Indonesia" who had made major contributions to the cultural field. Among the winners were Chairil Anwar (writer), Ismail Marzuki (composer) and Teguh Karya (movie and theatre director).

Sources: *Karya* (1979), back cover; "Dan Setelah Airmata: Mutu", *Tempo*, 6 April 1974, pp. 44–47; "Setelah Panggung", *Tempo*, 16 March 1974, p. 15; *TIM*, p. 23; Oemaryati, *Lakon*, p. 234; Riantiarno, ed. (1993), pp. 130–32.

Kasom TJOKROSAPUTRO. See **TJOKROSAPUTRO, Kasom**
KE Gui'an. See **HUTOMO, Suryo**
KE Quanshou. See **KWA Tjoan Sioe**
KE Xinbiao. See **UTOMO, Tirto**

KENCANAWATI, Cecillia (Xixiliya K. 茜茜丽亚; KIN Ai Tjin; JIN Aiqin 金爱钦, 1954?-)
Writer, reporter, better known as **Cecillia K**.

Born in Pekalongan, Java in 1954(?) and equipped with Chinese middle-school education, she worked as a reporter for the only Chinese newspaper, *Yindunixiya Ribao* (Harian Indonesia), in Jakarta during the New Order. Unlike writers of the older generation, most of her works were mainly published in the newspaper where she worked. She has published numerous poems and short stories and gained popularity among Indonesian Chinese readers. Reading her early short stories, one gets the impression that she was imitating Hong Kong pop writers such as Yi Da and Taiwanese writer Qiong Yao.

However, she is better known for her beautiful poems which were published not only in Indonesia but later also in Singapore, Hong Kong and Taiwan literary magazines. She has attended a few conferences for international Chinese writers in Malaysia and Singapore. In 1966, together with two other Indonesian Chinese women poets, they published a collection of their poems in *Sanren Xing* 三人行 (Three in a group). In 2001, she published a collection of her poems *Zhishi weile yige chengnuo* 只是为了一个承诺 (Only for a promise).

Sources: *Lianhe Zaobao* (Singapore), 15 April 1988, p. 15; *Dishanjie Yazhou Huawen Zuojia Huiyi Dahui Shouce* (1988), p. 92; Haryono (1988), p. 187; Dong Rui, *Lijin Jijie*, pp. 201–9; the compiler's notes.

KHARMAWAN, Byanti (KHOUW Bian Tie; XU Mianchi 许绵池, 1906–82)
Eminent financial expert

Born in Tegal on 1 June 1906, he received a Drs degree in Economics (cum laude, 1932) from Rotterdamsche Handels Hoogeschool. While in the Netherlands, he served as a member of the editorial board of the *CHHTC* in 1926–27 and as the editor in October 1929. After his return to Indonesia, he joined the CHH and in 1937–38 served as an executive member of the CHH central board.

In 1942 he was in private business. In 1949 he was a researcher at the Nederlands Economisch Institute, Rotterdam. In 1953 he became an Indonesian civil servant, serving as Economic Adviser at the Ministry of Economic Affairs and Ministry of Finance. He was also the Chief Economic Adviser and Deputy Governor at the Central Bank of Indonesia. From 1966 to 1968 he was appointed executive director of the Asian Development Bank; from 1968 to 1982 he was appointed by the RI government to serve as executive director of the International Monetary Fund (IMF) at Washington, DC. He died in Washington on 5 October 1982. His remains were flown back to Jakarta.

Sources: *CHHTC*, October–November 1926, title page; December 1927, inside cover; and February 1928, title page; Siauw, *Pantja Sila*, p. 27;

Hopper, *Winter 1971–72*, pp. 58, 66; *CHH 2de Lustrum*, p.7; *Who's Who in America* (vol. I), p. 1705; *International Who's Who (1978–79)*, p. 883; *Kompas*, 10 October 1982.

KHO Liang Ie (1927-) 许亮宜*
Interior designer

Born in Magelang in 1927, he migrated to the Netherlands in 1949. In 1963 he was the interior designer of the Netherlands National Travel Office in New York. He also designed for the Schiphol Airport in Amsterdam, Arfort showroom in Cologne, and other projects. He held an exhibition in Milan (1964) and in Amsterdam (1966 and 1968). From 1960 to 1968 he was appointed as a lecturer at Koninklijke Akademie Den Haag (the Hague).

Source: Kwee, "Tionghoa Luar Negeri", p. 52.

KHO Ping Hoo (Asmaraman SUKOWATI; XU Pinghe 许平和, 1926–94)
Kungfu novelist

Kho Ping Hoo was born on 17 August 1926 in Sragen (Surakarta). Educated in the "Dutch-Indigenous-School", he reads Dutch, Indonesian, as well as English. However, his knowledge of Chinese is extremely limited. Like **GAN K.L.**, after trying out various jobs, he eventually devoted himself to full-time writing. In fact, he first started writing short stories in 1952. Only in 1959 did he attempt to write *kungfu* novels. Most of his works were first serialized in local popular magazines such as *Selecta*, *Roman Detektip*, and *Monalisa* and later published in pocket book form. Many were published by Gema in Solo, which is his own printing press and publishing house. In the last thirty years he had completed writing more than one hundred titles. According to his own account, all his works, except *Si Teratai Emas*, were original. However, he also admitted that he read a lot of *kungfu* novels in Indonesian translation.

Kho's works are generally divided into *kungfu* novels, detective/ghost stories, Javanese "historical novels", and romances; but his *kungfu* novels are most numerous and popular. The plots were constructed from a variety of backgrounds in China, Japan, and Indonesia depending on the title. It might be true that Kho did not translate the works of other Chinese *kungfu* writers, but reading his novels, one gets the impression that he was very familiar with Chinese *kungfu* novels and was heavily influenced by them. The stories, book titles, and characters have strong Chinese *kungfu* novel flavour. Initially, most of his *kungfu* novels bore Chinese titles in Hokkien pronunciation. For instance, his first *kungfu* novel (1959) was called *Pek Liong Pokiam* ("Bai Long Baojian" in Mandarin) with an Indonesian subtitle: *Pedang Pusaka Naga Putih*. His 1962 work was also entitled *Ang Coa Kiam* ("Hong She Jian" in Mandarin) with an Indonesian subtitle: *Pedang Ular Merah*. But in his later years, he gradually dropped this practice and used only Indonesian titles, for example, *Kisah Bangau Putih* (1982) and *Tiga Naga Sakti* (1982).

His later works also include Chinese and non-Chinese characters. One good example is his *Kilat Pedang Membela Cinta*, published in 1981. The novel, consisting of nine volumes, is a love story in the Majapahit era. The main characters are a Chinese and a Javanese who fall in love with each other. At the end of the novel, Kho preaches intermarriage based on love. It seems that this is a new "tradition" in *kungfu* novel writing in Indonesia. His last *kungfu* novel is called *Hancurnya Kerajaan Han* [The fall of the Han dynasty], which was incomplete when he suddenly died on 22 July 1994. He is survived by two wives, twelve children, and thirty-three grandchildren.

In 2014 he was given the Satya Lencana Kebudayaan Award by the Indonesian government for his contribution to Indonesian culture.

Sources: Letter to the compiler, 1976; *Indonesian Monographs*, pp. 33–34; Suryadinata, *Kebudayaan*, pp. 141–44; *Suara Pembaruan*, 22 July 1994; *Kompas*, 22 July 1994; the compiler's notes.

KHO Sin Kie (?-1949) 许新基*
Tennis player

One of the earliest tennis players in Indonesia, Java-born Kho Sin Kie began to play tennis at the age of fourteen. In 1929 he won the Central Java tennis championship. In 1933 he took the men's singles title in the All-Java Championship. In the same year he was sent to China to participate in the "National Olympic Games". In 1935 he represented China in the Davis Cup competition in Mexico. The following year, he once again represented China in the Davis Cup competition in Europe. In 1939 he won the Bournmount Championship. Towards the end of 1939 he returned to Java. He continued defeating other tennis players in Java, where he lived, right up to Indonesia's independence. He died from tuberculosis in London in 1949.

Source: *Katili* (1973), pp. 163–67.

KHO Tjeng Lie. See SURIPTO, Ateng

KHO Tjoen Gwan (Wan?) 许俊源*
Ex-political party leader, merchant

A Brebes-born *peranakan* with no formal education, he began work as an office boy for *Perniagaan* (Jakarta). In 1916 he joined the editorial board of *Sinar Hindia*, a left-wing daily in Semarang. He wrote articles criticizing the Dutch Nationality Law in *Warna Warta*, which resulted in his arrest. After his release, he became more active in the PKI movement. In 1924 he became a leader of the PKI (Semarang branch). At about the same time he was the treasurer of Perserikatan Kaoem Boeroeh Goela. He was detained by the Dutch authorities for his involvement in the 1926–27 communist uprisings but was soon released. He later joined Hong Boen Hwee, a local Chinese secret society. In 1931 he was involved in racial conflicts in Pekalongan and was detained by the authorities. In the 1930s he attempted to set up the PTI branch in Kudus without success. His activities in the 1940s and 1950s are not known. In the early 1960s he served as an adviser to *Parama Arta*, a periodical on mysticism in Surabaya.

Sources: Tan, *Tionghoa*, pp. 115–16; McVey, *Communism*, p. 226; the compiler's notes.

KHO Wan Gie (GAO Huanyi 高焕义, 1908–83)
Cartoonist, painter

Born in 1908 in Indramayu (Java), he received Chinese primary and high-school education at his birthplace. After leaving high school he worked as a shopkeeper. Meanwhile he took a correspondence course from the Washington School of Cartooning and obtained a diploma in 1929. From 1935 to 1936 he also studied illustration under Percy V. Bradshaw at the Press Art School (London). From 1928 to 1965 he worked at the *Sin Po* Publishing House in Jakarta. The well-known cartoon character, *Put On* (which means "the man who worries"), a short, plump, and unlucky bachelor, was very popular in the 1950s. Ten volumes of *Put On* were published and 40,000 copies were sold out in months. He held a number of painting exhibitions in Jakarta during the 1950s and early 1960s. After 1965, Kho created other characters such as *Bandot* and *Itol* for popular magazines in Jakarta. He died in 1983.

Sources: *Sinar Harapan*, 11 November 1979; C.M. Hsu's notes; <http://id.wikipedia.org/wiki/Kho_Wan_Gie> (accessed 25 April 2013); the Compiler's notes.

KHOE A Fan (KHOE Siat Ting; QIU Yafan 丘亚樊)
Community leader, businessman

Born in China, he migrated to the Dutch East Indies and became a *luitenant* in Jakarta for at least twelve years. He was a founder and vice-president of the THHK (Jakarta) (1900–8).

He was also active in Soe Po Sia and was known as an ardent supporter of the revolutionary movement of Dr Sun Yat-sen.

Sources: Nio, *THHK*, pp. 203, 235–37, 270; Williams, *Nationalism*, pp. 105–6, 141–42; *Hari Ulang Ke-50 Tiong Hoa Hwee Koan Jakarta* (1950), p. 59.

KHOE Siat Ting. See **KHOE A Fan**
KHOE Soe Kiam. See **SASANASURYA**

KHOE Tjeng Tek (QIU Qingde 丘清德, 1875-?)
Community leader, businessman, majoor of Medan

Born in Medan in 1875, he was a founder of Hok Kian Hwee Koan (Medan) in 1906 and the Tionghoa Bank in Medan in the 1920s. In 1931 he helped to found Sudong Zhongxue, a large pro-KMT Chinese high school in Sumatra. In the 1950s he was the honorary president of Hok Kian Hwee Koan (Medan).

Sources: *Fujian*, pp. 38, 40, 115; Zhang, "Yinni Huaqiao", p. 82.

KHOE Woen Sioe (QIU Wenxiu 丘文秀, 1906–66)
Community leader, newspaperman, publisher

Born in Jakarta on 5 May 1906, he was educated at the THHT (Jakarta), a Bible school, MULO (Jakarta), and the AMS (Bandung). He began work at the age of eighteen, first with *Sin Po*, and later with *Keng Po*, eventually taking over the directorship of that newspaper. He was detained for three years (1942–45) during the Japanese Occupation. In 1946–48 he served as the president of Sin Ming Hui. Also in 1946, he began to publish *Star Weekly* (an influential *peranakan* journal, which survived until 1960) in addition to *Keng Po*, which ceased publication in 1958.

Khoe was active in the formation of the PT and became the editor of its official journal, *Sinar* (1949). When the PT was changed to the PDTI he served as an executive member of its central board and the temporary editor of its official journal *Berita P.D.T.I.* (1953–54). In March 1954 he was elected as one of the deputy chairmen of Baperki. He was known as the proprietor of PT Keng Po (later PT Kinta). He died in Jakarta on 6 June 1966.

Sources: Tan, *Tionghoa*, pp. 190–91; *Sinar*, 15 March 1949, p. 2; *Berita PDTI*, 15 October 1953, p. 1; Ojong, "Mengenangkan Khoe Woen Sioe (1906–66)"; *Kompas*, 5 June 1976; *SMH 10 Tahun*, p. 27.

KOO Bo Tjhan (1892-?) 许茂灿*
Entrepreneur, community leader

Born in Bondowoso on 6 August 1892, he was educated at the THHT (Bondowoso and Situbondo). He continued his studies at the CNHT (Nanking) and at Tokyo Agricultural University. As his intention was to apply what he had learned in school, he returned to China to run a small farm. But he failed in the venture and returned to Surabaya to become the director of the THHK (Surabaya), though he resigned from it shortly after. He made another attempt to run a small farm near Pasuruan, but again failed in the venture. Then for a while he took on the role of principal of the THHK (Tulungagung). He revisited China and worked in road construction in Fujian, but he was soon back in Java. In the 1930s he served as the principal of the THHK (Blitar) and the president of the HCTNH (Blitar).

Source: Tan, *Tionghoa*, pp. 64–65.

KHOUW Bian Tie. See KHARMAWAN, Byanti

KHOUW Hok Goan (XU Fuyuan 许福源)
Playwright, director

He was one of the founders of Seni Teater Kristen Jakarta in 1957. The following are plays he had directed: *Tigapuluh Keping Perak* [Thirty pieces of silver] (1958); *Tjawan* [The cup] (1958); *Dian Tak Menjala* [Candle without light] (1960); and *Pohon Djalar* [Creeping plant] (1962).

Sources: *Warta Bhakti*, 8 December 1962; Oemaryati, *Lakon*, p. 234.

KHOUW Ke Hien (XU Qixing 许启兴, 1907–38)
Aviator, proprietor of a large slaughter-house "Merbaboe"
Born in 1907 in Muntilan, he was educated at the ELS (Magelang) and MULO (Yogyakarta). He took over the Merbaboe Company from his father. He was the first Chinese aviator to obtain a diploma from the Department of Aviation, Dutch East Indies. In 1933 he graduated from the Netherlands Military Officers' Academy and later had advanced studies in aeronautics in England. In September 1935 he succeeded in making a long distance flight from Java to the Netherlands. Spurred by the success, he decided to undertake the Java-China flight "in order to study present conditions of his home country" in May 1937. During his stay in China he went to Nanking and conferred with the aviation authorities on the promotion of civil flying in China. The Nanking Government later bestowed him a wooden tablet with the following inscription: "National Salvation through Aviation". During the Sino-Japanese war, he was active in raising money for China before he died in a plane crash in 1938 in Jakarta during the training.

Khouw was known as a philanthropist. When Jang Seng Ie (later known as Husada) was established, he was a major contributor to that hospital's funds. According to one report, in 1934 he donated 15,000–18,000 guilders to build a pavilion at the hospital for X-ray and other facilities.

Sources: Tan, *Tionghoa*, pp. 189–90; *Straits Times*, 29 October 1936 and 22 August 1937; *Nanyang Nianjian* (1951), section on "huaqiao", pp. 158–59, Satyautama, *Tokoh-tokoh Etnis TH*, p. 126.

KHOUW Kim An (XU Jin'an 许金安, 1897–1945)
Community leader, leading businessman, shareholder of Bataviaasche Bank, son-in-law of **PHOA Keng Hek**
Born in Jakarta on 5 June 1897, he was educated at a Hokkien school but became fluent in Dutch. He was one of the founders of the THHK (Jakarta) in 1900. In 1905 he was appointed

as a *liutenant*, in 1908 promoted to *kapitein*, and in 1910 promoted further to *majoor*. From 1910 to 1930 he served as the president of the Chinese Council (Kong Koan) in Jakarta. During the period 1921–31 he was appointed by the Dutch as a member of the Volksraad. When the CHH was formed in 1928, he was involved in it and held an executive position in the CHH central board (1928–42). He was awarded medals by the Dutch Government for his services to the local community. In 1942 he was detained by the Japanese and died on 13 February 1945 while in a concentration camp.

Sources: Tan, *Tionghoa*, p. 140; Wal, *Volksraad*, vol. II, p. 715; Nio, *THHK* (plate no. 4).

KHOUW Thian Tong. See **SETIONO, Benny Gatot**
Ki Anan TANDIONO. See **TANDIONO, Ki Anan**
Ki Hadjar SUKOWIJONO. See **TAN Hong Boen**
Kiki BARKI. See **BARKI, Kiki**
KIN Ai Tjin. See **KENCANAWATI, Cecillia**

KO Hong An 高丰安*
Community leader, newspaperman

Born in Blitar, he was educated at the ELS and the HBS in Semarang before attending a commercial college in Rotterdam. After graduating from the college, he travelled widely in Europe, living in London for a year, Berlin for half a year, and Paris for half a year. He returned to Java and lived in Surabaya, where he served as the agent of the Be Biauw Tjwan Bank, a member of the executive board of the Darmo Town Council Hospital, and an executive member of the Annual Fair Committee. He later moved to Semarang and became the director of *Djawa Tengah* and *Djawa Tengah Review*. He was a supporter of the PTI in the 1930s. Among his interests was soccer.

Sources: Tan, *Tionghoa*, p. 134; the compiler's notes.

KO Kwat Oen (KOSASIH, S.T.L. 1917-) 高厥运*
Political party leader, pharmacist

Born in Cicalengka on 23 December 1917, he graduated from the Assistant Pharmacists' School in 1938. He was a council member of Tiong Hoa Kie Tok Kauw Hwee and was active in Sin Ming Hui (Bandung branch) in the 1950s. In 1955 (1954?) he served as the president of Sin Ming Hui (Bandung branch), the vice-president of Baperki (Bandung branch), and the vice-president of Parkindo (Bandung branch). From 1951 to the mid-1950s(?) he was a member of the DPRDS (Bandung). He participated in the 1955 general elections as a Baperki candidate but came into conflict with **SIAUW Giok Tjhan**, resulting in his departure from Baperki. He did not represent Parkindo in the DPR but the Chinese minority. However, he was later dismissed by Soekarno as he was considered to be anti-Baperki. Nevertheless, he continued to be a member of the Constituent Assembly, and after the 1965 coup, he became close to Sokowati, the ex-Golkar general chairman, and almost became a Golkar DPR candidate.

Sources: *Pedoman Kampanje*, p. 60; *Liberty*, 20 October 1956, p. 3; Letter to the compiler, December 1986; the compiler's notes.

KO Kwat Tiong (Mohamad SALEH; GAO Juezhong 高厥忠**, 1896–1970)**
Community leader, lawyer, son of a luitenant

Born in 1896 in Parakan, he was educated in the ELS (Magelang) and graduated from the HBS (Semarang) in 1914. Initially he worked for a Dutch company. Later he joined *Pelita*, a newspaper published in Yogyakarta, where he was active in the local Chinese organizations. He set up, without success, Centrale Vereeniging Tionghoa in Yogyakarta. In 1920 he went to the Netherlands to study law. Six years later he obtained a degree and returned to Java.

He first worked with another Chinese lawyer, **JAUW Keng Hong**, in Semarang. Later he shared an office with an Indonesian lawyer named Besar. He associated very closely with other Indonesian lawyers, and this enabled him to understand the feelings of the educated indigenous Indonesians.

He regarded the Dutch East Indies as the homeland of the *peranakan* and joined the CHH in 1928, but quickly became disillusioned with the organization and dissociated himself from it soon afterwards. He came into contact with **LIEM Koen Hian**. On Ko's initiative, the PTI (Semarang branch) was formed, as were other branches in Central Java. In 1934 he was elected as the president of the PTI central board. From 1935 to 1939 he represented the PTI in the Volksraad, but in 1939, before the elections of the Volksraad, he came into conflict with Liem Koen Hian, and this resulted in his expulsion from the PTI.

Soon after Indonesia's independence, he changed his name to Mohamad Saleh. He taught in a number of universities, especially the UNDIP. He died in Semarang on 17 June 1970.

Sources: *Sin Po*, 20 April 1926; Tan, *Tionghoa*, p. 135; Tjoa Tjie Liang, 25 September 1951, pp. 8–9, 25; Wal, *Volksraad*, vol. II, p. 715.

KO Swan Sik (1931-) 高宣锡*
Academician, lawyer, son of **KO Tjay Sing**

He was born in Magelang (Central Java) on 4 January 1931. After finishing the HBS (Semarang), he entered the FHUI in 1948 and obtained an SH degree in 1953. He then studied at Leiden University (1953–54), the University of Mainz (Germany, 1954–55), and the Hague Academy of International Law (Summer 1954). In 1957 he was awarded a PhD in Law (cum laude) by Leiden University after successfully defending his dissertation "Meervoudige Nationaliteit" [Plural nationality]. He returned to Indonesia and became Attorney-at-Law at Semarang from

1957 to 1963. In 1963 he moved to Jakarta to practise law. From 1959 to 1965 he was appointed as a senior lecturer of Public International Law, FHUI, and from 1961 to 1965 he served as a member of Lembaga Pembinaan Hukum Nasional (Institute for the Advancement of National Law). He left Indonesia in 1965 and since February that year has been living in the Netherlands, while retaining Indonesian citizenship. He served as Head of the Department of Public International Law at the Inter-University Institute for International Law (T.M.C. Asser Institute) in the Hague. In 1988 he assumed Professorship at the Erasmus University (Rotterdam) and retired in 1996. In 1989, together with Sri Lankan jurist M.C.W Pinto, he co-founded the Foundation for the Development of International Law in Asia (DILA Foundation). He also served as chairman of its governing board. As part of the DILA foundation activities, the *Netherlands Yearbook of International Law* was published. He passed the baton to the younger colleagues in the first decade of the 2000s. In 2001, he was elected into the membership of the Institut de Droit International (Institute of International Law, IDI) and became the only Asian member of the institute.

His publications include his doctoral dissertation, "Nietigheid en het Volkenrecht" [Nullity and international law, 1968], "The Establishment of Diplomatic Relations and the Scope of Diplomatic Immunity: The Dutch Experience with China" (1972), "Documentatie van Volkenrechtelijke Staatspraktijk" [Documentation of state practice in the field of international law] (1976), "Multi-System Nations and International Law with Special Reference to Dutch Practice" (1981), and *The Indonesian Law of Treaties 1945–1990* (co-editor: S Trifunovska, 1994).

Sources: *Optimis* (Semarang), 30 January 1958, p. 5; Letter to the compiler, 1976, 2015; *Asian Yearbook of International Law 3* (February 1995).

KO Tjay Sing (1903–85) 高财盛*
Lawyer, community leader, university professor, father of **KO Swan Sik,** *nephew of* **KO Kwat Tiong**

Born in Magelang in 1903, he was educated at the THHK (Magelang), the HCS (Magelang), and the HBS (Semarang). He later entered the RHS (Jakarta) and continued his studies at Leiden University, from which he obtained a law degree (Mr). While he was at the RHS, he helped to found Ta Hsioh Sing Hwee (1926) and became its first president.

After Ko had obtained a law degree, he returned to Indonesia and went into private practice, sharing an office with Sartono, a leading Indonesian nationalist. A year later he moved to Semarang. In 1932 he and Ko Kwat Tiong established the PTI (Semarang branch). He served as its secretary. Since 1950 he has been a state lawyer. In 1957 he became a lecturer and later Extraordinary Professor of Civil Law at Diponegoro University (Semarang). In 1978 he published a book entitled *Rahasia Pekerjaan Dokter dan Advocat* (Jakarta). He died in 1985.

Sources: *Sin Po*, 11 October 1926; Tan, *Tionghoa*, p. 134; Roeder, *Who's Who*, p. 184.

KOSASIH, S.T.L. See **KO Kwat Tiong**

KOSASIH, Tirtawinata (QIU Chengshao 丘成绍, 1925–2003)
Community leader, businessman, Hakka

Born in Jatinegara in 1925(?), he received high-school education in Guangdong (China). In the period 1955–58 he was in charge of Huaqiao Qingnian Tiyuhui (Jakarta), a KMT-associated youth association. In 1959 he was arrested by the Indonesian authorities for his affiliation with the KMT.

During 1967–69 he was appointed as a member of the BKUT. In 1968 he served as the vice-chairman of the NDC, a *totok* Chinese-dominated enterprise. From 1970 to 1975 he was chairman of the board of trustees of SNPC Chongde Xuexiao (Jaya Sakti).

Sources: Interview, 1970; *Huaqiao zhi*, p. 128; Jiang, "Yajiada", p. 16; Chung, *HCTYI*, p. 64; the compiler's notes.

KUO Lay Yen. See **TAN Tek Ho**

KURNIAWAN, Rudy Hartono (NIO Hap Liang; LIANG Hailiang 梁海量, 1949-)
Badminton player, older brother of **Utami DEWI**, *Protestant*

Son of a dairy farmer, he was born in Surabaya on 18 August 1949. After graduating from SMA (Surabaya) he studied economics at Universitas Trisakti (Jakarta). He started playing badminton at the age of ten; in 1964 he became Indonesia's Junior Badminton Champion. In 1967 he became the first singles player in the Indonesian Thomas Cup Team. The following year, he won the All-England Championship and continued to hold the title for seven years (up to 1974). From 1969 to 1974 he was twice elected by SIWO/PWI Jakarta as Indonesia's Best Sportsman. He accepted the offer to star in an Indonesian movie, *Matinya Seorang Bidadari* [Death of an angle] (1971). He was defeated by Svend Pri of Denmark in the All-England competition in 1975, but regained the title in 1976. He retired the following year. In 1980 he came out of retirement and participated in the Second World Badminton Championship in Jakarta. He won the men's singles title after defeating **LIEM Swie King**. Rudy was the key member of four Thomas Cup winning teams (1970–79). Sport commentators were of the view that he was "a complete player. Fit, fast and mentally strong, elegant and accurate. He capped it all with the most powerful smash the world had seen at the time. Virtually invincible during his heyday."

Sources: *Sterba*, 29 March 1972; *Merdeka*, 12 April 1972; *Topik*, 19 April 1972, pp. 14–21; "Siapa-Siapa Untuk 1974", *Tempo*, 11 January 1975, p. 43; "Gagal, Lalu Apa?", *Tempo*, 29 March 1975, pp. 44–47; *Straits Times*, 1 June 1980, 7 May 1994.

KUSUMA, Alan Budi. See BUDIKUSUMA, Alan

KUSUMA, Eddie (NG Soei Chong; WU Ruizhang 伍瑞章, 1958-)
Activist, politician, businessman, Buddhist

Born in Medan on 24 April 1958, he lost his father when he was six years old. Nevertheless, he was able to complete his high school and university education. He received a B.A degree from a teachers' training university in Medan and a law degree from the Universitas Sumatra Utara. While in Medan, he taught at the Supratman School, and between 1977 and 1983, he served as the headmaster of the same school. In 2009 he received a PhD from Pajajaran University (Bandung).

Kusuma is fluent in Chinese and Indonesian. He was active in various multi-ethnic organizations, including KNPI, PGRI, Bakom PKB, GPPI and Lions Club. He called himself "aktivis 'lintas batas'" (An activist who crosses boundaries) as he has been involved in many multi-purpose and multi-ethnic organizations. He contested in the DPD election in 2004 but was not successful. In 2007 he contested in the Jakarta governor election as a candidate for deputy governor, again he did not win. He later joined Gerindra party and contested the 2014 DPR election on the Gerindra ticket. He was not elected.

Kusuma established two educational foundations: one in Medan and the other in Jakarta. He is also an entrepreneur, being director of Domba Mas Group, CEO of Greenpalm Group, and director-general of Sakti Group.

He has published a few books, including *Etnis Tionghoa dalam politik Indonesia sebelum dan sesudah Reformasi* (as co-editor, 2006), *Suku Tionghoa dalam Masyarakat Majemuk Indonesia* (2006), and *Membangun Keutuhan Bangsa Indonesia dengan Memperkokoh Ketahanan Nasional* (2006).

Sources: *Youyi (Persahabatan)*, vol. 7 (April 2014), pp. 28–30; <http://caleg.kabarkita.org/31307-eddie-kusuma> (accessed 2 May 2014); Li Zhuohui 李卓辉, *Yinnicanzheng yu guojia jianshe* (2007), pp. 156–59; Eddie Kusuma & Satya Dharma, eds., *Etnis Tionghoa dalam Politik Indonesia Sebelum dan Sesudah Reformasi 1998* (Jakarta, 2006), pp. 207–8.

KUSUMA, Sugianto (A Guan; GUO Zaiyuan 郭再源, 1951-)
Property tycoon, philantropist

Also known as A Guan, he is a second-generation Indonesian Chinese who was born in Sumatra. Graduated from Jugang Zhongxue (Palembang Chinese High School), he has been in the property business since 1971. His Agung Sedayu Group had succeeded in building a megamall Harco Mangga Dua in Jakarta. He later worked in partnership with **Tomy WINATA** in building other mega real estate projects. In October 2001 A Guan came into contact with Ciji 慈济, a Taiwan-based Buddhist association, and became an ardent supporter of its activities. He officially joined the Ciji Branch in Indonesia in March 2002. Together with his wife Lin Liping (林丽萍), they contributed enomously to help the poor in Jakarta. One of the projects was to clean the Jakarta River.

Source: *Jiechu renwu minglu*, p. 272; 访印尼华商巨子郭再源: 慈悲为怀,济世助人, <http://www.people.com.cn/GB/guoji/1032/2421625.html> (accessed 4 March 2013); the compiler's notes.

KWA Kwie An. See HUTOMO, Suryo

KWA Khay Twan (1932-) 柯凯传*
Student leader, Protestant

Born in Pati on 25 July 1932, he was active in Chung Lien Hui while still at high school. He later entered FHUI but did not finish his studies. While at FHUI he served as the secretary of Working Committee, PPMI (Perhimpunan2 Mahasiswa Indonesia), member of BKSPM (Badan Kerjasama Pemuda-Militer), chairman of Perhimi (Jakarta Branch) and later, as chairman of the central board of Perhimpi (in the 1960s). He has also been active in GKI (Gereja Kristen Indonesia), serving as the chairman of Health section (Ketua Badan Kesehatan GKI, West Java).

Sources: Written information by Kwa Khay Twan; the compiler's notes.

KWA Sien Biauw. See UTOMO, Tirto

KWA Tjoan Sioe (KE Quanshou 柯全寿, 1893–1948)
Community leader, physician

Born in 1893 in Salatiga, he was first sent to a private Malay school and, at the age of eleven, he entered the ELS in Salatiga. In 1908 he was educated at the HBS (Semarang). In 1913 he went to the Netherlands where he obtained his medical degree in 1920. He spent one year at the Colonial Institute in Amsterdam specializing in tropical diseases. He was then sent to work at the General Hospital in Jakarta and, later, Instituut Pasteur (then also in Jakarta). In 1922 he went into private practice.

Kwa was active in politics. He held a pro-*Sin Po* view and was socialistic in his outlook. In 1924 he founded the Jang Seng Ie Hospital and became its first director. In 1926 he was suspected of being a member of the Comintern. Kwa was also a forceful critic of Chiang Kai-shek for breaking with the CCP (1927). In 1932 he arranged a meeting of the editors and directors of various *peranakan* Chinese newspapers in support of Indonesian nationalism. In 1934 he visited China. When Japan occupied Indonesia, Kwa was detained. He died in Jakarta in 1948. He had married twice — his first wife was a Dutch woman while his second wife (**LI Mei**) was a THHK (Jakarta) graduate. She returned to the PRC in the 1960s.

Sources: *National* (Bukit Tinggi), no. 1 (March 1928), p. 36; Tan, *Tionghoa*, pp. 191–92; McVey, *Communism*, pp. 334, 485; *Siang Po*, 29 December 1934; *Jang Seng Ie*, pp. I–II.

KWEE Bie Sin (GUO Meicheng 郭美丞, 1896–1959)
Community leader, leading businessman

Born in 1896 in Haideng (Fujian), he first came to Java in 1921, but returned to China after one year. In 1927 he came to Java again, this time for good. From 1927 to 1929 he served as the principal of a Chinese school in Solo. Later he moved to Jakarta and engaged in various businesses. Finally he ran the Nanyang Book Shop and Printing Press (Jakarta). Between 1944 and 1950 he served as the president of Hok Kian Hwee Koan (Jakarta). In 1946–50 he served as the president of Siang Hwee (Jakarta). In 1948 he was elected as the president of Shang Lian. In the 1950s he served as the chairman of the board of trustees of *Zhonghua Shangbao*, a pro-KMT Chinese daily in Jakarta. He was a member of the Overseas Chinese Affairs Committee, Taiwan, 1955. He died in Jakarta on 4 July 1959.

Sources: *Fujian*, p. 28; *Siang Hwee* (Chinese-language section), p. [37]; *Shangye Nianjian*, p. 334; the compiler's notes.

KWEE Djie Hoo (1904-?) 郭二和*
Community leader, newspaper editor, diplomat

Born in Tumpang in November 1904, he was educated at the THHT (Banyuwangi and Jember), the HCS (Malang), and the PHS (Jakarta) before going to the Nederlandsch Handels Hooge School (Rotterdam) where he received a Drs degree in Commerce. He returned to Indonesia and worked as a civil servant in Staats Spoorwagen for a year, then moved to Jakarta to work in a private firm. In 1933 he was invited by **PHOA Liong Gie** to edit *Siang Po*. He joined the CHH but left it in 1934 after a conflict with Phoa Liong Gie and **H.H. KAN**. During the Indonesian Revolution, he sided with the Republicans and in the early 1950s (1951–53) he was appointed Indonesian Consul-General in Hong Kong. He retired in Hong Kong.

Sources: Tan, *Tionghoa*, pp. 193–94; *Almanak Kempen 1952* (1952?), p. 506.

KWEE Eng Hoe(?). See **GUO Rongfu**
KWEE Han Tjiong. See **TJOKROSAPUTRO, Handoko**

KWEE Hin Goan (GUO Xingyuan 郭兴源, 1932-)
Architect, son of **KWEE Kek Beng**

Born on 4 June 1932 in Jakarta, he graduated from the HBS (Jakarta) in 1950 and received an Ir degree (in Architecture) from the Faculty of Technology, UI (Bandung branch), in 1958. He served as an assistant between 1951 and 1958 and a lecturer between 1958 and 1959 at the same faculty. Between 1959 and 1965 he was the director of an architecture firm in Bandung and Jakarta. In 1966 he worked as an architect at Heier and Monse Partners in Keulen and in 1966–92 at Kraijvanger Architekten in Rotterdam.

Before migrating to the Netherlands he was the co-founder of Ikatan Arsitek Indonesia (Indonesian Architects Association) and received numerous prizes for his designs. In 1956 he was awarded the first prize for the design of the National Monument in Jakarta. The selection committee was chaired by President Soekarno. In the following year he was awarded the first prize for his design of the Indonesian pavilion of the second Industrial Fair in Jakarta, and in 1959 he was awarded the first prize for the Mantrust Tinned Goods Factory of the Industrial Fair in Semarang. He was also the architect of various well-known projects in Indonesia, including the Press House, Cloverleaf Bridge Jembatan Semangi (Jakarta), and a number of villas for Soekarno's wife, son, and Adam Malik. After migrating overseas, he was involved in designing various office buildings and shopping centres in Holland. He published his memoirs in 2004, entitled *Bloeiende Bron: Een architactenleven* [The blooming source: the life of an architect].

Sources: "Curriculum Vitae" (1995); Kwee Hin Goan, *Bloeiende Bron: Een architactenleven* (Rotterdam, 2004).

KWEE Hing Tjiat (GUO Hengjie 郭恒节, 1891–1939)
Community leader, journalist

Born in Surabaya in 1891, he was educated at the BAS, a Dutch vocational school. After leaving school, he worked for Firma Kian Gwan. In 1913 he was attracted to journalism and published *Bok Tok*, a weekly newspaper based in Surabaya. In 1916 he was invited to Batavia where he was appointed as the editor-in-chief of *Sin Po*, which he used as the mouthpiece of Chinese nationalism. He was critical of the Dutch and was opposed to the idea of Defence of the Indies (Indie Weerbaar) on the grounds that the Chinese were aliens and hence should not serve in the Dutch Army. In 1918 he resigned and went to Europe for business but continued to write for *Sin Po*. In 1921 he published a book in Berlin entitled *Doea Kapala Batoe*, which told the story of the Chinese movement in Java before 1920. The arguments of the book clearly show that he still believed in Chinese nationalism for the Indies Chinese. In 1923 Kwee returned to the Dutch Indies but was barred from landing at Java by the Dutch colonial government. He was forced to live in Shanghai for ten-and-a-half years. By the 1930s he was allowed to return to the Indies on the guarantee of **OEI Tjong Hauw**, director of the Oei Tiong Ham Concern, who wanted to publish a newspaper to advance his business. The newspaper came into being in 1934 and was called *Mata Hari*. Apparently, Kwee had abandoned his Chinese nationalist orientation and became Indonesia-oriented. He advocated the idea of being "an Indonesian son" for the Indies Chinese in the sense of having the Indies Chinese completely assimilated with the Indonesian population. He died in 1939.

Source: Suryadinata, *Peranakan Politics*, pp. 149–51.

KWEE Kek Beng (GUO Keming 郭克明, 1900–75)
Journalist, community leader, writer, father of **KWEE Hin Goan**

Born on 16 November 1900 in Jakarta, he first went to the HCS in Jakarta and continued his education at the HCK (Jakarta). In 1922 he worked in Bogor as a schoolteacher. Four months later he was invited to work for *Bin Seng* and then transferred to the editorial board of *Sin Po*, which marked the beginning of his career as a professional journalist. In 1925 when **TJOE Bou San** died, he became the editor-in-chief of *Sin Po*. He retained the position until 1947. After he became the editor-in-chief of *Sin Po*, the editorials of the paper continued to reflect the Chinese nationalist point of view adopted by the late Tjoe Bou San. Kwee led *Sin Po* to be one of the most influential *peranakan* Chinese newspapers in the Indies.

In 1929 Kwee visited Singapore and Malaya. In 1932 he travelled again. This time he went to China, a place which he regarded as *tanah leluhur* (ancestral land). In China he was awarded a medal by the Red Cross of China for his role in raising funds for that organization.

As an ardent Chinese nationalist, he could not tolerate other *peranakan* Chinese who did not share *Sin Po*'s view. He differed with the Indies-oriented *Perniagaan* and later had a debate with **LIEM Koen Hian**, who identified himself with Indonesian nationalists. He advocated that *peranakan* should remain Chinese and hold Chinese citizenship. However, he was sympathetic to Indonesian nationalism. He served as an assistant to the PNI journal, *Soeloeh Indonesia Moeda* (1930s). He changed his view after Indonesia declared its independence and was critical of Indonesian policies towards the Chinese. However, he became an Indonesian citizen in 1950 and was criticized by other *peranakan* for being inconsistent. After Indonesia's independence, he continued to edit a number of journals and publish a few books. In his writings he continued to be China-oriented. He died in Jakarta on 31 May 1975. His works include *Beknopt Overzicht der Chineesche Geschiedenis* (Batavia, 1925); *Li Tai Po, Een Kleine Studie Over China's Grootsten Dichter* (Batavia, 1927); *Doea Poeloe Lima Tahon Sebagi Wartawan* (Batavia, 1948); *Ke Tiongkok Baru* (Jakarta, 1952); *Pendekar-Pendekar R.R.T* [Who's who in New China] (Jakarta, 1953); and *Kung Fu Tse* (Jakarta, 1955).

Sources: Suryadinata, *Peranakan Politics*, pp. 151–54; the above-mentioned books.

KWEE Oen Liam (GUO Yunlian 郭允廉, 1889–1978)
Physician, community leader

Born in 1889 in Tegal, Central Java, after graduating from the THHK school, he went to China. In 1920 he graduated from Tung-chi (Tongji) University (Shanghai) and received advanced training in Germany. In 1926 he graduated from the Universiteit Munich as a qualified physician. But his German degree was not recognized by the Dutch colonial government. As a result he had to study at STOVIA in order to practise medicine in Indonesia. He lived and practised medicine in Jakarta for more than fifty years. He worked in the Jang Seng Ie (now Husada Hospital). When **Dr KWA Tjoan Sioe** died in May 1950, Kwee was apoointed the director of the Jang Seng Ie to succeed him. He stayed in the position until March 1975. He was its honorary director when he died on 22 October 1978.

Sources: Zhang, "Yinni Huaqiao"; the compiler's notes.

KWEE Soen Tik (GUO Shunde 郭顺德, 1906-?)
Community and political party leader, businessman

Born in Malang on 3 May 1906, he was educated at the THHK for three years before transferring to the HCS (Malang) and later the HBS (Surabaya). Prior to World War II he was elected as the secretary of BABOH (Bond Auto Bus Ondernemers Hindia), an association of busowners in Indonesia. He was also appointed as the secretary of the Central Chung Hsioh.

In 1948 he moved to Denpasar (Bali) and became the cofounder of the CIP (Canning of Indonesian Products) together with **LIEM Sam Tjiang**. In 1951 he became a member of the PNI. In 1954 he served as a member of the PNI Sunda Kecil provincial council. Between 1951 and 1956 he was appointed as a member of the DPRD in Denpasar. In 1964 he served as the second chairman of Jajasan Pertanian Nasional (National Farmers Funds, Banyuwangi). In 1959 he moved to Banyuwangi where he established the NAFO (National Foodpackers), the first sardine cannery in Indonesia. In 1964 he was second chairman of "National Farmers Foundation" (Banyuwangi branch). He also established the first and only dispensary in Banyuwangi in 1965. In 1971 he moved back to Denpasar where he was elected as the president of the board of trustees of the CIP. In 1974 he retired and moved back to Malang.

Sources: *Tambahan Berita-Negara R.I.* (Tanggal 29/12-1950, Nr. 96); relevant documents; Letter to the compiler, 1979.

KWEE Som Tjok. See TJOKROSAPUTRO, Kasom

KWEE Swan Lwan (GUO Xuanluan 郭碹峦, 1892-?)
Community leader, businessman

Born in 1892, he first received MULO education in Jakarta. Later he went to Surabaya for a special course on the sugar industry. In 1936 he became the patron of various Chinese organizations in Cirebon. In 1943 he served as the president of the HCTH (Cirebon).

Source: *Djawa Nenkan* (1973), p. 464.

KWEE Tek Hoay (GUO Dehuai 郭德怀, 1886–1951)
Writer, journalist, community leader, father of **Mrs TJOA Hin Hoey**

Born in Bogor on 31 July 1886, he was educated in a traditional Chinese school but became fluent in English and *peranakan* Malay. When the Chinese nationalist awakening took place in Java, he got involved in the THHK movement and became the president of the THHK (Bogor) for more than twenty years. He developed an interest in the education of the Indonesian Chinese and was elected as the vice-president of Djawa Hak Boe Tjong Hwee for a number of years.

He wrote articles for *Sin Po* before he became the editor-in-chief of *Sin Bin* (1925), a newspaper which soon ceased publication. In 1926 he began to publish his own weekly newspaper, *Panorama*, which was critical of *Sin Po*. In 1931 he sold *Panorama* to **PHOA Liong Gie**, a Leiden-trained lawyer who was interested in politics. From then he rarely contributed articles to *Panorama* but began to devote himself to religious studies. Kwee developed an interest in Confucianism when he became involved in the THHK movement. He wrote articles on Confucianism and was critical of Confucian organizations. His disillusionment led to his founding of Sam Kauw Hwee in the 1930s. A monthly publication of Sam Kauw Hwee entitled *Sam Kauw Goat Po* was published under his editorship. He believed that Sam Kauw was more suitable than Khong Kauw for Indonesian

Chinese. Convinced that Indonesian Chinese needed a religion, he started preaching Sam Kauw. He devoted most of his time to writing articles on Buddhism, Taoism, and Confucianism. These articles were collected and published in book form in *Buddha Gautama* (Batavia, 1931–33); *Bhagavad Gita* (Batavia, 1935); *Hikajat Penghidoepan dan Peladjaran Khong Hoe Tjoe* (Batavia, 1935); and *Omong-omong tentang Agama Buddha* (Batavia, 1935).

In addition, he published a monthly on religion, mysticism, and philosophy, entitled *Moestika Dharma*, from 1932 to 1941, and a monthly *Moestika Panorama*, which was more general in content, from 1930 to 1932. *Moestika Panorama* became *Moestika Romans* in 1932 and continued to exist up to 1942. One of his major studies was "Atsal Moelahnja Timboel Pergerakan Tionghoa jang Modern di Indonesia" (an edited and abridged English translation was done by Lea E. Williams and published in 1969 by the Cornell Modern Indonesia Project as *The Origins of the Modern Chinese Movement in Indonesia*).

Kwee was also a prolific novelist. He wrote more than ten novels/dramas, including *Allah Jang Palsoe* (Batavia, 1919); *Boenga Roos Dari Tjikembang* (Batavia, 1927); *Drama Dari Krakatau* (Batavia, 1929); *Penghidoepannya Satoe Sri Panggoeng* (Batavia, 1930–31); and *Drama dari Boven Digul* (1938). He died in Cicurug (West Java) on 15 July 1951.

Due to his contribution to Indonesian culture, in November 2011 the president of Indonesia awarded him Piagam Penghargaan Bintang Budaya Parama Dharma (Hero of Malay Literature) and in September 2012, the Governor of Jakarta re-named the Chinatown area as Kawasan Chinatown Kwee Tek Hoay.

Sources: Tio, *Lie Kimhok* (c.1959), p. 89; "Kwee Tek Hoaij-Buitenzorg", *Hoakiao*, February 1926, inside cover; Museum Catalogue; *Gunadharma* (1975), pp. 3–8; Tjia Tjiep Ling, *Soeara Sam Kauw Hwee*, no. 3 (April 1935), pp. 2–5; Nio, *Sastera*, pp. 37, 77, 109, 151; *Star Weekly*, no. 290

(22 July 1951), pp. 25–26; Jamal D Rahman dkk., *33 Tokoh Sastra Indonesia Paling Berpengaruh* (Jakarta: KPG, 2014), p. 18.

KWEE Thian Hong (Daud BUDIMAN, 1910–97) 郭天丰*
Political participant in the Youth Pledge (1928)

Born in Palembang, he joined the indigenous-dominated organization Jong Sumatranen Bond (Organization of Young Sumatrans). He joined the Boy Scout section and served as a leader and a drum player. During the 1928 Youth Congress which resulted in the Youth Pledge (*Sumpah Pemuda*, 28 October 1928) in Jakarta, he was a student at the Eerste Gouvernements MULO Batavia (the First State Dutch Secondary School in Jakarta). He was influenced by Indonesian nationalism and attended the large gathering, together with his three other classmates who were also *peranakan* Chinese. In one of the activities related to the Congress, Kwee was arrested by the police but was soon released. Kwee later worked for Bank Niaga until he retired.

The Youth Pledge is considered to be the birth of the concept of a modern Indonesian nation during which the name and language of Indonesia emerged. The "Indonesia Raya" was also played at the Congress for the first time, the song was later made the Indonesian national anthem. The Congress was attended by almost all ethnic groups (except perhaps Papua).

Sources: Swd [Siswadhi], "Ada Juga Pemuda 'Non-Pri' dalam Sumpah Pemuda 1928", *Kompas*, 25 October 1978; Junus Jahja, *Peranakan Idealis* (2002), pp. 37–42.

KWEE Thiam Tjing (1900–74) 郭添清*
Community leader, journalist

Born in Pasuruan in 1900, he was educated at MULO (Malang). In 1925 he was a member of the editorial board of *Soeara Publiek* (Surabaya). In 1929 he joined Liem Koen Hian's newspaper,

Swara Publiek, also in Surabaya. Because of press law violation he was detained for ten months. When **LIEM Koen Hian** moved to *Sin Jit Po*, which was changed to *Sin Tit Po* in late 1929, Kwee followed him and served as an editor of *Sin Tit Po* and as its editor-in-chief in 1931. He was a founding member of the PTI (1932) and served as its secretary. He joined the *Mata Hari* in 1934. In 1946 he travelled to Malang where was hit by anti-Chinese riots. He described the events in great details in a book entitled *Indonesia dalem Api dan Bara* [Indonesia on Fire], using a pen-name: Tjamboek Berdoeri (Thorny Whip). Following his daughter, he lived in Kuala Lumpur for ten years from 1960–70. In 1970 he returned to Indonesia and began to write a series of articles for *Indonesia Raya* between 1971 and 1973. These articles were later collected and edited by Arief W. Djati and Ben Anderson and published under the title: *Menjadi Tjamboek Berdoeri: Memoar Kwee Thiam Tjing* (2008). Kwee died in Jakarta in May 2002.

Sources: *Sin Tit Po*, 26 September 1932; Tan, *Tionghoa*, pp. 135–36; *Tempo*, 2 June 2002); Arief W Djati and Ben Anderson, eds., *Menjadi Tjamboek Berdoeri: Memoar Kwee Thiam Tjing* (Jakarta: Kommunitas Bambu, 2002).

KWEE Tjoa Kwang. See **KARWANDY**
KWEE Yat Nio. See **TJOA Hin Hoey (Mrs)**

KWIK Djoen Eng (GUO Chunyang 郭春秧, 1895–1935)
Owner of a large trading company dealing with sugar, rice and tea before World War II

Born in 1895 in Tong'an district in Fujian, China, Kwik was a Taiwan *sekimin* (台湾籍民), that is, a Japanese subject who enjoyed European status in the Dutch colonies. Not much was known of his childhood and education. In 1876 when he was seventeen years old, he moved to Java with his uncle, Kwik Hoo Tong, who was engaged in the trading business in Java under a *kongsi* (company) named Gin Mo Ho. He learned the trade through travelling in the interior of Central Java.

In 1894, the Kwik family registered their *kongsi* as an unlimited company, NV Handelmaatschappij Kwik Hoo Tong (Trading Society Kwik Hoo Tong, KHT). KHT became one of the biggest Chinese trading companies in Semarang trading mainly in sugar, rice, tea, and other agricultural products. As a Taiwan *sekimin*, he had close relations with the Netherlands, Taiwan, Japan, and China which enabled the company to become multinational with an extensive network of branches and agencies all over East and Southeast Asia. He was also successful in the tea business and made use of his connections with Taiwan and Japan to gain access to Japanese shipping and banking credits. He was one of the foremost clients of de Javasche Bank (JB) owing to his stake in the sugar trade.

Kwik was chairman of the tea association in Taipei as well as adviser of the Japan China South Bank. He was also known as a charitable person who contributed to the building of schools and enhancing education. In 1927, the company suffered heavy losses through its sugar business, which led to its voluntary liquidation in 1934. The following year, he passed away in Taipei.

Source: Yuko Kudo, "Kwik Djoen Eng", in Suryadinata, ed., *Southeast Asian Personalities* (2012), pp. 469–71.

KWIK Kian Gie (GUO Jianyi 郭建义, 1935-)
Political leader, economist, businessman

Born in Juwana (Central Java) on 11 January 1935, he studied at the Faculty of Economics at UI, Jakarta, for a while before going to Holland. In 1963 he obtained a Drs degree from Nederlandsche Economische Hoogeschool, Rotterdam (presently called Erasmus Universiteit Rotterdam). While studying he married a Dutch woman, Edith Johanna de Wit. He worked in the Netherlands for a few years (including at the Indonesian embassy in the Hague) before returning to Indonesia.

He was active in business for twenty-five years but in 1989 he gave up business to concentrate on educational matters and politics. In 1987 he established Institut Bisnis Indonesia (IBII, after 2012 re-named Kwik Kian Gie School of Business) and became its director. Since 1993 the Institut was transformed into Sekolah Tinggi Ilmu Ekonomi IBBI. He has also been an executive committee member of the Trisakti University Foundation (Jakarta) since 1970. In 1983 he was one of the founders of the Management Institute of Prasetya Mulya and served as its director until 1988. From 1988 to 1992 he served as a member of the Supervisory Council of the Management Institute of Prasetya Mulya, and as the secretary of the Daily Committee of the Prasetya Mulya Foundation.

Kwik has been active in politics. Known as an effective speaker, he joined the PDI and participated in the 1987 parliamentary election but was defeated. Between 1987 and 1992 he was a member of the MPR working committee, representing the PDI. He was barred from participating in the 1992 parliamentary election due to late registration. He was the chairman of the Research and Development Body of the PDI (1991–93; 1993–98). He was also a chairman of the PDI central board (Ketua DPP PDI) in 1993–98. In October 1998 the PDI became PDIP (Partai Demokrasi Indonesia Perjuangan) and in 2000 Kwik was re-elected as one of the chairmen of the PDIP. In the 1999 election Kwik was elected as member of DPR (1999–2014) representing the PDIP. When Gus Dur became president, Kwik was appointed as Coordinating Minister for Economics and Finance (1999–2000) but he became unpopular among wealthy businessmen. Under pressure he was forced to resign. When Megawati became president, Kwik was made Minister of National Development Planning cum Head of Bappenas (National Planing Institute), again he continued to be outspoken during his term as minister and was a severe critic of corruption and nepotism.

Kwik has been a frequent contributor to *Kompas* and has published several books, including *Konglomerat Indonesia: Permasalahan dan Sepakterjangnya* [Indonesian conglomerates: its problems and behaviour] (Jakarta, 1991), as co-editor; *Saya Bermimpi Jadi Konglomerat* [I dream of becoming a tycoon] (Jakarta, 1993); and *Analisis Ekonomi Politik Indonesia* [Indonesia's political economy: an analysis] (Jakarta, 1994), *Praktik Busnis dan Orientasi Ekonomi Indonesia* [Business practice and economic orientation of Indonesia] (Jakarta, 1996), and *Ekonomi Indonesia dalam Krisis Transisi Politik* [Indonesian economics in the political transition crisis] (Jakarta, 1999).

Sources: *Apa & Siapa 1985–86*, pp. 428–19; the above-mentioned books; Suryadinata, ed., *Southeast Asian Personalities* (2012), pp. 472–74; *Wajah DPR 1999*, p. 60.

L

LAI Xixi. See **LOA Sek Hie**
LAKSANA, Jeanne. See **YUAN Ni**
Latif Harris TANOTO. See **TANOTO, Latif Harris**
LAUW Chuan Tho. See **JAHJA, Junus**

LAUW Giok Lan (LIU Yulan 刘玉兰, 1883–1953)
Journalist, writer

Born in Jakarta in 1883, he was educated at a Hokkien school in Jakarta and gained a reading knowledge of Dutch. He was first a member of the editorial board of *Sinar Betawi* in the 1900s. In 1910 he established *Sin Po* (Jakarta) and served as its editor-in-chief until 1912. In 1913 *Sin Po* was changed from a weekly to a daily. Lauw continued to serve as one of its editors until 1921. He also served as the editor-in-chief of *Penghiboer*, a weekly published in Jakarta in 1913. In 1923 he became the editor-in-chief of *Lay Po*, a monthly published in Bandung, and a regular contributor to *Keng Po*, a daily published in Jakarta. He died in Jakarta on 11 May 1953.

His publications include *Brilliant Jang Tertjoeri* (Bandung, 1924) and *Riwajat Hindia-Olanda* (Bandung, 1924).

Sources: *Sin Po*, 1 October 1910; *Keng Po*, 22 July 1923; Museum Catalogue; Tio's notes.

LAUWANI, Siegvrieda (LIU Ing Wen; LIU Yingwen 刘英文, 1967-)
Member of DPRD

Born in Jakarta on 16 August 1967, she received both a bachelor and master degree in law. She is a practising lawyer and teaches at the Faculty of Law, Unika Atmajaya. She is also a doctoral candidate. She contested in the 2014 DPRD election for Jakarta representing the PDIP and won the seat (2014–19).

Source: Pengurus Pusat Fordeka, *Buku Acuan 2014*, p. 176.

LEE Man Fong (LI Manfeng 李曼峰, 1913–88)
Artist, painter

Born on 14 November 1913 in Guangdong, he came to Singapore in 1917 and studied at the Anglo-Chinese School until 1929. He later migrated to Java and worked for Kolff, a Dutch printing and publishing company. In 1946 he was awarded a Malino scholarship by the Dutch Government to study in Holland. He stayed in Holland for three years and held many exhibitions there.

Later, Lee returned to Indonesia. From 1955 to 1961 he served as the chairman of Yinhua Meishu Xiehui (Society of Chinese Artists in Indonesia). From 1961 to 1966 he was appointed as a court-painter at the presidential palace of RI. In 1970 he migrated to Singapore. In the 1980s he suffered from kidney and heart diseases. He died in Jakarta on 3 April 1988.

One of his publications is *Paintings and Statues from the Collection of President Sukarno of Indonesia* (Tokyo, 1964), of which he was the chief editor.

Sources: C.M. Hsu, November 1953, pp. 6–8; *Who's Who in Malaysia*, p. 70; *Lianhe Zaobao*, 7 April 1988.

LEE Teng Hui (LI Denghui 李登辉, 1872–1947)
Educator

Born in Jakarta on 18 April 1872, he first received his education at a local school, then continued his schooling at the Anglo-Chinese School in Singapore, and later entered Ohio Wesleyan University. He transferred to Yale University and obtained a BA degree in 1899. He returned to Jakarta and headed the Yale Institute (1901). After resigning from it in 1903, he went to Shanghai where he founded Huanqiu Zhongguo Xuesheng Zonghui (World Chinese Students General Association) in 1905, and served as its president for ten years. From 1911 to 1913 he was the editor-in-chief of *Republican Advocate*. From 1913 to 1914 he worked for Zhonghua Shuju, a large publishing company and headed its English editorial section. In 1917 he was appointed the chancellor of Fudan University (Shanghai). In 1919 he was awarded an honorary doctoral degree in law by Saint John's University in Shanghai. From 1928 to 1930 he served as an executive member of the Chinese National Anti-Opium Committee. Lee died in Shanghai in 1947.

Sources: Chen Weilong, "Chengming qian zi Li Teng-hui xiansheng", *Nanyang Xuebao* (Singapore) 9, no. 2 (December 1953): 38–39; *Who's Who in China* (1936), p. 147.

LEMBONG, Eddie (ONG Joe San; WANG Youshan 汪友山, 1936-)
Community leader, social activist, leading pharmacist

Born on 30 September 1936 in Tinombo, Central Sulawesi, Lembong received his pre-university education in Manado, Sulawesi before continuing his studies at the Department of Pharmacy at Institut Teknologi Bandung (ITB), where he obtained his Drs degree in Pharmacy.

Lembong started work as a lecturer at ITB and as a pharmacist at Apotek Abadi in Bandung. About a decade later, he and his friends established PT Pharos, which soon won the recognition of members of the foreign pharmaceutical industry. The British "Welcome Foundation" entrusted his company with the production of Lanoxin, a medicine for heart diseases. He later set up PT Welcome Indonesia, which produces its own diarrhoea drug which became well-known in Indonesia. He was also actively involved in professional pharmaceutical organizations especially in the Central Federation of Pharmacy Entrepreneurs (1972–90) and the Pharmacy Department of Kadin (Indonesian Chamber of Commerce and Industry) (1978–99). It was during this time that he was given the responsibility of negotiating with the Indonesian government on pharmaceutical matters.

Lembong became a social activist and community leader after the fall of Soeharto in May 1998. He was one of the founding members of a large Chinese Indonesian social organization (Paguyuban Sosial Marga Tionghoa Indonesia or PSMTI), with a view to improving the situation of Chinese Indonesians. However, due to internal conflict, he and a number of PSMTI members left the organization and set up another social organization called Perhimpunan Indonesia Keturunan Tionghoa (INTI). Under his leadership, many branches of INTI were set up in Java and the Outer Islands. INTI was involved in improving ethnic relations in the country, especially the ethnic Chinese and so-called indigenous population. Aid was given to those in need and victims of natural disasters. He stepped down as the general chairman of INTI in 2005 and served as its honorary chairman.

In 2006 Lembong and his wife set up the Yayasan Nabil (Nation Building Foundation), organizing seminars, sponsoring publications, and giving awards to foreign and Indonesian scholars who have made contributions to nation building. The foundation was one of the major associations responsible for the success of making Chinese Indonesian Admiral **John LIE** alias Jahja Daniel Dharma the "Pahlawan Nasional" (National Hero) in 2009. Prior to this, no ethnic Chinese had been recognized as a national hero in Indonesia. In October 2011, his biography entitled *Eddie Lembong: Mencintai Tanah Air Sepenuh Hati* [Eddie Lembong: Loving the motherland wholeheartedly] was published.

In early 2014, he suggested to **Murdaya POO** that the Cabinet Presidium Circular No. 6 (1967) that introduced the derogatory term *Cina (Tjina)* for China and the Chinese had not been nullified and it was time for the president to do so. He also provided Poo with the necessary information. Poo acted as an intermediate between the Chinese groups and President Yudhoyono and eventually succeeded in persuading the president to promulgate the Keppres No. 12 (2014) which nullified the Cabinet Presidium Circular No. 6 (1967).

Sources: Leo Suryadinata, "Lembong, Eddie", Suryadinata, ed., *Southeast Asian Personalities* (2012), pp. 552–55; *Apa dan Siapa 1985–1986*, pp. 440–41; Bonnie, *Eddie Lembong: Mencintai Tanah Air Sepenuh Hati* (2011); Macintyre, *Business and Politics in Indonesia* (1991), pp. 142–94; *Perspektif*, 22–28 July 1999, pp. 14–15; "Sambutan Ketua Umum pada acara Peresmian berdirinya Perhimpunan INTI", 10 April 1999; Leo Suryadinata, *ISEAS Perspective*, no. 26/2014 (25 April 2014).

LESMANA, Hendrawan (Hendrick SIE, 1978–98) 施亨利*
Student leader, "Reform Hero"

Hendrawan (or Hendriawan according to *Gatra*) was born in 1978 in Balikpapan, East Kalimantan. He was the only son of Hendrick Sie (施) and Karsiah. In 1996 he finished his high school education in his birthplace and came to the University of Trisakti to study business management. Hendrawan was musically inclined. He played guitar well and was a good storyteller. On 12 May 1998 he joined the student demonstration against the Soeharto regime. Four students were killed by the military: he was one of the victims. This was the beginning of the larger demonstration which eventually forced President Soeharto to step down from office, ending the so-called New Order period (1966–98) in Indonesian political history.

Hendrawan Lesmana was later named as "Reform Hero" (Pahlawan Reformasi) together with three other students who were killed during the demonstration by the Indonesian press. It was also reported that the name of one street in his birthplace has been named after him.

Sources: "Selamat Jalan Pahlawan Reformasi", *Gatra*, 23 May 1998, pp. 36–37; Leo Suryadinata, "Etnis Tionghoa dan Konsep Bangsa Indonesia", *Tajuk*, 12–25 November 1998, pp. 32–33; Zhou Nanjing, *Huaqiao Huaren Baike Quanshu, Encyclopedia of Chinese Overseas* (2001), p. 182.

LI Bai. See **RIADY, James Tjahaja**
LI Chuan Siu. See **LIE Tjwan Sioe**

LI Chunming (李春鸣, 1894–1976)
Educationist

Born in August 1894 in China, he graduated from the Nanking Normal School in 1916. In 1919 he came to Singapore to teach at Huaqiao Zhongxue (Hua Zhong). His father died in 1923 and he had to return to China. In 1925 he came to Malaya to serve as the principal of K'uan-jou Chung-hsueh (Kuanrou Zhongxue, Johor). He later joined Hua Zhong (Singapore) again. Still in the 1920s, he went to Indonesia to work as a Chinese schoolteacher, first in Lombok, later in South Sumatra. From 1933 to 1939 he taught at the THHK school (Jakarta). In 1939 he and three Chinese teachers (including **ZHANG Guoji**) established Chung-hua Chung-hsueh (Zhonghua Zhongxue, also abbreviated as Hua Zhong), which later became the largest Chinese high school in Jakarta. He served as the principal of that school for many years. Between 1951 and 1966, he served as the vice-president of Qiao Zong (Jakarta). Hua Zhong (Jakarta) was closed down in April 1966 and in June he and his family returned to China. He died in Chungking on 5 January 1976.

Sources: *Dipingxian*, no. 15 (February 1981), pp. 4–6; *Jinian tekan*, pp. 24–25.

LI Demei. See **LIE Dharmawan**
LI Denghui. See **LEE Teng Hui**
LI Deqing. See **LIE Tek Tjeng**
LI Jianjin. See **LIE Kian Kim**
LI Jiedeng. See **ALI, Mohammad**
LI Jinfu. See **LIE Kim Hok**
LI Manfeng. See **LEE Man Fong**
LI Mei. See **LIE Mei**
LI Mindong. See **GOZELIE, Tellie**
LI Ningbiao. See **LIE Ling Piao, Alvin**
LI Ping'an. See **LIE Ping An**

LI Qing (犁青; XIE Zhongming 谢仲明, 1933-)
Poet, businessman

Born in Fujian in 1933, he migrated to Indonesia in 1948. He worked as a teacher at a Chinese school in Bandung and wrote a number of poems. In 1957 he founded the literary society, *Yedao* (Coconut Island), which published *Yedao Monthly*. After the 1965 coup he became a businessman and stopped writing for many years. He later migrated to Hong Kong and again became active in the literary world. He published two literary journals, *Wenxue Shijie* [文学世界 Literary world] and *Shi Shijie* [诗世界 World of poetry], but these lasted only a few years. He also published collections of his own poems, including *Li Qing Shanshui* [犁青山水 Poems on mountain and water by Li Qing].

Sources: Zou Fangjin, *Haixia Shikan*, 1993, pp. 33–35; the compiler's notes.

LI Quanshou. See **LIE Tjwan Sioe**
LI Quanxin. See **LIE Tjwan Sien**
LI Ruihua. See **WUISAN, Empie**
LI Shangda. See **LYMAN, Susanta**
LI Shuanghui. See **LIE Siong Hwie**
LI Shubao. See **LIYANTO, Abraham Paul**
LI Weikang. See **A Wu**
LI Wenming. See **GUNAWAN, Mu'min Ali**
LI Wenzheng. See **RIADY, Mochtar**
LI Xiangsheng. See **SADELI, Eddy**
LI Xinglian. See **LIE Hin Liam**
LI Xu. See **LI Xu'nan**

LI Xu'nan (李旭南; pen-name: LI Xu 李旭, 1925?–77)
Writer, translator

Born in 1925 (1927?), his father was a businessman in Solo. In 1954 he went to Sungailiat (Bangka) to teach but did not stay long because of conflict with the school principal. He moved to Jakarta to join Hua Zhong, a large Chinese secondary school, where he taught Chinese. He started writing in 1957, and translated numerous Indonesian short stories and novels into Chinese for local Chinese newspapers and magazines. Some were later published in book form. His jointly written novel, *Xidao Enchouji* (Jakarta, 1961), deals with the Chinese riot in the Bangka island during the Dutch colonial period. He left for China in 1966 and lived jobless in Shanghai. He died in 1977 after suffering from a heart disease.

Sources: Huang Kunzhang, "Caihua hengyi de Li Xu'nan laoshi", in Qian Ren, Liang Junxiang, eds., *Shenghuobao de huiyi* (Guangdong: Shijie tushu chuban Guangdongyouxian gongsi, 2013), pp. 410–11; the compiler's notes.

LI Yinghua. See **LIE, Ivanna**
LI Yingzheng. See **LIE Ing Tien**
LI Yonglong. See **ADIDHARMA**
LI Yuanli. See **SUWONDO, Gani**
LI Yudao. See **SUDJATMIKO, Prasasto**

LI Yunfu. See **LIE Oen Hock**
LI Yuxiao. See **SUDJATMIKO, Djoko**

LI Zhuohui (李卓辉; Bambang SURYONO, 1938-)
Journalist, former editor-in-chief of Guoji Ribao, writer

Born in 1938 in Indonesia, he probably received his primary education in a village. He went to Singapore for his high school education. In 1960 he returned to Indonesia and joined *Zhongcheng Bao* (忠诚报), the Chinese edition of *Warta Bhakti*, a leftist newspaper. In 1965, when General Soeharto came into power, all Chinese language newspapers were banned and he lost his job. He worked and later became the head of a paper manufacturing factory for the next twenty years while continuing to pay close attention to Indonesian politics and the Indonesian Chinese community, especially the Chinese-speaking community.

During the May 1998 riots, Li fled Jakarta for a while and started writing reports on the socio-political situation in Indonesia for Singapore's *Lianhe Zaobao* (联合早报), Malaysia's *Sin Chew Jit Poh* (星洲日报), and *Hu Sheng* (*Aspirasi*, Jakarta). The re-emergence of Chinese language newspapers in Indonesia enabled him to assume the role of editor-in-chief at the *Guoji Ribao* (国际日报) in 2001. Under the editorship of Li, *Guoji Ribao* developed into a large Chinese daily in Jakarta. The paper also collaborates with mainland Chinese newspapers and their "overseas editions" are distributed as *Guoji Ribao* supplements, enabling it to become an "international newspaper".

Li is a very prolific editor and writer, writing a number of essays and books on the history of the Chinese community in Indonesia, Indonesian Chinese pioneers in the socio-political and cultural fields, Indonesian Chinese leaders and Indonesian-Chinese culture and education. To date, he has published at least nineteen books. He is arguably the most well-known Chinese newspaper editor in Indonesia in the post-Soeharto era. Li left

Guoji Ribao in 2012, he is now editor-in-chief of *Yinhua Ribao* (印华日报).

Sources: Leo Suryadinata, "Suryono, Bambang", Suryadinata, ed., *Southeast Asian Personalities* (2012), pp. 1023–25; *Guoji Ribao*, 14 December 2007; *Husheng*, no. 26, May 2001.

LIANG Bingnong. See **NIO Peng Liong**

LIANG Chiu Sia (LIANG Qiuxia 梁秋霞, 1950-)
Badminton player, coach, sister of **TJUNTJUN**

Liang Chiu Xia was born in Cirebon, West Java, on 9 September 1950. She was interested in badminton and received her badminton training at the Sen Ho Se Club. In 1966 she went to China at the age of sixteen and entered the Sports Academy, Department of Badminton and graduated in 1972. She played singles in the PRC team but as the PRC was not yet a member of the IBF, she was unable to participate in official international competitions. Nevertheless, during 1974–79, she was able to play against many European and Japanese women badminton players and gained victory. The only international title that she got was Asian championship in 1976 after defeating **Verawaty FADJRIN**, an Indonesian player. She later moved to Hong Kong and married a ballet dancer. Nevertheless, she continued to promote badminton and served as a Hong Kong badminton coach. In 1982 when she accompanied the Hong Kong team to Indonesia, Chiu Sia was homesick. Her parents and younger brother **TJUNTJUN**, who was in the Indonesian national badminton team, wanted her to return. In 1985 she eventually returned to Indonesia and in 1986 she regained her Indonesian citizenship. She was given the task to coach the Indonesian women badminton team to prepare them for the 1986 Uber Cup in Jakarta. After coaching the Indonesian women players for eight years, Chiu Sia eventually succeeded in making them world class players. One of her trainees, **Susi SUSANTI** became the champion in badminton singles during the 1994 Olympic Games.

Source: Sabaruddin Sa., *Apa & Siapa sejumlah Orang Bulutangkis Indonesia*, pp. 142–44.

LIANG Hailiang. See **KURNIAWAN, Rudy Hartono**
LIANG Qiuxia. See **LIANG Chiu Sia**
LIANG Xiyou. See **LIONG Sit Yoe**
LIANG Youlan. See **NIO Joe Lan**
LIAO Chunhui. See **LIU Chun Wai**

LIAO Ziran (廖自然)
Newspaperman, university lecturer

Born in Aceh, he served as the editor-in-chief of *Tiansheng Ribao* (Jakarta) in the 1950s. Prior to 1959 he was a professor in the College of Humanities, Gamaliel University (Jakarta). He left Indonesia in 1959(?) for Taiwan and in the 1960s served as the editor and manager of *Yinni Qiaosheng*, a journal on the Overseas Chinese published in Taipei.

Sources: Liao, "Shehui Shi", p. 108; *Nanyang Yanjiu Zhongwen Ziliao Shuoying*, p. 13.

LIE Dharmawan (LIE Tek Bie; LI Demei 李德美, 1946-)
Thoracic and cardiovascular surgeon, social worker

Born on 16 April 1946, he is better known as Dr Lie. His early education from primary to senior high school was in Padang. In 1965, he moved to Jakarta where he enrolled at the Medical Faculty of the Res Publica University which was established by Baperki, an ethnic Chinese organization. Unfortunately in mid-October 1965, his university was burned down after his classes had started for only a few days. Lie then decided to study medicine abroad. He went to Free University in West Berlin in 1967 where he worked to support himself during his studies and graduated as a general practitioner in

1974. He continued to earn his Dr Med. (PhD) degree in 1978 and finished his specialization as a thoracic and cardiovascular surgeon six years later.

As a student, Lie was very active in various student organizations and continued his interest in social and organized activities after returning to Indonesia. Upon his return to Indonesia, he worked in a few hospitals before joining Husada Hospital in Jakarta in 1988. It was during this time that he was struck by the social conditions in Indonesia such as the big gap between rich and poor and the discrimination against ethnic Chinese. These impressions and memories motivated him to try to help the poor by providing free medical care and heart surgery whenever required. During the May 1998 riots, he assisted the victims of rioting, arson and gang rape of mostly ethnic Chinese women and girls in Jakarta. During that period, he worked with women's organizations, such as Kalyanamitra and Suara Ibu Peduli. He also worked with Tim Relawan untuk Kemanusiaan (Volunteers for Humanitarian Work) to alert the media with a report on the victims of the riots which contained revealing insights into the gang rapes. When the United Nations Special Rapporteur on Violence against Women, Rhadika Coomaraswami, visited Indonesia in November–December 1998 to compile a report on the May riots, Lie organized her meeting with some of the rape victims.

Lie continued his humanitarian work through his affiliation with Perhimpunan Indonesia Tionghoa (INTI), for which he heads its volunteer medical team. The team focuses on relief works in disaster-hit regions such as the earthquake and tsunami disaster areas in Aceh in 2004. It also assisted victims of earthquakes in Padang, Bengkulu, and Pangandaran as well as those of the landslide on Flores Island in 1992, and the 2007 major flood in Jakarta. In 2009 Lie established Indonesia's first Floating Hospital (Rumah Sakit Apung) and the Foundation of doctorSHARE to serve the poor in the remote areas.

Source: Mely G. Tan, "Lie, Dharmawan", in Suryadinata, ed., *Southeast Asian Personalities* (2012), pp. 565–67.

LIE Djin Kiong. See **LITELNONI, Benny Alexander**
LIE Eng Liong. See **ADIDHARMA**
LIE Giok Hauw. See **SUDJATMIKO, Djoko**
LIE Giok Tho. See **SUDJATMIKO, Prasasto**
LIE Guan Die. See **SUWONDO, Gani**

LIE Hin Liam (LI Xinglian 李兴廉)
Community leader, businessman

Born in China, he was a founder of the THHK (1900). He was interested in politics in China and was the host of Kang Youwei when this Hundred Day Reform leader visited Jakarta. In 1908 he was one of the founders of Siang Hwee (Jakarta) and its first president. He was appointed as a *luitenant* in Jakarta for a period of two years by the Dutch. In 1911 he supported Chinese revolutionaries in China.

Source: William, *Nationalism*, p. 141.

LIE Ing Hoa. See **LIE, Ivanna**

LIE Ing Tien (LI Yingzheng 李应徵, 1890–1958)
Community leader, physician

Born in Malang in 1890, he was educated at the THHK (Malang), the CNHT (Nanking), the T'ung-chi (Tongji) Medical School (Shanghai), and Berlin University, from where he received an MD in 1923. He returned to Java and lived in Surabaya. He was an executive member of the THHK (Surabaya) and Soe Soei Tiong Hoa Ie Wan (Surabaya Chinese Hospital). He later moved to Malang, and died in Lawang (near Malang) on 5 October 1958.

Sources: Tan, *Tionghoa*, p. 44; Chen Weilong's letter, 1969; Tio's notes.

LIE, Ivanna (LIE Ing Hoa; LI Yinghua 李英华, 1960-)
Badminton player

Born on 7 March 1960 in Bandung, she came from a poor family, and her mother was a dressmaker. She was interested in badminton since childhood. In 1975 she won a junior championship for West Java. In 1980 she joined the Mutiara Club, and three years later won the Indonesian Open Championship. In the same year she also won the SEA Games XII Badminton Championship in Singapore. In 1984 she was an Indonesian Uber Cup team member. She maintained that although she felt Indonesian, she had not been able to get Indonesian citizenship. Her case was publicized in the press, and this led to President Soeharto's intervention. Ivanna finally got her citizenship on 29 November 1982. A well-known Indonesian poet, Sitor Situmorang, wrote a poem dedicated to Ivanna and **TAN Joe Hok**, praising them as Indonesia's son and daughter who had made contributions to the nation.

Sources: *Apa & Siapa 1983–84*, pp. 318–19; *Pembauran*, no. 22 (August 1980), p. 10; *Sejumlah Orang Bulu Tangkis Indonesia*, pp. 144–46.

LIE, John. See LIE Tjeng Tjoan, John

LIE Khe Bo (1901-?) 李启茂*
Community leader

Born in Tegal on 15 September 1901, he was educated at the ELS (Tegal), the K.W. III (Jakarta), and the HBS (Semarang). He was an executive member of Chung Hsioh while studying in Jakarta. In the mid-1930s he served as the president of the Overseas Chinese Athletes Association and was a member of the Tegal Municipal Council. According to one source, he collaborated with the Japanese during the occupation. There is not much written information about him.

Sources: Tan, *Tionghoa*, p. 159; Letter of Sie Hock Tjwan, 11 November 2002.

LIE Kian Joe (1916-?) 李建佑*
Physician, university professor, brother of **LIE Kian Kim**

Born in Sukabumi on 25 November 1916, he obtained a PhD in medicine from Geneeskundige Hoogeschool (Jakarta) in 1941, and the degree of Doctor of Tropical Medicine & Hygiene from the London School of Hygiene & Tropical Medicine in 1950. In the 1950s he was appointed Professor of Parasitology and General Pathology, FKUI. Since 1960 he has been serving as Research Professor, School of Medicine, Hooper Foundation, Institute of Medical Research, Kuala Lumpur. He is a member of the WHO Expert Ad Hoc Panel on Parasitic Diseases. His publications include *Trichostrongy Iusinfecties bij den menschen de huisdieren op Java* (his dissertation, 1941); (as co-author) "Subcutaneous Phycomycosis: A New Disease found in Indonesia", *Annals of New York Academy of Science 89* (1960); and "Implications within Snail Hosts", *Transactions of the Royal Society of Tropical Medicine & Hygiene 62* (1968).

Sources: *Who's Who in Malaysia* (1969), p. 151; *Warta Bhakti*, 2 November 1962; *Selected Scholars*, p. 389.

LIE Kian Kim (LI Jianjin 李建金, 1915–50)
Community leader, lawyer, brother of **LIE Kian Joe**

Born in Sukabumi, he was educated at the RHS (Jakarta). In 1946 he helped to found Sin Ming Hui and served as its secretary from 1946 to 1947, and its president from 1948 to 1950. He was also the vice-president of the PT central board in 1949. He died in a car accident in May 1950.

Sources: *Sinar*, 15 March 1949, p. 7; *SMH 10 Tahun*, p. 34; Setyautama, *Tokoh-tokoh Etnis Tionghoa*, p. 174.

LIE Kiat Teng. See **ALI, Mohammad**

LIE Kim Hok (LI Jinfu 李金福, 1853–1912)
Writer, publisher, community leader

Born in Bogor on 1 November 1853, he started schooling at the age of eleven. He went to a Dutch missionary school where **PHOA Keng Hek**, the president of the THHK (Jakarta), was a classmate. His father, a house-painter, was familiar with some old Chinese traditions as well as fluent in Sundanese.

Towards the end of the 1870s, Lie started his own school for poor *peranakan* children. But his interest seemed to lie in writing and the publication business. He managed to get a *peranakan* to operate the school while he himself began to run a printing house. He published story books, children's books, and his own works: *Kitab Edja* (1884), *Sobat Anak-Anak* (1885), *Siti Akbari* and *Malajoe Batawi* (1886). *Malayoe Batawi* was the first modern Malay grammar book published in the Malay language.

In 1886 Lie moved to Batavia and worked for *Pemberita Betawi*, a daily newspaper edited by a Dutch *peranakan*. Lie later became a member of the editorial board as well as the publisher of the newspaper. But he soon left the newspaper and worked as a freelance writer. He was a regular contributor to *Hindia Belanda*.

Economic pressure caused him to work for a landlord as a "rice inspector". He spent his time translating Dutch and English works and writing a controversial book, *Hikajat Konghoetjoe* (1871), which was based on Dutch sources. His translation works (novels) were first serialized in *peranakan* newspapers and later published in book form. From 1883 to 1913 he published approximately twenty-five books.

Apart from his writing activities, he was involved in the pan-Chinese movement in Java. Together with PHOA Keng Hek and the other *peranakan*, he founded the first pan-Chinese organization (THHK) in 1900 and was elected as an executive member of the organization. In fact, he was in charge of matters dealing with customs and Confucianism. In 1909 he was awarded "Kung-pai" (a seventh grade medal) by the Chinese emperor. He died in Jakarta on 6 May 1912.

Source: Tio, *Lie Kimhok* (c.1959).

LIE Ling Piao, Alvin (LI Ningbiao 李宁彪, 1961-)
Politician, Catholic

Born in Semarang on 2 April 1961, his father was an owner of a local department store "Mickey Mouse". He was sent to Singapore for his education, first to the Anglo-Chinese School (1977) and later to Hwa Chong Junior College (1979). Later he went to Chattered Institute of Marketing (1990) and Strathclyde University, Glasgow, Scotland. He studied International Marketing and finished the course in 1997. After the fall of Soeharto, he was associated with many politicians in Central Java and became a founding member of PAN, a party established by Amien Rais. Alvin even contested in the 1999 election under the banner of PAN. He was elected as MP for two terms: 1999–2004 and 2004–9. Alvin was active in the DPR and was a member of the Budget Committee. He was involved in impeaching President Gus Dur for misusing the Bulog funds and the donation from the Sultan of Brunei, resulting in the resignation of Gus Dur.

Sources: Sudrajat, "Alvin Lie Ling Piao: Politisi Penjaja Jamu", in *Sepuluh Anggota DPR terbaik Pilihan Wartawan* (Jakarta: Millennium Publisher, 2001), pp. 40–58; Setyautama, *Tokoh-Tokoh Etnis Tionghoa*, p. 178.

LIE Mei (LI Mei 李梅, 1913–87)
Community leader, second (third?) wife of **Dr KWA Tjoan Sioe**

Born in 1913 in Guangdong, China, she was taken to Indonesia when she was a baby. She was among the first THHK Kao-chung (senior middle school) graduates in 1933. After World War II, she served as the president of the Chinese

Women's Association (Zhonghua Funü Xiehui), and an executive committee member of Qiao Zong. In 1950 she led a delegation to the PRC.

From April 1964 until the outbreak of the Cultural Revolution, she served as a member of ACROCA, a member of the Peking Returned Overseas Chinese Association, and a member of the 4th CPPCC. She died in 1987.

Sources: Fitzgerald, *Peking's Policy*, p. 203; Nio, *THHK*, p. 322; *Xinbao*, 6 August 1949; *Shenghuo Zhoubao*, 26 December 1964, p. 3; *Cidian*, p. 375.

LIE Men Dong. See GOZELIE, Tellie
LIE Mo Tie. See RIADY, Mochtar

LIE Oen Hock (LI Yunfu 李运福, ?-1966)
Lawyer, university professor

Born in Bukit Tinggi, he was educated at the HBS (Jakarta) and the RHS (Jakarta). He obtained an Mr degree from the University of Leiden and was active in Chung Hsioh and the HCTNH. He worked for the Native Court (Bukit Tinggi) upon his return to Indonesia from the Netherlands. In the mid-1930s he moved to Solo to practise law.

After World War II he moved to Jakarta and was appointed as a member to the Jakarta High Court. In the 1960s he served as Professor at the FHUI and Dean of the Faculty of Law, URECA. His publications include *Beberapa Tindjauan Ilmu Hukum* (Jakarta, 1960) and *Tjatatan Sipil di Indonesia* (Jakarta, 1961). He died in November 1966.

Sources: Tan, *Tionghoa*, pp. 149–50; *Organisasi Negara 1960*, p. 659; *Sinar Harapan*, 7 November 1966; the compiler's notes.

LIE Oen Sam (1918-?) 李运三*
Political party leader

Born in Padang on 3 October 1918, he graduated from Middelbare Handelsschool in Jakarta in 1937, and was active in local journalism. In 1953 he was elected as the chairman of Partai Katholik (Padang branch) and in 1954 he served as the vice-chairman of Baperki (Padang branch). He was nominated as a Baperki candidate in the 1955 general elections but left the organization in the same year(?).

Source: *Pedoman Kampanje*, p. 62.

LIE Ping An (LI Ping'an 李平安)
Community leader, journalist

Born in Surabaya, he was educated at the ELS and the HBS in Surabaya. In 1924 he served as a member of the Surabaya Municipal Council and in 1929 was appointed as a *wethouder* (assistant to mayor). At one time he also served as a member of the East Java Provincial Council. Upon his initiative, Tiong Hoa Keng Tjie Sia of Surabaya was reconstituted as the CHH Surabaya Section. A journal called *Peladjar* was published under his editorship. In the 1930s he moved to Jakarta and became a salaried secretary of the CHH central board. From 1936 to 1942 he was the editor-in-chief of *Pelita Tionghoa* (Jakarta), an official newspaper of the CHH.

Sources: Tan, *Tionghoa*, pp. 195–96; Suryadinata, *Peranakan Politics*, p. 110.

LIE Po Yoe. See DIPOJUWONO, Budi

LIE Siong Hwie (LI Shuanghui 李双辉, 1859-?)
Community leader, businessman

Born in Haideng (Fujian) in 1859, he came to Semarang in 1879 and worked in the commercial field. In 1891 he was employed by Kian Gwan (Yogyakarta branch) as a bookkeeper. In 1899 he returned to China to visit his relatives. When he resettled in Indonesia, he was made the deputy manager of Kian Gwan (Surabaya branch). In 1907 he was promoted to branch manager.

He was the founder and first chairman of Siang Hwee (Surabaya) in 1909(?). Interested in politics, he raised funds for the Chinese imperial government to buy warships (1909). Interestingly, he was also the vice-chairman of Soe Po Sia, a revolutionary organization in Surabaya. In 1916 he opposed Yuan Shih-k'ai and supported the revolutionaries.

Sources: Liu, *Gailan*, p. [91]; *Shangye Nianjian*, p. 339; Williams, *Nationalism*, p. 144.

LIE Siong Tay. See **LYMAN, Susanta**
LIE Soe Pau. See **LIYANTO, Abraham Paul**
LIE Tek Bie. See **LIE Dharmawan**

LIE Tek Tjeng (LI Deqing 李德清, 1931–2009)
Historian, lecturer, senior researcher

Born on 18 May 1931 in Palembang, he was educated at the Sinological Institute, FSUI, where he graduated with a BA degree in 1954. He went to Harvard and received his MA in Regional Studies (East Asia) in 1956 and a PhD in History and Far Eastern languages in 1962. Before obtaining his PhD he was a Rockefeller Research Fellow at the Institute of Humanistic Studies, Kyoto University, from March 1957 to September 1959.

He returned to Jakarta in 1963 and was appointed as a lecturer at the FSUI and later the head of the Department of Japanese Studies, FSUI. In September 1965 he was sent to Beijing by the Indonesian Ministry of National Research to the Academia Sinica. He stayed there until March 1966. In mid-1967 he was sent to Malaysia and Singapore by the Indonesian Army Staff and Command School to study racial problems. Between 1971 and 1980 he was the director of LRKN, LIPI. He has been Senior Researcher at LIPI since 1984. He taught at Lemhanas (National Defence Institute), the FIS-UI, and the Staff and Command School (SESKO).

He has many publications to his credit, including *An Indonesian View: The Great Proletarian Cultural Revolution* (Jakarta, 1970); *Masalah WNI dan Masalah Huakiau di Indonesia* (Jakarta, 1970); and *Studi Wilayah Pada Umumnya dan Studi Asia Tenggara Pada Khususnya*, vols. I and II (Bandung, 1977).

He suffered from heart attack and became paralyzed. He passed away in Jakarta on 12 January 2009.

Sources: Mely G. Tan, "Lie Tek Tjeng", in Suryadinata, ed., *Southeast Asian Personalities* (2012), pp. 569–71; Lie (1970), p. 25; *Indonesian Review of International Affairs*, July 1971, p. 2; Roeder, *Who's Who*, 2nd ed., p. 510; *Apa & Siapa 1985–86*, pp. 447–49; the compiler's notes.

LIE Tjeng Tjoan, John (Yahya Daniel DARMA; John LIE, 1911–88)
李清泉*
Admiral, national hero

Born on 9 March 1911 (1910, according to *Life*) in Kanaka, North Sulawesi, he received some Dutch education. Before World War II he spent fifteen years on a Dutch ship sailing between Durban and Shanghai. In 1946 he joined the Indonesian Navy and was stationed in Singapore to deal with arms supplies. He was promoted to Commander in 1949 due to his contribution during the Indonesian-Dutch conflicts. He was then well-known among Western correspondents as the "Guns and Bibles Smuggler". In 1960 he was promoted to *Laksamana Muda* (Admiral). In the same year he was appointed as a member of the DPR up to January 1961. In 1967 he changed his name from John Lie to Jahja Daniel Darma. Since that year he had been assigned the task of salvaging old ships. He died on 27 August 1988. He was the only Indonesian admiral of Chinese descent, as well as the only Chinese Indonesian who was awarded the title of "Pahlawan Nasional" (National Hero) in 2011.

Sources: Rowan, *Life*, 26 September 1949, pp. 49–52; *DPR 1971*, p. 638; *Sinar Harapan*, 12 March 1967; A. Dahana, "Lie Tjeng Tjoan, John", in Suryadinata, *Southeast Asian Personalities* (2012), pp. 571–73.

LIE Tjian Tjoen (李前俊, 1886–1964)
Social worker, community leader, husband of **AW Tjoei Lan**

Born into a *majoor* family in Jakarta, he was a co-founder of "Ati Sutji", a social institution set up to help orphans and deserted children. He was appointed as a *kapitein* by the Dutch and was awarded the Ridder Oranje Nassau by the Dutch Government for his contribution to the Indies society.

Sources: Tan, *Tionghoa*, p. 197. Satyautama, *Tokoh-Tokoh*, p. 188; picture of tombstone provided by Marius Roest, October 2013.

LIE Tjian Tjoen (Mrs). See AW Tjoei Lan

LIE Tjwan Sien (LI Quanxin 李全信, 1910–94?)
Physician, community leader

Born in Jombang (East Java) in 1910, he obtained an ARTS degree in Medicine at Geneeskundige Hoogeschool (Jakarta) in 1938. He also studied acupuncture and moxibustion at the Pyungnam and Red Cross Hospitals (in Pyongyang, North Korea). In the 1960s he was a lecturer at the Dental and Medical Faculty of URECA (Jakarta). He attended the Scientific Discussion, held in Beijing between 21 and 31 August 1964, during which he presented a paper "Man Frees Himself from Parasites". He was active in the Baperki central board, and was detained by the Indonesian authorities after the 1965 coup.

He wrote *Pengaruh Penyakit Parasit* (Jakarta, 1960).

Sources: *Sin Po*, 14 May 1957; *Zhongcheng Bao*, 26 August 1964; Letter to the compiler, 1979; Li Zhuohui, *Qingshan bulao haoqi changcun* (2008), p. 135.

LIE Tjwan Sioe (LI Chuan Siu; LI Quanshou 李全寿, 1914–98)
Indonesian and Malay language expert, writer, translator

Born in Surakarta in 1914, he was educated at the Chinese-English School in Semarang (1926–29), the Chip Bee Institute in Amoy, China (1930–33), and the FSUI (Jakarta), where he obtained a Drs degree in Sinology and Malay/Indonesian language and literature in 1953. After graduation he worked as a linguist and part-time lecturer at his alma mater while teaching Indonesian at the Kao Shang School (Jakarta). In 1955 he was appointed as an official Indonesian interpreter during the dual nationality negotiations between the PRC and Indonesia. During the 1950s he set up the Indonesian Language Academy (Jakarta).

From 1958 to 1964 he was appointed as a lecturer at Nanyang University (Singapore). In 1964 he migrated to Australia and took up a lectureship at Sydney University. In 1967 he was offered a professorship from Nanyang University for a three-year term but he preferred to stay at Sydney as a senior lecturer with a tenure position. In July 1979 he retired from the University and in the same year he was invited as Visiting Professor in the Academy of Foreign Languages in Beijing for a year. In 1980 he returned to Sydney. He continued to do some writings and taught Bahasa Indonesia. In 1992 he finished writing his memoirs which was later published as a book: *Dari Sinologi ke Indologi* (Kuala Lumpur: Pustaka Antara, 1994). After the publication of his memoirs, he continued to teach Indonesian for beginners once a week at the Workers Education Association Institute until December 1994. He only stopped teaching when his health deteriorated. He died in Sydney on 29 June 1998 at the age of eighty-three.

He published extensively, including Malay language textbooks for Chinese and Malays. His publications include "Yinni Huaqiao Jiaoyu Shi" [A history of Chinese education in Indonesia] (which was based on his academic exercise submitted to the University of Indonesia), in *Nanyang Xuebao* (1959); *Malaiyu Yufa* [Malay grammar] (Singapore, 1960); *Ikhtisar Sejarah Kesusasteraan Melayu Baru 1830–1945* [An Introduction to the New Malay Literature 1830–1945] (Kuala Lumpur, 1966; second printing, 1972); *Ikhtisar Sejarah Kesusasteraan Melayu Baru 1945–1965* [An Introduction to the History of New Malay Literature 1945–65] (Kuala Lumpur, 1967; reprinted, 1978); *An Introduction to the Promotion and Development of Modern Malay Literature* (Yogyakarta, 1975); and *Essentials of Indonesian Grammar* (Sydney, 1976). His translation works include: *Hidup Bagaikan Mimpi* [Shen Fu's Chapters from a Floating Life] (Kuala Lumpur, 1961); *Tiongkok* [An English book on Chinese history by Ping-chia Kuo] (Kuala Lumpur, 1965); and *Lampu yang tak kunjung Padam* [Selected short stories of Lu Xun] (Kuala Lumpur, 1984).

Sources: Tilman, *Specialists*, pp. 134–35; Hsu Yun-ch'iao, *Dongnanya Yanjiu I* (1965): 107–69; *Lie Tjwan Sioe* (1975), p. 9; *Dipingxian*, no. 14 (October 1980): 10–13; Li Chuan Siu, *Dari Sinologi ke Indologi* (1994); Sylvia Lie's letter to the compiler, 16 January 2014.

LIEM A Pat (1862-?) 林亚拔*
Community leader, businessman

Born in 1862, he was appointed as *luitenant* of Muntok in 1913 and later promoted to *kapitein*. During the period 1918–24, he was appointed as a member of the Volksraad, representing the Chinese minority.

Source: Wal, *Volksraad*, vol. II, p. 716.

LIEM Bian Khoen. See WANANDI, Albertus Sofjan
LIEM Bian Kie. See WANANDI, Jusuf
LIEM Boen Hwa. See HALIM, Boediharto

LIEM Boen Siang (LIN Wenxiang 林文祥)
Community leader, businessman

Prior to the 1965 coup, he was the president of Xinghua Huiguan (Hinghwa Association) and the vice-president of Qiao Zong (Jakarta).

Source: The compiler's notes.

LIEM Bwan Tjie (1891–1966) 林满志*
Founder of Indonesian Institute of Architects

Born on 6 September 1891 in Semarang, Liem completed his elementary school and basic technical education in Indonesia. His family was in the textile and draperies business and had good relations with many Dutch businessmen, who offered to help the Liem children to further their education in the Netherlands. He graduated from the Hogere Burgereschool (HBS) in Haarlem and upon graduation worked with various prominent architects.

In 1920, Liem pursued further studies in architecture at Delft Technical University where he engaged in social and spiritual debates which reminded him of his status as a second-class citizen in Indonesia. He went back in 1929 and started his own practice in Semarang. His works could be split into two periods: the Semarang (pre-World War II), and the Jakarta (post-World War II). In the former, the heavy influence of the Amsterdam School, which employed ornamentation reflecting the dynamic quality of life, was vividly expressed. The compact and organic organization of spaces flow into the second period, although the forms grew more solid and bereft of ornaments. The cubistic forms became more majestic in bigger buildings. As an architect, he blended three elements (dignity, prudence, and harmony) into a highly versatile creative power.

Liem had designed offices, sport facilities, shops, markets, and many houses and villas during his thirty-five year career in Indonesia. Some of his notable works include the headquarters for the Oei Tiong Ham Concern (OTH-C), the Leper Hospital in Tangerang, Institute for Mouth and Hoof Diseases in Surabaya, Teladan Sport Stadium in Medan, the Ministry of Agriculture building, the National Police Headquarters, the North Sulawesi University campus in Menado and the Hospital of Ambon. In 1959, he established the Indonesian Institute of Architect (IAI — Ikatan Arsitek Indonesia), the only organization for professional architects in Indonesia, He died at the Rijswijk Hospital on 28 July 1966.

Source: Sutrisno Murtiyoso, "Liem Bwan Tjie", in Suryadinata, ed., *Southeast Asian Personalities* (2012), pp. 573–76.

LIEM Eng Hway. See **NURIMBA, Adil A.**
LIEM Fung Sen. See **SALIM, Anthony**

LIEM Ho Ban 林和万*
Community leader

Born in Banjarmasin, he was educated at the ELS (Banjarmasin and Samarinda), the PHS (Jakarta), and a commercial school (Surabaya). At first he lived in Pasuruan where he was a member of the Municipal Council. In the 1930s he moved to Probolinggo, first serving as the chairman of the PTI (Probolinggo branch), later devoting his attention to the promotion of HCS education.

Source: Tan, *Tionghoa*, pp. 36–37.

LIEM Hok Liong. See **SOEJATMIKO, Basuki**

LIEM Hwie Giap (LIN Huiye 林徽业, 1900–48)
Community leader, businessman

He was born in 1900 in Pasuruan and was educated at the HBS (Surabaya), during which time he served as the chairman of Chung Hsioh. Before World War II he was the director (CEO) of the Surabaya branch of the Oei Tiong Ham Concern. In the 1930s he served as the chairman of the CHH (Surabaya branch) and was an executive member of Soe Soei Tiong Hoa Ie Wan (Surabaya Chinese Hospital). From 1937 to 1938 he served as an executive member of the CHH central board. In 1941 he was the chairman of the China Institute. Queen Wilhelmina knighted him to the Order of Oranje Nassau.

He was arrested by the Japanese during the Japanese Occupation and interned as a political prisoner in Cimahi for the duration of the war (1942–45), during which time he suffered from cancer and his health deteriorated. He was active in helping his fellow prisoners-of-war; for his aid to the British internees he received the British laurel leaf. For a short time, until 1946, he served as the director of Kian Gwan, Jakarta. During this time he also served as the president of the Jang Seng Ie Red Cross. However, his failing health made it necessary for him to seek treatment in Holland and in the United States. In 1948 he returned to Jakarta, where he died the same year.

Sources: Tan, *Tionghoa*, p. 45; *Jade 12*, no. 2 (1948): 1–2; *CHH 2 de Lustrum*, p. 7; information provided by Mrs Liem Hwie Giap and son Harold Lim, letter of Geok Po Oey, 3 March 1995.

LIEM Hwie Liat 林黴烈*
Community leader, businessman

Born in Pasuruan, he was educated at a Hokkien school (Pasuruan), the THHT (Surabaya), the ELS (Surabaya), and a private middle school. In the 1930s he served as an executive member of the CHH central board, a member of the East Java Provincial Council, a member of the executive committee of Soe Soei Tiong Hoa Ie Wan (Surabaya Chinese Hospital), and the Surabaya Soccer Association. He died in Surabaya.

Sources: Tan, *Tionghoa*, pp. 45–46; CHH 2 de Lustrum, p. 7; the compiler's notes.

LIEM K.D. (LIEM King Djwan) 林庆全*
Community leader, businessman

A long-time resident in Semarang, he was a member of the Semarang Municipal Council in the 1930s, a leading member of the CHH (Semarang branch) before World War II, and the secretary-general of Jajasan Sekolah Chung Hwa Hui (Semarang), 1950–60.

Sources: *CHH 2de Lustrum*, p. 7; the compiler's notes.

LIEM Kay Hoo. See KAMIL, Iskandar
LIEM Kek Tjiang. See LIM Kek Tjiang

LIEM Khiam Soen (LIN Qianshun 林谦顺, 1897-?)
Community leader, businessman

Born in 1897 in Tegal, he was educated at the ELS (Tegal) and the PHS (Jakarta). He had worked for the Kian Gwan Firm (Semarang) since 1921, and was promoted to the position of manager in charge of agricultural products in the Jakarta branch. In the 1930s he served as an executive member of Siang Hwee (Jakarta) and the president of the CHH (Jakarta branch).

Sources: Tan, *Tionghoa*, p. 199; Liu, Gailan, p. [34].

LIEM Khiem Yang (1933-) 林金扬*
Religious scholar, church activist

Born on 30 August 1933 in Semarang, after finishing the SMP in Semarang, he studied at Sekolah Tinggi Teologia (STT, Theologian College) in Jakarta between 1950 and 1956. Graduating as a clergyman, he returned to Semarang to become the church minister of Gereja Isa Almasih. Two years later he was sent to Rheinische Friedriech Wilhelm Universiteit at Bonn in West Germany. In 1964 he submitted a dissertation and obtained a PhD. Between 1964 and 1966 he worked as the translator of the New Testament at Lembaga Alkitab

Indonesia (Indonesian Bible Institute) at Bogor. He later returned to his alma mater (STT), first as a lecturer, and later as a professor. He also lectures at the Faculty of Law and the FISIP at the University of Indonesia.

Liem has been very active in Christian associations and church affairs. During his student days he was a student clergyman of the GMKI (Gerakan Mahasiswa Kristen Indonesia, Indonesian Christian Students Association). He is a committee member of the Indonesian church council and is involved in church publications.

Source: *Apa & Siapa 1985–86*, pp. 444–45.

LIEM Khing Hoo (pen-name: ROMANO; LIN Qinghe 林庆和, 1905–45)
Writer, novelist

Born in Welingi in 1905, he was educated at the THHT, but learned Chinese and Javanese classics from his father. His family background is reflected in his writings. In the early 1930s(?) he served as the editor-in-chief of *Tjerita Romans* (a journal of novels and short stories) and, from 1933 to December 1941, as the editor-in-chief of *Liberty*. Most of his novels and short stories were published in these two journals. The following are some of his better-known works: "Meledaknja Goenoeng Keloet" [The eruption of Kelud mountain] (June 1930); "Dewa-Dewa" [Deities] (November 1929); "Manoesia" [Human being] (April 1930); "Kembang Widjajakoesoema" [Wijayakusuma Flower] (October 1930); "Pengorbanan" [Sacrification] (August 1931); "Gelombang dari Laoetan Kidoel" [The wave of the southern sea] (April 1932); "Berdjoang" [Struggle] (April 1934); "Merah" [Red] (March 1937); and "Masjarakat" [Society] (May 1939). He also published an Indonesian translation of *San Guo* [The romance of the three kingdoms] before World War II. It was reported that he was detained by the Japanese and tortured in a concentration camp where he died on 4 April 1945.

Sources: Tan, *Tionghoa*, p. 46; Salah Satoe, *Liberty*, no. 167 (15 February 1946), pp. 23–24; "Toean Liem Khing Hoo", *Liberty*, no. 169 (15 March 1946), p. 15.

LIEM King Djwan. See LIEM K.D.

LIEM Koen Beng (LIN Qunming 林群明, 1909–83)
Prosecutor, younger brother of **LIEM Koen Hian**

Born on 29 June 1909 in Banjarmasin, he was educated at the HCS (Banjarmasin), the HCS (Surabaya), and the HBS (Surabaya). In 1927 he joined I-yung T'uan, a student troop consisting of Chinese youths from the Indies, which aimed at helping the southern government unite China. He could not withstand hardship in the student army and soon returned to Java. In 1934 he was appointed Prosecutor of the Raad van Justitie in Surabaya by the Dutch Governor-General. A member of the Indonesian Lawyers Association, he worked as a public prosecutor in Surabaya. He passed away on 13 November 1983.

Sources: Tan, *Tionghoa*, p. 45; *Liberty*, 19 November 1983, p. 8; the compiler's notes.

LIEM Koen Hian (LIN Qunxian 林群贤, 1896–1952)
Political leader, journalist, elder brother of **LIEM Koen Beng**

Liem Koen Hian was born in Banjarmasin (Kalimantan) in 1896. He received Dutch primary education and by self-study managed to pass the qualifying examination for the Law School in Jakarta.

Like many *peranakan* Chinese journalists, Liem was first a Chinese nationalist. He was the editor-in-chief of the following China-oriented newspapers: *Tjhoen Tjhioe* (1915–16), *Soo Lim Po* (1917), *Sinar Sumatra* (1918–21), and *Pewarta Soerabaia* (1921–25). He abandoned his Chinese nationalist view after the mid-1920s and declared himself an Indonesian nationalist. The ideas of Indonesian nationalism for *peranakan* Chinese were developed in the following newspapers of which he was the editor-in-chief: *Soeara Publiek* (Surabaya, 1925–29), *Sin Jit Po/Sin Tit Po* (Surabaya, 1929–32; 1939), and *Kong Hoa Po* (Jakarta, 1937–38). In September 1932 he and other *peranakan* Chinese succeeded in establishing a *peranakan* political party, Partai Tionghoa Indonesia (PTI), which sided with Indonesian nationalists in pursuing the goal of Indonesia's independence. Liem was the first president of that organization (1932–33). In 1939, when a left-wing Indonesian party (Gerindo) opened its membership to *peranakan*, Liem left the PTI and became a member.

Liem was against Japanese imperialism, and he published a book in 1938 denouncing it. He was detained when Japan occupied Java but was released soon after. In 1945 he was appointed as a member of the Investigative Committee for Indonesian Independence (BPUPKI) initiated by the Japanese (but headed by Soekarno and Hatta). After Indonesia gained its independence, Liem was appointed as a member of the Indonesian Central National Committee (1946). As time passed, he became more interested in the communist movement in China. He translated Gunther Stein's book, *The Challenge of Red China*, and published it in June 1949 predicting (in the preface) the victory of the communists over the Kuomintang. In 1950 he established a multiracial political party, Persatuan Tenaga Indonesia (the New PTI), advocating Indonesian nationalism but the party failed to develop. In 1951 he was arrested by the Sukiman government on suspicion of being a communist. Upon his release he repudiated Indonesian citizenship which he had advocated in the last twenty years. He became a businessman running a drug store. A year later (1952) he died in Medan.

Sources: Suryadinata, *Peranakan Politics*, pp. 161–65; Leo Suryadinata, *Mencari Identitas Nasioanal: Dari Tjoe Bou San sampai Yap Thiam Hien* (Jakarta: LP3ES, 1990), pp. 77–110.

LIEM Koen Seng (LIN Qunsheng 林群盛)
Community leader, lawyer

He was an executive member of the PDTI in 1953 and a leading member of Baperki (Jakarta) from 1954 to 1965. He visited the PRC in 1962.

Sources: *Berita P.D.T.I.*, 15 October 1953, p. 4; Kwee, *50,000 Kilometer*, p. 107; the compiler's notes.

LIEM Kwi Boen 林贵文*
Community leader, businessman

Born in Malang, he was educated at a Hokkien school and the THHT (Malang). He moved to Surabaya and was active in Chinese organizations. In the 1930s he was the chairman of the board of directors of Soe Soei Tiong Hoa Ie Wan (Surabaya Chinese Hospital), Boen Bio (Confucian temple), and the THHK (Surabaya). He was also an executive member of Siang Hwee (Surabaya).

Source: Tan, *Tionghoa*, p. 46.

LIEM, Lita. See SOEGIARTO, Lita
LIEM Oen Kian. See DJUHAR, Sutanto

LIEM Sam Tjiang (?-1978) 林三昌*
Community leader, journalist

Born in Tuban, he was educated at a private Dutch school, a Hokkien school (Tuban?), the HCS (Surabaya), the HBS (Surabaya), and NIAS (Surabaya). He left the medical school because of an illness. In the 1930s he served as the president of the following organizations: the PTI (Malang branch), Polikliniek Tiong Hoa Ie Sia (Malang), and Chung Hsioh (Malang). In 1937 he became the editor-in-chief of *Sin Tit Po*. He moved to Bandung where he was active in the formation of Sin Ming Hui (Bandung branch) and served as its vice-president in 1946. In 1948 he moved to Denpasar (Bali) to establish the Canning of Indonesian Products (CIP), of which he was the managing director until 1955. He died in Bandung on 14 December 1978.

Sources: Tan, *Tionghoa*, p. 27; *Buku Peringatan Sin Ming Hui 1946–56*, p. 29; the compiler's notes.

LIEM Seng Tee (LIN Shengdi 林生地, ?-1956)
Kretek cigarette king, grandfather of **Putera SAMPOERNA**

Born in Anxi (Fujian), he migrated to Surabaya when he was very young. He started working for a living as a worker for a *kretek* manufacturer at the age of twelve. He later established his own *kretek* factory. Djie Sam Soe, a well-known *kretek* brand, was owned by him. Liem was superstitious. He believed that nine was a lucky number, hence his phone number, car licence number, and name of his *kretek* cigarette were all related to "nine" (Djie Sam Soe, for instance, means two, three, and four, which equal nine). It was reported that during the colonial period he was sympathetic to Indonesian nationalists. He allowed his building to be used by Partindo for a conference (1932). Besides, he was also involved in the formation of the THHK school in Surabaya. He died in Surabaya on 10 August 1956.

Sources: Tan, *Tionghoa*, pp. 44–45; *Oen Tjhing Tiauw*, 25 August 1956, p. 15.

LIEM Sik Tjo (LIN Xizu 林锡祖, 1908-?)
Community leader, lawyer

Born in 1908 in Semarang, he graduated from Leiden University. At first he practised law in Jakarta; two years later he moved to Surabaya and worked as a lawyer there until 1958. In 1939 he was the chairman of the board of trustees of the Huaqiao Charity Hospital (Surabaya). In 1943 he became a member of Shugi In (Surabaya) and the vice-president of the HTCH (Surabaya). After 1945 he was the chairman of an orphanage, Tai Thong Bong Jan (Surabaya). In 1958 he moved to Koln to become the director of the Economics Section, Antara (Indonesian National News Agency). He retired in 1967 and lived in Amsterdam.

Sources: *Djawa Nenkan* (1973), p. 464; Letter of Dr Yusiu Lim, 12 January 1982.

LIEM Sioe Liong. See **SALIM, Soedono**
LIEM Soen Joe. See **WITARSA, Endang**
LIEM, Steve. See **KARYA, Teguh**

LIEM Swie King (LIN Shuijing 林水镜, 1956-)
Badminton player

Born in Kudus on 28 February 1956, he is a son of a bicycle dealer. He became the national champion in 1974 when he was still a secondary school student (SMA Negeri Kudus). In the following two years he continued to hold men's singles titles in Indonesian national championships. In 1976 and 1977 he was the runner-up in the All-England Badminton Competition but took the men's singles title in 1978. In 1979 he made a movie entitled *Sakura dalam Pelukan* [Sakura in his arms] and was criticized for not taking badminton seriously. He lost to Prakash Padukone of India in the 1980 All-England Competition but regained the title in 1981. His performance in the 1984 Thomas Cup was disappointing. He later played doubles and retired in 1988.

Liem re-emerged in 2009, not as a badminton player, but as the hero of an Indonesian movie entitled *Guntur* (the Indonesian name of Liem which he never used), which tells the story of Liem himself. The same year, a biography on him was published by Kompas Publishing, entitled *Panggil Aku King* (Just call me King). A forgotten badminton idol thus re-emerged in the news. According to the book, he married Lucia Alamsah in 1983 and went into the hotel business. He has one son and two daughters.

Sources: *Tempo*, 9 February 1974, pp. 44–45; *Topik*, 21 February 1974, pp. 28–29; *Apa & Siapa 1985–86*, pp. 446–47; Suryadinata, ed., *Southeast Asian Personalities*, pp. 579–80; the compiler's notes.

LIEM Tek Siang. See NURSALIM, Sjamsul

LIEM Thay Tjwan (1891-?) 林泰全*
Political party activist
Born in Jombang on 9 February 1891, he was educated at the THHT (Kediri) and the THHT (Mojokerto). He was first active in various Chinese organizations, including a local Chinese secret society and Keng Kie Hwee. After moving to Surabaya, he joined the ISDV and later Sarekat Rakjat. After the communist uprisings in 1926 he was arrested by the Dutch authorities and sent to Boven Digoel where he opened a shop. The shop went bankrupt and he was allowed to return to Java. In the mid-1930s he lived in Solo.

Source: Tan, *Tionghoa*, pp. 151–52.

LIEM Thian Joe (LIN Tianyou 林天佑, 1895–1962)
Journalist, local historian, writer
Born in Parakan in 1895, he was educated at the local THHK school. At the beginning of the 1920s he worked for Warna Warta, a *peranakan* daily in Semarang. In the early 1930s he joined the editorial staff of *Djawa Tengah* (Semarang), during which he wrote his well-known historical study, *Riwajat Semarang 1416–1931*, which was first published as a series in *Djawa Tengah Review* (March 1931–September 1933). He was also the unnamed author of *Boekoe Peringetan Tiong Hoa Siang Hwee 1907–37* (Semarang, 1937). From 1938 he was in charge of *Mimbar Melajoe*, a monthly published in Semarang. At the same time he contributed articles regularly to the weekly edition of *Sin Po*. His study on the *peranakan* Chinese press was serialized in that weekly (6 May–10 June 1939). His other works include *Pusaka Tionghoa* (Semarang, c.1952) and "Riwajat Kian Gwan"

(mimeograph, available at the ISEAS Library in Singapore). He died in Semarang in February 1962.

Sources: *Riwajat Semarang* ("Permoelaan Kata"); Tan, *Tionghoa*, p. 138; Liem Ek Hian's letter to the compiler; Coppel (May 1976).

LIEM Thwan Tek. See **LIEM Toan Tek**
LIEM Thwan Tik. See **LIEM Toan Tek**
LIEM Tien Pao. See **SAMPOERNA, Putera**

LIEM Tjae Le (LIN Caili 林财礼, 1907-?)
Community leader, physician

Born in Gorontalo on 29 October 1907, he was educated at Geneeskundige Hogeschool (Jakarta) and Gemeentelijke Universiteit (Amsterdam). In 1949 he was the vice-chairman of the Bangka Council and a member of the Indonesian delegation to the Round Table Conference representing Bangka. After Indonesia's transfer of sovereignty (1949) he became a doctor of the Bangka County as well as a high government officer attached to the Ministry of Health. He participated in the general elections of 1955 as a Baperki candidate.

Sources: *Pedoman Kampanje*, p. 71; *Xin Bao*, 6 August 1949.

LIEM Tjing Hien (1915–78?) 林清兴*
Community leader, lawyer, husband of **Kartini MULJADI**

Born in Gresik on 8 October 1915 in Gresik, East Java, he was a holder of an Mr degree from the FHUI (1954?). He served as the secretary of Sin Ming Hui (Jakarta) in 1950 and as its president in 1953–55. It was under his leadership that Sin Ming Hui began to open its membership to all ethnic groups in Indonesia. In 1958 he became the deputy editor-in-chief of *Pos Indonesia*. He passed away on 21 February 1978 (1973?) in Jakarta. He wife, **Kartini MULJADI,** was a judge in Jakarta.

Sources: *Buku Peringatan Sin Ming Hui 1946–56*, pp. 24–27; *Pos Indonesia*, 20 September 1958; Setyautama, *Tokoh-Tokoh Etnis TH*, p. 218; *Apa & Siapa 1985–86*, pp. 537–38; the compiler's notes.

LIEM Tjing Hien-Kho (Mrs). See **MULJADI, Kartini**
LIEM Tjoan Hok. See **KARYA, Teguh**

LIEM Tjong Hian (1917-?) 林宗贤*
Community leader, lawyer

Born in Palembang on 12 November 1917, he graduated from the RHS (Jakarta). In 1945–47 he served as a member of the High Court (Palembang) and the deputy head of the Ministry of Justice (RI) for South Sumatra. From 1948 onwards, he practised law and was a prosecutor, and concurrently the president of the Rubber Millers Association (Palembang). In 1954 he became a member of the Baperki central board and participated in the 1955 general elections as a Baperki candidate.

Source: *Pedoman Kampanje*, pp. 41–42.

LIEM Toan Tek (LIEM Thwan Tek; LIEM Thwan Tik; LIN Chuande 林传德**, 1895-?)**
Community leader, businessman

A fourth-generation *peranakan*, he was born in 1895 in Surabaya. In 1906 he graduated from the Surabaya Vocational School. In 1931 he began to engage in the cinema business. He was active in community service and was a committee member of a hospital and orphanage in Surabaya. During the Japanese Occupation he was the president of the HTCH (Surabaya). In 1943 he was appointed as a member of Tjuo (Chuo) Sangi In (1943–44).

Sources: *Djawa Nenkan* (1973), p. 464; Anderson, *Japanese Occupation*, p. 10.

LIEM Twan Djie (1913-) 林端裕* **(**林传如**)***
Economist, businessman, university professor

Born in Blitar on 23 May 1913, he obtained a PhD in Economics from Economische Hogeschool (Rotterdam) in 1947 for defending his dissertation, "De Distribueerende Tusschenhandel der Chineezen op Java". While in the Netherlands, he served as the editor of the *CHHTC* (1938) and the president of the CHH-Netherlands (1939).

He returned to Java and became the secretary-general of the East Java Rice Centre (1948). In 1949 he was elected as the chairman of Gabungan Perusahaan Rokok (Cigarette Business Federation) in Malang and in 1953, the chairman of Gappri (Indonesian Cigarette Business Federation). From 1953 to 1967 he became the head of Bank Tabungan Utama Malang. When Baperki was established, he served as an adviser of Baperki in Malang. He participated in the 1955 general elections as a Baperki candidate. In the 1960s he was a professor of economics at Airlangga University (Surabaya).

Sources: *Pedoman Kampanje*, p. 52; *CHHTC*, July–September 1938, title page and October–December 1939, title page; the compiler's notes.

LIEM Wan King. See **JAYA, David Herman**

LIM Hiong Tjheng (LIN Xiangchuan 林香串**, 1899–1970)**
Community leader, batik manufacturer

Born in 1899 at Jinjiang (Fujian), he migrated to Indonesia in 1923. He first worked as a shopkeeper in a *batik* workshop, and in 1927 established his own *batik* manufacturing enterprise. Prior to World War II, he served as an executive member of the Kuomintang (Jakarta branch) and Tih Yuk Hui. In the 1950s he served as the president of Hok Kian Hwee Koan in Jakarta. In 1958 he was detained by the Indonesian authorities for his affiliation with the Kuomintang, but was released in the same year for health reasons. He died in Jakarta on 25 April 1970.

Sources: Liu, *Gailan*, p. [50]; Ma, *Bian yu Luan*, p. 92; *Ribao*, 26 April 1970.

LIM Kek Tjiang (LIEM Kek Tjiang, LIN Kechang 林克昌**, 1928-)**
Violinist, conductor, husband of **TJIOK San Fang**

Born in Banjarmasin (Kalimantan) on 21 March 1928, Lim Kek Tjiang is an influential violinist and conductor who made an imprint beyond Indonesia. When he was a child, his father hired a local musician to teach him the violin. During the Japanese Occupation, he took violin lessons from Ivan Fedoroff, a Russian musician. He joined the Jakarta Radio Orchestra and at the age of sixteen he gave his first solo performance. He later became leader of the first violinists in the orchestra. After the Japanese surrender, he was awarded a Malino scholarship to study at the Netherlands Conservatorium (Amsterdam) before pursuing his music studies at the Conservatoire National de la Musique de Paris in France.

Lim became the director of the Indonesian Symphony Orchestra but left for China after his marriage in 1958. He was assigned to work at the Central Broadcasting Symphony Orchestra where he later became the head of the Orchestra. In 1963, he was transferred to the Central Music Academy (Zhongyang Yinyue Xueyan). Life was difficult for him during the Cultural Revolution and he left for Macao and sneaked into Hong Kong where he became Resident Conductor of the Hong Kong Philharmonic Orchestra. He introduced Chinese elements (including mainland Chinese compositions) into the repertoire of the orchestra; he was ahead of his time by twenty-five years! Despite his music achievements in Hong Kong, he could not get along with the authorities and was eventually asked to leave by the management. After unsuccessful stints in Australia and later in Hong Kong again, he was offered a position at the Music Academy in Taiwan where he taught many musicians, creating some sort of sensation. He was named "Karajan of the East" and "Beethoven of the Yellow Land".

Lim is currently retired with his wife in Australia. He was considered a musician who contributed to the music scene in mainland China, Taiwan and Hong Kong. Due to the turmoil in his life and his artistic temperament, he encountered a lot of difficulties as a violinist but his talent was eventually recognized and appreciated.

Sources: Leo Suryadinata, "Lim Kek Tjiang", in Suryadinata, ed., *Southeast Asian Personalities* (2012), pp. 628–31; *The Star* (Hong Kong), 11 December 1975; *Min Bao Zhoukan*, no. 511, 27 August 1978; *Huang Tudi Shang de Beiduofen: Lin Kechang Huiyi Lu* (2004); Writer's notes.

LIM Sin Tjoei. See **RAHARDJA, Subur**

LIM Sui Khiang (LIN Ruiqiang 林瑞强, 1960-)
Member of Parliament, Catholic

Lim Sui Khiang is also known as Suvianto. Born on 18 April 1960 in Pontianak, West Kalimantan, he received a Bachelor of Engineering degree from the University of Tanjungpura, Pontianak, in 1987. Prior to entering politics, he was director of CV Sari Pasifik (1996) and Planet I Hollywood (2008), both in Pontianak. He contested and won a parliamentary seat (in the West Kalimantan Constituency) under the Partai Demokrat (PD) banner in 2009. He contested in the 2014 election as a PD candidate again but failed to be elected.

Sources: *Wajah DPR & DPD 2009–14*, p. 76; the compiler's notes.

LIM Tek Tjun. See **DURIANTO, Darmadi**
LIN Caili. See **LIEM Tjae Le**
LIN Dechun. See **DURIANTO, Darmadi**

LIN Che Wei (1968-) 林志伟*
Leading financial analyst

Born in Bandung on 1 December 1968, he received his high school education (SMA) in Bandung. He later obtained his

Bachelor of Industrial Engeering degree from Trisakti University (1990) and MBA from NUS (1994). In 2006 he completed the Private Equity and Venture Capital Program developed and delivered by Harvard Business Colleage.

A leading economic/financial analyst in Indonesia, he was the presdir (president director) and director of Research SG Securities Indonesia up to April 2002. He was transferred to Singapore's headquarters when the Indonesian office was closed down. His position was director of Corporate Finance in SG Securities (Singapore). Apart from this, he was the CEO of Sampoerna Foundation (Indonesia), CEO of MNC Investment Banking (Societe Generale) and CEO of State Owned Enterprise Danareksa. He is the founder of Independent Research & Advisory Indonesia and founder of PT Katadata.

Lin is married to his SMA classmate Syenny Setiawan. They have two children.

During the May 1998 riots, his family lived in Liem Sioe Liong's residence in Gunung Sari. Liem's house was ransacked and Lin's wife got traumatized. SG Securities offered him the choice of either going to Singapore or Bali. He chose Singapore. He got a PR (permanent residential status) in Singapore but retained his Indonesian citizenship.

According to *Kompas*, he was invited by **KWIK Kian Gie** to join Bappenas, but Lin declined. He preferred to stay in the private sector and be given the freedom to write.

In 2002 he told *Kompas* that if he were no longer able to work as an analyst, he wanted to be a journalist.

Sources: "Lin Che Wei", *Kompas*, 28 April 2002; Setyautama, *Tokoh-Tokoh Etnis TH*, p. 226; <http://www.katadata.co/key.html> (accessed 13 February 2013); <http://www.irai.co.id/about/board-members/lin-che-wei-cfa> (accessed 13 February 2013).

LIN Chuande. See **LIEM Toan Tek**
LIN Dexiang. See **NURSALIM, Sjamsul**
LIN Fengsheng. See **SALIM, Anthony**

LIN Fuliang. See **SOEJATMIKO, Basuki**
LIN Guanyu. See **SUSANTO T.L.**

LIN Huiye. See **LIEM Hwie Giap**
LIN Kechang. See **LIEM Kek Tjiang**
LIN Mianji. See **WANANDI, Jusuf**
LIN Miankun. See **WANANDI, (Albertus) Sofjan**
LIN Qianshun. See **LIEM Khiam Soen**
LIN Qinghe. See **LIEM Khing Hoo**

LIN Qingshan (林青山)
Community leader

A leading member of the KMT (Palembang branch), he was the founder of Huaqiao Fuli Jijinhui (a welfare foundation for Overseas Chinese) in Palembang (March 1968) and the vice-chairman of SNPC Sumsel Jaya (Palembang) from 1969 to 1974.

Sources: *Ribao*, 23 March 1968, 19 June 1969, and 1 October 1969.

LIN Quanfu. See **KARYA, Teguh**
LIN Qunming. See **LIEM Koen Beng**
LIN Qunsheng. See **LIEM Koen Seng**
LIN Qunxian. See **LIEM Koen Hian**
Lin Ruiqiang. See **LIM Sui Khiang**

LIN Shaoliang. See **SALIM, Soedono**
LIN Shengdi. See **LIEM Seng Tee**
LIN Shuijing. See **LIEM Swie King**
LIN Tianbao. See **SAMPOERNA, Putera**
LIN Tianyou. See **LIEM Thian Joe**
LIN Wanjin. See **JAYA, David Herman**

LIN Wanli (林万里, 1938-)
Writer, translator

Born in 1938 in Bandung, he went to China to study Chinese at the Peking Teachers' Training College and graduated in

1962. On his return to Bandung, he became a businessman and began to write both essays and short stories in his spare time. After the 1965 coup he stopped writing for more than twenty years. He resumed writing in 1986 after being invited by the editor-in-chief of *Xianggang Wenxue* [Hong Kong literature] to contribute articles. He later collected his short stories and published them in book form, *Jiehun de Jijie* [Wedding season], which reflects life today in the Chinese community in Indonesia. The book was published in Singapore in 1990. He also translated the essays of Jakob Sumardjo, which are on *peranakan* literature, into Chinese.

Source: *Jiehun de Jijie* (1990), back cover, personal notes.

LIN Wenguang. See **ALIM, Markus**
LIN Wenhua. See **HALIM, Boediharto**
LIN Wenjing. See **DJUHAR, Sutanto**
LIN Wenxiang. See **LIEM Boen Siang**
LIN Xiangchuan. See **LIM Hiong Tjheng**
LIN Xizu. See **LIEM Sik Tjo**
LIN Yinghuai. See **NURIMBA, Adil A.**
LIN Yunhao. See **PRIBADI, Henry**
LIN Zhiqiang. See **YAN Weizhen**

LING Nanlong (凌南隆, 1917-)
Painter

Born in Pangkalpinang (Bangka) on 17 May 1917, he was educated at the China Institute of Arts (Hangzhou). Before World War II, he worked at the Guizhou Provincial Museum of Arts (China). He later returned to Indonesia. In 1951 he visited Holland and held a number of exhibitions. From the 1950s to 1965 he was a member of Yinhua Meishu Xiehui (Jakarta). In 1975 he received a bronze medal at the European Exhibition of Sculpture held in France.

Sources: C.M. Hsu's notes; the compiler's notes.

LING Yunchao (凌云超, 1915-)
Industrialist, calligraphist

Born in Jiangsu (China) on 9 February 1915, he was educated at the Lin Sin College of Accountancy in Shanghai (1941–43). In the 1940s he began to study the art of calligraphy under well-known calligraphers, including Zhang Daqian. Ling migrated to Indonesia and was active in the business world. He is presently president-director of Koflan Chemical Works Indonesia Ltd., managing director of Sederhana Holdent Tooth-Paste Factory, and director of Universal Corrugated & Cardboard Carton Factory.

Ling has also been active in the social and cultural fields: he is the chairman of Jiangsu and Zhejiang Clan Association (Jakarta) and the chairman of the Chinese Calligraphy and Painting Study Club (Jakarta). He has held a number of one-man exhibitions in Singapore, Hong Kong, Tokyo, Seoul, and Taipei.

Source: C.M. Hsu's notes.

LIONG Sit Yoe (LIANG Xiyou 梁锡佑, 1903–92)
Community leader, newspaperman, businessman

Son of a leading *totok* merchant who was once the chairman of Soe Po Sia (Jakarta), he was born in 1903 and received university education at the Lingnan Daxue 岭南大学 (China). In 1923 he began to run a business in the Dutch East Indies. In the 1930s he served as the vice-president of Soe Po Sia and the deputy director of *Tiansheng Ribao* (Jakarta).

He was engaged in various kinds of businesses, including trading in agricultural products, movie distribution, and running hardware stores. In the 1950s he served as an executive member of Huaqiao Gonghui 华侨公会 (Jakarta), the director of both the Gao Shang 高商 School (Jakarta) and *Ziyou Bao* 自由报. He participated in the Overseas Chinese Affairs Conference in Taipei (1952) and served as a member of the Overseas Chinese Affairs Committee (1950s). In May 1958 he was detained by the Indonesian Government for his affiliation with the KMT. In 1970 he served as the honorary director of SNPC Chongde Xuexiao 崇德学校 (Jatinegara, Jakarta).

He died in Jakarta in 1992.

Sources: Liu, *Gailan*, p. [53]; Zhong, *Huaqiao*, p. 60; interview with Hioe Njan Joeng, 1969; *Huaqiao Da Cidian*, pp. 862–63.

LITELNONI, Benny Alexander (LIE Djin Kiong, 1956-) 李仁强*
Politician, Christian

Not much information about him is available. Benny Alexander was born on 5 August 1956 in Timur Tengah Selatan, Nusa Tenggara Timur province. He has a law degree (SH). He has joined the local civil service since March 1980. He was an officer of Dinas PMD (Empowerment of Rural Society Agency) between 1980–2000. He then served as head of various local institutions. From 2009 to 2013, he was elected as the Deputy Bupati (Regent) of Timur Tengah Selatan, and since 2013 he has been elected as Deputy Governor of Nusa Tenggara Timur province (his term will expire in 2018).

Sources: Pengurus Pusat Fordeka, *Buku Acuan 2014*, p. 237; <http://id.wikipidia.org/wiki/Benny_Alexander_Litelnoni> (accessed 30 March 2014).

LIU Chun Wai (LIAO Chunhui 廖春慧, 1941?-)
Choreographer, dancer

Born in Jakarta in 1941(?), also known as Liao Chunyuan (廖春远?) or A Chun (阿春), she graduated from the Pa Hoa JPP School (also known as THHK school) in Jakarta in 1959. She has been active in studying various types of dances, especially Southeast Asian traditional dances from many leading dancers in the Southeast Asian region. Between 1957 and 1959 she was selected as member of the Indonesian artist delegation to participate in the World Youth (and Students) Festival in Moscow and member of Indonesian cultural delegation to Singapore. Furthermore, she was invited by President Soekarno to perform at the Presidential Palace. In 1968 she followed her husband to Hong Kong. In 1980 she established the Hong Kong Southeast Asian Dance Troupe. In 1992 she established the Jakarta Southeast Asian Dance Troupe and in 1993 she set up the Guangdong Southeast Asian Dance Troupe. She also served as president, artistic director and choreographer of the above-mentioned companies. Known as an enthusiast in promoting Southeast Asian dances, she has been invited to perform in many countries in the region.

Sources: "Liu Chun Wai", in *Buku Peringatan 100 Tahun Sekolah THHK/ PAHUA* (2001), p. 282; "liaochunhui 的个人资料", <http://www.cdanet.org/home.php?mod=space&uid=12281&do=profile> (accessed 30 June 2014).

LIU Jinduan (刘金端, 1904–95)
Community leader, teacher, wife of **SOETO Tjan**

Born in 1904 to a fisherman's family in Bagan Siapi-api (Sumatra), she left her hometown for teacher training at Nanyang Nüzi Zhongxue in Singapore while she was in her teens. After graduation, she became a teacher at the Palembang Chinese School in 1923. In the following year she married Soeto Tjan, the principal of the above-mentioned school.

In 1935 when Soeto Tjan became the principal of the Kuang-jen (Guang Ren) School, she was a teacher in the same school. During the Sino-Japanese war she and her husband joined the anti-Japanese movement. In October 1937 the China Charity Fund (in Jakarta) was set up to raise money for China during the Sino-Japanese war. Soeto Tjan served as the secretary while she served as the deputy chief of the women section.

In 1942 when the Japanese occupied Java, Soeto Tjan was arrested. Liu Jinduan continued to be active in the anti-Japanese movement. She was eventually arrested, together with her two sons. She was later sentenced to ten years' imprisonment.

In 1945 she and Soeto Tjan were released. She continued to assist her husband in establishing a Chinese secondary school. In 1955 she was elected as the president of Zhonghua Funü Xuehui (Chinese Women's Association) in Jakarta and a working committee member of Qiao Zong, also in Jakarta. In 1954 and 1959 she was invited by the Chinese Government to visit the PRC. In 1960 she and her husband returned to the PRC. She was active in Qiao Lian in Guangzhou. She died in Hong Kong on 12 March 1995.

Source: *Bazhong Huixun* (Hong Kong), 8 April 1995, p. 2.

LIU Lanfang. See **ERVINNA**

LIU Nam Sian (1912-) 刘南先*
Community leader, trade unionist
Born in Sungailiat (Bangka) on 10 May 1912, he was educated at Meixian Secondary School (Guangdong) and Jinan Daxue (Shanghai). He returned to Indonesia and worked in a tin mine (Bangka) from 1942 to the 1950s. In 1946 he was elected as the vice-chairman of Serikat Buruh Tambang Indonesia (Muntok branch) and held the position up to 1952. In 1954 he served as the chairman of Baperki (Muntok branch) and as secretary-general of Serikat Buruh Tambang Indonesia (Muntok branch). On 28 December 1954 he was elected as a member of the Muntok State Council. He participated in the 1955 general elections as a Baperki candidate.

Source: *Pedoman Kampanje*, p. 61.

LIU Quandao. See **JAHJA, Junus**
LIU Shunyan. See **WIJAYA, Eko**

LIU Yaozeng (刘耀曾, 1900–82)
Community leader, schoolteacher

Born in Guangdong in 1900, he received a BA degree in Education from Dongnan University (Nanking) and migrated to Java in 1931. He was a member of Huaqiao Gonghui (Jakarta), but sided with the pro-Beijing group, resulting in his departure from the association. In the late 1940s and 1950s he taught at the Pa Chung High School (Bacheng Zhongxue, also known as Ya Zhong) and served as the president of the Chinese School Teachers' Association (Jakarta). In the 1960s he was appointed as the principal of the Pa Chung and in 1963–65 served as the president of Qiao Zong in Jakarta. He returned to the PRC after the 1965 coup and lived in the village during the Cultural Revolution. He later served as the vice-chairman of Qiao Lian of Guangdong province. He died in Meixian on 3 June 1982.

Sources: *Zhongcheng Bao*, 1 October 1964; *Jinan tekan*, pp. 29–30.

LIU Ing Wen. See LAUWANI, Siegvrieda
LIU Yingwen. See LAUWANI, Siegvrieda
LIU Yulan. See LAUW Giok Lan

LIYANTO, Abraham Paul (LIE Soe Pau, LI Shubao 李树宝, 1956-)
Member of DPD, Christian

Born on 24 October 1956 in Kupang, Nusa Tenggara Timur (NTT), he received a Bachelor of Architecture degree from the Universitas Udayana (Denpasar, Bali) in 1986. He has served as chief director of a few companies, including PT Citra Desain Rekanusa (since 1987), PT Citra Bina Tenaga Mandiri (since 1998) and PT Citra Piala Timor Mandiri (since 2004). Between 1998 and 2009, he served as the president of Ikatan Nasional Konsultan Indonesia (Inkindo, Indonesian national consultants association), NTT, between 1999 and 2004, he served as treasurer, DPD I Golkar, NTT and between 2001–9, president of the Association of Manpower Service Companies,

NTT. He was elected as member of DPD in 2009–14 for NTT province and was re-elected as member of DPD in 2014–19 for the same province.

Sources: *Wajah DPR & DPD 2009–14*, p. 655; Pengurus Pusat Fordeka, *Buku Acuan 2014*, p. 112; the compiler's notes.

LO Siang Hien. See **GINTING, Lo S.H.**
LO S.H. GINTING. See **GINTING, Lo S.H.**

LOA Sek Hie (LAI Xixi 赖锡禧, 1898–1965)
Community leader, son of a landlord

Born in Jakarta in 1898, he was educated at the ELS (Jakarta), the HBS (Jakarta), and a commercial school (in Holland?). In 1927–31 he was appointed as a member of Volksraad. In 1924–51(?) he served as a member of the governing body of Jang Seng Ie. Before World War II, he was a member of the Jakarta Municipal Council. He joined the CHH and from 1928 to 1942 served as an executive member of the CHH central board. He died on 24 December 1965.

Sources: Tan, *Tionghoa*, p. 200; *Jang Seng Ie*, p. 12; Wal, *Volksraad*, vol. II, p. 717; the compiler's notes.

LOE Ping Kian (LÜ Bingjian 吕炳建, 1902–63)
Physician, community leader, married a Dutch woman

Born in Jombang in 1902, he was educated in Holland and graduated as a doctor specializing in skin diseases. He was the president of the CHH-Netherlands in 1929 and the president of the HCTNH in 1932. He worked for the Jang Seng Ie Hospital before World War II. Loe later specialized in nutrition. He became the director of Sumber Waras Hospital (sponsored by Sin Ming Hui) in Jakarta in the early 1960s. His published works include *Startling's Law of the Heart: Its Significance in Chronic Congestive Heart Failure* (Jakarta, 1961). He died in 1963.

Sources: *Shoudu Ribao*, 1 November 1963; *CHHTC* (October 1929), inside cover; *Zhongcheng Bao*, 2 November 1963; *SMH 10 Tahun*, pp. 42–45.

LOHANDA, Mona (1947-) 赖模娜*
Archivist, historian

She was born in Tangerang, West Java, in November 1947 into a Loa (赖) family. By her own admission, she is a "Cina Benteng" (a "Benteng Chinese"), a *peranakan* Chinese from Benteng (note: Benteng is another name for Tangerang, a Jakarta suburb). She got her B.A. from the University of Indonesia (1975) and an M.A. from SOAS, London (1994). She has been working at the Indonesian national archives (Arsip Nasional RI) for at least thirty-eight years. She also teaches history at the Department of History, University of Indonesia. Fluent in Dutch, English and Indonesian, she has published many books, two of which are in English: *The Kapitan Cina of Batavia 1837–1942: A History of Chinese Establishment in Colonial Society* (Jakarta: Djambatan, 1996) and *Growing Pains: The Chinese and the Dutch in Colonial Java, 1890–1942* (Jakarta: Yayasan Cipta Loka Caraka, 2002). Besides the books, she has also published many articles as book chapters. She received a Nabil Award for her contribution to Indonesian history (2010) from the Yayasan Nabil, Indonesia. In 2012 she was awarded by *Kompas*, a leading newspaper in Indonesia, as one of the Dedicated Intellectuals (Cendekiawan Berdedikasi) in Indonesia.

Sources: The above-mentioned books; *Peranakan Tionghoa Indonesia: Sebuah Perjalanan Budaya* (Jakarta, 2009), p. 350; Aimee Dawis, "Mona Lohanda: A humble national treasurer", *Jakarta Post*, 13 October 2010; "Kompas anugerahi 5 Cendekiawan Berdedikasi", *Kompas*, 29 June 2012; personal notes.

LÜ Bingjian. See **LOE Ping Kian**
LU Youying. See **LUKITA, Enggartiasto**

LUKITA, Enggartiasto (LU Youying 卢尤英, 1951-)
Politician, Christian

Lukita was born on 12 October 1951 in Cirebon, West Java. He graduated from IKIP Bandung in 1977. He joined Golkar in 1980 and served as an MPR member between 1997 and 1999. He served as an adviser to the Golkar Southern Jakarta Branch (1992–97) and deputy treasurer of Golkar (1998–2004). He was one of the two Golkar Chinese members of parliament from 1999 to 2009. When asked why there were not many Chinese MP from Golkar, he said that the selection of MP was rigid as Golkar only accepted those who were independent economically to represent Golkar in parliament.

Lukita was also re-elected as member of parliament as a Golkar candidate for the 2009–14 period but left Golkar and joined Nasdem party on the eve of the 2014 election. However, he did not contest in the 2014 election.

Lukita is well-known in the property business circle. He is the commissioner-general of PT Unicora Agung, Malang (since 1994), PT Rei Sewindu, Jakarta, and Intan Kemilau Utama Kediri, East Java (1995–2001).

Sources: Li Zhuohui 李卓辉, *Yinni canzheng yu guojia jianshe* (2007), pp. 194–95; 207–9; *Wajah DPR & DPD 2009–14*, p. 190; the compiler's notes.

LUNANDI, Andy (GOUW Loen An, 1934-) 吴伦安*
Writer, journalist

Born in Jakarta on 5 September 1934, he was educated at a Dutch middle school. Fluent in Dutch, Indonesian, and English, he began to write short stories in the mid-1950s. Most of his works were published in *Panorama, Star Weekly, Intisari, Keluarga,* and *Varia*. He first worked with a Dutch firm but later resigned and joined *Kompas* as a reporter (1965–71). It appears that he then stopped writing short stories. Lunandi entered Akademi Penerangan Bandung and obtained a bachelor degree in 1971. About the same time, he became interested in community development studies and worked for various international organizations. In the 1980s he lived in Sydney. His numerous short stories have never been published in book form. Nevertheless, since 1972 he has published a few general books: *Manusia Berkarya* [Community development] (Bandung, 1974); *Latihan Komunikasi* [Communication exercise] (Bandung, 1975); *Pendidikan Orang Dewasa* [Adult education methods] (Jakarta, 1980).

Source: Letter to the compiler, 28 May 1985.

LYMAN, Susanta (LIE Siong Tay; LI Shangda 李尚大, 1920–2008)
Businessman, community leader, philanthropist, Protestant

Born in Hutou (湖头), Anxi, Fujian, China in 1920, he was also known as Lie Siong Tay. He first went to Cishan (慈山) Primary School and continued his studies in various high schools in his village before graduating from Jinan University.

Lie became the school principal of Lanxi Middle School in Anxi before migrating to Indonesia. In Indonesia he established his own company SDR (Satya Djaya Raya) Group which dealt with trading and the timber business. The group was later renamed the Lyman Group, using Lie's Indonesian name and diversified its business into six lines, namely, timber, agriculture, building material, property distributor and telecommunication. The company has since become a multinational company with offices in Singapore, Hong Kong and the West.

Lie was also a community leader who was well known among the *totok* and a philanthropist who contributed substantially to the building of schools and universities in his original homeland in Southern China. In 1993, he worked hard to assist in the establishment of Jimei Daxue (Chip Bee University) following the footsteps of Tan Kah Kee. Unlike many overseas Chinese contributors who named the buildings that they donated after themselves, he named many of the buildings that he donated after his own teachers as his way of paying back. Lie died in Singapore in his sleep on 2 November 2008.

Sources: Leo Suryadinata, "Lyman, Susanta", in Suryadinata, ed., *Southeast Asian Personalities* (2012), pp. 733–35; *Kompas*, 17 November 2008, p. 39; *Guoji Ribao*, 17 November 2008.

MA Shuli. See **MAH Soo Lay**
MA Xuling. See **SULINDRO, Be**
MA Yongnan. See **WIJAYA, Nancy**

MAH Soo Lay (MA Shuli 马树礼, 1909–2006)
Journalist, politician

Born in Jiangsu (China) on 3 August 1909, he first went to Meiji University (Tokyo) to study Political Science and Economics and later, the University of Santo Tomas (Manila), where he graduated with a B.Sc. degree. In 1931–33 he served as the editor-in-chief of *Minguo Ribao*. In 1936–39 he was the editor of *New China Herald* (in Chinese) published in Manila. He later went to Indonesia and became the director and editor-in-chief of *Chung-hua Shang-pao* (Zhonghua Shangbao) (1953–58). He was detained by the Indonesian authorities in 1958 for his affiliation with the KMT, and expelled from Jakarta in 1959. In Taiwan, he became a member of the Legislative Council (Taiwan) and the head of the Third Section of the KMT Central Committee. His publications include *Yinni Duli Yundong Shih* [History of Indonesian independence movement] (Hong Kong, 1957) and *Yinni de Bian yu Luan* [Change and chaos in Indonesia] (Taipei, 1963). He died in Taipei on 19 July 2006.

Sources: *China Year Book 1969–70*, pp. 614–15; Zhong, *Huaqiao*, p. 60; the compiler's notes.

MANANSANG, Jansen (CAI Yasheng 蔡亚声, 1942–)
Recreation entrepreneur, conservationist

Born in Jakarta in 1942, he is the eldest son of Cai Jinxian (蔡锦贤 later known as Hadi Manansang, 1916–2003), who was the founder of the Oriental Circus Indonesia in 1965. Jansen, together with his two brothers, Frans Manansang (Cai Yaguang) and Tony Sumampau (Cai Yaxing), received rigorous training to become members of the circus. However, in the 1970s when the popularity of the circus began to wane, Jansen and his brothers, with the help of their father, jointly founded the wildlife park at Cisarua (West Java), known as Taman Safari Indonesia (TSI), in 1986. In 1999, they established another wildlife park called TSI Prigen (East Java) and later, TSI Gianyar and Marine Park in Bali as well.

Jansen received regular school education at Pah Tsung (a Chinese school in Jakarta) and graduated in 1962. He also received tertiary education and obtained Drs and Msc degrees. Jansen has become prominent in the wildlife park circles and in 2007, he was elected as chairman of the Southeast Asian Zoos Association. Jansen is also active in wildlife conservation. He has hosted several international meetings such as Conservation Breeding Specialist Group (CBSG) and has succeeded in saving various endangered species such as Sumatran tigers and elephants, orang utans and Bali's myna. In 2008, he was awarded a medal (Bintang Jasa Utama) by President Susilo Bambang Yudhoyono for his contribution to saving endangered species and protecting the environment.

It was reported that in mid-2015 Indonesia and China would swop two Komodo dragons and two panda bears as part of a diplomatic programme between the two countries. The pandas would be placed at the TSI when they arrive.

Sources: Li Zuohui, *Qingshan bulao, haoqi changcun*, 2008, pp. 4–9; <http://www.thejakartapost.com/news/2015/04/02/ri-china-resume-

talks-panda-komodo-exchange.html#sthash.p7dlLvHh.dpuf> (accessed 13 April 2015).

MARCHING, Soe Tjen (1971-) 黄淑贞*
Writer, academic, composer

Soe Tjen Marching was born on 23 April 1971 in Surabaya to a Chinese family. Her father is Oei Lian Bing and her mother is Juliana Susilo. According to her interview with Zara Majidpour, Soe Tjen's father was imprisoned and tortured during the New Order "because he was leftist and all of our property were confiscated". She was born after her father was out of the prison. Soe Tjen is talented and has been interested in music since childhood. In 1998 she won the national competition for Indonesian contemporary composers held by the German Embassy. In 2010 her work was selected as one of the best compositions on the international composition for avant-garde composers held in Singapore.

She received a PhD from Monansh University after submitting a thesis on "the discrepancy between the public and the private selves of Indonesian women", which was published as a book in 2007. She has also written several books, including *Mati Bertahun yang Lalu* [Dead for several years], a novel published by Gramedia in 2010; *Kisah di Balik Pintu* [Stories behind doors], published by Ombak in 2011; and *Kubunuh di sini* [I kill it here], a book which denotes her long struggle with cancer.

In 2009 she started a magazine called *Majalah Bhinneka* in Bahasa Indonesia which promotes critical thinking. She is married to a scholar Angus Nicholis. She has been frequently invited to give lectures in Australia, UK and Europe.

Sources: <http://zara-majidpour.blogspot.com/2012/07/my-music-and my writing-are both_05.html> (accessed 10 June 2014); <http://www.soetjenmarching.com/en/profile.html> (accessed 10 June 2014).

MARGA T. (TJOA Liang Tjoe; CAI Liangzhu 蔡良珠, 1943-)
Novelist, physician

Marga was born on 27 January 1943 in Jakarta. By her own admission, she has been interested in reading and writing since her schooldays. She received her primary and secondary education in Catholic schools. She went to a medical school at URECA but before finishing her course the URECA was burned down. She began to write short stories and novels. When the medical school was rebuilt and the university was renamed Trisakti University, she returned to the medical school and graduated in 1974 as a physician. Nonetheless, she did not practise as a physician but continued her literary life.

She became popular in the 1970s after publishing three novels: *Karmila* (Jakarta, 1973), *Badai Pasti Berlalu* (Jakarta, 1974), and *Gema Sebuah Hati* (Jakarta, 1975). The first two books have been made into movies, while the third deals with students' life before and after the 1965 coup with special reference to *peranakan* students in the URECA, the former name of her university. Its sequel, *Setangkai Edelweiss* (Jakarta, 1978), is not as good as the preceding part. In the 1980s she published more novels, all belonging to the genre of popular novels. She is a prolific writer and has published more than 100 short stories and at least fifty novels. Marga may be well-known for her popular novels, but nonetheless, she is interested in socio-political events. In her latest novel, *Sekuntum Nozomi*, which consists of five volumes, Volume 3 deals with the anti-Chinese riots which took place towards the end of Soeharto's rule, and describes how one of the protagonists witnessed not only the violence but also the anti-Chinese campaign engineered by some elements in Indonesian society. This was the first Indonesian novel to deal with the May 1998 event. From the perspective of a woman, Marga recounted the experiences of some Indonesians, especially urban Indonesian women, during the turbulence period. As such, she was also describing Indonesian society before the fall of Soeharto regime, capturing the atmosphere of those days.

Sources: Oemaryati (1979), pp. 138–39; Sumardjo (1979), pp. 132–34; the above-mentioned books; *Apa & Siapa 1985–86*, pp. 486–87; Suryadinata, ed., *Southeast Asia Personalities*, pp. 743–45.

Mari Cecelia PANG Hui Lan. See **PANGESTU, Mari Elka**
Mari Elka PANGESTU. See **PANGESTU, Mari Elka**
Maria TJUI. See **TJUI Maria**
Markus ALIM. See **ALIM, Markus**
Martha TILAAR. See **TILAAR, Martha**

MASAGUNG (TJIO Wie Tay; JIANG Weitai 蔣维泰, 1927–90)
Publisher, wealthy businessman

Born in Jakarta on 8 September 1927, he received a Dutch grammar school education (first in Jakarta and later in Bogor). He left school owing to the Japanese invasion of Java in 1942. He soon started a cigarette retail business and later went into bookselling and publishing. In 1953 he established a large publishing company and bookstore, Gunung Agung (Jakarta), which published semi-official biographies of Soekarno (1965), Soeharto (1970), Adam Malik (1979), Mohammad Hatta (1979), Sultan Hamengku Buwono IX (1979), and Ibnu Sutowo (1979). Tjio changed his name to Masagung in December 1962.

Initially he was a follower of Hindu Dharma, but from September 1976 he became a Muslim. After his conversion to Islam, he became active in promoting Islam and publishing Islamic books. Before 1987 he held the following positions: president of PT Gunung Agung (publishing, general trading), PT Sari Agung (bookselling, printing), PT Ayuman Gunung Agung (money exchange business), and PT Inti Idayu Press (printing); chairman of PT Windusurya and PT Inter Delta (Kodak products distribution); director of PT Jakarta Mandarin

Agung (hotels); chairman of the board of directors of Yayasan Idayu (foundation); and director of Jack Chia MPH Ltd. He relinquished his positions in 1986 and established an Islamic bookstore. He died in September 1990 after celebrating his sixty-third birthday. He had never celebrated his birthday previously, but on 8 September 1990 he did so because his youngest son, Ketut Abdurrahman Masagung, converted to Islam that night at the age of twenty.

Sources: Letters to the compiler, 1971, 1979; *Indonesia Raya*, 20 June 1970; *Sinar Harapan*, 24 June 1970; Arief, *Indonesian Business*, pp. 324–25; Song and Hsu, eds. (1981), pp. 219–23; Roeder, *Who's Who*, p. 507; *Tempo*, 29 September 1990, p. 44.

MAWIRA, Paul. See **TAN Goan Po**
Mayling OEY-GARDINER. See **OEY-GARDINER, Mayling**
mbah WONGSOREDJO. See **WONGSOREDJO, mbah**
Mely G. TAN. See **TAN, Mely G.**
Michael Bambang HARTONO. See **HARTONO, Michael Bambang**
Mingkie. See **SOESASTRO, M. Hadi**
Mira W. See **WIDJAJA, Mira**
MO Zhuangliang. See **MOCKTAR, Brilian**

MOCKTAR, Brilian (MOK Tjoang Liang; MO Zhuangliang, 莫壮亮, 1966-)
Member of DPRD
Born on 30 March 1966, place unknown. He obtained a Bachelor degree in economics. He joined the PDIP and won a seat in the 2014 DPRD election for North Sumatra (Sumatra Utara) representing the PDIP. He serves as a member of DPRD during 2014–19.

Mohamad SALEH. See **KO Kwat Tiong**
Mohammad ALI. See **ALI, Mohammad**
Mohammad ANTON. See **ANTON, Abah**
Mohammad Bob HASAN. See **HASAN, Mohammad Bob**

Mohammad HASSAN. See HASSAN, Hadji Mohammad
MOK Tjoang Liang. See MOCKTAR, Brilian
Mona LOHANDA. See LOHANDA, Mona
Monsieur d'AMOUR. See NJOO Cheong Seng
Mu You. See OEN Tek Hian
Muhammad AMIEN. See AMIEN, Muhammad
Mu'min Ali GUNAWAN. See GUNAWAN, Mu'min Ali

MULJADI (ANG Tjin Siang; WENG Zhenxiang 翁振祥, 1941-)
Badminton player

Born in Jember (East Java) on 11 September 1941, he won the Indonesian Badminton Championship in 1963, 1965, and 1967. In 1967, 1970, and 1973 he became a core member of the Thomas Cup Team representing Indonesia. In 1972 he retired after becoming the first runner-up in the All-England Badminton Championship.

Sources: "Regu Juara", *Topik*, 13 June 1973, pp. 26–27; "Menyorot Kasus Seorang Juara", *Topik*, 19 April 1972, pp. 14–19.

**MULJADI, Kartini (Mrs LIEM Tjing Hien-Kho; Fanny KHO, 1930-)
许芬尼***
Judge, notary, Buddhist

Born in Surabaya on 17 May 1930, she received her law degree from FHUI in 1958. She was appointed as a judge at the Jakarta Court and served there for thirteen years. Upon the demise of her husband, **LIEM Tjing Hien** who was also a lawyer, she resigned and set up her own law firm, initially specializing in land laws and regulations. The law firm was well developed, she later also went into cosmetic business, drug manufacturing and even advertisement. She is the owner and distributor of the products of PT Revlon, PT Tempo, and PT Roche. She also owns the advertising company PT Bates Indonesia. Before going into business, she published a book entitled, *Perdjandjian Dwikewarganegaraan RI-RRT dan pelaksanaannja* (Jakarta, 1961).

Sources: *Apa & Siapa 1985–86*, pp. 537–38; Setyautama, *Tokoh-tokoh Etnis TH*, p. 218, the above-mentioned book.

MURDAYA, Siti Hartati (CHOW Li Ing; ZOU Liying 邹丽英**, 1946-)**
Leader of Buddhist organization, wealthy businesswoman,
wife of **Murdaya Widyawimarta POO**

Born on 29 August 1946 in Jakarta into a Buddhist family, Hartati was exposed to Buddhism since childhood and was serious in pursuing Buddhist teachings before being stopped by her timber merchant father. After graduating from high school, she entered the Faculty of Economics at Ureca which later became Universitas Trisakti from where she graduated in 1969 with a Sarjana degree in business administration.

Hartati helped her father in the timber business and acquired her initial business experience. In 1971 she married **Murdaya Widyawimarta POO** (Poo Tjie Guan 傅志宽) and jointly established PT Kencana Sakti Indonesia dealing in electric appliances as well as providing services for lifts in multi-storey buildings. The two founded the Central Cipta Murdaya [CCM] Group, also known as Berca Group in 1990 which engaged in a wide range of businesses: electronics, timber, palm oil, shoes and property. She was listed as number 16 among the richest Indonesians on the Forbes 2006 list with a net worth of US$430 million.

Hartati was also active in socio-religious activities especially in the Buddhist community. During the Soeharto era, she supported the Indonesian Buddhist Council (Perwalian Umat Buddha Indonesia, abbreviated as Walubi) which was dominated by the pro-government Buddhists. After Soeharto was forced to step down, Walubi suffered an internal split and she became the leader of new Walubi (Perwakilan Umat Buddha Indonesia or the Indonesian Representatives of the Buddhist Community). She later became a member of the MPR (People's Consultative Council) from 1994–99 taking the only Buddhist community seat. She also serves as the general chairperson of Yayasan Kepedulian Sosial (Social Care Foundation), a charity organization.

Sources: "Apa dan Siapa — Siti Hartati Murdaya", Pusat Data dan Analisa Tempo; *Sinergi*, no. 11 (15 September–15 October 1999), pp. 15–19; Suryadinata, *Xian Jieduan de Yinni Huaren Zuqun* (2002), pp. 65–78; Suryadinata, "Murdaya, Siti Hartati", in Suryadinata, ed., *Southeast Asian Personalities* (2012), pp. 749–51.

Murdaya Widyawimarta POO. See **POO, Murdaya Widyawimarta**

NAGA, Dali Santun (YO Goan Li, YANG Yuanli 杨元利, 1934-)
Academic, university professor

Born in Tomini, Central Sulawesi, on 22 December 1934, he went to the THHK school at Gorontalo (1947–48). In 1949 he went to Jakarta and received his junior and senior school education at Pa Hoa (THHK school) and graduated in 1954.

After graduation he went to Bandung to teach English, algebra and geometry at Chiao Chung (school) and later at Ts'ing Hua (school). At the same time, he also enrolled in the Department of Electronics and Technology at ITB. He graduated in 1960. In 1965 he began to help out at IKIP. Since 1968 he officially joined IKIP (Jakarta) as a lecturer. In 1969 he became head of Electronical Technology at IKIP, and later served as deputy dean. He also established the computer centre and became its head (1981–99). He took the opportunity to do his PhD at IKIP and obtained his PhD after submitting his dissertation. In 1991 he was promoted to a full professor at IKIP. Between 1992 and 2000 he was appointed president (*rektor*) of Universitas Tarumanagara. He has published many books, including *Ilmu Panas* (PT Swasta, 1965); *Mekanika Tehnik pada Tititk Zat dan Benda Tegar* (year?) and *Elektronika Computer Digital* (1995).

Source: *Buku Peringatan 100 Tahun Sekolah THHK/Pahoa Centennial of the THHK School* (2001), p. 246.

NANGOI, T. (TENG Tjin Leng; DENG Zhenning 邓振宁, 1906-)
Community leader, lawyer, university professor

Born in Menado on 13 July 1906, he was educated at the RHS (Jakarta) and Leiden University, where he graduated with an Mr degree in 1933. In 1932 he left the CHH-Netherlands. Together with **TAN Ling Djie** and **TJOA Sik Ien**, he established the Sarekat Peranakan Tionghoa Indonesia. In 1934 he returned to Indonesia and practised law in Palembang. In 1939 he moved to Makassar. In 1946–49 he served as the deputy chairman of the Progressive Faction in Parliament of NIT. In 1949 he participated in the Round Table Conference in the Hague. From 1950 to 1956 he was a member of the DPRS. In 1951–52 he was a member and an adviser to the Indonesian delegation to the Conference on West Irian. In 1955–56 he was an adviser to the Indonesian delegation to the Conference on the Indonesia-Netherlands Union (Geneva). He was a member of Baperki but soon withdrew from it (in 1955?). Between 1958 and the 1970s he served as Extraordinary Professor at Hasanuddin University (UNHAS). In 1959–62 he was appointed as the secretary to the UNHAS Senate and in 1962–69 the chairman and honorary member of the Professors Council, UNHAS, and a member of the University Board of Trustees (UNHAS). In the 1960s he was an adviser to the PMKRI, an adviser to the ISKI, and the president of Atma Jaya Catholic University. Between 1980–86 he served as the president (*rektor*) of the Atmajaya Catholic University in Makassar.

Sources: Surayadinata, *Peranakan Politics*, p. 74; Roeder, *Who's Who*, p. 454; *Kompas*, 20 December 1993.

Nathanel, ISKANDAR. See ISKANDAR, Nathanel

NG Sim Kie (WU Shenji 吴慎机, 1896?–1985)
Community leader, newspaperman, Hakka

Born in 1896 (?) in Jiaoling, Guangdong, and a member of the KMT since the age of fourteen, he was educated at the Nanyang Zhongxue (Shanghai) and Tung-wu (Dong Wu) University (Suzhou, China). In 1919 he came to Jakarta, took over his father's business, and was engaged in selling Chinese products and distributing Chinese (Mandarin) movies.

In the late 1930s (1937?), he served as the director of *Tiansheng Ribao* (Jakarta), an executive member of both Kuomintang (Jakarta branch) and Siang Hwee (Jakarta). He was arrested by the Japanese and interned for several years. After the Japanese surrender, when *Tiansheng Ribao* was republished, he again served as its director (1945–55). In 1958 he was forced to leave Indonesia. He died in Taiwan in 1985.

Sources: Liu, *Gailan*, p. [28]; *Nanyang Nianjian* (1951), p. E107; *Huaqiao Da Cidian*, p. 820.

NG Soei Chong. See KUSUMA, Eddie
NIO Hap Liang. See KURNIAWAN, Rudy Hartono

NIO Joe Lan (Junus Nur ARIF; LIANG Youlan 梁友兰, 1904–72)
Journalist, writer

Born in Jakarta on 29 December 1904, he was educated at the HCS (Jakarta), the School met de Bijbel, and the KWS (Jakarta), where he graduated in 1924. He took private lessons in the Chinese language. He joined *Keng Po* at the invitation of **LAUW Giok Lan**, the uncle of his classmate **KHOE Woen Sioe**. In 1928 when **HAUW Tek Kong** died, Nio was appointed as the editor-in-chief of *Keng Po*. In 1935 when *Keng Po* was reorganized, he left *Keng Po* and joined the editorial board of *Sin Po* (Jakarta), where he stayed on until 1942. He was interned during the Japanese Occupation (1942–45). When *Sin Po* resumed publication after World War II, he rejoined it.

He resigned in 1958 and devoted most of his time to writing, primarily on Chinese history and culture.

He was active in Chinese organizations: he was the secretary of the THHK (Jakarta) before World War II, the president of Keng Kie Hwee in 1936, and an executive member of the Chinese Unemployment Funds Committee in the 1930s. In the period 1955–60 he was appointed as a lecturer in Chinese and Japanese History at a Teachers' Training College in Jakarta. In 1960 he was appointed as a member of Comite Sensor Film (Jakarta). He died in Jakarta on 13 February 1972.

His publications include *Riwajat 40 Tahon THHK Batavia* (Batavia, 1940), which he edited; *Dalem Tawanan Djepang* (Jakarta, 1946); *Peradaban Tionghoa Selajang Pandang* (Jakarta, 1961); *Sastera Indonesia-Tionghoa* (Jakarta, 1962); *Puntjak-Puntjak Kisah Tiga Negara* (Jakarta, 1963); and *Sastera Tiongkok Sepintas Lalu* (Jakarta, 1966).

Sources: Tan, *Tionghoa*, p. 201; *Gedenkboek THHK*, p. 6; interview, 1969.

NIO Peng Liong (LIANG Bingnong 梁炳农, 1873-?)
Community leader, entrepreneur

Born in 1873 in Zhongshan (Guangdong), he migrated to Java in 1895. In 1901 he established a machine factory and a motor service station and immediately became a leader in the field. In 1910 he represented the Chinese in Jakarta participating in the Nanyang Jianyehui exhibition in China. In 1911 he joined the 1911 Revolution. In 1926 he served as a member of the board of trustees of the Shanghai Commercial Bank. After the unification of China he returned to Java. From 1932 to 1934 he served as the president of Siang Hwee (Jakarta). In 1934 when Ho-yin Shang-lien Hui was formed, he served as the chairman of the Congress. In 1937 he served as the vice-president of the board of trustees of the Jang Seng Ie Hospital (Jakarta). He died in Jakarta.

Sources: Tan, *Tionghoa*, pp. 200–1; Liu, *Gailan*, p. 23.

NIO Pik Wan. See **DEWI, Utami**

NIO, Threes (1939–90) 梁丽丝*
Journalist, Catholic

She was born on 23 October 1939 in Banjarnegara, Central Java, but grew up in Semarang where she received her secondary school education. She continued her study in the Department of English Language at IKIP Santa Dharma. While finishing her university education she worked as a teacher for three years. During 1978–79 she studied at the Princeton University at the United States. Threes began to work for *Kompas* in 1966 and was well-known for her high quality reporting. She was known to many ministers such as Professor Widjojo Nitisastro, Radius Prawiro and Ali Alatas. Since 1982 she was sent to Washington, D.C. by *Kompas* as its special correspondent for eight years. She got a heart attack and died in New York on 14 December 1990. In 1995, *Kompas* collected her writings in *Kompas* and published it as a book entitled *Laporan Dari Lapangan* [Reports from the Field].

Sources: *Kompas*, 15 December 1990; also Sam Setyautama, *Tokoh-Tokoh Etnis Tionghoa*, p. 252.

NJOO Cheong Seng (pen-name: Monsieur d'AMOUR; YANG Zhongsheng 杨众生**, 1902–62)**
Writer, theatre-director, husband of **Fifi YOUNG**

Born in Surabaya on 6 November 1902, he was educated at the THHK school (Surabaya). He became interested in theatrical groups and in 1928 married Fifi Young, an actress. During the Japanese Occupation together with his wife, he formed Sandiwara Bintang Surabaja, a theatrical group. His works include short stories, novels, and film scripts: *Menika Dalem Koeboeran* [Wedding in the cemetery] (Surabaya, 1925); *Gagal* [Failure] (Surabaya, 1925); *Boeaja Soerabaja* [The bandit of Surabaya] (Surabaya, 1926); *Tjoekat Liang: Djojo Bojo Atawa*

Dari Manatah Asalnja Boemipoetra di Java? [Zhuge Liang: Joyoboyo or where were the origins of the indigenous population in Java?] (Surabaya, 1926); *Zoebaida* (Yogyakarta, 1940).

His film scenarios, among others, were *Kris Mataram* [The dagger of Mataram] (1940), *Airmata Ibu* [Tears of a mother] (1951), and *Mirah Gagaklodra* [Mirah, the mysterious hero] (1953). He died in Malang on 30 November 1962.

Sources: "Undangan" (Njoo Cheong Seng's invitation card to his fifty-first birthday celebration); Saleh, August 1954, p. 429; Museum Catalogue; "Fifi, Ibu Kita 1914–75", *Tempo*, 15 March 1975, pp. 36–37; *Catalogus*, pp. 399–40.

NJOO Han Siang (YANG Hanxiang 杨汉祥, 1930–85)
Film producer, banker

Born in Yogyakarta in 1930, he received Chinese primary education at his birthplace. In 1946 he went to Amoy (China) for secondary school education. When the communists came to power he left China and stayed in Hong Kong for a while. In 1950 he returned to Indonesia. After studying in the Academy of Journalism (established by Parada Harahap) for one year, he worked for the *Sunday Courier* (Jakarta) as a photographer-reporter. Two years later he joined a shipping company.

When he got tired of working in Jakarta, he returned to Semarang where he helped his brother run a business. He then became a businessman himself, selling agricultural products and cattle. In 1968 he came to Jakarta again and took over Bank Umum Nasional, a bank owned by members of the PNI. He was the president of that bank and the proprietor of the International Cine and Studio Center (laboratory for processing colour films) in the 1970s. In October 1973 he went to the United States as a member of the CSIS delegation. He was the producer of many movies, including *Meilan Aku Cinta Padamu* [Meilan, I love you], *November 1828* (co-produced with **Hendrick GOZALI**) and so forth. He died on 30 September 1985.

Sources: *Nusantara*, 13 February 1971; *Merdeka*, 12 February 1971; *Ribao*, 4 May and 6 June 1975; *Bangkok Post*, 28 January 1971; *Tempo*, 27 March 1976, p. 40, and 18 February 1978, p. 7; *Kompas*, 2 October 1985.

NOTOWIDJOJO, Suhendro (SIK Sian Han, 1931-) 施先汉*
Prominent businessman, Buddhist

Born in Indonesia on 11 April 1931, he was first educated at the HBS (Semarang) and later received a Master's degree in Business Administration (from France). He was in the textile business for seventeen years and later expanded into the steel manufacturing business. In the 1970s he was the managing director of PT Daya Manunggal, a large textile factory in Indonesia, and the president-director of the following enterprises: N.V. Sumera, Fumira, and PT Tagam Logam. He also served as chairman of Indonesian Galvanized Iron Sheet Manufacturers' Association, chairman (IV) of the Indonesian Steel Manufacturers' Association, and Plenary Council Member of Kadin (Indonesian Chamber of Commerce and Industry).

Sources: Arief, *Indonesian Business*, p. 398; Roeder, "Chinese 'Impudence'", p. 34; Roeder, *Who's Who*, 2nd ed., p. 198.

Nurdin PURNOMO. See **PURNOMO, Nurdin**

NURIMBA, Adil A. (LIEM Eng Hway; LIN Yinghuai 林英怀, 1922–2006)
Prominent businessman

Son of a local merchant, born in Bagan Siapi-api (Sumatra) on 23 May 1922, he was educated at the Chung Ling High School in Penang. In 1958 he moved to Jakarta. In 1963 he established PT Gesuri Lloyd. He was the president-director of PT Gesuri Lloyd, which is engaged in the shipping business.

He was also a shareholder of INBC (Indonesian Bulk Carriers), MOGES (Mitsui, OSK, Gesuri), Mutual International Finance Corporation, and the Five Ocean Shipping and Agencies Ltd. (Hong Kong).

Prior to his success, he used to make three trips a week across the Melaka Straits to transport export goods from North Sumatra to peninsular Malaysia and import goods from there to Indonesia. He attributed his success to hard work. He died in Tangerang, West Java on 17 August 2006.

Sources: "Dari Tongkang Ke Armada Internasional", *Ekspres*, 14 June 1971, pp. 16–18; Roeder, "Chinese 'Impudence'", *FEER*, 7 May 1973, p. 34; *Indonesia Raya*, 4 November 1972; Arief, *Indonesian Business*, p. 403; *Apa & Siapa 1985–86*, pp. 607–8; Setyautama, *Tokoh-tokoh Etnis Tionghoa*, p. 198; the compiler's notes.

NURSALIM, Sjamsul (LIEM Tek Siang; LIN Dexiang 林德祥, 1942-)
Businessman, banker

Born in 1942 in Lampung, Sumatra, he is the son of a pepper king. There are two versions of his Indonesianized Chinese name. *Apa & Siapa* gives it as Liem Tjoen Ho, while *Eksekutif* gives it as Liem Tek Siang. He probably had received Chinese education in Indonesia, but he also went to the United Kingdom to study. Not much is known about his earlier activities. In 1980 he salvaged Bank Dagang Nasional Indonesia, a bank which was founded by Indonesian independence fighters in Medan in 1945. He held 50 per cent of the shares while the other 50 per cent was owned by Sri Sultan Hamengku Buwono IX, the former vice-president of Indonesia. Nursalim is better known as an entrepreneur. He is the boss of PT Gajah Tunggal, which produces the Gajah (elephant) brand of tyres. His company was also in a joint venture to produce the Yokohama brand of tyres with Japan. He is the proprietor of Tuan Sing Tower, an office building in Singapore.

Sources: *Apa & Siapa 1985–86*, pp. 609–10; *Shijie Huaren Fuhao Bang*, p. 224; *Eksekutif*, no. 194 (August 1995), p. 36.

Obi DARMOHUSODO. See **DARMOHUSODO, K.R.T. Obi**

OE Siang Djie 邬祥如*
Community leader, lawyer, notary public
A Leiden-trained lawyer, in 1948–50 he served as the president of the PT (Surabaya) and in 1953 the president of the PDTI (Surabaya branch). In 1958 he was elected as a member of the DPRD (Surabaya) representing the Chinese minority.

Sources: *Sinar*, 1 April 1949; *Liberal*, 7 June 1958.

OEI Ek Tjhong. See **WIDJAJA, Eka Tjipta**

OEI Gee Hwat (HUANG Yifa 黄义发, 1915–48)
Member of "Illegal PKI", teacher
Born in Madiun in 1915, he went to a Christian school when he was young. He might have received Dutch education. In the 1930s, he was a member of the editorial board of *Sin Tit Po* and a teacher at the PTI school in Surabaya. He joined the labour movement and the illegal communist party. He participated in the Madium Affair in 1948 and was killed in the same year.

Sources: Suryadinata, *Peranakan Politics*, p. 134; Zhou Nanjing, ed., *Huaqiao huaren baike quanshu* (2001), p. 227.

OEI Gwie Siong. See **HARTONO, Michael Bambang**
OEI Gwie Tiong. See **HARTONO, Robert Budi**
OEI Hai Djoen Tj. See **OEY Hay Djoen**
OEI Hong Lan. See **WIDYONO, Benny**

OEI Hui Lan (Mrs Wellington KOO; HUANG Huilan 黄惠兰, 1899–1992)
Daughter of **OEI Tiong Ham**; *wife of Wellington Koo*

Born in 1899 in Semarang (Central Java), she was the second daughter of Oei Tiong Ham's first wife, Goei Bing Nio. Hui Lan was her father's favourite daughter and lived like a princess. She never went to formal school but received her education at home. Her father engaged tutors to teach her and her sister English, French and Dutch. Her home languages were Malay/Javanese which she learned from the servants and nurses. Hui Lan travelled to Beijing and Shanghai with her parents when she was a child. Later as a teenager she lived in Europe with her mother and her elder sister, and began to lead a social life in Paris.

In 1920 she was already well-known in the high society circles in Paris. It was in Paris that Hui Lan met a young Chinese diplomat Wellington Koo (1887–1985) who later became Chinese foreign minister for a short while and subsequently ambassador to France, UK and USA. They fell in love and got married in Belgium in 1921. Before World War II, she followed Wellington Koo to Beijing, Paris, and London and supported his diplomatic career. According to her story, Oei Tiong Ham bought beautiful mansions for her in various cities to support her luxurious life as a Chinese top diplomat's wife. After World War II, Wellington Koo moved to Washington, D.C. as the representative of the Republic of China. The couple later separated. In 1959 Wellington married another woman. According to Hui Lan's story, Hui Lan refused to be divorced and she claimed to have remained as the official Mrs Koo. She lived alone until she died in 1992.

In 1943 Hui Lan published her memoirs entitled *Hui Lan Koo (Madame Wellington Kook): An Autobiography as told to Mary van Rensselaer Thayer*, published in New York by the Dial Press. In 1975 she published another memoirs: *No Feast*

Lasts Forever (this time she collaborated with Isabella Taves, published by Quadrangle/The New York Times).

Sources: The above-mentioned books; Lim Tjwan Ling, *Raja Gula Oei Tiong Ham* (Surabaya, 1979), pp. 66–128; Agnes Davonar, *Kisah Tragis Oei Hui Lan: Putri Orang Terkaya di Indonesia* (Jakarta: AD Publisher, 2012); <http://en.wikipedia.org/wiki/V.K.Wellington Koo> (accessed 12 April 2014).

OEI Ik Tjoe (OEI Tjoe; HUANG Yizhu 黄奕住, 1868–1945)
Businessman, banker

Born in China in 1868, he left for Indonesia in 1900 when he was a poor young man. He made a fortune in Semarang dealing with various commodities and property. Unlike his contemporary, **OEI Tiong Ham**, who continued to live in the region, Oei Tjoe returned to China in 1919 and settled in Fujian province. Before leaving Indonesia he subscribed to one million shares of the Oversea Chinese Bank in Singapore. He also invested in telephone companies, electrical and water works, and railway lines in Fujian.

Sources: Chua, 23 March 1981; Suryadinata, ed. (1980), p. 45; Zhou Nanjing, ed., *Huaqiao huaren baike quanshu* (2001), pp. 227–28.

OEI Jong Tjioe (HUANG Yongzhou 黄涌洲, 1907–85)
Community leader, Indonesian nationalist, lawyer

Born in Tulungagung on 20 July 1907, he was educated at the HCS (Malang), the HBS (Surabaya and the Hague), and Leiden University, where he graduated with an "Mr" degree. In the 1930s he returned to Surabaya where he practised law and served as a member of the East Java Provincial Council, an executive member of both Soe Soei Tiong Hoa Ie Wan (Surabaya Chinese Hospital) and the THHK (Surabaya).

During the Japanese Occupation he was interned by the Japanese. He was closely associated with Indonesian nationalists, especially Mohammad Hatta. Oei was elected by the Republican government (in Yogyakarta) as a delegate to attend the Round

Table Conference in 1949. Between 1952 and 1956 he served as personal adviser (*penasehat pribadi*) to Mohammad Hatta, vice-president of Indonesia. Oei was instrumental in developing the Indonesian ceramic industry. He died in March 1985.

Sources: Tan, *Tionghoa*, pp. 47–48; *Xin Pao*, 1 August 1949; the compiler's notes; *Tempo*, 6 April 1985, p. 19; Junus Jahja, *Peranakan Idealis*, pp. 217–27.

OEI Kie Hok (1898–1959) 黄基福*
Newspaperman

Born in 1898, he received Dutch secondary school education. He served as the director of *Sin Po Oost Java Editie* (1922), *Nan Sing* (1930), and *Mata Hari* (Semarang, 1934). He died in Semarang on 1 May 1959.

Sources: *Nan Sing*, 18 March 1930; *Mata Hari*, 6 August 1934.

OEI Kim Tiang. See OEY Kim Tiang

OEI Liong Thay (HUANG Longtai 黄隆泰, 1914-)
Freelance journalist, political leader

Born in Lasem (Java) on 14 January 1914, he received his education at the HCS (Semarang) and the Handels School (Semarang). He was a freelance journalist who contributed articles to *Sin Po* and other *peranakan* newspapers before World War II. He was a member of the CHTCS (Chung Hua Ta Chung Sheh, Semarang), and the vice-chairman of the PNI (Semarang branch) (1948–53). In 1953 he represented the director and editorial board of the daily *Sin Min* in Semarang on a visit to the PRC. Between 1954 and 1965 he served as the deputy chairman of the World Peace Committee in Central Java, Semarang. He migrated to Holland after the 1965 coup and maintained contacts with fellow journalists in Indonesia. He contributed articles to *Merdeka* in the 1970s from Holland.

Sources: "Biodata", courtesy of C.M. Hsu; the compiler's notes.

OEI Tiang Tjoei. See **OEY Tiang Tjoei**

OEI Tiong Ham (HUANG Zhonghan 黄仲涵, 1866–1924)
Entrepreneur, community leader, millionaire, father of
OEI Tjong Hauw *and* **OEI Hui Lan**

Son of a migrant, Oei Tjie Sin, he was born in Semarang on 19 November 1866. In 1885 when he joined his father's company, Firma Kian Gwan, he was appointed *luitenant* by the Dutch authorities. In 1895 he was promoted to *kapitein* but he only held the position for two years after which he resigned due to business pressure. In 1901 he was appointed *titular Majoor*. In 1904 he became the first Chinese to obtain permission to cut his pigtail and wear Western dress. He made a fortune amounting to 18 million guilders out of the legal sale of opium in the period 1890–1903. Under his leadership, Kian Gwan expanded into various fields. It was involved in local products (especially sugar), banking, and the shipping business. In 1915 his income was said to amount to some two million guilders. He contributed generously to various Chinese scholars and educational institutions both in Java and Singapore, where he died on 6 June 1924. His property was inherited by the twenty-six sons and daughters of his eight wives.

Sources: *Nanyang Nianjian* (1951), section on "Huaqiao"; Panglaykim and Palmer (1970); Liem Thian Joe (1933), pp. 154, 182–83; Coppel (May 1976), mimeographed; Liem, *Raja Gula*, pp. 21–24.

OEI Tjeng Hien. See **KARIM, Hadji Abdul**
OEI Tjin San. See **WULLUR, Jahja**
OEI Tjo Iem. See **RIDWAN, Ignatius**
OEI Tjoe. See **OEI Ik Tjoe**

OEI Tjoe Tat (HUANG Zida 黄自达, 1922–96)
Political party leader, community leader, lawyer

Born in Solo in 1922, he graduated from the RHS (Jakarta) in May 1948. In the same year he joined a Jakarta law firm and was active in a number of Chinese and Indonesian organizations: in the 1950s he was an executive member of the Indonesian Red Cross, the THHK (Jakarta), and the UMS (a soccer association in Jakarta). From 1950 to 1953 he served as the president of Sin Ming Hui (Jakarta), and from 1950(?) to 1954 the vice-president of the PDTI central board. In 1954 he was one of the advocates for dissolving the PDTI and establishing Baperki. In the same year he was elected as the vice-president of the Baperki central board. In 1960 he joined Partindo and served on its executive committee. In December 1964 he was appointed Minister without Portfolio attached to the Cabinet Presidium by President Soekarno. In September 1964–65 he was appointed Minister of State, RI.

He was detained by the authorities after the 1965 coup. He was tried in March 1976 and was eventually released in December 1977 after the intervention of Foreign Minister Adam Malik. He reopened his law firm, but had to close it down in 1985 after suffering from a heart attack. In 1995 he published his memoirs entitled *Memoar Oei Tjoe Tat: Pembantu Presiden Soekarno* [The memoirs of Oei Tjoe Tat: President Soekarno's assistant]. The senior editor of the memoirs is a famous Indonesian novelist, Pramoedya Ananta Toer.

He died of cancer in 1996.

Sources: *Pedoman Kampanje*, pp. 37–38; *SMH 10 Tahun*, p. 27; Finch, *Cabinets*, pp. 53–54; *Berita Yudha*, 31 March 1976; *Oei Tjoe Tat's Memoir*; Suryadinata, ed., *Southeast Asian Personalities* (2012), pp. 798–800.

OEI Tjong Hauw (HUANG Zongxiao 黄宗孝, 1905–50)
Community leader, businessman, elder son of **OEI Tiong Ham**

The elder son of Oei Tiong Ham's fourth wife (Ong Mie Hwa Nio), he was born in Semarang on 20 January 1905 (*Risalah* noted that he was born in 1904) and educated at the HBS (Semarang). When Oei Tiong Ham died in 1924, the firm was given to Oei Tjong Swan and him to run. In 1927 he helped found the CHH and served on its executive committee. In 1934 he established *Mata Hari*, a daily newspaper published in Semarang. He served as an executive member of the CHH central board while in Shanghai (1937–38). During the Japanese Occupation, he was appointed as a member of "Tjuo Sangi In" representing Central Java, and a member of the BPUPKI (1945). He was in favour of declaring the ethnic Chinese in Indonesia as Chinese nationals (1945). He died in Jakarta on 21 January 1950 after suffering a heart attack.

Sources: Tan, *Tionghoa*, pp. 139–48; Yamin, *Naskah*, pp. 243–46; *CHH 2de Lustrum*, p. 7; Liem, *Raja Gula*, p. 130A; *Risalah Sidang*, n.p., *Konglomerat Oei Tiong Ham* (1991), p. 315.

OEI Tjong Ie (Jack OEI; HUANG Zongyi 黄宗诒, 1918–2007)
Anti-Japanese activist, businessman, son of **OEI Tiong Ham**

Oei Tjong Ie was born on 9 January 1918 in Semarang. He was the oldest son of Oei Tiong Ham's seventh wife, Ho Kim Hwa Nio (also known as Lucy Ho). He received primary school education in Semarang, but went to the Netherlands for his secondary school and tertiary education. He studied law and almost completed the course but was asked to return to Indonesia as he had to be properly installed as one of the shareholders of the Oei Tiong Ham Concern (OTHC). In February 1940 he married his Dutch fiancée, Maria Suzanna Matthysen and worked at Kian Gwan Surabaya Branch.

During the Japanese Occupation he joined the anti-Japanese resistance movement and in February 1943 he was arrested and sent to internment camp. He was sentenced to death for hiding KNIL (Dutch colonial soldiers) and financing the resistant network of Captain W.A. Meelhuysen. But according to his own admission, Oei Tjong Hauw, his brother, saved his life by donating 1.5 million guilders to the Japanese. His sentence was commuted to imprisonment for fifteen years. He spent two-and-a-half years in prison until the Japanese surrender. According to one source, in June 1946 he was appointed as the superintendent of police 1st class in Jakarta, specially assigned to capture escaped *kempei* (Japanese military police). When the Dutch recontrolled Indonesia he went to Singapore to head the OTHC Singapore. After Oei Tjong Hauw's untimely death in 1950, Oei Tjong Ie was made the chairman of the board of OTHC group, while his brother Oei Tjong Tjay headed the Indonesian branch. Tjong Ie later set up the Malayan Banking Corporation in Malaysia.

Sources: Yoshihara Kunio, ed., *Oei Tiong Ham Concern: The First Business Empire of Southeast Asia* (Kyoto University, 1989), pp. 148–85; Peter Post et al., ed., *The Encyclopedia of Indonesia in the Pacific War* (Brill, 2010), pp. 566–67.

OEI Tjong Swan (HUANG Zongxuan 黄宗宣, 1899–1943)
Community leader, leading businessman, son of **OEI Tiong Ham**

The son of Oei Tiong Ham's second wife (The Tjik Nio), he was born in Semarang on 19 January 1899. He and his brother Tjong Houw were given the task of running the Oei Tiong Ham Concern after 1924. In 1927 he was a founding member of the CHH and from 1928 to 1930 the president of Siang Boe (Chinese Chamber of Commerce in Semarang). In 1931 he suddenly sold all his shares to his brother and resigned from the Oei Tiong Ham Concern.

Sources: Suryadinata, *Peranakan Politics*, p. 141; the compiler's notes; Liem, *Raja Gula*, pp. 27, 167.

OEN Boen Ing. See DARMOHUSODO, K.R.T.

OEN Tek Hian (pen-name: Mu You 慕由; WEN Dexuan 温德玄, 1904–76)
Journalist, writer, community leader, Hakka

Born in 1904 in Singapore, he first received his education in Yin-hsin school (Singapore). In 1914 he migrated to Indonesia with his father, who was a hotel employee. He attended the THHK school in Jakarta and worked as a typesetter in *Xin Bao* (Chinese edition of *Sin Po*). When he graduated from the THHK school in 1933, he was promoted to a proofreader in the same newspaper. Later he was promoted again to the position of editor in charge of news from China.

During the Japanese Occupation (1942–45) he was interned. After World War II he was active in both the THHK (Jakarta) and Sin Ming Hui. He served as the Chinese language secretary of Sin Ming Hui in the 1950s. In the early 1960s he began to publish articles and books on the early history of local Chinese in Indonesia, including *Xijia Gongsi Zuzhi* 西加公司组织 [The organization of the Chinese *kongsi* in West Kalimantan] (Jakarta, 1961) and *Tiandi Hui* 天地会 (Jakarta, 1962). In 1963 when *Shoudu Ribao* was established, he served as the assistant director. He retired when the newspaper ceased publication on 1 October 1965. He died in Jakarta on 27 June 1976.

Sources: *SMH 10 Tahun*, p. 9; Chen, *Nanguan*, p. 37; *Shoudu Ribao*, 29 August 1963; interview, 1970.

OEN Tiong Hauw. See OETOMO, Dede

OEN Tjhing Tiauw (1900–81) 温清兆*
Community leader

Born in Malang on 29 May 1900, he received primary education at the THHK (Jombang). He left school at the age of thirteen and began to work for a living. He moved to Surabaya where he joined Hak Sing Swee, and served on the HCTNH central board. In the 1930s he worked as a member of the editorial board of *Sin Tit Po*. At the same time he became a member of the PTI as well as a commissioner of the PTI school. After World War II, he became active in *peranakan* politics. In 1946 he helped to establish the Servant of Society (SOS) in

Surabaya, a pro-Indonesian nationalist association, and was elected as the secretary of that organization.

In the 1950s he declined the invitation of **SIAUW Giok Tjhan** to join Baperki; instead he joined the PSI. Oen has been interested in Confucianism and Buddhism. In 1969 he became a patron of "Eka Dharma Loka", a Buddhist temple in Surabaya. He worked as a newspaper delivery agent. He died in March 1981.

Sources: Tan, *Tionghoa*, p. 49; interview, 1969; *Surabaya Post*, 21 March 1981.

OETOMO, Dede (OEN Tiong Hauw; WEN Zhongxiao 温忠孝, 1953-)
Linguist, university lecturer, gay activist, nephew of **Basuki SOEJATMIKO**

Born in Pasuruan, East Java, on 6 December 1953, he did his undergraduate work at the Institute of Teacher Training and Education (IKIP) in Surabaya, majoring in Teaching English as a Foreign Language, and obtained his Sarjana Pendidikan degree in 1978. He went to the United States in the same year to start graduate work in linguistics at Cornell University, where he obtained his MA (1982) and PhD (1984). While in the States, he taught Indonesian at Cornell University (1978–82) and the University of California, Berkeley (1979–80). He also joined the gay group on campus. He returned to Indonesia and joined the University of Airlangga as a lecturer. His dissertation is entitled "The Chinese of Pasuruan: A Study of Language and Identity in a Minority Community in Transition" (1984). He has also published a number of articles on the ethnic Chinese in Indonesia.

In 1987 Dede Oetomo established the Gaya Nusantara group in Surabaya to fight for gay and lesbian rights in Indonesia. Currently he chairs the Governing Board of the Asia Pacific Coalition on Male Sexual Health (2013–16) and is on the Advisory

Board of the Islands of Southeast Asia Network on Male and Transgender Sexual Health.

Sources: The above-mentioned dissertation; <http://angsamerahclinic.blogspot.sg/2013/08/dede-oetomo.html> (accessed 4 August 2014); <https://www.greenleft.org.au/node/20305> (accessed 4 August 2014); the compiler's notes.

OEY An Siok (Pita KALIANA, BOE Beng Tjoe; HUANG Anshu 黄安淑, 1915–87)
Kungfu novel translator

Born in 1915 in Tangerang, he was educated at the THHK school and Overseas Chinese Institute, both in Jakarta. In 1932 he passed the Junior Cambridge Local Examination and in the following year, the Senior Cambridge Local Examination. Initially he worked as an administrator at the Jang Seng Ie Hospital, and was later appointed director of the Administration of the Husada Hospital (the new name of Jang Seng Ie since June 1965).

Oey began to translate *kungfu* novels in the 1950s(?) using Boe Beng Tjoe as his pen-name (another *kungfu* novel translator, **OEY Kim Tiang**, also used the same pen-name). Both Oey An Siok and Oey Kim Tiang jointly translated *Sin Tiauw Hiap Lu*, a well-known *kungfu* novel by Jin Yong (Chin Yung). Oey An Siok himself later translated two other works by Jin Yong, *Ie Thian To Liong* and *Hoei Ho Gwa Toan*.

Apart from Jin Yong's novels, Oey An Siok also translated Liang Yusheng's novels into Indonesian: *Peng Tjoan Thian Lie* and *San Hoa Lie Hiap*. He died in a car accident.

Sources: Letter to the compiler, undated, received on 29 December 1984; C.M. Hsu's notes.

OEY-GARDINER, Mayling (HUANG Meiling 黄美玲, 1941-)
Demographer, executive director of Insan Hitawasana Sejahtera, professor

Born in Sukabumi (West Java) on 25 February 1941, Mayling, as she is usually called, went to the Dutch Santa Theresia elementary school and then the Santa Ursula Indonesian secondary school. Her education was postponed due to the discrimination against ethnic Chinese in getting into state universities. She managed to obtain a scholarship to study in the United States where she completed her BA in sociology in St. Xavier's College in Chicago in 1968. She then went on to the College of William and Mary in Williamsburg, Virginia and returned with an MA in sociology and a thesis on population growth patterns. She earned her PhD in demography from the Australia National University (ANU) in 1982.

Mayling founded Insan Hitawasana Sejahtera (IHS) with a number of colleagues in 1991, of which she is the executive director until today. IHS is an Indonesian company specializing in the provision of social science research covering a wide range of social, economic and demographic issues, and consulting services. She has produced a total of 117 titles in consultancies, both national and international. Her work included both primary (survey-based) data collection and analysis and is carried out not only in Indonesia, but also in Cambodia, Malaysia, Mongolia, the Philippines, Thailand, Timor Leste and Vanuatu.

Mayling has a number of "firsts". When there was an increase in population activities, including studies and scholarships in the 1970s, she was the first Indonesian individual applicant to receive the Ford-Rockefeller population research grant. The research became the basis of her dissertation and led her into becoming the first Indonesian to earn a PhD in demography. In 2001, she was the first woman to be appointed professor at the Faculty of Economics of the University of Indonesia (UI) in its fifty years of existence. In 2004 she was elected chair of the Academic Senate and secretary to the Board of Professors of the Faculty of Economics of UI in 2004–7.

Mayling is also active in civil society organizations (CSO): she was one of two international, non-Ford Foundation board members of the International Fellowship Program of the Ford Foundation; a member of the board of the Indonesian Centre for Strategic and International Studies (CSIS), a founding member as well as a board member of Transparency International-Indonesia. Her concern with women's issues led to her acceptance as board member of the Koalisi Perempuan (Women's Coalition). She is still active in research work at IHS and teaches intermittently at the Faculty of Economics of UI.

Source: Mely G. Tan, "Oey-Gardiner, Mayling", in Suryadinata, ed., *Southeast Asian Personalities* (2012), pp. 803–5.

OEY Hay Djoen (OEI Hai Djoen Tj; OEYHAYDJUN; HUANG Haichun 黄海春, 1929–2008)
Political party leader, writer

Born in Malang on 18 April 1929, he received his HCS education for seven years. But his education was interrupted due to Japanese invasion of Java. However he continued to read various books and became interested in Marxism. He joined the pro-Indonesian trade unionist movement and was detained for a year by the Dutch authorities. In 1950 he became the correspondent of Republik magazine, edited by **SIAUW Giok Tjhan**. Between 1950 and 1953 he served as the secretary of the Association of Cigarette Manufacturers in Semarang. He later moved to Jakarta and served as the journalist of *Harian Rakjat*. From 1956 to 1959, he was elected as a member of the Constituent Assembly, representing the PKI. According to one source, he was a member of DPR-GR (1960–66), also representing the PKI.

When Soeharto came to power, Oey was arrested and detained in Selemba (Jakarta) for four years (1965–69) and ten years in Buru Island (1969–79). After his release, he began to translate many books, including *Das Kapital* (by Karl Marx) and completed the Indonesian translation in October 2004. It was later published under the title of *Kapital: Sebuah Kritik Ekonomi Politik* [Capital: A Critic of Political Economy]. The book which consists of 929 pages was based on the English translation of *Das Kapital*, not from the German version. It was also confined to volume 1. The book was launched in 2005 and the former president of Indonesia, Abdurahman Wahid was the commentator of the book. He noted that the book was not easy to read. "In order to balance and understand the book of Karl Marx, one needs to read the books of two leading figures of Capitalism, David Racardo and Adam Smith." According to one report, Oey received the Gus Dur Award for his translation of *Das Kapital*. Oey's other publication includes *Perang Pembebasan Rakjat Vietnam Selatan* (translated from the work of Wilfred Burchett, Jakarta, 1965).

Sources: Somers, dissertation, p. 153; Anderson, *Bibliography*, p. 34; *DPR 1971*, pp. 622–28; Setyautama, *Tokoh-tokoh Etnis TH*, pp. 265–66; the compiler's notes.

OEY Hong Lee (HUANG Fengli 黄丰礼, 1924–92)
Former journalist, political scientist, university lecturer

Born in Sukabumi on 3 March 1924, he was educated at the HCS (Sukabumi, 1930–37), the HBS (Bandung, 1937–41), and Christelijk Lyceum (Bandung, 1946). In 1946 he was employed by the Recovery Allied Prisoners of War (RAPWI) in Bandung. Later in the same year he left for the Netherlands to study political science at the University of Amsterdam (1947–50). For a time he was the editor of *Tung Feng* [East wind], the organ of Chung San Hui, a *peranakan* student organization in Amsterdam that supported Indonesia's independence. In 1950–51 he spent a year at Universite de Paris (Sorbonne) and another year at Institut d'Etudes Politiques

(Paris, 1951–52). In 1952 he re-entered the University of Amsterdam for graduate study and obtained a Drs degree in 1955.

He returned to Indonesia to become a civil servant in the Ministry of Education, RI (1955–59). From 1956 to 1958 he also served as an editor of *Republik*, a Baperki daily newspaper published in Jakarta. In 1959 he was appointed as a lecturer at Akademi Penerangan (Academy of the Ministry of Information) in Jakarta. In 1960 he became a lecturer at Perguruan Tinggi Publisistik (College of Mass Communications). In 1961 he was appointed secretary of URECA and concurrently lecturer and head of the Mass Communications Department, FH and IS-UI (1961–65).

In 1965 he left Indonesia and became a research worker at Fakultat fur Journalistik, Karl-Marx Universitat (Leipzig, 1965–67). In 1971 he was awarded the Doctor Politieke Wetenschappen degree by the University of Amsterdam after successfully defending his dissertation on the Indonesian Government and the press during the period of Guided Democracy. He was a lecturer in Politics of Southeast Asia in the Department of Political Studies at the University of Hull and a staff member of the Centre for Southeast Asian Studies at the same university until the 1980s. He moved to Holland after his early retirement and died in Amsterdam in May 1992.

He published a large number of books and articles in scholarly journals. Among his books are *Naga dan Tikus: Kisah Perang Tiongkok-Djepang, 1937–45* (Jakarta, 1959); *Naga Bangkit: Kisah Kemenangan Mao Tse-tung, 1945–49* (Jakarta, 1960; 2nd ed., 1963); *Kisah Rahasia Perang Korea, 1950–53* (Jakarta, 1960; 2nd ed., 1962); *Asia Menang di Dien Bien Phu* (Jakarta, 1961); *Publisistik Pers* (Jakarta, 1965); *Publisistik Film* (Jakarta, 1965); *Indonesian Government and Press during Guided Democracy* (Zug, 1971); *Indonesia after the 1971 Elections* (London/Kuala Lumpur, 1974), which was edited by him; *Power Struggle in South-East Asia* (Zug, 1976); *Indonesia facing the 1980s* (Hull, 1979); and *War and Diplomacy in Indonesia: 1945–49* (Townsville, 1981).

Sources: The above-mentioned books; *Who's Who in Education* (1974); Letters to the compiler, 1976 and 1979; the compiler's notes.

OEY Hong Tjiauw (1893-?) 黄丰朝*
Community leader

Born in Cirebon in 1893, he was educated at the THHT (Bandung). Prior to 1935, he served as an executive member of the THHK (Tasikmalaya) and a temporary chairman of the PTI (Tasikmalaya branch). In the mid-1930s he was appointed as a zone-chief (Tasikmalaya) and a member of the Tasikmalaya Regency Council.

Source: Tan, *Tionghoa*, p. 232.

OEY Kian Hoei (HUANG Qianghui 黄强辉, 1930-)
Athlete/bodybuilder

Born in 1930 in Banten, he graduated from Pa Chung in 1951. After winning the "Mr Indonesia" title in 1951 and 1952, he went to study at Harbin Industrial University in China and became a leading weightlifter of China. He broke a number of world records for the lightweight category. He later became the chief trainer for weightlifting and was in charge of training ten weightlifters, five of them, including Liu Shoubin, won gold medals for China in the Olympic Games. Due to his achievement he was made a member of the 5th CPPCC. Nevertheless, he continued to work as a coach in bodybuilding and weightlifting. In 1988 he was invited to train Indonesian weightlifters for SEA Games. He stayed in Indonesia for six-and-a-half years and managed to train a few weightlifters. Lisa Rumbewas won a silver medal in the 2000 Olympic Games for weightlifting and another silver medal in the 2004 Olympic

Games. Triyatno and Eko Yuli Irawan won silver and bronze medals respectively in the 2012 Olympic Games. In 2013 Oey was invited again by the Indonesian Sport Council to train the younger generation of Indonesian weightlifters.

Sources: *Tempo*, 6 January 1979, p. 44; *Cidian*, p. 726; <http://www.tempo.co/read/news/2013/04/29/103476439/Huang-Qianghui-Bapak-Angkat-Besi-Cina> (accessed 9 October 2014); the compiler's notes.

OEY Kim Tiang (O.K.T.; HUANG Jinchang 黄金长, 1903–95)
Kungfu novel translator

Born in Tangerang in 1903, he was sent by his labourer father to the local THHK school. He received up to middle school education and when he graduated, he was already twenty years of age. Ong Kim Tiat, another *kungfu* novel writer, was his sworn brother. Oey Kim Tiang used to help Ong translate novels. Later Oey was invited to join *Keng Po* and began to translate Chinese novels regularly. His earliest translations were *Nona Badjoe Idjo* [Green dress lady] and *Kawanan Merah Hitam* [The red black group].

After World War II he became more productive. His translated works were serialized in *Keng Po, Weekblad Keng Po, Star Magazine,* and *Star Weekly*. All *kungfu* novels published in these newspapers/weeklies signed under O.K.T. were his works. Later he left *Keng Po* and began to work for *Mekar Djaja*, which published his translated works such as *Sia Tiauw Eng Hiong* (Memanah Burung Radjawali) and *Sin Tiauw Hiap Lie* (Radjawali Sakti). He also translated *Oey Eng Si Burung Kenari* [The Yellow Bird Huang Ying], which was based on a popular Hong Kong detective series. His latest work was *San Pek Ing Tay: Romantika Emansipasi Seorang Perempuan*, published in 1990. O.K.T. was his most often-used pen-name. However, among his other pen-names are Boe Beng Tjoe and Aulia. It is to be noted that his friend **OEY An Siok** also published some works under the name of

BOE Beng Tjoe. O.K.T. died on 8 March 1995 at the age of ninety-two.

Sources: Letters to the compiler, 19 May 1983; the above-mentioned books.

OEY Kwie Tek. See **DARMAWAN, Hendra**

OEY Liang Lee, Paulus Ignatius (1923–76) 黄良礼*
Economist, university professor

Born in Bogor in 1923, he received a Drs degree from the Netherlands School of Economics (Rotterdam) in Business Economics (1951) and an MBA degree in Business Management from the University of Michigan (1960). In the 1950s(?) he was appointed as a lecturer and in 1966 Professor of Business Economics at the Department of Economics, UGM. From 1960 he served as the chairman of the Department of Business Management, UGM.

He was politically active. In 1954 he was a founding member of Baperki but withdrew from it due to a disagreement with **SIAUW Giok Tjhan**. He later supported the LPKB (1960s). He died in Yogyakarta on 22 December 1976.

His publications include various articles in *Gajah Mada Monthly*: "Efforts made by the Catholic Church in Indonesia Toward Self-Support", *Pulsus 10* (1960), and "The Problem of Inflation in Indonesia", *Basis 1 and 2* (1963).

Sources: Roeder, *Who's Who*, p. 477; Tapingkae, ed., *Selected Scholars*, p. 506; the compiler's notes.

OEY Tiang Tjoei (HUANG Changshui 黄长水**, 1893–1970s)**
Newspaper director, community leader

Born in Jakarta in 1893, he received Dutch education. He was influenced by the concept of Pan-Asianism under the leadership of Japan. Before World War II, he served as the director of *Hong Po* (Jakarta, 1939–42). In 1941 he was arrested by the Dutch for his pro-Japanese activities. He later published a book (*Pangalaman Kita Dalem Pangasingan Garoet-Soekaboemi dan Noesakambangan*) on his experience in exile. During the Japanese Occupation of Indonesia, he was appointed as a member of Tjuo Sangi In (Chuo Sangiin) representing the Chinese of West Java, a member of the BPUPKI, and the president of the HCTH (Jakarta). He was also appointed director of the Malay edition of *Kung Yung Pao*. After Japanese surrender, he was detained by the British for a while. He died in Jakarta in the 1970s.

Sources: Anderson, *Japanese Occupation*, p. 10; Yamin, *Naskah*, pp. 242–43; *Djawa Nenkan* (1973), p. 464; Salmon, *Literature*, p. 278; Peter Post et al., ed., *The Encyclopedia of Indonesia in the Pacific War* (Brill, 2010), p. 567.

OEY Tong Pin (HUANG Dongping 黄东平, 1923–2014)
Writer

Better known in Mandarin as Huang Dongping, he had little formal education. Born in Kotabaru (Kalimantan) in 1923, he went to China when he was a child. During the Sino-Japanese war he and his mother lived in Hong Kong for more than two years. After the death of his mother he returned to Indonesia when he was still a teenager. This time he resided in Java where he later worked as a bookkeeper for various Chinese shops and firms. After the Japanese Occupation of Indonesia, he worked in Kalimantan, also as a bookkeeper. He eventually returned to Java.

A prolific writer, he began his creative writing in the 1950s. Initially writing poems, he later produced fables, essays, and short stories — most of which were published in local Chinese newspapers and Hong Kong/PRC magazines. In the 1970s he published three major works dealing with the story of Chinese migrants in colonial Indonesia: *Qizhouyang Wai* [Southeast Asia 七洲洋外], a novel (Hong Kong, 1973); *Lao Huagong* [老华工 The old Chinese labourer], a screenplay

(Hong Kong, 1974); *Chidao xian shang* [赤道线上 On the equator], a novel, sequel to *Qizhouyang Wai* (Hong Kong, 1979); and its concluding volume: *Lieri Dixia* [烈日底下 Under the Heat of the Sun], and *Duangao Yiji* [Short essays, vol. I] (Singapore, 1984); *Duangao Erji* [Short essays, vol. II] (Singapore, 1993).

After the fall of Soeharto, the Indonesian Chinese clan association of Jin Men decided to publish his entire works *Huang Dongping Wenji* (黄东平文集) in ten volumes. The last volume was published in 2003. He died in Solo on 26 December 2014.

Sources: The above-mentioned books; Huang Dongping, *Haiyang Wenyi*, no. 4 (1980): 68–73; Dong Rui, *Jing Bao*, no. 36 (10 September 1980): 33–34; Huang Dongping, *Xingzhou Ribao*, 21 June 1980; *Xianggang wenxue*, no. 1 (1985), inside cover; Leo Suryadinata, "Oey Tong Pin", in Suryadinata, ed., *Southeast Asian Personalities* (2012), pp. 807–10; the compiler's notes.

OEYHAYDJUN. See **OEI Hai Djoen Tj.**
OH Hong Boen. See **HARSONO, FX**
OH Sien Hong. See **HUSINO, M.H.**

OJONG, Petrus Kanisius (AUWJONG Peng Koen; OUYANG Bingkun 欧阳炳昆, 1920–80)
Journalist, publisher, lawyer, community leader, Catholic

Born in Bukit Tinggi on 25 June 1920, he received his primary education in Payakumbuh and MULO education in Padang (1934–37). After graduation he came to Java to attend the HCK. He graduated in 1940 and became a teacher in Jakarta for four years (1940–44). From 1946 to 1951 he worked for the editorial board of *Keng Po* (Jakarta) and *Star Weekly*. In 1946 he also enrolled at the FHUI where he obtained an Mr degree in 1951.

From 1951 to 1960 he served as the chief editor of *Star Weekly*. After the weekly was banned, he established PT Sakawidya, a printing and publishing firm. In 1963 he participated in publishing *Inti Sari*, a popular monthly magazine.

From 1964 to 1980 he was the general manager of the largest Indonesian daily, *Kompas*. From 1964 to 1968 he was a member of the Partai Katholik central board. From 1967 to 1969 he served as treasurer II of the Newspaper Publishers' Federation. From 1967 to 1980 he was treasurer of Yayasan Indonesia, a foundation which published *Horison*. From 1971 to 1980 he was a member of the Legal Aid Institute, Lembaga Bantuan Hukum, as well as the director of PT Gramedia, a large printing and publishing firm.

He was in favour of the assimilationist movement and was one of the ten Tokoh Asimilasi (1960). He died in Jakarta on 31 May 1980.

His publications include *Perang Pasifik 1941–45* (Jakarta, 1962); *Perkara-Perkara Kriminil Jang Termasjur* (Jakarta, 1962); and *Perang Dunia II* (Jakarta, 1963).

Sources: *Pedoman Kampanje* (1955), p. 43; *Topik*, 17 May 1972, p. 21; *Indonesian Monograph*, p. 6; *Liberal*, 24 September 1955, pp. 3, 8 October 1955, p. 3; Arief, *Indonesian Business*, pp. 408–9; *Kompas*, 1 June 1980.

ONG Ah Lok. See **BONG A Lok**
ONG, Charles. See **HIMAWAN, Charles**

ONG, Charles (1952-) 王查理*
Businessman, lecturer

Born on 20 February 1952 in Semarang, his late father is the director of Nyonya Meneer, a large herbs company in Indonesia founded by Charles Ong's grandmother. He himself at the age of twenty-five served as the marketing director of the same company. He received his education in Jakarta, and later went to the United Kingdom and the United States. In 1979 he received his PhD from Kensington University in California after submitting a dissertation entitled, "Jamu Awet Plays a Very Important Role in Expanding Sales of the Pharmaceutical & Herbs Industry 'Nyonya Meneer'".

Under his leadership, Nyonya Meneer has developed into a large company. The products have been exported to Singapore, Malaysia, Australia, Japan, and the Netherlands. Charles also lectures in various regional universities (Universitas Diponegoro and Universitas 17 Agustus).

Source: *Apa & Siapa 1985–86*, pp. 620–21.

ONG Eng Die (WANG Yongli 王永利, 1910-?)
Political party leader, economist

Born in Gorontalo (Sulawesi) in 1910, he graduated from the Faculty of Economics (Amsterdam University) in 1940, and obtained a PhD in 1943 after successfully defending his dissertation entitled, "Chineezen in Nederlandsch-Indie, een Sociografie van een Indonesische Bevolkingsgroep" (published in 1943). In 1945 he returned to Indonesia and worked at Bank Pusat Indonesia, Yogyakarta. In 1947–48 he served as a deputy finance minister (Menteri Muda Keuangan) in the Amir Sjarifoeddin Cabinet. During the Renville Negotiations he served as an adviser to the Indonesian delegation. In 1950 he established an accounting office. He joined the PNI and in 1955 served as Minister of Finance in the Ali Sastroamidjojo Cabinet. He was residing in the Netherlands.

Sources: Kempen, *K.P.*, p. 24; Ong's dissertation.

ONG Hok Ham (ONGHOKHAM; WANG Fuhan 王福涵, 1933–2007)
Historian, writer, university lecturer

Born into an established *peranakan* Chinese family in Surabaya in 1933, he was immersed in Javanese culture. He obtained a Sarjana Sastra degree in History from the FSUI after submitting a thesis on "Runtuhnja Hindia Belanda: Indonesia Dari 1940-Maret 1942" [The dissolution of the Dutch East Indies: Indonesia from 1940 to March 1942] (1968). In 1968 he went to Yale University to study history and received his PhD in 1975 after successfully defending his dissertation entitled,

"The Residency of Madiun: Priyayi and Peasant in the Nineteenth Century". Since his return from the United States, Ong had published extensively, especially in Indonesian magazines and journals, such as *Tempo* and *Prisma*. He published at least two books: *Negara dan Rakyat* (Jakarta, 1983) and *Runtuhnya Hindia Belanda* (1987). He continued to write until he got a stroke in 2001 when he was confined to a wheelchair. Since then Gramedia published collections of his articles.

While he was a student in Jakarta, he wrote many articles expressing his assimilationist view. He was a signatory of the "Piagam Asimilasi" and later a founder of the LPKB. Nevertheless, unlike most of the assimilationists, he did not change his Chinese name into an Indonesian name. He retired from the Department of History, FSUI (Jakarta). At one time, he was invited to serve as the director of a Buddhist school in Tangerang.

He died in Jakarta on 30 August 2007.

Sources: *Lahirnja Konsepsi Asimilasi*, pp. 22–23; Feith, *Thinking*, p. 477; Koentjaraningrat, ed. (1975), p. 158; interview, 1977; David Reeve, "Ong Hok Ham", in Suryadinata, ed., *Southeast Asian Personalities* (2012), pp. 823–26; the compiler's notes.

ONG Hok Lan (Wang Fulan 王福兰, 1898–1937)
Community leader, physician, father of **Kristoforus SINDHUNATHA**

Born in Banjarmasin on 21 December 1898, he received the ELS (Banjarmasin) and MULO education (Yogyakarta). After obtaining a medical degree from NIAS (Surabaya), he went into private practice in Tegal (1924–27). He was a participant in the 1927 Chung Hwa Congress in Semarang and was critical of the CHH. He later went to the Netherlands for further studies and returned to Java in the early 1930s. While he was a student he was active in a few organizations. He was a founder of Chung Hsioh in Jakarta and an executive member of the CHH-Netherlands. He died in May 1937.

Sources: Tan, *Tionghoa*, pp. 202–3; K.T.H., *Panorama*, 4 June 1927, pp. 5–6; *Sin Po*, 21 May 1937.

ONG Joe San. See **LEMBONG, Eddie**

ONG Liang Kok (WANG Liangguo 王良国)
Political leader, community leader, lawyer

Born in Blitar, he went to the THHT (Kediri), the ELS (Welingi, Blitar), and the HBS (Surabaya) and eventually graduated from the HBS (Bandung) in 1920. While at high school, he was the chairman of Chung Hsioh and the editor of *Orgaan Chung Hsioh*. He continued studying at the RHS (Jakarta) and later at Leiden University (Netherlands) where he was awarded an Mr degree in 1926. In the same year he returned to Indonesia, and joined the CHH in 1928. From September 1932 to February 1933 he served as treasurer of the PTI. In 1933 he had a disagreement with **LIEM Koen Hian** and withdrew from the PTI. In the 1930s he served as a member of the Surabaya Municipal Council and the East Java Provincial Council. Before 1935 he was also legal adviser to the Chinese Consulate in Surabaya.

Sources: *Sin Po*, 11 October 1926; Tan, *Tionghoa*, pp. 49–50; *Sin Tit Po*, 26 September 1932.

ONG Seng Keng. See **HUSNI, Arief**

ONG Siang Tjoen (WANG Xiangchun 王祥春, 1890s-)
Community leader, businessman

Born in the 1890s, he graduated from the HBS (Semarang). He resided in Surabaya, working as a car dealer and engaging in the tobacco industry. In 1942 he served as the president of the HTCH (Surakarta).

Source: *Djawa Nenkan* (1973), p. 465.

ONG Sin King. See **HUSNI, Arief**

ONG Siong Tjie (WANG Shangzhi 王尚志, 1900–92)
Community leader, KMT leader

Born in Jinmen, Fujian in 1900, he came to Jakarta at a young age. He was known as a businessman and was an executive member of the KMT (Jakarta) before World War II. After the war he served as the president of the CHTH (Jakarta), an executive member of Yinni Qiao Lian Zonghui (1950s), and the president of Hok Kian Hwee Koan (Jakarta, 1953–54). He was arrested by the Indonesian Government for his affiliation with the KMT in 1958. After his release he left Indonesia. When Soeharto came to power, Ong returned to Indonesia and continued his pro-KMT activities. He died in Jakarta in 1992.

Sources: *Shangye Nianjian*, p. 334; Zhong, *Yalong*; *Fujian*, p. 30; *Directory of Chinese Names*, p. 104; *Huaqiao dacidian*, pp. 794–95.

ONG Tek Bie. See **ESMARA, Hendra**
ONG Tjin Liong. See **WONGSOSEPUTERA, Jusuf**

ONG Tjoe Kim (WANG Ziqin 王梓琴, 1912–2009)
Prominent businessman

Born in China in 1912, he migrated to Indonesia at the age of fifteen. At the age of sixteen he stopped attending a Chinese school in Java and started working as a salesman, but not in his father's textile shop. At the age of forty-one he succeeded in opening his own shop in Surabaya. He came to Singapore in 1947 as the director of Aurora Ltd., and was with the firm until 1953 when he started his own business. He was the chairman of the Metro Group of Companies in Singapore and a chain of departmental stores in Hong Kong, Malaysia, and Indonesia.

He passed away on 11 August 2009.

Sources: Sharon Loo, "Ong Tjoe Kim", in Suryadinata, ed., *Southeast Asian Personalities* (2012), pp. 850–52; *Straits Times*, 27 May 1977.

ONG Tjong Hai. See **SINDHUNATHA, Kristoforus**
ONG Tjong Hauw. See **RAHMANATA, A.M.**
ONGHOKHAM. See **ONG Hok Ham**
Otje HONORIS. See **HONORIS, Otje**
Oto SUASTIKA. See **SIAUW Tik Kwie**
OU Cuilan. See **AW Tjoei Lan**
OUW Tjoei Lan. See **AW Tjoei Lan**
OUYANG Chunmei. See **SIDHARTA, Myra**

P.L. GOUW. See **GOUW Peng Liang**
PAN Guochang. See **SUPRANA, Jaya**
PAN Jinghe. See **PHOA Keng Hek**
PAN Liangyi. See **PHOA Liong Gie**
PAN Wanxin. See **WISAKSANA, Panji**
Panji WISAKSANA. See **WISAKSANA, Panji**
PANG Lay Kim. See **PANGLAYKIM, Jusuf**
PANGESTU J. See **PANGLAYKIM, Jusuf**

**PANGESTU, Mari Elka (Mari Cecelia PANG Hui Lan;
FENG Huilan 冯慧兰)**
Economist, cabinet minister, daughter of **J. PANGLAYKIM**,
Catholic

Born in 1956 in Jakarta, she received an MA in Economics from the Australian National University (1980) and a PhD in Economics from the University of California, Davis (1986). She was Head of the Department of Economics at the CSIS, and a coordinator of the PECC Trade Policy Forum. She taught at the Faculty of Economics, UI (1986–2004), and at the Graduate School of Management Prasetya Mulya (1990–2004). She was also a consultant for the World Bank and other international organizations. Her areas of specialization are international trade, especially with regard to trade policy and ASEAN, foreign investment, and development economics.

After Soeharto stepped down, qualified Indonesian Chinese began to be appointed to cabinet minister positions. Mari was appointed as Minister of Trade in the President Yudhoyono cabinet between 2004 and 2009, and reappointed by Yudhoyono in 2009 to the same position until October 2011 when she was moved to a newly created position of Ministry of Tourism and Creative Economy.

She has published a few monographs and numerous articles on the above areas: *The Role of the Private Sector in Indonesia: Deregulation and Privatization* (CSIS, November 1990); chapters in *Growth Triangle: The Johor-Singapore-Riau Experience* (ISEAS, 1991), edited by Lee Tsao Yuan; and *Pacific Initiatives for Regional Trade Liberalization and Investment Co-operation: Role and Implications for the Private Sector* (CSIS, 1993), which she edited. She is also a frequent contributor to Indonesian newspapers and journals.

Sources: The above-mentioned books; *Indonesian Quarterly XXI*, no. 4 (1993): 510; *XXII*, no. 4 (1994): 381; Mely G. Tan, "Pangestu, Mari", in Suryadinata, ed., *Southeast Asian Personalities*, pp. 869–71.

PANGESTU, Prajogo (PHANG Djun Phen; PENG Yunpeng 彭云鹏, 1944-)

Tycoon, timber king

Born on 13 May 1944, he was the son of a rubber tapper in Desa Sungai Sambas, Kabupaten Sambas, West Kalimantan. To supplement his income, his father, Phang Sui On, also worked as a tailor at the Sungai Betung market.

Prajogo used to help his father before going to school. After graduating from a local Chinese junior middle school (SMP Nan Hua) in Singkawang, he went to Jakarta to look for a job. Unsuccessful in securing a job, he returned to Kalimantan and worked as a public transport driver between Singkawang and Pontianak. This did not last long. He then began to run a small business with friends — selling shrimp paste and salted fish.

He started getting to know Bong Swan An in the early 1960s. Bong is known as **Burhan URAY**, boss of the Djajanti Group. The Djajanti Group later moved to Banjarmasin. In 1975 Boerhan appointed Prajogo as the general manager of the PT Nusantara Plywood in Surabaya. One year later, Prajogo became independent. He bought the CV Pacific Lumber Company and changed its name to PT Barito Pacific Lumber Company. The company developed rapidly. According to the Anatomy of Indonesian Conglomerates, the Group now has fifty-eight companies. But according to *Forbes Zibenjia* it has 120 companies. He has diversified his business, ranging from lumber, banking (Andromeda Bank), chocolate plantation (PT Lestari Unggul Jaya), paper manufacturing, to petrochemicals.

Prajogo formed a partnership with Mrs Siti Hardianti Rukmana (Mbak Tutut), the eldest daughter of President Soeharto, called PT Tanjung Enim Pulp dan Kertas. In May 1990 Prajogo, **Henry PRIBADI** (Lin Yunhao of the Napan Group), and Bambang Trihatmodjo (second son of Soeharto and the boss of PT Bimantara) established Andromedia Bank. Later, the three of them set up PT Chandra Asri, the largest petrochemical company in Indonesia.

In September 1991, Prajogo and the Kuok brothers of Malaysia jointly established a hotel on Sentosa Island. He also formed a joint company with the Salim Group in Bintan to develop tourism. In the same year he had a joint venture with Taiwan to set up a plywood company in Jiangsu (mainland China). When the Summa Bank of Soeryadjaya was in trouble, Prajogo and other tycoons moved in to take over the bank. Hence he became one of the largest shareholders of the Astra Group, which used to be controlled by **SOERYADJAYA'S** family. Prajogo was one of the richest businessmen who responded to Soeharto's appeal to give away some of his shares to cooperatives. In 1996 he had become one of the top ten billionaires in Indonesia with assets worth US$2.2 billion.

During the 1997–98 financial crisis, Prajogo's companies, with high exposure to foreign debt, were among the worst affected. Andromeda Bank was liquidated in 1997, and Prajogo's companies underwent massive debt restructuring. But he was able to bounce back in 2007, acquiring a majority stake in PT Chandra Asri and in 2008 PT Tri Polyta, thus consolidating his holdings in the petrochemical industry. In 2010, the two companies merged as Chandra Astri Petrochemical with assets worth US$1.5 billion. Prajogo also has a stake in Star Energy. He has become a major player in the petrochemical and energy industries as well as in the timber industry. By the end of 2010, Forbes listed Prajogo as the 40th richest person in Indonesia with assets worth US$455 million.

Sources: *Tempo*, 26 October 1991, pp. 31–32; *FEER*, 12 March 1992, pp. 42–46; *Forbes Zibenjia*, October 1991, p. 67, and June 1995, pp. 82–83; *Shijie Huaren Fuhao Bang*, pp. 208–10; Hui Yew-Foong, "Pangestu, Prajogo", in Suryadinata, ed., *Southeast Asian Personalities*, pp. 871–73.

PANGLAYKIM, Jusuf (J. PANG Lay Kim; Jusuf PANGESTU; FENG Laijin 冯来金, 1922–86)
Banker, economist, former university professor, father of
Mari PANGESTU, *Catholic*

Born in Bandung in 1922, he received his education at Harvard University (where he obtained a certificate in Advanced Management in 1957) and at the FEUI (where he obtained a PhD degree in Economics in 1963). He taught at the FEUI and since 1967 has been appointed Associate Professor of Economics at the FEUI. In the same year (1967) he also served as the director of the Institute of Management, UI. In 1967–68 he was awarded a senior research fellowship by the ANU (Canberra). In 1970 he was made Professor of Economics at Nanyang University and held the position until 1972. From 1972 to 1973 he was appointed Professor of

Business Administration at the University of Singapore. He later returned to Indonesia and went into banking. He was a member of the board of directors, CSIS; the president of PT Sejahtera Bank Umum; the director of PT Pakarti Yoga; and the chairman of various enterprises, including the PT Mutual International Finance Corporation (Jakarta) and PT Lloyd Indonesia. He died in Jakarta in 1986.

His publications include *The Indonesian Economy: Facing a New Era* (Rotterdam, 1966), as co-author; *Indonesia Exports: Performance and Prospects, 1950–70* (Rotterdam, 1967), as co-author; *Indonesia Today: Transition to Economic Development* (Melbourne, 1968); *Persoalan Masa Kini: Perusahaan-perusahaan Multinational* [The problem of today: multinational corporations] (Jakarta, 1974); *Business Relations between Indonesia and Japan* (Jakarta, 1974); *Trends in Marketing* (Jakarta, 1974); *Indonesia's Economic and Business Relations with ASEAN and Japan* (Jakarta, 1977); and *Bisnis Keluarga* (Yogyakarta, 1984).

Sources: Tilman, *Specialists*, pp. 175–76; *Nanyang University Calendar 1970–71*; *CSIS*, pp. 3, 17; the above-mentioned books; the compiler's notes.

PATROS, Asmin (TAI Yun Ming; DAI Yunming 戴运明, 1963-)
Member of DPRD

Born in Dabo Singkep on 13 March 1963, he received a Master's degree in Law from UGM. He was elected as a member of DPRD, Batam City (2009–14) representing Golkar. In 2014 he contested and won the DPRD seat for the Riau Archipelagos, also representing Golkar (2014–19).

Sources: Pengurus Pusat Fordeka, *Buku Acuan 2014*, p. 169; the compiler's notes.

Paul MAWIRA. See TAN Goan Po
PEK Pang Eng. See WONGSOREDJO, mBah

PENG Yunpeng. See **PANGESTU, Prajogo**
Peter SIE. See **SIE, Peter**
Petrus Aang SURYADI. See **SURYADI, Petrus Aang**
Petrus Kanisius OJONG. See **OJONG, Petrus Kanisius**

PHANG Djun Phen. See **PANGESTU, Prajogo**

PHOA Keng Hek (PAN Jinghe 潘景赫, 1857–1937)
Community leader, son of a kapitein, father-in-law of **KHOUW Kim An**

He was born in Bogor in 1857, son of a wealthy *kapitein*. He received his education at a Hokkien school and a Dutch mission school (in Cianjur) where he came to know **LIE Kim Hok**. He later continued his education at the ELS (Bogor). After marrying the daughter of a *luitenant* in Jakarta he settled down in that town and was involved in the agricultural products business. Because of his good command of Dutch, he was able to move in Dutch circles. He was outspoken and became the spokesman of the local Chinese community. In 1900 he and other ethnic-conscious *peranakan* formed the THHK, the first pan-Chinese association in Indonesia, and he served as its president up to 1923. He was critical of Dutch discriminatory policies against the Chinese and published articles in *Perniagan* on this matter using Hoa Djin (huaren means "Chinese person") as his pen-name (1900s). In 1904 he leased a piece of private land in Bekasi (West Java) and managed to ban gambling in that area. He was knighted by the Netherlands Crown in 1937 a short while before he died in Jakarta.

Sources: Kwee Tek Hoay, *Moestika Romans* 7, no. 80 (August 1936): 776–78, 9, no. 98 (February 1938): 85–88; Phoa Kian Sioe, *Mingguan Sadar* VIII, no. 20 (19 August 1956): 40–45; Nio, *THHK*, plate 1.

PHOA Kok Tjiang. See **SUPRANA, Jaya**

PHOA Liong Gie (PAN Liangyi 潘良义, 1904-?)
Community leader, journalist, lawyer

Born in Bandung on 4 June 1904, he was educated at the ELS (Garut), the HBS (Jakarta), the RHS (Jakarta), and Leiden University where he obtained an Mr degree in 1925. In 1926–27 he was the editor of the *CHHTC*. In 1927 he returned to Bandung to work for a Dutch lawyer. One year later he moved to Jakarta and opened his own office. In 1930 he bought *Siang Po* and served as the director of that daily newspaper. He also joined the CHH and emerged as one of its national leaders. In 1934 he came into conflict with **KAN Hok Hoei**, resulting in his departure from the CHH. In 1939 he was appointed as a member of the Volksraad. He later migrated to Switzerland.

Sources: *CHHTC* (October–November 1926, December 1927), title page; Tan, *Tionghoa*, pp. 204–5; Suryadinata, *Peranakan Politics*, pp. 90–91; Zhang, "Yinni Huaqiao", p. 81.

Pita KALIANA. See OEY An Siok

POEY Kok Gwan (1886–1964) 方国源*
Community leader, journalist

Born in Bandung on 18 December 1886, he took private lessons from a Hokkien teacher and became a local expert on Confucianism. In 1923 he established Khong Kauw Tjong Hwee in Bandung and served as its president. He also served as the director of *Sin Bin*, Bandung (1925), a member of the Bandung Regency Council, and the president of Siang Hwee (Bandung) (in the 1930s?). He died in Bandung on 3 May 1964.

Sources: *Officieel Verslag dari Conferentie Khong Kauw Tjong Hwee* (1924), pp. 4–5; Tan, *Tionghoa*, p. 180; Tio's notes.

POO, Murdaya Widyawimarta (POO Tjie Guan; FU Zhikuan 傅志宽, 1941-)
Businessman, politician, community leader, husband of
Siti Hartati MURDAYA

Born on 12 January 1941, Blitar, Poo received his secondary school education at Malang Zhongxue (Malang). After graduation he went to study Economics at UI from which he received a bachelor (S-1) degree in 1966.

He has been successful in business. He is the owner of Berca Retail Group and the founder and owner of the PT Central Cipta Murdaya Group since 1970. He is also the owner of a hospital, Rumah Sakit Yayasan Paramita. Poo and his wife were listed number 16 among the richest Indonesians on the Forbes 2006 list with a net worth of US$430 million.

After the fall of Soeharto, Poo joined the PDI-P and contested in the 2004 DPR elections on the PDI-P ticket and got elected. He served as the chairman of the Field of Funds and Sources of the PDI-P Central Board from 2005–10. He also contested the 2009 election on the PDI-D ticket, again he got elected, but only stayed until February 2010 as he was expelled from the party for his close association with President Susilo Bambang Yudhoyono of the Partai Demokrat. Poo did not support Megawati, who was from his PDI-P party, during the 2009 presidential election. His vacant parliamentary seat was filled by Ichsan Soelistio. When Poo was still in DPR, he was chairman of a committee on the citizenship law which resulted in the emergence of the new Indonesian citizenship law. In 2014, Poo was also accredited for his intermediate role between the Chinese group and President Yudhoyono on the promulgation of the Keppres no. 12 (2014) which nullified the Cabinet Presidium Circular no. 6 (1967) that introduced the derogatory term *Cina* (*Tjina*) for China and the Chinese.

Poo has been the honorary chairman of the Indonesian Chinese Businessman Association (Perhimpunan Pengusaha Indonesia Tionghoa); a member of the Advisory Council of Kadin (Kamar Dagang dan Industri Indonesia); adviser to the Indonesian Hakka Association (Keshu lianyi hui), and a member of Honorary Council, Perwakilan Umat Buddha Indonesia (Walubi).

Sources: *Wajah DPR & DPD 2009–14: Latar Belakang Pendidikan dan Karier* (Jakarta: Penerbit Buku Kompas, 2010), p. 313; Li Zhuohui 李卓辉,《印华参政与国家建设》(雅加达: 联通, 2007), pp. 195–96; <http://us.politik.news.viva.co.id/news/read/110827-murdaya_poo_dipecat_karena-tak...> (accessed 28 March 2014); Leo Suryadinata, "An end to discrimination for China and the Chinese in Indoneisia?" *ISEAS Perspective*, no. 26 (25 April 2014).

POO Tjie Guan. See POO, Murdaya Widyawimarta

POUW Kioe An (SASTRADJAJA, pen-name: ROMO; BAO Qiu'an 包求安, 1906–81)
Journalist, writer

Son of a rice-mill owner, he was born in Cianjur on 3 January 1906. After leaving the ELS (Cianjur), he worked for *Perniagaan* in 1923 and later for *Lay Po* (Bandung), a newspaper edited by **TIO Ie Soei**. In 1925 he went to Semarang to join *Warna Warta* but did not stay long. He then moved to Surabaya and served on the editorial board of *Soeara Publiek* and later of *Pewarta Surabaya* (daily) for six years. In 1933 he served as an editor of *Sin Tit Po*. In 1935 he established his own bi-weekly, *Terang* (Semarang). In March 1937 he was appointed as the editor-in-chief of *Djawa Tengah*, a position he held until June 1937.

After World War II he joined the editorial board of a short-lived daily, *Sedar* (Jakarta, 1949). From the early 1950s to 1966(?) he served as the editor-in-chief and later, deputy editor-in-chief, of the *Malang Post*. Since September 1953 he regularly contributed articles to *Liberty* (known as *Liberal* before 1959, a Surabaya weekly).

Pouw was active in the local community. He served as the *jiko* (vice-chairman) of Ang Hien Hoo-Malang, a mutual help social organization for *peranakan* Chinese. His publications include *Katja Rasa (oleh Romo)* (Tasikmalaja, 1934); *Boeat Apa Hidoep* (Malang, 1937); *O, Prempoean!* (Malang, 1937); *Karma ...?* (Malang, 1938); *Api Jang Tidak Bisa Dibikin Padam* (Malang, 1946); *198 Hari Dalam Kungkungan Kempeitai* (Malang, 1946); *Siapa Kuat dan Siapa Lemah* (Semarang, 1965); *Panca Yoga (oleh Sastradjaja)* (Semarang, 1972); *Pikiran Berkuasa* (Semarang, 1974), as editor; *Horoscoop Umum* (Semarang, 1976); and a number of novels published in *Tjerita Romans* (before World War II). He died in Malang on 25 March 1981.

Sources: Tan, *Tionghoa*, pp. 140–41; *Djawa Tengah*, 6 March 1937, 28 June 1937; *Sinar* (Jakarta) I, no. 6 (15 June 1949): 8; *Ekspres*, 29 August 1970, p. 4; Letter to the compiler, 1976; *Kompas*, 27 March 1981.

PRAWIROHUSODO (YAP Kie Tiong; YE Jizhong 叶基忠, 1915–69)
Physician, son of **YAP Hong Tjoen**

Born in Leiden (Netherlands) on 18 March 1915, he received his education at the ELS (Yogyakarta), the HBS (Semarang), and the Medical School (Jakarta). He later continued his studies at the University of Utrecht from which he obtained a doctorate in Medicine, specializing in eye diseases (1948). He had contributed numerous articles to various academic journals. In 1942–46 he served as his father's assistant at "Dr Yap Hospital" in Yogyakarta. In 1949 he headed the hospital. In 1957–59 he was appointed assistant head of the Eye Disease Section of the University of Utrecht. In August 1960 Yap was appointed the Indonesian Government's First-Class Doctor. He committed suicide in Yogyakarta on 10 January 1969.

Source: *Sinar Harapan*, 13 January 1969.

PRIBADI, Henry (LIN Yunhao 林运豪, 1948?-)
Developer, banker, cousin of **Djuhar SUTANTO**

Born in Malang in 1948(?), he was educated at a local Chinese school (Malang Chinese School?). Initially he worked in the cement factory founded by **LIEM Sioe Liong** and **Djuhar SUTANTO** (Lin Wenjing). Later he became independent and established Arga Karya Prima Industry and Branta Mulia. He eventually established the Napan Group, of which he is the president.

According to *Forbes Zibenjia*, he worked closely with **Prajogo PANGESTU** and Bambang Trihatmodjo (President Soeharto's son), as evidenced in the establishment of the PT Chandra Astri, the largest petrochemical company in Indonesia, if not in Southeast Asia.

PT Tri Polyta, a company under the Napan Group, has been listed on the New York stock exchange. Pribadi has also cooperated with Thai Chinese merchants, Xu Zenan and Li Shicheng, to establish a company in Bangkok.

Sources: *Shijie Huaren Fuhao Bang* (1994), p. 219; the compiler's notes.

PURNAMA, Basuki Tjahaja. See **TJAHAJA PURNAMA, Basuki**

PURNOMO, Nurdin (GO Nen Pin; WU Nengbin 吴能彬, 1948-)
Political party leader, community leader

Nurdin Purnomo was born in Jakarta on 15 August 1948 into a Hakka family. He went to a Chinese school (Pah Tsung), also in Jakarta. After the school was closed down in early 1966, he went to Hong Kong to attend St. Stephen's College. After returning from Hong Kong he began to engage in travel business. In 1976 he purchased the First Setia Diamond Travel Servive Ltd. and developed it into a large travel service company.

In 1998 following the fall of Soeharto, he and his friends set up the Partai Bhinneka Tunggal Ika Indonesia (PBI) and he served as its president. The party contested the 1999

Indonesian parliamentary election and gained one parliamentary seat won by **Sutanto L.T.** (Lin Guanyu). Later there was a crisis within the PBI, those who disagreed with him formed PBI-Perjuangan. Due to internal struggle, both PBI and PBI-Perjuangan were unable to contest the 2004 election as both sides did not meet the election requirements.

It was reported that Purnomo also established a Chinese daily called *Heping Ribao* (和平日报) when Chinese newspapers were allowed to be published after the end of the New Order. But the paper did not last. Purnomo also set up the Indonesian General Association of Hakkas (印尼客属总会) and later, the ASEAN General Association of Hakkas.

Sources: Zhou Nanjing, *Huaqiao huaren baike quanshu* (2001), p. 538; *Chinese Consumer Directory & Lifestyle Indonesia*, p. 273; Luo Yingxiang 罗英祥, *Yindunixiya de kejia*《印度尼西亚的客家》(广西师范大学, 2011), p. 276; Zhang Yonghe 张永和, *Qiandao zaoxia* 千岛朝霞 (Jakarta, 2002), p. 99.

QIU Chengshao. See **KOSASIH, Tirtawinata**
QIU Hanxing. See **QIU Zheng'ou**
QIU Qingde. See **KHOE Tjeng Tek**
QIU Siqian. See **SASANASURYA**
QIU Wenxiu. See **KHOE Woen Sioe**
QIU Yafan. See **KHOE A Fan**
QIU Yuanrong. See **HIOE Njan Joeng**

QIU Zheng'ou (丘正欧; CH'IU Han-hsing; QIU Hanxing 丘汉兴, 1904–2001)
Newspaperman, community leader

Born in Guangdong in 1904, he graduated from Peking University before World War II. He migrated to Indonesia after the establishment of the PRC. In 1950 he served as the editor-in-chief of *Tiansheng Ribao*, a KMT daily in Jakarta. In 1957–58 he was also acting principal of Zhongshan Zhongxue (Jakarta) and dean of the Faculty of Arts (Humanities) of Gamaliel University (Jakarta). He was detained by the Indonesian authorities in 1958 for his affiliation with the KMT and was released in 1959. He lived in Taipei. One of his books is entitled, *Hua-ch'iao Wen-t'i Yen-chiu* [Studies of Overseas Chinese problems] (Taipei, 1965).

Sources: Interview with Hioe Njan Joeng, 1969; Ma, *Bian yu Luan*, p. 82; Liao, "Shehui Shi", p. 93; Chung, *HCTYN*, p. 62; Li Zhuohui, *Xiezuo jingying fendou fengyu rensheng* (2010), pp. 38–42.

Rachman HAKIM. See **HAKIM, Rachman**
Rachman HALIM. See **HALIM, Rachman**

RAHARDJA, Hendra (TAN Tjoe Hien; CHEN Zixing 陈子兴, 1943–2003)
Businessman, brother of **Eddy TANSIL**

He was born in 1943 in Ujungpandang (Sulawesi) where his father was a motorcycle dealer. He came to Jakarta in the 1950s to attend a Chinese school. When Chinese schools were closed in the mid-1960s, he started selling motorcycles with financial help from his family and friends. He first sold Vespa scooters and other brands of motorcycles. Only in 1966 did he begin to sell Yamaha motorcycles. He later became known as the "Yamaha King". Initially he imported the motorcycles, later 60 per cent of the components were made locally, his target was to manufacture the entire motorcycle in Indonesia.

Rahardja sold about 100,000 units per year and made S$25 million annually. He also obtained the Dutsun Forklift franchise for Indonesia. With money pouring in, Rahardja began to diversify his business. He formed the Harapan Group and in 1974 began to move into real estate. He owned several big plazas in Jakarta and a few small banks in Medan and Surabaya.

In 1980 the Harapan Group moved into Hong Kong and established the Unistock Financial Company. Earlier (1977) he established the Town & City Properties Ltd. in Singapore and invested heavily in the hotel business. It was reported that he invested 1,600 million dollars in the Lion City. His concentration in building major hotels earned him the title of "Hotel King". Nevertheless, recession and the oversupply of hotels in Singapore caused some difficulties with his project. *Insight* reported that his close indigenous associates were Generals Sudjono Humardani and Ali Murtopo, personal assistants of President Soeharto, and General Sumitro.

He eventually completed building three hotels. However, these hotels were later sold to clear his debts. In 1987 he returned to Indonesia and moved into the property business, from which he made a lot of money. Within a few years his Harapan Group revived. The Group also had three banks — Bank Harapan Santosa, Bank Guna, and Bank Sake — with 250 branches all over Indonesia.

Like many wealthy *totok* Chinese, in recent years he invested in China. In 1993 he built both an airport and a commercial complex in Fuzhou, Fujian. However, Rahardja was involved in illegal transcations with the Central Bank of Indonesia involving a large sum of money and refused to return to Indonesia. He was brought to court and sentenced to life imprisonment in absentee. Rahardja left Hong Kong for Australia and was detained by the Australian immigration. Nevertheless, he refused to be deported to Indonesia and died in prison in Sydney on 26 January 2003.

Sources: Steidtmann and Waworuntu, July 1982, pp. 6–12; Huang Shuling (1984), pp. 15–17; Lee, *Straits Times*, 26 March 1984; *Apa & Siapa 1985–86*, pp. 661–63; *Forbes Zibenjia*, July 1994, pp. 29–30; Jamie Mackie, "Rahardja, Hendra", in Suryadinata, ed., *Southeast Asian Personalities* (2012), pp. 919–20.

RAHARDJA, Subur (LIM Sin Tjoei, 1919–86) 林新水*
Kungfu instructor

Born in Indonesia in 1919 (another source says that he was born on 4 April 1925), he began to learn *kungfu* from the age of six, initially from his father and later from various famous martial arts teachers, including a Javanese. On 25 December 1952 he established the Persatuan Gerak Badan Bangau Putih (White Crane Martial Arts Association), a *kungfu* school in Bogor. In the early 1980s the association had over 5,000 members and had branches not only in Indonesia but also in the United States, West Germany, Australia, and England. Many leading Indonesian personalities such as Adnan Buyung Nasution (lawyer), W.S. Rendra (poet and playwright), and Hardi (artist) were registered as his students. According to *Tempo*, many intellectuals joined his group to learn not only *kungfu* but also philosophy and sometimes also for medical treatment. He also had many American students in his Bogor school. Subur Rahardjo, who received MULO education, was fluent in English and Dutch. He died in a car accident on 1 January 1986.

Sources: "Sang Bangau Ke Mana-mana", *Tempo*, 6 June 1981, pp. 20–21, 18 January 1987, p. 17.

RAHMANATA, A.M. (ONG Tjong Hauw, 1926-) 王宗孝*
Leader of the assimilationist movement, lawyer

Born in Banjarmasin on 17 November 1926, he obtained an Mr degree from Leiden University in 1954. He returned to Indonesia and joined Baperki in 1954 but withdrew from the organization in 1957. He later became a leader of the LPKB and in 1965–67 served as the chairman of that organization's Banjarmasin branch. Since 1958 he has been appointed as a lecturer in law at Lambung Mangkurat University (Banjarmasin).

Source: The compiler's notes.

Rama Moorti van Java. See **TAN Tik Sioe Sian**
RAO Boji. See **DJIAUW Pok Kie**

RAO Jian (饶简, 1894–1976)
Community leader, KMT activist

Born in Meixian, Guangdong, in 1894, he first received traditional Chinese school education. He went to Penang to study, later returned to China and joined the KMT. When his father-in-law in Indonesia fell ill, he went to Indonesia and stayed there. In 1928 he established *Mianlan Xin Zhonghua bao* (棉兰新中华报) and also set up a KMT branch in Medan to recruit KMT members. He was later invited to Meixian by the local government to take charge of education and finance matters for six months but eventually returned to Sumatra. He served as the president of the Chinese Chamber of Commerce in Medan. He was also a founder of Sudong Zhongxue in Medan (苏东中学), the largest Chinese high school in Sumatra. He died in 1976.

Source: *Huaqiao Da Cidian*, pp. 965–66.

RAO Yaowu. See **ADMADJAJA, Usman**

RIADY, James Tjahaja (LI Bai 李白, 1957-)
Banker, Christian, son of **Mochtar RIADY**

He was born in 1957 in Jakarta. After graduating from Melbourne University (in Accountancy and Economics), he became a trainee in the Irving Trust and Investment Bank in the United

States. In 1979 he returned to Jakarta and helped his father at the BCA. Later he was asked to take over PT Basuki Indah (manufacturer of TVs) and was successful in revitalizing the company. He then took over PT Multi Polar, which produced, among other things, video games, which had a large market in the United States and Europe. The decline of the video game industry as a result of Indonesia's regulations caused James Riady to move into Bank Perniagaan Indonesia (BPI), the backbone of the Lippo Group, a grouping of various companies, led by his father **Mochtar RIADY** (Li Wenzheng). Total assets of the BPI amounted to 100 billion rupiah in 1983, and it had three branches and 550 employees.

In 1984 James Riady moved to the United States and became the president of Worthen Bank of Arkasas. He also became close friends with Bill Clinton and his wife Hilary Clinton. In fact, James had known Bill Clinton since he was doing an internship at Little Rock, when Bill Clinton was the state-attorney general of Arkansas. Moreover, when James was the president of the Worthen Bank, Hilary served as the bank attorney. Bill Clinton became the president of the United States in 1993 and James and his father were invited to attend the inauguration ceremony. James continued the close relationship and he even contributed to the Democratic Party for the 1996 US presidential elections which was later found to be unlawful.

In fact, James had returned from the US in 1987 and became the chief executive officer of the Lippo Group. When Soeharto stepped down and anti-Chinese riots were rampant, many Chinese business people moved their capital overseas, but the Lippo group remained. President B.J. Habibie appointed him as "business ambassador" to win back foreign capital and gave Lippo Bank the first call in recapalization funds in 1999. James was able to bring the Lippo Group to a comeback from the verge of collapse in the beginning of 2000.

Sources: "James T. Riady", *Eksekutif*, January 1984, pp. 18–24; *Apa dan Siapa 1985–1986*, pp. 713–14; Hoon Chang Yau, "Riady, James Tjahaja", in Suryadinata, ed., *Southeast Asian Personalities*, pp. 923–25.

RIADY, Mochtar (LIE Mo Tie; LI Wenzheng 李文正, 1929-)
Banker, tycoon, father of **James RIADY**, *Christian*

Born in East Java in 1929, he received Chinese education, first in Java and later in China. During his student days in Java, he joined the anti-colonial movement under the leadership of Major Imam Soekardjo. In those days he was often sent to Surabaya to get medical supplies and other materials for Indonesian guerrillas. Riady was then the president of the East Java Overseas Chinese Students Association and often participated in anti-Dutch demonstrations. He was arrested and jailed together with other friends. In 1947 he was deported to China, and there he entered the University of Nanking. Before the communist takeover he fled to Hong Kong and only returned to Indonesia in 1950 with the assistance of Soekardjo.

Between 1950 and 1960 he was involved in various kinds of businesses. Initially he worked in a provision shop, then he ran an import firm together with his Surabaya friends. Later he moved into the shipping business and became a shipping agent. In 1960 he was able to join a small bank, and that marked the start of his banking career. He was able to revitalize a few small banks and in 1975 succeeded in fusing three small banks into the Pan-Indonesian Bank or Panin Bank.

A decade after **LIEM Sioe Liong** had bought the Bank Central Asia (BCA), he invited Riady to join him. Riady was offered 17.5 per cent (one source says 19.8 per cent) of the shares in the BCA. Although not a major shareholder, Riady was given executive and management power. He was chief executive director of BCA (Jakarta), vice-chairman of Central Asia Capital Corp. Ltd. (Hong Kong), and director of Bank Buana Indonesia (Jakarta).

In 1990, Riady exchanged his BCA shares with Liem Sioe Liong for his shares in the Lippo Group. As a result Liem became the largest shareholder in the BCA while the Riady family controlled the Lippo Group. The Lippo Group focused its development on property and finance. It established the Lippo City and Lippo Village in Jakarta. It has also transformed itself into a multinational corporation. One of the largest bases outside Indonesia was Hong Kong and later Singapore, which were manned by his son Stephen Riady (Li Zong), while his other son, **James RIADY** (Li Bai), was in charge of the Indonesian operation.

Mochtar Riady is not only seen as a financial magnate but also a visionary. As the founder and chairman of the Lippo Group he has been able to develop his educational institutions. Apart from the Christian University Pelita Harapan and Ma Chung University, he also donated generously to Singapore tertiary education. He has also authored at least three books: *Mencari Peluang di tengah Krisis* [Searching for opportunities amidst crisis] (1999), *Nanotechnology Management Style* (2004), and *Filsafat Kuno dan Manajemen Modern* [Ancient philosophy and modern management] (2006).

Sources: *Eksekutif*, February 1982, pp. 8–14, January 1984, pp. 18–24; *Apa & Siapa 1983–84*, pp. 684–86; *Forbes Zibenjia*, July 1994, p. 25; Hoon Chang Yao, "Riady, Mochtar", in Suryadinata, ed., *Southeast Asian Personalities*, pp. 926–27.

RIDWAN, Ignatius (OEI Tjo Iem, 1941-) 黃佐音*
Community leader, political party leader

Born in Yogyakarta on 26 February 1941, he obtained an SH degree from UNDIP (Semarang) in 1966. In 1967 he served as the secretary of the LPKB (Central Java) before its dissolution. In 1969 he was elected as the secretary of Partai Katholik (Central Java Section). Presently he practises law in Semarang.

Source: The compiler's notes.

Robby TJAHJADI. See TJAHJADI, Robby
Robert Budi HARTONO. See HARTONO, Robert Budi
ROMANO. See LIEM Khing Hoo
ROMO. See SASTRADJAJA
Roumi'ou ZHENG. See ZHENG, Roumi'ou
Rudianto TJEN. See TJEN, Rudianto
Rudy GUNAWAN. See GUNAWAN, Rudy
Rudy Hartono. See KURNIAWAN, Rudy Hartono

SADELI, Eddy (LI Xiangsheng 李祥胜, 1940-)
Community leader, member of parliament, lawyer

Born in 1940 in Jakarta, he graduated from FIS, UI in 1964. He later studied law and graduated from the FH (Faculty of Law), UI in 1985. He was active in the student movement. Between 1964 and 1967, he was secretary-general of Gerakan Mahasiswa 45, and about the same time, he also worked as a reporter for *Majalah Perekonomian Nasional* in Jakarta. After receiving a law degree he set up a law firm.

He has been outspoken against anti-Chinese laws and regulations in Indonesia. In 1998 he founded the legal section in the PSMTI and served as its legal expert. He later joined Partai Demokrat, contested the 2009 election, and got elected as a member of parliament (2009–14). In 2014 he contested in the DPD election but failed to be elected.

He has been interested in Indonesian Chinese affairs and has published a few books on the subject. He edited a book entitled: *Kewarganegaraan Republik Indonesia berikut peraturan pelaksanaannya* (Jakarta: LPPTM-TI, 2006).

Sources: *Wajah DPR & DPD 2009–14*, p. 43; *Jiechu renwu minglu*, p. 280; the compiler's notes.

SALEH, Mohamad. See KO Kwat Tiong

SALIM, Anthony (LIEM Fung Sen; LIN Fengsheng 林逢生, 1949-)
Tycoon, entrepreneur, third son of **Soedono SALIM**

Born in 1949 (according to *Tempo*, 1950) in Jakarta, he was educated at Sin Hwa, a Chinese primary and junior high school in his birthplace. He also received high school education in Singapore before going to a college in London for two years. Upon graduation in 1971, he returned to Jakarta to help his father in his business.

It appears that Salim senior had quietly selected Anthony as the successor of his business empire. The 1970s were learning years for Anthony. Under the tutelage of his father, he became familiar with the Indonesian business world. However, due to his overseas education he also started expanding the Salim Group business overseas. He helped set up the First Pacific of Hong Kong as the Salim Group overseas business base, the company which also invested in mainland China and other countries.

In the 1980s, Anthony was responsible for the expansion of the Indofood under the Salim Group. He was also involved in the public offering of the PT Indocement Tunggal Prakarsa, another major company under the Salim Group. This public offering upset many businessmen because the company got a waiver of the Finance Ministry rule in order to sell shares.

The Salim group was seriously affected by the 1997 financial crisis. The collapse of rupiah resulted in banking crisis and the BCA, the pillar of the Salm Group, left Salim saddled with more than US$5 billion in debt. The situation became worse after Soeharto stepped down as many of Salim's enemies want to destroy the Salim Group. Salim senior was ill and Anthony was the one who negotiated with the authorities. To settle the debt, Anthony gave stakes in 108 companies to the government, which sold them. He managed to save the Indofood but lost two of the Salim Group's pillars: BCA and Indocement. He shifted the majority ownership of Indofood to First Pacific of Hong Kong, in which Anthony was the biggest shareholder. In 2004, he became the Indofood president-director. In the same year, he also received a "release and discharge" document saying that he had met his obligations. He went on to rebuild the Salim Group, which is now under his full control. He has been able to expand his business to China and the Philippines again. In 2013 he was listed by Forbes as the third richest Indonesian with a net worth of US$6.3 billion.

During the New Order period, Anthony was chairman of the Budget and Treasury Department of Kadin (Indonesian Chamber of Industry and Commerce). Between 1987 and 1993, he was appointed as a member of the MPR.

Sources: *Jakarta Program Magazine*, July 1994, p. 65; *Forbes Zibenjia*, July 1994, p. 21; *Apa & Siapa 1985–86*, pp. 765–66; Richard Borsuk and Nancy Chng, "Salim, Anthony", in Suryadinata, ed., *Southeast Asian Personalities*, pp. 933–35.

SALIM, Soedono (LIEM Sioe Liong; LIN Shaoliang 林绍良, 1916–2012)

*Tycoon, entrepreneur, Hokchia, father of **Anthony SALIM***

Born in 1917 (1916?) in Fuqing, Fujian, he was the second son of a small farmer. After receiving a traditional Chinese education, at the age of sixteen he operated a noodle shop in his village. When the Chinese civil war broke out, many of his fellow villagers left China for Southeast Asia. In 1925 his eldest brother, Liem Sioe Hie, and his brother-in-law, Zheng Xusheng, went to Indonesia to do business. In 1936 Liem Sioe Liong joined them. He first lived in Kudus (Central Java) helping his brother in his clove and peanut oil trading business. During the 1945–49 period he came into contact with members of the Indonesian Army, who were still fighting for independence. He supplied the Indonesian Armed Forces with medical supplies. According to an English source, he also supplied the Republican Army with arms, but Liem strongly denied this allegation.

In 1952 he left Kudus for Jakarta and began to expand his business. His brother, Liem Sioe Hie, remained in Kudus. In Jakarta, Liem succeeded in establishing relations with Chinese businessmen in Singapore and Hong Kong. This helped his newly established import-export business. He also set up a soap factory, and using his connections, was able to become a supplier of soap to the armed forces. During this early Jakarta period, he moved into textiles (Muliatex in Kudus and Tarumatex in Bandung) and banking (PT Bank Windu Kencana and Bank Central Asia). The Bank Central Asia (BCA) later became the largest private bank in Indonesia, with Soeharto's children, elder daughter Tutut and eldest son Sigit, owning 30 per cent equity in the bank.

Nevertheless, his business really became successful only after the New Order came to power. In 1968 his PT Mega together with another firm, PT Mercu Buana, received the monopoly right on clove importation. In the following year, he together with another Hokchia businessman established PT Bogasari Flour Mill, which later developed into the largest flour producer in Indonesia. These two companies provided him with the capital to establish his giant cement company (Indocement) in 1973.

Liem's own major company was PT Salim Economic Development Corporation. His third son, London-trained **Anthony SALIM**, was the executive director of this company. Like most other major entrepreneurs, Liem did not confine his business to Indonesia. He set up companies in Singapore and Hong Kong. The headquarters of his company was still in Jakarta, but Hong Kong had been used for investment purposes. This was partly due to Indonesian regulations which did not allow a company to make direct investments overseas. In 1982 he bought Shanghai Land (established in 1888) which was transformed into the First Pacific Holding. It was through this First Pacific Holding that the Liem Group invested in the United States and the PRC. The first Pacific Holding acquired Hibernia Bancshares Corporation, a small bank in San Francisco (United States) and a well-known Dutch company, N.V. Hagemayer (Netherlands). It was also in Hong Kong that Liem's company was able to sign a contract of US$552 million for the PT Cold Rolling Mill, Indonesia.

Liem's acquaintance with President Soeharto had facilitated his phenomenal expansion. He had acknowledged that he had known President Soeharto since the 1950s, but had denied that this connection has helped his ventures.

In the 1980s, like many other Chinese businesses, Liem's various companies were owned by his family and Chinese partners. Even his senior staff members were "still mainly non-indigenous (that is, Chinese) but the middle management and below are staffed by both ethnic Chinese and indigenous Indonesians at the 50–50 ratio". It is also worth noting that Liem had business connections with ethnic Chinese businessmen outside Indonesia, for instance, the owner of the Bangkok Bank. In Indonesia, apart from Soeharto's family, his major Chinese partner was **DJUHAR Sutanto** (Liem Oen Kian). However, Liem began to retreat to the background in the 1990s and **Anthony SALIM** was the one who takes over the leadership from him.

Liem died on 10 June 2012 in Singapore and was buried at the Choa Chu Kang Chinese cemetery, Singapore.

Sources: Richard Borsuk and Nancy Chng, "Salim, Anthony", in Suryadinata, ed., *Southeast Asian Personalities* (2012), pp. 935–38;

Verchere, *Insight*, May 1978, pp. 8–16; Rowley, *FEER*, 7 April 1983, pp. 44–56; *Tempo*, 31 March 1984, pp. 66–72; *Swasembada*, August 1985, p. 68; Lin Shaokang (1985), p. 53; *Shijie Huaren Fuhao Bang*, pp. 204–6; Richard Borsuk and Nancy Chng, "Salim, Soedono", in Suryadinata, ed., *Southeast Asian Personalities*, pp. 935–39.

SAMPOERNA, Putera (LIEM Tien Pao; LIN Tianbao 林天宝, 1947-)
Wealthy businessman, grandson of **LIEM Seng Tee**

Born in 1947 in Schiedam (Holland), he attended school in Hong Kong and Australia, and later went to the United States to receive his university education. His grandfather is Liem Seng Tee, a clove cigarette king. Seng Tee passed on his business to his son Aga Sampoerna. In 1980 Aga passed the business to Putera, who became the general chairman of PT Hanjaya Mandala Sampoerna, the manufacturer of the fourth largest clove cigarette producer (Djie Sam Soe and Sampoerna) in Indonesia. Apart from clove cigarette, it also moved into the printing and transport business.

Source: *Forbes Zibenjia*, July 1994, p. 28.

SANJAYA, Christiandy (BONG Hong San; HUANG Hanshan 黄汉山, 1964-)
Deputy governor, Protestant

Born on 29 March 1964 in Singkawang, he was elected deputy governor of West Kalimantan between 2008–13. The governor was Cornelis M.H., an indigenous Indonesian.

In September 2011, Sanjaya who is a university graduate, joined the Partai Demokrat of President Susilo Bambang Yudhoyono. Four months later, he was appointed as head of the Assessment Council of DPD Partai Demokrat West Kalimantan Branch. Sanjaya was a teacher before getting involved in politics.

Sources: <http://id.wikipedia.org/wiki/Chrisandy_Sanjaya> (accessed 30 June 2014); the compiler's notes.

SASANASURYA (KHOE Soe Kiam; QIU Siqian 丘思谦, 1915-)
Religious leader, community leader, social geographer, Tridharma

Born in Semarang on 18 August 1915, he graduated from the HBS (Semarang) in 1935. After World War II he studied at Amsterdam Gemeente Universiteit (1946–52) where he obtained a Drs degree in Social Geography. In 1953 he returned to Indonesia and taught at a normal school in Jakarta. From 1953 to 1960(?) he was appointed as a regular lecturer (*dosen tetap*) at the IKIP (Jakarta).

Khoe has also been active in the Chinese community. He was a founder of Sin Ming Hui and served as its vice-president from 1953 to 1955 and its president from 1955 to 1956. He was especially active in the *peranakan* religious movement. In 1953 he was elected as the president of Sam Kauw Hwee (or Gabungan Tridharma after the 1965 coup) and continued to hold the position until 1970.

His publications include various articles published in *Tri Budaja* (journal of Sam Kauw Hwee) and *Sendi-Sendi Sosiologi: Ilmu Masjarakat* (Jakarta, 1963).

Sources: Interview, 1970; *SMH 10 Tahun*, pp. 9, 24.

SASTRADJAJA. See **POUW Kioe An**

SATJADININGRAT, TKP (TAN King Po, 1915–69) 陈庆宝*
Physician

Born in Yogyakarta on 1 October 1915, he received a medical degree from Leiden University(?). From 1958 to 1969 he served as a physician in the Indonesian Army, Siliwangi division, and was awarded medals for his service. In the 1950s he was the deputy director of Jang Seng Ie (Jakarta), and in the 1960s he was a lecturer at the UKRIDA (Jakarta). He died in Jakarta on 17 September 1969.

Source: *Sinar Harapan*, 29–30 September 1969.

SATYAWARDAYA, Anang. See **TJOA Tjie Liang**

SETIABUDI, Natan (TAN Tiong Ien, 1940-) 陈忠延*
Religious leader, Protestant

Born on 30 August 1940 in Magelang, Central Java, he went to study at the Theological College (Sekolah Theologia Tinggi) in Jakarta in 1960 and graduated in 1966. While studying he was elected chairman of the Students' Union. After graduation he served as the clergyman in GKI (Gereja Kristen Indonesia) Tangerang (1967–73) and later chairman of GKI Klasis Bandung (1978–82; 1992–94). He has been active in the Christian movement in Indonesia. He was one of the leaders who unified the Christian churches in West, Central and East Java. He served as the chairman of the Federation of Indonesian Churches (Persatuan Gereja-Gereja di Indonesia, PGI) from 2000–5. In November 2011 when there were religious and ethnic tensions in Indonesia, Natan, together with ten other religious leaders and social activists, jointly organized the Gerakan Integritas Nasional (GIN), promoting tolerance and national integrity in Indonesia.

Natan has also been active internationally. He was a frequent participant in international seminars/conferences. He was also elected as a member of the Central Committee of WCC from 1998–2004. His thirst for knowledge led him to leave for the United States for further education and he obtained his PhD from the Department of Theology, the Graduate School of Arts and Sciences, Boston College in 1995. The title of his dissertation was "The Christian Chinese Minority in Indonesia, with special reference to the Gereja Kristen Indonesia: A Sociological and Theological Analysis".

Natan is a prolific writer. He started publishing books since 1975 and to date has published at least twelve books. His earliest work is entitled *Benih yang tumbuh: sebuah self-study GKI Jabar* [The seed which grows: a self-study of the

Indonesian Christian Church of West Java] (1975); one of his latest books is *Sikap dan Pemikiran Krtisis Pdt Natan Setiabudi Ketum PGI Menjelang dan Pasca Pelimu* [The critical attitude and thinking of Clergyman Natan Setiabudi, the general chairman of the Federation of Indonesian Churches before and after the General Election] (2004).

Sources: Leo Suryadinata, *Negara dan Etnis Tionghoa: Kasus Indonesia* (Jakarta LP3ES, 2002), p. 286; <http://www.tokohindonesia.com/biografi/article/285-ensiklopedi/82-pelayan-lintas-wak...> (accessed 12 April 2014); <http://www.tempo.co/read/news/2011/01/11/078305473/Prihatin-Kondisi-Bangsai-11> (accessed 12 April 2014); Sam Setyautama, *Tokoh-tokoh Etnis TH*, pp. 390–91.

SETIAWAN, Chandra (HUANG Jinquan 黄金泉, 1961-)
Religious leader, Confucian

Born in Pangkal Pinang, Riau, in 1961, his father was a goldsmith. During his school age, there was no Chinese medium school. He went to Yogyakarta to study in the high school, and entered an Islamic University to study economics. After graduation he studied at UGM and received a Master of Management degree. He later obtained two doctoral degrees, one of which was from the Universiti Putra Malaysia (2011).

When Chandra was in high school he was already active in the Khonghucu circle. He joined Matakin and eventually served as its chairman in 1993 after **Suryo HUTOMO**, the first Matakin chairman, passed away. Chandra held the position until 2002. During that period Confucian religion was not recognized by the Soeharto regime since 1979. Nevertheless, he continued to maintain contacts with various groups. When Soeharto stepped down he managed to hold a congress, using the premises of the Ministry of Religious Affairs, indicating the good relationship between Matakin and the religious group. Matakin under the leadership of Chandra was able to gain permission to celebrate Lunar New Year (often called Chinese New Year) in 2000,

President Abdurrahman Wahid (Gus Dur) and his ministers attended the celebration.

In 2002–7 Chandra was appointed as a member of KOMNAS HAM (Indonesian human rights commission). Between 2001–6 he served as rector (president) of the IBII (Institute of Business and Informatics Indonesia). Since 2012, he has been appointed as rector of the President University, a private university located in West Java.

Sources: Liao Jianyu, *Yinni kongjiao*, p. 77; Wang Aiping, *kongjiao yanjiu*, pp. 131–33.

SETIAWAN, Daniel Budi (何明良, 1956-)
Politician, Protestant

Born on 28 October 1956 in Semarang, Central Java, he completed his primary and high school education in Semarang. After finishing high school in 1974, he was admitted to ITB where he studied mechanical engineering and graduated in 1980. Sixteen years later he got an M.A degree in management from the Universitas Diponegoro in Semarang.

Daniel has worked as a manager in various companies, one of them was PT Siba Surya in Semarang, which had 700 trucks. He later got involved in a few organizations. In 1999 he was elected as member of parliament (1999–2004) for Kabupaten Karanganyar, Central Java, representing PDIP.

Source: *Wajah Dewan Perwakilan Rakyat Republik Indonesia: Pemilihan Umum 1999* (Penerbit Buku Kompas, 2000), p. 19.

SETIONO, Benny Gatot (KHOUW Thian Tong; XU Tiantang 许天堂, 1943-)
Community leader, writer

Born on 31 October 1943 in Kuningan, West Java, he is a community leader and head of INTI, the Chinese Indonesian Association, the Jakarta Branch. He is also the writer of *Tionghoa Dalam Pusaran Politik*, published by Elkasa in Jakarta in

2003, with an introduction by Daniel S. Lev, the late American political scientist who was a specialist on Indonesian political history from the Washington University in Seattle. Setiono received the Wertheim Award 2008 from Wertheim Stichting (Wertheim Foundation) in Leiden-Amsterdem for his efforts and work for freedom in the Indonesian nation.

Source: Thung Ju Lan, "Setiono, Benny Gatot", Suryadinata, ed., *Southeast Asian Personalities* (2012), pp. 954–56.

Shannu (TAN To; ZHAN Hu; CHEN Zhanhu 陈展湖; CHEN Shanhu 陈善湖, 1934–2013)
Translator

Born in Siantar, Sumatra, in 1934, he received Chinese education in his birthplace. After finishing his senior secondary school education he went to Jakarta where he continued his study. In the early 1950s he taught Indonesian in a Chinese school in Sumatra. At the end of the 1950s he moved to Jakarta and worked as an editor of *Juexing Zhoukan* 觉醒周刊 and part-time journalist of daily *Xin Bao* 新报 and later, *Zhongcheng Bao* 忠诚报.

He compiled a few Indonesian Chinese dictionaries and translated many left-wing Chinese literary works into Indonesian. The most well-known was the novel of Yang Mo, *Nyanyian Remadja* [The Song of Youth, 青春之歌] (Jakarta: Jajasan Pembaruan, 1961). He also translated the collected works of Lu Xun: *Pilihan Tulisan Lu Sin* (Jajasan Sadar, 1965) which includes Lu Xun's well-known novel *The True Story of Ah Q* 阿Q正传.

After the 1965 coup, he went to China and worked for the Foreign Languages Publication Department (Pustaka Bahasa Asing Beijing) as a translator, and later, Radio Beijing (Indonesian section). He died on 22 January 2013 in the United States while visiting his son who worked there.

Sources: Zhou Nanjing, ed., *Huaqiao huaren baike quanshu* (2001), p. 66; "In Memoriam Shannu, Kolom Ibrahim Isa, Rabu, 23 Januari 2013" (accessed 2013); Jennifer Lindsey and Maya H.T. Liem, *Heirs to World Culture* (2012), p. 170; Ye Yuan 叶原,《飞跃沧桑, 北京重逢》, *Siantar People.Org website* (accessed January 2014).

SHEN Ailing. See JUSUF, Ester Indahyani

SHEN Demin (SHEN Teh Min 沈德民, 1936-)
Physician, community leader

Born in Jakarta on 24 September 1936, his father ran a printing office. After finishing his secondary education at a Chinese-medium high school in Bandung, Demin went to Jakarta to study medicine at the FKUI and graduated in 1960. Initially he worked for Jang Seng Ie (Husada) Hospital in Jakarta; one year later he moved to Bandung to work for Chung Hwa Hospital. He then went overseas for graduate studies at the University of Pennsylvania. He specialized in cardio-thoracic surgery at St. Vincent Hospital (Cleveland Clinic, according to another source). In 1970 he returned to Bandung and worked at Hasan Sadikin Hospital, setting up and heading an intensive care unit.

In 1975 together with fellow physicians he set up the "Bandung Humanity Foundation", which later established Radjawali Hospital, of which he is the director.

Shen was interested in medical research. He enrolled in the PhD programme of IPB (Institut Pertanian Bogor) to do research on heart related diseases and submitted a dissertation on the influence of EDTA on atherogenesis in high risk monkeys. He obtained his PhD from IPB in 1991. In 1998 he also obtained a master's degree in Healthcare Management from UGM.

Shen felt that he was still discriminated as a member of a minority group. He is internationally recognized as a cardiac surgeon and has been invited to various countries for his expertise, yet he was not given a professorship in Indonesia although a professorship was conferred on him by the Peking Union of Medical College in 1995. This has not deterred him from advocating meritocracy for all Indonesians, regardless of their ethnicity, working together for the success of Indonesia.

After Soeharto stepped down he joined INTI and more recently he was elected as chairman of the INTI West Java branch (2010–14). In 2011, a group of Chinese Indonesians who had received some Chinese education decided to establish an ASEAN Nanyang International University, and he served as the chairman of the preparatory committee.

Shen is married to Geraldine Waligorski, an American anaesthetist whom he met when he was studying in the United States. They have one son and one daughter.

Sources: *Apa & Siapa 1985–86*, pp. 831–32; Song and Hsu, eds. (1981), pp. 131–36; Suryadinata, *Southeast Asian Personalities*, pp. 959–61.

SHEN Ji'ai. See **SIM Ki Ay**
SHEN Miniang. See **SIEM Piet Nio**
SHEN Teh Min. See **SHEN Demin**
SHI Furen. See **BUDIMAN, Arief**
SHI Fuyi. See **SOE Hok Gie**
SHI Libi. See **SOE Lie-Piet**
SHI Shengfang. See **TJIOK San Fang, Elsie**
SHI Wenlian. See **SIE Boen Lian**

SIAUW Giok Bie (XIAO Yumei 萧玉美, 1918–93)
Community leader, younger brother of **SIAUW Giok Tjhan**

Born in Surabaya on 27 February 1918, he was educated at the ELS, MULO(?), and a radio/electric technical school. He was detained by the Japanese in 1943. In 1945 he began to be active in Indonesia's independence movement and was elected as the chairman of Angkatan Muda Tionghoa (East Java). In the 1950s he was a member of the Presidium of GAPPERSON (the Federation of the National Cigarette Industry Association) in Malang, the deputy president of Baperki (Malang branch), and later the president of Baperki (East Java). He was also chairman of Ang Hien Hoo, a social association in Malang, from 1961 to 1965. The association later changed its name to Perkumpulan Sosial Panca Budhi. Ang Hien Ho was well-known for its Wayang Orang group, a traditional Javanese theatre owned and performed by the *peranakan* Chinese, which started in the 1950s.

Siauw was detained by the Indonesian authority after the 1965 Coup. After his release he lived in West Germany. He died in Koln, Germany on 23 May 1993.

Sources: *Pedoman Kampanje*, p. 47; Melani Budianta, "Malang Mignon: Cultural Expression of the Chinese 1940–1960", in Jennifer Lindsay and Maya H.T. Liem, *Heirs to World Culture* (2012), pp. 255–81; the compiler's notes.

SIAUW Giok Tjhan (XIAO Yucan 萧玉灿, 1914–81)
Community and political leader, journalist

He was born on 23 March 1914 in Surabaya. He received ELS (Dutch Primary School for Europeans) and HBS (Dutch Secondary School) education at his birthplace. In the 1930s he became acquainted with **LIEM Koen Hian** and joined the PTI. He worked for a pre-war *peranakan* daily, the *Mata Hari*, from 1934 to 1942. His leftist orientation appeared during this period.

Siauw went underground when the Japanese occupied Indonesia. During the Indonesian Revolution, Siauw sided with the Indonesian nationalists. He was appointed as a member of the BPKI (Indonesian Central National Committee) in 1946 and, in the following year was made Minister without Portfolio for Peranakan Affairs.

Siauw had established close relationship with **TAN Ling Djie** since 1939 when Tan was the editor-in-chief of *Sin Tit Po*. One source noted that Tan was the political mentor of Siauw. Siauw also joined the Socialist Party with Tan after World War II. In 1948, Tan was arrested after the Communist rebellion known as the Madiun Affair while Siauw was suspected of having been involved in the PKI rebellion and was imprisoned by the Indonesian authorities. He was soon released and became active again in Indonesian politics. He was first appointed, and later elected as a member of the Indonesian Parliament representing the Chinese minority from 1950 to 1966. He was officially dismissed from this position because of his alleged involvement in the 1965 coup.

Siauw's career as a journalist after World War II is not well-known. He edited *Liberty* (Malang, 1946) and *Pemuda* during the Indonesian Revolution. Between July 1951 and October 1953 he served as the director of *Harian Rakjat*, the official organ of the PKI. He also edited *Republik*, the official newspaper of the Baperki in the 1950s. In 1954 he participated in the formation of Baperki, the most influential *peranakan* socio-political organization during the "Guided Democracy" period and was elected as the chairman of its central board. He retained this position until 1965 when Baperki was banned.

He was detained for thirteen years soon after the 1965 coup. When released he went to the Netherlands. His memoirs, *Lima Jaman: Perwujudan Integrasi Wajar* [Five eras: formation of natural integration] was published in May 1981 in Holland. Its Chinese and English editions were later published in Hong Kong and Australia. Siauw died in Leiden on 20 November 1981.

Sources: *Pedoman Kampanje*, p. 35; *Harian Rakyat*, 31 October and 2 November 1953; Parlaungan, *Tokoh Parlemen*, pp. 321–22; Somers, dissertation, p. 36; *DPR 1971*, pp. 533, 597, 616, 628, and 646; Hindley, *PKI*, p. 67; *Dipingxian*, no. 14, December 1980, pp. 9, 75; *Kompas*, 23 November 1981; Letter from Sie Hok Tjwan, 11 November 2002; Siauw Tiong Djin, *Siauw Giok Tjhan*, 1999, pp. 59–60.

SIAUW Tik Kwie (Oto SUASTIKA; XIAO Degui 萧德贵, 1913–88)
Painter, illustrator, designer

Born in Solo (Java) on 23 June 1913, he received Chinese primary school education at his birthplace (1920–27). In 1932–33 he studied art at Bataviasche Kunstkring (Jakarta) and from 1934 to 1935 took a correspondence course from the Press Art School (London). Before World War II he worked as a designer for various companies in Jakarta. After the war he was a regular contributor of comic strips to *Star Weekly* (Jakarta, 1954–60) and other periodicals. He held one-man exhibitions at the Cultural Council (Jakarta) in 1965, 1968, 1969, and 1971.

Sources: *Sinar Harapan*, 10 May 1971; *Tempo*, 5 June 1971; *Intisari*, no. 78 (January 1971); C.M. Hsu's notes.

SIDHARTA, Myra (EW YONG Tjhoen Moy; OUYANG Chunmei 欧阳春梅, 1927-)
Psychologist, university lecturer, writer, wife of **Priguna SIDHARTA**, *Protestant*

Born in Tanjung Pandan (South Sumatra) in 1927, she received ELS education at her birthplace but her education was interrupted during the Japanese Occupation. After World War II she went to the Netherlands to continue her education, and obtained an HBS diploma (1948) from Amsterdam and a Drs degree in Psychology from Rijks Universiteit in Leiden (1958). She got married to **SIE Pek Giok** (Priguna Sidharta) while studying and they eventually returned to Indonesia. Initially she taught at the Faculty of Psychology, UI (1958–69). Between 1968 and 1971 she was a lecturer at the University of Malaya. She has published a number of books on psychology, including *Menuju Kesejahteraan Jiwa* (6th ed., 1984), as co-author; *Kepribadian dan Perubahannya* (5th ed., 1984), as co-author; *Rumah Sakit Dalam Cahaya Jiwa* (1983); and *Penilaian Psikologis terhadap Anak-Anak dengan Brain Disfunction* (1973).

After returning from Malaysia, she became interested in Chinese studies and joined the Department of Sinology at the FSUI as an adjunct lecturer (1977–). She has conducted research on *peranakan* literature and society and has published a number of papers, including "The Making of the Indonesian Chinese Women", "Contemporary Peranakan Women Writers", and "Tan Hong Boen: A Man of Many Faces". She has also edited a book on a leading *peranakan* intellectual, titled *100 Tahun Kwee Tek Hoay*; authored a book of biographies of some *peranakan* writers, *Dari Penjaja Tekstil Sampai Ke Pendekar Pena* (Jakarta, 1989); and published a biography of a Dutch priest entitled *M.A.W. Brouwer, Antara Dua Tanah Air: Perjalanan Seorang Pastor* (Jakarta, 1994).

Sources: *Apa & Siapa 1985–86*, pp. 838–39; *100 Tahun Kwee Tek Hoay*, p. 331.

SIDHARTA, Priguna (SIE Pek Giok; XUE Biyu 薛碧玉, 1924–2003)
Physician, university professor, husband of **Myra SIDHARTA,** *Protestant*

Born on 18 December 1924 in Indramayu, his father was a petty merchant in the market. After finishing primary education at a mission school (1931–38), he attended Hollands-Inlandse Kweekschool in Solo (1938–41) and the HBS in Jakarta (1946–47). From 1949 to 1954 he studied medicine at Rijks Universiteit (Leiden). In 1956 he received his doctoral degree from the same university. From 1962 to 1963 he did post-doctoral work at the Montreal Neurological Institute, Canada.

From 1955 to 1956 he worked at Rijks Universiteit as special assistant and from 1956 to 1958 as acting head of the Neuropathology section. From 1959 to 1968 he was a senior lecturer at the FKUI. From 1968 to 1970 he was appointed as a senior lecturer in the Department of Medicine, University of Malaya. He returned to Jakarta and served as a volunteer doctor in Persahabatan Hospital. Between 1973 and 1986 he was senior lecturer at the Faculty of Medicine, Universitas Katholik Atma Jaya (Jakarta). In October 1987 he was promoted to Professor of Neurology at the same university. In 1993 he published his memoirs entitled *Seorang Dokter Dari Losarang: Sebuah Otobiografi* [A physician from Losarang: an autobiography].

He has published numerous research papers and more than ten medical books, including *Localization of Fibre Systems within the White Matter of the Medulla Oblongata and Cervical Cord in Man* (Leiden, 1956), his dissertation; *Neurologi Dasar* [Basic Neurology] (Jakarta, 1967); *Pengobatan Penyakit Saraf* [Treatment for Neurological Illness] (Jakarta, 1968); *Neurologi Klinis Dasar* [Basic Clinical Neurology] (Jakarta, 1978); *Neurologi Klinis dalam Praktek Umum* [Clinical Neurology in General Practice] (Jakarta, 1980); Ketegangan dan Akibatnya [Tension and Its Consequences] (1981); *Kembali Hidup Dengan Cacat* [Living again with handicap] (1981); and *Encok-Remetik* [Rheumatics] (1983).

Sidharta died in Jakarta on 3 July 2003. He was survived by his wife Myra Sidharta, daughters Sylvia and Julie, and son Amir.

Sources: Leo Suryadinata, "Sidharta, Priguna", in Suryadinata, ed., *Southeast Asian Personalities* (2012), pp. 975–77; "Curriculum Vitae" (1980); *Apa & Siapa 1985–86*, pp. 839–40; his autobiography.

SIE Boen Lian (SHI Wenlian 施文连, 1902–70)
Physician, community leader

Born in Madiun on 24 August 1902, he received his education at the HCS (Madiun) and later at NIAS (Surabaya). He continued his advanced medical education in Jakarta and in Prague, specializing in eye diseases. After graduation he returned to Indonesia to join **Dr YAP Hong Tjoen**'s hospital in Yogyakarta. In 1935 he moved to Jakarta.

He was interested in Chinese culture. While at high school he was active in Chung Hsioh and served as its president in 1948. Between 1957 and 1966 he served as the president of the Jajasan Pendidikan dan Pengajaran (JPP, the Education & Teaching Foundation), a foundation which established the Sekolah Pa Hoa JPP in 1957 to accommodate the students from the THHK school who were Indonesian citizens.

When Soekarno was still in power, Dr Sie was Soekarno's private doctor. In April 1966 he went to the Netherlands to work for the University of Amsterdam Hospital. In 1969 he fell ill and died in Amsterdam, the Netherlands, on 9 November 1970.

Sources: Tan, *Tionghoa*, p. 205; *Jade* XII, no. 2 (1948): 43; Kwee, "Tionghoa Luar Negeri", p. 53; Zhang, "Yinni Huaqiao", p. 81; Sie Chin Ling and Sie Liang Hai, "Ayahku, Dokter Sie Boen Lian", *Buku Peringatan 100 Tahun Sekolah THHK/Pahoa Centennial of THHK School* (Jakarta, 2001), pp. 169–70; also p. 34.

SIE, Hendrawan. See **LESMANA, Hendrawan**
SIE Pek Giok. See **SIDHARTA, Priguna**

SIE, Peter (SIE Thiam Ie, 1929-) 施添宜*
Dress designer

Peter Sie was born on 28 December 1929 in Bogor (West Java), the younger son of Sie Tjeng Hay, owner of a food shop. Peter finished his primary school education in Bogor. At the age of fifteen he decided to be a dressmaker. Two years later his brother-in-law Kho Han Gao took him to the Netherlands. He studied at the Volkschool voor Kleermaker en Coupeuse in the Hague (1947–53) and returned to Jakarta in 1954, beginning his career as a trendy dressmaker. Initially his clients were Chinese ladies among his neighbours and gradually he became well-known beyond his neighbourhood. He introduced the latest fashion from the West, especially from Paris. Ladies in Indonesian high society came to him to order dresses. In 1959 he had an exhibition at the Hotel Des Indies, Jakarta. He was named as one of the first dress designers in Indonesia, not simply a dressmaker. He was also active in welfare. In 1984 in connection with his thirty-year career as a designer, he staged a fashion design exhibition, and raised 62 million rupiahs which he donated to the Indonesian children welfare fund.

Source: *Apa & Siapa 1985–86*, pp. 842–43.

SIE Thiam Ie. See **SIE, Peter**
SIE Tjia-Ie. See **TJAHJADI, Robby**

SIE Tjin Gwan (1908-?) 施振源*
Journalist, writer

Born in Jakarta in 1908, he received MULO education in Medan and Jakarta. He first worked for *Keng Po* (Jakarta), and in the late 1920s and early 1930s joined the editorial board of *Perniagaan/Siang Po*. In 1932 he was appointed as the editor-in-chief of *Panorama*, a Jakarta weekly owned by **PHOA Liong Gie**. In 1933 he became the editor-in-chief of *Sin Tit Po* (Surabaya), a paper closely linked with the PTI. During the Japanese Occupation, he worked for Tjoa Sik Ien Printing House in Surabaya. One source says that after World War II he worked as a reporter for *Antara* in Bonn.

Sources: Tan, *Tionghoa*, p. 50; Tio's notes (on Sie's activities after World War II).

Siegvrieda LAUWANI. See **LAUWANI, Siegvrieda**

SIEM Piet Nio (SHEN Miniang 沈泌娘**; pen-name: HONG Le Hoa, circa 1907–80s)**
Writer, feminist

Born in 1907 in Purbolinggo (Probolinggo?), East Java, Siem received her education at the Sekolah Bethel, a missionary school. She is most known for using her literacy skills to promote women's emancipation in Indonesia. Soon after graduation, she founded the Ping Min Niu Sze Hui (平民女子会) or Association for Women masses. In the late 1920s she moved to Banyumas (Central Java) and began to contribute articles to various magazines such as *Panorama* and *Liberty*.

In 1928, Siem published a short article "Persatoean jang diharap" [The Federation which we expect] in an issue of *Panorama* under her pen-name, Hong Le Hoa. According to her, "women who were able to write should use their literary skills to help enlighten other members of their sex." She also argued that "women were mainly responsible for themselves in the struggle for their emancipation. They were the only ones who were able to give a clearer view of women's lives — men could not do so, as they often criticized women with contempt or created an inaccurate picture of women." It was well received and within a few weeks gathered enthusiastic letters from seven women's association based in Java. She launched the first issue of her magazine entitled, *Soeara Persatoean Kaoem Prampoean Tionghoa Indonesia* [The Voice of the Federation of Indonesian Chinese Women]. It was apparently the first Sino-Indonesian feminist magazine to be published in the Malay language and was concerned with the improvement of the social status of women. She passed away in Sukabumi in the 1980s.

Source: Claudine Salmon, "Siem Piet Nio", in Suryadinata, ed., *Southeast Asian Personalities* (2012), pp. 977–79.

SIK Sian Han. See **NOTOWIDJOJO, Suhendro**

SILALAHI, Harry Tjan (TJAN Tjoen Hok; ZENG Chunfu 曾春福, 1934-)
Politician, lawyer, Catholic
Born in Yogyakarta on 11 February 1934, he was son of a male nurse. Besides his two years at the HCS, he was educated

in Indonesian schools. He finished the SMP and the SMA in Yogyakarta. While at high school, he joined Chung Lien Hui, a *peranakan* Chinese student association in Java. At the same time, he was also a member of the IPPI, an Indonesian student and youth organization.

In 1952 he served as the chairman of Chung Lien Hui. Under his leadership the name Chung Lien Hui was changed to Perkumpulan Peladjar Sekolah Menengah Indonesia (PPSMI). Besides the student movement, he was active in cultural activities. He played a major role in a number of plays produced by Sin Ming Hui (Jakarta) and the Catholic University Students Association (PMKRI): *Penuntutan* (adapted from "Witness for the Prosecution", 1956, produced by PMKRI); *Mawar Hutan* (1958), directed by himself and produced by Sin Ming Hui; *Taufan* (1958), directed by Steve Lim and produced by Sin Ming Hui.

He joined the FHUI in 1955 and graduated in 1962. During his student years, he was active in the PMKRI and was elected as the chairman of the PMKRI-Pusat in 1961–62. He went to the United States four times, this included his visits to the States and Canada in 1962 to attend student conferences representing the PPSMI, of which he was the vice-chairman.

In the educational field, he was involved in converting the Chinese-medium school at Jakarta-Kota into an Indonesian-medium school, with him as the appointed principal. Since 1966 he has served as an executive member of the Trisakti University Foundation.

In 1965 he was elected as the secretary-general of the Front Pantjasila, a federation of anti-communist mass and political organizations. He was also one of the forerunners of the assimilationist movement. In June 1965 he joined Partai Katholik. In 1967 he was adopted by the Silalahi family and hence took on Silalahi as his surname. From 1967 to 1971 he was appointed as a member of the DPR and the chairman of the "Commission 1" in charge of Information on Higher and Non-Departmental Institutions. In 1971 he participated in the general elections as a candidate of Partai Katholik, but was not elected. He left Partai Katholik and joined the CSIS, serving as the vice-chairman of the board of directors. In 1978 he was appointed as a member of the DPA (Dewan Pertimbangan Agung) by President Soeharto. In 1989(?) he was appointed as the chairman of Bakom. He has published a number of articles and monographs, one of which is *Konsensus Politik Nasional Orde Baru* (Jakarta, 1990).

Sources: *Star Weekly*, 16 February 1956, p. 8; *Sin Ming Hui 12 1/2 Tahun* (1958); *Inti Masalah* "Minorita" (c.1962), p. 29; interview, 1976; Letter to the compiler, 1977.

SIM Ai Ling. See JUSUF, Ester Indahyani

SIM Ki Ay (SHEN Ji'ai 沈基爱)
Physician, community leader

Born in Probolinggo, he was educated at the ELS (Temenggung), the HBS (Surabaya and Semarang), and Amsterdam University. In 1917 he was active in the CHH-Netherlands. He returned to Java after obtaining his degree in Medicine. With other ex-CHH-Netherlands leaders, he founded the CHH in 1927–28. He was later sympathetic to Indonesia's independence movement and remained in Yogyakarta during the Indonesian-Dutch conflict. He served the local population and established friendship with the "Republicans" headed by Soekarno-Hatta-Sjahrir. He was appointed as a member of the RI delegation to the Round Table Conference. He probably died in Bandung.

Sources: *Sinar*, 20 September 1949, p. 3; *Xin Pao*, 6 August 1949; Suryadinata, *Peranakan Politics*, p. 62; the compiler's notes.

SINDHUNATHA, Kristoforus (ONG Tjong Hai; WANG Zonghai 王宗海, 1933–2005)
Leader of the assimilationist movement, lawyer, business consultant, Catholic

Son of a physician, he was born in Jakarta on 20 March 1933 and was active in the PMKRI during his student days. He graduated from the FHUI in 1961, and in the same year began active service in the Indonesian Navy. While in the Navy he served as a staff member of the Law Section of the Navy in 1961–63, and a staff member of the G-V of KOTI from 1963 to 1967. In 1963 when the LPKB was instituted, he was appointed as its (acting?) chairman, a position he held until its dissolution in 1967. In 1967–69 he was appointed Acting General Secretary of the National Naval Defense Command of the Department of Defense.

After he left the Navy in 1970 he established the Industrial and Legal Consultants (Indulexco/ILO) firm and became its director. In 1975 he became the president of the same company. During the 1970s he held the following positions: board member of the Association of Indonesian Consultants (since 1973); board member of the National Private Entrepreneurial Development Foundation (since 1975); vice-chairman of the Municipal Board of the Committee for the Development of National Unity (BPKB-DKI) (since 1974); and vice-chairman of Trisakti University Foundation. In 1983 as the vice-president of the Indonesia-France Friendship Association, he was awarded Chevalier de l'Ordre National du Merite by the French Government for his contribution to Jakarta-Paris relations. He was also awarded Bintang Mahaputra Pratama in August 1998. He has served as the chairman of Bakom since 1977.

He died in Jakarta on 16 August 2005 of lung cancer and complications from other diseases. After a requiem mass led by the Jakarta Catholic archbishop, he was buried with naval military honours at the Kalibata Heroes' Cemetery. He is survived by his wife, Hudiani Sutikna (Kiem Hoey), and their three children.

Sources: Charles A. Coppel, "Sindhunatha, Kristoforus", in Suryadinata, ed., *Southeast Asian Personalities* (2012), pp. 991–94; Roeder, *Who's Who*, pp. 363–64; "Curriculum Vitae"; *Apa & Siapa 1985–86*, pp. 852–53.

Singgih D. GUNARSA. See GUNARSA, Singgih D.
Siti Hartati MURDAYA. See MURDAYA, Siti Hartati
SITU Meisheng. See SOETO Meisen
SITU Zan. See SOETO Tjan
Sjamsul NURSALIM. See NURSALIM, Sjamsul
SOE Hok Djin. See BUDIMAN, Arief

SOE Hok Gie (SHI Fuyi 史福义, 1942–69)
Political activist, college instructor, former student leader, younger brother of **Arief BUDIMAN**, *son of* **SOE Lie-Piet**

Born in Jakarta in 1942, he was educated at the FSUI, where he was awarded the *Sarjana Sastra* degree in History in 1969. He was active in the LPKB Group and served as de facto editor of its journal, *Bara Eka* (1964–65). After the 1965 abortive coup, he was active in student politics. He had contributed significantly to the student campaign which helped overthrow the Soekarno government. During that time, he was also the editor of *Mahasiswa Indonesia* (a militant students' paper published in Bandung). In 1968–69 he served as the chairman of the students' union, FSUI. After Soekarno was overthrown he was the first Indonesian who wrote publicly about political prisoners and corruption. He contributed articles to a number of Jakarta newspapers including *Sinar Harapan* and *Kompas*. His critical writings were later (1995) put together by Stanley and Aris Santoso and published as a book under the title: *Zaman Peralihan* [Transitional Era]. Apart from political and social activities, he loved mountain climbing, which was the cause of his death on 16 December 1969. Prior to his death, he held the position of an instructor at the Department of History, FSUI. His publications include *Kisah Penumpasan "RMS"* (Jakarta, 1965); *Demonstrasi Mahasiswa Djanuari 1966* (Jakarta, 1966); and *Catatan Seorang Demonstran* (Jakarta, 1983). His Sarjana Muda thesis ("Dibawah Lentera Merah — Riwajat Sarekat Islam Semarang 1917–20") was published in 1991 but was immediately banned because it "could spread communism and socialism, which was against the Pancasila state ideology". Soedjatmoko, a leading Indonesian intellectual, made the following remarks about Soe: "To me, he exemplified the possibility of a new type of Indonesian, of a truly Indonesian Indonesian. It is this message that his brief life contains for us."

To commemorate the fortieth anniversary of his death, his friends published a book titled, *Soe Hok-gie, Sekali Lagi* [Soe Hok Gie, Once More] (2009). In 2005, his life story was made into a motion picture entitled, *Gie*, which was nominated in twelve categories in the Festival Film Indonesia (Indonesian Film Festival) and won three awards: Best Picture, Best Actor and Best Cinematography. Professor A. Dahana said that "Soe Hok Gie has become an icon of young, courageous, and idealist Indonesians, regardless of their racial origins."

Please note that his surname Soe in Chinese character is 史 (shi), not 苏 (Su) as commonly cited in Chinese publications.

Sources: *Kompas*, 22 December 1970; *Ekspres*, 7 June 1970, p. 22; Anderson, *Indonesia* (April 1970), pp. 225–27; Soedjatmoko, *Asia* (1969/70), p. 7; Bachtiar (1975), p. 76; *Straits Times*, 13 September 1991, p. 16; A. Dahana, "Soe Hok Gie", in Suryadinata, ed., *Southeast Asian Personalities of Chinese Descent* (2012), pp. 996–99.

SOE Lie-Piet (Salam SUTRAWAN, SHI Libi 史立笔, 1904–88)
Writer, newspaper editor, father of **Arief BUDIMAN** *and* **SOE Hok Gie**

Born on 18 June 1904 in Jakarta, he received a THHK education in Jakarta. He died in September 1988. He was the editor of various *peranakan* daily newspapers and periodicals: *Tjin Po* (Medan, 1922–26); *Panorama* (Jakarta, 1925); *Hwa Po* (Palembang, 1927); *Liberty* (Bandung, 1930); *Hong Po* (Jakarta, 1933); *Kung Yung Pao* (Jakarta, 1942); *Min Pao* (Jakarta, 1945–47); and *Sadar* (a daily in Jakarta, 1950). Before Indonesia's independence, he published approximately ten novels, some of which were serialized in two journals: *Tjerita Roman* and *Penghidoepan*. Some of his major works are *Bidadari dari Telaga Toba* (1928), *Uler Jang Tjantik* (1929), *Djadi Pendita* (1934), *Lejak* (1935), *Dimana Adanja Allah?* (1940), and *Gadis Kolot* (1941).

Sources: "Bio-data Soe Lie-Piet" (courtesy of C.M. Hsu); Nio, *Sastera*, pp. 79–80, 124–25; the compiler's notes.

Soe Tjen MARCHING. See MARCHING, Soe Tjen

SOEGIARTO, Lita (LIEM, Lita, 1946-) 林丽达*
Tennis player, Protestant

Born in Leiden (Holland) on 27 February 1946, her father is an ethnic Chinese (physician) while her mother is a Dutch woman. From a very young age she has been very keen in sports, and was trained by a professional when she was at high school in Bandung at the age of sixteen. Two years later (in 1962) she became the Indonesian National Champion. In 1966 she received the Satya Lencana Kebudayaan Award from the Indonesian government for her contribution in sports. In 1972 she married another tennis player Soegiarto. In 1974 she was elected Best Sports Woman of the Year by the PWI. A natural left-hander, she was the former champion of Asian Games Tennis Championship.

Sources: *Topik*, 17 May 1972; *Straits Times*, 21 October 1992, p. 34; *Apa & Siapa 1985–86*, pp. 746–47; Setyautama, *Tokoh-Tokoh Etnis Tionghoa*, p. 207.

SOEJATMIKO, Basuki (LIEM Hok Liong; LIN Fuliang 林福良, 1939–90)
Editor, leader of the assimilationist movement

Born in Pasuruan on 5 October 1939, he graduated from the SMA in 1959. Soon after graduation he joined *Liberty* (Surabaya). He later became the deputy director/editor (*wakil pemimpin*) of *Liberty*. He won the best journalist writing awards of the PWI (East Java branch) in 1978 and 1979. Apart from essays, he also wrote novels which were serialized in *Liberty*. Two of his novels also appeared in book form: *Bunga Mawar Kuning Tercinta* (1978) and *Nyonya Sita* (1979). His latest novel, *Sinyo Sipit*, was serialized in *Jawa Post* (Surabaya), a paper he edited before his demise.

He was active in the assimilationist movement since 1962. From 1966 to 1967 he served as acting head of the LPKB, East Java section. Since 1977 he was active in Bakom (East Java division). He died on 17 June 1990.

Sources: Letter to the compiler, 1980; *Jawa Pos*, 18 June 1990.

SOEMANTO, Agoes (TANN Sing Hwat; CHEN Shengfa 陈盛发, 1918–80s)

Journalist, writer, screenplay writer, movie director

Born on 5 January 1918 into a poor family in Pasuruan, East Java, he attended the THHK school for less than two years. In 1934, at the age of sixteen, he began to write short stories. When Ong Ping Lok was the editor-in-chief of *Liberty*, he contributed articles to the magazine. Later he worked as a bookkeeper for a company and got involved in the conflict between the workers and the Dutch authorities, which resulted in his arrest. In 1940 he was sentenced to two years' imprisonment for writing articles deemed insulting to the Dutch.

After the Japanese invasion in 1942 he joined the Indonesian guerrilla movement. He was arrested by the Japanese but was later released. In 1944 he came to know **NJOO Cheong Seng** from whom he learned to write screenplay. He also performed the leading role in one of Njoo's plays. At the same time he contributed articles to various *peranakan* newspapers (such as *Keng Po* in Jakarta and *Pewarta Soerabaja* in Surabaya). He was involved in the revolutionary movement and was detained again in 1948 by the Dutch.

In 1949 he was released and in 1950, through the introduction of Fred Young, a *peranakan* movie-director, Tann worked for various movie companies. Between 1950 and 1961 he worked for Bintang Surabaya Film Company, Golden Arrow Film Company, and Sanggabuana Film Company. In 1962 he worked as a freelance director and directed movies for Gema Masa Film Company.

Probably due to his association with Lekra, a PKI cultural association, he was unable to write again after the 1965 coup. According to his own account, he worked as a *bemo* (motor-operated tricycle) driver for nine years. However, during the 1970s he began to write again and produced a number of TV dramas. He either wrote the screenplays or directed at least nineteen movies (including *Bawang Merah Bawang Putih*, *Gadis Tiga Zaman*, *Butet*, and *Sing Sing So*). He died in the late 1980s.

Sources: Letter to the compiler, 2 April 1985; the compiler's notes.

SOERYADJAYA, William (TJIA Kian Liong; XIE Jianlong 谢建隆, 1922–2010)
Wealthy businessman, Christian

Born in 1922 in Majalengka (West Java), his father (Tjia Tjio Bie) was a trader dealing in agricultural products and the owner of a small transport company called Sindang Kasih. His parents died when he was young. After having completed his Dutch secondary school education at the age of nineteen he went into business. At first he sold used papers, then he went into his late father's business — selling agricultural products. In 1947 he went to the Netherlands for vocational training and business courses. In 1949 he returned to Indonesia and set up a leather factory, but was forced to close it down because he could not compete with his *totok* counterparts who controlled the leather business.

After 1952 he moved into the import-export business, dealing in general commodities. In 1957, together with his younger brother, Drs Tjia Kian Tie, and a friend called Liem Peng Hong, he established PT Astra International Inc. Initially the company was involved in the marketing of soft drinks and the export of agricultural products. This firm later developed into a big company. At one time Astra was affiliated with General Ibnu Sutowo, the director-general of Pertamina, the state oil company. Since the inception of Astra, Soeryadjaya served as the managing director of the company. Starting from 1968 he was also a member of the board of trustees of the National Road Builders and Construction Company, the president of Gaya Motor Company, and the president-director of Astra International Inc.

PT Astra International Inc. under his leadership had developed into one of the largest automobile companies with almost fifty affiliated companies. His brother TJIA Kian Tie also assisted him in managing the company. After the death of Tjia Kian Tie, he installed his youngest brother, B.A. Soeryadjaya (Tjia Kian Yoe), a graduate from a Dutch university, as the president-director. He was assisted by two other engineers in the running of the companies. His sons were also involved in the business. Unlike many ethnic Chinese companies, Astra International Inc. employed many indigenous Indonesians at the management level and was considered an example of an "assimilated company". In one of the branches, for example, 90 per cent of the staff members were *pribumi* Indonesians.

The development of Astra led to the expansion of its business activities: it entered into agribusiness, banking, real estate, and construction. Soeryadjaya's business empire got into serious trouble in 1993 when Summa Bank, which was originally a subsidiary of the Astra International Inc., suffered a great loss due to investments in the wrong areas. Its managing director, Edward Soeryadjaya (formerly Tjia Han Sek), was his eldest son. William Soeryadjaya was forced to sell his shares to others (one of them was **Prajogo PANGESTU**) in order to meet his debt, and with that he was no longer the largest shareholder in Astra. He passed away in 2010.

Sources: Jamie Mackie, "Soeryadjaya, William", in Suryadinata, ed., *Southeast Asian Personalities* (2012), pp. 999–1002; Roeder, *Who's Who*, p. 105; *Apa & Siapa 1983–84*, pp. 909–12; *Expo 2*, no. 2 (4 January 1984): 24–25; Panglaykim (1984), pp. 62–66; *Insight Indonesia*, March 1993, p. 17; the compiler's notes.

SOESASTRO, M. Hadi (Martinus Yosefus Marwoto Hadi SOESASTRO; TAN Yueh Ming; CHEN Yueming 陈月明, 1945–2010)
Economist, community leader, Catholic

Also known as Mingkie, he is the son of a printer from East Java. Born in Malang on 30 April 1945, after completing his secondary education in his hometown, he went to West Germany to attend Technische Hochschule at Aachen. In 1963, upon the advice of B.J. Habibie, Hadi transferred to the Department of Aeroplane Construction and graduated in 1971. While studying, he was the president of the Indonesian Students' Association in West Germany (Perhimpunan Pelajar Indonesia, 1966–68).

He returned to Indonesia to join the CSIS in Jakarta. Later he studied at the Rand Graduate Institute at the University of Santa Monica (California, United States), specializing in policy analysis, and obtained a PhD degree after submitting a dissertation entitled, "Policy Analysis for the External Financing of Indonesia's Development".

He was the executive director of the CSIS, and was a columnist in *Tempo* and *Eksekutif*. He co-edited several books, including *Pacific Economic Co-operation: The Next Phase* (1983); *ASEAN Security and Economic Development* (1984); and *Sino-Indonesian Relations in the Post-Cold War Era* (1992). His influential articles include: "ASEAN during the Crisis" (1999); "The Political Economy of Trade in Indonesia" (with M. Chatib Basri, 2005); and "Regional Integration in East Asia: Achievements and Future Prospects" (2006).

He passed away in Jakarta on 4 May 2010 after a long illness.

Sources: Mely G. Tan, "Soesastro, Hadi Marwoto", in Suryadinata, ed., *Southeast Asian Personalities* (2012), pp. 1002–4; *Apa & Siapa 1985–86*, pp. 975–58; the above-mentioned books.

SOETANTYO, Tegoeh (TAN Kiong Liep; CHEN Gongli 陈恭立, 1918-)
Businessman, Buddhist

Born in Yogyakarta on 30 April 1918, he received MULO education (in Yogyakarta?). He was the president-director of PT Mantrust/Maxim Company, a large enterprise with business activities in general trade and agroindustry in the 1970s.

Sources: Arief, *Indonesian Business*, p. 591; Roeder, "Chinese 'Impudence'", p. 34; Roeder, *Who's Who*, p. 515.

SOETO Meisen (SZE TU Mei Sen; SITU Meisheng 司徒眉生, 1928–2010)
Community leader, journalist, son of **SOETO Tjan**

Born in Sukabumi in 1928, he was educated at Hua Zhong (Jakarta). During the Japanese Occupation he joined Fuxing She, an anti-Japanese underground organization, and was captured and detained by the Japanese authorities (1943–45). After World War II, he worked for *Tiansheng Ribao* as a reporter. In the 1950s he was a member of the editorial board of *Xin Bao* (*Sin Po*, Chinese edition). In the 1960s he served as a personal interpreter of President Soekarno. From 1963 to 1965 he became the director of *Shoudu Ribao* (Jakarta). He left Indonesia after the 1965 coup, and resided in Macao.

When he was in Macao, he kept close contact with Indonesian leaders, including Adam Malik (then Soeharto's foreign minister). Meisen was Adam Malik's messenger to Beijing prior to the meeting of the UN General Assembly, conveying the latter's intention to facilitate the PRC's entrance to the UN.

In 2003/4, with the support of President Megawati, Meisen and two of his sons started a new business to introduce traditional Chinese medicine to Indonesia. Meisen passed away in Macao on 13 October 2010.

Sources: Chen, *Nanguan*, p. 44; Xu Jingxian (1953), p. 64; *Almanak Pers Indonesia 1954–55* (1955), p. 223; *Shoudu Ribao*, 29 August 1963; Liu Hong, "Soeto Meisen", in Suryadinata, ed., *Southeast Asian Personalities* (2012), pp. 1005–6; the compiler's notes.

SOETO Tjan (SITU Zan 司徒赞, 1900–78)
Community leader, teacher, father of **SOETO Meisen**, *husband of* **LIU Jinduan**

Born in 1900 into a hawker family in Kaiping (Guangdong), he lost his father in 1908. In 1911 he came to Kuala Lumpur to join his uncle. In 1915, at the age of fifteen, he returned to China to study, first at Shanghai, later at the CNHT (Nanking) in the Teachers' Training Section. In 1919, after graduation, he came to Indonesia to assume the position of principal of a Chinese school (in Muntilan) sponsored by Guangzhao Huiguan (Cantonese Association). Between 1922 and 1934 he travelled widely in Indonesia and served at various Chinese schools. In 1935 he settled down in Jakarta, taking on the role of principal of Guang Ren School, which was also sponsored by Guangzhao Huiguan. From 1935 to 1942 he was the chairman of Batavia's Chinese Schools Federation.

During the Sino-Japanese war, he was active in raising funds for China as well as for Fuxing She, an anti-Japanese organization. He and his son, **SOETO Meisen**, were later detained during the Japanese Occupation of Java.

In 1945, after the Japanese surrender, he and his friends established Lianhe Zhongxue (United Secondary School) in Jakarta. The following year the school's name was changed to Pa-ch'eng Chung-hsueh (Pa Chung or Pah Tsung) and he became its principal. Under his leadership, Pa Chung developed into one of the largest secondary schools in Indonesia.

From 1945 to 1951 he was the chairman of the Chinese School Teachers' General Association. In 1951 he was the deputy chairman of the Association for Fostering Overseas Chinese Unity in Jakarta. In April 1953 when the association changed its name to Qiao Zong, he continued to serve as its deputy president. In 1957 he was elected as its president. In January 1960 he was expelled from Indonesia for his criticism of Indonesian Chinese policy. From that year onwards, he lived in the PRC, holding a number of positions: deputy director of the Institute of Southeast Asian Studies at Jinan University (Canton, 1960–78), committee member of China's Afro-Asian Association, member of the Guangdong Returned Overseas Chinese Association, and trustee of the Guangdong Overseas Chinese Investment Board. When he died on 14 March 1978, he was a committee member of the 5th CPPCC. His publications include *Nanyang Holing Dongyindu Dili* [Geography of Dutch East Indies] (Nanking, 1922), *Nanyang Hoyin Dili Keben* [Textbook of Dutch East Indies geography] (Batavia, 1930), and *Zhong Ri Youji* [Travels in China and Japan] (Batavia, 1935).

Sources: The above-mentioned publications; *Yasheng* (February 1980), pp. 9–11; Suryadinata, *Pribumi*, p. 107; *Jiniankan*, pp. 22–23.

Sofyan TAN. See **TAN, Sofyan**
Sofjan WANANDI. See **WANANDI, Sofjan**
Soetopo JANANTO. See **JANANTO, Soetopo**

SONG Zhongquan (宋中铨, 1905–62)
Community leader, teacher, journalist
Born in Meixian (Guangdong) on 25 March 1905, he had received high school education in Jakarta for two years before returning to China. He graduated from the Central University at Nanking from which he received a BA degree. In 1932 he returned to Java and worked first as editor and later editor-

in-chief of *Xin Bao* (*Sin Po*, Chinese edition). In 1958 he also served as the president of Qiao Zong (侨总, Jakarta). In 1960 Chinese newspapers were closed down, and he was invited to be the principal of the THHK school (also known as Pa Hwa 八华 Jakarta) until his death in Jakarta on 4 December 1962.

Sources: *Buku Peringatan Sekolah Tiong Hoa Hwee Koan 1963* (1963), p. B-1; *Warta Bhakti*, 5 December 1962; Chen, *Nanguan*, p. 45; *Nanyang Nianjian* (1951), p. E-107; Li Zhuohui, *Baorong kuanda, fengyutongzhou* 包容宽大, 风雨同舟 (Jakarta, 2013), pp. 183–86.

SRIMULAT, Teguh (Teguh Slamet RAHARDJO; KHO Tjien Tiong; 许坚忠, 1926–96)*
Leading comedian

Teguh Srimulat's Indonesian name is Teguh Slamet Rahardjo, but he is better known by Teguh Srimulat, the name of the legendary comedy group that he established with his first wife. In fact, Srimulat is the name of his first wife. Born as Kho Tjien Tiong in Klaten, Central Java in 1926, he was adopted by the Go (Wu) family who ran a printing company. Kho graduated from the THHK, a local Chinese school in Solo. While working at his father's printing press in 1942, he became exposed to music and began to learn to play the guitar and violin. Together with his peranakan friends he formed a *keroncong* (a form of popular Indonesian music) group. The group was later dissolved. He joined the indigenous Indonesian group and in 1946, he met Raden Ayu Srimulat, a Javanese stage artist (1905–68), and they performed together. In 1950, Kho married Srimulat and established Gema Malam Srimulat, a travelling troupe. This husband-and-wife team performed regularly in Surabaya and became popular.

In 1963 the name of the group was changed to Aneka Ria Srimulat and it started to perform regularly in four cities: Surabaya, Solo, Semarang and Jakarta where they had their own stage. Their comedian performances were welcomed by the local audience and many considered the Srimulat Group as the pioneer of Indonesian popular comedy. The climax of their success was during the 1960s to the 1980s. They not only performed on stage but also appeared on Indonesian televisions regularly. In 1968, Teguh's wife RA Srimulat passed away. In 1970 he remarried to Jujuk (Djudjuk, 1947–2015), a member of the group who was also a leading comedian.

Teguh was the leader of the group (at one time about 300 members) and very influential in the Indonesian comedy scene. He not only led the group but also wrote the scripts. In 1996 he suffered from a heart attack and died in Solo. With his passing, the Srimulat group declined.

Sources: Herry Gendut Janarto, *Teguh Srimulat: Berpacu dalam komedi dan melodi* (Jakarta: Gramedia, 1990); Teguh (Srimulat)-wikipedia bahasa Indonesia, id.wikipedia.org/wiki/Teguh(Srimulat) (accessed 15 April 2015); "Obituary: Godmother of Srimulat passes away", *Jakarta Post*, 7 February 2015 (accessed 15 April 2015).

Stephen TONG. See **TONG, Stephen**
Steve LIEM. See **KARYA, Teguh**

SUASTIKA, Oto. See **SIAUW Tik Kwie**
Subur RAHARDJA. See **RAHARDJA, Subur**
Sudargo GAUTAMA. See **GAUTAMA, Sudargo**
Suhargo GONDOKUSUMO. See **GONDOKUSUMO, Suhargo**

SUDIN (TJOA Soei Leng; CAI Ruilong 蔡瑞龙, 1964-)
Member of Parliament, Buddhist

Sudin was born in Lampung on 15 November 1964. He graduated from the SMA Tanjung Karang in 1985. He later studied Business Management and received a degree. After leaving school he worked as area manager of PT Sungai Budi (Jakarta) for several years (1986–89). Since 1993 he was appointed as director of Gindo Jaya Mitra Abadi (Jakarta). He has also been the director of PT Cahaya Dewata Persada (Jakarta) since 1999. Sudin later joined PDIP and served as its treasurer of the PDIP Lampung branch. He was elected as member of parliament for two periods: 2009–14; 2014–19.

Sources: *Wajah DPR dan DPD (2009–14)*, p. 336; Pengurus Pusat Fordeka, *Buku Acuan 2014*, p. 119.

SUDJATMIKO, Djoko (LIE Giok Hauw; LI Yuxiao 李玉孝, 1944-)
Former student activist, political party leader, brother of **Prasasto SUDJATMIKO,** *Catholic*

Born on 6 April 1944, he graduated from the Bandung Institute of Technology in 1965. While studying he was active in the PMKRI and KAMI. He was the chairman of KAMI (Bandung branch) in 1966 and the chairman of PMKRI (Bandung branch) for the period of 1967–68. He joined Golkar and contested in the 1971 and 1978 general elections. He was elected as a member of the DPR (1971–76) and re-elected for the period 1977–82, 1982–87, and 1987–92. He also served as the chairman of the Intellectuals and Foreign Relations Department, central board of Golkar (1988–93). He was a member of the Board of Management of some private manufacturing and trading companies. He was also a member of the Board of Trisakti University Foundation, member of the Board of Trustee, Atma Jaya University.

Sources: *Who's Who in Parliament, 1971–76*, p. 63; *Memperkenalkan Anggota-Anggota Hasil Pemilihan Umum* (1971), p. 168; *Tempo*, 24 August 1991, p. 40; Letter to the compiler.

SUDJATMIKO, Prasasto (LIE Giok Tho; LI Yudao 李玉道, 1937-)
Former student activist, lawyer, brother of **Djoko SUDJATMIKO,** *Catholic*

Son of a retail trader, he was born in Pati on 12 December 1937. While studying at the university, he was active in the PMKRI.

He was the chairman of the PMKRI (Jakarta branch) in 1960–61, and from 1962 to 1963 he was the chairman of the PMKRI central board as well as the vice-chairman of the PPMI.

When the LPKB was established he joined the organization and soon became its leading figure. In 1966–67 he served as the chairman of the LKPB (Jakarta branch). He was a member of Partai Katholik and an executive member of the ISKI.

Source: The compiler's notes.

SUDYATMIKO, Basuki. See **SOEJATMIKO, Basuki**
Sugianto KUSUMA. See **KUSUMA, Sugianto**
Suhendro NOTOWIDJOJO. See **NOTOWIDJOJO, Suhendro**
Sukanta TANUDJAJA. See **TANUDJAJA, Sukanta**
Sukanto TANOTO. See **TANOTO, Sukanto**
SUKOWATI, Asmaraman. See **KHO Ping Hoo**
SUKOWIJONO, Ki Hadjar. See **TAN Hong Boen**

SULINDRO, Be (MA Xuling 马须铃)
Businessman, community leader

There is little information available on him. He was born in either Central or East Java and graduated from the Chinese High School in Malang. He served as a member of the Presidium of the IBC (Jakarta) and was the director of the NDC (Jakarta) in the 1960s.

Sources: *Huaqiao Nianjian* (section on Indonesia), p. 15; *Ribao*, 4 July 1968.

SUN Peng Yen. See **SUNUR, Eliaser Yentji**

SUNUR, Eliaser Yentji (SUN Peng Yen) 孙炳炎*
Bupati

No information is available on his family background. He is known as Yance Sunur and in 2009 participated in the DPRD election for Bekasi (West Java) under the banner of PDIP. The result is unknown. In 2011 he was elected as Bupati of Kabupaten Lembata NTT (2011–16). His wife is Margyati Kandou.

Sources: Pengurus Pusat Fordeka, *Buku Acuan 2014*, p. 237; <https://www.blogger.com/profile/08982058735100760865> (accessed 9 October 2014).

SUPRANA, Jaya (PHOA Kok Tjiang; PAN Guochang 潘国昌, 1949-)
Cartoonist, pianist, businessman, Protestant

Born in Denpasar, Bali, on 27 January 1949, his grandfather was the founder of the Jamu Jago (rooster brand of Indonesian medicinal herbs). After his primary and secondary education in Semarang, he went to West Germany to study music and arts. In 1975 he was elected as the president of the PPI (Indonesian Students' Association) in Muenster, West Germany. In 1976 he returned to Indonesia and worked in his father's medical herbs company. In 1983 he took over the company from his father and became its general chairman. A wealthy businessman, he is better known as a pianist and a cartoonist. He frequently performs in public and he is the first Indonesian cartoonist who has held a solo exhibition.

Sources: *Apa & Siapa 1985–86*, pp. 1054–55; *Intisari* (July 1987), pp. 11–19.

SUPRATIKNO, Hendrawan (OEI Tjin Tik 黄正德, 1960-)
Politician, academic, Protestant

Hendrawan was born on 21 April 1960 in Cilacap, Central Java. Information on his pre-university education is not available. He received his first university education at the Universitas Kristen Satya Wacana, majoring in economics. He later went to Belgium to get an M.A. and a PhD from the Vrije Universiteit Amsterdam, the Netherlands. He returned to his alma mater to teach. He was later appointed as assistant dean and eventually dean of the Faculty of Economics (1989–2004). At the same time he was also the president-director of IEU School of Business (1990–93). Between 2004 and 2008, he served as the director of Postgraduate Studies, IBII, Jakarta (2004–8).

Hendrawan was a member of GMKI (Gerakan Mahasiswa Kristen Indonesia) in 1978. He joined PDIP in 2004 and was elected as member of parliament for two periods: 2009–14; 2014–19.

Sources: *Wajah DPR & DPD 2009–14*, p. 292; Pengurus Pusat Fordeka, *Buku Acuan* 2014, p. 149.

SURIPTO, Ateng (KHO Tjeng Lie, 1942–2003) 许正理*
Movie actor, comedian

Born on 8 August 1942 in Jatinegara (suburb of Jakarta), he is better known as Ateng. His talent for acting as well as his short physical stature has gained him popularity as a comedian. He has regularly appeared on Indonesian TV and in a number of movies such as *Ateng Minta Kawin* [Ateng wants to have a wife], *Ateng Sok Tahu* [Ateng pretends to know], and *Ira Maya dan Kakek Ateng* [Ira Maya and Grandpa Ateng]. Formerly known as Ateng KHO Tjeng Lie, he assumed the name Ateng Suripto on 30 August 1978. He died in Jakarta on 6 May 2003.

Sources: *Tempo*, 16 September 1978; *Pembauran*, no. 1 (October 1978), p. 3; *Topik*, no. 93 (29 March 1980), p. 31.

Surya WONOWIDJOJO. See WONOWIDJOJO, Surya

SURYADI, Petrus Aang (ANG Hian Liang, 1921-) 洪贤良*
Mathematician

Born on 12 September 1921 in Semarang, he was educated at the ITB and the University of California, where he received a PhD in statistics. From 1946 to 1948 he was a high schoolteacher in Semarang. From 1950 to 1953 he was an assistant lecturer at the ITB. In 1953 he was promoted to lecturer and in 1961, professor of Mathematics and Statistics. Apart from holding the above-mentioned positions, he has also been the president of Maranatha Christian University (Bandung) since 1965. He has published several textbooks on analytic geometry and statistics.

Sources: Roeder, *Who's Who*, p. 28; Roeder, *Who's Who*, 2nd ed., p. 33.

SURYADJAYA, William. See **SOERYADJAYA, William**

SURYAWAN, Yoza (YANG Zhaoji 杨兆骥, 1933-)
Printer, publisher, writer

Born in 1933 in Sumbawa, he received Chinese middle school education in Surabaya (Xinhua 新华) and senior school education in Jakarta (Huazhong 华中). After graduation in 1957 he taught at Zhen Qiang 振强 Chinese School (1957–61) in Jakarta. While teaching in school, he also studied the Indonesian language at the Universitas Nasional in Jakarta. He graduated in 1960. Between 1961 and 1964 he and his friends established Yayasan Kebudayaan Jamrud in Jakarta (翡翠文化基金会) to publish numerous Chinese books, including *Yinni yu xuexi yuekan* [Learning Indonesian Language Monthly]. He himself also compiled two Chinese-Indonesian dictionaries. In 1964 (1966?) he established PT Pantja Simpati, a printing and publishing company. In 1971 he moved to Singapore together with his family. In 1979 he became the agent of British Linguaphone products. In 1981 he established a modern printing company in Singapore. He eventually returned to Indonesia.

From 1994 he was elected as deputy chairman of the Indonesian Printing Association. In 2000 he participated in the Indonesian International Book Exhibition, importing Chinese books from China and Taiwan. In 2001 he established Lian Tong Chinese bookstore (联通书局) in Surabaya, publishing and selling Chinese books. In the same year he opened the second Chinese bookstore in Jakarta and in 2002, the third bookstore in Medan. After a few years, the bookstores in Surabaya and Medan were closed down. The only one still standing today is in Jakarta. In 2010 Lian Tong Bookstore organized an exhibition on Chinese books.

Sources: *Jiechu renwu minglu*, p. 295; Li Zhuohui, *Qundao xinghuo guangmang shanyao* (2010), pp. 248–51.

Suryo HUTOMO. See **HUTOMO, Suryo**
SURYONO, Bambang. See **LI Zhuohui**
Susanta LYMAN. See **LYMAN, Susanta**

SUSANTI, Susi Lucia Francisca (WANG Lianxiang 王莲香, 1971-)
Badminton player

Born on 11 February 1971 in Tasikmalaya, she has been ranked by the International Badminton Federation as the top seed female singles player for many years. She joined the Jaya Raya Club in Jakarta. In 1989, when she was only eighteen years old, she emerged as the finalist in the All-England Competition. Although only 161 cm in height, she is regarded as an all-round player. She won the All-England women's singles championship in the years 1990, 1991, 1993, and 1994. She also won the women's singles in the 1992 Olympics. She was placed as the first singles player in the Indonesian Uber Cup team in 1994, which was the year when Indonesia won the Cup. She is married to another Indonesian badminton champion, **Alan BUDIKUSUMA**.

Sources: *Media Karya*, June 1994, p. 54; *Sejumlah Orang Bulutangkis Indonesia* (1994), pp. 299–304; the compiler's notes.

SUSANTO, T.L. (LIN Guanyu 林冠玉, 1942-)
Member of DPR, pharmacist, Catholic

Born in Sekadau, West Kalimantan, on 2 January 1942, he received his primary school education at SD Michael (1950–56) and junior middle school education SMP Bruder (1956–59), both in Pontianak, and senior secondary school education at SMA St. Albertus, Malang (1959–62). He later entered the Department of Pharmacy, Institute of Technology Bandung (ITB) in 1962 and graduated in 1968. He worked as a pharmacist after graduation and since 1993 also worked as a car dealer. He was active in two foundations: Yayasan Suci and Yayasan Halim. After the fall of Soeharto, he joined the PBI when it was first established and participated in the 1999 DPR election as a PBI candidate. He was elected and served in the parliament from 1999 to 2004. In 2000 he was elected as the general chairman of the PBI for the period of 2000–5. He only served one term in the DPR.

Source: *Wajah Dewan Perwakilan Rakyat Republik Indonesia Pemilihan Umum 1999* (Jakarta: Kompas, 2000), p. 446.

Susi SUSANTI. See SUSANTI, Susi
Susilo WONOWIDJOJO. See WONOWIDJOJO, Susilo

SUTANU, Tommie (CHEN Binghuang 陈炳煌, 1940–2014)
Philantropist

Tommie Sutanu whose Chinese name was Chen Binghuang was born on 29 July 1940 in Manado (Sulawesi). He received Chinese school education at his birthplace and went to Pah Tsung, Jakarta for his high school education. During the PP 10 (1959) he was still studying at Pah Tsung Senior High School (second year), but decided to go to China where he completed his high school education. He later applied to study at the English language department of the Shanghai Foreign Trading Institute and graduated in 1965.

After graduation he was sent to Beijing Film Corporation to be a translator. During the Cultural Revolution (1966–69) he was forced to work in the rural areas. In 1972 he moved to Hong Kong. Initially he engaged in small business and later set up the International Trading Odyssey, which imported fertilizers and chemicals from the United States and Canada to mainland China via Hong Kong. His business was successful and in 1992 he immigrated to Hawaii and in 1998 he became a US citizen.

In fact, since 1990 Tommie often returned to his birthplace. In 1995 he came to be acquainted with Bhikku Dr Dharma Surya Mahastavira who worked for a local society. Tommie was moved by Bhikku's dedication to the unfortunate. Tommie also wanted to help the poor and the old folks, especially the orphans in Manado regardless of their racial and religious backgrounds. He then established a foundation called Yayasan Dharma Bakti, under which there are two institutions: Panti Asuhan Prajapan (for orphans) and Panti Werda (for old folks).

In 1999 Tommie also established the Universitas Sariputra Indonesia Tomohon (UNSRIT) in his birthplace. Usually people built universities in developed areas but Tommie had a different view. He would like to establish a university in the less developed area to promote local education. The university has so far produced 2,000 graduates. Many of them were orphans and after getting higher degrees they returned to the area to serve. Due to Tommie's contribution to local education, in 2013 he was awarded a certificate by the Indonesian ministry of education culture "in recognition of an outstanding effort and action in promoting … education for the remote area of which he has served with excellence."

Tommie died in Hong Kong on 22 July 2014.

Sources: Chen Binghuang (Tommie Sutanu), 爸B的故事 (*Papi's Story*), n.p.; Rank Books <www.rankbooks.com>, 2013; <http://www.qiao-you.com/index.php/article/detail/uid/20090.html> (accessed 9 May 2014); the compiler's notes.

Sutanto, DJUHAR. See **DJUHAR, Sutanto**
SUTRAWAN, Salam. See **SOE Lie-Piet**

SUTRISNO, Slamet (TJOE Tit Fat; ZHU Difa 朱迪发, 1913–70)
Businessman, publisher

Born in Guangdong on 12 August 1913, he was a major shareholder of *Shoudu Ribao* (a Chinese daily in Jakarta) from 1963 to 1965. After the 1965 coup he served as the director of Asia Bowling Investment Company Ltd. (Hong Kong and Jakarta). He died in Jakarta on 5 February 1970.

Sources: *Ekspres*, 15 August 1970, p. 7; *Ribao*, 6 February 1970; the compiler's notes.

Suwandi HAMID. See **BONG A Lok**

SUWONDO, Gani (LIE Guan Die; LI Yuanli 李源利, 1965-)
Member of DPRD (Provincial Parliament)
Born in Bagan Siapi-api on 26 June 1965, Gani received a Bachelor of Law degree (SH). He is a businessman and contested the 2014 DPRD election for Jakarta representing the PDIP and won a seat (2014–19).

Sources: Pengurus Pusat Fordeka, *Buku Acuan 2014*, p. 175; the compiler's notes.

SZE TU Mei Sen. See **SOETO Meisen**

Tahir (WENG Junmin 翁俊民, 1952-)
Banker, philanthropist, son-in-law of **Mochtar RIADY,** *Christian*
Born on 26 March 1952 in Surabaya, he received Chinese school education in his birthplace. He obtained his B.A. in Business Administration from the Chinese-medium Nanyang University (Singapore, 1976), an MBA from the Golden Gate University (California, 1987), and an Honorary Doctor degree from the "Universitas Tujuhbelas Augustus" (Surabaya, 2008). He married the daughter of **Mochtar RIADY** (LI Wenzheng); they have three daughters and one son.

In 1990 he founded the Mayapada Bank and served as its chairman and president-commissioner, and after 17 October 2011, its vice-chairman. He has also been the chairman of the Mayapada Group since its inception. In 2008 with the technical assistance from the National Healthcare Group Singapore, he founded Mayapada Healthcare Group and has since served as its chairman. Since 2010 he has become a major shareholder of *Guoji Ribao*, a large Chinese language daily newspaper in Jakarta.

According to one report, in 2009 he donated generously to Indonesian universities such as ITB, UI, and Surabaya State University. Between 2006 and 2010, he gave a total of S$3 million to set up scholarships and bursaries at NUS Business School and the University Town. In 2012 he donated S$30 million to NUS medical school to advance education and research; the largest amount of donation that an Indonesian Chinese ever gave to NUS. It was also reported that in April 2014, the Bill & Melinda Gates Foundation announced its plan to work with Tahir in Indonesia, its first major private donor partnership. Tahir's foundation is putting up US$100 million to focus initially on polio eradication, then TB, malaria, HIV/AIDS and family planning.

Tahir made his fortune in banking and real estate through the Mayapada Group. He recently opened a luxurious beachside hotel Regent Bali and a second Mayapada Hospital in Jakarta.

Tahir is a Hokchia and a Christian. He has been the president of the Indonesian Table Tennis Association and chairman of Hua Shang Zonghui (华商总会), an Indonesian Chinese businessmen association.

Sources: "跑单帮小子变巨人", *Lianhe Zaobao*, 14 October 2012, p. 25; <http://www.forbesasiaconferences.com/forbesglobalceoconference2012/speaker/dr-tahir-0> (accessed 14 December 2012); 翁俊民: 白手起家写传奇, 倾力回报美名传, <http://hongqiwang.net/detail12.asp?id+66> (accessed 14 December 2012); "Indonesian tycoon makes $30m donation to NUS", <http://www.asiaone.com/News/Latest+News/Singapore/Story/A1Story20120101-319334.html> (accessed 14 December 2012); <http://www.forbes.com/profile/tahir/> (accessed 10 June 2014).

TAI Yun Ming. See **PATROS, Asmin**

TAN Beng Yauw (1900s-?) 陈明耀*
Community leader

Born in the 1900s, he operated a *warung*. He was first active in the CHTH (Sukabumi) and eventually served as its chairman.

From 1956 to 1957 he was the chairman of Baperki (Sukabumi branch).

Source: Tan Giok Lan (1963), p. 245.

TAN Boen Aan (ISMANTO, Adil; CHEN Wen'an 陈文安, 1918–89)
Political party leader, engineer, Protestant

Born in Banjarnegara on 14 August 1918, he was first educated at the HCS and the HBS (Jakarta), and later the THS, where he obtained an engineering degree. In 1940 he served as the chairman of Ta Hsioh (Bandung). From the Japanese Occupation to 1948 he worked as an engineer at the Department of Public Works (in charge of irrigation). In 1948–50 he went into business in the private sector. In 1945 he served as a member of the Komite Nasional Pusat representing the Chinese minority. In 1948–49 he was the chairman of the PT (Surabaya branch). From 15 February to 16 August 1950 he was a member of parliament, representing Negara Jawa Timur. From 16 August 1950 to 26 March 1956 he served as a member of the DPR/MPRS, first representing the PT and later, the PSI. He was converted to Christianity in the 1980s and was active in the gospel group.

Sources: *Berita PDTI*, 15 November 1953, p. 2; *Sinar 1*, no. 8 (20 September 1949): 9; *Sinar 1*, no. 2 (1 April 1949): 8; *Ta Hsioh Tsa Chih*, September 1940, inside cover; Kempen, *KP*, p. 133; *DPR 1971*, pp. 582–83, 589–99; interview, 22 June 1984; Junus Jahja, p. 187.

TAN Boen Kim (CHEN Wenjin 陈文金, 1887–1959)
Writer, journalist

Born in Jakarta in 1887, he received no formal education. In the 1910s he published a number of novels, including *Nona Gan Jan Nio: Pertjinta'an Dalem Rasia* [Miss Gan Jan Nio: secret love] (Batavia, 1914); *Nona Kim Lian* [Miss Kim Lian] (Batavia, 1916); *Nona Fientje de Feniks atawa Djadi Korban dari Tjemboeroean* [Miss Fientje de Feniks or victim of jealousy] (Batavia, 1917); *Boenga Berdjiwa* [A living flower] (Batavia, 1919); and *Nona Lan-im* [Miss Lan-im] (vol. 1, Batavia, 1919). In the 1920s he published *Peroesoehan di Koedoes* [Riots in Kudus] (Batavia, 1920), a report based on the racial conflicts in Kudus in 1918, and *Tiga Millioen Satenga* [Three-and-a-half million] (Weltevreden, 1923), a novel. He served as an editor of *Ien Po* (Jakarta) in 1917 and the editor-in-chief of *Kiao Pao* (Palembang) in 1926–27. He died in Jakarta on 2 May 1959.

Sources: *Museum Catalogue*; Tio's notes; Nio, *Sastera*, p. 30; *Catalogus*, pp. 537–38.

TAN Boen Soan (CHEN Wenxuan 陈文宣, 1905–52)
Journalist

Born in Sukabumi on 25 June 1905, he was educated at the HCS (Sukabumi) and the KWS (Jakarta). As a student he was active in Chung Hsioh (Sukabumi). After his graduation from the KWS he worked for Staats Spoorwagen in Jakarta. He later returned to Sukabumi where he began to write articles for *Sin Po* and *Perniagaan*. In the mid-1920s he was a member of the editorial board of *Sin Bin* (Bandung), in 1931–32 he served as the editor-in-chief of *Warna Warta*, and in 1939–42, the editor-in-chief of *Soeara Semarang*. After World War II, he became the editor-in-chief of *Sin Min* (Semarang, 1947–52). He died in West Java on 12 August 1952.

Sources: Tan, *Tionghoa*, pp. 230–31; *Sin Min*, 14 August 1952; the compiler's notes.

TAN Eng Hoa (CHEN Yinghua 陈英华, 1907–49)
Politician, lawyer

Born in 1907 in Semarang, his parents owned a grocery store. He finished HBS (1925) in Semarang and studied at RHS in Jakarta (Batavia) from which he received a law degree (1932). He practised as a lawyer. In 1934 he acquired a European status. He was attracted to the idea of an "Asia for Asians" and during the Japanese Occupation he was head of the Film Censor Department of the Barisan Propaganda (Propaganda Team). He became the secretary of Kakyo Sokai (HCTH or Huaqiao Zonghui), a Japanese sponsored overseas Chinese association. The chairman of Kakyo Sokai was **OEY Tiang Tjoei**. When BPUPKI was established he was appointed as a member, together with Oey Tiang Tjoei, **OEI Tjong Hauw** and **LIEM Koen Hian**. It was reported that he was the one who proposed to include "freedom of organization in a free and independent Indonesia" in the new Indonesian constitution. Interestingly his brothers joined the Royal Netherlands East Indies Army (Koninklijk Nederlands Indisch Leger, KNIL). Tan Eng Hoa suffered from cancer and died in 1949.

Sources: *Risalah Sidang*, n.p.; Kwartanada (2013); Peter Post et al., *The Encyclopedia of Indonesia in the Pacific War* (Brill, 2010), p. 607.

TAN Eng Hong 陈英丰*

He was a *peranakan* member of the DPR, representing the Chinese minority from December 1956 to 1959.

Source: *DPR 1971*, p. 618.

TAN Eng Tie (CHEN Yingzhi 陈英智**, 1907–2003)**
Community leader, physician

Born in Lampegan (Cianjur) on 19 July 1907, he was first educated at Instituut Kooiman in Sukabumi. While studying at the K.W. III (Batavia) he served as an executive member of the HCTNH. In 1925 he attended Leiden University where he was awarded a medical degree in 1932. He returned to Java to work in the Jang Seng Ie Hospital (Jakarta) and the General Hospital (Jakarta). After Indonesia's independence he was elected as the president of the PDTI (1953). He was a founding member of Baperki and an executive member of the Baperki central board (1954–56). He died in May 2003.

Sources: Tan, *Tionghoa*, p. 216; *Pedoman Kampanje*, p. 63; the compiler's notes.

TAN Giok Lan. See **TAN, Mely G.**

TAN Giok Sin (CHEN Yuxin 陈玉信)
Community leader, teacher

A member of the KMT, he came to Java as a teacher before World War II. In the 1950s he established Tzu-yu Hsueh-hsiao in Jatinegara, during which period he also served as an executive member of Hok Kian Hwee Koan. In 1967–69 he was appointed as a member of the BKUT. He was involved in the establishment of SPNC Chongde Xuexiao in 1970.

Sources: *Fujian*, p. 34; Jiang, "Yajiada", p. 15; the compiler's notes.

TAN Goan Po (CHEN Yuanbao 陈源宝; Paul MAWIRA, 1913–78)
Economist, university professor

Born in Ulu Siau, Kepulauan Sangihe Talaud, North Sulawesi in 1913, he was sent to Manado for his primary school education and to Jakarta for his AMS education. After graduation he went to the Netherlands and entered the Nederlandsche Economische Hoogeschool (now Erasmus School of Economics) in Rotterdam. He received a Drs degree in November 1942.

Soon after Indonesia's independence he joined the PSI, and became close to Sutan Sjahrir, Soedjatmoko, Hasjim Ning and Soemitro Djojohadikusumo. Together with Soemitro, he lectured at the FEUI until 1954. In 1955 he served as the secretary of the FEUI under Professor Sumitro Djojohadikusumo. In 1956 he was appointed as a professor (*Gurubesar Tetap*) specializing in economic theory. He had many students who later became well-known, including **THEE Kian Wie**, **PANGLAYKIM**, Widjojo Nitisastro, and Ali Wardhana. In 1958 he was involved in the Regional Rebellion and left the FEUI together with Professor Sumitro.

Tan Goan Po lived in many countries and in 1961 he eventually returned to Indonesia. He was immediately detained by the authorities upon his return due to his involvement in the Regional Rebellion. During the New Order period he changed his name to Paul Mawira. In the 1970s he served as dean of the Faculty of Economics, Universitas Krisnadwipayana, one of the oldest private universities in Jakarta. He was also appointed as Extraordinary Professor (*Professor Luarbiasa*) of the Academy of Military Law. Tan died in Jakarta in 1978.

Sources: *Pedoman Fakultas Ekonomi Universitas Indonesia 1953–54*, p. 7; *Pedoman Fakultas Ekonomi Universitas Indonesia 1965–58*, p. 7; Bachtiar (1975), p. 40; Setyautama, *Tokoh-tokoh Etnis Tionghoa*, pp. 353–54.

TAN Goan Tiang. See ISKANDAR, Nathanel
TAN Hian Wie. See WINARTA, Frans Hendra

TAN Hin Hie (CHEN Xingyan 陈兴砚, 1891–1969)
Community leader, businessman, owner of Loka Sari (Recreation Park in Jakarta)

Born in 1891 in Fujian, he migrated to Indonesia before 1911. He ran a salted fish and agricultural product business in Cianjur. He later moved to Jakarta where he was associated with the KMT (Jakarta branch). He served in a number of Chinese organizations in Java: he was the president of Huaqiao Zhiyu Hui (pre-World War II), the vice-chairman of the China Charity Fund (1930s), the president of Hok Kian Hwee Koan (Jakarta, 1950s), and the vice-president of the board of trustees of the Kao Shang School (Jakarta, 1950s). He was detained by the Indonesian Government in 1958 on account of his affiliation with the KMT. He died in Jakarta in 1969.

Sources: Liu, *Gailan*, p. [36]; *Fujian*, p. 28; the compiler's notes.

TAN Hoe Teng (CHEN Fuding 陈富定, 1892–1951)
Leading businessman

Born in Jakarta on 12 September 1892, he received Malay education at the primary school level. At first he operated a *grobak* business; later he moved into leather processing. In 1929 he established the first leather-processing factory in West Java, which earned him the reputation of "Captain of the Leather Industry". He died in Jakarta in 1951.

Sources: Tan, *Tionghoa*, p. 209; *Directory of Chinese Names*, p. 85; the compiler's notes.

TAN Hong Boen (pen-name: IM Yang Tjoe; IM Jang Tju; Ki Hadjar SUKOWIJONO; CHEN Fengwen 陈丰文, 1905–83)
Writer, mystic

Born in Slawi on 27 February 1905, not much is known about his education. He published more than ten novels in the 1920s and early 1930s, including *Soepardi dan Soendari* (Surabaya, 1925); *Oh, harta* (Surabaya, 1928); *Koepoe-koepoe di dalam Halimoen* (Semarang, 1929); *Soerat Resia di Tangkoeban-Praoe* (Bandung, 1930); *Ketesan Aer Mata di Padang-lalang* (Bandung, 1930); *Gelap Goelita Lantaran Sajapnja Kampret dari Yomani* (Bandung, 1931); and *Angin Pagoenoengan, Koemandangnja Soemoer Djalatoenda* (Bandung, 1931). Most of these novels were published in *Penghidoepan, Boelan Poernama* and *Tjantik*.

In 1935 he compiled *Orang-Orang Tionghoa Jang Terkemoeka di Java*, the first biographical dictionary of the Chinese in Java. After World War II, he published *Riwajat Ejang Djugo Penembahan Gunung Kawi* (Surabaya, 1953), a book on a leading Chinese mystic in East Java. He died in Slawi (Central Java) on 15 September 1983.

Sources: The above-mentioned books; *Catalogus*, pp. 198–99, 539; *Sinar Harapan*, 19 September 1985; Sidharta (1993), pp. 64–72.

TAN Hwat Tiang (1912-) 陈发长*
Community leader, engineer

Born in Solo in 1912, he received an Ir degree from the ITB (Bandung) in 1937. In the 1950s he was active in the social and commercial fields. He was the president of PRETEX (Priangan Textile Business Federation) in 1950, the president of GAPO (Bus Transportation Association, West Java) and IPPOI (Indonesian Bus Transport Business Federation) in the 1950s, and the director of Kantor Insinjur dan Arsitek Puntjak (an architectural and engineering firm in Bandung). In the 1950s he also served as the president of Baperki (West Java Region), a member of the DPRDS (West Java), and an adviser to Sin Ming Hui (Bandung).

Source: *Pedoman Kampanje*, pp. 45–46.

TAN Joe Hok (Hendra KARTANEGARA; CHEN Youfu 陈友福, 1938-)
Badminton player

Born in Bandung on 11 August 1938, he was educated at Nanhua Xuexiao and Huaqiao Zhongxue (both in Bandung), and Baylor University (Texas, 1959–63). He began playing badminton at the age of twelve and was the first Indonesian who won the All-England Championship in 1959. In 1958, 1961, and 1964 he represented Indonesia in Thomas Cup competitions. In 1970 he worked as a coach in Hong Kong and Mexico. He returned to Indonesia in 1972 to engage in business. In 1982 he became a coach again, and in 1983 he was appointed as the coach of the Indonesian Thomas Cup Team. Indonesia won the Thomas Cup again in 1984.

In 1967 when the Soeharto regime introduced name changing regulations, Tan, who was already well-known by his Chinese name, was asked to use a new name. An army general suggested "Hendra" for his first name, and he himself created Kartanegara as his surname. He felt a bit unhappy about the name changing as Ferry Sonneville, another Thomas Cup player who was of Dutch Indonesian descent, did not have to change his Western name to Indonesian sounding name. Apparently only Chinese Indonesians were required to change their names.

Tan Joe Hok felt that there was racial discrimination. After the fall of Soeharto, together with many well-known Chinese Indonesians he appealed to the new Indonesian government to abolish laws and regulations which were discriminatory in nature.

Sources: *Apa & Siapa 1985–86*, pp. 389–90; Suryadinata, *Southeast Asian Personalities*, pp. 1073–75; the compiler's notes.

TAN Kang Ho. See TANOTO, Sukanto

TAN Kang So (CHEN Jiangsu 陈江苏)
Leading banker, industrialist, nephew of TAN Pia Teng

He is the owner of a zinc factory in Jakarta and a local bank in Jakarta (Bank Buana).

Source: The compiler's notes.

TAN Kian An. See TANDIONO, Ki Anan

TAN Kian Lok (CHEN Jianlu 陈建禄, 1920-)
Lawyer

Born in Batu (Malang) on 20 November 1920, he was awarded an LL D from Leiden University in 1949. He did his post-doctoral work at Faculte de Droit (Paris) in 1950. From 1947 to 1951 he served as a teaching assistant to Professor R.D. Kollewijn. In 1951 he returned to Indonesia and practised law in Jakarta. He participated in the 1955 general elections as a Baperki candidate.

Source: *Pedoman Kampanje*, p. 50.

TAN Kim Bo (1872–1935) 陈金茂*
Community leader, journalist

Born in Jakarta in 1872, he was educated at the ELS (Jakarta?). He worked for the KPM for thirty-nine years and was awarded a medal by the Dutch Government for his service in that company. From 1902 to 1903 he served as the deputy secretary to the THHK (Jakarta) and from 1904 to 1921 as its secretary. In 1904 he also served as an editor of *Kabar Perniagaan* (Jakarta). He died in Jakarta on 20 May 1935.

Sources: Tan, *Tionghoa*, p. 206; Nio, *THHK*, p. 277.

TAN Kim Hong (CHEN Jinfeng 陈金丰, 1897–1964)
Physician

Born in 1897 in Tangerang, he was first educated at the THHK (Jakarta). He later graduated from the University of London and returned to Indonesia. In 1949 he served as the president of Jang Seng Ie Hospital. He died in Jakarta on 12 August 1964.

Source: The compiler's notes.

TAN Kim Kian (CHEN Jinjian 陈金建, 1903-?)
Community leader

Born in Jakarta in 1903, he was educated at the THHK (Jakarta), the Anglo-Chinese School in Singapore, and the University of Iowa (majoring in Commerce). He returned to Java and served as an executive member of the THHK (Tasikmalaya) and, in the 1930s, as a member of the Tasikmalaya Regency Council.

Source: Tan, *Tionghoa*, p. 223.

TAN Kim Liong. See **HASSAN, Hadji Mohammad**
TAN Kim Nio. See **YOUNG, Fifi**

TAN Kim San (CHEN Jinshan 陈金山, 1873-?)
Community leader

Born in 1873 in Jakarta, he was educated at a local Hokkien school (Jakarta) and an English school (Singapore). A founder of the THHK (Jakarta) in 1900, he served as its secretary from 1900 to 1902 and was its master of ceremonies from 1904 to 1916. In 1911 he was sent by the THHK to attend a conference on "The Malaysia Mission of Methodist Episcopal Church" in Singapore, where he tried but was unsuccessful in recruiting an English teacher for the THHK high school. In 1915 he was appointed the director of the THHK school.

Sources: Nio, *THHK*, p. 275; Williams, *Nationalism*, p. 140; the compiler's notes.

TAN King Po. See SATJADININGRAT, TKP
TAN Kiong Liep. See SOETANTYO, Tegoeh

TAN Koen Swie (1894-?) 陈群瑞*
Writer, mystic, publisher

Born in 1894 in Wonogiri. A student of Mas Ngabei Mangoenwidjojo in Wonogiri, he was well-versed in Javanese literature. When he was young he worked in Sie Dhian printing house in Solo. He later moved to Kediri, where he established his own printing press and bookstore called Boekhandel Tan Khoen Swie. He published numerous books in Javanese and Malay, especially the Javanese *primbon*, similar to the Chinese *tongshu*. He published a catalogue every year to announce the new publications of his company.

He was well-known as a philosopher and a mystic. Wearing long hair and sporting a moustache, he looked like a present-day hippie. He was a close friend of **TAN Tik Sioe Sian** (Ramamoerti), who was also a well-known mystic. Tan Khoen Swie himself built a cave in the yard of his house for meditation. It was beautifully built and many people had visited his cave.

Tan Khoen Swie was active in the local Chinese society. He was a committee member of the THHK and the HCTNH in Kediri. He was also an advocate of Hoe Lie Hiap Hwee (Women Association), of which his wife was the chairperson.

Sources: *Pandji Poestaka 62* (5 August 1927): 1075; Tan, *Tionghoa*, p. 89; *Catalogus* (Boekhandel Tan Khoen Swie-Kediri, 1937).

TAN Kong Tam 陈光谭*
Community leader, businessman

A Dutch-educated Semarang-born Chinese, he served as the director of the Indische Lloyd (before World War II) and was a member of the Semarang Municipal Council in 1934.

Source: The compiler's notes.

TAN Lian Houw. See ANANTA, Aris

TAN Liep Tjiauw (1922–63) 陈立超*
Tennis player

Born on 2 February 1922 in Pare, Kediri (East Java), he is the son of a businessman. He began playing tennis at the age of thirteen. In 1940 he won the Bandung tournament and began to dominate the Indonesian tennis world for almost a decade. In the 1950s he was sent to Wimbledon to participate in international competitions. In 1956 and 1957 he represented Indonesia in the Interport Championships in Singapore. In 1956 he won the men's singles title in the Open Malaya Championship.

It is interesting to note that Tan was the tennis partner of General Abdul Haris Nasution, an army general known for not being friendly with the Chinese community. Their relationship was so good that Tan was mentioned in Nasution's memoirs twice, and a picture portraying their conversations was also included.

Tan married a woman who is also a tennis player. He died in November 1963.

Sources: Katili (1973), pp. 163–67; AH Nasution, *Memenuhi Panggilan Tugas: Masa Kebangkitan Orde Baru*, vol. 6, CV Haji Masagung, 1989?, p. 32 (coutersy: Didi Kwartanada).

TAN Ling Djie (CHEN Linru 陈粦如, 1904–69)
Political party leader

Born in Surabaya in 1904, he attended the RHS (Jakarta) and Leiden Law School. Originally active in the CHH-Netherlands, in 1932 he broke away from the student organization and founded Sarekat Peranakan Tionghoa Indonesia (in the Netherlands). He served as the secretary of this new organization. In 1933 he served as an editor and a correspondent of *Sin Tit Po* in Europe, and from 1939 to 1942 as the editor-in-chief of the newspaper. After Indonesia declared its independence, he became a leader of the PSI (1946) and a member of the KNIP. From September 1948 he was also a member of the Politburo PKI. In 1949–51 he served as the secretary-general of the PKI. He came into conflict with the Aidit group and was criticized by the group for his "Tan-ling-djieisme", resulting in his expulsion from the Politburo in October 1953. A close friend of **SIAUW Giok Tjhan**, he lived in Siauw's house from 1951–65. He was detained by the authorities after the 1965 coup and died in 1969 while still in detention. (Siauw Tiong Djin in his book noted that Tan died in detention at the age of sixty-five.)

Sources: Aidit, *Pilihan Tulisan 1* (1962): 292; Anderson, *Java*, pp. 452–53; *Sin Tit Po*, 16 December 1939; Hindley, *PKI*, pp. 63–64; Jacques Leclec, "Kondisi kehidupan partai: Kaum revolusioner Indonesian dalam mencari identitas (1928–1948)", *Prisma* 8 (August 1979), p. 49, Siauw Tiong Djin, *Siauw Giok Tjhan* (Jakarta: Hasta Mitra, 1999), pp. 59–60.

TAN Liong Houw. See **TANOTO, Latif Harris**

TAN, Mely G. (TAN Giok Lan; CHEN Yulan 陈玉兰, 1930-)
Sociologist, university lecturer, better known as **Mely Tan**, *Catholic*

Born in Jakarta in 1930, she graduated from the Department of Sinology, FSUI, in 1959. After receiving an MA degree in Sociology from Cornell University (1961), she returned to Indonesia and worked as a lecturer at Atma Jaya University (1962–63). In 1963 she joined LEKNAS as a research assistant. She was soon awarded a scholarship to study at the University of California (Berkeley), from which she obtained a PhD degree (Sociology) in 1968. She returned to Indonesia in the same year and became the head of the Social Sciences Division of LEKNAS in LIPI (1968–78) and remained in LIPI until 1997. She was a lecturer at the FIS-UI, the secretary-general of Himpunan Indonesia Untuk Pengembangan Ilmu Ilmu Sosial, co-chairperson of the board of directors of Atma Jaya Research Centre (1997–2002), and a member of the BPKB-DKI (from 1974).

Between 1986 and 1987 she was Visiting Research Scholar at the Center for Southeast Asian Studies, University of Kyoto, Japan. She was often invited to participate in international conferences. After the fall of Soeharto, she was one of the founders and a Commisioner of the Komisi Nasional Anti-Kekerasan Terhadap Perempuan [National Commision of Anti-Violence against Women]. She has been awarded several medals by the government of Indonesia for her service and contribution to Indonesian society.

Her publications include *The Chinese in Sukabumi* (Ithaca, 1963); *The Chinese in the United States: Social Mobility and Assimilation* (Taipei, 1971); *The Social and Cultural Context of Family Planning in Indonesia* (Jakarta, 1971); as well as *Golongan Etnis Tionghoa di Indonesia* (Jakarta, 1979), and *Perempuan Indonesia: Pemimpin Masa*

Depan (Jakarta, 1991), which she edited. In 2008, coinciding with her 78th birthday, the Yayasan Obor Indonesia published the selected writings of Mely Tan entitled: *Etnis Tionghoa di Indonesia: Kumpulan Tulisan*. The book consists of 12 articles on Chinese Indonesians, 9 in English and 3 in Indonesian.

Sources: The above-mentioned publications; interview, 1970; *Tempo*, 25 May 1974, p. 28; "Keputusan Gubernur" (mimeographed); *Pusat Penelitian Atma Jaya Annual Report 1975* (1975), p. 29.

TAN Pia Teng (CHEN Bingding 陈丙定, 1887–1940s)
Community leader, leading businessman

Born in Fujian in 1887, he received a traditional Hokkien education in China. He came to Java in 1902(?), initially living in Serang and later moving to Jakarta where he joined Tongmeng Hui and Soe Po Sia. He served as the president of Siang Hwee (Jakarta) in 1919–20 and again in 1922–24. In 1924–25 he also served as the president of the THHK (Jakarta). He returned to China in the 1940s and probably died in Shanghai.

Sources: *Fujian*, p. 26; *Siang Hwee* (Chinese-language section), pp. [43–44].

TAN Ping Liem (?-1960s) 陈炳林*
Trade unionist, community leader

Born in Mojosragen, he was educated at the HCS and MULO (Surakarta). He worked for *Warna Warta* as a curator and later for *Djawa Tengah* as an administrator. He was active in the local Chinese trade union. In the 1930s he joined the PTI, served as the chairman of Persatoean Kaoem Boeroeh Tionghoa (Chinese Trade Union), and as the editor of its newsletter. He probably died in Semarang in the early 1960s.

Sources: Tan, *Tionghoa*, p. 143; the compiler's notes.

TAN Ping Tjiat (CHEN Bingjie 陈秉节, 1885?–1964)
Political activist, community leader

Born in Surabaya in 1885(?), he had no formal education. In 1924 he was attracted to the radical movement and joined the PKI. In the same year he became an executive member of the SPPL, a PKI-sponsored Seamen's and Dockers' Union. After the 1926–27 communist uprisings, he was arrested and was about to be sent to Boven Digoel with the other communist leaders when he changed his political conviction and remained in Java. He later became involved in the CHH and was the president of the CHH (Malang branch) (1934?). He was appointed as a zone chief (*wijkmeester*) by the Dutch and was detained by the Japanese in 1942. He died in Batu (near Malang) on 5 July 1964.

Sources: Tan, *Tionghoa*, p. 28; McVey, *Communism*, pp. 334, 485; the compiler's notes.

TAN Po Goan (CHEN Baoyuan 陈宝源, 1911–85)
Politician, lawyer

Born in Cianjur on 24 October 1911, he was educated at the AMS (Bandung) and the RHS (Jakarta), from where he obtained an Mr degree in 1937. He practised law in Makassar in 1937–38 and in Surabaya in 1939. In 1939 he joined *Sin Po*, and from 1942 to 1945 he was interned by the Japanese. In 1946–47 he was appointed Minister of State in the Sjahrir Cabinet (III) and was active in Sin Ming Hui's Labour Section. In 1947 he served as a member of the KNIP and was appointed as a member of the DPR from 1950 to 1956. He joined the PDTI and in 1953 became a member of the PSI (one source says that he joined PSI in 1946). He was to participate in the general elections of 1955 as a Baperki candidate, but withdrew before the elections took place. In 1959(?) he left Indonesia and returned to it after the fall of Soekarno. In 1977 he contributed short articles on his experiences during the colonial period to *Intisari*, a monthly published by P.K. Ojong. He later migrated to Australia and died in Sydney in November 1985.

Sources: *Pedoman Kampanje*, p. 54; *Liberal*, 24 September 1955, p. 3; Kempen, *KP*, p. 134; *Directory of Chinese Names*, p. 87; *Intisari*, no. 168 (July 1977): 57–64; *Intisari*, no. 169 (August 1977): 89–94; *Tempo*, 23 November 1985, p. 21; the compiler's notes.

TAN Siang Lian (CHEN Xianglian 陈祥连, 1906-?)
Community leader

Born in Brebes on 2 June 1906, he was educated at the ELS (Tegal), MULO (Bandung and Purwokerto), and at a commercial college (Jakarta). He was an editor of *Warna Warta* (Semarang) before serving as the secretary of the Rice Millers Association (Jember) and the president of the CHH (Tegal, 1930s). In 1949 he served as the deputy president of the PT (central board), and as a member of the East Java Provincial Council.

Sources: Tan, *Tionghoa*, p. 161; *Sinar*, 20 September 1949, p. 10; *Sinar*, 1 April 1949, p. 8.

TAN Siong Kie (CHEN Xiangji 陈祥基, 1916-)
Prominent businessman

Born in Semarang on 20 November 1916, he was educated at the Chinese-English High School, Semarang, and at St. John's University, Shanghai, from which he obtained a BA degree in Economics. Residing in Jakarta, he is the owner of PT Roda Mas, the sole agent for imported glass in Indonesia and a "Panda" air-conditioner manufacturer.

Sources: C.M. Hsu, *Java Critic*, no. 11 (August 1949): 16; *Indonesia Raya*, 4 November 1972; the compiler's notes.

TAN Soe Lin. See DANANJAYA, James

TAN, Sofyan (TAN Kim Yang; CHEN Jinyang 陈金扬, 1959-)
Educator, physician, member of parliament, Buddhist

Born on 25 September 1959 in Singgal, near Medan, his father was originally a tailor. While studying in the Medical Faculty of Universitas Methodis Indonesia in Medan, Sofyan financed himself by giving private tuition to secondary school students. After graduation, he did not practise medicine and instead set up a racially and religiously mixed school in Singgal, his hometown.

He introduced the adoption programme requesting rich businessmen to sponsor children from poor indigenous and Chinese families. The school, which is known as Perguruan Sultan Iskandar Muda, named after the first king of Aceh, is noted for producing well-trained graduates and its reputation continues to grow. Sofyan received support from both domestic and foreign organizations, especially the Ashoka Foundation from Washington, D.C. He was highly praised by indigenous Indonesian leaders: the Governor of North Sumatra awarded him the "Youth of Pioneer" medal in 1990, while Professor B.J. Habibie donated funds to the school and noted (in 1994) that what Sofyan did was the work of a "son of the [Indonesian] nation" (*putra bangsa*).

Sofyan has attempted to use education as a means to bring about integration/assimilation. He also believes that integration/assimilation should be implemented in the economic field, especially in small and medium enterprises (Usaha Kecil dan Menengah, or UKM). Not surprisingly he has become an entrepreneur himself and has also been involved in the local *Koperasi* (cooperative) to improve the economic condition of the poor. He served as chairman of the Forum Nasional UKM (National Forum for SMEs, 2002–4). In addition to this, he was interested in local politics and contested in the 2004 election for a seat in DPRD but lost. In 2010 he also contested the mayoral election of Medan as deputy mayor but was defeated. In the election he was supported by PDIP. Tan contested in the 2014 election for a parliamentary seat (2014–19) for Northern Sumatra on the PDIP ticket, this time he was elected.

Sources: *Kompas*, 6 August 1995, p. 2; Suryadinata, *Southeast Asian Personalities*, pp. 1108–10; the compiler's notes.

TAN Swan Bing (CHEN Xuanming 陈宣明, 1906-?)
Community leader, newspaperman

Born in Kediri on 11 November 1906, he was educated at the HBS (Bandung and Surabaya) and the Nederlandsch Handels Hooge School (Rotterdam). In 1927–28 he served as the editor of the *CHHTC* (Holland). In 1933 he returned to Java to join the editorial board of *Siang Po* (Jakarta) and later became its director. He worked as a salaried secretary of the CHH central board in 1934(?), and as an administrator for *Mata Hari* in 1935(?).

Sources: Tan, *Tionghoa*, p. 141; the compiler's notes.

TAN Tay Kang. See TANUDJAJA, Sukanta

TAN Tek Heng (CHEN Deheng 陈德恒, 1906-?)
Economist, university professor, community leader

Born in Menado on 4 May 1906, he was educated at the PHS (Jakarta) and Economische Hogeschool (Rotterdam). He obtained a Drs degree in Economics from Amsterdam University in 1937. In 1938–40 he was a member of Makassar Municipal Council. In 1940–42 he taught at the HBS in Makassar. His activities during the Japanese Occupation are not known. From 1947 to 1950 he was appointed Minister of Finance of the NIT and from 1950 to 1952 as a senior officer in the Ministry of Economics, RI. He was later (1952–53) appointed deputy director of the Biro Perantjang Negara (State Budget Bureau). In 1953 he served as the director of Jajasan Kopra (Copra

Foundation) and from 1955 he was professor of Economics at the FEUI and director of Bank Persatuan Dagang Indonesia (United Commercial Bank of Indonesia Ltd.). He participated in the 1955 general elections as a Baperki candidate.

Source: *Pedoman Kampanje*, p. 53.

TAN Tek Ho (pen-name: KUO Lay Yen; CHEN Dehe 陈德和, 1894–1948)
Community leader, writer

Born in Jakarta in 1894, he was educated at the THHK (Jakarta and Bandung), the CNHT (Nanking), and the China Institute (Shanghai). He returned to Java and became a businessman in Bandung where he was also involved in the THHK (1917) movement. Unsuccessful in his business, he went to Bali to work. Meanwhile he became interested in journalism and began to write articles for *Sin Po*. He worked for *Sin Po Oost Java Editie* (Surabaya). He engaged in a polemic with **LIEM Koen Hian**, resulting in a fight. He returned to Bandung after *Sin Po Oost Java Editie* ceased publication. He began writing *kungfu* stories for *Sin Po*, and in the 1930s he edited a monthly on *kungfu* novels called *Tjerita Silat*. His better known works are *Tiga Djago Silat* (Bandung, 1930) and *Tay Beng Kie Hiap* (Bandung, 1932). He died in Bandung in 1948.

Sources: Tan, *Tionghoa*, pp. 181–82; *Sin Po*, 9 June 1928; *Museum Catalogue*; Salmon, *Literature*, pp. 327–28.

TAN Tek Peng (CHEN Zebing 陈泽炳, 1896–1969)
Community leader, leading businessman

Born in Bandung in 1896, he attended the ELS (Bogor), the HBS (Jakarta), and graduated from the PHS (Jakarta) in 1917. In the same year he joined Kian Gwan and was promoted to a director within three years. In 1923–25 he served as a member of the Semarang Municipal Council. In 1927 he and other Dutch-educated *peranakan* organized the Chung Hwa

Congress, which led to the formation of the CHH in 1928. He served as an executive member of the CHH until 1942. In 1934 he was elected as a member of the Central Java Provincial Council. In 1935 he served as the president of Siang Hwee (Siang Boe) (Semarang). He moved to Jakarta after World War II and continued to be the chairman of the directors of Kian Gwan (Indonesia) and the Oei Tiong Ham Concern (Jakarta). In 1946–49 he again served as the president of Siang Hwee (Semarang). In 1952 he became the governor of Rotary International (Indonesia district), and in 1955 he was elected as the treasurer of the board of directors of the Indonesian Red Cross. He participated in the general elections of 1955 as a Baperki candidate. He died in Amsterdam on 24 November 1969.

Sources: Tan, *Tionghoa*, p. 142; Liu, *Gailan*, p. [62]; *Pedoman Kampanje*, p. 57; *Shangye Nianjian*, p. 339; the compiler's notes.

TAN Thiam Hok. See TANZIL, Haris Otto Kamil

TAN Tik Sioe Sian (CHEN De Xiu Xian 陈德修仙; Rama Moorti van Java, 1884–1929)
Mystic, Taoist

Born in Surabaya in 1884, he was a son of a rice trader. He worked in a ship and visited many Asian cities. At the age of twenty-one he was well-known as a hermit and meditated on Mount Wilis and Mount Sumber Agung (both in East Java). Later, he moved to Penang and took up domicile at the White Crane Cave (present name: Hundred Bats Cave, Penang). He wrote several books on Javanese philosophy, Chinese prescription, mysticism, and charms. He died in Penang in 1929.

Sources: *Liberty*, no. 626 (4 September 1965); *Liberty*, no. 629 (25 September 1965); C.M. Hsu's notes; Salmon, *Literature*, p. 330.

TAN Tiong Ien. See SETIABUDI, Natan

TAN Tiong Khing (CHEN Zhongqing 陈忠庆, 1894–1937)
Community leader, businessman

Born in Semarang on 18 January 1894, he was educated at the ELS and MULO (Semarang) and a commercial school in Amsterdam. After working with Unie Bank (Amsterdam) for a year, he got a job with Java China Japan Lijn (JCJL). He later left for Semarang and worked for Lindeteves Stokvis (a Dutch firm). In the 1920s he worked as the secretary of Siang Boe (Semarang). He was a founding member of the CHH (1927–28) and a member of the Semarang Municipal Council in the 1930s. He probably died in Semarang in 1937.

Sources: Tan, *Tionghoa*, p. 143; the compiler's notes.

TAN Tjan Hok. See **DARMAWAN, Hari**

TAN Tjeng Bok (ITEM; CHEN Qingmu 陈清木, 1899–1985)
Actor, comedian

Born in 1899 in Jakarta, his father was a Chinese and his mother a native Indonesian. He had no formal education. At the age of sixteen, he joined a travelling drama troupe. First, he worked as a janitor and later as a supporting actor. Around 1918–19 he joined Dardanella, a well-known travelling drama troupe, and changed his name from Item to Tan Tjeng Bok. His star was rising and soon he became known as the "Douglas Fairbanks van Java" (the Douglas Fairbanks of Java).

His popularity led him from stage to screen. Up to 1954 he made more than one hundred movies (one source says that he acted in fifty movies until 1975). However, the decline of the Indonesian movie industry after 1954 led to his retirement. In 1969 he became active again, and in 1970 he played a leading role in the comedy, *Ardjuna Kesiangan* [The ugly Arjuna]. He later appeared in a number of movies and TV shows. He died in February 1985 in Jakarta after a heart attack.

Sources: *Ekspres*, 3 October 1970, p. 25; *Kompas*, 27 March 1975; "Fifi, Ibu Kita 1914–75", *Tempo*, 15 March 1975, pp. 36–38; "Di Panggung, Tidak di Tempat Lain", *Tempo*, 8 May 1976, pp. 14–16; *Jakarta Post*, 16 February 1985.

TAN Tjien Lien (CHEN Zhenlin 陈振霖, 1916–73)
Community leader, businessman, Protestant

He was born in Semarang on 24 July 1916. His father, who was originally from Padang where his family had lived for a few generations, owned a gold and jewellery shop.

Tan Tjien Lien was educated at St. Stephen's College (Hong Kong) and St. John's University (Shanghai), where he majored in economics. He returned to Indonesia and became an agent for a life insurance firm (1937). In 1947 he established the Union Trading Company dealing with imports and exports. He was a member of the board of directors of Kuang Po (Semarang) in 1952. In the same year he attended the Overseas Chinese Affairs Conference in Taipei. In 1954 he became a member of Baperki but soon withdrew from it. (According to another source, he was on the Baperki planning board but when Baperki was officially established, he resigned.) He was active in various commercial and social organizations in Indonesia, including the CHTH and Siang Hwee (Semarang). In January 1959 the whole family moved to Hong Kong. He died in Tilburg (Holland) on 8 October 1973.

Sources: Willmott, *Semarang*, pp. 154–56, 163, 167; *Shangye Nianjian*, p. 339; Huang, *Geming*, p. 266; Letter of Tan Tjien Lien's son, 1979.

TAN Tjin Beng. See **TANUWIBOWO, Budi S.**
TAN Tjioe Hak. See **KARTAJAYA, Hermawan**
TAN Tjiok Sien. See **BUDIANTA, Melani**
TAN Tjoe Hien. See **RAHARDJA, Hendra**
TAN Tjoe Hong. See **TANSIL, Eddy**

TAN Tjoen Hay (1888-?) 陈春海*
Community leader, physician

Born in Bogor in 1888, he was educated at the ELS (Bogor), the HBS (Holland), and Amsterdam University where he obtained a medical degree. He was a founding member and the first president of the CHH-Netherlands (1911–12). He returned to Java and lived in Bandung as a physician of both the Shiong Tih Hui Polyclinic and the THHT.

Source: Tan, *Tionghoa*, p. 183.

TAN Tju Fuan. See TANSIL, Eddy
TAN Yueh Ming. See SOESASTRO, M. Hadi

TANDIONO, Ki Anan (TAN Kian An; CHEN Chien-An; CHEN Jian'an 陈建安, 1931-)
Writer, cartoonist, translator

Born on 31 July 1931 in Jombang (East Java), he received Dutch and Indonesian secondary education. He has also obtained various diplomas, including certificates in English and Dutch.

Initially he wrote short stories which were published in various Indonesian magazines (including *Star Weekly* and *Pantjawarna*, both published in Jakarta). He later wrote children's and detective stories. He also drew cartoons for newspapers, mainly those published in Surabaya, where he now lives. The books he published include *Pertemuan* (Taskimalaja, c.1950); *Gadis Pudjaanku* (Tasikmalaja, 1956); and *Majat Menjanji?* (Jakarta, 1963).

Sources: Letter to the compiler, 23 February 1985; Salmon, *Literature*, pp. 163, 322.

TANG Chongrong. See TONG, Stephen
T'ANG Leang-Li. See THUNG Liang Lee

TANG Liangli. See **THUNG Liang Lee**
TANG Xinniang. See **THUNG Sin Nio, Betsy**
TANG Youlan. See **THUNG Ju Lan**
TANG Yu. See **TONG Djoe**
TANN Sing Hwat. See **SOEMANTO, Agoes**

TANNOS, W.P.A. (YANG Wie Pin; YANG Weibin 杨伟彬, 1918-early 1970s)
Community leader, leading businessman, Hakka, Protestant

Born in Muara Enim (Sumatra) on 19 March 1918, he was a major shareholder of *Tiansheng Ribao* in the late 1950s and was active in banking. In 1970 he served as the chancellor of Solomon University in Jakarta. He died in the early 1970s.

Sources: *Indonesian Raya*, 21–24 October and 5–6 November 1969; the compiler's notes.

TANOESOEDIBJO, Hary (CHEN Mingli 陈明立, 1965-)
Media tycoon, politician, Christian

Born in September 1965 in Surabaya, Hary Tanoe's father is a businessman. Hary went to the SMAK St. Louis, a Christian high school in his birthplace. After graduation, he went to Canada for tertiary education. He received a Bachelor of Commerce degree from Carleton University, Ottawa, Canada in 1988, and an MBA from the University of Ottowa, also in Canada, the following year. After graduation he returned to Indonesia to start a stock brokerage firm Bhakti Investama. The firm went public in 1997. He was friendly with **Anthony SALIM** but regularly denied that he was Salim's proxy. In 2001 Hary won the Salim convenience store chain Indomaret and later bought over Salim's oleochemicals assets, but he soon sold the assets and from 2002 began to focus on his media business. He is the boss of the MNC (Media Nusantara Citra) Group which controls three television stations: RCTI, MNCTV and GlobalTV.

Initially he joined the Partai Nasional Demokrat (Partai Nasdem), a party established by another media tycoon Surya Paloh. But in January 2013, he joined the Partai Hati Nurani Rakyat (Hanura Party) and became the vice-presidential candidate of General (retired) Wiranto, the chairman of the Hanura Party, for the 2014 presidential election. The Hanura Party was unable to gain much votes and hence unable to contest the presidential election. Hary decided to support Prabowo as the presidential candidate while Wiranto rendered his support to Jokowi. As a result, Hary left Partai Hanura.

Sources: <http://www.orangterkayaindonesia.com/profil-hary-tanoesoedibjo-orang-super-kaya-di-i> (accessed 2 April 2014); Ulla Fionna and Alexander Aifianto, "Getting to know the contestants of the 2014 Indonesian Parliamentary Elections", *ISEAS Perspective*, no. 14 (10 March 2014); "2014 nian daxuan zhengdang — Minxin Dang", *Qiandao Ribao*, 3 March 2014; Borsuk and Chng, *Liem Sioe Liong's Salim Group*, pp. 438–40.

TANOTO, Latif Harris (TAN Liong Houw; CHEN Longhu 陈龙虎, 1930-)
Soccer player

Born on 26 July 1930, Surabaya, he was educated at the Middlebare Technisch School (Jakarta). While he was young he joined Chung Hua Tsing Nien Hui (Perkumpulan Olahraga & Sosial Tunas Jaya, Jakarta) and was selected as a player of Voetbal Bond Batavia & Omstreken. In 1950 he was selected to play for Persatuan Sepakbola Seluruh Indonesia (PSSI, All-Indonesian Football Union) and won the reputation of "Macan Bola" (Soccer Tiger). In the following year he was a member of the PSSI team in four Asian Games and the Olympic Games in Melbourne, Australia. He is now a businessman.

Source: "Biographical Data of Tan Liong-Houw" (courtesy of C.M. Hsu).

TANOTO, Sukanto (TAN Kang Ho; CHEN Jianghe 陈江河, 1949-)
Tycoon, lumber king

Born in Belawan, North Sumatra on 25 December 1949, he received Chinese primary school education in his birthplace but went to Medan for Chinese high school education. In 1966 his father, who ran an automobile shop, was ill and Sukanto had to take over the family business. However, he did not confine the business only to automobile. When plywood was in demand, he formed CV Karya Pelita in 1972 in Medan dealing with plywood business. The business developed rapidly and in 1973 the company was renamed PT Raja Garuda Mas, which later became PT Raja Garuda Mas International or Royal Golden Eagle International (REGI) in English. In 1976 he established a construction company called PT Bina Sarana Papan. His business expanded to Malaysia and in 1980 he set up PT Inti Indosawit Sejati dealing with palm oil business.

According to one source, in 1997 Sukanto moved his company's headquarters to Singapore. His REGI Group has a total asset of US$15 billion across several primary business areas: pulp and paper, agro industry, dissolving wood pulp, and energy resources development.

(Note: *Shijie huaren fuhao bang 94*, a book published by *Forbes Zibenjia* in Hong Kong in July 1994, mistook Tan Tay Kang 陈大江 as Tan Kang Ho 陈江河.)

Sources: *Apa dan Siapa 1985–86*, pp. 1109–10; *Forbes Zibenjia*, July 1994, p. 28; <http://en.wikipedia.org/wiki/Sukanto_Tanoto> (accessed 30 June 2014); the compiler's note.

TANUDJAJA, Sukanta (TAN Tay Kang; CHEN Dajiang 陈大江, 1926-)
Garments king

Born in Fujian, China, he came to Indonesia when he was a child. His father ran a shop selling clothes in Purwokerto. He moved to Batavia (Jakarta) to study at the THHK (Pa Hoa) up to Junior Middle school as it was closed down when the Japanese occupied Java. He returned to Purwokerto to help his father. Upon encouragement from two merchant friends, he went to Pintu Kecil, Jakarta, to learn trading. In 1957 he set up a shop, CV Sahabat, to import clothes from overseas. In 1973 he had a joint venture with Japan and established the textiles factory Kanisatex. In the following year, together with Sutopo Jananto, they set up a tire factory Bridgestone. In 1976 he established PT Great River Garment Industry. (His Chinese name Tay Kang or Dajiang means "Great River".) In 1987, it was developed into PT Great River International. The company not only manufactured its own clothes but also held the licence of fifty well-known brand shirts, including Arrow and Triumph. In 1997 he and Djaja Ramli jointly set up the Bali Bank. He was made deputy president of the bank. He later stepped down when Djaja Ramli passed away.

(Note: *Shijie huaren fuhao bang 94*, a book published by *Forbes Zibenjia* in Hong Kong in July 1994, mistook Tan Tay Kang 陈大江 as Tan Kang Ho 陈江河.)

Sources: Setyautama, *Tokoh-Tokoh Etnis TH*, p. 384; *Jiechu renwu minglu*, p. 272.

TANUWIBOWO, Budi S. (TAN Tjin Beng; CHEN Qingming 陈清明, 1960-)

Leader of Religious Organization, community leader, Confucian

Born on 31 March 1960 in Tegal, central Java, he received his high school education in his birthplace. Budi obtained his B.A. from Institut Pertanian Bogor (IPB) in 1984 and M.A. in Management from UI (1993–95). In 1993 he came to know Chandra Setiawan and joined Matakin. Between 1998 and 2002 he served as the secretary-general of Matakin; between

2002 and 2010, he served as the chairman of Matakin. From 2010 and 2014 he became president and secretary of Dewan Rohaniwan Matakin (Matakin Clergy Council). Between 2005 and 2013 he was elected as secretary-general of Perhimpunan INTI. Budi has published a book entitled *Bertambah Bijak Setiap Hari* [Becoming clearer each day] (Gramedia, 2013).

Sources: <http://www.spocjournal.com/berita/101-dialog-dengan-ws-budi-s-tanuwibowo.html> (accessed 26 June 2014); Liao Jianyu, *Yinni Kongjiao*, pp. 77–78; Wang Aiping, *Kongjiao yanjiu*, pp. 136–40.

TANSIL, Eddy (TAN Tju Fuan; TAN Tjoe Hong; CHEN Zihuang 陈子煌, 1934-)
Wealthy businessman, brother of **Hendra RAHARDJA**, *Hokchia*

Information about his romanized Chinese name and his date of birth varies according to different accounts. According to *Tempo*, his passport states that Eddy Tansil, alias Tan Tju Fuan, was born on 2 February 1934 in Ujungpandang. His education is unknown. In the 1970s as the sole agent for *bajaj* (three-wheel taxi) he made a fortune. However, when the government banned *bajaj* as a means of public transport, he became the agent for Kawasaki. He found that he could not compete with Suzuki and Honda, and later moved into other businesses. In 1983 he formed PT Rimba Subur Sejahtera to manufacture Beck's Beer, which is called "Bir Kunci" (Key's Beer) in Indonesia. His partner was a retired general, Koesno Achzan Jein. The beer did not sell well in Indonesia, and he moved his production to Fujian, China. The business took off well and he was known as "the Father of Fujian Beer". Tansil renamed his Indonesian company Golden Key and upon the suggestion of Admiral Sudomo, the former security chief, Golden Key moved into the petrochemical field. Initially it was quite successful. But over expansion and "mismanagement" became major problems. The company later was unable to repay bank loans and that became an issue, but what eventually brought Tansil down was his loans from Bapindo (Bank Pembangunan Indonesia). According to newspaper reports, he applied for loans from Bapindo between December 1989 and June 1992 to set up a US$476.6 million petrochemical complex in Cilegon, West Java. The funds obtained were instead used for other purposes. A few high government officers were implicated in the fraud. Tansil was sued in court and sentenced to seventeen years of jail. He was also fined US$21,000 and ordered to pay US$350 million in compensation to Bapindo Bank. His assets in Indonesia were seized.

Sources: *Tempo*, 19 February 1994, pp. 24–26; *Forbes Zibenjia*, July 1994, p. 30; *Straits Times*, 16 August 1994, p. 18.

TANZIL, Haris Otto Kamil (TAN Thiam Hok; CHEN Tianfu 陈添福, 1923-)
Professor of Medicine

Born in Surabaya on 16 July 1923, he received a Dutch education from 1929 to 1942. He entered Geneeskundige Hoogeschool in 1946. From 1953 to 1955 he suffered from pulmonary tuberculosis. He received a PhD in 1957, and an MD (Doctor of Medicine) in 1959, and became a Specialist in Microbiology in 1960. He taught at the Department of Microbiology of the Medical Faculty (UI) from 1957. In 1967 he was appointed professor, and in October 1974 professor emeritus.

He has published 184 scientific papers both in Indonesia and overseas. The Tan Thiam Hok Staining Method for staining acid-fast (tubercle) bacilli and the Tan Thiam Hok Test for differentiating bovine from human tubercle bacilli are well-known in tuberculosis bacteriology.

Sources: Roeder, *Who's Who*, pp. 450–51; "Biodata" (courtesy of C.M. Hsu).

TEDJOSUWITO (THE Tjhoen Swie, 1912-) 郑俊瑞*
Playwright, director, Protestant

Born in Surabaya in 1912, he was educated at a local English school. Before World War II he joined the HCTNH (Surabaya) and was active in the local drama scene. After World War II he wrote plays for local charity shows. His first drama, *Menjerah* [Surrender], was produced in 1949. Between 1949 and 1976 he wrote and directed more than fifty plays, the better known of which were the following: *Tikungan Berbahaya* [Dangerous curve], 4 Acts, produced by Sawahan Chung Hwa Hui, 1954; *Huang Lung* (Surabaya, November 1962); *Gunung Agung Tragedy* [The tragedy of Gunung Agung], 3 Acts, produced by a local Catholic university, February 1970; *The Cross atau Memikul Salib*, produced by GKI East Java, Surabaya, November 1971; *Manusia Tak Bertuhan* [A man without god], 3 Acts, produced by GKI East Java, July 1974; *Kasih Tak Sampai* [One-sided love], produced by GGS, Surabaya, June 1976.

It is worth noting that his last plays were more religious than his earlier ones.

Sources: Interview, 31 May 1976; newspaper clippings and photo albums of Tedjosuwito.

Tedy JUSUF. See **JUSUF, Tedy**
Teguh KARYA. See **KARYA, Teguh**
Teguh Slamet RAHARDJO. See **SRIMULAT, Teguh**
Teguh SRIMULAT. See **SRIMULAT, Teguh**
Tellie GOZELIE. See **GOZELIE, Tellie**

TENG, Benny (DENG Tongli 邓通力, 1936?-)
Journalist, writer

Born in Indonesia, he graduated from the Taiwan National University in 1960. When the Chinese language was banned in Soeharto's Indonesia, he started a Chinese magazine *Yinni yu Dongxie* (印尼与东协, Indonesia and ASEAN). The magazine, which began publication in 1990, was registered in Hong Kong but distributed in Indonesia and became a popular magazine among the Chinese-educated readers. After Soeharto stepped down, he got involved in the planning of the publication of *Heping Ribao* and *Shijie Ribao* in Jakarta.

It was reported that in 2003 he planned to retire and migrate to the United States, but when he heard that *Yinni yu Dongxie* had some problems, he returned to Jakarta and re-establish *Xin Yin Dong* (新印东 New Indonesia and ASEAN).

Source: *Jiechu renwu minglu*, p. 299.

TENG Sioe Hie 邓寿喜*
Community leader, physician

Born in Surabaya, he was educated at the HBS (Surabaya) and Leiden University where he obtained a medical degree. He was the president of the CHH-Netherlands in 1915–16, a founding member of the CHH in 1928, and a member of the Surabaya Municipal Council in the 1930s.

Source: Tan, *Tionghoa*, p. 53.

TENG Tjin Leng. See NANGOI, T.
THE Bwan An. See JINARAKKHITA, Bhikku Ashin

THE Goan Tjoan (1907-?) 郑源全*
Community leader

Born in Bandung on 15 May 1907, he was educated at the ELS (Sukabumi), MULO, and the AMS (Bandung). While at high school he served as the chairman of Chung Hsioh, the secretary of the THHK (Bandung), and an executive member of two soccer associations: Bandoengsche Voetbal Bond and Hwa Nan. When he was first elected as a member of the Bandung Municipal Council he could not assume office owing to his youth. Only in the 1930s was he able to serve in organizations as the president of Sarikat Boeroeh Tionghoa (Bandung) and the president of Federatie Kaoem Boeroeh Tionghoa.

Source: Tan, *Tionghoa*, pp. 183–84.

THE Hong Oe (ZHENG Hongyu 郑宏宇, 1896-?)
Community leader, businessman

A second-generation *peranakan*, he was born in 1896 in Yogyakarta. In 1908 he graduated from the Zhonghua Xuexiao (Yogyakarta). He was in the *batik* business and was active in the local Chinese community. He was the president of the HCTNH and a committee member of a local Chinese school and hospital. In 1942 he served as the president of the HCTH (Yogyakarta). In 1955 he represented Baperki in the general elections.

Sources: *Djawa Nenkan* (1973), p. 465; *Pedoman Kampanje*, p. 66.

THE Kian Seng. See HASAN, Mohammad Bob

THE Kian Sing (ZHENG Jiancheng 郑坚成, 1880–1937)
Community leader, newspaperman, businessman

Born in Surabaya in 1880, he was educated at a Hokkien school in Surabaya but had knowledge of Dutch. In the 1910s he served as the president of various Chinese organizations in Surabaya, including Hua Kiauw Tjong Hui (Surabaya). In 1917 he advocated Chinese nationalism for the Indies Chinese at the largest Chinese conference held in Semarang. He was not in favour of *peranakan* Chinese participation in local political institutions. In 1927 he favoured Dutch education and became the proponent for the conversion of THHK schools to Dutch schools. He served as the director of *Pewarta Soerabaia* from 1917 to the 1920s. He died in Lawang (near Malang) on 22 September 1937.

Sources: Tan, *Tionghoa*, pp. 20–21; Suryadinata, "Education", pp. 58–59.

THE Kian Wie. See **THEE Kian Wie**

THE Liang Gie (ZHENG Liangyi 郑良义**, 1932-)**
Former university lecturer, writer

Born in Yogyakarta on 25 August 1932, he obtained a Sarjana degree in International Relations from the UGM (July 1956), and a graduate certificate in Public Administration from the University of Utah (Salt Lake City, July 1960). Soon after his graduation from the UGM, he worked for the Jakarta Municipal Government in the Legal Affairs Division. In December 1958 he was appointed as a lecturer at the School of Political and Social Sciences, UGM. From 1964 to 1966 he taught at Tjendrawasih University Law School (Irian Jaya). In February 1965 he was also appointed as the director of the Institute of State Administration Development of the same university. In January 1967 he returned to UGM and became a lecturer in the School of Social and Political Sciences. From January 1968 to 1972 he was appointed as a lecturer at the Institute of Administration Development, UGM.

He is a prolific writer with an impressive list of publications including *Pemerintahan Daerah di Indonesia* [Local government in Indonesia] (Jakarta, 1958); *Sedjarah Pemerintahan Kota Jakarta* [A history of the municipal government of Jakarta] (Jakarta, 1958); *Pengertian, Kedudukan dan Perintjian Ilmu Administrasi* [On administration] (UGM, 1963); *Pertumbuhan Pemerintahan Propinsi Irian Barat dan Kemungkinan2 Perkembangan Otonominja dikemudian Hari* [The growth of West Irian province and possibilities of its autonomy in the future] (UGM, 1968), as co-author; *Bibliografi Ilmu Administrasi dalam Bahasa Indonesia* [Bibliography of administration in the Indonesian language] (Tjenderawasih University, 1966); *Pertumbuhan Pemerintahan Daerah di Negara Republik Indonesia: Suatu Analisa tentang Masalah^2 Desentralisasi dan Tjara^2 Penjelesaiannja* [The development of local government in RI: an analysis of its decentralization problems and solutions] (Jakarta, 1967–68), 3 volumes; *Ilmu Politik* [Political science] (UGM, 1970).

In 1973 he shifted his field to philosophy and was subsequently transferred to the Faculty of Philosophy (UGM). His works after 1973 include *Kamus Logika* [A dictionary of logic] (Yogyakarta, 1975); *Garisbesar Esterik* [An outline of aesthetics] (Yogyakarta, 1976); *Suatu Konsepsi Ke Arah Penertiban Bidang Filsafat* [A conception towards the systematization of philosophy] (Yogyakarta, 1971). In 1979 he left UGM and concentrated on his own research on science and technology. He was a visiting scholar at the MIT (United States) from 1980 to 1989 (for sixteen months). He retired from UGM in 1986. In fact, since 1989 he has served as the chairman of Yayasan Studi Ilmu dan Teknologi (Science and Technology Studies Foundation), Yogyakarta.

In 1990 he received a PhD from Columbia-Pacific University (San Francisco). His dissertation is entitled, "Managing the Building of Science in a Developing Country: Science Policy for Indonesia's National Development". One of his latest publications is *Keadilan Sebagai Landasan Bagi Etika Administrasi Pemerintahan Dalam Negara Indonesia* [Justice as the foundation of public administration ethics in Indonesia] (Yogyakarta, 1993).

Sources: Letters to the compiler, 1971, 1977, and 1995; the above-mentioned books; *Ensiklopedi Administrasi*, pp. 336–37.

THE Neng King (ZHENG Nianjin 郑年锦, 1931-)
Tycoon, Hokchia

Born in Bandung on 20 April 1931, he was educated in a local Chinese school. After completing his secondary education, he assisted his father in the textile business. In 1949 he accompanied his father to Jakarta but a few years later he left for Salatiga, Central Java, to establish his own textile factory.

After many years his Daya Manunggal Textile (Damatex) became one of the largest textile business groups in Indonesia. He later established Argos Manunggal, which has thirty-six companies, engaging in a wide range of businesses: textiles, steel, property, bicycle, electronics, and chemicals. He is a council member of the Shijie Fuqing Shetuan Lianyihui (International Federation of Futsing [Fuqing] Clan, based in Singapore).

Sources: *Forbes Zibenjia*, June 1993, p. 89; *Rong Qing*, no. 17 (15 September 1993): 2–3.

THE Sin Tjo (?-1971) 郑信作*
Community leader, wealthy businessman

Born into a Semarang *kapitein* family, he received an HBS education in his birthplace. In 1927 he was involved in the founding of the CHH. In the 1930s he was elected as a member of the Semarang Municipal Council and the Central Java Provincial Council. In 1948 he became an executive member of the PT and represented it in the Central Java Provincial Council. In 1954 he was an adviser to the PDTI (Semarang branch). He died in Semarang on 20 December 1971.

Sources: Tan, *Tionghoa*, p. 144; *Sinar 1*, no. 2 (April 1949): 8; *Sinar 1*, no. 8 (September 1949): 10; *Berita PDTI*, no. 5 (15 February 1954): 5; *Sinar Harapan*, 23 December 1971.

THE Teng Chun (EDERIS or IDRIS Tahyar; ZHENG Dengjun 郑登俊, ?-1977)
Movie producer

Born in Surabaya into a rich businessman's family, The Teng Chun was sent to the United States in 1920 to study commerce, but instead he learned scenario-writing at the Palmer Play Theatre in New York. Five years later, he went to Shanghai and got involved in the movie business. In 1930 he returned to Jakarta where he began the production of his first movie, *Boenga Roos dari Tjikembang* [The beauty from Tjikembang], which was also the first Indonesian motion picture with sound. However, this first movie was not appreciated by the press. Nevertheless, he continued to produce more movies: *Sam Pek Eng Tai* [Sam Pek and Eng Tai]; *Ouw Pe Tjoa* [Black and white snakes]; *O, Iboe* [O, Mother]; *Gadis Terdjoeal* [A girl who was sold]; and *Alang-Alang* [Grass].

In 1940 (1935?) he established the Java Industrial Film Company, which was the largest and most modern studio in Indonesia. The company produced many Indonesian movies such as *Matjan Berbisik* [The whispering tiger], *Rentjong Atjeh* [The dagger of Aceh], and *Kartina*. The company ceased productions during the Japanese Occupation. In 1950 he and Fred Young (a *peranakan* Chinese movie director) founded a new company called Bintang Surabaja. In 1962 the movie industry crisis had its effect on the studio and it was closed down. The Teng Chun then made his living by giving tuition in English. In 1967 he changed his name to Tahyer Idris. He died in Jakarta on 26 February 1977.

Sources: Pane, *Indonesia*, January–February 1953, pp. 16–17; *Tempo*, 12 March 1977, p. 10; "Filmographic Indonesienne", *Archipel*, no. 5 (1973): 53–64.

THE Tjhoen Swie. See TEDJOSUWITO

THEE Kian Wie (DAI Jianwei 戴建伟, 1935–2014)
Senior Economist, researcher, Buddhist

Born in Jakarta on 20 April 1935, he graduated from the SMA (Jakarta) in 1952. In the same year he entered the FEUI, from which he obtained a Drs degree in Economics in 1959. He first joined the MIPI, the former name for LIPI and worked as a staff member. In 1962 he became a research staff of

LEKNAS-LIPI. In the following year he was sent to further his studies in the United States. He obtained an M.S. (in Economics) in 1964 from the University of Wisconsin and a PhD in 1969 from the same university.

He returned to LEKNAS after completing his studies and in 1974 was promoted to the position of assistant director, a position he held until 1978. From 1974 to 1978 he was also the head of the project on the long-term perspective of Indonesia (*Indonesia Jangka Panjang*). From 1986 to 1990 he was head of the Centre for Economic and Development Studies, LIPI. He was Visiting Fellow at the Department of Economics, Research School of Pacific Studies at the Australian National University in 1982–83 and 1990–91.

He published extensively. His books include *Beberapa Masalah Ekonomi Internasional* (Jakarta, 1971); *Plantation Agriculture and Export Growth: An Economic History of East Sumatra* (Jakarta, 1977); *Japanese Direct Investment in Indonesia: Findings of an Experimental Survey* (Tokyo, 1978), as joint author; *Pemerataan, Kemiskinan, Ketimpangan Beberapa Masalah Pertumbuhan Ekonomi-Kumpulan Esei* [Equity, poverty and disparities: some problems of economic growth — a collection of essays] (Jakarta, 1981); *Industrialisasi Indonesia-Analisis dan Catatan Kritis* [Indonesian industrialization: analysis and critical notes] (Jakarta, 1988); *Industrialisasi, Teknologi, dan Penanaman Modal Asing di Indonesia* [Industrialization, technology and foreign investment in Indonesia] (Jakarta, 1993); and *Indonesia's Economy since Independence* (Singapore, 2013).

Thee dedicated his life to economic research. He was also active in training and educating younger scholars at LIPI and beyond. Professor Hal Hill of Australian National University said that "Dr Thee Kian Wie is without doubt the foremost Indonesian economic historian of his generation with a profound understanding of the current Indonesian economy."

Thee died in Jakarta on 8 February 2014.

Sources: *Prisma 4*, no. 6 (December 1975): 84; *Prisma* 5, no. 7 (July 1976): 92; "Curriculum Vitae"; "Thee Kian Wie disemayamkan di kantor pusat LIPI", <http://www.antaranews.com/print/418171/thee-kian-wie-...> (accessed 12 February 2014); the above-mentioned publications.

THIO In Lok (1905?–70s) 张印禄*
Community leader, teacher, journalist

Born in Sukabumi in 1905(?), he was educated at the HCK and was active in the COB before World War II. In 1947 he became the editor-in-chief of *Sin Po* (Jakarta), and in 1949 the editor-in-chief of *Sedar* (Jakarta). He was a member of the Indonesian delegation to the Round Table Conference (at the Hague) in 1949 and was active in the PT and the PDTI in the late 1940s and early 1950s. In 1956 he was an adviser to Baperki (Sukabumi branch). He died in Jakarta probably in the early 1970s.

Sources: Tan Giok Lan (1963), p. 245; *Sinar*, 1 May 1949, p. 8; the compiler's notes.

THIO Soei Sen (ZHANG Ruisheng 张瑞生, 1888–1967)
Journalist

Born in 1888 in Jakarta, he was educated at the ELS (Jakarta?). From 1911 to 1924 he worked as an editor for *Sin Po*. After leaving *Sin Po*, he was engaged in business, and later worked as the chief of the Jakarta Section for Assurantie Lloyd Combinatie. In the 1930s he returned to the journalistic world serving as the editor-in-chief of *Djawa Tengah* (Semarang). In the 1950s he became the editor-in-chief of *Sin Min* (Semarang). He died in Semarang(?) in 1967.

Sources: Tan, *Tionghoa*, p. 144; *Djawa Tengah*, 7 September 1932; the compiler's notes.

THIO Thiam Tjong (ZHANG Tiancong 张添聪, 1896–1969)
Community leader, wealthy businessman

He was born on 4 April 1896 into a wealthy *peranakan* family. His father was the owner of an import-export firm in Semarang, Firma Seng Liong, which Thio Thiam Tjong inherited and expanded after his father had retired.

Thio was Dutch-educated, first in Semarang, and later in the Delft Technical College (in Holland). Before graduating he returned to Java, presumably to take over his father's business. He became very active in the local Chinese community. In 1927 he and other Dutch-educated *peranakan* organized the Chung Hwa Congress, which led to the formation of the CHH in 1928. Thio was elected to its central board. He was also elected as president of the Semarang branch in the 1930s and served as a member of the Provincial Council of Central Java.

His role in local business circles was widely recognized. From 1930 to 1934 he was elected as the chairman of Semarang Siang Hwee ("Siang Boe"). He was also concerned with the social and educational affairs of the Chinese community. In 1936 he became the chairman of the School Board of Semarang Zhonghua Xuexiao, and in 1928, of the Chinese-English School (Huaying Zhongxue) as well.

Thio had a business office in China. He visited China several times and was active in the anti-Japanese movement. He was the chairman of "Jiuguo Houyuan Hui" [Save the country from the back line] and later the China Charity Fund (Semarang branch). It was reported that for every donation drive his Seng Liong Company was always the largest donor. Before the Japanese invasion of Java, the Dutch Government organized a local defence force in which he was appointed as the chief commander. He even retreated to Ambarawa when the Japanese conquered Semarang.

Thio was detained in a concentration camp together with other Chinese leaders (1942–45). It was during his detention that he began to study Mandarin. He also became acquainted with many Chinese leaders. This laid the foundation for his national leadership after his release. The Dutch reoccupied Java after the Japanese surrender and Thio was invited to Jakarta to serve as the personal adviser of Governor-General van Mook. Apparently, van Mook recognized Thio's popularity among the Indonesian Chinese and his moderate view in political affairs. In 1948 Thio established Persatuan Tionghoa (PT) with the aim of organizing Indonesian Chinese in readiness for the changing situation. Thio was popular for a short while. Nevertheless, the complete withdrawal of the Dutch forces and the coming to power of indigenous Indonesians diminished Thio's influence. His past record as van Mook's adviser made him unpopular among radical Indonesian nationalists. Thio's PDTI (the new name of the PT after 1950) was declining and was eventually replaced by Baperki. Although Thio remained as a member of the central board, he was no longer influential. He became inactive after the 1965 coup and died in the Netherlands on 22 September 1969.

Sources: Li Min, *Nanyang Post*, 14 February 1947; Willmott, *Semarang*, pp. 153–54; Tan, *Tionghoa*, p. 145; interview, 1969.

THIO Tiauw Siat (ZHANG Zhaoxie 张肇燮 alias ZHANG Bishi 张弼士, 1841–1916)
Merchant, planter, industrialist, consul of Chinese Government

Born in 1841 into a poor family in Dapu district, Guangdong, not much was known of Thio's childhood and education background. He immigrated to Batavia (now Jakarta) of the Dutch East Indies in 1858 to earn a living. Initially, he worked in a rice shop owned by an overseas Chinese and spent his spare time observing the local economic circumstances and learning the local languages. His studious bent and diligence were highly commended by a neighbouring Hakka shop owner, Wen, who married his daughter to Thio and financially supported him to open a new rice shop. When Wen passed away, Thio inherited his father-in-law's assets and expanded the business and opened a wine shop.

Through his good rapport with the Dutch officials, he managed to win some tax farming contracts. In 1866, he undertook the project of clearing and developing wasteland adjacent to Batavia and his work drove the development and prosperity of the surrounding areas. He also diversified into the plantation industry by opening up coconut, rubber and tea plantations. He jointly established the Deli Bank to monitor the monetary condition as well as to facilitate the cash remittance of overseas Chinese to their homeland. His ever expanding business led him to develop shipbuilding and navigation to solve the transport problems. He also made huge investments throughout Southeast Asia with business bases in Penang, Malacca, Bentong of British Pahang, Selangor and Klang.

Thio also made huge investments in China such as the famous Zhang Yu Pioneer Wine Company (张裕酿酒公司). He was also involved in setting up the first Chinese-owned bank, i.e the Imperial Bank of China (later known as Commercial Bank of China (中国通商银行). In return for his support and adherence to the economic policy of the late Qing Dynasty, he was granted audiences by the Empress Dowager Cixi and Emperor Guangxu as well as conferred titles of "First Rank Dingdai" (头品顶戴) and "Taipusi Zhengqing" (太仆寺正卿). It was unprecedented for the Qing Government to give such eminent honours to a migrant. After the founding of the Republic of China, he became the adviser for President Yun Sikai (袁世凯), adviser for the Ministry of Commerce & Industry, etc. He was also conferred various prestigious titles and appointments in Southeast Asia and China.

Apart from his notable accomplishment in politics and businesses, Thio also contributed to the educational and cultural development in Southeast Asia. He established Penang Chung Hwa School (槟榔屿中华学堂) and the Singapore Yin Sin School (新加坡应新学堂). The Penang Chung Hwa School was the pioneer for modern Chinese education in Malaya and also the first school to adopt Mandarin as a medium of instruction, establishing the foundation for the development of Chinese education in Malaysia. Thio passed away in Batavia in 1916.

Source: Chong Siou Wei, "Thio Tiauw Siat", in Suryadinata, ed., *Southeast Asian Personalities* (2012), pp. 1174–76.

THIO Tjin Boen (ZHANG Zhenwen 张振文, 1885–1940)
Writer, journalist

Born in Pekalongan in 1885, he was an editor of *Taman Sari*, a daily published in Jakarta in 1890 and the editor-in-chief of *Perniagaan* from 1927 to 1929. His novels include *Oey Se* (Solo, 1903), *Njai Soerimah atawa Pertjintahan Jang Kekal* (Batavia, 1917), and *Tan Fa Lioeng atawa Moestadjabnja Sinshe Hong Soei* (Weltevreden, 1922). He probably died in Bandung in 1940.

Sources: Nio, *Sastera*, pp. 44–45; the compiler's notes; *Museum Catalogue*; Salmon, *Literature*, pp. 337–38.

THUNG Ju Lan (TANG Youlan 汤友兰, 1958-)
Researcher, academic

Thung Ju Lan was born in Jakarta in 1958 but received her primary and secondary school education at Bogor, West Java. She first went to study at the Department of Sinology, the University of Indonesia and graduated in 1982. She shifted to

Sociology for her post-graduate study: she received her MA in Sociology from Purdue University (Indiana-USA, 1989), and a PhD in Sociology from La Trobe University, Victoria-Australia (1998) after submitting her dissertation on "Identities in flux: Young Chinese in Jakarta".

Ju Lan joined LIPI since 1983 after her graduation and she is currently a senior research fellow (Peneliti Ahli) at the same institute. She taught part-time at the FSUI (now FIB) from 1998–2004, lecturing a course on the position of ethnic Chinese in Indonesian society. Since 2010 she has taught courses related to China, ethnic Chinese in Indonesia etc. at the Faculty of Literature, Al Azhar University (Jakarta). She has actively participated in national and international seminars/conferences.

Ju Lan has published at least 81 research papers, which includes "Chinese in Jakarta after 1965" (La Trobe, 1998); "Rethinking the 'Chinese Problem'" (Adelaide, 2001), "Ethnicity and Civil Rights Movement in Indonesia" (Singapore, 2004), and "Redefinisi Etnisitas dalam Konteks Kebudayaan Nasional" [Redefinition of ethnicity in the context of national culture] (Jakarta, 2006). She also co-edited (with I. Wibowo) a book entitled, *Setelah Air Mata Kering: Masyarakat Tionghoa Pasca-Peristiwa Mei 1998* [After tears dry: Chinese society after the May 1998 affair] (Jakarta: Penerbit Buku Kompas, 2010).

Sources: CV Thung, May 2013; email to the compiler, 20 June 2014; *Setelah Air Mata Kering*, p. 247.

THUNG Liang Lee (Tubagus Pranata TIRTAWIDJAJA; T'ANG Leang-Li; TANG Liangli 汤良礼, 1901–75)
Politician, writer, businessman

Born into a landowning family in Bogor in 1901 (1902?), he attended the HBS (Jakarta) and the University of London, where he was awarded a B.Sc. degree in Economics. He also studied at the University of Vienna. In 1929 he was the principal correspondent in Europe for the KMT Central Executive

Committee; in the following year he served as a correspondent in China for *Sozial-demokratischer Pressedienst Deutschlands* (Berlin), *Daily Herald, New Leader* (both in London), and *Sin Po* (Jakarta). He was also the *New York Times'* correspondent in Beijing. From 1931 to 1938 he was the managing director of *China United Press* and the editor of *People's Tribune*, and concurrently a political associate and English secretary of Wang Ching-wei. In 1934 he served as Minister without Portfolio, China. Prior to his appointment, he wrote regularly for *Sin Po* (Jakarta). In 1950, he formed the Persatuan Tenaga Indonesia with **LIEM Koen Hian**. He then worked for the Ministry of Information, RI. After the 1965 coup he and other intellectuals established the Indonesian Institute of International Affairs (Jakarta) and he was a member of its board of directors. He was also the editor of the Institute's journal, *Indonesian Review of International Affairs*, published since 1969. He died in 1975.

His publications include *China in Revolt* (London, 1927); *Foundation of Modern China* (London, 1928); *The Inner History of the Chinese Revolution* (London, 1930); *Wang Ching-wei: A Political Biography* (Peiping, 1931); *The New Social Order in China* (Shanghai, 1936); and *China's New Currency System* (Shanghai, 1937).

Sources: *Who's Who in China* (1936), p. 222; Woodhead, ed. (1938), p. 179; *Library of Congress Catalog*, vol. 145 (1945), pp. 574–75; *Indonesian Review of International Affairs* 1, no. 1 (July 1970), back cover; Mary Somers Heidhues and Leo Suryadinata, "T'ang Leang-Li", in Suryadinata, ed., *Southeast Asian Personalities* (2012), pp. 1133–35.

THUNG Liang Tjay (1903-?) 汤良才*
Community leader

Born in Jatinegara on 15 October 1903, he was educated at a Dutch school in Bogor, Instituut Kooiman in Sukabumi, and K.W. III in Jakarta. In 1924 he studied at the Handels Hooge

School (Rotterdam). In the 1930s he served as the president of the CHH (Sukabumi branch) and a member of the Sukabumi Municipal Council.

Source: Tan, *Tionghoa*, pp. 231–32.

THUNG Sin Nio, Betsy (TANG Xinniang 汤新娘, 1902–96)
Physician, community leader, sister of **THUNG Liang Lee**

Born in 1902 in Batavia, Thung received Dutch primary education before attending the Prins Hendrikschool and the Hollandsch Chineesche Kweekschool (Dutch-Chinese Teachers' College) in Jatinegara district, where she received her degree. In 1925, she went to Holland to study economics at the Handels Hoge School in Rotterdam and was inspired by Aletta Jacobs, the first Dutch woman physician and active feminist. She then became active on the issues of employment and matrimonial laws and was a member of the Chung Hwa Hui (中华会) from 1926 to 1933.

Thung went on to study medicine in Amsterdam and opened her practice in the family house in Salemba in 1938. She specialized in women's and children's health, as well as regular health control of infants. She was also employed as a school doctor in the Ministry of Education from 1945–51. In 1948–49, she became the first woman member of the Jakarta Council to represent the Persatuan Tionghoa (PT) or Chinese Union. She decided to carry out her political activities on her own as an independent candidate for the 1955 national elections.

In 1968, in relation with the implementation of an assimilation policy, Thung left Indonesia for Holland and continue to work as a part-time physician. She received her knighthood (RIdder in de orde van Oranje Nassau) on 29 April 1983 as a reward for "her efforts to emancipate women". She died in 1996 at the age of ninety-four.

Sources: Claudine Salmon, "Thung Sin Nio, Betsy", in Suryadinata, ed., *Southeast Asian Personalities* (2012), pp. 1176–78; *Sinar 1*, no. 2 (1 April 1949): 8; *CHH Statuten en Reglementen* (1928).

THUNG, T.H. See **THUNG Tjeng Hiang**
THUNG Thay Tung. See **ARIEF, Jackson**

THUNG Tjeng Hiang (T.H. THUNG, 1897–1960) 汤清香*
Academician

Born on 8 May 1897, he went to a Dutch primary school at Sukabumi (West Java). After secondary school (HBS) at Jakarta, he studied agriculture and plant diseases at the Agricultural University of Wageningen (the Netherlands) and later at Berlin and Paris (at the "Institut Pasteur").

In Holland he worked with the Phytopathological Service and the Agricultural University from 1925 to 1928, after which he returned with his family (Mrs Thung-Willekes MacDonald, a son, and a daughter) to colonial Indonesia. He worked from 1929 to 1939 as a phytopathologist with "Proefstation voor Vorstenlandse Tabak" (experimental station for tobacco culture in the autonomous areas Surakarta/Yogyakarta) at Klaten (Central Java).

From November 1939 he was head of the Mycological Department of the Institute for Plant Diseases at Bogor. After the war, in 1947, he was appointed Professor of Phytopathology with the Faculty of Agricultural Sciences (at Bogor) of the University of Indonesia. In 1949 he became head of the Department of Virology of the new Institute for Phytopathological Research at Wageningen and at the same time Extraordinary Professor of Virology at the Agricultural University, Holland. In 1957 he was appointed full Professor of Virology and head of a new Virological Laboratory of the Agricultural University. He died in November 1960.

He visited China for the first time in 1921. While living in Europe he continued to advocate the study of Chinese culture. He was an executive member of the CHH-Netherlands (1930s). Together with **TJAN Tjoe Som** and other friends he established China Instituut (1930s?). Shortly before he died he visited China (PRC) again (in 1960).

Sources: Somers, dissertation, p. 70; his son's letter to the compiler, 6 April 1982; the compiler's notes.

TILAAR, Martha (TJHIE Pwee Giok, 1937-) 徐培玉*
Leader in jamu and cosmetic industry

Born in Gombang, Kebumen (Java) on 4 September 1937, she is recognized as the leader in both *jamu* (Indonesian traditional herbs) and cosmetic industry in Indonesia. After finishing her teachers' training education (IKIP) in Jakarta, she went to teach at a primary school. When her husband went to the United States to do a PhD, she went with him and took a course at the Bloomington Academy of Beauty and Culture in Indiana. In 1970 she returned to Indonesia with her husband and started a beauty salon in her parents' garage. It was very successful. Soon she opened the second salon. Within a short period of time she was able to open sixteen salons and four beauty schools under the name of Sari Ayu. In 1977, with Theresia Harsini Setiady, she established PT Martina Berto to produce *jamu* and herbal cosmetics. She continued to learn about her field, travelling to many countries and expanded her business. In 1993 she acquired cosmetics factory PT Cedefindo and two other factories. In 1996 her factory gained the ISO 9001 Certificate for R&D, manufacturing and system of management, this is the first Indonesian factory to obtain such a recognition. In 1999 she was able to purchase all the shares of PT Martina Berto and formed the Martha Tilaar Group of Companies. Martha Tilaar has become the leading figure in the Indonesian *jamu* and cosmetic industry. In 2008 she established the Organic Jamu Village (Kampoeng Djamoe Organik Martha Tilaar) to grow various plants needed by the industry; in 2014 she set up a museum of *jamu* to propagate *jamu* culture.

Sources: *Apa & Siapa 1985–86*, pp. 1123–24; Theresa C.Y. Liong, "Industri jamu dan kosmetika Indonesia Abad XIX sampai kini", unpublished paper for the Yayasan Nabil project.

TIO Hian Sioe 赵贤修*
Community leader

Born in Surabaya, he received a Dutch education. In 1933 he served as the secretary of the PTI (Surabaya branch) and, from 1937 to 1942, as the president of the PTI (Surabaya branch). In the 1930s, upon the support of the PTI, he became a member of the Surabaya Municipal Council. After World War II, he was active in socio-religious organizations in Surabaya.

Sources: Tan, *Tionghoa*, pp. 53–54; interview, 1969; the compiler's notes.

TIO Ie Soei (ZHAO Yushui 赵雨水, 1890–1974)
Journalist, writer

Born on 22 June 1890 in Jakarta, he received a private Dutch school education. At the age of fifteen he joined *Perniagaan* (Jakarta), and remained with the newspaper until 1920. Tio's style of writing was influenced by **GOUW Peng Liang**, the editor-in-chief of *Perniagaan* (1909–16). For health reasons, Tio moved to Lembang (Bandung) to grow potatoes. Meanwhile he continued to contribute articles to various *peranakan* newspapers. In 1926 he was invited to Banjarmasin to edit *Bintang Borneo*. In 1927 he returned to Java and was appointed as the editor of *Pewarta Soerabaia*, a position he held until 1942. During the Japanese Occupation, he went into hiding. He became active again in the press after 1948. In 1952–54, he served as the first secretary of Perwitt (Surabaya), and in 1953 was elected as the president of Persatuan Wartawan Surabaya. He died in Jakarta on 29 August 1974.

He wrote and translated many books, including *Badjak* [Pirate] (Surabaya, 1922), *Pieter Elberveld* (Weltevreden, 1924), *Saltima* [Miss Saltima] (Bandung, 1925), and *Lie Kimhok 1853–1912* (Bandung, 1959).

Sources: Interview, 1969; Tan, *Tionghoa*, p. 54; PKA, *Liberty*, no. 1098 (21 September 1974), pp. 23, 37.

TIO Kiang Sun (1910-) 赵江顺*
Community leader

Born in Sintang (West Kalimantan) on 1 November 1910, he was educated at the HBS (five years). In the period 1938–49 he served as an administrator at a rubber estate in Sintang. In 1949–51 he was appointed head of the Chinese Affairs Office in West Kalimantan. In 1951–52 he became acting head of the Chinese Section in the Ministry of the Interior (in charge of *peranakan* and alien affairs). In 1952–54 he worked for the Municipal Government of Jakarta Raya. On 27 March 1954 he was appointed as a member of the DPR, representing the Chinese minority.

Source: Kempen, *KP*, p. 135.

TIO Oen Bik (ZHAO Wenbi 赵温毕, 1906–70?)
Political activist, physician

Born in Bojonegoro (East Java) on 27 January 1906, Tio Oen Bik (also known as Bi Daowen 毕道文) studied medicine at NIAS, Surabaya. In 1920 he went to the Netherlands for further studies, but did not complete the course. Instead he was influenced by left-wing movement and joined Communist International in the Netherlands. During the Anti-Fascist War in Spain (1937–39) he joined the Spanish Aid and served as a physician at Mahora to assist the anti-Fascist group. During the anti-Japanese movement he went to China to support the Chinese communists. He also helped in the world organization in combating epidemic in China. After World War II he continued to live in China and later travelled to Eastern Europe. His friend, **Dr TJOA Sik Ien**, wanted him to remain at WHO, but he was not interested. In 1953 he returned to Indonesia and worked as a doctor. Because of his temperament he was unable to stay in the job for long. He later went to Maluku. He died at his birthplace in 1970(?).

Source: Zhou Nanjing, *Nushantala huayi zongheng* 努山塔拉华裔纵横 (Random Notes on Indonesians of Chinese descent), Hong Kong Press for Social Sciences LTD. 2011, pp. 61–79.

TIRTAWIDJAJA, Tubagus Pranata. See **THUNG Liang Lee**
Tirtawinata KOSASIH. See **KOSASIH, Tirtawinata**
Tirto UTOMO. See **UTOMO, Tirto**

TJAHAJA PURNAMA, Basuki (A Hok; ZHONG Wanxue 钟万学, 1966-)
Politician, businessman, geologist, Christian

Born in Manggar, Belitung Timur, on 29 June 1966, Basuki who is also known as A Hok (Ahok), received his primary school and SMP (junior middle school) education in his hometown before going to Jakarta to receive his SMA (senior high school) education. He graduated from the Faculty of Mineral Technology, Department of Geological Technics at the Universitas Trisakti, Jakarta with a degree in 1990. In 1994 he obtained a Master of Management (M.M.) degree from the Sekolah Tinggi Manajeman Prasetya Mulia in Jakarta.

Basuki worked for a few years before returning to his hometown and began to be interested in politics. He joined a minor party, Partai Pembangunan Indonesia Baru (PPIB) and was elected as a local MP (DPRD) in 2004. He then stood for the regency election for the Regent (*Bupati*) the following year and was elected as Regent. The living conditions of the local population improved as he managed to introduce free health and free education for the Belitung Timur residents. He also practised clean government and rejected kickbacks.

In the mid-2000s, Basuki was selected as one of ten Indonesian figures who changed Indonesia (*Tokoh yang mengubah Indonesia*) by *Majalah Tempo*, a leading Jakarta news weekly. In 2007, he was awarded the title of Anti-Corruption Leader (*Tokoh Anti-Korupsi*) by the Gerakan Tiga

Pilar Kemitraan. He contested and was elected as Deputy Governor of Jakarta in a heatedly contested election on 20 September 2012. He is the first Chinese Indonesian in the history of the Republic of Indonesia to become Deputy Governor of Jakarta. Many political analysts are of the view that his electoral victory, as an ethnic Chinese as well as a Christian, signifies a change in Indonesian racial politics. In 2014, when Joko Widodo, the Governor of Jakarta, contested the presidential election, Basuki was made acting Jakarta Governor. Joko Widodo was elected as the 7th president of Indonesia and has assumed the presidency since 20 October 2014. Since then Basuki has also become Jakarta Governor.

Sources: Leo Suryadinata, "Tjahaja Purnama, Basuki", in Suryadinata, ed., *Southeast Asian Personalities* (2012), pp. 1395–97; *Jakarta Post*, 12 September 2012; *Straits Times*, 26 August 2012; *Wajah DPR & DPD 2009–14: Latar Belakang Pendidikan dan Karier* (2010), p. 173; *Merubah Indonesia: The Story of Basuki Tjahaja Purnama* (2008).

TJAHAJA PURNAMA, Basuri (ZHONG Wanyou 钟万友, 1967-)
Bupati, younger brother of **Basuki Tjahaja Purnama**, *Christian*

Born in Tanjung Pandan, Belitung on 1 December 1967, he received his primary and SMP education at Gantung, Belitung, but went to Jakarta for his SMA education (1983–86). He received his tertiary education at the Catholic University of Atmajaya (1986–95) and UI (Jakarta, 2003–7). Basuri worked as a physician at Puskemas, Manggar (Belitung, 2001–3), and RSUD Belitung Timur (2003–8). In 2010 he was elected as Bupati of Belitung Timur (2010–15), following the footsteps of his eldest brother, Basuki, who was the Bupati of Belitung Timur between 2005 and 2006.

Sources: Basuri Tjahaja Purnama-Wikipedia Bahasa Indonesia (accessed 6 October 2014); Profil Kepala Daerah-Basuri Tjahaja Purnama (accessed 6 October 2014).

TJAHJADI, Robby (also spelt as Robbi CAHYADI; SIE Tjia-Ie, 1943-) 施佳宜*
Wealthy businessman, also known as **Robby SIE**

Born in Solo in 1943 and Chinese-educated, he has been identified as a *cukong* who became rich through car smuggling. In the early 1970s he imported hundreds of expensive cars without paying import duties. When that became a scandal, he was charged in court and sentenced to seven-and-a-half years' imprisonment, but was released after only two-and-a-half years. Fifteen years later he re-emerged as a successful textile businessman. He established Kanindo Success Textile (Kanindotex) in Semarang, a company specializing in twine-making. In October 1990 he launched an export drive of twine to Europe and received support from the Indonesian authorities. In 1991 the Kanindo Group established a factory producing twine. It needed 380 billion rupiahs, of which 35 per cent came from the Kanindo Group itself, while the rest came from Bank Pembangunan Indonesia and Bank Bumi Daya. According to *Tempo*, one of his business partners was retired Indonesian security chief General Sumitro, who was made the president-commissioner of the Group. Later the Group expanded into the property business and in 1993 started building a shopping complex, Century Centre. In April 1993, he invited a leading Taiwanese star Lin Qingxia to promote the sale of Century Centre Shopping Complex. However, the Kanindo Group became deeply in debt and was unable to repay its loans; it subsequently went bankrupt in September 1994.

Sources: *Matahari*, May 1979, p. 36; *Apa & Siapa 1985–86*, p. 586; *Tempo*, 13 October 1990, p. 94 and 17 April 1993, p. 39; "Robby Tjahjadi: Si 'Raja Benang'", *Sinar*, 31 January 1994, pp. 64–66; *Forum*, 15 September 1994, pp. 100–4.

TJAN I.D. See TJAN Ing Djiu

TJAN Ing Djiu (TJAN I.D.; ZENG Yingqiu 曾荧球, 1949-)
Kungfu novel translator

Tjan Ing Djiu first emerged in the late 1960s and became well-known in the 1970s. Between the late 1960s and the early 1980s he translated about seventy titles, most of them were works of Gu Long, Qing Hong, Gudu Hong, and Chen Chingyun. It is interesting to note that because of the popularity of Gu Long among readers, the publishers preferred to print the novels under the name of Gu Long (Indonesian spelling: Khu Lung), although Tjan's name appeared as translator in an equally prominent position. Therefore Tjan's name became well-known after being associated with Gu Long's novels.

Tjan is a *peranakan* Chinese. Born in 1949, he received Chinese primary education. His mother was a Chinese schoolteacher. When Chinese schools were closed, Tjan transferred to an Indonesian school. After finishing secondary school, he entered a private university in Semarang. However, he had to terminate his studies due to financial difficulties. His interest in reading *kungfu* novels led him to translate the novel called *Tiancan Qiding* by Bai Hong into Bahasa Indonesia: *Tujuh Pusaka Rimba Persilatan*. This was done in the 1960s after he left the university. The translation was published in 1969. After the success of his first venture, he became a professional translator. His latest works were *Darah Pahlawan* (Lu Ding Ji) by Jin Yong and *Pedang Tetesan Airmata* (Yingxiong Wulei) by Gu Long. He has now stopped translating *kungfu* novels.

Source: Suryadinata, *Kebudayaan Minoritas Tionghoa*, p. 132.

TJAN Kiem Bie (1885?–1960?) 曾金美*
Journalist, community leader

Born in Kraksaan in 1885(?), he received ELS education in Surabaya(?). From 1915 to 1916 he served as the editor-in-chief of *Tjhoen Tjhioe* (Surabaya). One source says he also wrote articles for *De Locomotief*, a Dutch daily newspaper in Semarang.

In the 1930s he joined the PTI and was nominated a PTI candidate for the Volksraad election in 1939. He died in 1960(?).

Sources: Suryadinata, *Peranakan Politics*, p. 115; the compiler's notes.

TJAN Som Hay (1884–1961) 曾森海*
Community leader, lieutenant (titular), businessman, landlord

Born in Bogor in 1884, he was educated at a local Hokkien school and later at a private Dutch school. He served as the president of the THHK (Bogor) and the CHH (Bogor) in the 1930s(?). He died in Bogor on 8 March 1961.

Sources: Tan, *Tionghoa*, p. 218; the compiler's notes.

TJAN Tian Soe (ZENG Tianci 曾天赐, 1896-?)
Community leader, soap manufacturer

Born in Batang in 1896, he was educated at a local Hokkien school, the THHK (Bandung and Jakarta), the PHS (Jakarta), and a commercial school (Jakarta). He returned to Batang where he became a leader of the THHK (Batang). In 1931 he moved to Garut and served as the director and co-owner of the Nansen Soap Manufacturing Company. In the 1930s he also served as the president of the CHH (Garut branch).

Source: Tan, *Tionghoa*, p. 223.

TJAN Tjoe Siem (ZENG Zuqin 曾祖沁, 1909–78)
Professor of Javanese culture and Islamology, younger brother of **TJAN Tjoe Som**, *Muslim*

Born in Solo on 3 April 1909, he was a son of a well-established *peranakan* Muslim family. One of his ancestors served in the Solo court and received an award from Mangkunegara III because of his merit in the Diponegoro War (1825–30).

Tjan's grandfather was knowledgeable in Javanese culture while Tjan's father was an *imam*. Naturally, Tjan was immersed in both cultures. After finishing Dutch secondary school education, he went to the Netherlands to attend Leiden

University. He was awarded a PhD in Oriental Studies in 1938 after successfully defending his dissertation on "Hoe Koeroepati Zich Zijn Vrouw". While in the Netherlands he served as the editor-in-chief of the *CHHTC* (1930s). On his return to Indonesia, he initially worked as a language teacher, and later taught at the FSUI. From 1954 to 1958 he was Professor of Modern Javanese, FSUI; from 1960 to 1965 he served as Dean of the Faculty of Arts, URECA (Jakarta); from 1968 to 1973 he served as Professor of Malay Studies at Nanyang University (Singapore). He retired in 1973 and returned to Jakarta. In 1978 he was appointed Extraordinary Professor of the State Institute of Islam (IAIN Sunan Kali Jaga) in Yogyakarta. He died in Jakarta on 30 December 1978.

Sources: *CHHTC*, January–March 1935, title page; September 1936, title page; interview, 1969; *Nanyang University Calendar 1970–71*, p. 138; Suryatmoko, *Intisari*, no. 189 (April 1979), pp. 129–35.

TJAN Tjoe Som (ZENG Zusen 曾祖森, 1903–69)
Sinologist, brother of **TJAN Tjoe Siem,** *Muslim*

Born in Surakarta in 1903, the son of a well-established Muslim family. He attended the HCS (Surakarta) and the AMS (Yogyakarta), but before finishing high school he returned to Surakarta to take over his father's business. However, he continued to learn through self-study and was well-known for his knowledge on Sinology and Islamology. He was one of the founders of "China Instituut".

In 1935 he went to the Netherlands and in the following year he entered Leiden University to read Sinology. In 1949 he received a PhD degree and was appointed as a professor at the same university. He returned to Indonesia in 1952 to head the Department of Sinology, FSUI.

During the period of "Guided Democracy" he was associated with left-wing intellectuals. He joined the HSI and accepted the appointment of director of UNRA in 1958. In 1959 he was appointed as a member of the Dewan Perancang Nasional (National Plan Council) by the Indonesian Government, representing scientists and intellectuals. In 1963–65 he was the adviser of *Zhongcheng Bao* (Chinese edition of *Warta Bhakti*). He died in Bandung in February 1969.

He published numerous articles and books, including his dissertation, "Po Hu T'ung: The Comprehensive Discussions in the White Tiger Hall" (Leiden, 1949–52), *Sardjana Sastra dan Pembangunan Kebudajaan Nasional: Sebuah Prasaran* (Jakarta, 1961), and *Tao-te Tjing* [Daode Jing] (Jakarta, 1962).

Sources: *Bintang Timur*, 8 December 1958; *Zhongcheng Bao*, 26 March and 17 December 1964; *Kompas*, 12 July 1969; Tan, *Tionghoa*, pp. 155–56; *Organisasi*, p. 591; interview, 1967.

TJAN Tjoen Hok. See **SILALAHI, Harry Tjan**

TJANDINEGARA, Wilson (CHEN Donglong 陈冬龙, 1946-)
Writer, translator, photographer

Born in Makassar, Sulawesi, in 1946, he received Chinese middle school education. Since 1970 he began to run a bookshop until 1995. In 1996 he moved to Tangerang, West Java, and started his literary life. He published his first collection of Indonesian poems: *Puisi Untukmu* (Poems for you) in 1995. In 1999 he published another collection of bilingual poems in both Indonesian and Chinese entitled, *Rumah Panggung di Kampung Halaman* [House in the village]. However, most of his works are translations. He has translated and published at least six books from Chinese to Indonesian, including *55 Puisi Cinta Mandarin* (1998), *Kumpulan Cerpen Mini Yin Hua* (1999), and *101 Puisi Mandarin* (2000). He noted that he wanted to serve as a bridge between indigenous Indonesians and Chinese Indonesians.

He is a council member of Komunitas Sastra Indonesia (KSI, Indonesian Literary Community) and member of Yin Hua Zuoxie (Indonesian Chinese Writers Association). Since 1998, he started taking photographs of poor Chinese in Indonesia and had exhibitions in at least eight Indonesian cities.

Sources: "Biodata", in *101 Puisi Mandarin*, pp. 116–17; *Jiechu renwu minglu*, p. 297.

TJEN Djin Tjong (1889-?) 曾仁宗*
Community leader, businessman

He was born in Blinyu (Bangka) on 17 November 1889. After receiving a two-year Hakka education (Muntok), he went to the ELS (Muntok), the HBS (Jakarta?, three years), and a commercial school (Jakarta). After marrying a daughter of Lieutenant Tan Joen Liong, he moved to Bandung. In 1912 he was elected as a member of the Bandung Regency Council and the Bandung Municipal Council. From 1928 to the 1930s he served as a *wethouder* (assistant to mayor) of Bandung and the acting deputy of the West Java Provincial Council.

Source: Tan, *Tionghoa*, p. 184.

TJEN, Rudianto (TJEN Tjau Tjen; ZENG Zhaozhen 曾昭真, 1958-)
Politician, Protestant

Tjen was born in Bangka on 27 May 1958. When he was young he worked as a technician and technical supervisor in various foreign companies in Indonesia. In 1987 he graduated from the Mechanical Engineering Department, Universitas Kristen Krida Wacana (Jakarta). He continued to work for foreign companies in Indonesia, until 1997 when he began to run his own business. He joined PDIP and contested in the local election in 1999. He was elected Member of Local Parliament (DPRD, Bangka) for 1999–2004, representing the PDIP. Since 2004 he contested and won in three general elections and served as member of parliament, representing PDIP for three periods: 2004–9, 2009–14, and 2014–19. He has served as treasurer of DPD PDIP Bangka-Belitung Branch (2001–6) and treasurer of DPD PDIP (date unknown).

Sources: *Wajah DPR & DPD 2009–14*, p. 328; Pengurus Pusat Fordeka, *Buku Acuan 2014*, p. 117.

TJEN Tjau Tjen. See **TJEN, Rudianto**
TJHIE Pwee Giok. See **TILAAR, Martha**

TJHIE Tjay Ing (Hs) (XU Zaiying 徐再英, 1935-)
Religious leader, Confucian

Born in 1935 in Blora, he was educated at a local primary Chinese school. He later moved to SMP (Junior Middle School), also in Blora. In 1954 he went to study at SGA (teachers' training school) in Solo and in the same year, he became interested in Confucianism. In 1955, he and his friends established Pemoeda Agama Khonghoetjoe Indonesia (Young Confucian Religion Council). In the same year he graduated from SGA and became a primary school teacher at Sekolah Tripusaka in Solo. In the following year he was appointed as the principal of the school. He later resigned and since 1960 became a full-time Confucian religion teacher. In 1967 he was elected Haksu (Hs.) or a senior Confucian priest of the Agama Khonghucu in Indonesia. He also served as the first deputy chairman of Matakin in charge of religious matters. *Tempo* misreported that he was the chairman of Matakin. At one time he taught a course at the UGM (Universitas Gadjah Mada) on Confucian religion and has been active in promoting the religion. In 2003 he received a special Yan Hui 颜回 Award (Anugerah Gan Hui) from Matakin in recognition of his contribution to the development of the Confucian religion in Indonesia. He is the most senior Haksu in Matakin.

Sources: The compiler's notes; *Tata Agama & Tata Laksana Upacara Agama Khonghucu* (1975?), p. 1; Hutomo, comp., "Sejarah Singkat Perkembangan Agama Khonghucu di Indonesia", mimeographed; *Tempo*, 11 July 1994, p. 88; Setyautama, *Tokoh Tokoh Etnis TH*, pp. 437–38.

TJHO Lian Sin (CAO Lianxin 曹联信, 1908?–1970s)
Leading physician

Born in Blinyu (Bangka) in 1908(?), he was educated at the ELS (Blinyu) and the HBS (Jakarta). After receiving a medical degree from a university in Amsterdam, he went into practice in Tegal to replace **Dr SIM Ki Ay**, who went abroad for further studies. In the 1960s he served as the director of the Sumber Waras Hospital (Jakarta), a private hospital financed by Sin Ming Hui. He went overseas for a few years, but eventually returned to Jakarta where he died in the 1970s.

Sources: Tan, *Tionghoa*, p. 161; the compiler's notes.

TJIA Eng Tong 谢英堂*
Community leader

A MULO student from Cirebon, he was a founding member of Chung Hsioh (Cirebon?). In the 1930s he served as a member of both the Cirebon Municipal Council and the Cirebon Regency Council.

Source: Tan, *Tionghoa*, p. 221.

TJIA Giok Thwan (Basuki HIDAYAT; XIE Yuduan 谢玉端, 1927–82)
Physician, guerrilla fighter

Born in 1927, he was eighteen years of age when he joined Corps Mahasiswa Djawa Timur (CMDT, East Java Students Corps) fighting for Indonesia's independence. He resigned from the CMDT after Indonesia had achieved independence. On 5 October 1958 he received the independence medal (Satya Lencana Perang Kemerdekaan Dua). On 29 January 1959 he was awarded another medal (Satya Lencana Gerakan

Operasi Militer Kesatu). He was also a member of the Legiun Veteran RI. He graduated as a physician from Universitas Airlangga (Surabaya) in the early 1960s. Since 1967 he served as the head of Rumah Sakit Jiwa Sumerporong, a mental hospital. He died on 1 March 1982 at the age of fifty-five. Due to his contribution to Indonesia's independence, he was buried in the Surapati National Hero Cemetery in Malang. In fact, there was another Chinese who also received the independence medal and was qualified to be buried in the cemetery, but his relatives declined.

Source: *Kompas*, 30 March 1982.

TJIA Kian Liong. See SOERYADJAYA, William

TJIA, May On (XIE Meian 谢梅安, 1934-)
Scientist, university professor

Born in Probolinggo (East Java) on 25 December 1934, his father was a schoolteacher. Tjia May On finished his SMP and SMA in Malang and entered ITB (Bandung) from which he obtained a Sarjana degree in 1962. In 1963 he went to the Northwestern University in the United States and received a PhD in 1969. His dissertation was entitled, "Saturation of Chiral Charge-Current Commutator". He also received a few fellowships, one of which was from the International Center for Theoretical Physics (Trieste, Italy, 1974) and another from The Japan Society for Promotion of Science for doing research at Osaka University (Japan, 1980).

After returning from the United States, Tjia returned to his alma mater (ITB) to teach. He devoted his life to teaching and research. He has published two textbooks and more than 200 research papers in various international journals. Tjia was respected as he was a serious researcher and dedicated teacher. He stayed in Indonesia and continued to do research under poor condition. He belongs to the first generation of

Indonesian scientists who have contributed to the development of science. On 5 February 2005, when he was seventy years old, the ITB held a celebration for him to commemorate his dedication and contribution to research culture in the university. In 2012 he received the Bakrie Award for Science.

Sources: *Apa dan Siapa Ilmuwan dan Teknokrat Indonesia* (Jakarta: Pustaka Kartini, 1989), pp. 159–60; "Penghargaan Achmad Bakrie X 2012 untuk Negeri" (pamphlet, 2012); Ye Han 叶晗, "Yinni kexuejia Xie Meian", 印尼科学家谢梅安, *Dipingxian* 地平线, no. 7 (July 2002): 32–33.

TJIA Tjeng Siang (1879-?) 谢清祥*
Community leader, businessman, majoor in Pontianak

Born in Pontianak on 20 August 1879, he was educated at the ELS (Pontianak). He was also a holder of a "diploma for minor civil servant". Initially working as a clerk in the Department of Home Affairs in Dutch Borneo, he later held various positions. In 1911 he was appointed *kapitein* (Pontianak) and later, *majoor*. From 16 May 1927 to 1935 he was appointed as a member of Volksraad representing the PEB. He was awarded a medal by the Dutch Government for his services.

Sources: *Volksraad*, 1829–29, p. 165; Wal, *Volksraad*, vol. II, p. 724.

TJIAM Djoe Khiam, Fredericus Christophorus (ZHAN Yuqian 詹裕谦, 1904–83)
Lawyer, Catholic

Born on 16 February 1904 in Kebumen (Central Java), he attended the RHS (Jakarta), and later Rijks Universiteit, Leiden (the Netherlands), from which he obtained an Mr degree in 1937. He returned to Indonesia and in 1938 was appointed as an advocate and a lawyer at the Supreme Court of the Netherlands Indies. From 1947 to 1950 he served as legal juridical counsellor of the Department of Economic Affairs in the Netherlands Indies. Since 1951 he has been practising law privately, serving as Legal Counsel to the Ministry of

Information, RI, and the Dasaad Musin Concern (a large indigenous enterprise involved in the import-export business). After the 1965 coup, he was appointed Legal Counsel to Brigadier-General Supardjo.

Sources: Roeder, *Who's Who*, p. 516; "Tjiam dan Ali Baba", *Topik*, 17 May 1972, p. 25; Zhou Nanjing, ed., *Huaqiao huaren baike quanshu* (2001), p. 660.

Tjiangdra WIDJAYA. See **WIDJAYA, Tjiangdra**
TJIE Tjin Hoan. See **TJIPUTRA**

TJIO Tiang Soey 蒋长瑞*
Community leader, businessman, owner of Firma Lauw Tjin (import-export firm in Jakarta)
Born in Jakarta, he was educated at the ELS (Jakarta), the HBS (Jakarta), and the RHS (Jakarta). In the 1930s he served as a member of the Jakarta Municipal Council, an executive member of both the CHH and the Chinese Importers' Association.

Source: Tan, *Tionghoa*, p. 211.

TJIO Wie Tay. See **MASAGUNG**

TJIOK San Fang, Elsie (Mrs Elsie TJIOK-LIM; SHI Shengfang 石圣芳, **1935-)**
Ballerina, pianist, married to **LIM Kek Tjiang**
She was born in Magelang in September 1935 (but in her authobiography, she states that she was born in Shanghai in 1936). After studying at the Puck Meijer Dancing School in Jakarta for three years, she continued her training at the Legat School (in Tunbridge Wells, Kent), England, and joined the Legat Dancing Group, travelling to England, France, Belgium, and the Netherlands. In 1953 she returned to Indonesia, giving a few performances. She later studied at and graduated from

the Royal Academy of Music in London. In 1956 she returned to Indonesia and was asked by the Indonesian government to start a ballet school. In 1958 she married **LIM Kek Tjiang**. In May 1959 the couple went to Beijing. She got sick and in October 1959 began to teach ballet at the Ballet Academy of Beijing. During the Cultural Revolution she was involved in training ballerinas for the performance of "The Red Detachmen of Women", one of the few ballet pieces that were allowed to be performed. She fell ill due to stress and long working hours. She suffered from thyroid disorder and her neck became swollen, but she refused to have an operation in Beijing. In 1969 she and her husband left for Hong Kong. They worked for several years and in 1975 migrated to Sydney and later moved to Melbourne. In 1984 she was invited to teach ballet in Hong Kong. While in Hong Kong she met the founder of a ballet school in Taiwan, Lin Huaimin, who invited her to teach at his school. Her husband went with her and they stayed in Taiwan for seven years until both retired. In 1998 they returned to Australia.

Sources: "Elsie San Fang Tjiok", *Pantjawarna*, no. 61 (October 1953), p. 6; *Southeast China Morning Post* 18(?), September 1970; Suryadinata, ed., *Southeast Asian Personalities*, pp. 1189–91; the compiler's notes.

TJIOK-LIM, Elsie. See **TJIOK San Fang, Elsie**

TJIPUTRA (also spelt as CIPUTRA; TJIE Tjin Hoan; XU Zhenhuan 徐振焕, 1931-)
Entrepreneur, architect

Born in Parigi (Central Sulawesi) on 24 August 1931, he graduated from the Department of Architecture at the ITB (Bandung). Initially, together with two other architects (Ismail Sofjan and Lie Toan Hong), he set up Dajatjipta, an architect firm in Bandung and Medan. Later they formed Pembanguanan Jaya. He is the president-director of PT

Pembangunan Jaya, a conglomerate of twenty-odd corporations involved in real estate, steel trade, aluminum, gas, among others. His other important position is perhaps as chairman (*ketua*) of the Pembangunan Jaya Group, which has many subsidiary companies and employs more than 10,000 workers. PT Pembangunan Jaya is owned by the Jakarta government and the governor of Jakarta is automatically its president-commissioner. Governor Ali Sadikin, the first powerful president-commissioner of the company, is a personal friend of Ciputra. In fact, just before Ali Sadikin stepped down, Sadikin granted "Model Entrepreneur Awards" to ten outstanding Indonesian citizens. Ciputra was one of the recipients. He was closely associated with Sadikin but he was also able to get along well with the other Jakarta governors after Sadikin.

Ciputra's business continued to expand. It was reported that he has shares in many major companies, including the Metropolitan Development and PT Cold Rolling Mill Indonesia Utama. The above-mentioned companies were also associated with the **LIEM Sioe Liong** Group. Ciputra is a successful entrepreneur. He has also been interested in education in Indonesia. He has been involved in the development of the Taruma Nagara University and Prasetya Mulya School of Management. In 2006 after he attended an international conference on entrepreneurship and education in Singapore, he established the "Universitas Ciputra Entrepreneurship Center" in Surabaya. Apparently he is eager to train Indonesians to be entrepreneurs and provide Indonesian entrepreneurs with further training.

[Note: In the past, the Chinese characters of Tjie Tjin Hoan were given as 徐清华 (or 徐振环), in fact, the correct ones should be 徐振焕.]

Sources: *Apa & Siapa 1985–86*, pp. 145–47; *Tempo*, 16 July 1977, p. 58; *Expo 2*, no. 1 (4 January 1984): 13–14; information provided by Professor Dali Naga, October 2013.

TJOA Hin Hoey (Mrs) (maiden name: KWEE Yat Nio; GUO Yueniang 郭悦娘; Buddhist name: Visakha Gunadharma, 1906–93)
Religious and community leader, daughter of **KWEE Tek Hoay**, *mother of* **Effie TJOA Keng Loan**

Born in Bogor in 1906, she was educated at the THHK and the Methodist English School (Bogor), where she graduated in 1924. She became a schoolteacher at the same English school. After getting married in 1925, she moved to Jakarta and taught at the Batavia English School (Jakarta). From 1932 to 1940 she served as the chairperson of the Zhonghua Funühui (Chinese Women's Association) in Jakarta; from 1934 to 1938 she was the secretary of the Batavia Buddhist Association (Jakarta); from 1934 to the 1950s she was elected as the chairperson of Sam Kauw Hwee (Jakarta) and the deputy chairperson of Gabungan Sam Kauw (Federation of Trireligion Associations) in Indonesia; from 1935 to 1942 she edited *Istri*, a weekly for married women; from 1952 to 1956, she was the general manager of *Tribudaja*, a journal of Gabungan Sam Kauw Indonesia; in 1956 she was chairperson of the Baperki Women Section (Jakarta). She died on 26 September 1993.

Sources: "Riwajat Hidup Nj. Tjoa Hin Hoey", *Berita Baperki Tjabang Jogya II* (February 1956): 57; *Kompas*, 28 September 1990.

TJOA Ing Hwie. See WONOWIDJOJO, Surya

TJOA Keng Loan, Effie (CAI Qingluan 蔡庆鸾, 1931–2007)
Professional singer, daughter of **Mrs TJOA Hin Hoey**

Born in Surabaya on 6 June 1931, she was educated at a music college in Holland and later in Beijing. In the early 1950s, she won the first prize for the "Best Dramatic Soprano" in an international contest in Italy. She has since held numerous concerts in Indonesia and around the world, including the United States, the Netherlands, China, Japan, Korea, Hong

Kong and Singapore. When Soekarno was in power, she was a regular performer at the Palace. At the age of seventy, she won the gold medal in classical vocal performance at a singing competition for seniors. During the late 1950s and early 1960s she was a woman cadre of Baperki. After the 1965 coup, she left for the Netherlands and lived there until she passed away on 16 March 2007.

Sources: *Auwj* (November 1958), p. 2; Saleh, *Sumbangsih* (1956), p. 16; Siauw, *Pantja Sila*, p. 13; Letter to the compiler, 1995; "Eulogy for our beloved — Effie Tjoa", private correspondence, 14 March 2007.

TJOA Liang Tjoe. See MARGA T.

TJOA Sie Hwie (CAI Xihui 蔡锡辉, 1907–79)
Political party leader, lawyer

Born in Pasuruan (East Java) on 6 February 1907, he obtained an Mr degree from Leiden University in 1938. After graduation, he returned to Indonesia and practised law in Surabaya. From 1945 to 1947 he was appointed Judge of Surabaya. He later worked for the Rice Centre (East Java) and the Textile Industry (Surabaya). From 1948 to 1949 he was a committee member of the PT (Surabaya branch). In the 1950s he joined the PNI. During the RIS period he was appointed as a member of the DPR representing East Java, and from August(?) 1950 to 1956, he served as a member of the DPR representing the PNI. He died in 1979.

Sources: *Sinar*, 20 September 1949, p. 9; Kempen, *KP*, p. 132; the compiler's notes.

TJOA Sik Ien (CAI Xiyin 蔡锡胤, 1907–87)
Political party leader, physician

Born in Surabaya in 1907, he was educated at Amsterdam University. In 1932 he and two other *peranakan* students (**TAN Ling Djie** and **TENG Tjin Leng**) founded Sarekat Peranakan

Tionghoa Indonesia in opposition to the CHH-Netherlands. After finishing medical school, he returned to Indonesia and was active in local politics. In 1939 he served as the president of the PTI central board and the director of *Sin Tit Po*. During the Indonesian Independence Movement in 1946 he was involved in the SOS, taking the side of the Indonesian Republicans. Between 8 December 1947 and 17 January 1948 he was a member of the Indonesian delegation in the Renville negotiation led by Amir Sjarifoeddin. In 1949 he was a delegate of the RI to the United Nations. From 1950 to an unknown date he served as the director of *Republik* (Surabaya). In 1959 he was appointed as a member of Dewan Perancang Nasional (National Planning Council), representing Indonesian citizens of foreign descent. In 1964 upon the invitation of Siauw Giok Tjhan, he rejoined Baperki and was active in the East Java branch. He left Indonesia for Europe and died in Vienna in 1987.

Sources: Suryadinata, *Peranakan Chinese*, p. 134; *Almanak Organisasi*, p. 592; Anderson, *Bibliography*, p. 34; Junus Jahja, *Peranakan Idealis*, p. 61; Setiono, *Tionghoa Dalam Pusaran Politik* (2002), p. 633; Cui Yisheng 崔一生,〈蔡锡胤和国籍协商会〉,刊载于李卓辉编,《五湖四海殊途同归〉(雅加达: 联通, 2011), p. 308; the compiler's notes.

TJOA Soei Leng. See **SUDIN**

TJOA Tjie Liang (Anang SATYAWARDAYA; CHUA Chee Liang; CAI Zhiliang 蔡志良, 1913–2006)
Journalist, political party leader, Protestant

Born in Banjarmasin on 1 May 1913, he moved to Java and became interested in journalism. Although without formal education, he managed to become an editor of *Sin Tit Po* (Surabaya) in 1932–33. In 1933 he was elected as the secretary of the PTI. In 1933–34 he served on the editorial board of *Soeara Oemoem* (Surabaya), an Indonesian nationalist newspaper. In 1935 he worked for *Mata Hari* and in the following year he worked for *Siang Po*. He returned to *Mata Hari* in 1937 and stayed there until 1942. From 1942 to 1945 he was interned by the Japanese. He joined the PNI and was active in the Central Java branch. In 1951 he worked for *Sin Min* and from 1953 to 1965 he became the publisher and editor-in-chief of *Kuang Po*, a Semarang-based Indonesian daily. The newspaper was later renamed *Sinar Indonesia* and ceased publication in August 1965 due to political pressure.

He was active in the assimilationist movement and was a signatory of Piagam Asimilasi in 1961. In 1996 when he was eighty-three years old, he completed his memoirs denoting his life story from an infant at two years old to the closure of *Sinar Indonesia*, which was taken over by the military and renamed *Berita Yudha* (Central Java edition). In 2003 his daughter Cherry, edited the manuscript and published it under the title: *Dari Banjarmasin Hingga Surabaya*. He died on 5 November 2006 and was buried in Ambarawa, Central Java.

Sources: Tjoa Tjie Liang, *Nusaputra*, 25 September 1951, p. 8; *Lahirnja Konsepsi Asimilasi* (1962), p. 24; Letter to the compiler, 1971; Anang Satyawardaya (n.p., 2003); the compiler's notes.

TJOE Bou San (ZHU Maoshan 朱茂山, 1891–1925)
Journalist, community leader

Born in 1891 in Jakarta, he received some Dutch education. Largely through self-taught, he was able to read and write Malay, English, and probably Chinese. In 1909 he became the editor-in-chief of *Hoa Tok Po*, a Jakarta-based weekly in *peranakan* Malay, which had close links with a Chinese revolutionary association called Soe Po Sia [Reading Club]. A few years later he left *Hoa Tok Po* for Surabaya, where he became the editor-in-chief of *Tjhoen Tjhioe* until June 1917. He then went to China to work as a *Sin Po* correspondent.

In 1918 he returned to Jakarta and was appointed as the editor-in-chief of *Sin Po* and, in 1919, the director as well.

Before he led *Sin Po*, Tjoe was known as a novelist who published his works under the pseudonym Hauw San Liang. His well-known works include *Satoe Djodo Jang Terhalang* (1917) and *The Loan Eng* (1922). Nevertheless, Tjoe was better known as a community leader and a journalist.

It was under his leadership that *Sin Po* became one of the most influential political forces in the Chinese communities before World War II. Because of his Chinese nationalist viewpoint, he was very critical of P.H. Fromberg, a Dutch lawyer, who advocated the identification of the local Chinese with an "Indies nation" by accepting Dutch nationality.

Tjoe soon came into conflict with *peranakan* Chinese leaders who did not agree that the solution to the problem of the Indies Chinese was Chinese nationalism. His main opponent in the press was **GOUW Peng Liang**, the editor-in-chief of *Perniagaan*, who actively advocated cooperation with the Dutch authorities and the popularization of Dutch education among the *peranakan* Chinese.

Tjoe contracted tuberculosis which led to his premature death in 1925 at the age of thirty-four.

Sources: Ang, *Sin Po*, 26 December 1925, pp. 614–22; Salmon, *Literature*, pp. 362–63.

TJOE Siauw Hoei (1871–1947) 朱晓辉*
Publisher, father-in-law of **TIO Ie Soei**

Born in Jakarta on 30 March 1871, he was educated at a local Hokkien school (Jakarta). He was a major shareholder of Ho Siang In Kiok (a printing press in Jakarta) and the director of *Perniagaan* (Jakarta) from 1907 to 1918. He died in Jakarta on 7 February 1947.

Source: Tio Ie Soei's notes.

Biographies

TJOE Tit Fat. See **SUTRISNO, Slamet**

TJOENG Lin Sen 钟林生*
A *peranakan* from Kalimantan Barat, he was a member of the DPR-RIS from February to August 1950, and a member of the DPR from 1950 to 1953.
Source: *DPR 1971*, p. 599.

TJOENG Tin Jan (ARSADJAJA, Jani; ZHONG Dingyuan 钟鼎远**, 1919–84)**
Political party leader, lawyer, Catholic
Born in Sungaislan (Bangka) on 9 February 1919, he was educated at the RHS (Jakarta) and later the University of Rijks (Leiden), where he received an Mr degree. Before he was appointed as the deputy head of the state court in Pangkal Pinang, he worked for a telephone company. He later went into private practice working as a prosecutor. He was also a legal adviser to a Chinese school in Pangkal Pinang.

In 1949 he founded the PT Bangka branch and served as its chairman. From February to August 1950 he was appointed as a member of the DPR-RIS representing the Bangka region. From 1950 to 1953 he was a member of the DPR representing the PDTI. In 1953 he joined Partai Katholik and represented the party in the DPR (up to 1960). From 1953 to 1959 he served as a member of the central board of Partai Katholik and from 1956 to 1958, second deputy general chairman of Partai Katholik (Jakarta). From 1958 to 1979 he was a member of the Board Council of Church Foundation and Papa Santa Ignatius Fund.

From 1955 to 1961 he was the director of Perusahaan Pembangunan Pertambangan, PT Tambang Emas Cikotok, and PT Logam Emas; from 1961 to 1968, the director of General

Board, state mining companies; and from 1968 to 1974, the financial director of PN Aneka Tambang.

Tjoeng was an advocate of assimilation for the Chinese Indonesian. In 1960 he was known as one of the ten assimilation leaders in the *Star Weekly*. He was critical of Yap Thiam Hien's argument. Tjoeng died in Jakarta in 1984.

Sources: *Sinar 1*, no. 4 (1 May 1949): 7; Kempen, *KP*, p. 133; *DPR 1971*, pp. 579–701; Roeder, *Who's Who*, 2nd ed., p. 52; Junus Jahja, pp. 179–85.

TJOKROSAPUTRO, Handoko (KWEE Han Tjiong, 1949-) 郭汉将*
Businessman, son of **KWEE Som Tjok**

Born in Surabaya on 29 September 1949, he finished his secondary school in Semarang. Between 1967 and 1969 he studied mechanical engineering at the ITB. In 1970 before completing his studies, he became the director-general of PT Batik Keris, the *batik* factory which was established by his father. He took over the company when his father passed away in 1976. The company continued to develop under his leadership and is now a leading *batik* manufacturer in Indonesia. In the 1980s he had 4,600 workers. The sister company, PT Dian Laris, which was run by his younger brother Handiman (Kwee Han Liem) had 2,900 workers.

Source: *Apa & Siapa 1985–86*, pp. 1134–35.

TJOKROSAPUTRO, Kasom (KWEE Som Tjok, 1929–76) 郭森作*
Leading batik businessman

Born in Semarang in 1929, he was the managing director of PT Batik Keris, a leading Indonesian *batik* manufacturer. He died in Sydney on 29 December 1976.

Source: Roeder, "Chinese 'Impudence'", p. 34; *Sinar Harapan*, 4 January 1977.

TJONG A Fie (TJONG Yiauw Hian; ZHANG Yaoxuan 张耀轩; ZHANG Hongnan 张鸿南, 1860–1921)
Businessman, community leader, younger brother of **TJONG Jong Hian**

Born in 1859 (1861, according to another source; 1860, according the most recent publication) in Meixian (Guangdong), he came to Deli in 1880. In 1888 he was made *luitenant*, and later promoted to *kapitein*, and in 1911 he became *majoor*. In the following year he was awarded the Ridder Oranje Nassau by the Dutch Government for his services to the Dutch East Indies. He owned a vast amount of residential property in Medan and was associated with many important industrial concerns. He owned a copra factory at the Brayan Island and controlled all the opium farms in the district. Together with his elder brother, he also invested in the Swatow Railway (southern China) and the Deli Bank (in Medan). One of the shareholders of the Deli Bank, **THIO Tiauw Siat** (alias Zhang Bishi or Chang Pi-Shih 张弼士) of Penang, was Tjong's uncle. Tjong A Fie also helped a few Chinese *opsir* (Dutch-appointed officers) in Batavia (Jakarta) set up the Batavian Bank (1904). He held 200 shares out of the 600 shares in the bank. Tjong A Fie and his brother, Tjong Jong Hian, were responsible for the import of a large number of Chinese coolies from China. In the 1910s he succeeded Tjong Jong Hian to become the president of Siang Hwee (Deli).

After the death of Tjong Jong Hian, Tjong A Fie managed to develop the business further for a while. (When THIO Tiauw Siat died, Tjong A Fie bought over Thio's bonds and shares of the Deli Bank from Thio's concubine at a low price and became the major shareholder of the bank.) However, Tjong A Fie's business encountered difficulties when the recession hit Dutch and British colonies. His various businesses —

plantation, tin-mining, shipping, and banking — began to decline, affecting his bank's reserves. Tjong A Fie was not able to honour a cheque of 300,000 guilders that the Deli Bank issued. When the news spread, customers began to rush to the bank to withdraw their deposits. Unable to face the reality, Tjong A Fie committed suicide, thus marking the decline of the Tjong business empire.

Tjong was a close associate of the Sultan of Deli. He also contributed significantly to the local welfare. He built markets, hospital and bridge (known as Chen Tek bridge 成德桥 or Virtuous Bridge to commemorate his elder brother) for the local communities. Unofficially called "the king of Medan", large crowd attended the funeral ceremony when he died in 1921.

Sources: Li (1984), pp. 183–202; Chang (1981), pp. 59–62.; Mary Somers Heidhues, "Tjong A Fie", in Suryadinata, ed., *Southeast Asian Personalities* (2012), pp. 1196–99; Rebecca Chandra, ed., *Tjong Yong Hian: Legacy of a Great Leader* (Medan 2011, privately published), pp. 68–69, 112).

TJONG Hioen Nji (ZHANG Xunyi 章勋义, 1901–72)
Community leader, grocer, Hakka

Born in Guangdong in 1901, he had been active in the KMT since pre-World War II. In 1939 he served as *ta-ko* (*dage*, chairman) of the Hong Yi Shun (a *totok* Chinese secret society) and regained the title in 1952. In the early 1950s he was elected as the president of the CHTH (Jakarta) and Yanong Gonghui (亚弄公会, Jakarta). In 1953 he came into physical conflict with pro-Beijing Chinese within Yanong Gonghui, resulting in his expulsion from Indonesia by the Indonesian authorities. He was received as a hero by the Taiwan authorities and awarded the title of "Honorary Citizen" by the Taiwan municipality upon his arrival in Taipei. In the mid-1960s he moved to Bangkok and worked in a Chinese restaurant owned by his friend. After 1966 he returned to Indonesia and established a foundation called Jajasan Intisari, of which he was the deputy director. The director was a retired Indonesian general. He died in Jakarta in 1972.

Sources: *Huaqiao zhi* (1961), pp. 128–32; Jiang, "Yajiada", p. 14; Zhong, *Yanong*; *Directory of Chinese Names*, p. 100; *Huaqiao Da Cidian*, pp. 861–62.

TJONG Jok Nam. See **TJONG Jong Hian**

TJONG Jong Hian (TJONG Jok Nam; ZHANG Rongxuan 张榕轩; ZHANG Yunan 张煜南, 1850–1911)
Businessman, community leader, elder brother of **TJONG A Fie,** *Hakka*

Born in Meixian (Guangdong) in 1855 (1851, according to another source; 1850 according to the most recent publication), he is a son of a poor farmer. Jong Hian was a small rice trader in his village before he came to Jakarta where he engaged in various occupations — at one time he was a licensed pawnbroker. In 1880 he left Jakarta for Sumatra. In 1884 he was made *luitenant* in Medan. In 1893 he was promoted to *kapitein* and in 1898 to *majoor*. He was also a member of the Native Court (Landraad) in Medan. A wealthy property owner in Sumatra, he was the director of the Deli Bank and a major shareholder of the Swatow Railway (Chao-shan Railway 潮汕铁路 China). Under his initiative, Siang Hwee (Deli) was formed, and he was its first president.

Tjong made significant contributions to Imperial China, especially his investment in the Swatow Railway. He met Emperor Guangxi and Empress Dowager and received several awards and accolades from them. In 1903, Empress Dowager bestowed gifts (such as a scroll, a *paiting* and a piece of jade) to him on his birthday. He also built schools, orphanages, and old folks homes in Medan. Tjong died on 11 September 1911. He was buried in Kebun Bunga (known as Mao Rong Yuan 茂榕园 in Chinese) around Jalan Kejaksaan, Medan. In 2013 the Mayor of Medan renamed Bogor Street to Tjong Yong Hian Street to commemorate both the Tjong brothers' contribution to the local community. The street had been changed from Jalan Tjong Yong Hian to Jalan Bogor in 1960.

Sources: Wright, *Impression*, pp. 580–81; *Shangye Nianjian*, p. 338; Chang, "Memories"; Li Songan (1984); Rebecca Chandra, ed., *Tjong Yong Hian: Legacy of a Great Leader* (Medan 2011, privately published), pp. 42, 60–63; Rao Ganzhong 饶淦中〈还原华族先贤贡献国家的历史〉, *Diping xian*, December 2013, pp. 4–11.

TJONG Yiauw Hian. See **TJONG A Fie**

TJOO Tik Tjoen (CAO Dechong 曹德崇, 1921-)
Politician, former schoolteacher

Born in Surabaya on 15 April 1921, he was educated at Tung-chi (Tongji) University in China for a year (before World War II). From February to August 1941 he was the headmaster of a THHK school in Lawang. His activities during the Japanese Occupation are unknown. From January to December 1946 he became a teacher at the Sin Hwa High School in Surabaya. In January 1949 he moved to Lombok to teach at a THHK school (Ampenan). In July 1947 he returned to Surabaya to serve as the deputy director of a trading firm, Pyramid.

He began to be active in politics after the Japanese capitulation. From 1945 to 1946, he was chairman of the *totok*-dominated youth section of Ta-Chung Sze (Surabaya).

He was against the formation of Poh-An Tui during the Dutch-Indonesian conflicts. From 1948 to January 1950 he was detained by the Dutch authorities and, from August 1951 to September 1952 he was imprisoned by the Sukiman government for his left-wing political activities. In 1954, he was elected as the secretary of Baperki (Surabaya branch). In April 1956 he formally joined the PKI. In fact, before this he had participated in the 1955 general elections on the PKI ticket. He was elected as a member of the DPR in 1956 and held the position until 1964. He was detained after the 1965 coup.

Sources: Parlaungan, *Tokoh Parlemen*, pp. 309–10; DPR 1971, pp. 619, 653, 672.

TJUI, Maria (TJUI Mauw; CUI Miao 崔妙, 1934-)
Painter

Born in 1934 in Pariaman, West Sumatra, she wanted to be a painter since childhood. She left her birthplace to look for inspiration and applied to enter ASRI (Akademi Seni Rupa Indonesia) in Yogyakarta. But her application was rejected as she only had an SMP (Junior high school) diploma. She then joined the Indonesian Young Artists group (Senirupa Indonesia Muda) under the tutelage of a leading Indonesian painter S. Soedjojono from 1953–59. In 1961 she applied to ASRI again and this time she was accepted. She graduated in 1963. As she had studied under S. Soedjojono and also Affandi, her paintings have been influenced by these two Indonesian masters. She had produced more than 3,000 paintings, many of which have been collected by the wives of Indonesian presidents (Mrs Soeharto and Mrs Habibie) and their dignitaries. One of her favourite objects is sunflower and she has painted more than a hundred of them. Maria lived in Bali for twenty-five years and later moved to Puncak, West Java.

Source: Setyautama, *Tokoh-tokoh Etnis TH*, pp. 466–67.

TJUI Mauw. See **TJUI, Maria**

TJUNG See Gan (ZHUANG Xiyan 庄西言, 1885–1965)
Community leader, businessman

Born in 1885, Nanjing (南靖 Fujian), he migrated to Indonesia in 1905 and joined Tongmeng Hui 同盟会 (later the KMT) in Jakarta.

In 1913 he served as the president of Siang Hwee (Jakarta). In 1917 he established the Tjoan Bie Textile Company. He was active in promoting investment by Overseas Chinese in China. From 1928 to 1932 he again served as the president of Siang Hwee (Jakarta) and from 1935 to 1937, the vice-president of the THHK (Jakarta). He was appointed as a member of the Chinese Parliament representing the Overseas Chinese prior to World War II. From 1943 to 1945 he was detained by the Japanese authorities. In the 1950s he became active again in Shang Lian, serving as the vice-chairman of the Shang Lian–sponsored Kao Shang School Board. He died in Hong Kong in 1965.

Sources: Liu, *Gailan*, pp. [21–22]; *Fujian*, p. 27; the compiler's notes.

TJUNTJUN (1952-) 梁俊俊*
Badminton player, younger brother of **LIANG Chiu Sia**

His Chinese surname is Liang. Born in Cirebon on 4 October 1952, he had a secondary school education. He played the men's doubles with **Johan WAHYUDI** and won the All-England title six times (1974, 1975, 1977, 1978, 1979, and 1980). He was also a member of the Indonesian Thomas Cup Team for three times (1973, 1976, and 1979).

Sources: *Apa & Siapa 1981–82*, p. 816; *Sejumlah Orang Bulutangkis Indonesia*, pp. 347–49.

Tommie SUTANU. See **SUTANU, Tommie**

TONG Djoe (TANG Yu 唐裕, 1926-)
Businessman, community leader

Born in Medan (Pematang Siantar?) in 1926, he was a son of a migrant shopkeeper. He received his Chinese school education in Singapore. In 1943 he joined a small shipping firm owned by his brother. During the independence movement, he supplied rice, medicine and military equipment to the Indonesian Republican army. It was during this period that he became acquainted with Indonesian nationalists (A.K. Gani and Ibnu Sutowo) who later became leaders after Indonesian independence.

Tong and his brother were invited by A.K. Gani to assist in the establishment of the National Shipping Company (PELNI) after 1949. In 1953 Tong Djoe himself formed a shipping company. Towards the end of the 1950s, he became the Pertamina (the Indonesian state oil company) overseas representative and agent in Singapore. The chief of Pertamina was Ibnu Sutowo. In 1961 Tong Djoe established the Tunas Company with its headquarters in Singapore. Later it was developed into the Tunas Group, whose business spread to Indonesia and Hong Kong. The Group continued to engage in shipping, travelling and tourism. However, his business started to decline because of over expansion. He was the president of the Singapore Shipowners' Association and Anxi Huiguan in Singapore.

Tong has succeeded in developing his networks between Singapore, Indonesia and China. He has contributed to the re-establishment of Indonesia-PRC diplomatic ties and gained a medal from the Indonesian government in August 1998.

Sources: *Nanyang Shangbao*, 9 October 1977; *Progres*, no. 136 (February 1978): 16–18; the compiler's notes; *Tempo*, 1 December 1973, p. 40; *Straits Times*, 7 February 1993, p. 3; Liu Hong, "Tong Djoe", in Suryadinata, *Biographical Dictionary* (2012) pp. 1201–4.

TONG, Stephen (TANG Chongrong 唐崇荣, 1940-)
Reformed evangelist

Stephen Tong was born in 1940 on Gulangyu island of Fujian, China, a foreign (western) enclave since 1842 and was therefore heavily influenced by western cultures, including Christianity. His family suffered great economic hardship after his Chinese-Indonesian mother was widowed at the age of thirty-two and had to raise seven siblings and Tong himself. The family went back to Indonesia at a time when a number of prominent Chinese evangelists fled China and focused on preaching evangelism among the ethnic Chinese in the world outside, especially in Southeast Asian countries and North America.

Tong decided to dedicate his life to evangelism in 1957 at the age of seventeen when his mother brought him to a youth conference that was conducted by the Southeast Asia Bible Seminary (SABS) Madrasah Alkitab Asia Tenggara in Malang. On 9 January, the last day of the conference, Andrew Gih (许志文) gave a revival sermon, and Tong became a Christian. He began to share the Gospel and taught children in Christian schools. In 1960, he enrolled in SABS, and later graduated with a Bachelor of Theology in 1964. He then joined SABS's faculty, and taught theology and philosophy classes from 1964 to 1988. In 1979 he started his own worldwide evangelistic ministry — Stephen Tong Evangelistic Ministry International (STEMI). In 1982, he received his ordination as pastor. He served at GKT (Gereja Kristus Tuhan, "Christ, the Lord Church"), and later ministered in GKA (Gereja Kristen Abdiel, "Servant Christian Church"). He has conducted services in Mandarin and Indonesian, but some of his speaking engagements have been in Hokkien and English.

He became one of the most influential figures among the Chinese-speaking ethnic Chinese Christian communities in Indonesia. His Gereja Reformed Injili Indonesia (GRII, or Reformed Evangelical Church of Indonesia) churches are found in a number of predominantly Chinese neighbourhoods in Jakarta and other big cities in Java and Sumatra. In some de facto "ethnic Chinese only" residential areas, the sermons are often conducted in Mandarin and translated into Bahasa Indonesia. In fact his GRII church branches even extend beyond major cities in Indonesia — there are GRII churches in Singapore, Germany, Australia, America, Malaysia, Taiwan,

China and Switzerland, mainly serving the Indonesian diaspora and students. In recognition of Tong's life work in Christian ministries, the Westminister Theological Seminary in Philadelphia awarded him an Honorary Doctorate of Divinity in 2008 and established the Stephen Tong Chair of Reformed Theology in 2011.

Source: Susy Ong, "Tong, Stephen", in Suryadinata, ed., *Southeast Asian Personalities* (2012), pp. 1204–6.

Tony WEN. See **WEN, Tony**

TSAI, Frans (CAI Huaxi 蔡华喜, 1941-)
Political activist, physician
Born in Singkawang, West Kalimantan, on 12 July 1941, he first received his primary and junior middle school education at his birthplace, but went to Jakarta to attend the SMA Kanisius for his high school education. In 1962 he received a scholarship and went to Switzerland for his tertiary education. He graduated from the University of Zurich (according to another source: Fribourg University, also in Switzerland) in 1971 as a physician. While in Switzerland, he served as a secretary of the Indonesian Students Association (PPI). After graduation he worked at the Lakewood Hospital, Cleveland, Ohio (USA) for a year.

When he returned to Indonesia he worked in various pharmaceutical companies. After the fall of Soeharto, he joined PDIP and contested in the 1999 parliamentary election but was not elected. He left PDIP and established the Partai Bhinneka Tunggal Ika Perjuangan (PBI-Perjuangan) in 2001 together with **SUSANTO, T.L.**, but the party failed to meet the requirements of the Election Commission. He later joined Partai Demokrat (PD) and participated in the 2004 parliamentary election, but was not elected. However, in January 2009 he was sworn in as a member of parliament to replace Yusuf Perdamea of North Sumatra constituency.

Sources: <http://www/epochtimes.com/gh/3/1/16/n266515...> (accessed 22 October 2014); <https://groups.yahoo.com/neo/groups/singkawang/conversations/messages/7004> (accessed 22 October 2014); Setyautama, *Tokoh-Tokoh Etnis Tionghoa*, pp. 469–70.

UMBOH, Wim (1933–96) 林炎荣*
Movie director

His original Chinese name is still unresolved. One source says that his former Chinese surname was Lam (Lin in Mandarin and Liem in Hokkien; in the Wikipedia, it was given as Liem Yan Yung) but another says that it was Oen (Wen). Born on 26 March 1933 (Archipel says it was 1932) in Minahasa (Sulawesi), he came to Jakarta to join a Chinese film studio, the Golden Arrow, where he started from a low position. He acquired the technics and know-how about movie-making while working in the studio. He was later promoted to the position of a director. His first well-known movie was *Terang Bulan Terang Dikali* [Moonlight on the river] produced in 1956. In 1959 he and Mdm. A. Mambo formed the Aries Film. Some of his better-known movies were *Istana Jang Hilang* [The lost palace] (1960), *Bintang Ketjil* [The little star] (1963), *Matjan Kemajoran* [The tiger of Kemajoran] (1965), *Sembilan* [Nine] (1967), *Laki-Laki Tak Bernama* [A man without a name] (1969), and *Dan Bunga-Bunga Berguguran* [And the flowers are dropping] (1970). His movie *Pengantin Remadja* [Young bride] (1971) won the Golden Harvest Award for the Best Picture of the Year in the 17th Film Festival in Asia (Taipei, 1971). In 1972 he directed *Mama*, one of the most expensive movies in Indonesian film history, which became another hit. In 1973 he was awarded Best Director for his motion picture, *Perkawinan* [Wedding] in the Indonesian Film Festival. The film also won the Best Picture of the Year award. His other films which won Best Picture Awards were *Senyum di Pagi Bulan Desember* [Smile in the morning of December] (1975) and *Cinta* [Love] (1976). His 1979 production *Pengemis dan Tukang Becak* [Beggar and becak driver] was chosen as the Second Best Picture in the 1970 Indonesian Film Festival. He died in Jakarta in 1996.

Sources: *Kompas*, 3 February 1980; *Topik IV*, no. 9 (1975): 25–26; Lombard (1973), pp. 126–27; *Top* (Jakarta), no. 105 (June 1979: 12–13; Gunawan, *Kompas*, 4 February 1979; <http://en.wikipedia.org/wiki/Wim_Umboh> (accessed 30 June 2014); the compiler's notes.

URAY, Burhan (BONG Swan An; BONG Sun On; HUANG Shuang'an 黄双安, 1931-)
Timber king, community leader, Hokchia

He was born on 13 November 1931, but there were a number of versions regarding his birthplace. According to Taiwan's *Kuanghua Magazine* (also known as *Sinorama Magazine*) published in 1991, he was born into a very poor family in southern China and came to Indonesia in his teens. But according to a book published by *Zibenjia* (Chinese edition of *Forbes*), he was born to a poor farmer's family in Kuching, Sarawak, and went to Indonesia in his teens. The recently published biography (in Chinese) by his Taiwanese wife, Bai Jiali, has resolved the issue. Burhan was born in Minqing (Fujian) to a poor family and went to Sibu (Sarawak) at the age of six with his parents. He moved to Indonesia at a later date.

Burhan received little formal education. After working with a local timber company in Sarawak, he moved to Indonesia in 1956 and entered the timber business. Due to good relations with the government, he obtained forest concessions and his business began to expand in the 1960s. Within thirty years he emerged as a timber king of Indonesia. Currently his Djajanti Timber Group is the second largest timber company in Indonesia.

In 1975 (1973?) President Soeharto officiated at the opening of the PT Nusantara Integrated Woodworking Industry in Gresik, near Surabaya, an affiliated company of the Djajanti Timber Group. Burhan is the boss of this company.

The Group has obtained concessions for four million hectares of timber in Kalimantan and Irian Jaya, and a number of affiliated companies in the timber supply and processing business. In 1992 the Group was reorganized and one of the affiliated companies, PT Artike Optima Inti, was scheduled to go public. But this did not materialize. However, in 1994 he sold 31.5 per cent of the company's shares to the Karamat Tin Dredging Company of Malaysia, and in return obtained 25 per cent of the shares of the Karamat Tin Dredging Company.

Burhan has received many medals and been honoured with a number of positions overseas. In 1990 he was awarded a Dato' Seri title by the Sultan of Trengganu, Malaysia. In 2005 he was awarded a medal by the Sarawak head of state. He was also the honorary chairman of China's Wildlife Foundation and honorary chairman of the Fuzhou Overseas Association. He is also a permanent honorary chairman of the Muara Karang Foundation which was established by the Jakarta Fuzhou Clan Association in 1986. He was also interested in promoting Chinese language and culture in Indonesia. In 2010 he offered three to four storeys of his Djajanti building in the centre of Jakarta for the venue of the Institute of Pusat Bahasa Mandarin.

Burhan married a Taiwanese TV celebrity, Bai Jiali (Betty), in September 1977.

Sources: Chen Hantong, *Nanyang Shangbao*, 2 September 1976; *World Star* (Jakarta) 1, no. 2 (September 1976): 35–36; *Silat Weekly* (in Chinese), no. 70 (22 September 1977): 2; Liu Li Chen (1991), pp. 130–37; *Shijie Huaren Fuhao Bang*, pp. 212–13; *Forbes Zibenjia*, June 1995, pp. 84–85; Suryadinata, *Southeast Asian Personalities*, pp. 1229–31.

Usman ADMADJAJA. See **ADMADJAJA, Usman**
Utami DEWI. See **DEWI, Utami**

UTOMO, Tirto (KWA Sien Biauw; KE Xinbiao 柯新标, 1930–94)
Entrepreneur, pioneer of mineral water in Indonesia, Protestant

Born in Wonosobo, Central Java, on 9 March 1930, he received SD and SMP education in his hometown and went to Malang for his SMA education (Saint Albertus). In 1959 he received a law degree (SH) from the University of Indonesia. After graduation, he worked for Pertamina, the state oil company, for about eighteen years (1960–78). He was then head of the foreign relations of the company. In one of the negotiations with the American delegation in 1971, the wife of the delegation head suffered from stomachache as a result of drinking dirty water. He began to think of producing mineral water in Indonesia. In 1974 he succeeded in producing mineral water *Aqua* (meaning: water). Initially it was a small business, but gradually it developed into a big business. His company, PT Aqua Golden Mississippi, had approximately 1,000 employees by 1984. Apart from producing *Aqua*, he also managed two large restaurants in Jakarta.

Tirto was also active in the Indonesian badminton association. He served as its treasurer and raised funds for the association. He passed away suddenly on 16 March 1994.

Sources: Sabaruddin Sa, *Orang Bulu Tangkis Indonesia*, pp. 357–59; *Apa & Siapa 1985–86*, pp. 1152–53.

Verawaty FADJRIN. See **FADJRIN, Verawaty**
Verawaty WIHARJO. See **FADJRIN, Verawaty**
Visakha Gunadharma. See **TJOA Hin Hoey (Mrs)**

WAHYUDI, Johan (ANG Yu Liang 洪友良, 1953-)
Badminton player

Born in Malang on 10 February 1953, initially he attended primary and secondary schools in his hometown. He later went to Surabaya to continue his secondary education; he joined the Radjawali Club where he met **ANG Tjin Siang** and **Rudy Hartono KURNIAWAN**, two well-known badminton players. He and **TJUNTJUN** won the All-England title six times (1974, 1975, 1977, 1978, 1979, and 1980). He was a member of the Indonesian Thomas Cup Team in 1973, 1976, and 1979.

Sources: *Apa & Siapa 1981–82*, pp. 845–46; *Sejumlah Orang Bulutangkis Indonesia*, pp. 360–61; Setyautama, *Tokoh-Tokoh Etnis TH*, pp. 13–14.

WANANDI, (Albertus) Sofjan (LIEM Bian Khoen; LIN Miankun 林绵昆, 1941-)
Former student leader, political activist, businessman, younger brother of **Jusuf WANANDI**, *Catholic*

Born in Sawahlunto (West Sumatra) on 3 March 1941, he received primary and junior high school education in Padang (1948–57). In 1957 he moved to Jakarta to attend the SMA (senior high school) and graduated in 1960. He first studied at Pajajaran University in Bandung (1960–61). A year later he transferred to the FHUI and remained a student until 1968. While studying, he was active in the Catholic students movement and served as an executive member in the PMKRI. From 1965 to 1968 he served as an executive member of KAMI (Jakarta branch). From February 1967 to October 1971 he represented the students group in the DPR and MPRS. From 1967 to 1974 he served as assistant to Major-General Soedjono Hoemardani, who was Personal Assistant to President Soeharto for Economic Affairs. From 1974 he was vice-president of PT Dharma Kencana Sakti, which was established by the Kostrad (Army Strategic Reserve Command) Foundation. There were three companies under him: PT Garuda Mataram, PT Mandala Airways, and PT Dharma Putera Film. He was also managing director of PT Pakarti Yoga from 1974 and later president of the Gembala Group. After Soeharto stepped down, Sofjan was appointed by President Gus Dur as chairman of the Economic Rehabilitation Committee. In 2003, he was elected as the general chairman of the Indonesian Entrepreneurs' Association.

Sources: Letter to the compiler, 1971; *Topik*, nos. 18–19 (October 1978): 11; *Apa & Siapa 1985–86*, pp. 1165–66.

WANANDI, Jusuf (LIEM Bian Kie; LIN Mianji 林绵基, 1937-)
Politician, lawyer, brother of **Sofjan WANANDI***, Catholic*

Born in Sawahlunto (West Sumatra) on 15 November 1937, he was brought up as a Catholic and received his secondary school education at a Catholic high school (Canisius). He later studied law at the University of Indonesia in Jakarta, from which he obtained an Indonesian law degree (SH) in 1960.

Liem was first active in the PMKRI. He soon became the most prominent leader in that organization. Under his leadership, the PMKRI was able to play a major role in the Indonesian Students Action Front (KAMI) formed before the downfall of Soekarno. He then became acquainted with the powerful Army General Ali Murtopo, and later became his assistant. When Soeharto became president, Murtopo was appointed personal assistant to President Soeharto for Special Affairs. Liem was made Murtopo's assistant.

Between 1967 and 1971 Liem was appointed as a member of the Indonesian Parliament (DPR) and the People's Consultative Assembly (MPRS). When the government party, Golkar (Functional Groups), was organized prior to the 1971 general elections, Liem played a notable role and became the deputy secretary-general of its central board. In 1971 he and other pro-Army intellectuals established the Centre for Strategic and International Studies (CSIS or Yayasan Proklamasi). The organization, with the support of Murtopo, has been engaged in research for the Indonesian Government. In May 1973 Liem and other prominent members of the Centre toured the United States defending Soeharto's various policies. He was a member of the MPR (1972–87) and a member of the foreign affairs section of the DPP Golkar (1982–87). He is currently a Senior Fellow at the CSIS and Vice-Chairman of the CSIS Foundation.

Sources: *Ekspres*, 6 September 1971, p. 21; *Washington Post*, 24 July 1975; *CSIS*, p. 3; *Asian Survey XVIII*, no. 8 (August 1977): 792; *Apa & Siapa 1985–86*, pp. 1162–63; *Indonesian Quarterly XXII*, no. 4 (1994): 381.

WANG Chengqing. See **HUSNI, Arief**
WANG Demei. See **ESMARA, Hendra**
WANG Fuhan. See **ONG Hok Ham**
WANG Fulan. See **ONG Hok Lan**

WANG Jiyuan (王纪元, 1910–2001)
Journalist

Born in Zhejiang in 1910, he was educated in Japan. He first worked in Shanghai, and went to Hong Kong in 1936. In 1940 he and other Chinese writers came to Singapore. Before the Japanese invasion, he escaped to Indonesia. From 1945 to 1951 he was the director of *Shenghuo Bao*, a pro-Chinese communist newspaper in Jakarta. In August 1951 he was arrested by the Sukiman government for his left-wing activities and was eventually expelled from Indonesia. From October 1951 up to the occurrence of the Cultural Revolution of China he served as the deputy director of the Education and Cultural Propaganda Office, OCAC, the deputy director of the Chinese News Service, and the deputy secretary-general of the All-China Returned Overseas Chinese Association. In 1964 he was elected as a member of the 4th CPPCC. In 1979 he served as a leader in the China News Agency. He died in Beijing in 2001.

Sources: *Shenghuo Zhoubao*, 26 December 1964; *Nanyang Nianjian* (1951), p. E-107; Fitzgerald, *Peking's Policy*, p. 205; *Cidian*, pp. 71–72; Li Zhuohui, *Yinni xiezuo jingying* (2010), pp. 21–23; the compiler's notes.

WANG Liangguo. See **ONG Liang Kok**
WANG Lianxiang. See **SUSANTI, Susi Lucia Francisca**

WANG Renshu (王任叔; pen-name: Ba Ren 巴人, 1901–72)
Political activist, Chinese diplomat, writer

Born in Zhejiang in 1901, he was active in journalism in China prior to 1941. In 1941 he came to Singapore and became the principal of the Nanqiao Normal School. When Japan invaded Singapore in 1942, he escaped to Indonesia. In 1945 he became the editor of a Chinese daily in Indonesia called *Democratic Daily News*. In 1947 he was involved in the General Overseas Chinese Association (Sumatra). In September 1949 he was arrested and deported to China by the Dutch authorities. From 1949 to 1954 he was a member of the Overseas Chinese Affairs Commission. From August 1950 to November 1954, he served as the PRC ambassador to Indonesia. He was replaced by Huang Zhen in 1955. In 1960 he was criticized for being a revisionist. He died in 1972.

His publications which relate to Indonesia include *Yindunixiya zhi Ge* [Song of Indonesia] (composed in 1944; first published in 1984), *Wu Ge Bei Diao Shih de Kuli* [Five coolies who were hung] (written in 1946; published in 1985), *Lun Yinni de Fandi Douzheng* [On the Indonesian struggle against imperialism] (Shanghai, 1947), *Yinni Shehui Fazhan Gaiguan* [The outline of development of Indonesian society] (Singapore, 1948), *Qundao zhi Guo: Yinni* [A nation of islands: Indonesia] (Shanghai, 1949), and *Linren Men* [Our Indonesian neighbours] (Beijing, 1950).

Sources: *Who's Who in Communist China*, pp. 678–79; *Indonesian Monographs*, p. 72; *Cidian*, p. 71.

WANG Shangzhi. See **ONG Siong Tjie**
WANG Xiangchun. See **ONG Siang Tjoen**
WANG Yalu. See **HAMID, Suwandi**
WANG Yongli. See **ONG Eng Die**
WANG Youshan. See **LEMBONG, Eddie**
WANG Ziqin. See **ONG Tjoe Kim**
WANG Zonghai. See **SINDHUNATHA, Kristoforus**
WEI Chaofeng. See **GOEY Tiauw Hong**
WEI Fuyi. See **GUNAWAN, Andrew H.**
WEI Renfang. See **BUDIKUSUMA, Alan**

WEN Bei'ou (温悲鸥; WEN Peor, 1920–2007)
Painter, ex-schoolteacher

Born on 28 December 1920 in Padang, he was first educated at a Chinese primary school in Padang (1926–33). In 1934 he went to China for his secondary education, first in Kwangya School (Canton, 1934–36), later at Ginlin (Chinling?) University (Nanking, 1936–38). He returned to Indonesia in 1938 and became the headmaster of a Chinese school in Sawah Lunto (1939–40). In 1941 he moved to Jakarta where he worked for a leading advertising agency, TATI. In the following year he became interested in painting.

During the Japanese Occupation (1943) he was detained for a few weeks. When the Indonesian Revolution broke out, he stayed in Yogyakarta, associating himself with leading Indonesian painters such as Affandi, Hendra, and Sudarso. In 1947 he returned to Jakarta and had his first joint exhibition with a *peranakan* artist, Chia Choon-kui. While in Jakarta, he served as the technical head of the Art Section of Sin Ming Hui. In 1952 he moved to Bukit Tinggi to become the headmaster of a Chinese school again, but did not stay long. In 1955 he returned to Jakarta to work as an artist. He served as an executive member of Yin-hua Mei-shu Hsieh-hui (Yinhua meishu xiehui), and was a member of the Lekra, a PKI-dominated artists' and writers' association. He worked in Yogya with left-wing artists and helped young Indonesian painters.

After the 1965 coup in Indonesia, he went to China again. This was during the Cultural Revolution in China and Wen was assigned to work in an overseas Chinese farm. In 1973 with the help from a woman artist Xiao Shufang, he joined the Guangdong Academy of Painters. He was able to hold several exhibitions.

In 1980 he left for Hong Kong where he became productive again. While in Hong Kong he held several exhibitions. In 1987 he participated in the painting exhibition in Jakarta organized by Bank Central Asia (BCA). In 1988 he went to Indonesia again and held painting exhibitions.

It was reported that while in Hong Kong, Wen donated significantly to the Chinese disasters victims and Xiwang Xuexiao (School of Hope), a project to help poor students in China.

Wen died in Hong Kong on 18 March 2007.

Sources: *Xin Bao*, 15 September 1949; C.M. Hsu, *Sin Tjun*, no. 3 (1958), pp. 102–3; "Wen Peor, Pelukis Tionghoa kelahiran Padang telah meninggal dunia pada tgl 18 Maret 2007", HKSIS website (accessed 2007).

WEN Dexuan. See **OEN Tek Hian**
WEN Peor. See **WEN Bei'ou**

WEN, Tony (BOEN Kim [Kin] To, 1911–63) 温金道／温庆道*
Political party leader, sportsman

Born in Bangka in 1911, he was Chinese-educated and was a teacher at the THHK school in Patekoan, Jakarta. He was an active member of an Indonesian Chinese football association, the Union Makes Strength (UMS) in Jakarta, and became an idol of young football fans. He was sympatethic to the Indonesian idependence movement. In 1948 while the Indonesian revolution was still on, he was appointed by the Yogyakarta-based Indonesian Finance Minister Miramis to smuggle opium to Singapore in order to raise fund for the Republic. In 1952 he joined the PNI and in the 1950s was appointed as a member of Comite Olympiade Indonesia. From August 1954 to March 1956, he was appointed as a member of the DPR, representing the PNI. He died on 30 May 1963 and was buried in Menteng Pulo, Jakarta.

Sources: *DPR 1971*, p. 603; "Tony Wen dan John Lie", in H. Junus Jahja, ed., *Catatan Orang Indonesia* (Jakarta: Komunitas Bambu, 2009), pp. 93–94; Iwan Santoso, *Tionghoa dalam Sejarah Kemiliteran: Sejak Nusantara sampai Indonesia* (Jakarta: Penenrbit Buku Kompas, 2014), pp. 172–75; the compiler's notes.

WEN Zhongxiao. See **OETOMO, Dede**
WENG Junmin. See **TAHIR**
WENG Zhenxiang. See **MULJADI**

WIBISONO, Christianto (HUANG Jianguo 黄建国, 1945-)
Journalist, business consultant, Protestant

Born in Semarang on 10 April 1945, he graduated from the Faculty of Political and Social Sciences, UI, in 1977. He began writing during the student demonstration in 1966 and was a member of the editorial board of *Harian Kami* (a major student newspaper after the 1965 coup) and the president of Indonesian University Students' Press Federation. He was a founder and the deputy director of *Ekspres* (a leading Jakarta news magazine) in 1970 and *Tempo* (a major news magazine in Jakarta) from 1970 to 1974. Between 1977 and 1985 he served as an executive member of the Bakom-PKB Pusat. In 1980 together with Adam Malik and **NJOO Han Siang** he established Pusat Data Business Indonesia. He was the president-director of the Indonesian Business Data Centre (Jakarta), a consulting firm.

In May 1998 his family was affected by the riots in Jakarta. He moved to the United States with his family but continued to contribute regularly to major Indonesian newspapers and magazines. He also served as a lobbyist in Washington, D.C. for President Abdurrahman Wahid and President Bill Clinton in 1999. In 2007 he returned to Indonesia and on 10 April of that year he established Global Nexus Institute (GNI) which serves as a research centre to study geopolitics that affects Indonesian national interests.

His publications include *Aksi-Aksi Tritura: Kisah Sebuah Partnership* [Partnership of students and the military] (Jakarta, 1970); *Wawancara Imajiner dengan Bung Karno* [Imaginary interview with Bung Karno] (Jakarta, 1977); *Kearah Indonesia Incorporated* [Towards Indonesia Corp.] (Jakarta, 1985), in two volumes; *Menelusuri Akar Krisis Indonesia* [The roots of Indonesia's crisis] (Jakarta, 1998); and *The Global Nexus* (Jakarta, 2007).

Sources: The above-mentioned books; Arief, *Indonesia Business*, revised ed., pp. 926–27; *Apa & Siapa 1985–86*, pp. 1178–79.

WIDJAJA, Eka Tjipta (OEI Ek Tjhong; HUANG Yicong 黄奕聪, 1923-)
Tycoon, Hokkien

Born on 29 October 1923 in Quanzhou, Fujian, he came to Indonesia at the age of nine, together with his father, who opened a small provincial shop in Ujung Pandang (Makassar). He was educated in a local Chinese school, but left at the age of fifteen to work as a hawker. During the Japanese Occupation, he was jailed for two weeks by the Japanese because of "non-cooperation". He was then nineteen years old.

He began to engage in business — he opened a small coffeeshop and sold agricultural products. His business empire started in 1955 when he became a copra trader in North Sulawesi. But Eka Tjipta became well-known only after he had set up PT Bitung Manado Oil Indonesia, specializing in cooking oil in 1969. His company catered up to 50 per cent of the demand in the Indonesian cooking oil market. He expanded his business into paper manufacturing, real estate, finance, and agroindustry under his new giant company, Sinar Mas.

He went into joint ventures with the Salim Group (**LIEM Sioe Liong**) in the cooking oil business but they split in 1990. Eka Tjipta's son, Oei Hong Liong, was a businessman based in Singapore, who had been active in Hong Kong and China.

Eka Tjipta was considered as the second richest tycoon in Soeharto's Indonesia. After the fall of Soeharto, Eka Tjipta is still listed by Forbes as the second richest Indonesian in Indonesia.

Sources: *Sinar*, 17 January 1994, pp. 65–66; *Shijie Huaren Fuhao Bang*, pp. 206–8.

WIDJAJA, Mira (1949-) 黄美拉*
Writer, physician, better known as **Mira W.**

Born in Jakarta on 13 September 1949, she graduated from the medical school of Trisakti University in 1979. Daughter of a film producer whose Chinese surname is Oey (or Wong?), she emerged as a popular writer in the 1970s. She is a teaching staff at the Dr Prof Moestopo University in Jakarta and also works as a university physician. However, she is better known as a popular novel writer.

She began to write short stories in 1975. Her first work was published in *Femina* magazine. In 1977 she wrote her first novel, *Dokter Nona Friska*, which was serialized in *Dewi* magazine. (However, *Kompas* says that her first novel was *Cinta tak Pernah Berhutang*, published in 1978.) It was later published in book form with a new title: *Kemilau Kemuning Senja*. Her second novel, *Sepolos Cinta Dini* [As pure as Dini's love] was serialized in *Kompas*, and later also published as a book.

Her most popular novel was perhaps *Di Sini Cinta Pertama Kali Bersemi* [Love first blooms here] (1980). However, her better novel is *Relung-Relung Gelap Hati Sisi* [Dark side of the heart] (1983), a story about lesbians. Her recent works include *Masih Ada Kereta Yang Akan Lewat* [There is still a train which will pass] (1989?) and its sequel, *Biarkan Kereta Itu Lewat, Arini* [Let the train go, Arini] (1990). The book tells the story of an elderly woman who falls in love with a young man. She has published more than forty novels, many of which have been made into movies.

Sources: The above-mentioned books, especially *Biarkan Kereta itu Lewat, Arini* (1990), pp. 293–94; *Apa & Siapa 1985–86*, pp. 1187–88; *Kompas*, 30 October 1993.

WIDJAJA, Nancy. See **WIJAYA, Nancy**

WIDJAYA, Tjiangdra (HUANG Songchang 黄松长, 1957-)
Politician, Catholic

Born in Ujung Pandang (Makassar) on 20 March 1957, Tjiangdra completed his primary school, junior middle school and senior middle school (Catholic High School) in his birthplace. He continued his further education in Berlin, Germany in 1977 and entered the TFH Berlin the following year. In 1983 Tjiangdra graduated and returned to Indonesia. He worked as the director of Bumi Serpong Indah, and later became director of various large companies such as PT Kepahyang Indah and PT Sinar Surya Pelangi Permai. All of these companies are in the property business. However, he began to be active in the Indonesian Real Estate Organization in 1996–99 and Himpunan Kerukunan Tani Indonesia (Indonesian peasants solidarity association) in 1999–2004.

Tjiangdra joined the PDIP and participated in the 1999 parliamentary election. He won a DPR seat for the 1999–2004 period. In 2004 he contested in the elections again and got re-elected but did not complete the term. There was a split in PDIP and Tjiangdra left PDIP before the 2014 election.

Sources: *Wajah Dewan Perwakilan Rakyat Republik Indonesia: Pemilihan Umum 1999* (Penerbit Buku Kompas, 2000), p. 141; Li Zhuohui 李卓辉, *Yinhua canzheng yu guojia jianshe* (Jakarta, 2007), pp. 204–6.

WIDYONO, Benny (OEI Hong Lan; HUANG Honglan 黄鸿栏, 1936-)
Economist

Born on 16 October 1936 in Magelang, he received a Drs degree in 1959 from the FEUI, an MA degree from the University of Kansas (Lawrence) in 1961, and a PhD from the University of Texas in 1963 after submitting his dissertation, "Petroleum Resources and Economic Development: A Comparative Study of Mexico and Indonesia".

From 1963 to 1975 he was an officer at the UN ECAFE. From 1975 to 1977 he was in the UN ECLA (Santiago, Chile) as a Transnational Corporations Officer in the Joint Unit on Transnational Corporations. Between 1973 and 1976 he was also on short-term assignments as UN Adviser to the Indonesian Government on Planning. Since 1977 he has served as chief, Joint CTC/ESCAP Unit on Transnational Corporations, Office of the Executive Secretary. While in Bangkok, he was guest lecturer on the Annual Economic Development Course, Chulalongkorn University (1963–79). In 1981 he was posted to the UN Secretariat, New York. He has published a few papers on Indonesia as well as on transnational corporations.

Sources: Letter to the compiler, 1980; Bachtiar, *Directory*, p. 38.

WIHARJO, Verawaty. See FADJRIN, Verawaty

WIJAYA, Eko (LIU Shunyan 刘顺严, 1981-)
Member of Parliament

Eko was born in Pangkal Pinang on 20 November 1981. He finished his high school education at SMA Santo Yosef, Pangkal Pinang. He is the director of PT Essex Field Venture Ltd. He joined Partai Demokrat, contested the 2014 election, and won a seat for Bangka-Beltung. He is a DPR member for the period of 2014–19.

Sources: Pengurus Pusat Fordeka, *Buku Acuan 2014*, p. 115; the compiler's notes.

WIJAYA, Nancy (also spelled as WIDJAJA, MA Yongnan 马咏南, 1945-)
Community leader, social activist, Buddhist

Born in 1945 in Garut (West Java), she received a Chinese school education in Bandung. After graduation, she studied at the Res Publica University in Jakarta but did not finish her education because the university was closed down after the 1965 coup. She went into business together with her husband.

When Soeharto stepped down she joined other Chinese Indonesians to found the Paguyuban Sosial Marga Tionghoa Indonesia (PSMTI) in 1998. There was a split in the new organization and a group of board members left PSMTI. In February 1999 they established another Chinese NGO: Perhimpunan Keturunan Tionghoa Indonesia (known as INTI), with **Eddie LEMBONG** as its general chairman. She served first as the Chinese language secretary of INTI (1999–2001), and later chief of Chinese education section (2001–3). Starting from end of 2003 she became the chairperson of the women section and held the position for ten years.

Nancy has been conscious with the position of Chinese Indonesian women and is interested in enhancing their social position. She has also encouraged Chinese women to integrate into the mainstream Indonesian society. Under her leadership, the INTI women section participated in anti-violence and human rights activities. It also helped Indonesians, especially women and children, who were victims of natural disasters.

Being a Chinese Indonesian who was educated in Chinese when she was young, she is also active in promoting the learning of the Chinese language which was banned during the Soeharto era. She and her friends set up a Chinese language centre in Jakarta to promote Mandarin learning. In addition, she has also been generous in donating money to build classrooms for several schools.

Nancy herself has never stopped studying. In early 2000 she joined the NUS Business School Chinese Program. Later she set up a Foundation of the NUS Business School Alumni in Indonesia and was elected as its chairperson. In order to know more about the foundation and the various laws, she eventually enrolled at the Law School of the Universitas 17 Agustus in Jakarta in 2008. She graduated in 2012 with a law degree.

Sources: Li Lei 李磊, 黄旭云,〈勤俭自强爱国爱家奋斗崛起: 马咏南带领银华妇女部走向辉煌〉, in Li Zhuohui 李卓辉,《印华写作精英奋斗风雨人生》(2010), pp. 252–57; interview, 2012.

WIJAYAKUSUMA, Hembing (ZHANG Xinming 张鑫铭, 1940–2011)
Acupuncturist, writer on traditional medicine, Muslim

Born in Medan, North Sumatra, he finished high school education at his birthplace. He later went to Hong Kong for further studies and graduated from the Chinese Acupuncture Institute (Hong Kong) and Chinese Medical College (also in Hong Kong) in 1970. He returned to Medan to start the Wijayakusuma Acupuncture Centre (1970–78). In February

1976 he was made a professor in Eastern Medicine at the Won Kwang University, South Korea. In the same year, he founded the acupuncture department at the Universitas Islam Sumatra Utara where he served as head (1976–78). In 1978 he moved to Jakarta and established the Acupuncture Institute. He was active in the international acupuncture circles and was elected as deputy president of the World Academy Society of Acupuncture in Seoul, South Korea (1975-?).

His publications include *Impotensi* [Impotence] (1979); *Pengobatan Murah* [Cheap medication] (1985); *Latihan Penapasan Qi Gong Pencegahan, Penyembuhan Penyakit juga Melawan Kanker* [Qi Gong as a means to prevent and cure illness; to combat cancer] (1985); *Tanaman Berkhasiat Obat di Indonesia* [Plants which can be used for medicine in Indonesia] (1992); and many more popular books on traditional medicine. Hembing also served as Senate Gurubesar (Senate of Professors) of Universitas Bung Karno (Jakarta). He died suddenly in 2011 and his Wijayakusuma Centre is now run by his sons.

Sources: *Apa & Siapa 1985–86*, pp. 1190–91; <http://id.wikipedia.org/wiki/Hembing_Wijayakusuma> (accessed 30 June 2014).

Wilson TJANDINEGARA. See **TJANDINEGARA, Wilson**
Wim UMBOH. See **UMBOH, Wim**

WINARTA, Frans Hendra (TAN Hian Wie; CHEN Xianwei 陈贤伟, 1943-)
Human rights lawyer

Born on 17 September 1943 in Bandung, Winarta spent most of his junior to senior high school education in Christian Schools in Bandung. He continued his studies at the Law Faculty of Parahyangan Catholic University in Bandung and graduated in 1970. He later obtained his Master's degree in criminal law from the University of Indonesia in 1999 and earned his PhD from Padjadjaran University in 2007. He is most known as a human rights lawyer who often speaks on the issue of discrimination against Chinese Indonesians as well as civil rights and crimes against humanity during the Soeharto regime and the post-Soeharto era.

In 1981, Winarta started to work as an attorney and set up his own office, Frans Winarta and Partners, in Jakarta. He became close with **YAP Thiam Hien**, an outspoken human rights lawyer, and started to broaden his knowledge of human rights. In 1985, he joined IKADIN (Ikatan Advokat Indonesia — the Indonesian Bar Association) and was later appointed chairman of international relations in the Central Board of IKADIN. He started to become a human rights activist in 1988 by joining Lembaga Pembela Hak Asasi Manusia or, the Institute for the Defense of Human Rights. Since 1989, he has also been actively involved in Yayasan Lembaga Bantuan Hukum Indonesia (YLBHI — the Indonesian Legal Aid Foundation) as a member of the Board of Trustees.

Winarta's work mainly focused on criminal, civil and business laws, commercial arbitration, and human rights issues. He contributed and was involved in various local and international organizations that deal with legal, arbitration and anti-discrimination matters. He lobbied for the implementation of human rights in Indonesia during the Soeharto regime in the late 1980s and the 1990s, constitutional rights of the poor to obtain legal aid, and the political rights of the ethnic Chinese in Indonesia in the post-Soeharto era. He is currently the founding partner of his law firm and Winarta IP Practice which he established in 2005.

Source: Thung Ju Lan, "Winarta, Frans Hendra", in Suryadinata, ed., *Southeast Asian Personalities* (2012), pp. 1271–73.

WINATA, Tomy (GUO Shuofeng 郭说锋, 1958-)
Tycoon, philanthropist

Born in 1958 in Pontianak, Kalimantan, Tomy only received junior middle school education. At the age of fifteen he began to work. His major breakthrough was in 1988 when he rescued Bank Propelat that belonged to the Siliwangi Division. The bank was re-named Artha Graha Bank. The second breakthrough was in 1999 when he took over Jakarta International Hotel Development. His Artha Graha group also developed Sudirman Central Business District. Within thirty years or so he has emerged as a very wealthy and influential businessman. He is involved in banking, mining, agriculture, real estate, and IT communication. Some commented that his success was due to his connection with the military but he denied it. In 2002 he came into conflict with the Tempo magazine on the report of his intention to rebuild the Tanah Abang shopping centre.

In 2013 he gave a rare interview to the CNBC in which he talked about his life, business and dream. He wanted to build bridges to connect Indonesian islands. The first plan was to build the Sunda Strait Bridge linking Java and Sumatra islands. The bridge which would cost US$23 billions, if approved, would take ten years to complete.

Tomy also visited mainland China and wanted to enhance China–Indonesia relations. In 2012, he gave an interview to CRI Meeting Hall (CRI huike ting), noting that China is technologically more advanced than Indonesia and he hoped that there would be a technological transfer.

Tomy also set up Artha Graha Peduli Foundation, aimed at doing philanthropic works. He was keen in forest conservation and has saved Sumatran tigers which are endangered species.

Sources: Sam Stetyautama, *Tokoh-tokoh etnis Tionghoa*, pp. 152–53; "Tomy Winata on CNBC managing Asia 2013 with Christine Tan", 27 August 2013; CRI Online: CRI 会客厅: 华人故事系列访谈, 17 November 2014, <Big5. cri.cn/gate/big5/gb.cri.cn/.../1427s4767565.htm> (accessed 8 April 2015).

WIRANATA, Ardi (1970-) 王阿迪*
Badminton player

Born on 10 February 1970 in Jakarta, he was the youngest son of the Wang family. He was the champion in the Japan Open (1991, 1992, 1994), All-England (1991), and the runner-up of the All-England Competition in 1994. In the 1994 Thomas Cup Competition, he was defeated by **ARBI Haryanto**. However, he played the second men's singles and defeated Malaysia's Ong Ewe Hock.

Sources: *Media Karya*, June 1994, p. 52; *Zaobao*, 16 May 1994, p. 24; *Sejumlah Orang Bulutangkis Indonesia*, pp. 368–70.

WISAKSANA, Panji (PAN Wanxin 潘万鑫, 1925-)
Entrepreneur

Born in Bandung on 27 June 1925, he went to the THHK and English schools in Bandung. His schooling was interrupted by the Japanese Occupation. After the war, he studied at Universitas Nasional (Jakarta) and Universitas 17 Agustus (Jakarta), and he received a Sarjana degree from the latter. He is known as the first person who introduced plastic pipes into Indonesia. He is the director-general of the PT Pioneer Plastics Ltd. and the New Asia Industry. He also serves as district governor of the 307 Lions Club International, general chairman of Yayasan Panji Sejahtera (a welfare foundation), and deputy chairman of Yayasan Universitas Trisakti (a university foundation). He was also one of the founders of Bank Mata DKI Jaya (Eyes Bank of Jakarta). In 1977 he was given a Model Entrepreneur Award by the Jakarta Governor. In 1983 he received the Satya Lencana Pembangunan medal from the Indonesian Government.

Sources: *Apa & Siapa 1983–84*, pp. 1145–47; *Apa & Siapa 1985–86*, pp. 1212–13.

WITARSA, Endang (LIEM Soen Joe, 1916–2008) 林順佑*
Soccer player, coach, dentist

Born in Kebumen on 4 October 1916, he became interested in soccer when he was a child. At the age of twelve he moved to Malang, and later to Surabaya, where he graduated from a dental school in 1936. Even after becoming a dentist, he still played soccer. He was a member of the Hooge Bouw Stand and Surabaya Voetbal Bond (SVB). He represented the SVB in the Nederlandsch Indie Voetbal Unie Competition during the colonial era.

In 1946 he moved to Jakarta. As late as 1948 he still participated in football competitions representing Persidja (Perserikatan Sepakbola Djakarta). Towards the end of the 1940s he retired and became a coach in the UMS (Union Makes Strength) Club. He was responsible for training a number of national football players such as Djamiat Dhalhar, Thio Hin Tjiang and Kwee Kiat Sek, who became soccer stars in the 1950s.

Since 1978 he stopped practising as a dentist and concentrated on soccer-coaching in his UMS 80 Club. His wife is also a dentist.

Sources: *Kompas*, 12 October 1980; <http://id.wikipedia.org/wiki/Endang_Witarsa> (accessed 24 March 2013).

WONG Kam Fu. See WONGSOREDJO, mBah

WONGSOREDJO, mBah (WONG Kam Fu; PEK Pang Eng; BAI Bangying 白邦英, 1898–1984)
Astrologer, publisher, former journalist

Son of a sugar, coffee, and textile merchant, he was born in Gresik on 27 November 1898. Originally known as **PEK Pang Eng**, he used **WONG Kam Fu** as his professional name. He was educated at the HCS. Before finishing the HCS, he visited Amoy

(China). At the age of nineteen, he worked for *Tjhoen Tjhioe* (Surabaya) as a reporter. In 1924 he set up his own printing press and published *Hoa Po* (Gresik). In the mid-1920s he made a short trip to China. In 1926 he published a number of popular magazines, including *Soeara Baroe* (Semarang, 1926) and *Doenia Baroe* (Medan, 1926). In 1935 he began to be interested in astrology, which led him to Hong Kong to study the subject under two leading astrologers in the island. After returning to Surabaya he was in charge of the Horoscope column in *Pewarta Soerabaia*. In the 1940s he edited a number of magazines (such as *Min Pao, Soeara Rakjat*, and *Soerabaia*). In the 1950s he ran a bookstore and published a number of popular weeklies: *Tjermin, New Look, Bintang Surabaja*, and *Indah*, which were banned during the Guided Democracy (1959–65) period. In each weekly, there was a section on astrology. After Soeharto came to power, he published *Parama Arta*, a weekly on astrology and mysticism. He died in Batu, Malang on 31 December 1984. Before he died he worked as an astrological consultant for many magazines and operated a private practice as well.

Sources: *Tempo*, 21 June 1975, pp. 45–48; *Tempo*, 12 January 1985, p. 15; the compiler's notes.

WONGSOSEPUTERA, Jusuf (ONG Tjin Liong) 王振龙*
Community leader, former political party leader

He was associated with Baperki but left it in 1955. His activities were largely confined to East Java. He was at one time the deputy chairman (Ketua II) of Partai Katholik (East Java). From 1963 to 1964 he served as the deputy chairman of the LPKB (East Java branch) and in 1966–67, the chairman of the LPKB (East Java branch).

Source: The compiler's notes.

WONOWIDJOJO, Surya (TJOA Ing Hwie; CAI Yunhui 蔡云辉, 1925–85)
Kretek cigarette manufacturer, father of **Rachman HALIM** *and* **Susilo WONOWIDJOJO**

Tjoa Ing (Jien) Hwie alias Surya Wonowidjojo was the *kretek* cigarette king. He died on 29 August 1985. His case exemplified Chinese control over the cigarette industry in Indonesia. Born in China in 1925 he came to Indonesia as a child. A Hokchia, he first lived in Madura, where his father ran a small provision store. After the death of his father he moved to Kediri in East Java. He first worked for his uncle, a *kretek* manufacturer, in the factory of "93" (the brand name of the cigarette). In 1956 he left his uncle and established his own company, Gudang Garam. In the 1980s Gudang Garam became the largest producer of *kretek* cigarette in Indonesia. At one time, 30 per cent of all *kretek* products were from Gudang Garam. At its peak, Gudang Garam was reported to have made US$700 million sales per year and in 1983 alone the profit (after tax) was US$80 million. The company has fully mechanized and it can produce one million cigarettes per day. This is one of the most modern and largest cigarette manufacturers in Indonesia. But in 1984 and 1985, Djarum, another giant *kretek* industry founded by the late Oei Wie Ghwan, increased its production and posed a challenge to Gudang Garam. TJOA Ing Hwie, who retired because of a heart problem, returned to work. Unlike many big businessmen in Indonesia, Tjoa did not diversify his business. Only later did he and Probosutedjo (who is linked to the Soeharto family) opened a factory manufacturing cigarette paper (PT Zig Zag). It was reported that Tjoa was not comfortable in over-expanding his business beyond his own expertise.

Gudang Garam employed 42,000 workers in Kediri and was important for the livelihood of the population there. Tjoa himself was also known as a philanthropist and was a major contributor to the local welfare. However, with his sudden departure in 1985, the responsibility is now with his local-born sons. In fact, they were already in the business when Tjoa was still alive.

Sources: *Tempo*, 29 June 1985, pp. 52–56; *Tempo*, 7 September 1985, p. 71; *Sinar Harapan*, 2 September 1985; *Lianhe Zaobao*, 7 September 1985; *Harian Indonesia* (Yindunixiya Ribao), 2 September 1985. Sondang wrongly identified the owner of Gudang Garam as Tjai Ko Tjiang alias Th.D. Rachmat. See *Expo 2*, no. 1 (4 January 1984): 17–18.

WONOWIDJOJO, Susilo (CAI Daoping 蔡道平, 1955-)
Kretek cigarette manufacturer, son of **Surya WONOWIDJOJO**, *brother of* **Rachman HALIM**

Born in Kediri in 1955, he was the third son of **Surya WONOWIDJOJO** alias Tjoa Ing Hwie, the founder of Gudang Garam. He succeeded his brother **Rachman HALIM** when he died in 2008 and assumed the president director of the Group. Under his leadership, the Gudang Garam Group continued to develop. In 2013 Susilo Wonowidjojo's family was listed as the fourth richest Indonesian family in the country.

Sources: <http://www.orangterkayaindonesia.com/profil-SusiloWonowidjojo ...> (accessed 20 October 2014); <http://www.forbes.com/profile/susilo_wonowidjojo...> (accessed 20 October 2014).

WU Bingliang. See **GOUW Peng Liang**
WU Jiaxiong. See **GONDOKUSUMO, Suhargo**
WU Nengbin. See **PURNOMO, Nurdin**
WU Qingfu. See **GOH Tjing Hok**
WU Qixiang. See **GUNARSA, Singgih D.**
WU Ruiji. See **ANGKOSUBROTO, Dasuki**
WU Ruizhang. See **KUSUMA, Eddie**

WU Shenji. See **NG Sim Kie**
WU Yingliang. See **GO Ing Liang**

WU Weikang (吴伟康, 1883-?)
Political party leader, newspaperman

He was born in Jiaoling (Guangdong) in 1883. Before going to France, he was educated at the Officers' Training School in Guangdong sponsored by the Imperial Government of China. In 1907 he migrated to Java and joined T'ung-meng Hui (Tongmeng Hui) in Jakarta. In 1908(?) he established Soe Po Sia (*Huaqiao Shubaoshe*, Jambatan Batu, Jakarta) and served as its chairman. From 1928 to the 1930s he became the general manager of *Tiansheng Ribao* and an executive member of the KMT (Dutch East Indies branch).

Sources: Liu, *Gailan*, p. [27]; Wu (1939), section two, p. 30.

WU Xiehe. See **GOZALI, Hendrick**
WU Yinquan. See **GO Gien Tjwan**
WU Yixiu. See **GO Ik Sioe**
WU Yuxiang. See **GAUTAMA, Sudargo**
WU Zhaoyuan. See **GO Tiauw Goan**

WUISAN, Empie (LI Ruihua 李瑞华, 1950-)
Table tennis player

Born in 1950 in Jakarta, he received a few years of Chinese school education. He won a number of national and international championships, including the men's singles title in the Southeast Asian Games in 1977 (Kuala Lumpur). His wife, Diana Wuisan, also won the women's singles title in the Southeast Asian Games in 1982 (Manila). He works as a trainer and lives in Kediri.

Sources: *Xingzhou Ribao*, 29 September 1979; *Apa & Siapa 1985–86*, pp. 1218–19.

WULLUR, Jahja (OEI Tjin San) 黄振山*
Leader of the assimilationist movement, psychologist
In the 1960s he was the president of the LPKB (West Java), a leading member of the GKI (West Java), and a senior lecturer at the Department of Psychology, UNPAD (Bandung).

Sources: *Pedoman UNPAD* (1969), p. 159; Mackie, *Five Essays*, pp. 225–26.

XIAO Degui. See **SIAUW Tik Kwie**
XIAO Yucan. See **SIAUW Giok Tjhan**
XIAO Yumei. See **SIAUW Giok Bie**
XIE Jianlong. See **SOERYADJAYA, William**
XIE Meilan. See **TJIA, May On**

XIE Yuduan. See **TJIA Giok Thwan**
XIE Zhongming. See **LI Qing**

XIE Zuoshun (谢佐舜**, 1899?–1986)**
Journalist, writer, elder brother of **XIE Zuoyu**, *Hakka*
Born in 1900 (1899?) in Guangdong, he went to Indonesia at the age of twelve. In 1917 he returned to China for his primary and secondary school education. In 1922 he came to Indonesia again to serve as a teacher in Jakarta and Probolinggo. Two years later he returned to China again to attend Dongnan University; he graduated in 1929. In that year he re-entered Indonesia to become the editor-in-chief of *Xin Bao*, the Chinese edition of *Sin Po* (Jakarta). During the Japanese Occupation he went into hiding. After the Japanese surrender, he returned to *Xin Bao* to serve as the editor of its supplementary section. Between 1961 and 1966 he was appointed as the school principal of Qinghua Zhongxue, a pro-Beijing school in Bandung. In 1966 he returned to China, living with his daughter

in Beijing. He published extensively in the local newspaper using the following pen-names: N.H., Jingfu, and Lao Song. He died in Beijing on 19 March 1986.

Sources: Information supplied by Zou Fangjin; Li Zhuohui (2013), pp. 168–72.

XIE Zuoyu (谢佐禹, 1901-?)
Journalist, younger brother of **XIE Zuoshun**, *Hakka*

Born in Guangdong in 1901, he was educated at a university in China and went to the United States for further studies. In 1927–29 he served as the editor-in-chief of *Xin Bao*. He later joined the KMT newspaper which affected his relationship with his brother. After 1958 he went to Taiwan.

Sources: *Ulang Tahun THHK Yang ke-50*; *Sin Po 25 Tahun*; the compiler's notes.

XIONG Deyi. See JUSUF, Tedy
Xixiliya K. See KENCANAWATI, Cecillia

XU Baozhang (徐保璋, 1905-)
Community leader

Born in Fujian in 1905, he came to Indonesia in the 1920s. In 1942–45 he was detained by the Japanese for his anti-Japanese activities. During the Indonesian Revolution, he served as adviser to the Chinese Consul in Medan. In 1948 he served as treasurer of Shang Lian, and in the 1950s as a member of the board of directors of Kao Shang (Gao Shang) School (Jakarta).

Sources: *Shangye Nianjian*, p. 334; *Fujian*, p. 117; *Siang Hwee* (Chinese-language section), p. [34].

XU Fucai. See HIE Foek Tjhoy
XU Fuyuan. See KHOUW Hok Goan

XU Huazhang (徐华璋 1899-?)
Businessman

Born in Guangdong in 1899, he served as the president of Siang Hwee (Medan) after World War II and later (in the 1950s) as the director of Kao Shang School.

Source: *Siang Hwee* (Chinese-language section), p. [35].

XU Jin'an. See KHOUW Kim An

XU Juqing (徐琚清; C.C. HSU, 1908–99)
Community leader, leading businessman, newspaperman

Born in Guangdong in 1908, he came to Batavia with his father when he was only four years old, and returned to China at the age of seven. He was educated at Yen-ching (Yanjing) University (Beijing). In 1929 he came to Batavia to work in the editorial board of *Tiansheng Ribao*, a Kuomintang daily, and later served as its editor-in-chief. He later returned to China again. Between 1933–35 he studied in Japan, but continue to write for *Tiansheng Ribao*. In 1938 he returned to Batavia and became the editor of *Tiansheng Ribao* again. During the Japanese Occupation he was arrested and was released in 1945. In 1950 he became an executive member of Shang Lian while concurrently holding the directorship of both the Kao Shang School and a KMT daily, *Ziyou Bao*. In 1958 Taiwan was involved in the Indonesian rebellion, he as a member of KMT was detained by the Indonesian authorities and expelled to Taiwan in August 1959. He later migrated to Canada and died in 1999.

Sources: Li Zhuohui, *Yinhua xiezuo jingying fendou fengyu rensheng*, pp. 49–58; the compiler's notes.

XU Mianchi. See KHARMAWAN, Byanti
XU Pinghe. See SUKOWATI, Asmaraman
XU Qixing. See KHOUW Ke Hien

XU Tiantang. See **SETIONO, Benny Gatot**
XU Tingzhou. See **DJIE Ting Tjioe**
XU Zaiying. See **TJHIE Tjay Ing (Hs)**
XU Zhenhuan. See **TJIPUTRA**

XU Zhongming (许仲铭; C.M. HSU, 1914-)
Artist, writer, painter

Born in Tegal on 31 July 1914, he was educated both in Indonesia and China. From 1935 to 1938 he studied at the China Institute (Shanghai) and from 1937 to 1938 at the Shanghai College of Fine Arts. He also lectured at that college from 1940 to 1941. In 1942 he returned to Indonesia and worked for various newspapers (such as *Min Pao* and *Sin Po*) and companies (Lintas Limited, Rodamas Companies Group, and so forth). He was a personal art adviser to President Soekarno (1952–66), the secretary of Yin-hua Mei-shu Hsieh-hui (1956–62), and an associate editor of the publication *Paintings and Statues from the Collection of President Sukarno of the Republic of Indonesia* (Tokyo, 1964). He was a lecturer in the Department of East Asian Studies, UI (1975-).

Sources: *International Who's Who in Art & Antiques* (1972–76), p. 239; Letter to the compiler, 1979.

XUE Biyu. See **SIDHARTA, Priguna**

YAN Guoliang. See **GAN K.L.**

YAN Weizhen (严唯真; real name: LIN Zhiqiang 林志强, 1933–2008)
Writer, promoter of Chinese literature

Born in Indonesia, probably in Bandung in 1933, Yan Weizhen, whose real name in Lin Zhiqiang, only receive a secondary school education. He became a full-time Chinese schoolteacher in Bandung (West Java) and part-time journalist writing for Chinese language newspapers published in Jakarta prior to Soeharto's coming to power.

Yan was a talented writer and had begun writing when he was fifteen years old. He was particularly good at writing poems and dominated the Indonesian Chinese poetry world in the 1950s and early 1960s with another poet Li Qing. Some of Yan's better known poems include "Bandung — Beautiful City in the Bright and Glorious Days" (秀丽的山城一万隆，在光辉灿烂的时日里), "Fatherland, You are so far away yet you are with me" (祖国，你是那么遥远，但又在我身边), "O Good, the Other Side of Mount Tangkuban Perahu" (好啊，覆舟山的那一边), etc.

Yan lost his job after the 1965 coup eradicated the "three pillars" of Chinese culture. His love of Chinese writing and culture took him back to writing Chinese and he continue to produce poems, short stories, translations, essays and other forms of writing. In 1995, his poem "I want to live a life of poetry in my old age" (愿有个诗的晚年) shows the change in Yan's ideology from being China-oriented to being Indonesian-oriented, and his attempt to reconcile the past. Yan passed away in Bandung on 25 August 2008.

Sources: Leo Suryadinata, "Yan Weizhen", in Suryadinata, ed., *Southeast Asian Personalities* (2012), pp. 1306–8; *Yan Weizhen Shiwen Xuan* (1998); Wang, eds., *Dongya Huawen Wenxue* (1989), pp. 86–104; *Shenghuo Bao Shi Zhounian Jinian Tekan* (1955), pp. 120–23.

YANG Chunmei. See YO Soen Bie
YANG Guibin. See YEO Kuei-pin
YANG Hanxiang. See NJOO Han Siang
YANG Mingyue. See INJO Beng Goat
YANG Weibin. See TANNOS, W.P.A.
YANG Wie Pin. See TANNOS, W.P.A.

YANG Xinrong (杨新容, 1907–82)
Educationist, community leader

Born in 1907 in Longhai, Fujian, he attended Jimei Normal School between 1923 and 1926 where he began to get involved in the revolutionary movement. He joined the Chinese Communist Party in 1927. Between 1928 and 1932, Yang studied in Shanghai but continued to get involved in the movement. In 1932 to 1934 he taught at a primary school in Fujian. From 1934 he came to Indonesia. During World War II he taught at Huaqiao Gongxue 华侨公学 in Solo and Xinhua School (新华 Sin Hwa) in Jakarta where he served as the principal until 1951. In August 1951 he was arrested by the Sukiman government for left-wing activities. He was later released and expelled to China. He was soon appointed as the principal of Huaqiao Buxiao (华侨补校 Preparatory School for Overseas Chinese Students). In 1964 he was elected as a member of the 4th CPPCC representing Overseas Chinese. He died in 1982.

Sources: *Shenghuo Zhoubao*, 26 December 1964; Zhou Nanjing, ed., *Cidian*, p. 353; the compiler's notes.

YANG Xiulian (杨秀莲, 1917-)
Community leader, teacher

Born in Fujian, China in 1917, she received a junior middle school education. When the Japanese entered Fujian, she followed her father to Surabaya (Indonesia). She worked as a teacher at a local Cantonese school. She later moved to Malang and then to Jakarta to teach at a Hokkien school. In 1942 Jakarta fell into the Japanese hands. In 1943 she married a China-born newspaper man and schoolteacher Wang Dajun (1914–2007) and took refuge in Bandung. After the Japanese surrender, she taught at Sin Hwa School in Jakarta. In the 1950s she was active in Qiao Zong and in 1952 was elected as the president of Funü Xiehui (Chinese

Women's Association, which was pro-Beijing) in Jakarta until 1965.

Sources: *Zhongcheng Bao*, 8 March 1965; *Xin Bao*, 8 March 1949; Xiao Ya 小雅,〈看近百老人长寿的精神秘诀〉, Li Zhuohui, ed., 李卓辉编,《赤道火花自强不息: 印华写作精英风雨人生第三集》(雅加达, 2011), pp. 232–33; the compiler's notes.

YANG Yuanli. See **NAGA, Dali Santun**
YANG Zhaoji. See **SURYAWAN, Yoza**
YANG Zhongsheng. See **NJOO Cheong Seng**

YAP A Siong (ABDUSSOMAD, H.; YE Yaxiang 叶亚祥, 1885–1984)
Religious leader, Muslim

Born in Guangzhou in February 1885, he came to Indonesia in 1894. He lived in Medan among the Malays and became a Muslim in 1929. In 1931 he went to Mecca and became a *haji*. From 1936 he was involved in the Islamic movement. Together with other Chinese Muslims he formed Persatuan Islam Tionghoa (PIT) in Medan, the purpose was to prevent Chinese Muslims from becoming beggars as "this degrades the religion that we believe in". The first president of the PIT was Liem Kian Gie (Abdullah Rasyid), the vice-president was So Kien Hoa (Usman), and the secretary was Yap A Siong (Abdussomad) himself.

Yap married three times. His first wife, a Chinese, died in 1934; his second marriage, to a woman from Banjarmasin, ended in divorce in 1938; and his third wife was a Javanese girl whom he married in 1939. In the 1970s, he managed the "As-Salam" Mosque in the Bintang Tujuh Complex (Jakarta). The director-general of Bintang Tujuh was another Chinese Muslim, H. Moh. Husein, who died in late 1980. Yap died on 20 October 1984.

Sources: "Profil Seorang Ulama Islam Tionghoa", *Pelita*, 2 January 1979; *Pelita*, 3 November 1980; Jahja, ed. (1989), p. 164.

YAP Hong Tjoen (YE Hongjun 叶鸿俊, 1885–1952)
Physician, community leader, father of **YAP Kie Tiong**

Born in Yogyakarta in 1885, he first went to a local Hokkien school but soon transferred to the ELS. He received his HBS education in Semarang and then studied medicine in Leiden, specializing in eye diseases. He worked for four years in the Netherlands after graduating and returned to Java after World War I.

While in the Netherlands, Yap was active in student organizations. He was one of the founders of the CHH-Netherlands and also the second president of that organization (1912–13?). Probably because of his educational background and the people he met, he began to believe in racial harmony. In 1921 **KWEE Hing Tjiat** criticized Dr Yap for being an admirer of the anti-Chinese nationalist lawyer, Fromberg. According to Kwee, Dr Yap did not involve himself in the pan-Chinese movement and therefore could not understand what was really happening to the Indies Chinese. Kwee pointed out that there was no real communication between Dr Yap and the Indies Chinese.

Dr Yap ran a clinic in Bandung after he returned to Java. Later he went to Yogyakarta to open an eye clinic, where he gained high professional reputation. However, the name of the clinic, Prinses Juliana Gasthuis voor Ooglijders (Princess Juliana Hospital for Eye Patients), annoyed the Chinese nationalists. Dr Yap did not dissociate himself from the Chinese movement in Java, as assumed by many contemporary observers. The formation of the CHH was one of his efforts. He also set up a Dutch school for the Chinese, named after his brother. He highly valued Dutch education for he himself was a product of that education. In his opinion, Chinese education in the Dutch East Indies was not practical. Dutch education, on the contrary, provided the Chinese with a means to prosperity and modernization. After the formation of the CHH, Yap virtually left *peranakan* Chinese politics and concentrated solely on medicine. He died at the Hague in the Netherlands on 20 November 1952.

Source: Suryadinata, *Peranakan Politics*, pp. 160–61.

YAP Kie Tiong. See PRAWIROHUSODO
YAP Li Cheng. See YUAN Ni

YAP Lip Keng (YE Ligeng 叶立庚, 1906–74)
Community leader, leading businessman, political party (KMT) leader

Born in Fuqing (Fujian) in 1906, he came to Indonesia in 1925. He first resided in Banjarmasin (Kalimantan), but moved to Surabaya in 1930. In 1938 he was elected as a representative of the Chinese in Surabaya to attend an Overseas Chinese conference in Singapore. He went into hiding during the Japanese Occupation. From 1946 to 1949(?) he served as the director of a pro-KMT newspaper, *Qingguang Ribao* (Surabaya). In 1947 he was an executive member of Siang Hwee (Surabaya); from 1948 to 1958 he was the president of the CHTH (Surabaya). In 1952 he participated in the Overseas Chinese Affairs Conference in Taipei. In 1958 he was arrested by the Indonesian authorities for his active role in the KMT. After his release he continued to live in Surabaya. He died in Surabaya in 1974, honoured by the KMT.

Sources: Huang, *Geming*, p. 266; Liu, *Xunian biao*, p. 65; *Shangye Nianjian*, p. 339; Liu, *Gailan*, p. [90]; the compiler's notes.

YAP Loen (1874-?) 叶仑*
Community leader, landlord

Born in 1874 in Jakarta, he went to China at the age of seven and returned to Java at the age of twelve. He moved to Bandung and became engaged in trade. He made a fortune during World War I and bought over 130 houses in Pasar Andir (Bandung).

He was a founding member of the THHK (Bandung) and served four times as president of that organization. He was also a co-founder of Siang Hwee (Bandung) and in the 1930s served as a member of the Bandung Regency Council.

Source: Tan, *Tionghoa*, p. 185.

YAP Soei (Swie) Kie. See **JANANTO, Soetopo**
YAP Soetopo. See **JANANTO, Soetopo**

YAP Thiam Hien (YE Tianxing 叶添兴, 1913–89)
Lawyer, community leader, human rights activist, Protestant

Born on 25 May 1913 in Banda Aceh (North Sumatra), he was first educated at a Dutch-Chinese Teachers' School in Jatinegara (a suburb of Jakarta). He then entered the Law School in Jakarta and continued his law training at the University of Leiden (Holland) from which he obtained a Dutch law degree (Mr) in 1947.

Before practising law, Yap taught at various Christian high schools (1934–42). His Christian background made him an activist in the Christian movement, especially in Tiong Hoa Kie Tok Kauw Hwee (Chinese Christian Association) in West Java. He was the co-founder and chairman of the Indonesian Church Education Board from 1950 to 1957. Nonetheless, his activities were not limited to Christian organizations. In 1954 he participated in the formation of Baperki and in 1955 he was the fourth deputy chairman of the Baperki central board. From 1956 to 1960 he served as the first deputy chairman. In 1960 he came into conflict with **SIAUW Giok Tjhan**, the chairman of Baperki, over Baperki's policy and stepped down from his position, but remained in that organization as a member.

Yap had a long career as a lawyer. From 1950 to 1953 he worked with John Karwin, who established a law firm together with Mochtar Kusumaatmadja. From 1953 to 1970 he worked with various partners including **TAN Po Goan**, **LIE Kian Kim**, and **OEI Tjoe Tat**. In 1970 he established his own law firm.

Yap was well-known in his profession. He became a controversial figure when he served as Defence Counsel of Liem Koe Nio, a pro-KMT millionaire, during the left-wing Soekarno period. In 1966 he was in the headlines again. This time he accepted the appointment of Defence Counsel for Soekarno's first Deputy Prime Minister, Dr Subandrio, offered by the new Indonesian authorities. Yap received international recognition for his courage and brilliant performance during the trial.

Yap was outspoken on Indonesian social ills and was concerned with problems on law and human rights. In 1966, together with other Indonesian intellectuals, he appealed to the authorities to release political detainees. As a follow-up, they formed Lembaga Pembela Hak-hak Asasi Manusia (Institute for the Defence of Human Rights), of which he was once more the secretary. From 1968 to 1976 he served as a committee member of the CICAWSRUS (Commission on Inter-Church Aid, World Service, and Refugees). And from 1975 onwards he served as a committee member of the CCIA (Church Commission on International Affairs), which also comes under the World Council of Churches. His term on that committee ended in 1983.

He was a member of the International Commission of Jurists (Geneva) and Lembaga Bantuan Hukum (Legal Aid Institute), which was formed together with Adnan Buyung Nasution and the Indonesian Lawyers' Association. On 11 January 1980 he was awarded an honorary doctoral degree in Law by Vrije Universiteit (the Netherlands) for his outstanding achievements in the field. He died on 24 April 1989 while attending an international conference.

Sources: Lasut, *Mutiara*, 20 February 1980, pp. 16–17; Roeder, *Who's Who*, pp. 518–19; *Pedoman Kampanje*, p. 36; Ward, *Review of Indonesian and Malayan Affairs*, January–March 1968, pp. 1–16; *Sin Po*, 24 December 1956; *Harian Kami*, 5–6 January 1968; Suryadinata, *Mencari*, pp. 186–209.

YAP Tjoen Soe (YE Cunxu 叶存淯, 1922-)
Leading businessman, community leader

Born in Fujian (China) in 1922, he received Chinese primary education. In 1937 he came to Surabaya and started a textile business. From 1961 to 1965 he served as the chairman of Zhonghua Qiaolianhui (Surabaya). He was the manager/director of a large textile company in the 1970s.

Source: Interview, 1976.

YAP Tjwan Bing (YE Quanming 叶全明, 1910–88)
Political party leader, pharmacist

Born in Surakarta on 31 October 1910, he obtained a Drs degree in Pharmacy from Amsterdam University in 1939. During colonial rule, he was the director of both Cativo (Centraal Textiel In-En Verkoop Kantoor) and a dispensary in Bandung. He was active in the Indonesian Independence Movement. In August 1945 he was a member of the Indonesian Independence Preparatory Committee (PPKI), representing the Chinese minority. In May 1948 he was a founder of the PT. When the Pasundan Cabinet (a Sundanese state based in West Java) was announced in the early 1950s, Yap declined the offer to become its Minister of State. From February to August 1950 he served as a member of the DPR-RIS representing the Republican government. In August 1950 when the Provisional DPR was formed, he remained as a member, but this time to represent the PNI. He was replaced by **Tony WEN** of the PNI on 18 August 1954. He was a founder of Bank Union Nasional. Due to his son's illness, his wife decided to migrate to the United States. He eventually left Indonesia for California in 1963, and also left politics. He wrote his memoirs entitled, *Meratas Jalan Kemerdekaan: Otobiografi seorang Pejuang Kemerdekaan*, which was published in 1988. He died on 26 January 1988.

Sources: Kempen, *KP*, p. 137; *Ensiklopedie Indonesia*, vol. III, p. 1437; *DPR 1971*, p. 137; *Merdeka*, 11 January 1950; Somers, dissertation, p. 109; Yap's memoirs; *Kompas*, 26 February 1988.

YAP Yun Hap (YE Yunhe 叶运合, 1977–99)
Student leader, "Reform Hero"

Yap Yun Hap was born in Pangkal Pinang (Bangka) on 17 October 1977, the elder son of Yap Pit Sing and Ho Kim Nio. He was a top student in Chemistry during high school and won the championship for a Chemistry competition for the entire Jakarta City. After graduation he studied Electrical Technology at the University of Indonesia and was a member of Keluarga Besar Universitas Indonesia (KBUI, Indonesian University Large Family). On 19 September 1999 he joined the student demonstration at the Sudirman Road against the Law of Crisis Resolution (Undang-undang penanggulangan keadaan bahaya) and was killed by an unidentified bullet. His body was later taken to the University of Indonesia (UI) and was sent off by the president of UI for burial. A large number of students saw him off forming a line about one kilometer long. He was also given the title of "Pahlawan Reformasi" by the Indonesian Press, together with four Trisakti students who were killed. The main road to UI Depok campus is named as Jalan Yap Yun Hap.

Sources: *Sinergi*, 12/1999; Setyautama, *Tokoh-Tokoh Etnis TH*, p. 490.

YAPUTRA, Albert S. (YE Cing Piaw; YE Jinbiao 叶锦标, 1951-)
Member of Parliament, businessman, Buddhist

Born on 8 October 1951 in Jakarta, first educated in Shie Hoo (协和) school, he completed his high school education at SMA Kosgoro in 1973. According to one source, he received a B.A. in Political Science and an MA in Computer Science (Magister Ilmu Komputer), name of the university is unavailable.

Yaputra was director-general of PT Komoditi Mas (Gold commodity, 1984–86); director-general of PT Prima Sistematika Jakarta (1987–89); director-general of Parner Sejati Garment (since 2000). He joined Partai Demokrat and served as deputy treasurer, Central Board of Partai Demokrat (2001–3); chairman of Central Board of Partai Demokrat (2004–6); treasurer and coordinator of the Success Team for presidential candidates SBY-JK (2004); treasurer of Partai Demokrat Faction in Parliament (2009–14); coordinating director for group cooperation with the PRC in Parliament (2009–14). He contested in the 2014 election as a PD candidate but was not elected.

Sources: *Wajah DPR & DPD 2009–14*, p. 16; Pengurus Pusat Fordeka, *Buku Acuan 2014*, p. 162; name card of Albert Yaputra S.

Yahya Daniel DARMA. See **LIE Tjeng Tjoan, John (John LIE)**
YE Cing Piaw. See **YAPUTRA, Albert S.**
YE Cunxu. See **YAP Tjoen Soe**
YE Hongjun. See **YAP Hong Tjoen**
YE Jinbiao. See **YAPUTRA, Albert S.**
YE Jizhong. See **PRAWIROHUSODO**
YE Lizhen. See **YUAN Ni**
YE Ligeng. See **YAP Lip Keng**
YE Quanming. See **YAP Tjwan Bing**
YE Ruiji. See **JANANTO, Soetopo**
YE Tianxing. See **YAP Thiam Hien**
YE Yaxiang. See **YAP A Siong**
YE Yunhe. See **YAP Yun Hap**
Yenni. See **YUAN Ni**

YEO Kuei-pin (YANG Guibin 杨圭斌, 1954-)
Pianist, Musician

Born in Jakarta on 24 April 1954, she started piano lessons at the age of five. She enrolled at Yayasan Pendidikan Musik Jakarta in 1968 and received a diploma in 1970. In 1973 she enrolled at the Manhattan School of Music, New York, in the United States, and obtained a bachelor degree in music in 1976. Two years later she received an MA degree, and in 1979, a Master of Music Education degree from the same school after submitting her thesis, "A Guide for the Choral Pianist". In 1980 she received the Doctor of Musical Arts degree from the same school after submitting her dissertation on "Modest Moussorgsky: Pictures at an Exhibition".

She has received numerous awards and honours, including the second place winner of Concourse Piano Jakarta in 1970, the Harold Baurer Award for "outstanding accomplishment" from the Manhattan School of Music (New York) in 1979, and the University of Maryland International Piano Competition, Loren Eisley Memorial Prize Winner in 1981.

She made her first public performance at the age of eight and had extensive experience as a solo recitalist, soloist with orchestras, as well as a chamber music player in Asia, Canada, and the United States. Her performances have been praised by the *New York Times*.

In June 1995 she was invited to the international music festival in Bergen (Norway) where she performed for an hour. Apart from playing the works of Western composers, she also played those of Mochtar Embut, an Indonesian composer. She is currently the director of Sekolah Musik Jakarta.

Source: "Dr Kui-Pin Yeo" (courtesy of C.M. Hsu), *Gatra*, 24 June 1995, p. 66.

YO Goan Li. See **NAGA, Dali Santun**

YO Heng Kam (1897–1959?) 杨恒甘*
Community leader, political party leader, leading businessman

Born in Jakarta on 7 May 1897, he was educated at the ELS (Jakarta), the PHS (Jakarta), and a commercial college at the Hague. After returning to Indonesia, he worked for the Javasche Bank for two years, and later joined his father, who worked as a supplier of food for ships. In 1918 he joined the PEB and retained his membership until 1942. Because of his affiliation with the PEB, he was not accepted as a member of the CHH. In 1925 he was appointed *luitenant*, and in 1927 *kapitein,* by the Dutch. In 1925 he also served as the chairman of the board of management of a large Chinese hospital in Jakarta, Jang Seng Ie. From 1927 to 1942 he was elected as a member of the Volksraad, largely owing to the support of a cigarette merchants' association in Java. In 1949 he was a member of the Jakarta Municipal Council. He died on 6 March 1959 (or 1958?), probably in Jakarta.

Sources: Tan, *Tionghoa,* pp. 212–13; *Jang Seng Ie,* p. 12; Wal, *Volksraad,* vol. II, p. 726; *Sinar,* 1 April 1949, p. 8; *Volksraad,* 1828–29, p. 166.

YO Soen Bie (YANG Chunmei 杨纯美, 1875–1968)
Businessman, community leader

Born in 1875 in Zhangpu (Fujian), he received two years of old-style Chinese education in China. In 1891 he migrated to Indonesia. In 1895 (1900, according to *Djawa Nenkan*) he began his textile business, which became very successful. He was awarded a medal by the KMT government. Prior to World War II he was the president of Siang Hwee (Bandung) and helped finance the Chunmei High School in his birthplace. During the Japanese Occupation, he was appointed the president of the HCTH (Priangan).

Sources: Liu, *Gailan,* p. [59]; *Djawa Nenkan* (1973), p. 465; <http://baike.baidu.com/view/4434148.htm> (accessed 24 March 2013).

YOE Tjoe Ping (YOU Ziping 游子平, 1895?–1970)
Community leader, manufacturer of Chinese medical preparation under the name of Tai An Ho (Da An He) in Jakarta

Born in 1895 (or 1905?) in Yongding (Fujian), he migrated to Indonesia when he was young. In the 1950s he became a leading member of Huaqiao Gonghui (Jakarta) and the treasurer of Hok Kian Hwee Koan (Fujian Huiguan). He died in Jakarta on 29 August 1970.

Sources: *Fujian,* p. 32; *Siang Hwee,* p. 30, *Chinese-language section,* p. [10]; the compiler's notes.

YOU Ziping. See **YOE Tjoe Ping**

YOUNG, Fifi (TAN Kim Nio; CHEN Jinniang 陈金娘, 1915–75)
Actress, wife of **NJOO Cheong Seng**

Born in Aceh on 12 February 1915 (1914, according to another source), she had a Chinese mother and a French father who died when she was only forty days old. She received no formal education. At the age of fourteen she married **NJOO Cheong Seng**, a *peranakan* theatre director and writer, and remained as his wife until he died in 1959.

Fifi Young ("Young" is pronounced as "Nyo" in Hokkien) studied Indonesian dances from Abdulhadi. In the late 1920 she followed her director husband who led "Miss Ribut Orion", a travelling drama troupe, touring West Malaysia and Singapore. She began to appear on the stage when her husband led Moonlight Crystal Follies in Penang. In the 1930s, her husband joined Dardanella, a well-known travelling drama troupe in Indonesia. Fifi then became a leading star. They travelled widely in Indonesia, Singapore, and India. The success eventually led them to form their own travelling drama troupe called Fifi Young's Pagoda.

During the Japanese Occupation, they founded Sandiwara Surabaya (a drama troupe) together with Dahlia, a movie queen prior to World War II. Fifi played a leading role in the movie *Kris Mataram* (1940). Up to 1977 she had taken part in about fifty-five movies. Her most successful role was that of a mother, a role she first played in *Air Mata Ibu* [Tears of a mother], a movie produced in 1951 based on a work by her husband. In 1954 (one source says it was 1955) she starred as a mother again in Tarmina, for which she was given the Best Actress award. From then Fifi became the symbol of Indonesian mother on the screen. Her last picture, *Ranjang Pengantin* [The wedding], made in 1975, still portrayed her as a mother. She died in Jakarta on 5 March 1975.

Sources: *Archipel*, no. 5, 1970; *Kompas*, 6 March 1975; "Fifi, Ibu Kita 1914–75", *Tempo*, 15 March 1975, pp. 36–37.

YU Chunxiang. See **IE Tjoen Siang**
YU Yuling. See **DAWIS, Didi**
YOU Ziping. See **YOE Tjoe Ping**
Yoza SURYAWAN. See **SURYAWAN, Yoza**

YUAN Ni (袁霓 Jeanne LAKSANA; Yenni; YAP Li Cheng; YE Lizhen 叶丽珍, 1956-)
Writer, community leader, Hakka

Born in Jakarta in 1956, her original name is Yap Li Cheng and her Indonesian name is Jeanne Laksana, but she is better known as Yuan Ni among the Chinese speaking community. When the Chinese school she was attending was closed down, she was only in Primary 5. She learned Chinese through self-study and private tuitions. After the fall of Soeharto, she enrolled at the Xiamen University for overseas students and eventually obtained a bachelor degree.

Since 1972, she began to send her works to the only Chinese newspaper in Indonesia, *Yindunixiya Ribao*. She wrote short stories, mini short stories and poems. She has published a few collections: *Hua Meng* (花梦 Dream of Flowers, collection of short stories), *Yuan ni wenji* (袁霓文集 collected essays of Yuan Ni), *Nanren shi yifu hua* (男人是一幅画 A man is a picture, bilingual poems in Chinese and Indonesian) and *Sanren xing* (三人行 Three walking in group, collected poems with **Cecillia KENCANAWATI** and Xie Menghan). She has been very active in the Chinese Indonesian community. She is president of Indonesian Chinese Writers' Association (Yinhua xiezuozhe xiehui or Perhimpunan Penulis Tionghoa Indonesia), deputy chairwoman of Jakarta Chinese Language Education Coordinating Executive Body, and deputy chairwoman of World Mini Short Stories Association (Shijie huawen weixing xiaoshuo yanjiuhui).

Sources: Li Zhuohui, *Yinni xiezuo jingying*, 2010, pp. 186–93; *Jiechu renwu minglu*, p. 297

ZENG Chunfu. See **SILALAHI, Harry Tjan**
ZENG Tianci. See **TJAN Tian Soe**
ZENG Tiansu. See **TJAN Tian Soe**
ZENG Yingqiu. See **TJAN Ing Djiu**
ZENG Zhaozhen. See **TJEN, Rudianto**
ZENG Zuqin. See **TJAN Tjoe Siem**
ZENG Zusen. See **TJAN Tjoe Som**
ZHAN Yuqian. See **TJIAM Djoe Khiam, Fredericus Christophorus**
ZHANG Bingwen. See **HEI Ying**
ZHANG Bishi. See **THIO Tiauw Siat**

ZHANG Guoji (张国基, 1894–1992)
Educationist, community leader

Born in Yiyang (Hunan) in 1894, he attended a normal school at the age of fifteen. In 1918 he joined the New People Society. During the May Fourth Movement (1919) he served as the vice-chairman of the Federation of Hunan Province Students Association. In 1920 he was sent by the New People Society to teach at Daonan School, Huaqiao Zhongxue, and Nanyang Nüzhong in Singapore. In 1922 he went to Indonesia to take on the post of the principal of a Chinese school in Pekalongan. In 1926 he returned to China to participate in the Northern Expedition. In the following year he was invited by Mao Zedong to serve as a lecturer at the Peasants Movement Institute. In the same year he joined the Chinese Communist Party and got involved in the Nanchang Uprising. After the failure of the uprising he went overseas again. In 1939 he founded Zhonghua Zhongxue (also known as Hua Zhong) in Jakarta. First serving as the deputy principal, he later became its principal. He taught in that school for almost twenty years. In the 1950s he served as an executive member of Qiao Zong (Ch'iao Tsung). In 1958 he returned to the PRC and headed Huaqiao Buxiao (Preparatory School for Overseas Chinese students before they enter a university in China) in Beijing. He was also elected as a member of the 4th CPPCC and later the president of Qiao Lian (Federation of Overseas Chinese Associations). He died in 1992.

Sources: Song Zhongchuan, *Yindunixiya yu xuexi*, no. 5 (1962), p. 4; Huang Kunzhang, *Dipingxian*, no. 10 (April 1980), pp. 44–45; *Cidian*, p. 420.

ZHANG Hongnan. See **TJONG A Fie**
ZHANG Ie Hao. See **JOHAN, Daniel**
ZHANG Rongxuan. See **TJONG Jong Hian**
ZHANG Ruisheng. See **THIO Soei Sen**
ZHANG Tiancong. See **THIO Thiam Tjong**
ZHANG Xinming. See **WIJAYAKUSUMA, Hembing**
ZHANG Xunyi. See **TJONG Hioen Nji**
ZHANG Yaoxuan. See **TJONG A Fie**
ZHANG Youjun. See **HEI Ying**
ZHANG Yuhao. See **JOHAN, Daniel**
ZHANG Yunan. See **TJONG Jong Hian**

ZHANG Zhan'en (张沾恩)
Community leader, timber businessman

A local KMT leader who once served as an executive member of the CHTH (Jakarta), he served as the vice-president of Guang Zhao Huiguan in 1958. In the same year he was arrested by the Indonesian authorities for activities related to his affiliation with the KMT. One year and eight months later, he was released. In 1967–69 he was appointed as a member of the BKUT. In 1970 he was involved in the establishment of SNPC Chongde Xuexiao.

Sources: *Yinni Zainan* (1959), p. 24; *Huaqiao zhi*, p. 131; Zhong, *Huaqiao*, p. 63; Jiang, "Yajiada," p. 15.

ZHANG Zhaoxie. See **THIO Tiauw Siat**
ZHANG Zhenwen. See **THIO Tjin Boen**
ZHANG Zhenxun. See **THIO Tiauw Siat**

ZHANG Zhusan (张祝三, 1897-?)
Community leader, grocery shop owner
Born in Guangdong in 1897, he was active in the *totok* Chinese community in Jakarta. In 1952 he was elected as the chairman of the pro-KMT Yanong Gonghui and Hong Yi Shun. In 1958 he served as the vice-chairman of the board of trustees of Zhongshan Zhongxue (Jakarta). He was arrested in 1958 for his affiliation with the KMT and was expelled to Taiwan.
Sources: Zhong, *Huaqiao*, p. 63; Zhong, *Yanong*.

ZHAO Chunling. See **CHIAO, Evelyn**
ZHAO Wenbi. See **TIO Oen Bik**
ZHAO Yushui. See **TIO Ie Soei**
ZHENG Dengjun. See **IDRIS, Tahyar**
ZHENG Hongyu. See **THE Hong Oe**
ZHENG Jiancheng. See **THE Kian Sing**
ZHENG Jiansheng. See **HASAN, Mohammad Bob**
ZHENG Liangyi. See **THE Liang Gie**
ZHENG Man'an. See **JINARAKKHITA, Bhikku Ashin**
ZHENG Nianjin. See **THE Neng King**

ZHENG Roumi'ou (柔密欧·郑; ZHENG Zhiping 郑志平, 1924–95)
Writer, teacher
Born in 1924 in Riau island, he received Chinese education in Singapore. He had published his poems in Chinese newspapers and literary magazines in Singapore. Two collections of his poems had been published: one was entitled, *Yue Qi* 跃起 [To jump up] (1979) and the other is an edited work entitled, *Xin He* 新荷 [New lotus] (1984), which includes works of other Indonesian Chinese writers. The third book was *Xiyang Hong Shang Bai Tou Lai* 夕阳红上白头来 [Until the sun sets

and hair becomes grey] (1995), a collection of essays, and the last one was a collection of his short stories: *Suizhe Lianyi Sanqu le de Jiangsheng* 随着涟漪散去了的桨声 [Following the disappearance of rowing sound after ripple] (Singapore, 1995). He died in Jakarta on 22 September 1995.

Sources: The above-mentioned books; Li Zhuohui, ed., *Qundao xinghuo guangmang shanshuo* (2010), pp. 195–209.

ZHENG Zhiping. See **ZHENG, Roumi'ou**
ZHONG Dingyuan. See **ARSADJAJA, Jani**
ZHONG Wanxue. See **TJAHAJA PURNAMA, Basuki**
ZHONG Wanyou. See **TJAHAJA PURNAMA, Basuri**
ZHU Changdong. See **CHU Chong Tong**
ZHU Difa. See **SUTRISNO, Slamet**
ZHU Maoshan. See **TJOE Bou San**
ZHUANG Xiyan. See **TJUNG See Gan**

ZOU Fangjin (邹访今, 1921–99)
Newspaper editor, writer, Hakka

Born in April 1921 in Guangdong, he came to Indonesia in 1938. Initially he worked as an apprentice and labourer. After World War II he became involved in various Indonesian Chinese associations. He served as the secretary of Zhonghua Zonghui 中华总会 (Chinese General Association) in Bima, and Zhonghua Laogong Zonghui 中华劳工总会 (Chinese Workers Union) in Belitung. He also served as the editor of *Gong Sheng* 工声 (Voice of Labourers), a trade union newspaper, and was a correspondent of *Xin Bao* 新报 and *Shenghuo Bao* 生活报. In 1950 he was arrested by the Sukiman government as he was suspected to have been involved in communist activities. He was released in 1952.

Between 1955 and 1960 he served as the editor of the Supplement of *Shenghuo Bao*, and between 1963 and 1965 he served as the editor of the Supplement of *Huoju Bao* 火炬报.

He wrote regularly for the local Chinese newspapers using the following pen-names: Chang xizi 常习之, Xia Feishuang 夏飞霜, Linxia ren 林下人, and so forth. He published a book entitled, *Wulidong Huagong Shiji* 勿里洞华工事迹 [The historical records of Chinese labourers in Belitung, Jakarta] (1963). He returned to China after the 1965 coup. During the Cultural Revolution, he was sent to a village to work in the farm. After Deng Xiaoping re-emerged, he was sent to live in a farm in Fujian specially established for the returned overseas Chinese. He continued to write and his works were eventually collected in a book form entitled, *Qiandao Chunhen* 千岛春痕 [The Marks of Spring in the Thousand Islands], published in late 2013, the collection of his earlier works was also published at the same time under the title of *Zou Fangjin wenxuan* 邹访今文选 [Selected works of Zou Fangjin].

Sources: The above-mentioned book and the compiler's notes.

ZOU Liying. See MURDAYA, Siti Hartati

ABBREVIATIONS AND GLOSSARY

ACROCA (All-China Returned Overseas Chinese Association) — an organization in the PRC

AMS (Algemeene Middelbare School) — Dutch secondary school in the Dutch East Indies

Antara — Indonesian National News Agency

asimilalsi — assimilation (Indonesian). See also pembauran

Bakom or Bakom PKB (Badan Komunikasi Penghayatan Kesatuan Bangsa) — Communicating Body for Appreciation of National Unity, a new LPKB-type organization formed in December 1977 under the auspices of the Ministry of Home Affairs.

Bank Central Asia — one of the largest private banks in Jakarta, at one time owned by the Salim (Sudono Salam, i.e. Liem Sioe Liong) Group.

Baperki (Badan Permusjawaratan Kewarganegaraan Indonesia) — Indonesian Citizens Consultative Body, a socio-political organization formed in March 1954 aimed at protecting Chinese minorities who were Indonesian citizens. Banned after the 1965 coup

Bapilu (Badan Pengendali Pemilihan Umum) — Control Body of the General Elections

Bara Eka — the official journal of the LPKB

BAS (Burgeravondschool) — a Dutch trade school located in Surabaya

Batavia — the old name of Jakarta during the Dutch colonial rule

BFO (Bijeenkomst voor Federaal Overleg) — Federal Consultative Assembly established in 1948 with the formation of the RIS to which the Dutch transferred sovereignty in December 1949.

Bintang Tujuh — a large Indonesian Chinese company located in Jakarta producing various kinds of medicinal products such as ointments and pills.

BKUT (Badan Kontak Urusan Tjina) — Liaison Committee for Chinese Affairs, established by the Soeharto government in 1967 to serve as a bridge between the government and the Chinese (especially the alien Chinese). Dissolved in 1969

BPKB-DKI (Badan Pembina Kesatuan Bangsa dalam Wilayah DKI Jakarta) — the body for the Development of National Unity in the National Capital, Jakarta, established by Ali Sadikin in August 1974.

BPKI (Badan Persiapan Kemerdekaan Indonesia) — the Committee for the Preparation of Indonesian Independence, a committee established soon after the Japanese surrender. Often seen as a continuation of BPUPKI

BPS (Biro Pusat Statistik) — Central Bureau of Statistics

BPUPKI (Badan Penyelidik Usaha-usaha Persiapan Kemerdekaan Indonesia) — Investigating Committee for the preparation of Indonesian independence, initiated by the Japanese.

Soekarno and Hatta were two leading figures on the Committee. There were four ethnic Chinese representatives in the sixty-member committee.

BULOG — National Logistics Board, established in the late 1960s, concerned with trading in essential commodities (especially rice).

bumiputra — son of the soils, another term for *pribumi*. See also *pribumi*

BUMN (Badan Usaha Milik Negara) — State Operations Agency (Indonesia)

Cavito (Central Textiel voor In-en Verkoop Kantoor) — Central Office for Buying and Selling Textiles, during the time of the Dutch East Indies

CHH (Chung Hwa Hui 中华会 Zhonghua Hui) — Chinese Association, a political organization in Java set up in 1928 by Dutch-educated *peranakan* Chinese intellectuals and businessman. Dissolved in 1942

CHH-Netherlands (Chung Hwa Hui-Netherlands) — a *peranakan* Chinese students' association in the Netherlands, formed in 1911. Oriented culturally towards China but politically towards the East Indies.

CHHTC (Chung Hwa Hui Tsa Chih 中华会杂志) — a journal of the CHH-Netherlands

Chih-nan Hsueh-t'ang (Jinan Xuetang). See JNXT

China Charity Fund — a fund established to raise money during the Sino-Japanese war by Indonesian Chinese

China Instituut — China Institute, an organization formed in Indonesia before World War II, aimed at promoting Chinese studies, dominated by Dutch-educated *peranakan* intellectuals.

CHTH (Chung Hua Tsung Hui, Zhonghua Zonghui 中华总会) — Chinese Central Organization, established after World War II in various major cities in Indonesia. Dominated by *totok* Chinese and gradually controlled by pro-Beijing groups. Dissolved in 1965

CHTNH (Chung Hua Tsing Nien Hui, Zhonghua Qingnianhui 中华青年会) — Chinese Youth Association (Indonesia)

Chung Hsioh (Zhongxue 中学) — an association of secondary school students which consisted of Dutch-educated *peranakan* Chinese before Indonesia's independence.

Chung Hua Tsung Hui. See CHTH

Ciji (慈济) — a Taiwanese-based Buddhist association. Active in Southeast Asia

COB (Chinese Onderwijzers Bond) — a Dutch-educated *peranakan* Chinese teachers' association, active before World War II

CPPCC — Chinese People's Political Consultative Conference, Beijing

CSIS (Centre for Strategic and International Studies) — also known as Yayasan Proklamasi, a private research institute established in 1971

cukong (zhugong 主公) — a Hokkien term for "boss" or "master", commonly used to mean a wealthy Chinese businessman who collaborates with the Indonesian power élite.

Dewan Kesenian Jakarta — Arts Council of Jakarta City, established in 1968 by the Jakarta Mayor Ali Sadikin

Djawa Hak Boe Tjong Hwee 爪哇学务总会 — General Educational Association of Java, active before World War II

Djawa Tengah — a pre-war *peranakan* Chinese daily published in Semarang

DPD (Dewan Perwakilan Daerah) — Regional Representative Council, created in 2004. Members of DPD are elected during the general election, together with members of DPR (parliament), to form the MPR.

DPR (Dewan Perwakilan Rakyat) — People's Representative Council, which is the Indonesian Parliament

DPRD (Dewan Perwakilan Rakyat Daerah) — Regional People's Representative Council Indonesia. Assembly at provincial, regional and municipal level. Usually used to refer to Representative Council of the Provincial Level, i.e. DPRD I.

Drs (Doctorandus) — a Dutch university degree, equivalent to either MA or PhD preliminary. Its Indonesian equivalent is Sarjana (in the old system).

Dwi Fungsi (Dual Function) — Indonesian military doctrine

Eisaikantyo — a regional health department during the Japanese Occupation

ELS (Europeesche Lagere School) — European Primary School, a school specially designed for Dutch children in the Dutch East Indies

Era Reformasi — the reform period, it refers to the period after the fall of Soeharto since 21 May 1998.

FEUI (Fakultas Ekonomi Universitas Indonesia) — Faculty of Economics, University of Indonesia

FHUI (Fakultas Hukum Universitas Indonesia) — Faculty of Law, University of Indonesia

firma — Dutch term for "firm"

Firma Kian Gwan — another name for the Oei Tiong Ham Concern

FIS-UI (Fakultas Ilmu-Ilmu Sosial Universitas Indonesia) — Faculty of Social Sciences, University of Indonesia

FKUI (Fakultas Kedokteran Universitas Indonesia) — Faculty of Medicine, University of Indonesia

FPUI (Fakultas Psikologi) — Faculty of Psychology, University of Indonesia

FSUI (Fakultas Sastra Universitas Indonesia) — Faculty of Arts, University of Indonesia

G-30-S (Gerakan Tigapuluh September) — 30th September Movement, also known as Gestok or Gestapu, a coup which took place on 1 October 1965 leading to the fall of Soekarno, the liquidation of the PKI, and the emergence of the military-dominated New Order.

Gandi (Gerakan Anti Diskriminasi) — Anti-Discrimination Movement (Indonesia)

Gao Shang (Kao Shang 高商) (Yinni Huaqiao Gaoji Shangye Xuexiao 印尼华侨高级商业学校; Yin-ni Hua-ch'iao Kao-chi Shang-yeh Hsueh-hsiao) — a Chinese commercial high school in Jakarta, established by Shang Lian in 1950. Closed in 1958

GAPO (Gabungan Pengusaha Otobis) — Bus Owners' Union

GAPPERSON (Gabungan Perserikatan Perusahaan Rokok Nasional) — Federation of National Cigarette Companies

Gappri (Gabungan Perusahaan Rokok Seluruh Indonesia) — All-Indonesia Cigarette Manufacturers Federation

Gerindo (Gerakan Rakyat Indonesia) — Indonesian People's Movement, formed in 1937. The first pre-World War II nationalist party opening its membership to *peranakan*; a left-wing movement.

GKI (Gereja Kristen Indonesia) — Indonesian Christian Church

Golkar (Golongan Karya) — the Functional Groups, the largest political group, consisting of military and civil servants

Abbreviations and Glossary 415

under the New Order. The ruling party between 1971–98. After the fall of Soeharto, the name was changed to Partai Golkar.

Guided Democracy — refers to Indonesian historical period from 1959–65 during which President Soekarno held tremendous power

Guoji Ribao (《国际日报》) — a large Chinese daily published in Jakarta, Indonesia, after the fall of Soeharto

halal — permissible (often refers to food prepared in a certain way for Muslims)

Harian Ibukota. See *Shoudu Ribao*

Harian Indonesia. See *Yindunixiya Ribao*

Harian Kompas — the largest circulation Indonesian daily newspaper in Jakarta

Harian Rakjat — the PKI's daily newspaper, banned in 1965

Hatta, Mohamad. See Mohammad Hatta

HBS (Hoogere Burger School) — Dutch Secondary School, established by the Dutch Indies Government. Although open to all ethnic groups, its clientele was overwhelmingly Dutch. There were two types: the HBS III (three years) and HBS V (five years).

HCK (Hollandsch Chineesche Kweekschool) — Dutch-Chinese Teachers' College for HCS schoolteachers

HCS (Hollandsch Chineesche School) — Dutch Elementary School for the Chinese

HCTH (Hua Ch'iao Tsung-hui, Huaqiao Zonghui 华侨总会) — General Association of Overseas Chinese, an organization sponsored by the authorities during the Japanese Occupation. The Japanese name for this organization is *Kakyo Sokai*.

HCTNH (Hua Ch'iao Tsing Nien Hui, Huaqiao Qingnianhui 华侨青年会) — Overseas Chinese Youth Association, established by *peranakan* Chinese students before World War II

Henghua (or Xinghua 兴化) — a district in Fujian, which also constitutes a speech group

HIS (Hollandsch-Inlandsche School) — Dutch Elementary School, for Indigenous Indonesians

Ho In Hoa Siang Lian Hap Hwee (Ho Yin Huashang Lianhehui 荷印华商联合会) — Federation of Chinese Chambers of Commerce, formed in 1934 in Jakarta with the encouragement of the Chinese Government. It consisted of various Siang Hwees in the Dutch East Indies and was dominated by *totok*.

Ho Yin Huashang Lianhehui. See Ho In Hoa Siang Lian Hap Hwee

Hokchia (福清) — Fuqing-speaking Chinese

Hokkien School — a Chinese private school established before the twentieth century, with Hokkien as its teaching medium (instead of Putonghua 普通话) and Confucian classics as its main curriculum.

Horison — a literary publication published monthly in Jakarta after the 1965 coup

HSI (Himpunan Sarjana Indonesia) — Indonesian Scholars' Society, a left-wing intellectuals' organization prior to the 1965 coup

Hsin Pao. See *Xin Bao* 新报

Hua Zhong 华中 or Zhonghua Zhongxue 中华中学 (Chinese High School) — established in 1939, it was one of the largest Chinese high schools in Jakarta after World War II. Being pro-Beijing, it was closed in 1966.

Hua-ch'iao Kung-hui. See Huaqiao Gonghui

Hua-ch'iao Tsung Hui. See HCTH

Huaqiao Gonghui (华侨公会) — a Hakka-dominated association, consisting of pro-KMT Chinese. Banned in 1958

Huaqiao Lianhehui 华侨联合会. See Qiao Lian

Huayi Zonghui (华裔总会) — a Chinese term of INTI

IBC (International Business Center) — an organization aimed at promoting business with Taiwan. Established in 1968, it consisted of pro-Taiwan *totok* businessmen and some Indonesian officials. This organization later formed a body called the National Development Corporation (NDC).

ICMI (Ikatan Cedekiawan Muslim se Indonesia) — Association of Indonesian Muslim intellectuals, established during the Soeharto period

IDI (Ikatan Dokter Indonesia) — Indonesian Physicians' Association

IKIP (Institut Keguruan Ilmu Pendidkan) — Teachers' Training Institute

IMF — International Monetary Fund

Inpres (Instruksi Presiden) — Presidential Instruction (Indonesia)

International Federation of Futsing [Fuqing] Clan — a federation of Hokchia associations, first established in Singapore in 1988 with the name of Shijie Fuqing Tongxiang lianyihui. In 2009 its name was changed to Shijie Fuqing shetuan lianyihui.

INTI (Perhimpunan Indonesia-Tionghoa) — also known as Perhimpunan Indonesian Keturunan Tionghoa, a large social organization established after the fall of Soeharto. Known also as Huayi Zonghui

IPPI (Ikatan Pemuda Pelajar Indonesia) — Association of Indonesian Youth and Students

IPPOSI (Ikatan Perserikatan Pengusaha Otobis Seluruh Indonesia) — All-Indonesia Bus Owners' Association

Ir (Ingenieur) — a Dutch (also Indonesian) degree awarded to a graduate of the School of Engineering; a qualified engineer

ISDV (Indische Sociaal-Democratische Vereeniging) — Indies Social Democratic Organization, formed in 1914; it changed its name to Partai Komunis Indonesia (PKI) in 1920.

ISKI (Ikatan Sarjana Katholik Indonesia) — Indonesian Catholic Scholars' Association

ITB (Institut Teknologi Bandung) — Institute of Technology at Bandung

Jakarta — the capital city of the Republic of Indonesia

Jang Seng Ie (or Yang Sheng Yuan 养生院) — a Chinese-sponsored hospital in Jakarta established in 1924. It changed its name to Rumah Sakit Husada on 1 June 1965.

Jinan Xuetang. See JNXT

JNXT (Jinan Xuetang 暨南学堂) — also known as Kay Lam Hak Tong, a school designed for Overseas Chinese. First established in Nanking (Nanjing) around 1906. It ceased operations in 1911, but was re-established in Shanghai as Jinan Xuexiao and eventually developed into a university. The Jinan University is now located in Guangzhou, Guangdong.

kabupaten — district, regency (Indonesia)

Kadin (Kamar Dagang dan Industri) — Indonesian Chamber of Commerce and Industry

Kakyo Sokai. See HCTH

KAMI (Kesatuan Aksi Mahasiswa Indonesia) — Indonesian Students Action Front, a powerful anti-communist students' association which emerged after the 1965 coup.

Kao Shang. See Gao Shang 高商

Kapitein — a Dutch term for "Captain", a rank given to a Chinese leader in the Indies by the Dutch authorities. Also spelled as Kapitan. See Kapitan

Kay Lam Hak Tong. See JNXT

Keng Po — an Indonesian-language daily published by *peranakan* in Jakarta in 1923. It changed its name to *Pos Indonesia* in 1958 and ceased publication in the 1960s. The largest *peranakan* newspaper besides *Sin Po*.

Khong Kauw Tjong Hwee (or Kongjiao Zonghui 孔教总会) — General Association of Confucian Societies in Indonesia, established in Bandung in 1923

Kiai — Islamic teacher and community leader (Indonesia)

Kitab yang Empat — Four Books (四书), the basic teachings of Confucius in Indonesian, used as the bible of the Confucian Religion in Indonesia

KMT (Kuo Ming Tang 国民党) — (Chinese) Nationalist Party, established by Dr Sun Yat-sen in 1912

KNI (Komite Nasional Indonesia) — Indonesian National Committee

KNIP (Komite Nasional Indonesia Pusat) — Indonesian Central National Committee, formed shortly after Indonesia's independence in 1945

Komnas HAM (Komisi Nasional Hak Asasi Manusia) — National Commission for Human Rights (Indonesia)

Kompas. See *Harian Kompas*

Kongjiao Zonghui. See Khong Kauw Tjong Hwee

Kostrad — Komando Cadangan Strategis Angkatan Darat — Army Strategic Reserve (Indonesia)

KOTI (Komando Operasi Tertinggi) — Supreme Operation Commando

kungfu (or gongfu 功夫) — a Chinese martial art

Kwik Kian Gie School of Business — In 1987 Kwik Kian Gie established the Institut Bisnis Indonesia (IBII). In 2012 the IBBI was renamed Kwik Kian Gie School of Business.

KWS (Koningin Wilhelmina School) — Queen Wilhelmina School, a vocational institution established in Jakarta before World War II

LBH (Lembaga Bantuan Hukum) — Legal Aid Institute (Indonesia)

LEKNAS (Lembaga Ekonomi dan Kemasyarakatan Nasional) — Institute of Economics and Social Research, a section of LIPI

Lekra (Lembaga Kesenian Rakjat) — People's Arts Council, established by pro-PKI artists and writers in August 1950. Banned in 1965

Liberal Democracy — also known as Constitutional Democracy, it refers to the Indonesian historical period from 1950–58 during which political parties were in power. In fact, by 1957, the political system was moving toward Guided Democracy.

LIPI (Lembaga Ilmu Pengetahuan Indonesia) — Indonesian National Science Council, a government-sponsored body for scientific research

Lithang (Litang 礼堂) — literally means ceremonial hall, it is now used by Matakin and Makin as Sino-Indonesian Confucian Church.

LPKB (Lembaga Pembinaan Kesatuan Bangsa) — Institute for the Development of National Unity, a *peranakan*-dominated organization supported by the army, and rival of Baperki. Advocated assimilation of the Indonesia Chinese. Consisted of anti-communist elements. Formed in 1963 and dissolved in 1967.

LRKN (Lembaga Research Kebudayaan Nasional) — National Institute for Cultural Studies, a body of LIPI

Majoor — a Dutch term for "Major", the highest rank for a Chinese leader in the Dutch East Indies appointed by the Dutch authorities

Makin (Majelis Agama Khonghucu Indonesia) — Indonesian Confucian Council

Manikebu (Manifes Kebudajaan) — Cultural Manifesto, initiated in 1963 by Indonesian anti-communist writers and artists. Banned by Soekarno

Mata Hari — a pre-World War II *peranakan* daily in Semarang, sponsored by Oei Tiong Ham Concern

Matakin (Majelis Tertinggi Agama Khonghucu Indonesia) — the Highest Council of Confucian Religion in Indonesia. There are many Makin under Matakin.

Mohammad Hatta (1902–80) — The first Deputy President of the Republic of Indonesia (1945–56). Both Soekarno and Hatta jointly signed the proclamation of Indonesian independence on 17 August 1945 representing the Indonesian people. Leader of pre-war independence movement

MPR (Majelis Permusyawaratan Rakyat) — People's Consultative Assembly, the highest organ of state and the body to which the president is responsible under the 1945 Constitution. Members of the DPR are also members of the MPR.

MPRS (Majelis Permusyawaratan Rakyat Sementara) — Provisional People's Consultative Assembly, the interim body appointed in 1960 to function as the highest organ of the state pending the formation of the elected MPR.

Mr (Meester in de Rechten) — a Dutch law degree. FHUI now offers Sarjana Hukum (SH) instead of Mr.

Muhammadiyah — a Muslim socio-cultural organization formed in 1912

MULO (Meer Uitgebreid Lager Onderwijs) — Junior High School (literally: More Comprehensive Elementary Education)

N.V. (Naamloze Vennootschap) — limited liability company

NDC (National Development Corporation) — IBC-sponsored body which aims at mobilizing Chinese capital for the development of Indonesia after the 1965 coup

New Order (Orde Baru) — it refers to Soeharto rule from 1965–98. Also known as Oancasila Democracy

NGO — non-government organization

NIAS (Nederlandsch Indische Artsen School) — Dutch East Indies Medical College, located in Surabaya

NIT (Negara Indonesia Timur) — an East Indonesian state, formed by the Dutch according to the agreement of the Den Pasar Conference in 1946

NU (Nahdlatul Ulama) — Muslim Ulama Party, formed in 1926 as a non-political party. Became a political party in August 1952. Fused with three other Muslim parties in 1973 and formed the Partai Persatuan Pembangunan (PPP, United

Development Party). Withdrew from the PPP after the 1982 election

OCAC (Overseas Chinese Affairs Commission) — a body under the Foreign Ministry in the PRC, dissolved after the Cultural Revolution

Oei Tiong Ham Concern — the largest Chinese commercial firm in Indonesia before World War II. Originally based in Semarang. See also Firma Kian Gwan

Old Order (Orde Lama) — the term used by the Soeharto government to refer to the Soekarno period

Orde Baru. See New Order

Orde Lama. See Old Order

Pa Chung (巴中 Pa-ch'eng Chung-hsueh, Bacheng Zhongxue 巴城中学, the original spelling used by the school was Pah Cheng Tsung Shueh) — a major Chinese high school in Jakarta before the 1965 coup. First established in 1945, gradually dominated by pro-Beijing Chinese; changed its name to Ya-ch'eng Chung-hsueh or Yacheng Zhongxue 雅城中学 (Ya Chung or Ya Zhong 雅中) in 1960(?). It is often misspelled as Pah Tsung.

Pah Tsung (Pah Cheng Tsung Shueh). See Pa Chung

PAN (Partai Amanat Nasional) — National Mandate Party, a political party led by Amien Rais established in 1998 after the fall of Soeharto.

Pancasila Democracy — It refers to the Soeharto period from 1965–98. It is also known as the New Order period, in opposition to the Soekarno period which was called the Old Order period.

Pancasila — Five principles of the Indonesian state, also known as Indonesian state ideology developed by Soekarno in 1945 on the eve of Indonesian independence.

Panorama — a *peranakan* weekly published in Jakarta before World War II.

Parkindo (Partai Kristen Indonesia) — Indonesian Christian Party (Protestant). Formed in 1945, it became part of the PDI (Partai Demokrasi Indonesia) in 1973.

Partai Demokrat — Democrat Party, a party established in 2001 by pro-Susilo Bambang Yudhoyono (SBY) activists to support him to be the president of Indonesia. SBY later became the chairman of the PD.

Partai Gerindra (Gerakan Indonesia Raya) — The Great Indonesian Movement Party, established by retired general Probowo Subianto in 2008.

Partai Golkar. See Golkar

Partai Hanura (Partai Hati Nurani Rakyat) — The People's Conscience Party, a new party established by retired general Wiranto in 2006 after he resign from Golkar. Supported by the Soeharto family

Partai Nasdem (Nasional Demokrat) — the National Democrat Party, a new party established in 2011 by a media mogul Suryo Paloh.

Partindo (Partai Indonesia) — the Indonesian Party, a left-wing party first formed in 1931, banned by the Dutch authorities in 1936, revived in the 1950s(?), and banned again after the 1965 coup.

PD. See Partai Demokrat

PDI (Partai Demokrasi Indonesia) — Indonesian Democratic Party, a fusion of the PNI, Parkindo, Partai Katholik, Murba, and IPKI. Officially established in January 1973. Megawati eventually controlled the PDI but was not recognized by the Soeharto regime. In 1998 Megawati renamed the party as PDIP. See PDIP

PDI-P (Partai Demokrasi Indonesia-Perjuangan) — Indonesian Democratic Party-Struggle, Megawati-led Indonesian nationalist party. Based on PDI

PDTI (Partai Demokrat Tionghoa Indonesia) — Democratic Party for the Indonesian Chinese, a continuation of PT, formed in March 1950. Dissolved in 1954 upon the formation of Baperki

PEB (Politiek Economische Bond) — Political Economic Association formed in 1919 by Dutch businessmen and with membership consisting of *peranakan* Chinese and indigenous Indonesian traders. Very conservative

pembauran — originally means "mixing", another term for "assimilation" in Indonesian

peranakan (*peranakan* Tionghoa) — a term used to refer to Indonesian-born Chinese who use Malay or one of the indigenous dialects as their medium of communication. Culturally they are partly adapted to the indigenous community. Some *peranakan* Chinese do speak Chinese (Mandarin), but as their second language.

Perhimi (Perhimpunan Mahasiswa Indonesia) — Indonesian University Students' Association, a new name of Ta Hsueh Hsueh Sheng Hui (Daxue Xueshenghui 大学学生会) in the 1960s. Banned after the 1965 coup

Perhimpunan Penulis Tionghoa Indonesia. See Yinni Zuoxie

Perniagaan — a *peranakan* daily in Jakarta published before World War II. The name was changed to *Siang Po* in 1930. Pro-CHH

Perwitt (Persatuan Warga Negara Indonesia Turunan Tionghoa) — Association of Indonesian Citizens of Chinese Origin formed in Surabaya in 1952. Dissolved upon the formation of Baperki

Pesantren — Islamic boarding school (Indonesia)

PHS (Prins Hendrikschool) — Prince Hendrik School, a vocational school located in Jakarta which operated before World War II

Piagam Asimilasi — Piagam of Assimilation, a declaration made in 1960 by prominent *peranakan* advocating Chinese assimilation into the indigenous Indonesian community.

PIT. See PITI

PITI (Persatuan Islam Tionghoa Indonesia) — Association of Indonesian Chinese Muslims, first formed in 1936 in Medan. Originally called the Persatuan Islam Tionghoa (PIT), it became the Persatuan Islam Tionghoa Indonesia after World War II when its activities spread to Java. The name was changed again to Persatuan Iman Tauhid Islam in 1974(?).

PKB (Partai Kebangkitan Bangsa) — The National Awakening Party, established in 1998 with the endorsement of Abdrrahman Wahid (Gus Dur), often considered as an NU party.

PKI (Partai Komunis Indonesia) — Indonesian Communist Party. Formed in May 1920, suppressed in 1927, but re-emerged after Indonesia's independence, it was banned after the 1965 coup.

PMKRI (Perhimpunan Mahasiswa Katholik Indonesia) — Indonesian Catholic University Students Union

PMSTI (Paguyuban Sosial Marga Tionghoa Indonesia) — the social organization of Indonesian Chinese, also known in Chinese as Yinhua Baijiaxing Xiehui. The first Chinese Indonesian social organization set up by the Chinese community after the fall of Soeharto.

PNI (Partai Nasional Indonesia) — Indonesian Nationalist Party, formed by Soekarno in July 1927 and dissolved in 1930.

Abbreviations and Glossary 427

Revived after Indonesia's independence. Merged with the PDI in 1973

Poh An Tui (Bao'an Dui 保安队) — Peace Preservation Corps, first established in Medan in 1945 by some Chinese under the instruction of the Chinese consul, aimed at protecting Chinese property and life during the Indonesian conflict with the Dutch. Armed by the Dutch, it was unpopular with leftist Chinese and Indonesian nationalists.

PP-10 (Peraturan Presiden No. 10) — Presidential Regulation no. 10 issued in 1959 prohibiting aliens from engaging in retail trade in Indonesia. It was reported that 102,000 Chinese left Indonesia for China after its enactment.

PPP (Partai Persatuan Pembangunan) — United Development Party, a fusion of four Islamic parties (NU, Partai Muslimin Indonesia, PSII, Perti), formed officially in January 1973.

PPSMI (Persatuan Pelajar Sekolah Menengah Indonesia) — Indonesia Secondary School Students Union, a continuation of pre-World War II Chung Hsioh

pribumi — indigenous Indonesian

PT (Persatuan Tionghoa) — Chinese Union, a political party formed in 1948. It changed its name to the PDTI in 1950.

PT (Perseroan Terbatas) — a limited company

PT Gunung Agung — one of the largest bookstores and publishing houses in Indonesia. It has published biographies of Soekarno and Soeharto.

PTI (Partai Tionghoa Indonesia) — Indonesian Chinese Party, a *peranakan* political party formed in Surabaya in 1932. It supported Indonesia's independence and advocated nationalism among *peranakan* Chinese. Dissolved during the Japanese Occupation

Qiao Lian 侨联 (Huaqiao Lianhehui 华侨联合会) — Overseas Chinese Federation in the PRC.

Qiao Lian 侨联 (Yin-ni Hua-ch'iao Lien-ho-hui; Yinni Huaqiao Lianhehui 印尼华侨联合会) — Federation of Indonesian Chinese Associations, formed in Jakarta by pro-KMT *totok* Chinese in the 1950s. Banned in 1958

Qiao Zong 侨总 (or Zhonghua Qiaotuan Zonghui 中华侨团总会) — Federation of Chinese Associations, established in April 1952 in Jakarta. It consisted of pro-Beijing organizations closely connected with the consulate of the PRC. Dissolved after the 1965 coup

RC — Republic of China, Taiwan

RHS (Rechts Hoogeschool) — a law school established in Jakarta before World War II. It changed its name to FHUI after Indonesia's independence.

RI (Republik Indonesia) — Republic of Indonesia

RIS (Republik Indonesia Serikat) — United States of the Republic of Indonesia, a form of government in accordance with the Hague agreement, abolished in 1950.

RRI (Radio Republik Indonesia) — Radio of the Republic of Indonesia

RRT (Republik Rakjat Tiongkok) — People's Republic of China

Rumah Sakit Husada. See Jang Seng Ie

rupiah – Indonesian currency unit

Sam Kauw (san jiao 三教) — three religions (a combination of Confucianism, Taoism and Buddhism (Indonesia)

Sam Kauw Hwee (Sanjiao hui 三教会) — Buddhist-Taoist-Confucianist Society, the Association of Three Religions in Indonesia. First established in various major cities in Java before World War II. It changed its name to Tri Dharma in the late 1950s.

Sarekat Rakyat — People's Union, a front organization of the PKI in the 1920s

Seskoad (Sekolah Staf Komando Angkatan Darat) — Indonesian Army Staff and Commanders School, located in Bandung

SH (Sarjana Hukum) — Master of Law, Indonesian equivalent for Meester in de Rechten ("Mr")

Shang Lian 商联 (Yinni Zhonghua Shanghui Lianhehui 印尼中华商会联合会) — Federation of Chinese Chambers of Commerce in Indonesia in the late 1940s and the 1950s. Dominated by pro-KMT businessmen

Sheng Hwo Pao (*Shenghuo Bao*《生活报》) — a pro-Beijing Chinese daily published in Jakarta, 1945–65

Shenghuo Bao. See *Sheng Hwo Pao*

Shijie Fuqingshetuan lianyihui. See International Federation of Futsing Clan

Shoudu Ribao (*Harian Ibukota*《首都日报》) — a large Chinese daily in Jakarta, 1963–65. Pro-Beijing

Shou-tu Jih-pao. See *Shoudu Ribao*

Siang Hwee (Shang Hui 商会) — the abbreviation of Tiong Hoa Siang Hwee (Zhonghua Shanghui), which means Chinese Chamber of Commerce, established in Java in the early twentieth century at the time of the Chinese nationalist awakening. Most well-known of them were the Siang Hwee in Jakarta (1908), the Siang Boe (商务) in Semarang (1907), and the Siang Hwee in Surabaya (1909?).

Siang Po — the name of Perniagaan after July 1930. Representing the CHH before 1934

Sin Ming Hui (新明会) — a *peranakan*-dominated social organization established in 1946 with its headquarters in Jakarta. In the late 1950s it changed its name to Tjandra Naja (or Candra Naya).

Sin Po — an Indonesian daily newspaper published by *peranakan* Chinese in Jakarta (1910–59). It held a Chinese nationalist point of view and constituted a major stream in *peranakan* Chinese politics before World War II. It changed its name to Warta Bhakti in 1959 and was banned in 1965.

SIWO/PWI (Seksi Wartawan Olahraga-Persatuan Wartawan Indonesia) — Sport Reporters' Section of the Indonesian Journalists' Union

SMA (Sekolah Menengah Atas) — Indonesian Senior Middle School

SMP (Sekolah Menengah Pertama) — Indonesian Junior Middle School

SNPC (Sekolah Proyek Nasional Chusus) — Special Project National School, a school system established under the sponsorship of private groups within the Chinese community supervised by the Indonesian Government after the 1965 coup. Its aim was to provide alien Chinese children with an education in Indonesian since no Chinese medium schools were allowed to operate after the coup. In 1975, all SNPC were converted to regular Indonesian schools.

Soe Po Sia (Shubao she 书报社) — Reading Club, a Chinese revolutionary organization affiliated with the KMT

Soe Soei Tiong Hoa Ie Wan (泗水中华医院) — Surabaya Chinese Hospital

Soekarno (Sukarno, 1901–70) — The first president of the Republic of Indonesia (1945–65). Both Soekarno and Hatta jointly signed the proclamation of Indonesian independence on 17 August 1945 representing the Indonesian people. Leader of pre-war independence movement

Abbreviations and Glossary 431

SOS (Servants of Society) — a *peranakan* political group based in Surabaya, formed shortly after Indonesia's independence. It supported Indonesians in their struggle against the Dutch.

SPPL (Sarekat Pegawai Pelabuhan dan Lautan) — Indonesian Seamen's and Dockers' Union, established by the PKI in 1924

Stovia (School tot Opleiding van Inlandsche Artsen) — School for the Training of Indigenous Doctors before World War II, located in Jakarta

Sumber Waras — a hospital sponsored by Sin Ming Hui, located in Jakarta. See also Sin Ming Hui

Su-tung Chung-hsueh (Sudong Zhongxue 苏东中学) — probably the largest Chinese high school in Indonesia before 1958, located in Medan. It was founded in 1931 and run by a pro-KMT group.

T'ien-ti Hui (Tiandi Hui 天地会) — a Chinese secret society

Ta Chung Sze (Dazhong she 大众社) — *totok*-dominated social and recreational society during the pre-Soeharto's period

Ta Hsioh Sing Hwee. See Ta Hsueh Hsueh Sheng Hui (Daxue Xueshenghui 大学学生会)

Ta Hsueh Hsueh Sheng Hui. See Perhimi

taoke. See *toke*

The 1965 Cup. See G-30-S

THHK (Tiong Hoa Hwee Koan; Zhonghua Huiguan 中华会馆) — Chinese Association, the first pan-Chinese organization in Java, formed in Jakarta in 1900. Initially involved in social, religious, and educational reforms of the Chinese, it gradually became an educational organization with branches throughout Indonesia. It went into a decline after Indonesia's independence and eventually disappeared.

THHT (Tiong Hoa Hak Tong; Zhonghua Xuetang 中华学堂) — Chinese School, the name of early Chinese schools established by the THHK

THS (Technische Hoogeschool) — Dutch Technical College, usually with reference to the one in Delft

Tiansheng Ribao (or *Thien Sung Yit Po*《天声日报》) — The largest pro-KMT Chinese daily published in Jakarta, 1921–58. A major rival of *Xin Bao*.

Tiong Hoa Keng Kie Hwee (Zhonghua Jingji Hui 中华经纪会) — Chinese Employees' Association, dominated by *peranakan*, established in 1909. Dissolved after Indonesia's independence

Tiong Hoa Kie Tok Kauw Hwee (Zhonghua Jidujiao Hui 中华基督教会) — Chinese Christian Church, a *peranakan* organization

Tiong Hoa Siang Hwee. See Siang Hwee

Tiong Hoa Tih Yuk Hui 中华智益会 (Tih Yuk Hui) — a pro-KMT *totok*-dominated organization, active before World War II

Tjuo Sangi In — Central Advisory Council, created by the Japanese in 1943, in many respects resembling the Volksraad, except that it was not allowed to criticize the regime.

TNI — Tentara Nasional Indonesia: Indonesian National Army

toke — Chinese boss, another spelling for *taoke*

totok (*totok* Tionghoa) — a term used to refer to China-born Chinese residing in Indonesia. *Totok* still speak a Chinese dialect or Mandarin. Their immediate descendants, though Indonesian-born, are still considered *totok* if their mother tongue is still Chinese.

Tridharma. See Sam Kauw Hwee

Tzu-yu Pao (*Ziyou Bao*《自由报》) — a pro-KMT daily published in Jakarta during the 1950s

UGM (Universitas Gadjah Mada) — the oldest national university in Indonesia, located in Yogyakarta

UI (Universitas Indonesia) — University of Indonesia, located in Jakarta and Depok

UKRIDA (Universitas Kristen Indonesia Djakarta Raya) — Jakarta Indonesian Christian University

UMS (Union Makes Strong) — name of a Chinese soccer organization in Jakarta prior to World War II

UNDIP (Universitas Diponegoro) — a Semarang-based university

Universitas Trisakti. See URECA

UNPAD (Universitas Pajajaran) — a Bandung-based university

UNRA (Universitas Rakjat) — People's University, PKI's university established in Jakarta in September 1958

UNTAR (Universitas Tarumanegara) — a private university in Jakarta, established by the Chinese community, a large number of the student population is ethnic Chinese.

URECA (Universitas Res Publica) — a university established by Baperki in the 1960s. Taken over by a committee appointed by the Indonesian Government in 1965 and given a new name, Universitas Trisakti

Volksraad — People's Council, an advisory body (later also assuming semi-legislative functions) in the Dutch East Indies established in 1918 by the Dutch

Walubi (Perwalian Umat Buddha Indonesia) — Indonesian Buddhist General Association, representatives of Indonesian Buddhist Community *warung* — a type of small grocery shop frequently run by *totok*. Also known as yanong 亚弄 in Mandarin

WHO — World Health Organization

Xin Bao (Hsin Pao《新报》) — Chinese edition of *Sin Po*, the largest Chinese language newspaper before 1959. First published in Jakarta in 1921, its Malay edition was the champion of Chinese nationalism before World War II.

Ya Chung (雅中). See Pa Chung

Ya Zhong (雅中). See Pa Chung

Yanong (亚弄). See *warung*

Yindunixiya Ribao — An Indonesian Chinese language newspaper controlled by the Indonesian army established during the New Order period. It usually consisted of eight pages, half was in Indonesian. After the fall of Soeharto, the newspaper was sold to *Sin Chew Jit Poh* group in Malaysia. While retaining the Indonesian name *Harian Indonesia*, the Chinese name has become *Yinni Xingzhou Ribao* (《印尼星洲日报》).

Yinhua Baijiaxing Xiehui (印华百家姓协会) — the Chinese name of PSMTI

Yin-hua Meishu Hsieh-hui (Yinhua Meishu Xiehui 印华美术协会) — Indonesian Chinese Fine Arts Association, established after Indonesia's independence, dominated by *totok* artists.

Yin-ni Hua-ch'iao Kao-chi Shang-yeh Hsueh-hsiao (印尼华侨高级商业学校). See Gao Shang

Yinni Huaqiao Gaoji Shangye Xuexiao. See Gao Shang

Yinni Xingzhou Ribao. See *Yindunixiya Ribao*

Yinni Zhonghua Shanghui Lianhehui. See Shang Lian

Yinni Zuoxie (印尼作协; 印尼写作者协会), formed in 1999 in Jakarta after the fall of Soeharto. Its Indonesian name is Perhimpunan Penulis Tionghoa Indonesia.

YLBHI (Yayasan Lembaga Bantuan Hukum Indonesia) — Indonesian Legal Aid Foundation

Yueh Po She (Yue Bo She 月波社) — a social and recreational club in Jakarta affiliated with the pro-KMT group

Zhongcheng Bao (《忠诚报》) — pro-Beijing Chinese edition of *Warta Bhakti* (Jakarta). Banned in 1965

Zhonghua Qiaotuan Zonghui. See Qiao Zong

Zhonghua Shanghui. See Siang Hwee

Zhonghua Zhongxue. See Hua Zhong

SELECT BIBLIOGRAPHY

"#16 Murdaya Poo and Siti Hartati Cakra". Available at <http://www.Forbes.com> (accessed 2 December 2011).

"2014 nian daxuan zhengdang — Minxin Dang" 2014年大选政党 — 民心党. *Qiandao Ribao* 千岛日报, 3 March 2014.

A La 阿拉. "Lin Kechang Riben Guanpian Zhihui Guilai Toulu…" 林克昌日本灌片指挥归来透露… *Mingbao Zhoukan* 明报周刊, no. 511–27 August 1978.

Abdul Hadi W.M. See Hadi, Abdul WM

"About Lyman Group". In Puspa Iptek. Available at <http://www.thebiggestsundial.com/php/thebiggestsundial/main_aboutus.php?id=11> (accessed 13 October 2011).

Abun Sanda. See Sanda, Abun

Aidit, D.N. "Tentang Tan Ling Djieisme". *Pilihan Tulisan* (Jakarta) 1 (1962): 292.

Almanak Kempen 1952. Jakarta: Kementerian Penerangan, 1952(?).

Almanak Organisasi Negara RI. Jakarta: Lembaga Administrasi Negara, 1960(?). [Cited as *Organisasi RI*]

Almanak Pers Indonesia 1954–55. Jakarta: Yayasan Lembaga Pers dan Pendapat Umum, 1955. [Cited as *Almanak Pers*]

"Alumnus in Conversation: Mr Alim Markus". NUS Business School website. Available at <http://bizalum.nus.edu.sg/featuredalumi/featurealumnidetails.aspx?id=44> (accessed 26 January 2012).

Anderson, Benedict R.O'G. *Bibliography of Indonesian Publications: Newspapers, Non-Government Periodicals and Bulletins 1945–58*. Ithaca: Modern Indonesia Project, Cornell University, 1959. [Cited as Anderson, *Bibliography*]

―――. *Some Aspects of Indonesian Politics under the Japanese Occupation 1944–45*. Ithaca: Modern Indonesia Project, Cornell University, 1961. [Cited as Anderson, *Japanese Occupation*]

―――. "In Memoriam: Soe Hok Gie". *Indonesia*, no. 9 (April 1970): 225–27.

―――. *Java in a Time of Revolution: Occupation and Resistance 1944–46*. Ithaca: Cornell University Press, 1972. [Cited as Anderson, *Java*]

Ang Jan Goan. "Almarhoem Tjoe Bou Sam". *Sin Po Wekelijksche Editie*, 26 December 1925, pp. 614–22.

Anggraeni, Dewi. "Arief Budiman: Defying the Chinese Stereotype". *Jakarta Post*, 2 June 2008.

"Apa dan Siapa — Siti Hartati Murdaya". Pusat Data dan Analisa Tempo (accessed 2 December 2011).

Apa dan Siapa Ilmuwan dan Teknokrat Indonesia. Jakarta: Pustaka Kartini, 1989.

Apa dan Siapa Orang Film Indonesia 1926–1978. Jakarta: Yayasan Artis Film & Sinematek Indonesia, 1979.

Apa & Siapa Sejumlah Orang Bulutangkis Indonesia. See Sabaruddin Sa

Apa & Siapa Sejumlah Orang Indonesia, 1981–1982, 1983–1984, 1985–1986. Jakarta: Grafiti Pers (various years). [Cited as *Apa dan Siapa 1981–1982*, or *1983–1984, 1985–1986*]

Archipel, Vol. 5 (1973).

Arditya, Andreas D. "It's Fauzi vs Jokowi on Sept 20". *Jakarta Post*, 12 September 2012.

Arief, Sritua, ed. *Who's Who in Indonesian Business*. Jakarta: Sritua Arief Associates, 1975; 2nd ed., 1977. [Cited as Arief, *Indonesian Business*]

Arifin Suryo Nugraho dkk. See Nugroho, Arifin Suryo

Assimilasi dalam Rangka Pembinaan Kesatuan Bangsa. Jakarta: Kempen, 1964(?). [Cited as *Assimilasi*]

Auwj. "Inkonsekwensi Jang Merugikan Negara". *Berita PDTI*, no. 2 (November 1958): 2.

Bachtiar, Harsja. *Universitas Indonesia 1950–75*. Jakarta: LIPI, 1975.

———. *Directory of Social Scientists in Indonesia*. Jakarta: Indonesia Institute of Sciences, 1976. [Cited as Bachtiar, *Directory*]

Bai Jiali 白嘉莉. *Ai zai Lin Shenchu: Qingqian Huang Shuang'an* 爱在林深处: 情牵黄双安. Fuzhou 福州: Haixia Shuju 海峡书局, 2011.

"Bangkitnya Klenteng Tirtowinoto". *Tempo*, 29 March 1975, p. 16.

Berita PDTI (Jakarta)

Berita Yudha (Jakarta), 31 March 1976

Bintang Timur (Jakarta)

"Biographical Data of Tan Liong-Houw"

Bonnie, Triyana. *Eddie Lembong: Mencintai Tanah Air Sepenuh Hati*. Jakarta: Penerbit Buku Kompas, 2011.

Borsuk, Richard and Nancy Chng. *Liem Sioe Liong's Salim Group: The Business Pillar of Suharto's Indonesia*. Singapore: Institute of Southeast Asian Studies, 2014.

Brown, Iem. "Contemporary Indonesian Buddhism and Monotheism". *Journal of Southeast Asian Studies* XVIII, no. 1 (March 1987): 108–17.

Budiman, Arief. *Chairil Anwar: Sebuah pertemuan*. Jakarta: Pustaka Jaya, 1976.

———. "The Inaugural Professorial Lecture". Melbourne: Institute of Asian Languages and Societies, the University of Melbourne, 1999.

Buku Pedoman Universitas Katholik Indonesia 1971. Jakarta: Universitas Katholik Indonesia, 1971.

Buku Peringatan 100 Tahun Sekolah THHK/Pahoa Centennial of the THHK School. Jakarta: 2001.

Buku Peringatan Sekolah Tiong Hoa Hwee Koan 1963. Jakarta: Tiong Hoa Hwee Koan, 1963.

Buku Peringatan Sin Ming Hui 10 Tahun 1946–56. Jakarta: Sin Ming Hui, 1956. [Cited as *SMH 10 Tahun*]

Centre for Strategic and International Studies, 1975. Jakarta: Centre for Strategic and International Studies, 1975. [Cited as *CSIS*]

Chang, Queeny. "Memories". *Star* (Malaysia), 20 March 1977. [Cited as Chang, "Memories"]

———. *Memories of a Nonya*. Singapore: Eastern University Press, 1981.

Chen Fencheng 陈奋澄. *Nanguan Baigan Lu* 南冠百感录 [Recollections on the Japanese Occupation]. Batavia: n.p., 1948. [Cited as Chen, *Nanguan*]

Chen Hantong 成汉通. "Reyandi muye jituan" 惹炎帝木业集团. *Nanyang Shangbao* 南洋商报 (Singapore), 2 September 1976.

CHH Statuten en Reglementen. Hague: Chung Hwa Hui, 1928.

Chua Leong Kian. "The Other Rich Oei Whom Few Knew …". *Straits Times*, 23 March 1981.

Chung Hwa Hui 2de Lustrum. Batavia: Chung Hwa Hui, 1938. [Cited as *CHH 2de Lustrum*]

Ci Shan Xuexiao 慈山学校. "Li Shangda Shengping Shiji — Jinian Ci Shan Xuexiao Xiaozhu" 李尚大生平事迹 — 暨南慈山学校校主. Available at <http://web.axcsxx.cn:2010/zt/sd/zysd/200811/20081105093248.htm> (accessed 14 October 2011).

Coppel, Charles. "Liem Thian Joe's Unpublished History of Kian Gwan". Paper presented at ASAA conference in May 1976. Mimeographed.

CRIonline. "Yinni Qiaoling Lin Wenguang he ta de qiaoxiang touzi zhi lu" 印尼侨领林文光和他的侨乡投资之路. Available at <http://gb.cri.cn/1321/2009/07/29/542s2576992.htm> (accessed 3 December 2011).

Crouch, Harold. "Generals and Business in Indonesia". *Pacific Affairs* 48, no. 4 (Winter 1975–76): 534–35.

"Curriculum vitae" (provided by Sarasin Viraphol).

Daftar Alamat dan Nomor Telepon Pemimpin Partai-Partai Politik dan Sekber Golkar. Jakarta: Sekbar Golkar, n.d. [Cited as *Daftar Golkar*]

Davonar, Agnes. *Kisah Tragis Oei Hui Lan: Putri Orang Terkaya di Indonesia*. Jakarta: AD Publisher, 2012.

Dewi Anggraeni. See Anggraeni, Dewi

Dipingxian 地平线 (Hong Kong)

Directory of Chinese Personal Names in Indonesia. External Research Paper no. 110. Jakarta: Office of Intelligence Research, Department of State, October 1953. [Cited as *Directory of Chinese Names*]

Dishanjie Yazhou Huawen Zuojia Huiyi Dahui Shouce 第三届亚洲华文作家会议大会手册. Kuala Lumpur: Yazhou Huawen Zuojia 亚洲华文作家, 1988.

Djawa Nenkan. First published, 1944. Reprinted, Tokyo: Biburio, 1973.

Dong Rui 东瑞. "Huang Dongping ji qi Qiaoke" 黄东平及其侨歌. *Jing Bao* 镜报 (Hong Kong), no. 36 (10 September 1980), pp. 33–34.

———. "Miusi zhi Zi de Xinling Luo Ge" 缪斯之子的心灵裸歌. In *Yan Weizhen Shiwen Xuan* 严唯真诗文选. Hong Kong: Huoyi Publisher 获益出版社, 1998.

———. "Jiechu de Yin Hua Zuojia Huang Dongping — *Qiao Ge* he qita" 杰出的印华作家黄东平 —《侨歌》和其他. In *Liujin Jijie* 流金季节. Hong Kong: Huoyi Publisher 获益出版社, 2000.

Editor (Jakarta)

Ekspres (Jakarta)

"Elsie San Fang Tjiok". *Pantjawarna*, no. 61 (October 1953), p. 6.

Email interview with Sarasin Viraphol, July 2011.

Expo (Jakarta)

Far Eastern Economic Review [Cited as *FEER*]

Feith, Herbert and Lance Castles, eds. *Indonesian Political Thinking 1945–65*. Ithaca: Cornell University Press, 1970. [Cited as Feith, *Thinking*]

"Filmographic Indonesienne". *Archipel*, no. 5 (1973): 53–64.

Finch, Susan. *Republic of Indonesia Cabinets 1945–65*. Ithaca: Modern Indonesia Project, Cornell University, 1965. [Cited as Finch, *Cabinets*]

Fitzgerald, Stephen. *China and the Overseas Chinese: A Study of Peking's Changing Policy 1949–70*. Cambridge: Cambridge University Press, 1972. [Cited as Fitzgerald, *Peking's Policy*]

Forbes Zibenjia 资本家 (Hong Kong)

Forum Keadilan (Jakarta, weekly) [Cited as *Forum*]

Fujian National University website 福建师范大学网站. "Yinni Alazha Daxue Kongzi Xueyuan Hanyu Shizi Peiyang Zhongxin Hezuo Beiwanglu Qianshu Yishi zai Yajiada Juxing", 14 January 2011. Available at <http://iccs.fjnu.edu.cn/n740c18.aspx> (accessed 3 December 2011).

"Gagal, Lalu Apa?". *Tempo*, 29 March 1975, pp. 44–47.

General Catalogue of Jakarta Museum Library [Cited as *Museum Catalogue*]

Go, Tik Swan. *Jawa Sejati: Otobiografi Go Tik Swan Hardjonagoro* (Seperti yang dituturkan kepada Rustopo). Jakarta: Penerbit Ombak, 2008.

Gunadharma, Visakha. "In Memoriam". In *Keterangan Singkat Agama Buddha*, by Ven. Narada Maha Thera. Jakarta, 1975.

Gunawan, Indra. "Berkenalan Dengan Tokoh-Tokoh Non-Pribumi". *Kompas*, 4 February 1979.

Guoji Ribao 国际日报. 14 December 2007. Speech by Li Zhuohui 李卓辉 at Konkuk University.

———. "Xieqi" 谢启, 17 November 2008.

———. "Yecheng Xiamen Anxi San Di Wan Ren Zhi'ai Daonian" 椰城厦门安溪三地万人致哀悼念, 17 November 2008.

———. "Dongmeng Nanyang Daxue Chouweihui Zhengshi Chengli" 东盟南洋大学筹委会正式成立, 8 June 2011.

Hadi, Abdul W.M. *Potret Panjang Seorang Pengunjung Pantai Sanur*. Jakarta: Pustaka Jaya, 1975.

Hamdy L. Gumanti, ed. *Masagung: Sukaduka Anak Jalanan*. Jakarta: Serial Usahawan, Sukses, Karena Allah S.w.t. Jakarta: PT Pitoko, c.1982.

Hari Ulang Ke-50 Tiong Hoa Hwee Koan Jakarta. Jakarta: Tiong Hoa Hwee Koan, 1950.

Harsono, FX. "CV FX Harsono 2011" (courtesy of FX Harsono).

———. "Washed Away Memories: FX Harsono" (courtesy of FX Harsono).

Haryono, Inny C. "Pemakaian Bahasa Indonesia oleh Masyarakat Cina di Indonesia Dalam Kurun waktu 20-th Terakhir". *Bahasa Indonesia Tahun 2000*. Depok: FSUI, 1988.

Hindley, Donald. *The Communist Party of Indonesia 1951–1963*. Berkeley and Los Angeles: University of California Press, 1964. [Cited as Hindley, *PKI*]

Hopper, Richard H. "Petroleum in Indonesia: History, Geology and Economic Significance". *Asia*, no. 24 (Winter 1971–72): 58, 66.

Hsu C.M. "Lee Man Fong dan Senilukisnya". *Pantjawarna*, no. 62 (November 1953).

———. "Buah-tangan dan Riwajat Hidup Wen Peor". *Sin Tjun*, no. 3 (1958): 102–3.

Hsu Yun-ch'iao 许云樵. "Nanyang Wenxian Xulu Xubian" 南洋文献叙录续编. *Dongnanya Yanjiu* 东南亚研究 I (1965): 107–69.

Huang Dongping 黄东平. "Toujia yanli de ..." 头家眼里的 ... *Xingzhou Ribao* 星洲日报 (Singapore), 21 June 1980.

———. "Yi muqin" 忆母亲. *Haiyang Wenyi* 海洋文艺, no. 4 (1980): 68–73.

———. "Wo yu Qiao Ge" 我与侨歌. In *Duangao Yi Ji* 短稿一集. Singapore: Jiaoyu Publisher 教育出版社, 1984.

Huang Dongping Zuopin Shumu 黄东平作品书目 (draft copy), provided by the author.

Huang Fuluan 黄福銮. *Huaqiao yu Zhongguo Geming* 华侨与中国革命 [Overseas Chinese and Chinese revolution]. Hong Kong: Asia Publishing House, 1954. [Cited as Huang, *Geming*]

Huang Kunzhang 黄昆章. "Huiyi Yajiada Zhonghua Zhongxue" 回忆雅加达中华中学. *Dipingxian* 地平线, no. 10 (April 1980): 44–45.

Huang Shuling 黄叔麟. "Gao motuoxika qijia defuhao 搞摩托西卡起家的富豪". *Lianhe Wanbao* 联合晚报, 26 March 1983. Reprinted in *Da chuji* 《大出击》, pp. 15–17. Singapore: SNPL Book Publication Department, 1984.

Huang Yongyu 黄永玉. "Weixiao. Hanshui. Jiayuan — Dao Li Shangda Xiong" 微笑·汗水·家园 — 悼李尚大兄. Available at <http://blog.sina.com.cn/s/blog_60d380b40100gf8r.html> (accessed 14 October 2011).

Huaqiao Bianweihui 华侨编委会 [Overseas Chinese Annals Editorial Committee]. *Yinni Huaqiao zhi* 印尼华侨志 [Indonesia: an Overseas Chinese annal]. Taipei: Huaqiao zhi bianweihui 华侨志编委会, 1961. [Cited as *Huaqiao zhi*]

Huaqiao Da Cidian 华侨大词典 (Taipei: Huaqiao xiehui zonghui 华侨协会总会, 2000).

Huaqiao yu Huaren 华侨与华人 (Guangzhou)

Husheng 呼声 (Jakarta), no. 26 (May 2001).

Hutomo, Suryo, comp. "Sejarah Singkat Perkembangan Agama Khonghucu di Indonesia". Mimeographed.

Indonesia Raya (Jakarta)

Indonesian Monographs on Microfiche 1945–68. Zug: Inter Documentation, 1975. [Cited as *Indonesian Monographs*]

Indonesian Quarterly XXI, no. 4 (1993); XXII, no. 4 (1994).

Indonesian Review of International Affairs (Jakarta)

Insight Indonesia (Australia)

Interviews with Oei Tjoe Tat, 1984.

Inti Masalah "Minorita". Jakarta: LPKB, c.1962.

Intisari (Jakarta, weekly)

Ishwara, Helen. *P.K. Ojong: Hidup Sederhana Berpikir Mulia*. Jakarta: Penerbit Buku Kompas, 2001.

Jahja, Junus, ed. *Kisah-Kisah Saudara Baru*. Jakarta: Yayasan Ukhuwah Islamiah, 1989.

———. *Nonpri Di Mata Pribumi*. Jakarta: Yayasan Tunas Bangsa, 1991.

———. *Peranakan Idealis: Dari Lie Eng Hok sampai Teguh Karya*. Jakarta: KPG, 2002.

———. *Catatan Orang Indonesia*. Jakarta: Komunitas Bambu, 2009.

Jakob Oetama. *Kawan Kami: Myra 'Moy' Sidharta*. Jakarta: privately printed, 2004.

Jalan Demokratis Ke Sosialisme: Pengalaman Chili dibawah Allende [Democratic Way to Socialism: Chili under Allende]. Jakarta, 1987.

"James T. Riady". *Eksekutif*, January 1984, pp. 18–24.

Jang Seng Ie Jubileum 25 Tahun. Jakarta: n.p., c.1951. [Cited as *Jang Seng Ie*]

Ji Huiqi 纪辉琦. "Meikuang juzi, jiashe zhongyin jingmaucaiqiao" 煤矿巨子, 架设中印经贸彩桥. Available at <http://www.hongqiwang.net/detail12.asp?id=635> (accessed 14 December 2012).

Jiang Nan 江南. "Yajiada Qiri Xiaozhu" 雅加达七日小驻 [Short stay in Jakarta as a reporter]. *Xinwen Tiandi* 新闻天地, 10 May 1969, pp. 14–16. [Cited as Jiang, "Yajiada"]

Jiechu renwu minglu 杰出人物名录 [List of prominent personalities]. In *Yinni huawen gongshang yu shenghuo zhinan* 印尼华文工商与生活指南 [English title: Chinese Consumer Directory & Lifestyle Indonesia]. Jakarta: Yinni huawen gongshang yu shenghuo zhinan chubanshe, 2005. [Cited as *Jiechu renwu minglu*]

Juangari, Edij. *Menabur Benih Dharma: Riwayat Singkat Bikkhu Ashin Jinarakkhita*. Bandung: Yayasan Penerbit Karaniya, 1995.

K.T.H. (Kwee Tek Hoay). "Sikepnja Dr Ong Hok Lan". *Panorama*, 4 June 1927, pp. 5–6.

Karya, Teguh. *November 1828*. Jakarta: Sinar Harapan, 1979.

Katili, A.A. *Olahraga Tennis*. Jakarta, 1973.

Kementerian Penerangan R.I. *Kami Perkenalkan* ... Jakarta: Kementerian Penerangan, c.1954. [Cited as Kempen, *KP*]

"Kisah Sukses Alim Markus Pendiri Maspion". Available at <http://www.martinwijaya.net/my-experience/kisah-sukses-alimmarkus-pendiri...26/01/2012> (accessed 4 January 2012).

Koentjaraningrat, ed. *The Social Sciences in Indonesia*, vol. 1. Jakarta: Indonesian Institute of Sciences, 1975.

Kolesnikov-Jessop, Sonia. "FX Harsono's Rebellious, Critical Voice Against 'Big Power' in Indonesia". *New York Times*, 11 March 2010.

Kompas (Jakarta)

Ksp, Robert Adhi. *Panggil Aku King*. Jakarta: Kompas, 2009.

Kwartanada, Didi. *Hilangnya Tokoh-tokoh Tionghoa dalam Buku Acuan Sejarah Nasional Indonesia: Kasus BPUPKI (1945)*. Photocopy, December 2013.

Kwee Kek Beng. *25 Tahon Sebagi Wartawan*. Batavia: Kuo-Batavia, 1948. [Cited as Kwee, *Wartawan*]

———. *50,000 Kilometer Dalam 100 Hari*. Palembang: Lauw Putra, 1965. [Cited as Kwee, *50,000 Kilometer*]

———. "Orang Tionghoa dari Indonesia di Luar Negeri". *Buku Peringatan HUT Hoo Hap Semarang 1923–73*. Semarang: Hoo Hap Hwee Kwan, 1973. [Cited as Kwee, "Tionghoa Luar Negeri"]

"Kwee Tek Hoaij-Buitenzorg". *Hoakiao*, February 1926.

Kwee Tek Hoay. "Atsal Moelahnja Timboel Pergerakan Tionghoa jang Modern di Indonesia". *Moestika Romans* 7, no. 80 (August 1936): 776–78; 9, no. 98 (February 1938): 85–88.

Lahirnja Konsepsi Asimilasi. Jakarta: Panitia Penjuluh Asimilasi Pusat, 1962.

Lasut, Yopie. "Yap Thiam Hien, Tak Pandai Bersiasat". *Mutiara* (Supplement to *Sinar Harapan*), 20 February 1980, pp. 16–17.

Lee, Alan. "Hendra to Change Tack?". *Straits Times*, 26 March 1984.

Lee Khoon Choy. *Indonesia between Myth and Reality*. Singapore: Times, 1976.

Lembaga Pemilihan Umum. *Memperkenalkan Anggota-Anggota Dewan Perwakilan Rakjat Hasil Pemilihan Umum 1971*. Jakarta: Lembaga Pemilu, n.d. [Cited as *DPR 1971*]

Li Chuan Siu. *Dari Sinologi ke Indologi*. Kuala Lumpur: Pustaka Antara, 1994.

Li Min 李敏. "Fanmuke Fudu Zhengzhi Guwen Zhang Tiancong Xiansheng" 樊慕克副督政治顾问张添聪先生. *Nanyang Post* (Jakarta), 14 February 1947.

Li Qing 犁青. "Jianku Chengzhang de Yindunixiya Huaren Wenxue" 艰苦成长的印度尼西亚华人文学. In *Dongnanya Huawen Wenxue* 东南亚华文文学, edited by Wang Runhua 王润华 and Bai Haoshi 白豪士. Singapore: Zuojia Xiehui yu Gede Xueyuan 作家协会与歌德学院, 1989.

Li Song'an 李松庵. "Nanyang Jugu Zhang Shi Xiongdi" 南洋巨贾张氏兄弟 [Big businessmen in Nanyang: the Tjong brothers]. In *Huaqiao Cangsang Lu* 华侨沧桑录. Guangdong: Guangdong Remin Chubanshe 广东人民出版社, 1984.

Li Weimin 李尉民 and Li Shengmu 李圣穆. "A wise leader of an overseas Chinese Guo Yuxiu 一代侨贤郭毓秀". In *Gaige kaifang yu Fujian huanqiao huaren* 改革开放与福建华侨华人, edited by Yang Xuelin 杨学潾. Amoy: Xiamen University Press, 1999.

Li Zhuohui 李卓辉. *Yinjie Luodishenggen Shidai* 迎接落地生根时代. Jakarta: Liantong Shuju 联通书局, 2003.

———. *Youtuoyuenuo de Jiyu yu Tiaozhan* 尤托约诺的机遇与挑战. Jakarta: Liantong Shuju 联通书局, August 2005.

———. *Yin Hua Canzheng yu Guojia Jianshe* 印华参政与国家建设. Jakarta: Liantong Shuju 联通书局, 2007.

———. *Qingshan bulao haoqi changcun* 青山不老浩气长存. Jakarta: Liantong Shuju, 联通书局, 2008.

———. Qundao xinghuoguangmang shanyao: Yin Hua Xiezuo Jingying Fengyu Fendou Rensheng Di San Ji (2) 群岛星火光芒闪耀: 印华写作精英风雨奋斗人生第二集. Jakarta: Lian Tong Shuju 联通书局, 2010.

———. *Yin Hua Xiezuo Jingying Fengyu Rensheng* (1) 印华写作精英风雨人生. Jakarta: Liantong Shuju 联通书局, 2010. [Cited as *Yinhua xiezuo jingyin*].

———. Chidao Huohua Ziqiangbuxi: Yin Hua Xiezuo Jingying Fengyu Rensheng Di San Ji (3) 赤道火花自强不息: 印华写作精英风雨人生第三集. Jakarta: Liantong Shuju 联通书局, 2011.

———. *Zhonghua Qing Yinni Meng* 中华情印尼梦. Jakarta: Liantong Shuju 联通书局, 2011.

Lianhe Zaobao 联合早报 (Singapore)

———. *Xian Jieduan de Yinni Huaren Zuqun* 现阶段的印尼华人族群. Singapore: NUS Chinese Department & World Scientific, 2002.

———. *Yinni kongjiao chutan* 印尼孔教初探. Singapore: Chinese Heritage Centre 华裔馆, April 2010. [Cited as Liao Jianyu, *Yinni kongjiao*]

Liao Ziran 廖自然. "Yinni Huaqiao Shehui Shi" 印尼华侨社会史 [A social history of the Overseas Chinese]. In *Huaqiao Shi Lunwenji* 华侨史论文集 [Papers on Overseas Chinese history], edited by Gao Xin 高信. Taipei: Guofang Yanjiu Yuan 国防研究院, 1963. [Cited as Liao, "Shehui Shi"]

Liberty (Surabaya)

Library of Congress Catalog, vol. 145 (1945).

Lie Tek Tjeng. *An Indonesian View: The Great Cultural Revolution*. Jakarta: LIPI, 1970.

Lie Tjwan Sioe. *An Introduction to the Promotion and Development of Modern Malay Literature*. Yogyakarta: Kanisius, 1975.

Liem Gwan Ging. "Djurnalistik Tionghoa-Melaju di Masa Lampau". *Pos Indonesia*, 23–27 August 1971.

Liem Thian Joe. *Riwajat Semarang*. Semarang: Ho Kim Yoe, 1933.

———. "Joernalistiek Tionghoa-Melajoe". *Sin Po Wijkelijksche-Editie*, 10 June 1939. [Cited as Liem, "Joernalistiek"]

Liem Tjwan Ling. *Raja Gula Oei Tiong Ham*. Surabaya: privately published, 1979.

Lin Kechang (dictate) 林克昌口述, Yang Zhongheng 杨忠衡 and Chen Xiaozhen 陈效真. *Huang Tudi shang de Beiduofen: Lin Kechang Huiyilu* 黄土地上的贝多芬: 林克昌回忆录. Taipei: Shibao Wenhua 时报文化, 2004.

Lin Shaokang 林绍康. "Lin Shaoliang de qingshaonian shidai" 林绍良的青少年时代. *Huaren* 华人 (Hong Kong), no. 10 (1985): 53.

Lin Wanli 林万里. *Jiehun Jijie* 结婚季节. Singapore: Daoyu Wenhua she 岛屿文化社, 1990.

Lindsay, Jennifer and Maya H.T. Liem. *Heirs to World Culture: Being Indonesian 1950–1965* (Verhandelingen 274). Leiden: KITLV Press, 2012.

Liu Huanran 刘焕然, ed. *Heshu Dongyindu Gailan* 荷属东印度概览 [Netherlands East Indian sketch]. Singapore: Nanyang Baoshe 南洋报社, 1939 [Cited as Liu, *Gailan*]

Liu Lizhen 刘丽真. "Huang Shuang'an yu Bai Jiali" 黄双安与白嘉莉. In *Jie zai Yixiang de Guoshi: Jiaodian Huaren* 结在异乡的果实: 焦点华人. Taipei: Guanghua Huabao Zazhishe 光华日报杂志社, 1991. (The original article was published in *Guanghua Zazhi* [光华杂志], May 1990 issue.)

Lombard, Denys. "Images Des Cinemas Indonesien Et Malaysien". *Archipel*, no. 5 (1973): 126–27.

Luo Yingxiang 罗英祥. *Yindunixiya de kejia*《印度尼西亚的客家》. 广西师范大学, 2011.

Ma Shuli 马树礼. *Yinni de Bian yu Luan* 印尼的变与乱 [Change and turbulence in Indonesia]. Taipei: Haiwai Chubanshe 海外出版社, 1963. [Cited as Ma, *Bian yu Luan*]

Macintyre, Andrew. *Business and Politics in Indonesia*. Sydney: Allen and Unwin, 1991.

Mackie, J.A.C., ed. *The Chinese in Indonesia: Five Essays*. Honolulu: University Press of Hawaii in association with the Australian Institute of International Affairs, 1976. [Cited as Mackie, *Five Essays*]

Matahari (Jakarta), May 1979.

McDonald, Hamish. *Soeharto's Indonesia*. Victoria: Fontana/Collins, 1980.

McVey, Ruth. *The Rise of Indonesian Communism*. Ithaca: Cornell University Press, 1965. [Cited as McVey, *Communism*]

Media Karya (Jakarta)

Memoar Oei Tjoe Tat: Pembantu Presiden Soekarno. Jakarta: Hasta Mitra, 1995.

"Mengenang Yang Arya Mahabhiksu Ashin Jinarakkhita". Phamplet, 2002.

"Menyorot Kasus Seorang Juara". *Topik*, 19 April 1972, pp. 14–19.

Merdeka (Jakarta)

Merubah Indonesia: The Story of Basuki Tjahaja Purnama. Jakarta: Center for Democracy and Transparency, 2008.

Mingguan Sadar (Jakarta)

Mira W. *Biarkan Kereta itu Lewat, Arini*. Jakarta: Gramedia, 1990.

Moerthiko. *Riwayat Klenteng, Vihara, Lithang, tempat Ibadat Tridharma Se Jawa*. Semarang: Sekretariat Empeh Wong Kam Fu, 1980.

Morais, J. Victor, ed. *Who's Who in Malaysia and Singapore 1971–72*. Petaling Jaya: Who's Who Publications, 1972. [Cited as *Who's Who in Malaysia*]

Musyawarah Keluarga Besar Paguyuban Sosial Marga Tionghoa Indonesia. Kota Batam, 28 November–2 December 2000, pp. 22–26.

Nanyang Nianjian 南洋年鉴 [Nanyang year book]. Singapore: Nanyang Baoshe 南洋报社, 1951.

Nanyang Shangbao 南洋商报 (Malaysia)

Nanyang Shangbao 南洋商报 (Singapore)

Nio Joe Lan. *Riwajat 40 Taon dari Tiong Hoa Hwe Koan-Batavia*. Batavia: Tiong Hoa Hwee Koan, 1940. [Cited as Nio, *THHK*]

———. "Gouw Tiauw Goan". *Pantjawarna*, no. 91 (April 1956): 42.

———. *Sastera Indonesia-Tionghoa*. Jakarta: Gunung Agung, 1962. [Cited as Nio, *Sastera*]

Nugoho, Arifin Suryo dkk. *10 Tokoh Tionghoa Paling Populer di Indonesia*. Yoyakarta: Bio Pustaka, 2009.

Nugraha, Arifin Surya dkk. *10 Orang Terkaya Indonesia*. Yogyakarta: Pustaka Timur, 2007.

Nurhayati, Nunuy. "Tan Joe Hok Perintis di Pentas Bulu Tangkis". Available at <http://majalah.tempointeraktif.com/id/arsip/2009/09/14/MEM/mbm.20090914.MEM131359.id.html> (accessed 5 October 2011). *Guoji Ribao* (Jakarta), 24–25 May 2009.

Ockeloen, G. *Catalogus van Boekenen en Tijdschriften uitgegeven in Ned. Oost-Indie*, vol. 2. Amsterdam: Swets and Zeitlinger, 1966. [Cited as *Catalogus*]

Oemaryati, Boen S. *Bentuk lakon dalam sastra Indonesia*. Jakarta: Gunung Agung, 1971. [Cited as Oemaryati, *Lakon*]

———. "Social Issues in Recent Indonesian Literature". In *Southeast Asian Affairs 1979*, edited by Leo Suryadinata. Singapore: Institute of Southeast Asian Studies, 1979.

Oen Tjhing Tiauw. "Dari Buruh Rokok Mendjadi Radja Rokok". *Star Weekly*, 25 August 1956, p. 15.

Oey, Abdul Karim. *Mengabdi Agama, Nusa Dan Bangsa: Sahabat Karib Bung Karno*. Jakarta: Gunung Agung, 1982.

Officieel Verslag dari Conferentie Khong Kauw Tjong Hwee. Bandung: Khong Kauw Tjong Hwee, 1924.

Ojong P.K. "Mengenangkan Khoe Woen Sioe (1906–66)". *Kompas*, 5 June 1976.

Optimis (Semarang)

Pan Changan 潘长安. Fenzhiwujin, mianjinzili, 奋志无矜, 勉勤自励, Fujian qiaoxiang《福建侨报》. Available at <http://www.com/Fujian_w/news/fjqb/031024/1_17.html> (accessed 25 January 2014).

Pan Yadun 潘亚墩, ed. *Lunyi shang de zhange* 轮椅上的战歌. Guangzhou: Jinan daxue, 1995.

Pandji Poestaka 62 (5 August 1927).

Pane, Armijn. "Produksi Film Tjerita di Indonesia". *Indonesia*, January–February 1953, pp. 16–17.

Pane, Sanusi. *Indonesia*, January–February 1953, pp. 16–17.

Panglaykim, J. *Bisnis Keluarga*. Yogyakarta: Penerbit Andi Offset, 1984.

Panglaykim, J. and I. Palmer. *Entrepreneurship and Commercial Risks: The Case of a Schumpeterian Business in Indonesia*. Singapore: Nanyang University, 1970.

Pantja Warna (Jakarta)

Parera, Frans M. "P.K. Ojong: Intelektual yang Menganut Sosialisme Fabian". *Prisma*, no. 7 (1985).

Parlaungan. *Hasil Rakjat Memilih Tokoh-Tokoh Parlemen*. Jakarta: Gita, 1956. [Cited as Parlaungan, *Tokoh Parlemen*]

Pedoman Fakultas Ekonomi Universitas Indonesia 1953–54

Pedoman Fakultas Ekonomi Universitas Indonesia 1965–58

Pedoman Kampanje Perdjoangan Badan Permusjawaratan Kewarganegaraan Indonesia (Baperki) dalam Pemilihan Umum. Jakarta: Pengurus Harian Pusat Baperki, 1955. [Cited as *Pedoman Kampanje*]

Pembauran (Jakarta)

"Pengantar Redaksi". *Pantjawarna*, 15 September 1956, p. 1.

Pengurus Pusat Fordeka. *Buku Acuan Pemilihan Legislatif Bagi Caleg-Caleg DPR RI, DPD RI, DPRD Provinsi, DPRD Kabupaten/Kota Periode 2014–2019 Keluarga Suku Tionghoa Indonesia*. Jakarta: no publisher, December 2013. [Cited as Pengurus Pusat Fordeka, *Buku Acuan 2014*]

Peresmian Pusat Kesenian Jakarta "Taman Ismail Marzuki". Jakarta: Pusat Kesenian Jakarta, 1968. [Cited as *TIM*]

Peringetan Tiong Hoa Siang Hwee Batavia Berdiri 40 Taon 1908–48. Batavia: Tiong Hoa Siang Hwee, 1948. [Cited as *Siang Hwee*]

Perspektif. "Kami sudah lama tidak ikut politik", 22–28 July 1999, pp. 14–15.

Phoa Kian Sioe. "Phoa Keng Hek Sia". *Mingguan Sadar* VIII, no. 20 (19 August 1956): 40–45.

Pikiran Rakyat (Bandung). "Pluralisme Itu Obat", 7 February 2010.

"Pilgub Jakarta: Foke-Nara Kalah, Partai Pendukung Tak Mahu Disalahkan". Available at <http://www.harianjogja.com/baca/2012/09/21/pilgub-jakarta-foke-nara-kalah-partai-pendukung-tak-mau-disalahkan-331400?utm_source=twitterfeed&utm_medium=twitter> (accessed 5 October 2012).

PKA (Pouw Kioe Aan). "In Memoriam: Tio Ie Soei". *Liberty*, no. 1098 (21 September 1974): 23, 37.

Post, Peter et al., eds. *The Encyclopedia of Indonesia in the Pacific War*. Brill, 2010.

Prasetyo, Budi. "Buku Pengusaha Bob Hasan Untuk Biayai PASI dan Pertuni". Tribunnews website, 30 October 2011. Available at <http://www.tribunnews.com/2011/10/30/bukupengusaha-bob-hasan-untuk-biayai-pasi-dan-pertuni> (accessed 7 February 2012).

"Presdir Maspion Group, Alim Markus". Available at <http://www.sinarharapan.co.id/ekonomi/ceo/2002/04/4/ceo01.html> (accessed 4 January 2012).

Pringgodigdo, A.G. and Hassan Shadily, eds. *Ensiklopedi Umum*. Jakarta, 1973.

Prisma (Jakarta)

private communications, April 2012.

"Prof DR Dr Demin Shen menjawab, 10 Juni 2009". Available at <http://4rief-online.blogspot.com/2009/06/prof-dr-dr-demin-shen-menjawab.html> (accessed 4 January 2012).

"Profil Seorang Ulama Islam Tionghoa". *Pelita* (Jakarta), 2 January 1979.

PT Maspion. Available at <http://www.maspion.com/company/index.php?act=history> (accessed 26 January 2012).

Pusat Data dan Analisa Tempo. "Apa dan Siapa-Bob Hasan". Available at <http://www.pdat.co.id/ads/html/B/ads.20030617-20,B.html> (accessed 14 December 2011).

———. "Apa dan Siapa-Demin Shen". Available at <http://www.pdat.co.id/ads/html/D/ads,20030618-32,D.html> (accessed 2 December 2011).

Pusat Penelitian Atma Jaya Annual Report 1975. Jakarta: Atma Jaya, 1975.

Qian Ren 千仞 and Liang Junxiang 梁俊祥, eds. *Shenghuobao de huiyi* 生活报的回忆. Guangdong: Shijie tushu chuban Guangdong youxian gongsi 世界图书出版广东有限公司, 2013.

Rath, Amanda Katherine, Hendro Wiyanto, Seng Yu Jin, Tan Siuli. *Re: Petition/Position/FX Harsono*. Magelang, Central Java: Langgeng Art Foundation, 2010.

"Regu Juara". *Topik*, 13 June 1973, pp. 26–27.

Riantiarno, ed. *Teguh Karya dan Teater Populer 1968–93*. Jakarta, 1993.

"Riwajat Hidup Nj. Tjoa Hin Hoey". *Berita Baperki Tjabang Jogya* II (February 1956): 57.

"Robby Tjahjadi: Si 'Raja Benang'". *Sinar*, 31 January 1994, pp. 64–66.

Roeder, O.G. "Chinese 'Impudence'". *FEER*, 7 May 1973, p. 34.

―――. *Who's Who in Indonesia*. Jakarta: Gunung Agung, 1st ed., 1971; 2nd ed., 1980. [Cited as Roeder, *Who's Who*]

Rong Qing (Singapore)

Rowan, Roy. "Guns-Bibles are Smuggled to Indonesia". *Life*, 26 September 1949, pp. 49–52.

Rowley, Anthony. "Birth of a Multinational". *FEER*, 7 April 1983, pp. 44–56.

"Rudy Hartono Kurniawan: Kunci Sukses Berdoa". In *Ensiklopedi Tokoh Indonesia*. Available at <http://TokohIndonesia.com> (accessed 10 October 2011).

Sabaruddin Sa. *Apa & Siapa Sejumlah Orang Bulutangkis Indonesia*. Jakarta: Jurnalindo Aksara Grafika, 1994.

Said, Salim. *Profil Dunia Film Indonesia*. Jakarta: Grafitipers, 1982.

Salah Satoe Sobatnja. "Liem Khing Hoo". *Liberty*, no. 167 (15 February 1946): 23–24.

Saleh, Boejoeng. "Beberapa Pandangan Tentang Kebudajaan Indonesia". *Indonesia* (Jakarta), August 1954, p. 429.

———. "Kata Pengantar Sdr. Boejoeng Saleh". In *Simposion Baperki tentang Sumbangsih: Apakah jang Dapat Diberikan oleh Warganegara2 Indonesia Keturunan Asing kepada Pembinaan dan Perkembangan Kebudajaan Nasional Indonesia*. Jakarta: Baperki, 1956. [Cited as Saleh, *Sumbangsih*, 1956]

Salmon, Claudine. *Literature in Malay by the Chinese of Indonesia: A Provisional Annotated Bibliography*. Paris: Etudes Insulindiennes-Archipel: 3, Maison des Sciences de l'Homme, 1981. [Cited as Salmon, *Literature*]

Sanda, Abun, ed. *Sofjan Wanandi: Aktivist Sejati*. Jakarta: Penerbit Buku Kompas, 2011.

Santosa, Iwan. *Tionghoa dalam Sejarah Kemiliteran: Sejak Nusantara sampai Indonesia*. Jakarta: Penenrbit Buku Kompas, 2014.

Sarasin Viraphol. See Viraphol, Sarasin

Satyawardaya, Anang (Tjoa Tjie Liang). *Dari Banjarmasin Hingga Surabaya*. Jakarta: privately printed, 2003.

Schwarz, Adam. *A Nation in Waiting: Indonesia in the 1990s*. NSW: Allen and Unwin, 1994.

"Sekilas Mengenal Marga T". In *Sekuntum Nozomi*, vol. 5, by Marga T. Jakarta: Gramedia, 2007.

Senematek Indonesia. *Apa dan Siapa: Orang Film Indonesia 1926–1978*. Jakarta: Yayasan Artis Film, 1979.

Seperempat Abad Dewan Perwakilan Rakjat Republick Indonesia. Jakarta: Sekretariat DPR, 1970. [Cited as *DPR 1970*]

Setiono, Benny G. *Tionghoa Dalam Pusaran Politik*. Jakarta: Elkasa, 2002.

Setyautama, Sam. *Tokoh-Tokoh Etnis Tionghoa di Indonesia*. Jakarta: KPG bekerjasama dengan Chen Xinghu Foundation, 2008. [Cited as Setyautama, *Tokoh-Tokoh Etnis TH*.]

Shen Demin. "Pengaruh EDTA terhadap aterogenesis pada kera ekor panjang (Macaca Fascicularis)". Disertasi, Facultas Pasca Sarjana, Institut Pertanian Bogor, 1991.

Shenghuo Bao Shi Zhounian Jinian Tekan 生活报十周年纪念特刊. Yecheng 椰城: Shenghuo Bao 生活报, 1955.

Shenghuo Zhoubao 生活周报 (Jakarta)

Shijie Huaqiao Nianjian 1969 世界华侨年鉴 1969 [1969 Universal Chinese Directory]. Hong Kong, 1970(?). [Cited as *Huaqiao Nianjian*]

Shijie Huaren Fuhao Bang 世界华人富豪榜 [World Chinese millionaires]. Hong Kong: Sansi Chuanbo 三思传播, 1994.

Siang Po 商报 (Jakarta)

"Siapa-Siapa Untuk 1974". *Tempo*, 11 January 1975, p. 43.

Siauw Giok Tjhan. *Pantja Sila Anti Rasialisme*. Jakarta: Baperki, c.1962. [Cited as Siauw, *Pantja Sila*]

Siauw Tiong Djin. *Siauw Giok Tjhan*. Jakarta: Hasta Mitra, 1999.

Sidharta, Myra. "Tan Hong Boen: A Man with Many Faces". *Asian Culture*, no. 17 (1993): 64–72.

———, ed. *100 Tahun Kwee Tek Hoay*. Jakarta: Pustaka Sinar Harapan, 1989.

Sidharta, Priguna. "Curriculum Vitae", 1980.

———. *Seorang Dokter Dari Losarang: Sebuah Otobiografi*. Jakarta: PT Temprint, 1993.

Sin Ming Hui 12 1/2 Tahun. Jakarta: Sin Ming Hui, 1958.

Sin Po 新报 (Jakarta)

Sin Po Jubileum Nummer 1910–35. [Cited as *Sin Po 25 Tahun*]

Sin Tit Po 新直报 (Surabaya)

Sinar (Jakarta, pre-World War II)

Sinar (Jakarta, weekly, first published in 1993)

Sinar Harapan (Jakarta)

Sinematek Indonesia. *Apa dan Siapa Orang Film Indonesia 1926–1979*. Jakarta: Yayasan Artis Film dan Sinematek Indonesia, 1979.

Sinergi (Media Sinenrgi Bangsa), no. 11 (15 September–15 October 1999): 15–19.

Singapore Futsing Association. *Singapore Futsing Association 70th Anniversary Souvenir (1910–80)*. Singapore, 1980.

Singgih D. Gunarsa. *Psikologi Olahraga: Teori dan Praktik*. Jakarta: BPK Gunung Mulia, 1996.

———. *Melintas Batas Cakrawala: Kisah Ketangguhkan Menembus Rintangan & Meraih Prestasi*. Jakarta: Libri, 2011.

Siregar, Sori Ersa and Kencana Tirta Widya. *Liem Sioe Liong: Dari Futching Ke Manca negara*. Jakarta: Pustaka Merdeka, 1988.

"Siti Hartati Murdaya — Berbisnis Berlandasan Ajaran Buddha-Direktori T…" Available at <http://www.tokohindonesia.com/biografi/article/286-direktori/3543-berbisnisberland> (accessed 8 December 2011).

Soedjatmoko. "The Intellectual in a Developing Nation". *Asia*, no. 17 (1969/70): 7.

Soeprobo, Satyagraha Hoerip, comp. *Antologi esei tentang Persoalan Sastra*. Jakarta: Gramedia, 1969.

Somers, M.F.A. "Peranakan Chinese Politics in Indonesia". Dissertation, Cornell University, 1965. [Cited as Somers, dissertation]

Song Zhongchuan 宋中铨. "Qiao Zong Shinian" 侨总十年. *Yindunixiya yu xuexi* 印度尼西亚语学习, no. 5 (1962): 4.

South China Morning Post, 18(?) September 1970

Star Weekly (Jakarta)

Steidtmann, Nancy and Dantje Waworuntu. "Harapan Takes Pols Position in Singapore Hotel Stakes". *Insight*, July 1982, pp. 6–12.

Sterba, James P. "Badminton Champion is Indonesia's Hero". *New York Times*, 29 March 1972.

Straits Times (Singapore)

Suara Pembaruan (Jakarta)

Sumardjo, Jakob. *Novel Indonesia Mutakhir: Sebuah Kritik*. Yogyakarta: Nur Cahaya, 1979.

Sung, Chek Mei 宋哲美 and C.M Hsu 许仲铭. *Who's Who in Indonesia* 印度尼西亚人物志, vol. I, no. 1 (1981): 185–86.

Suryadinata, Leo. "Indonesian Chinese Education: Past and Present". *Indonesia*, no. 14 (October 1972): 49–71. [Cited as Suryadinata, "Education"]

⸻. *Peranakan Chinese Politics in Java 1917–42*. Singapore: Singapore University Press, 1976. [Cited as Suryadinata, *Peranakan Politics*]

———. *Pribumi Indonesians, the Chinese Minority and China: A Study of Perceptions and Policies*. Kuala Lumpur: Heinemann Asia, 1978. [Cited as Suryadinata, *Pribumi*]

———. *Peranakan Chinese Politics in Java 1917–1942*, 2nd ed. Singapore: Singapore University Press, 1980.

———. "Bukan Kisah Seoroang Politisi". *Tempo*, 9 April 1988.

———. *Kebudayaan Minoritas Tionghoa di Indonesia*. Jakarta: Gramedia, 1988. [Cited as Suryadinata, *Kebudayaan Minoritas Tionghoa*]

———. *Mencari Identitas Nasional: Dari Tjoe Bou San Sampai Yap Thiam Hien*. Jakarta: LP3ES, 1990.

———. *Peranakan's Search for National Identity: Biographical Studies of Seven Indonesian Chinese*. Singapore: Times Academic Press, 1993.

———. *Kompas*, 22 January 1995.

———. *Prominent Indonesian Chinese: Biographical Sketches*. Singapore: Institute of Southeast Asian Studies, 1995.

———. *The Culture of Indonesian Chinese Minority*. Singapore: Times Academic, 1997.

———. *Negara dan Etnis Tionghoa: Kasus Indonesia*. Jakarta LP3ES, 2002.

———, ed. *Pemikiran Politik Etnis Tionghoa Indonesia 1900–2002*. Jakarta: LP3ES and INTI, 2005.

———, ed. *Political Thinking of the Indonesian Chinese*. Singapore: Singapore University Press, 1980.

Suryatmoko, Hari. "In Memoriam of Prof. Dr Tjan Tjoe Siem". *Intisari*, no. 189 (April 1979): 129–35.

Susunan Kabinet Republik Indonesia. Jakarta: Departemen Penerangan, 1970. [Cited as *Kabinet*]

Tan Giok Lan. *The Chinese of Sukabumi*. Ithaca: Modern Indonesia Project, Cornell University, 1963.

Tan Hong Boen. *Orang-Orang Tionghoa Jang Terkemoeka di Java*. Solo: Biographical Publishing Centre, 1935(?). [Cited as Tan, *Tionghoa*]

"Tan Tjeng Bok (1899–1985): Seniman Tiga Zaman". In *Peranakan Idealis: Dari Lie Eng Hok sampai Teguh Karya*, by Junus Jahja. Jakarta: KPG, 2002.

Tan Tjoei Hok and Evi Fadjari. "Tan Tjeng Bok 'Buaya Keroncong'". In *Pelangi Cina Indonesia*. Jakarta: Inti Sari, 2002.

Tapingkae, Amnuay, ed. *Directory of Selected Scholars and Research in Southeast Asia*. Singapore: Regional Institute of Higher Education and Development, May 1974. [Cited as Tapingkae, ed., *Selected Scholars*]

Tata Agama & Tata Laksana Upacara Agama Khonghucu. Sala: Matakin, 1975(?).

Tedy Jusuf. *Sekilas, Budaya Tionghoa di Indonesia (PSMTI)*. Jakarta: Bhuana Ilmu Pupuler, 2000.

Teeuw, A. *Sastera Baru Indonesia*. Kuala Lumpur: Penerbit Universiti Malaya, 1970.

Tempo (Jakarta)

Tempo. 9 February 1974, pp. 44–45.

———. 12 March 1977, p. 10.

———. "Perginya Alumnus Glodok-Senen-Kwitang", 29 September 1990, p. 44.

———. "Aktivis dari Tanah Abang". Available at <http://majalah.tempointeraktif.com/id/arsip/2010/10/25/MEM/mbm.20101025> (accessed 2 November 2010).

The Jakarta Post. "Timber tycoon 'Bob' Hasan sent to jail", 14 February 2001. Available at <http://www.thejakartapost/news/2001/02/14/timber-tycoon-039bobo39-hasansent-jail.html> (accessed 7 February 2012).

———. "Bob Hasan Freed on Parole", 21 February 2004. Available at <http://www.thejakartapost.com/news/2004/02/21/bob-hasan-freed-parole.html> (accessed 7 February 2012).

———. "The Voice of Jusuf Wanandi", 23 December 2008. Available at <http://www.thejakartapost.com> (accessed 10 September 2011).

The Star (Hong Kong), 11 December 1975.

Thoeng family genealogy (stencil, Riddekerk NL).

Tilman, Robert. *Directory of Southeast Asian Specialists*. Ann Arbor, Michigan: Association of Asian Studies, 1969. [Cited as Tilman, *Specialists*]

Tio Ie Soei. *Lie Kimhok 1853–1912*. Bandung: "Good Luck", c.1959.

Tiong Hoa Keng Kie Hwee. *Gedenkboek Tiong Hoa Keng Kie Hwee 1909–39*. Batavia: Tiong Hoa Keng Kie Hwee, 1940. [Cited as *Gedenkboek THKKH*]

Tjahaja Purnama, Basuki. *Merubah Indonesia: The Story of Basuki Tjahaja Purnama*. Privately published, 2008.

Tjia Tjiep Ling. "Prihal Sam Kauw dengan Bangsa Tiong Hwa". *Soeara Sam Kauw Hwee* (Kediri), no. 3 (April 1935): 2–5.

"Tjiam dan Ali Baba". *Topik*, 17 May 1972, p. 25.

Tjoa Tjie Liang. "Satu Bangsa Jang Homogeen". *Nusaputra*, 25 September 1951, pp. 8–9, 25.

"Toean Liem Khing Hoo". *Liberty*, no. 169 (15 March 1946): 15.

Topik (Jakarta)

Tyler Rollins Fine Arts Exhibitions. "FX Harsono: Writing in the Rain". Available at <http://trfineart.com/exhibitions/29> (accessed 10 April 2012).

"Ucapan Terimakasih". *Kompas*, 17 November 2008, p. 39.

Ulang Tahun Tiong Hoa Hwee Koan Jang ke-50. Jakarta: Tiong Hoa Hwee Koan, 1950. [Cited as *THHK 50 Tahun*]

Ulla Fionna and Alexander Aifianto. "Getting to know the contestants of the 2014 Indonesian Parliamentary Elections". ISEAS Perspective, no. 14 (10 March 2014).

Umesh Pandey. "Contending with giants". *Bangkok Post*, 30 October 2006.

van der Wal, S.L., ed. *De Volksraad en de Staatkundige Ontwikelling van Nederlands-Indie*. 2 vols. Groningen: J.B. Wolters, 1963. [Cited as Wal, *Volksraad*]

Verchere, Ian. "Liem Sioe Liong: Suharto's Secret Agent". *Insight*, May 1978, pp. 8–16.

Viraphol, Sarasin. *Tribute and Profit: Sino-Siamese Trade 1652–1853*. Cambridge, Massachusetts: Harvard University Press, 1977.

―――. "The Emergence of China's Economic Power and Its Implications for Chinese Business in Southeast Asia". In *Southeast Asia's Chinese Businesses in an Era of Globalization: Coping with the Rise of China*, edited by Leo Suryadinata. Singapore: Institute of Southeast Asian Studies, 2006.

Volksraad: Overzicht Betreffende het Zittingjaar 1928–29. Weltevreden, 1929. [Cited as *Volksraad, 1928–29*]

Wajah Dewan Perwakilan Rakyat Republik Indonesia, Pemilihan Umum 1999. Jakarta: Penerbit Harian Kompas, July 2000. [Cited as *Wajah DPR 1999*]

Wajah DPR & DPD 2009–14: Later Belakang Pendidikan dan Karier. Jakarta: Kompas Penerbit Buku, 2010. [Cited as *Wajah DPR & DPD 2009*]

Wanandi, Jusuf. "The Road Ahead". *Far Eastern Economic Review*, 30 July 1998.

———. *Global, Regional and National: Strategic Issues & Linkages*. Jakarta: CSIS, 2005.

Wang Aiping 王爱平. Yindunixiya kongjiao yanjiu 印度尼西亚孔教研究. Beijing: Zhongguo wenshi chubanshe 中国文史出版社, October 2010. [Cited as Wang Aiping, *Kongjiao yanjiu*]

Ward, Ken. "Upholding the Rule of Law — The Yap Affairs". *Review of Indonesian and Malayan Affairs*, January–March 1968, pp. 1–16.

Warta Bhakti (Jakarta)

"Wei Xiong Jin Feng, Qiao Jian Hexie: Lin Wenguang" 伟雄金峰, 瞧见和谐: 林文光". In *Quanqiu Jiechu Huaren Huazhuan* 全球杰出华人画传 [Global Outstanding Chinese Biography]. Beijing: Zhongguo Wenxian Publisher 中国文献出版社, 2011.

"Welcome to Jakarta International Expo". Available at <http://www.jiexpo.com/hom.php?menu=8&id=4> (accessed 10 December 2011).

Wen Guangyi 温广益. "Situ Zan" 司徒赞. In *Guangdong Ji Huaqiao Mingren Zhuan* 广东籍华侨名人传, edited by Wen Guangyi 温广益. Guangzhou: Guangdong Renmin Publisher 广东人民出版社, 1988.

Who's Who in China (Biographies of Chinese Leaders). 5th ed. Shanghai: China Weekly Review, 1936.

Who's Who in Education. London: Mercury House Business Publications, 1974.

Who's Who in Parliament: A List of Short Biographies of the Members of the House of People's Representatives 1971–76 of the Republic of Indonesia. Jakarta: Departemen Penerangan, [1976]). [Cited as *Who's Who in Parliament 1971–76*]

Williams, Lea E. *Overseas Chinese Nationalism: Genesis of Pan-Chinese Movement in Indonesia 1900–16.* Glencoe: Free Press, 1960. [Cited as Williams, *Nationalism*]

Willmott, Donald E. *The Chinese of Semarang: A Changing Minority Community in Indonesia.* Ithaca: Cornell University Press, 1960. [Cited as Willmott, *Semarang*]

Woodhead, H.G.W., ed. *The China Year Book.* Shanghai, 1938.

World Star (Jakarta). "Data About PT Nusantara Plywood Integrated Wood Working Industries at Gresik (Surabaya)". vol. 1, no. 2 (September 1976): 37.

Wright, A. *Twentieth Century Impression of Netherlands India.* London: Lloyd's Greater Britain Publishing, 1909. [Cited as Wright, *Impression*]

Wu Gongpu 吴公辅. "Tiansheng Ribao Shih Zhou Nian Ji-nian-kan de Shu-wang Chih-lai" 天声日报十周年纪念刊的述往知来. In *Heshu Dongyindu Gailan* 荷属东印度概览 [Netherlands East Indian sketch], by Liu Huanran 刘焕然, section two, p. 30. Singapore: Nanyang Baoshe 南洋报社, 1939.

"Wu Xiehe Xishuo Rensheng" 吴协和戏说人生 manuscript, June 2006.

Xin Bao 新报 (Jakarta)

Xu Jinghan 许经汉. "Huang Dongping Jianli" 黄东平简历. In *Huang Dongping Wenji: Qita Wengao* 黄东平文集: 其它文稿, vol. 10. Jakarta: Jinmen Huzhu Jijinhui Wenhuabu 金门互助基金会文化部, 2003.

Xu Jingxian 徐竞先. *Yinni Shinian* 印尼十年. Jakarta: Xing Qi Ri Baoshe 星期日报社, 1953.

Ya Sheng 雅生. "Yi Situ Zan" 忆司徒赞. *Dipingxian* 地平线 (Hong Kong), February 1980, pp. 9–11.

Yamin Muhammad, ed. *Naskah Persiapan Undang-Undang Dasar 1945*. Vol. 1. Jakarta: Prapantja, 1959. [Cited as Yamin, *Naskah*]

Yan Weizhen Shiwen Xuan 严唯真诗文选. Hong Kong: Huoyi Publisher 获益出版社, 1998.

Yap, Tjwan Beng. *Meratas Jalan Kemerdekaan: Otobiografi seorang Pejuang Kemerdekaan*. Jakarta: Gramedia, 1988.

Yecheng Fujian Zhongxiao Xuexiao Sanshi Zhounian Jinian Tekan 椰城福建中小学校三十周年纪念特刊 [The commemorative issue of the thirtieth anniversary of Fujian primary and high school in Jakarta]. Jakarta: Fujian Huiguan 福建会馆, 1955. [Cited as *Fujian*]

Yindunixiya Ribao 印度尼西亚日报 (Harian Indonesia) (Jakarta). [Cited as *Ribao*]

Yinni Huaqiao de Zainan 印尼华侨的灾难 [The catastrophe of the Overseas Chinese in Indonesia]. Taipei, 1959. [Cited as *Yinni Zainan*]

Yinni Shangye Nianjian 印华商业年鉴 [Indonesian commercial almanac]. Jakarta: Zhonghua Shangbaoshe 中华商报社, 1955. [Cited as *Shangye Nianjian*]

"Yongyuan de Li Shangda" 永远的李尚大. Available at <http://blog.sina.com.cn/s/blog_60d380b40100gemv.htm> (accessed 14 October 2011).

Yoshihara, Kunio. *Oei Tiong Ham Concern: The First Business Empire of Southeast Asia*. Kyoto University, 1989.

Yuan Houchun 袁厚春. Yi ge "Canyu Chuangzao Lishi" de Huaren: *Situ Meisheng Chuanqi* 一个"参与创造历史"的华人: 司徒眉生传奇. Hong Kong: Sanlian Shudian 三联书店, 2005.

Yusrinlie's blog. "dr. Sofyan Tan's Assimilation Style". Available at <http://yusrinlie.wordpress.com/2010/01/27/dr-sofyantans-assimilation-style/> (accessed 4 January 2012).

Zakir Hussain. "Jakarta removes racist video, hunts for culprit". *Straits Times*, 26 August 2012.

Zhang Tieshan 张铁山. "Yinni Huaqiao Sishinian de Cangsang" 印尼华侨四十年的沧桑 [Violent changes in the Indonesian Overseas Chinese society in forty years]. *Ming Bao* 明报 (Hong Kong), March–April 1971. [Cited as Zhang, "Yinni Huaqiao"]

Zhang Yonghe 张永和. *Qiandao zaoxia* 千岛朝霞. Jakarta, 2002.

Zhong Guangxing 钟广兴. *Huaqiao zai Yinni* 华侨在印尼. Taipei, 1959. [Cited as Zhong, *Huaqiao*]

Zhong Xing. *Yejiada Huashang Yanong Gonghui Hongyishun Gonghui Fangong Douzheng jishi* 椰加达华商亚弄公会洪义顺公会反共斗争纪实 [Jakarta Chinese *warung* association and Hung I Hsun association and their struggle against the communists]. Jakarta: n.p., 1952. [Cited as Zhong, *Yanong*]

Zhongcheng Bao 忠诚报 (Jakarta)

Zhou Nanjing 周南京. *Nushantala huayi zongheng* 努山塔拉华裔纵横 [Random Notes on Indonesians of Chinese descent]. Hong Kong Press for Social Sciences Ltd., 2011.

———. *Huaqiao Huaren Baike Quanshu: Renwu juan* [English title: *Encyclopedia of Chinese Overseas, volume of Who's Who* 华侨华人百科全书: 人物卷]. Beijing: Zhongguo Huaqiao Chubanshe, 2001.

———. *Shijie Huaqiao Huaren Cidian* 世界华侨华人辞典 [Dictionary of Overseas Chinese]. Beijing: Peking University, 1993. [Cited as *Cidian*]

Zou Fangjin 邹访今. "Li Qing ji qi Shanshui Si" 犁青及其山水诗. *Haixia Shikan* 海峡诗刊, no. 12 (September 1993): 33–35.

INDEX

A
A Guan, 108
A Hok, 329–30
A WU, 1–2
ABC battery, 33
ABDUSSOMAD, H., 392
Abiturient, 44
ACROCA, 139
Adam Malik, 112, 178, 265, 370
Adi Buddha concept, 81
ADIDHARMA, 2
ADMADJAJA, Usman, 3–4
Affandi, 368
Aga Sampoerna, 239
AI Huina, 35
A.K. Gani, 357
Akademi Teater Nasional Indonesia, 91
ALI, Mohammad, 4
Ali Murtopo, 365
Ali Sadikin, 88, 343
ALIM, Markus, 5
All-England badminton competition, 106, 275, 380
AMIEN, Muhammad, 6

Anang SATYAWARDAYA, 346–47
ANANTA, Aris, 6–7
ANG Ban Tjiong, 7–8
ANG Hian Liang, 273
ANG Jan Goan, 8–9
ANG Tjiang Liat, 9
ANG Tjin Siang, 180, 364
ANG Yu Liang, 364
Angkatan Muda Tionghoa, 41, 246
ANGKOSUBROTO, Dasuki, 10
Antara, 250
Anthony SALIM, 237, 238, 303
anti-Chinese riots, 59
anti-Dutch law, 64
anti-KMT campaign, 31, 68
ANTON, Abah, 10–11
Apa & Siapa, 3
ARBI, Haryanto, 11, 380
Argos Manunggal, 314
Arief BUDIMAN, 258–60
ARIEF, Jackson, 11–12
Arifin, Bustanil, 10
ARSADJAJA, Jani, 349–50

Asia-Pacific Economic
  Co-operation (APEC)
  Secretariat in Singapore, 35
Asian Games, 11, 36
Asian Games Tennis
  Championship, 260
Asmaraman SUKOWATI, 94
Association of Indonesian
  Muslim Intellectuals (ICMI),
  77
Astra International Inc., 263
AUWJONG Peng Koen, 209–10
AW Tjoei Lan, 12

B
BA Ren, 367
BAI Bangying, 381–82
Bai Jiali, 361, 362
Bakom, 87, 256, 257, 261
Bakom-PKB, 370
Bambang SURYONO, 130
Bambang Trihatmodjo, 217,
  225
Bandung Municipal Council,
  336
Bandung Regency Council, 336,
  395
Bangkok Bank, 10, 238
Bank Asia Afrika, 3, 31
Bank Central Asia (BCA), 232,
  233, 237
Bank Danamon, 3
Bank Perkreditan Rakyat
  (BPR), 80
Bank Susila Bhakti, 26
Bank Windu Kencana, 237
BAO Qiu'an, 223–24

Baperki, 9, 37, 41, 43, 44, 79,
  99, 102, 140, 247, 319, 345,
  354, 395
Bapilu (Badan Pengendali
  Pemilihan Umum), 74
BARKI, Kiki, 13
Basuki HIDAYAT, 338–39
Batik Keris, 350
BCA. *See* Bank Central Asia
  (BCA)
Be Biauw Tjwan Bank, 14, 101
BE Kwat Koen, 14
BE Tiat Tjong, 14
Berca Group, 181
Berkat Group, 78
Bintang Mahaputra Utama, 77
Bir Kunci, 307
B.J. Habibie, 264
BKUT, 405
Blora Regency Council, 42
BOE Beng Tjoe, 200, 206–7
Boekhandel Tan Khoen Swie,
  289
BOEN Kin To, 369–70
BONG A Lok, 15
BONG Hong San, 239
BONG Sun On, 361–62
BONG Swan An, 361–62
Bong Tjhai Bun, 16
BPKB-DKI, 77, 87, 257
BPKI, 247
BPR. *See* Bank Perkreditan
  Rakyat (BPR)
Bridgestone Tyres Corporation,
  78
Brigadier-General Supardjo, 341
BUASAN, Bahar, 16

Buby CHEN, 21
BUDIANTA, Melani, 16–17
BUDIKUSUMA, Alan, 17
BUDIMAN, Arief, 17–19
BULOG, 10, 73
Burhan URAY, 217

C
CAI Daoping, 384
CAI Daoxing, 54–55
CAI Huaxi, 359
CAI Liangzhu, 177–78
CAI Qingluan, 344–45
CAI Ruilong, 269–70
CAI Xihui, 345
CAI Xiyin, 345–46
CAI Yasheng, 175–76
CAI Yunhui, 383–84
CAI Zhiliang, 346–47
CAO Dechong, 354–55
CAO Lianxin, 338
C.C. HSU, 388
CCP, 109
Cecillia K., 92, 403
Central Bank of Indonesia, 93
Central Chung Hsioh, 115
Central Cipta Murdaya (CCM) Group, 181
Central Java Provincial Council, 42
Chairani, Leila, 18–19
CHAN Kok Cheng, 20
Charles ONG, 66–67
CHEN Baoyuan, 294–95
CHEN Bingding, 293
CHEN Binghuang, 276–77
CHEN Bingjie, 294

CHEN, Bubi, 21
CHEN Chien-An, 302
CHEN Dajiang, 305–6
CHEN De Xiu Xian, 299
CHEN Dehe, 298
CHEN Deheng, 297–98
CHEN Donglong, 335–36
CHEN Fengwen, 285
CHEN Fuding, 285
CHEN Gongli, 265
CHEN Jian'an, 302
CHEN Jianghe, 305
CHEN Jiangsu, 287
CHEN Jianlu, 287
CHEN Jinfeng, 288
CHEN Jinjian, 288
CHEN Jinlong, 63–64
CHEN Jinniang, 402–3
CHEN Jinshan, 289
CHEN Jinyang, 296–97
CHEN Lianhu, 6–7
CHEN Linru, 291
CHEN Longhu, 304
CHEN Mingli, 303–4
CHEN Qingming, 306–7
CHEN Qingmu, 300–1
CHEN Qiuxue, 89
CHEN Shanhu, 244–45
CHEN Shengfa, 261–62
CHEN Shilin, 25–26
CHEN Tianfu, 308
CHEN Wenjin, 280–81
CHEN Wenxuan, 281
CHEN Xiangji, 295
CHEN Xianglian, 295
CHEN Xianwei, 377–78
CHEN Xingyan, 284

CHEN Xuanming, 297
CHEN Yinghua, 281–82
CHEN Yingzhi, 282–83
CHEN Youfu, 286–87
CHEN Yuanbao, 283–84
CHEN Yuanchang, 76
CHEN Yueming, 264–65
CHEN Yulan, 292–93
CHEN Yuxin, 283
CHEN Zebing, 298–99
CHEN Zhanhu, 244–45
CHEN Zhenlin, 301
CHEN Zhenwen, 6
CHEN Zhongqing, 300
CHEN Zihuang, 307–8
CHEN Zixing, 227–29
CHENG, David G., 23
CHH. *See* Chung Hwa Hui (CHH)
CHH-Netherlands, 14, 57, 183, 256, 291, 302, 325, 346, 393
CHHTC, 93
Chiang Kai-shek, 109
CHIAO, Evelyn, 23–24
China Charity Fund Committee, 67, 318
China News Agency, 366
Chinese Communist Party, 391
Chinese Muslim organization, 10
Chinese Women's Association, 138–39
CH'IU Han-hsing, 226–27
CHOW Li Ing, 181–82
CHTCS, 193
CHTH, 15, 68, 301, 352, 394, 405
CHU Ch'ang-tung, 24

CHU Chong Tong, 24
CHU Kok Seng, 33
CHUA Chee Liang, 346–47
Chung Hsioh, 135, 139, 252, 338
Chung Hwa Hui (CHH), 14, 32, 46, 57, 85, 86, 93, 101, 111, 140, 196, 221, 256, 294, 299, 314, 318, 333, 341, 393–94, 400
Chung Lien Hui, 109, 255
CIPUTRA, 342–43
Cirebon Regency Council, 338
Clinton, Bill, 231, 371
C.M. HSU, 389
CNHT, 42, 99, 134, 266
Confucianism, 75
Conservation Breeding Specialist Group (CBSG), 175
Coopa, N.V., 73
CPPCC, 139, 366, 405
CSIS, 256, 264, 365
CUI Miao, 355
Cultural Revolution, 139, 276
CV Berkat Paper Manufacturing Company, 78

D

DAI Jianwei, 315–17
DAI Yunming, 219
Dalai Lama, 81
Damatex, 314
DANANJAYA, James, 25–26
Dardanella, 402
DARMADI, Jan, 26–27
DARMAPUTERA, Eka, 27
DARMAWAN, Hari, 28
DARMAWAN, Hendra, 28

Index

DARMOHUSODO, K.R.T. Obi, 29
Dasaad Musin Concern, 341
Daud BUDIMAN, 118
Davis Cup competition, 96
DAWIS, Didi, 29–30
Deli Bank, 351–53
DENG Tongli, 309–10
DENG Zhenning, 183
Department of Economics (NUS), 7
Dewan Perancang Nasional, 335, 346
Dewan Pertimbangan Agung (DPA), 256
DEWI, Utami, 30–31
Dharmala Group, 44–45
Diguo de nuer, 65
DIPOJUWONO, Budi, 31
Djajanti Group, 217, 362
Djarum Group, 60, 61
Djawa Hak Boe Tjong Hwee, 116
DJIAUW Pok Kie, 31–32
Djie Sam Soe, 239
DJIE Ting Liat, 32
DJIE Ting Tjioe, 32
DJOJONEGORO, Husain, 33
Djoko HARJONO, 31–32
Djoko SUDJATMIKO, 270–71
Djuhar SUTANTO, 33–34, 225, 238
dokter keresidenan, 4
DPA. *See* Dewan Pertimbangan Agung (DPA)
DPR, 9, 31, 40, 63, 102, 107, 255, 270, 328, 345, 349, 350, 355, 364, 370

DPR-RIS, 397
DPRD, 37, 115
DPRDS, 102
DURIANTO, Darmadi, 34
Dutch Nationality Law, 57, 64

E

East Java Provincial Council, 140
Eddy TANSIL, 227–29
Edward Soeryadjaya, 263
Elsie TJIOK-LIM, 341–42
ERVINNA, 35
ESMARA, Hendra, 35–36
EW YONG Tjhoen Moy, 249–50

F

Faculty of Law at Universitas Indonesia (FHUI), 83, 103–4
FADJRIN, Verawaty, 36
Fanny KHO, 180–81
Farindo Investments, 61
Federation of Siang Hwees, 86
FENG Huilan, 215–16
FENG Laijin, 218–19
FEUI, 76
FHUI. *See* Faculty of Law at Universitas Indonesia (FHUI)
FIQ, 78
First Pacific Holding, 238
FOK Jo Jau, 26–27
Forbes Zibenjia, 62
Fred Young, 262
Fu Sunming, 75
FU Zhikuan, 222
Funü Xiehui, 391
Fuxing She, 265, 266

G

GAN Choo Ho, 37
GAN Fafu, 85
GAN K.L., 37–38, 94
GAN Koen Han, 38–39
GAN Kok Liang, 37–38
GAO Huanyi, 97
GAO Juezhong, 102–3
Gao Shang School, 67
Gatot Subroto, 62
GAUTAMA, Sudargo, 39–40
Gembala Group, 365
General Sumitro, 331
Gesuri Lloyd, 188–89
GINTING, Lo S.H., 40
GKI, 386
Global Nexus Institute (GNI), 371
GMKI, 27
GO Ge Siong, 47–48
GO Gien Tjwan, 41–42
GO Ing Liang, 42
GO Ka Him, 44–45
GO Nen Pin, 225–26
GO (GOUW) Tiauw Goan, 42
GO Tik Swan, 57–58
GO Tjoe Bin, 43
Goei Hing An, 10–11
GOEI Hok Gie, 48–49
GOEI Poo Aan, 43, 48–49
GOEY Tiauw Hong, 43–44
GOH Tjing Hok, 44
Golkar, 102, 270, 365
Golongan Putih, 18
GONDOKUSUMO, Suhargo, 44–45
GOUW Giok Siong, 39–40
GOUW Peng Liang, 45–46, 327, 348
GOW Swie Kie, 10
GOZALI, Hendrick, 46–47
GOZELIE, Tellie, 47
Gu Long, 37–38, 332
Guang Ren, 266
Guangzhao Huiguan, 266
Gudang Garam, 54–55, 383–84
GUNARSA, Singgih D., 47–48
GUNAWAN, Andrew H., 43, 48–49
GUNAWAN, Mu'min Ali, 49–50
GUNAWAN, Rudy, 50
GUO Chunyang, 119–20
GUO Dehuai, 116–18
GUO Hengjie, 112–13
GUO Hongyuan, 50
GUO Jianyi, 120–22
GUO Keming, 113–14
GUO Liangjie, 50–51
GUO Meicheng, 110
GUO Rongfu, 51
GUO Shunde, 115
GUO Shuofeng, 379
GUO Xingyuan, 111
GUO Xuanluan, 116
GUO Yueniang, 344
GUO Yunlian, 114–15
GUO Yuxiu, 51–52
GUO Zaiyuan, 108

H

Habibie, B.J., 231
HADI, Abdul W.M., 52–53
HADINATA, Christian, 53
Hagemayer, N.V., 238

HAKIM, Rachman, 53–54
HALIM, Boediharto, 54
HALIM, Rachman, 54–55
HAN, Awal, 55–56
HAN Haoquan, 55–56
HAN Hoo Tjwan, 55–56
HAN Tiauw Tjong, 56–57
HAN Zhaozong, 56–57
Hancurnya Kerajaan Han, 95
Harapan Group, 228
HARDJONAGORO, Kanjeng Raden Tumenggung, 57–58
HARSONO, FX, 59–60
HARTONO, Michael Bambang, 60–61
HARTONO, Robert Budi, 60–61
HASAN, Mohammad Bob, 62–63
HASSAN, Hadji Mohammad, 63–64
Hauw San Liang, 348
HAUW Tek Kong, 64, 184
HCTH, 32, 116, 401
HCTNH, 99, 309
HE Chunlin, 69
HE Longchao, 68
He Xiaokun (Ho Sioe Koen, Samadikun Hartono), 69
HE Zhenkang, 68–69
HE Zhi, 69
HEI Ying, 64–65
Hendra KARTANEGARA, 286–87
Hendrick GOZALI, 188
Hendrick SIE, 126–27
Henry PRIBADI, 217
Heping Ribao, 226
H.H. KAN, 57, 86–87, 111–12

Hibernia Bancshares Corporation, 238
HIDAYAT, Basuki, 66
HIE Foek Tjhoy, 66
HIM Tek Ji, 84
HIMAWAN, Charles, 66–67
HIOE Njan Joeng, 67–68
HO Liong Tiauw, 68
HO Tjek, 69
Hok Kian Hwee Koan (Medan), 98, 110, 401
HONG Abi, 11
Hong Boen Hwee, 96
HONG Le Hoa, 253–54
HONG Yuanyuan, 8–9
HONORIS, Charles, 68–69
HONORIS, Otje, 69
HOO Eng Djie, 69–70
HOU Deguang, 64
HU Fengwen, 59–60
Hua Zhong, 128, 265
HUANG Anshu, 200
HUANG Changshui, 207–8
HUANG Dongping, 2, 208–9
HUANG Fengli, 203–5
HUANG Haichun, 202–3
HUANG Hanshan, 239
HUANG Honglan, 374
HUANG Huilan, 191
HUANG Huixiang, 60–61
HUANG Huizhong, 61
HUANG Jianguo, 370–71
HUANG Jinchang, 206–7
HUANG Jinquan, 242–43
HUANG Longtai, 193
HUANG Meiling, 200–2

HUANG Qianghui, 205–6
HUANG Qingxing, 87
HUANG Shaofan, 88–89
HUANG Shuang'an, 361–62
HUANG Songchang, 373–74
HUANG Yicong, 371–72
HUANG Yifa, 190
HUANG Yizhu, 192
HUANG Yongzhou, 192–93
HUANG Yurong, 71–72
Huang Zhen, 367
HUANG Zhonghan, 194
HUANG Zida, 194–95
HUANG Zongxiao, 195–96
HUANG Zongxuan, 197
HUANG Zongyi, 196–97
Huaqiao Buxiao, 391
Huaqiao Gonghui, 401
Huaqiao Zhongxue, 30
Hundred Day Reform, 134
HUO Zuoyou, 26–27
Husada Hospital, 48, 133
HUSINO, M.H., 72–73
HUSNI, Arief, 73
HUTOMO, Suryo, 73–74

I

Ibnu Sutowo, 178, 263, 357
ICMI. *See* Association
  of Indonesian Muslim
  Intellectuals (ICMI)
IE Tjoen Siang, 74
Ikatan Akontan Indonesia, 28
Ikatan Arsitek Indonesia, 111
IKIP, 326
IM Jang Tju, 285
IM Yang Tjoe, 285

IMF. *See* International Monetary
  Fund (IMF)
Indocement, 237
Indonesian Association of
  Architects (IAI), 56
Indonesian Central Bank, 4
Indonesian Chinese society, 1
Indonesian economy, 63
Indonesian Plywood
  Association, 62
INJO Beng Goat, 75
Institute for the Defence of
  Human Rights, 396
International Monetary Fund
  (IMF), 93
IRAWAN, Bingky, 75
Iriani Dewi Karim, 88
ISKANDAR, Nathanel, 76
Islamic community, 75
ISMANTO, Adil, 280
Istiqal Mosque Project, 87
ITEM, 300–1
Ivana LIE, 61

J

Jack OEI, 196–97
JAHJA, Junus, 77–78
Jakarta Municipal Council, 341,
  401
Jamu Jago, 272
Jan Darmadi Group, 26
JANANTO, Soetopo, 78–79
Jang Seng Ie, 100, 115, 240, 245,
  401
JAUW Keng Hong, 79, 103
JAYA, David Herman, 79–80
Jeanne LAKSANA, 403

JI Mingfa, 53
JI Qihui, 13
JIAN Fuhui, 86–87
JIANG Weitai, 178–79
JIN Aiqin, 92–93
Jin Yong, 332
Jinan University, 267
JINARAKKHITA, Bhikku Ashin, 81–82
JNXT, 8
JOHAN, Daniel, 82
Johan WAHYUDI, 356
John LIE, 142
Johor Sultan, 78
Junus Nur Arif, 184–85
JUSUF, Ester Indahyani, 83
Jusuf PANGESTU, 218–19
JUSUF, Tedy, 84

K

Kadin, 236
KAM Hwat Hok, 85
KAMI, 270, 364
KAMIL, Iskandar, 85
KAN Hok Hoei, 86–87, 221
Kang Youwei, 134
Kangjeng Raden Tumenggung (KRT), 29
Kanindotex, 331
Kao Shang, 356, 387–88
KARIM, Hadji Abdul, 87–88
KARMAN, Hasan, 88–89
KARTAJAYA, Hermawan, 89–90
KARWANDY, 90
Karwin, John, 395
KARYA, Teguh, 91–92

K.C. CHAN, 20
KE Gui'an, 73–74
KE Quanshou, 109–10
KE Xinbiao, 363
KENCANAWATI, Cecillia, 92–93
Keng Po, 64, 75, 123, 184, 206
K.H. JAUW, 79
KHARMAWAN, Byanti, 93–94
KHO Liang Ie, 94
KHO Ping Hoo, 94–96
KHO Sin Kie, 96
KHO Tjeng Lie, 273
KHO Tjien Tiong, 268–69
KHO Tjoen Gwan (Wan), 96–97
KHO Wan Gie, 97
KHOE A Fan, 97–98
KHOE Siat Ting, 97–98
KHOE Soe Kiam, 240
KHOE Tjeng Tek, 98
KHOE Woen Sioe, 98–99, 184
Khong Kauw, 116
KHOUW Bian Tie, 93
KHOUW Hok Goan, 99
KHOUW Ke Hien, 100
KHOUW Kim An, 100–1, 220
KHOUW Thian Tong, 243–44
Ki Hadjar SUKOWIJONO, 285
Kian Gwan, 140
KIN Ai Tjin, 92–93
KNIP, 294
KO Hong An, 101
KO Kwat Oen, 102
KO Kwat Tiong, 79, 102–3, 105
KO Swan Sik, 103–5
KO Tjay Sing, 103, 105

KOO Bo Tjhan, 99
Koo, Wellington, 191
KOSASIH, S.T.L. 1917, 102
KOSASIH, Tirtawinata, 105–6
Kostrad, 365
kungfu novel, 38, 94–95, 229
KUO Lay Yen, 298
Kuomintang (KMT), 15, 67, 230, 352, 355, 388, 394, 401
KUSUMA, Eddie, 107–8
KUSUMA, Sugianto, 108
KWA Khay Twan, 109
KWA Kwie An, 73–74
KWA Sien Biauw, 363
KWA Tjoan Sioe, 109–10, 115, 138–39
KWEE Bie Sin, 110
KWEE Djie Hoo, 110–11
KWEE Eng Hoe, 51
KWEE Han Liem, 350
KWEE Han Tjiong, 350
KWEE Hin Goan, 111–13
KWEE Hing Tjiat, 112–13, 393
KWEE Kek Beng, 9, 42, 111–14
KWEE Oen Liam, 114–15
KWEE Soen Tik, 115
KWEE Som Tjok, 350
KWEE Swan Lwan, 116
KWEE Tek Hoay, 116–18, 344
KWEE Thiam Tjing, 118–19
KWEE Thian Hong, 118
KWEE Tjoa Kwang, 90
KWEE Yat Nio, 344
KWIK Djoen Eng, 119–20
KWIK Kian Gie, 120–22

L
Las Tiga, 79

LAUW Chuan Tho, 77
LAUW Giok Lan, 122–23, 184
LAUWANI, Siegvrieda, 123
LEE Man Fong, 123–24
LEE Teng Hui, 124
Lekra, 262, 368
Lembaga Bantuan Hukum, 396
Lembaga Pembinaan Hukum Nasional, 104
LEMBONG, Eddie, 54, 124–26, 375
Lemhanas, 141
LESMANA, Hendrawan, 126–27
Lev, Daniel S., 244
LI Bai, 230–32
LI Chunming, 127–28
LI Demei, 132–33
LI Denghui, 124
LI Deqing, 141–42
LI Jianjin, 136
LI Jiedeng, 4
LI Jinfu, 137–38
LI Manfeng, 123–24
LI Mei, 110, 138–39
LI Mindong, 47
LI Ningbiao, 138
LI Ping'an, 140
LI Qing, 128
LI Ruihua, 385
LI Shuanghui, 140–41
LI Weikang, 1–2
LI Wenming, 49–50
LI Wenzheng, 232–33
LI Xiangsheng, 234
LI Xinglian, 134
LI Xu, 129
LI Xu'nan, 129

LI Yinghua, 135
LI Yingzheng, 134
LI Yonglong, 2
LI Yuanli, 278
LI Yudao, 270–71
LI Yunfu, 139
LI Yuxiao, 270
LI Zhuohui, 130–31
LIANG Bingnong, 185
LIANG Chiu Sia, 131–32, 356
LIANG Hailiang, 106
LIANG Qiuxia, 131–32
LIANG Youlan, 184–85
Liang Yusheng, 37
LIAO Ziran, 132
LIE Dharmawan, 132–34
LIE Eng Liong, 2
LIE Giok Hauw, 270
LIE Giok Tho, 270–71
LIE Guan Die, 278
LIE Hin Liam, 134
LIE Ing Hoa, 135
LIE Ing Tien, 134
LIE, Ivanna, 135
LIE Khe Bo, 135
LIE Kian Joe, 136
LIE Kian Kim, 136, 395
LIE Kiat Teng, 4
LIE Kim Hok, 137–38, 220
LIE Ling Piao, Alvin, 138
LIE Mei, 138–39
LIE Men Dong, 47
LIE Mo Ming, 49–50
LIE Mo Tie, 232–33
LIE Oen Hock, 139
LIE Oen Sam, 139–40
LIE Ping An, 140

LIE Po Yoe, 31
LIE Siong Hwie, 140–41
Lie Soen Liang, 2
LIE Tek Bie, 132–33
LIE Tek Tjeng, 141–42
LIE Tjeng Tjoan, John, 142
LIE Tjian Tjoen, 12, 143
LIE Tjwan Sien, 143
LIE Tjwan Sioe, 144–45
LIEM A Pat, 145
LIEM Bian Khoen, 364–65
LIEM Bian Kie, 365–66
LIEM Boen Hwa, 54
LIEM Boen Siang, 146
LIEM Bwan Tjie, 146–47
LIEM Eng Hway, 188–89
LIEM Fung Sen, 235–36
LIEM Ho Ban, 147
LIEM Hok Liong, 260–61
LIEM Hwie Giap, 147–48
LIEM Hwie Liat, 148
LIEM K.D., 149
LIEM Khiam Soen, 149
LIEM Khiem Yang, 149–50
LIEM Khing Hoo, 150–51
LIEM Koe Nio, 396
LIEM Koen Beng, 151
LIEM Koen Hian, 103, 114, 119,
  151–52, 213, 247, 282, 298, 323
LIEM Koen Seng, 153
LIEM Kwi Boen, 153
LIEM, Lita, 260
LIEM Oen Kian, 33–34, 238
Liem Peng Hong, 263
LIEM Sam Tjiang, 115, 153–54
LIEM Seng Tee, 154, 239
LIEM Sik Tjo, 154–55

Liem Sioe Hie, 236, 237
LIEM Sioe Liong, 30, 33, 225, 232, 236–39, 343, 372
LIEM Soen Joe, 381
LIEM Swie King, 61, 106, 155–56
LIEM Tek Siang, 189–90
LIEM Thay Tjwan, 156
LIEM Thian Joe, 156–57
LIEM Tien Pao, 239
LIEM Tjae Le, 157
LIEM Tjing Hien, 157, 180
LIEM Tjing Hien-Kho, 180–81
LIEM Tjoan Hok, 91
LIEM Tjong Hian, 158
LIEM Toan Tek, 158
LIEM Twan Djie, 158–59
LIEM Wan King, 79–80
LIM Hiong Tjheng, 159
LIM Kek Tjiang, 160–61, 341–42
LIM Sin Tjoei, 229
LIM Sui Khiang, 161
LIM Tek Tjun, 34
LIN Che Wei, 161–62
LIN Dechun, 34
LIN Dexiang, 189–90
LIN Fengsheng, 235–36
LIN Fuliang, 260–61
LIN Guanyu, 275–76
LIN Mianji, 365–66
LIN Miankun, 364–65
LIN Qingshan, 163
LIN Quanfu, 91
LIN Shaoliang, 236–39
LIN Tianbao, 239
LIN Wanjin, 79–80

LIN Wanli, 163–64
LIN Wenguang, 5
LIN Wenhua, 54
LIN Wenjing, 33–34
LIN Yinghuai, 188–89
LIN Yunhao, 225
LIN Zhiqiang, 389–90
LING Nanlong, 164
LING Yunchao, 165
LIONG Sit Yoe, 165–66
LIPI, 141, 292, 315, 316, 322
LITELNONI, Benny Alexander, 166
LIU Chun Wai, 166–67
LIU Ing Wen, 123
LIU Jinduan, 167–68, 266–67
LIU Lanfang, 35
LIU Nam Sian, 168
LIU Quandao, 77
LIU Shunyan, 375
LIU Yaozeng, 169
LIU Yingwen, 123
LIU Yulan, 122–23
LIYANTO, Abraham Paul, 169–70
LO Siang Hien, 40
LOA Sek Hie, 170
LOE Ping Kian, 170–71
LOHANDA, Mona, 171
LPKB, 77, 257, 261, 271, 386
LRKN, 141
LUKITA, Enggartiasto, 172
LUNANDI, Andy, 172–73
LUO Xiangxing, 40
LYMAN, Susanta, 173–74

M
MA Xuling, 271

MAH Soo Lay, 174
Majelis Agama Khonghucu Indonesia (Matakin), 74
Majelis Ulama Indonesia, 77, 87
MANANSANG, Jansen, 175–76
Mangkunegoro VII, 14
Mantrust/Maxim Company, 265
Mao Zedong, 404
MARCHING, Soe Tjen, 176
MARGA T., 177–78
Mari Cecelia PANG Hui Lan, 215–16
MarkPlus, 89
Markus, Alim, 5
Martinus Yosefus Marwoto Hadi SOESASTRO, 264–65
MASAGUNG, 178–79
Masjumi, 87
May Fourth Movement, 404
Mayapada Group, 278, 279
Mingkie, 264
MO Zhuangliang, 179
Mochtar RIADY, 49–50, 230–33, 278–79
MOCKTAR, Brilian, 179
Modern Group, 69
Mohamad SALEH, 102–3
Mohammad ANTON, 10–11
Mohammad Hatta, 178
MOK Tjoang Liang, 179
Monsieur d'AMOUR, 186–87
MPR, 236
MPRS, 364, 365
Mu You, 197–98
Muhammadiyah, 77, 87
MULJADI, 180
MULJADI, Kartini, 180–81

Murdaya POO, 126
MURDAYA, Siti Hartati, 181–82, 222–23
Murdaya Widyawimarta POO, 181–82, 222–23
Muslim Friendship Association, 6

N
NAGA, Dali Santun, 182–83
NANGOI, T., 183
NDC, 15, 271
NG Sim Kie, 184
NG Soei Chong, 107
Niciren Syosu, 12
NIO Hap Liang, 106
NIO Joe Lan, 184–85
NIO Peng Liong, 185
NIO Pik Wan, 30–31
NIO, Threes, 186
NJOO Cheong Seng, 70, 186–87, 261, 402–3
NJOO Han Siang, 47, 187–88, 370
NOTOWIDJOJO, Suhendro, 188
NU, 10, 63, 64
NURIMBA, Adil A., 188–89
NURSALIM, Sjamsul, 189–90
Nyonya Meneer, 210–11

O
OCAC, 366
OE Siang Djie, 190
OEI Ek Tjhong, 371–72
OEI Gee Hwat, 190
OEI Gwie Siong, 60–61
OEI Gwie Tiong, 61

OEI Hai Djoen Tj, 202–3
OEI Hong Lan, 374
Oei Hong Liong, 372
OEI Hui Lan, 191–92
OEI Ik Tjoe, 192
OEI Jong Tjioe, 192–93
OEI Kie Hok, 193
OEI Liong Thay, 193
OEI Tiong Ham, 191–92, 194–97
Oei Tiong Ham Concern, 32, 113
OEI Tjeng Hien, 87
OEI Tjin San, 386
OEI Tjin Tik, 272–73
OEI Tjo Iem, 233
OEI Tjoe, 192
OEI Tjoe Tat, 194–95, 395
OEI Tjong Hauw, 113, 195–96, 282
OEI Tjong Ie, 196–97
OEI Tjong Swan, 197
OEI Tong Pin, 2
OEN Boen Ing, 29
OEN Tek Hian, 197–98
OEN Tiong Hauw, 199–200
OEN Tjhing Tiauw, 198–99
OETOMO, Dede, 199–200
OEY An Siok, 200, 206
OEY Hay Djoen, 202–3
OEY Hong Lee, 203–5
OEY Hong Tjiauw, 205
OEY Kian Hoei, 205–6
OEY Kim Tiang, 200, 206–7
OEY Kwie Tek, 28
OEY Liang Lee, Paulus Ignatius, 207

OEY Tiang Tjoei, 207–8, 282
OEY Tong Pin, 208–9
OEY-GARDINER, Mayling, 200–2
OEYHAYDJUN, 202–3
OH Hong Boen, 59–60
OH Sien Hong, 72–73
OJONG, Petrus Kanisius, 209–10
O.K.T., 206–7
Olympic Games, 205–6
ONG Ah Lok, 15
ONG, Charles, 210–11
ONG Eng Die, 211
Ong Ewe Hock, 380
ONG Hok Ham, 211–12
ONG Hok Lan, 212–13
ONG Joe San, 124–26
ONG Liang Kok, 213
ONG Seng Keng, 73
ONG Siang Tjoen, 213
ONG Sin King, 73
ONG Siong Tjie, 214
ONG Tek Bie, 35–36
ONG Tjin Liong, 382
ONG Tjoe Kim, 214
ONG Tjong Hai, 256–57
ONG Tjong Hauw, 229–30
ONGHOKHAM, 211–12
Oto SUASTIKA, 249
OU Cuilan, 12
OUW Tjoei Lan, 12
OUYANG Bingkun, 209–10
OUYANG Chunmei, 249–50

P
Pa Chung, 266

Pa Hwa, 84
Paguyuban Sosial Marga Tionghoa Indonesia (PSMTI), 84, 375
PAN Guochang, 272
Pan Indonesia Bank (Panin), 26, 49
PAN Jinghe, 220
PAN Liangyi, 221
PAN Wanxin, 380
Pancasila, 27, 81, 259
PANGESTU, Mari, 218–19
PANGESTU, Mari Elka, 215–16
PANGESTU, Prajogo, 216–18
Pangkal Pinang Conference, 43
PANGLAYKIM, Jusuf, 215–16, 218–19, 283
Panitia Penjuluhan Asimilasi, 77
Pantjawarna, 42
Pantoen Melajoe Makassar, 8
Pao-an Tui, 354
Parama Arta, 97
Parkindo, 102
Partai Katholik, 40, 140, 255–56, 271, 349, 382
Partai Kebangkitan Bangsa, 82
Partai Muslimin Indonesia, 87
Partai Tionghoa Indonesia (PTI), 97, 101, 103, 105, 119, 247, 253, 327, 333, 346
Pasar Swalayan Hari-Hari, 28
PASI, 62, 63
PATROS, Asmin, 219
Paul MAWIRA, 283–84
PDI, 121
PDTI, 9, 75, 98, 195, 294, 314, 318, 319, 349

PEB, 340, 400
PECC, 366
Pek Liong Pokiam, 95
PEK Pang Eng, 381–82
Pembangunan Jaya, 343
Pemoeda Agama Khonghoetjoe Indonesia, 337
PENG Yunpeng, 216–18
peranakan community, 46, 78, 86
Perbuddhi, 81
Perhimi, 48, 109
Perkumpulan Peladjar Sekolah Menengah Indonesia (PPSMI), 255
Perniagaan, 95
Persatuan Islam Tionghoa Indonesia (PITI), 10, 87
Persatuan Tionghoa (PT), 314, 318, 319, 324
Persatuan Wartawan Surabaya, 327
Persekutuan Gereja Indonesia, 27
Perserikatan Kaoem Boeroeh Goela, 96
Perserikatan Perhimpunan2 Mahasiswa Indonesia (PPMI), 48
Persidja, 381
Pertamina, 263, 357
Perwitt, 327
P.H. Fromberg, 348
PHANG Djun Phen, 216–18
PHOA Keng Hek, 100, 137, 220
PHOA Kok Tjiang, 272
PHOA Liong Gie, 111, 116, 221, 253

Piagam Asimilasi, 44, 77
Pin Tiong, 3
Ping Min Niu Sze Hui, 254
Pita KALIANA, 200
PITI. *See* Persatuan Islam Tionghoa Indonesia (PITI)
PKI, 96, 248, 262, 354–55, 368
P.L. GOUW, 45–46
PMKRI, 255, 257, 270, 365
PNI, 31, 63, 114, 345, 370, 397
POEY Kok Gwan, 221
Poh An Tui, 66
POO Tjie Guan, 222
POUW Kioe An, 223–24
PPI, 272
PPSMI. *See* Perkumpulan Peladjar Sekolah Menengah Indonesia (PPSMI)
Prajogo PANGESTU, 225, 264
Prasetya Mulya, 121
PRAWIROHUSODO, 224
PRIBADI, Henry, 225
Priguna SIDHARTA, 249
Probosutedjo, 383
PSI, 73, 294
PSII, 4
PSMTI. *See* Paguyuban Sosial Marga Tionghoa Indonesia (PSTMI)
PT, 98–99, 319
PT Bina Sarana Papan, 305
PT central board, 136
PURNOMO, Nurdin, 225–26
Pusat Organisasi Buruh (POB), 73
PWI, 260

Q

Qiao Lian, 24, 405
Qiao Zong, 51, 128, 267, 268, 405
Qinghua Zhongxue, 386
Qiong Yao, 92
QIU Chengshao, 105–6
QIU Hanxing, 226–27
QIU Qingde, 98
QIU Siqian, 240
QIU Wenxiu, 98–99
QIU Yafan, 97–98
QIU Yuanrong, 67–68
QIU Zheng'ou, 226–27

R

Rachman HALIM, 383, 384
RAHARDJA, Hendra, 227–29, 307
RAHARDJA, Subur, 229
RAHMANATA, A.M., 229–30
Rama Moorti van Java, 299
Ranggawarsita, 81
RAO Boji, 31–32
RAO Jian, 230
RAO Yaowu, 3–4
Rashid Sidek, 11
Rhoma Irama, 11
RIADY, James Tjahaja, 230–33
RIADY, Mochtar, 49–50, 230–33, 278–79
Ridder Oranje Nassau, 351
RIDWAN, Ignatius, 233
Robbi CAHYADI, 331
Robby SIE, 331
ROMO, 223–24

Round Table Conference, 183, 256
RRI Orchestra, 2
R.T. Sumantri, 23
Rudy Hartono KURNIAWAN, 30–31, 106–7, 364
Rumah Sakit Mohammad Husni, 4

S
SADELI, Eddy, 234
Sai Baba, 81
Salam SUTRAWAN, 259–60
SALIM, Anthony, 235–36
Salim Economic Development Corporation, 237
SALIM, Soedono, 33–34, 61, 235–39
Sam Kauw Hwee, 81, 116, 240, 344
SAMPOERNA, Putera, 239
SANJAYA, Christiandy, 239
Santa Maria, 59
SASANASURYA, 240
SASTRADJAJA, 223–24
SATJADININGRAT, TKP, 240
Satya Lencana Kebaktian Sosial medal, 4
Satyalencana Kebudayaan, 25
S.E.A. Write Award, 52
Semarang Municipal Council, 14, 314
Seni Teater Kristen Jakarta, 99
SESKO, 141
SETIABUDI, Natan, 241–42
SETIAWAN, Chandra, 242–43

SETIAWAN, Daniel Budi, 243
SETIONO, Benny Gatot, 243–44
Shang Lian, 67, 110, 387
Shannu, 244–45
SHEN Ailing, 83
SHEN Demin, 245–46
SHEN Ji'ai, 256
SHEN Miniang, 253–54
SHEN Teh Min, 245–46
SHI Furen, 17–19
SHI Fuyi, 258–59
SHI Libi, 259–60
SHI Shengfang, 341–42
SHI Wenlian, 251–52
Siang Hwee, 9, 50–51, 67, 74, 110, 134, 141, 301, 318, 351, 353, 356, 388, 401
SIAUW Giok Bie, 246–47
SIAUW Giok Tjhan, 102, 199, 202, 207, 246–48, 291, 395
SIAUW Tik Kwie, 249
SIDHARTA, Myra, 249–51
SIDHARTA, Priguna, 250–51
SIE Boen Lian, 251–52
SIE Pek Giok, 249–51
SIE, Peter, 252–53
SIE Thiam Ie, 252–53
SIE Tjia-Ie, 331
SIE Tjin Gwan, 253
SIEM Piet Nio, 253–54
Sigit Harjojudanto, 62
SIK Sian Han, 188
SILALAHI, Harry Tjan, 254–56
SIM Ai Ling, 83
SIM Ki Ay, 256, 338
Sin Hwa, 235, 391

Sin Ming Hui, 98, 102, 136, 240, 255, 256, 338
Sin Po, 42, 46, 64, 97, 112, 116, 122, 317, 348, 389
Sin Tit Po, 43, 119, 247
SINDHUNATHA, Kristoforus, 212–13, 256–57
Singara Kulla-Kullawa, 70
Sitor Situmorang, 135
SITU Meisheng, 265–66
SITU Zan, 266–67
SMA Bhineka Tunggal Ika, 79
SNB. *See* Solidaritas Nusa Bangsa (SNB)
Social Welfare Association, 38
SOE Hok Djin, 17–19
SOE Hok Gie, 17–19, 258–60
SOE Lie-Piet, 258–60
Soe Po Sia (*Huaqiao Shubaoshe*), 98, 141, 347, 385
Soe Soei Tiong Hoa Ie Wan, 134
Soedjatmoko, 259
Soedjono Hoemardani, 364
SOEGIARTO, Lita, 260
Soeharto, 1, 30, 32, 41, 54, 59, 61–63, 135, 178, 181, 202, 216, 231, 238, 242, 256, 286, 359, 362, 364, 372
SOEJATMIKO, Basuki, 199–200, 260–61
Soekarno, 17, 23, 24, 44, 70, 102, 111, 178, 252, 258, 265, 389, 396
SOEMANTO, Agoes, 261–62
SOERYADJAYA, William, 262–64
SOESASTRO, M. Hadi, 264–65
SOETANTYO, Tegoeh, 265

SOETO Meisen, 265–67
SOETO Tjan, 265–67
Solidaritas Nusa Bangsa (SNB), 83
Solo Court, 29
SONG Zhongquan, 267–68
Southeast Asian Games, 385
Special Project National Schools (SNPC), 68, 106, 405
SPMJ, 79
SPNC, 32
Sri Susuhunan Solo, 14
SRIMULAT, Teguh, 268–69
Steve LIEM, 91
"Sub-Rosa", 20
Subandrio, 396
Sudarso, 368
SUDIN, 269–70
SUDJATMIKO, Djoko, 270
SUDJATMIKO, Prasasto, 270–71
Sukabumi Municipal Council, 324
Sukiman, 407
SULINDRO, Be, 271
Sultan Hamengku Buwono IX, 178
Summa Bank, 263
SUN Peng Yen, 271–72
Sun Yat-sen, 46, 98
SUNUR, Eliaser Yentji, 271–72
SUPRANA, Jaya, 272
SUPRATIKNO, Hendrawan, 272–73
Surabaya Municipal Council, 327
SURIPTO, Ateng, 273
SURYADI, Petrus Aang, 273–74

SURYAWAN, Yoza, 274
SUSANTI, Susi Lucia Francisca, 275
SUSANTO, T.L., 275–76, 359
Susi SUSANTI, 17, 61, 131
Susilo Bambang Yudhoyono, 239
Susuhunan Paku Buwono XII, 58
Sutanto L.T., 226
SUTANU, Tommie, 276–77
SUTRISNO, Slamet, 277
Suwandi HAMID, 15
SUWONDO, Gani, 278
Suyanto, 45
Swatow Railway, 351, 353
SZE TU Mei Sen, 265–66

T
Ta Hsioh Sing Hwee, 72, 75
Ta-Chung Sze, 354
Tahir, 278–79
TAI Yun Ming, 219
Taman Safari Indonesia (TSI), 175
TAN Beng Yauw, 279–80
TAN Boen Aan, 280
TAN Boen Kim, 280–81
TAN Boen Soan, 281
TAN Eng Hoa, 281–82
TAN Eng Hong, 282
TAN Eng Tie, 282–83
TAN Giok Lan, 292–93
TAN Giok Sin, 283
TAN Goan Po, 283–84
TAN Goan Tiang, 76
TAN Hian Wie, 377–78

TAN Hin Hie, 284
TAN Hoe Teng, 285
TAN Hong Boen, 285
TAN Hwat Tiang, 286
TAN Joe Hok, 135, 286–87
TAN Kang Ho, 305
TAN Kang So, 287
TAN Kian An, 302
TAN Kian Lok, 287
TAN Kim Bo, 288
TAN Kim Hong, 288
TAN Kim Kian, 288
TAN Kim Liong, 63–64
TAN Kim Nio, 402–3
TAN Kim San, 289
TAN Kim Yang, 296–97
TAN King Po, 240
TAN Kiong Liep, 265
TAN Koen Swie, 289–90
TAN Kong Tam, 290
TAN Lian Hou, 6–7
TAN Liep Tjiauw, 290–91
TAN Ling Djie, 183, 247, 291, 345
TAN Liong Houw, 304
TAN, Mely G., 292–93
TAN Pia Teng, 287, 293
TAN Ping Liem, 293
TAN Ping Tjiat, 294
TAN Po Goan, 294–95, 395
TAN Siang Lian, 295
TAN Siong Kie, 295
TAN Soe Lin, 25–26
TAN, Sofyan, 296–97
TAN Swan Bing, 297
TAN Tay Kang, 305–6
TAN Tek Heng, 297–98

TAN Tek Ho, 298
TAN Tek Peng, 298–99
TAN Thiam Hok, 308
TAN Tik Sioe Sian, 289, 299
TAN Tiong Ien, 241
TAN Tiong Khing, 300
TAN Tjan Hok, 28
TAN Tjeng Bok, 300–1
TAN Tjien Lien, 301
TAN Tjin Beng, 306–7
TAN Tjioe Hak, 89
TAN Tjiok Sien, 16–17
TAN Tjoe Hien, 227–29
TAN Tjoe Hong, 307–8
TAN Tjoen Hay, 302
TAN Tju Fuan, 307–8
TAN To, 244–45
TAN Yueh Ming, 264–65
TANDIONO, Ki Anan, 302
TANG Chongrong, 357–59
T'ANG Leang-Li, 322–23
TANG Liangli, 322–23
TANG Xinniang, 324
TANG Youlan, 321–22
TANG Yu, 356–57
TANN Sing Hwat, 261–62
TANNOS, W.P.A., 303
TANOESOEDIBJO, Hary, 303–4
TANOTO, Latif Harris, 304
TANOTO, Sukanto, 305
TANSIL, Eddy, 307–8
TANUDJAJA, Sukanta, 305–6
TANUWIBOWO, Budi S., 306–7
TANZIL, Haris Otto Kamil, 308
Teater Populer, 91

TEDJOSUWITO, 309
Teguh Slamet RAHARDJO, 268–69
Tempo, 62
TENG, Benny, 309–10
TENG Sioe Hie, 310
TENG Tjin Leng, 183, 345
T.H. THUNG, 325–26
THE Bwan An, 81–82
THE Goan Tjoan, 310–11
THE Hong Oe, 311
THE Kian Seng, 62–63
THE Kian Sing, 311
THE Liang Gie, 312–13
THE Neng King, 313–14
THE Oen Hien, 27
THE Sin Tjo, 314
THE Teng Chun, 314–15
THE Tjhoen Swie, 309
THEE Kian Wie, 283, 315–17
THHK, 8, 9, 14, 42, 73, 74, 85, 97–101, 110, 137, 195, 198, 261, 268, 298, 333, 354, 356, 395
THHT, 42
THIO In Lok, 317
THIO Soei Sen, 317
THIO Thiam Tjong, 318–19
THIO Tiauw Siat, 319–21, 351
THIO Tjin Boen, 321
Thomas Cup, 11, 50, 53, 106, 356, 364, 380
THUNG Ju Lan, 321–22
THUNG Liang Lee, 322–24
THUNG Liang Tjay, 323–24
THUNG Sin Nio, Betsy, 324

Index   491

THUNG Thay Tung, 11–12
THUNG Tjeng Hiang, 325–26
TILAAR, Martha, 326
TIO Hian Sioe, 327
TIO Ie Soei, 223, 327
TIO Kiang Sun, 328
TIO Oen Bik, 328–29
Tiong Hoa Im Gak Hwee, 85
Tiong Hoa Kie Tok Kauw Hwee, 102, 395
Tionghoa Bank, 98
TJAHAJA PURNAMA, Basuki, 329–30
TJAHAJA PURNAMA, Basuri, 330
TJAHJADI, Robby, 331
TJAN Ing Djiu, 332
Tjan Khay Sing, 57
TJAN Kiem Bie, 332–33
TJAN Som Hay, 333
TJAN Tian Soe, 333
TJAN Tjoe Siem, 333–35
TJAN Tjoe Som, 325, 333–35
TJAN Tjoen Hok, 254–56
TJANDINEGARA, Wilson, 335–36
TJEN Djin Tjong, 336
TJEN, Rudianto, 336–37
TJEN Tjau Tjen, 336–37
TJHIE Pwee Giok, 326
TJHIE Tjay Ing, 337–38
TJHO Lian Sin, 338
TJIA Eng Tong, 338
TJIA Giok Thwan, 338–39
TJIA Kian Liong, 262–64
Tjia Kian Tie, 263

Tjia Kian Yoe, 263
TJIA, May On, 339–40
TJIA Tjeng Siang, 340
TJIAM Djoe Khiam, Fredericus Christophorus, 340–41
TJIE Tjin Hoan, 342–43
TJIO Tiang Soey, 341
TJIO Wie Tay, 178–79
TJIOK San Fang, Elsie, 341–42
TJIPUTRA, 342–43
TJOA Hin Hoey, 116–18, 344–45
TJOA Ing Hwie, 383–84
TJOA Keng Loan, Effie, 344–45
TJOA Liang Tjoe, 177–78
TJOA Sie Hwie, 345
TJOA Sik Ien, 183, 328, 345–46
TJOA Soei Leng, 269–70
TJOA Tjie Liang, 346–47
TJOA Toh Heng, 54–55
TJOE Bou San, 8–9, 113, 347–48
TJOE Siauw Hoei, 348
TJOE Tit Fat, 277
TJOENG Lin Sen, 349
TJOENG Tin Jan, 349–50
TJOKROSAPUTRO, Handoko, 350
TJOKROSAPUTRO, Kasom, 350
TJONG A Fie, 351–54
TJONG Hioen Nji, 352–53
TJONG Jok Nam, 353–54

TJONG Jong Hian, 351–54
TJONG Yiauw Hian, 351–52
TJOO Tik Tjoen, 354–55
TJUI, Maria, 355
TJUI Mauw, 355
TJUNG See Gan, 355–56
TJUNTJUN, 53, 131–32, 356, 364
Tjuo Sangi Kai, 87
Toko De Zon, 28
TONG Djoe, 356–57
TONG, Stephen, 357–59
Tongmeng Hui, 355, 385
Tony WEN, 397
Trisakti University Foundation, 255, 257, 270
TSAI, Frans, 359
Tubagus Pranata TIRTAWIDJAJA, 322–23

U
Uber Cup, 135
UGM, 40, 52, 312–13
UMBOH, Wim, 360–61
UNDP, 374
Universitas Katholik Atma Jaya, 251
Universitas Sariputra Indonesia Tomohon (UNSRIT), 277
University of Malaya, 249, 250
UNPAD, 76
UNRA, 335
UNSRIT. *See* Universitas Sariputra Indonesia Tomohon (UNSRIT)
URAY, Burhan, 361–62
URECA, 41, 139, 334

Urusan Pembinaan Kesatuan Bangsa, 77
Utami DEWI, 106
UTOMO, Tirto, 363

V
van Mook, 319
Verawaty FADJRIN, 131
Verawaty WIHARJO, 36
Visakha Gunadharma, 344
Volksraad, 86, 340

W
Wahid, Abdurrahman, 5, 243, 371
WAHYUDI, Johan, 356, 364
Walubi, 82
WANANDI, Jusuf, 364–66
WANANDI, (Albertus) Sofjan, 364–66
WANG Chengqing, 73
Wang Ching-wei, 323
WANG Demei, 35–36
WANG Fuhan, 211–12
WANG Fulan, 212–13
WANG Jiyuan, 65, 366–67
WANG Liangguo, 213
WANG Lianxiang, 275
WANG Renshu, 367
WANG Shangzhi, 214
WANG Xiangchun, 213
WANG Yalu, 15
WANG Yongli, 211
WANG Youshan, 124–26
WANG Ziqin, 214
WANG Zonghai, 256–57
Warta Bhakti, 9, 130

WEI Bao'an, 43
WEI Chaofeng, 43–44
WEI Fuyi, 48–49
WEI Renfang, 17
WEN Bei'ou, 368–69
WEN Dexuan, 197–98
WEN Peor, 368
WEN, Tony, 369–70, 397
WEN Zhongxiao, 199–200
WENG Junmin, 278–79
WENG Zhenxiang, 180
West Java Provincial Council, 336
WHO, 38
WHO Expert Ad Hoc Panel on Parasitic Diseases, 136
WIBISONO, Christianto, 370–71
WIDJAJA, Eka Tjipta, 371–72
WIDJAJA, Mira, 372–73
WIDJAYA, Tjiangdra, 373–74
Widodo, Joko, 26, 330
WIDYONO, Benny, 374
WIJAYA, Eko, 375
WIJAYA, Nancy, 375–76
WIJAYAKUSUMA, Hembing, 376–77
wijkmeester, 77, 85
WINARTA, Frans Hendra, 377–78
WINATA, Tomy, 379
WIRANATA, Ardi, 380
WISAKSANA, Panji, 380
WITARSA, Endang, 381
WONG Kam Fu, 381–82
WONGSOREDJO, mBah, 381–82

WONGSOSEPUTERA, Jusuf, 382
WONOWIDJOJO, Surya, 54–55, 383–84
WONOWIDJOJO, Susilo, 383, 384
WU Bingliang, 45–46
WU Dexuan, 57–58
WU Jiaxiong, 44–45
WU Nengbin, 225–26
WU Qingfu, 44
WU Qixiang, 47–48
WU Ruiji, 10
WU Ruizhang, 107
WU Shenji, 184
WU Weikang, 385
WU Xiehe, 46–47
WU Yingliang, 41
WU Yinquan, 41–42
WU Yuxiang, 39–40
WU Zhaoyuan, 42
Wuisan, Diana, 385
WUISAN, Empie, 385
WULLUR, Jahja, 386

X
XIAO Degui, 249
XIAO Yucan, 247–48
XIAO Yumei, 246–47
XIE Jianlong, 262–64
XIE Meian, 339–40
XIE Yuduan, 338–39
XIE Zhongming, 128
XIE Zuoshun, 386–87
XIE Zuoyu, 386–87
Xin Bao, 386
XIONG Deyi, 84

Xixiliya K., 92–93
XU Baozhang, 387
XU Fucai, 66
XU Fuyuan, 99
XU Huazhang, 388
XU Jin'an, 100
XU Juqing, 388
XU Mianchi, 93
XU Pinghe, 94
XU Qixing, 100
XU Shijing, 53–54
XU Tiantang, 243–44
XU Tingzhou, 32
XU Zaiying, 337–38
XU Zhenhuan, 342–43
XU Zhongming, 389
XUE Biyu, 250–51

Y

Yahya Daniel DARMA, 142
YAN Guoliang, 37–38
YAN Weizhen, 389–90
YANG Chunmei, 388, 401
YANG Guibin, 399–400
YANG Hanxiang, 187–88
YANG Mingyue, 75
YANG Weibin, 303
YANG Wie Pin, 303
YANG Xinrong, 391
YANG Xiulian, 391–92
YANG Yuanli, 182–83
YANG Zhaoji, 274
YANG Zhongsheng, 186–87
Yanong Gonghui, 352
YAP A Siong, 392
YAP Hong Tjoen, 224, 251, 393–94
YAP Kie Tiong, 224, 393–94
YAP Li Cheng, 403
YAP Lip Keng, 394
YAP Loen, 394–95
YAP Soei (Swie) Kie, 78–79
YAP Soetopo, 78–79
YAP Thiam Hien, 83, 378, 395–96
YAP Tjoen Soe, 397
YAP Tjwan Bing, 397
YAP Yun Hap, 398
YAPUTRA, Albert S., 398–99
Yayasan Ukuwah Islamiah, 77
Yayasan Universitas Trisakti (Trisakti University Foundation), 380
YE Cing Piaw, 398–99
YE Cunxu, 397
YE Hongjun, 393
YE Jinbiao, 398–99
YE Jizhong, 224
YE Ligeng, 394
YE Lizhen, 403
YE Quanming, 397
YE Ruiji, 78–79
YE Tianxing, 395–96
YE Yaxiang, 392
Yenni, 403
YEO Kuei-pin, 399–400
Yi Da, 92
Yindunixiya Ribao, 92
Yin-hua Mei-shu Hsieh-hui (Yinhua meishu xiehui), 368
Yinhua Meishu Xiehui, 123
YO Goan Li, 182–83
YO Heng Kam, 400–1

YO Soen Bie, 401
YOE Tjoe Ping, 401
YOU Ziping, 401
YOUNG, Fifi, 402–3
YU Chunxiang, 74
YU Yuling, 29–30
YUAN Ni, 403–4
Yuan Shih-k'ai, 141

Z

ZENG Chunfu, 254–56
ZENG Tianci, 333
ZENG Yingqiu, 332
ZENG Zhaozhen, 336–37
ZENG Zuqin, 333–34
ZENG Zusen, 334–35
ZHAN Hu, 244–45
ZHAN Yuqian, 340–41
ZHANG Bingwen, 64–65
ZHANG Bishi, 319–21
ZHANG Guoji, 127, 404–5
ZHANG Hongnan, 351–52
ZHANG Le Hao, 82
ZHANG Rongxuan, 353–54
ZHANG Ruisheng, 317
ZHANG Tiancong, 318–19
ZHANG Xinming, 376–77
ZHANG Xunyi, 352–53
ZHANG Yaoxuan, 351–52
ZHANG Youjun, 64–65
ZHANG Yuhao, 82
ZHANG Yunan, 353–54
ZHANG Zhan'en, 405
ZHANG Zhaoxie, 319–21
ZHANG Zhenwen, 321
ZHANG Zhusan, 406
ZHAO Chunling, 23–24
ZHAO Wenbi, 328–29
ZHAO Yushui, 327
ZHENG Dengjun, 314–15
ZHENG Hongyu, 311
ZHENG Jiancheng, 311
ZHENG Jiansheng, 62–63
ZHENG Liangyi, 312–13
ZHENG Man'an, 81–82
ZHENG Nianjin, 313–14
ZHENG Roumi'ou, 406–7
ZHENG Zhiping, 406–7
ZHONG Dingyuan, 349–50
ZHONG Wanxue, 329–30
ZHONG Wanyou, 330
Zhonghua Shangbao, 15
ZHU Changdong, 24
ZHU Difa, 277
ZHU Guosheng, 33
ZHU Maoshan, 347–48
ZHUANG Xiyan, 355–56
Zibenjia, 361
ZOU Fangjin, 407–8
ZOU Liying, 181–82

www.ingramcontent.com/pod-product-compliance
Lightning Source LLC
Chambersburg PA
CBHW052045290426
44111CB00011B/1626